THE RECONQUEST OF BURMA
VOLUME II
June 1944—August 1945

P. N. KHERA, M.A.
S. N. PRASAD, PH.D.

OFFICIAL HISTORY OF THE INDIAN ARMED FORCES
IN THE SECOND WORLD WAR
1939-45

THE RECONQUEST OF BURMA
Volume II

COMBINED INTER-SERVICES HISTORICAL SECTION
(INDIA & PAKISTAN)
1959

The Naval & Military Press Ltd

Published by

The Naval & Military Press Ltd
Unit 5 Riverside, Brambleside
Bellbrook Industrial Estate
Uckfield, East Sussex
TN22 1QQ England

Tel: +44 (0)1825 749494

www.naval-military-press.com
www.nmarchive.com

In reprinting in facsimile from the original, any imperfections are inevitably reproduced and the quality may fall short of modern type and cartographic standards.

ERRATA

Page   25, line 18: *for* 53 Column *read* 55 Column
Page   27, line 2 from bottom: *for* Batalions *read* Battalions
Page   39, line 20: *for* 22 July *read* 22 June
Page   56, line 16: *for* abondoned *read* abandoned
Page 146, line 26: *for* Kelewa *read* Kalewa
Page 193, line 6 from bottom: *for* south-east *read* south-west
Page 279, line 11: *for* 25 February *read* 25 January
Page 406, line 5: *for* companies *read* platoons
Page 432, line 20 and page 447 lines 3 and 4: *for* Paungdi *read* Paungde
Page 445, line 5 from bottom: *for* Paungda *read* Paungde

TO ALL WHO SERVED

ADVISORY COMMITTEE

Chairman
SECRETARY, MINISTRY OF DEFENCE, INDIA

Members

DR TARA CHAND
DR S. N. SEN
PROF K. A. NILAKANTA SASTRI
PROF MOHAMMAD HABIB
DR R. C. MAJUMDAR
GENERAL K. S. THIMAYYA
LIEUT-GENERAL SIR DUDLEY RUSSELL
LIEUT-GENERAL S. P. P. THORAT
MILITARY ADVISER TO THE HIGH COMMISSIONER
    FOR PAKISTAN IN INDIA

Secretary
DR BISHESHWAR PRASAD

CAMPAIGNS IN THE EASTERN THEATRE

CAMPAIGNS IN SOUTH-EAST ASIA 1941-42

RETREAT FROM BURMA 1941-42

ARAKAN OPERATIONS 1942-45

RECONQUEST OF BURMA 1942-45, TWO VOLUMES

POST-WAR OCCUPATION FORCES: JAPAN AND SOUTH-EAST ASIA

PREFACE

This is the second volume of the campaigns in Burma, leading to its reconquest by the British in 1945. This volume, a continuation of the first volume, takes up the story from June 1944 to the month of August 1945, when Japan surrendered to the Allies. It deals mainly with the operations of the Fourteenth Army during the monsoon of 1944, the crossings of the Irrawaddy, the capture of Meiktila and Mandalay, and the double thrust to Rangoon down the river and the railway axes. In addition, there is a chapter on the capture of Rangoon by a seaborne and airborne operation known as 'Dracula'. Finally, the account of the mopping-up operations against the Japanese escaping to the east of Burma has also been given.

This volume, together with the three already published, namely, the *Retreat from Burma*, the *Arakan Operations*, and the first volume of the *Reconquest of Burma*, completes the story of the Japanese occupation of Burma and their expulsion from that land, which was at one time part of the British Indian Empire. In all these campaigns the India Command and the Indian people were intimately concerned, because the presence of the Japanese so close to the eastern frontier of India, and occasional glimpses of their aggressive intentions on that frontier, did create symptoms of alarm in the country. There was perfect unanimity in India about the need of protecting the Indian frontiers and saving the country from foreign aggression, and though there was difference of opinion between the Government and the political parties in regard to the method of achieving it, the resources of the country both in men and material were harnessed to the object of expelling the hostile forces from the Indian border.

Our object, as in the previous volumes, has been to present an accurate and objective account emphasising the strategic and tactical plans which influenced the operations in the area. There is, therefore, greater stress on the strategic planning, policies and events than on personalities. There is no attempt also to narrate the story of the achievements of any particular units, except when they fought independently and their part was a significant one in contributing to the execution of the strategic or tactical plan. In this campaign large masses of troops were converged at certain points and, therefore, the story proceeds mainly on the basis of corps or divisions, rather than battalions or companies. The land forces were receiving ample support from the air forces of the United States and the United Kingdom, whose part in the campaign has been adequately traced.

The Indian troops fought alongside their British, Chinese and African comrades under the supreme command of Lord Mountbatten. Therefore, this account is more that of the achievements of the Allied powers in Burma than of the Indian units separately. Of course, the Indian units have been given a more detailed treatment in the progress of the fighting, but the contribution of the other elements has not been minimised. As historians we have kept objectivity as our guiding motive, and to this we have tried invariably to conform.

The history of the Indian armed forces in the Second World War has been produced by the Combined Inter-Services Historical Section (India & Pakistan), which is a joint organisation of the Governments of India and Pakistan and was established for the purpose of producing a detailed history of the operations in which the Indian armed forces were involved.

This volume has been seen in the typescript by Admiral the Lord Louis Mountbatten of Burma, Field Marshal Sir William Slim, General Sir Frank Messervy, General Sir Geoffry Scoones, Lieut.-Gen. Sir Montagu Stopford and Major-General Sir Douglas Gracey to whom we are greatly indebted. Their comments have been of great value in resolving doubts and making the story clear and coherent. I am also grateful to General K. S. Thimayya and Lieut.-Gen. S. P. P. Thorat who read the volume as members of the Advisory Committee and offered valuable suggestions. I am also thankful to the Historical Section of the Government of Pakistan for their suggestions which have been incorporated. I must also acknowledge my deep gratitude to Brigadier H. B. Latham and his colleagues in the Historical Section of the Cabinet in the United Kingdom for their ready assistance and valuable suggestions.

This volume has been written by two of my colleagues, Dr. S. N. Prasad who has contributed the first four chapters, and Shri P. N. Khera who has written the rest. Their co-operation has been of great value to me in preparing this volume. I am also thankful to Shri T. D. Sharma, Cartographer, for the maps which he has prepared. For the views and opinions expressed in this volume I take full responsibility. The Government of India had placed all the available records at our disposal, but have no connection with the views expressed herein.

In conclusion I thank the Ministries of Defence of the Government of India and the Government of Pakistan for their valued assistance which has made my task lighter.

BISHESHWAR PRASAD

New Delhi
December 1958

CONTENTS

		Page
INTRODUCTION		xix

CHAPTER

		Page
I.	HIGHER STRATEGY AND PLANS	1
II.	THE NORTHERN SECTOR—ALLIED OFFENSIVE AND THE RECAPTURE OF UKHRUL	12
III.	TAMU REGAINED	38
IV.	THE PURSUIT TO TIDDIM AND KALEMYO	63
V.	ALLIED PLANS—NOVEMBER 1944	108
VI.	FOURTEENTH ARMY CROSSES THE CHINDWIN (NOVEMBER—DECEMBER 1944)	127
VII.	IV CORPS ADVANCE TO THE IRRAWADDY	160
VIII.	XXXIII CORPS ADVANCE TO THE IRRAWADDY	193
IX.	XXXIII CORPS ADVANCE TO THE IRRAWADDY (CONTD.)	215
X.	CROSSING THE IRRAWADDY	255
XI.	MEIKTILA RECAPTURED	289
XII.	TO THE CITY OF THE KINGS	342
XIII.	THE DASH TO RANGOON—XXXIII CORPS	366
XIV.	THE DASH TO RANGOON—IV CORPS	388
XV.	OPERATION 'DRACULA' AND THE FALL OF RANGOON	411
XVI.	COMPLETING THE CONQUEST	428
APPENDICES		461
BIBLIOGRAPHY		529
INDEX		531

APPENDICES

		Page
1.	CHAIN OF COMMAND—AFTER THE CREATION OF HEADQUARTERS ALLIED LAND FORCES SEAC—12 NOVEMBER 1944	463
2.	ORDER OF BATTLE—33 INDIAN CORPS—1 AUGUST 1944	465
3.	4 CORPS OPERATION INSTRUCTION No. 100—23 JUNE 1944	481
4.	5 INDIAN DIVISION LOCATION STATEMENT—19 AUGUST 1944	482
5.	WITHDRAWAL BEHIND THE IRRAWADDY, 1944 (JAPANESE VIEW AS DISCLOSED IN INTERROGATIONS)	485
6.	TASKS OF THE LUSHAI BRIGADE—33 IND CORPS OPERATION INSTRUCTION No. 20 DATED 6-10-44	487
7.	33 INDIAN CORPS OPERATION INSTRUCTION No. 23, DATED 1-12-44	488
8.	TASKS OF 33 INDIAN CORPS—DECEMBER 1944	490
9.	33 IND CORPS OPERATION INSTRUCTION No. 24, DATED 17-1-45	491
10.	APPRECIATION OF THE SITUATION BY COMMANDER 4 CORPS—19 JANUARY 1945	495
11.	DECEPTION SCHEME "CLOAK"	499
12.	33 CORPS PLAN FOR CAPTURING MANDALAY—33 CORPS OPERATION ORDER No. 13, DATED 2-2-45	503
13.	4 CORPS OPERATION INSTRUCTION No. 125, DATED 5 FEBRUARY 1945	508
14.	JAPANESE STRENGTH—15TH ARMY, MARCH 1945	512
15.	63 BRIGADE OPERATION INSTRUCTION No. 1, DATED 9 MARCH 1945	514
16.	4 CORPS DECEPTION SCHEME "CONCLAVE"	515
17.	ORDER OF BATTLE—33 IND CORPS—31 MARCH 1945	518
18.	4 CORPS OPERATION INSTRUCTION No. 139, DATED 5 APRIL 1945	519
19.	33 CORPS OPERATION ORDER No. 21, DATED 30 APRIL 1945	521
20.	ORDER OF BATTLE—33 IND CORPS—1 MAY 1945	524
21.	EXTRACT FROM INTELLIGENCE SUMMARY No. 15, DATED 18 MAY 1945	525
22.	JAPANESE PLAN FOR BREAK-OUT—JULY 1945	526

MAPS

Burma (Central and Lower)	facing page	1
The advance on Ukhrul, 27 June—8 July 1944	page	21
Reopening of the Ukhrul road, 1-10 July 1944	,,	30
The Tengnoupal positions on the Palel-Tamu Road April-July 1944	,,	46
The thrust to Sibong, 24-28 July 1944	facing page	51
The outflanking march by 123 Ind. Inf. Bde., 30 August—14 September 1944	page	85
Operations of 5 Ind. Div. against Vital Corner and Fort White, 2-8 November 1944	,,	102
Drive to the Chindwin, June-November 1944	,,	106
Fourteenth Army Plans, December 1944	facing page	133
Allied and Japanese dispositions, 24 December 1944	,, ,,	161
Allied dispositions (February 1945) prior to advance on Meiktila and Mandalay	,, ,,	191
Allied advance to the Irrawaddy, January-February 1945	,, ,,	215
The crossing of the Irrawaddy by 19 Indian Div. Mid-January to 20 February 1945	page	220
20 Ind. Div. Operations to clear the north bank of the Irrawaddy, January-February 1945	,,	231
2 British Div. Operations to clear the north bank of the Irrawaddy, January-February 1945	,,	241
Crossings of the Irrawaddy, January-February 1945	facing page	255
Crossing of the Irrawaddy by 20 Ind. Div., 13 February 1945	,, ,,	259
The crossing of the Irrawaddy by 2 British Div., 24 February 1945	page	277
The crossing of the Irrawaddy by 7 Ind. Div., 14 February 1945	,,	285
Capture of Meiktila, 1-5 March 1945	facing page	295
17 Div. consolidation in Meiktila, March 1945	,, ,,	319
Operation in Mandalay Area, March-April 1945	page	351
Advance of Fourteenth Army to Rangoon, 26 December to 3 May 1945	,,	368
Exploitation Phase, situation 7 April 1945	facing page	373
Battle of the Sittang bend, 7-10 July 1945	page	449
Japanese break-out from Pegu Yomas, 20 July to 4 August 1945	,,	456
Burma	at the end	

ILLUSTRATIONS

Admiral the Lord Louis Mountbatten of Burma, Supreme Allied Commander, South-East Asia Command	*Facing page*	4
Lieut.-General Sir Oliver Leese, Commander ALFSEA	*Following page*	4
Lieut.-General (later Field Marshal) Sir William Slim, Commander Fourteenth Army	" "	4
Lieut.-General Sir Geoffry Scoones, Commander IV Corps (16 Nov. 43—8 Dec. 44)	*Facing page*	5
Lieut.-General R. A. Wheeler (U.S. Army), Deputy Supreme Allied Commander	" "	5
Lieut.-General Sir Montagu Stopford, Commander XXXIII Corps	" "	12
Lieut.-General Sir Frank Messervy, Commander IV Corps (8 Dec. 44—1 Nov. 45)	" "	12
Air Marshal Sir John Baldwin, Air Commander Third Tactical Air Force	*Following page*	12
Rear-Admiral B. C. S. Martin, Flag Officer Force "W"	" "	12
Lieut.-General F. I. S. Tuker, Commander IV Corps (14 July 45—18 Aug. 45)	" "	12
Major-General C. G. G. Nicholson, Commander 2nd British Division	" "	12
Major-General G. C. Evans, Commander 7th Indian Division (29 Dec. 44—7 Feb. 46)	*Facing page*	13
Major-General C. C. Fowkes, Commander 11th East African Division	" "	13
Supply mules cross a mountain stream in Imphal area	" "	42
Looking back from Scraggy to Malta Hill from which the famous feature was attacked by the Gurkhas	" "	42
Aircraft dropping supplies on Tiddim Road	" "	43
General view of the "Chocolate Staircase" showing some of its 39 hairpin bends	" "	88
Vehicles move along the muddy Tiddim Road	" "	88
Troops of 4th J & K Infantry move up to consolidate the newly won position on the Kennedy Peak	" "	89
Major-General T. W. Rees, Commander 19th Indian Division	" "	112

Brigadier P. C. Marindin, Commander Lushai Brigade	*Facing page*	113
Major-General F. W. Festing, Commander 36th British Division	,, ,,	150
Major (later Major-General) Sarda Nand Singh of 5th Indian Division and Major E. Wilson V.C. of 11th East African Division meet at Kalemyo to mark the closing of the pincers	,, ,,	150
Major-General D. D. Gracey, Commander 20th Indian Division	,, ,,	151
Gurkhas advance cautiously in outskirts of a village during Fourteenth Army advance prior to crossing the Irrawaddy river	,, ,,	151
A section of well armed Chin Levies with one of their trophies—a Japanese flag	,, ,,	176
Budalin in flames being attacked	,, ,,	176
Jat machine-gunners support the advance of 14th Punjabis to Monywa	,, ,,	177
4/10 Gurkhas attack a burning Burmese village	,, ,,	177
General view of one of the starting points on the river bank	,, ,,	264
Stuart tanks move up to cross the river	,, ,,	264
Men of 4/6 Gurkha and other Indian troops cross the Irrawaddy during drive on Mandalay	*Following page*	264
Hoisting a section of the bridge into position in mid-stream	,, ,,	264
Gurkha patrol advances in Pakokku village area	,, ,,	264
Trucks go across the river on rafts as advance continues in Pagan area	,, ,,	264
Lieut. Karamjeet Singh Judge V.C., 4/15 Punjab	*Facing page*	265
Naik Gian Singh V.C., 4/15 Punjab	,, ,,	265
Captain Michael Allmand V.C., 3/6 G.R.	,, ,,	265
Major Frank Gerald Blaker V.C., 3/9 G.R.	,, ,,	265
Men of 4/12 Frontier Force Regiment charge burning remnants of a village during drive on Meiktila	,, ,,	304
3.7" Howitzer gun of 6 Jacob Mountain Battery, in action against the Japanese south of Meiktila	,, ,,	304
Rifleman Tulbahadur Pun V.C., 3/6 G.R.	,, ,,	305
Rifleman Lachhiman Gurung V.C., 4/8 G.R.	,, ,,	305
Naik Fazal Din V.C., 7/10 Baluch	,, ,,	305
Jemadar (acting Subedar) Ram Surup Singh V.C., 2/1 Punjab	,, ,,	305
Major-General D. T. Cowan, Commander 17th Indian Division (16 Nov. 43—30 May 45)	,, ..	354

3" Mortars near Madaya open fire on Japanese position north of Mandalay	*Facing page*	354
Brigadier (later General) K. S. Thimayya, Commander 36th Indian Infantry Brigade . . .	,, ,,	355
Men of the 1st Sikh Light Infantry crawl up a nullah prior to dislodging the Japanese from a hill position south of Pyawbwe	,, ,,	390
Allied convoys driving on Rangoon frequently met with blown-up bridges. They forded the rivers helped by bull-dozers	,, ,,	390
Major-General E. C. Mansergh, Commander 5th Indian Division	,, ,,	391
Tanks and troops of 4/7 Rajput advance on a village during Fourteenth Army drive on Rangoon	,, ,,	391
Troops of 10th Gurkha search Pegu, last big town taken before the recapture of Rangoon . . .	,, ,,	412
Part of the force consisting of warships of the Royal Indian Navy on their way to the mouth of the Rangoon river	,, ,,	412
Civilians help in disposal of supplies dropped by air to liberated Rangoon	*Following page*	412
The first paratroop jumps—some have already landed and others are swarming down to the ground	,, ,,	412
Jemadar Parkash Singh V.C., 14/13 Frontier Force Rifles	,, ,,	412
Jemadar Abdul Hafiz V.C., 3/9 Jat	,, ,,	412
Major-General H M. Chambers, Commander 26th Indian Division	*Facing page*	413
Major-General W. A. Crowther, Commander 17th Indian Division (22 June 45—31 May 46) . . .	,, ,,	413

ABBREVIATIONS

AA guns	Anti-Aircraft guns.
AFO	Anti-Fascist Organisation.
AITM	Army in India Training Memorandum.
ALFSEA	Allied Land Forces South-East Asia.
Appx	Appendix.
A/Tk	Anti-Tank.
BDA	Burma Defence Army.
Bde	Brigade.
BNA	Burma National Army.
Bty.	Battery.
CCRA	Chief Commander Royal Artillery.
CIGS	Chief of Imperial General Staff.
CIS	Combined Inter-Services.
CRA	Commander Royal Artillery.
Cs-in-C	Commanders-in-Chief.
DCO	Director Combined Operations.
D Day	The day on which an operation is planned to begin.
DF	Defensive Fire.
DG	Prince of Wales's Dragoon Guards.
Div	Division.
DLI	Durham Light Infantry.
EA	East African.
F/Bs	Fighter Bombers.
Fd. Arty	Field Artillery.
Fd Regt	Field Regiment.
FFR	Frontier Force Regiment.
FF Rif	Frontier Force Rifles.
FIC	French Indo-China.
F/R	Fighter Reconnaissance.
GOC	General Officer Commanding.
GR	Gurkha Rifles.
GS	General Staff.
HAA (Regt)	Heavy Anti-Aircraft (Regiment).
HM Govt	His Majesty's Government.
HMS	His Majesty's Ship.
HP	Horse Power.
HQ	Headquarters.
IAF	Indian Air Force.
IMB	Independent Mixed Brigade.
INA	Indian National Army.
Ind	India or Indian.
Isum	Intelligence summary.
IWT	Inland Water Transport.
JPS	Joint Planning Staff.
KAR	King's African Rifles.
KOSB	King's Own Scottish Borderers.
LAA (Regt)	Light Anti-Aircraft (Regiment).
LMG	Light Machine-Gun.

MG Coy	Machine-Gun Company.
MMG	Medium Machine-Gun.
MS	Milestone.
MT	Mechanical Transport.
MT Regt	Mountain Regiment.
NCAC	Northern Combat Area Command.
NRR	Northern Rhodesian Regiment.
OO	Operation Order.
OPs	Observation Posts.
Op Instr	Operation Instruction.
PBF	Patriotic Burmese Forces.
POL	Petrol Oil and Lubricants.
Pt.	Point.
RA	Royal Artillery.
RAC	Royal Armoured Corps.
RAF	Royal Air Force.
R Berks	Royal Berks.
Recce	Reconnaissance.
Regt	Regiment.
R Horse	The Royal Deccan Horse (9th Horse).
RIASC	Royal Indian Army Service Corps.
RS	Royal Scots.
RWF	Royal Welch Fusiliers.
SAC SEA	Supreme Allied Commander South-East Asia.
SEAC	South-East Asia Command.
SEATIC	South-East Asia Translation and Interrogation Centre.
Sitrep	Situation Report.
S Lan R	South Lancashire Regiment.
Tac/R	Tactical Reconnaissance.
Tp.	Troop.
USAAF	United States Army Air Force.
VC	Victoria Cross.
VCP	Visual Control Post.
VJ Day	Victory over Japan Day.
WD or W/D	War Diary.
Worc R	Worcestershire Regiment.

INTRODUCTION

The process of recovering Burma from Japanese occupation, began in 1943, had reached a stage in the summer of 1944 from where the spring into Upper Burma was easy. The last of the attempts of the Japanese forces to acquire a foothold on the Indian soil had failed with the deliverance of Imphal and Kohima from their stranglehold. The Indian and British troops had been hastily concentrated on the outskirts of Kohima, and the garrison was succoured mainly by recourse to air-droppings and intercepting the Japanese line of communication. Their retreat had been cut off and it was with tremendous effort that the Japanese invaders were able, with decimated strengths, to retire into Burma and cross back the Chindwin. The danger to India was over ; the Long Range Penetration Groups had shown the way of advance and scoured the forests and hills in the rear of the Japanese forces. The India Command had organised supplies and trained new forces to take the offensive with troops who had been initiated into the mysteries of jungle warfare. The war in Europe was nearing its end ; the African and West Asian theatres had ceased to be live fields of action any more ; the Russians were hammering back the Nazi armies ; and in the Pacific the United States forces were island-hopping and drawing the ring closer to Japan. The Chinese had regained their confidence and the British people were once again able to mobilise their war industries. The South-East Asia Command was now bubbling with enthusiasm and its Supreme Commander was forging a new strategy to push back the Japanese from the north of Burma and free the land from alien occupation. The story in this second volume of the Reconquest of Burma is a tale of successes of the Indo-British forces and the steady repulse and retreat of the Japanese, leading to the fall of Rangoon and its possession by the British.

The actual commencement of the forward operations, however, was delayed by the uncertainty of plans, the indefiniteness of objective and the prolonged resistance by the German forces in Europe. From the time that the South-East Asia Command had been set up, discussions had continued between the operational command, the Chiefs of Staff in the United Kingdom and the Combined Chiefs of Staff in Washington as to the direction of the thrust in the east which would bring the Japanese to their knees. There was the inevitable difference in the outlook of two Allies, the British and the Americans, and this divergence in their views, fundamental in its nature, was reflected primarily in the planning in South-East Asia and the character of campaign in Burma. To the United States, the primary purpose of military operations on the Indian borders of Burma was to keep China in the list by transporting supplies through India across the Hump or by reopening the Burma-China road. The main attack on Japan was to be administered by the American naval forces from the islands of the Pacific and the air forces based on the mainland of China. In this strategy, the Combined Chiefs of Staff had no place for British collaboration and viewed with disfavour any concentration of energies or resources by the latter on any operations which did not have for their main object the building up of the base in China. The British, on the other hand, were not content with playing the second fiddle and were definitely concerned about the retrieval of their empire in South-East Asia. To them, therefore, the operations in northern Burma directed towards the mere opening of the new China road or the defence in depth of the airfields in India had no attractions. Their heart was set upon an amphibious operation directed against Sumatra or Malaya which would replace them as rulers in these strategic regions. Mr. Churchill was extremely keen about such a move and the South-East Asia Command had been asked to plan for it. The British Chiefs of Staff were also eager to participate in the final hammering of Japan and had offered their fleet for co-operation, which was cold-shouldered by the Joint Chiefs of Staff. The United States frowned upon any diversion of the military, naval or air forces for schemes primarily related to the restoration of the British Empire, while the British were reluctant to commit their land forces solely for the object of helping China and guarding the air routes and the landing places—at best a secondary operation of a police character. This division of objective continued to figure for nine months and contributed to the uncertainty of planning and delay in the commencement of definite, decisive operations.

Conditions in China were verging on the desperate, and poverty of the people was appalling. "The level of wholesale price index in Chungking was more than two hundred times as high as in 1937. The production of war material, despite able technicians was almost completely hamstrung by lack of financial control. As a result, the Chinese soldier was, by western standards, almost incredibly ill-armed, ill-clothed and ill-fed." In spite of this estimate of John Ehrman, the official historian of the United Kingdom, the United States military authorities assessed the strategic value of China rather high and in any plans of campaigns in the East gave first priority to the supplies to China. To the American Chiefs of Staffs, China was a valuable asset ; and in the words of Ehrman, "at the least, as a sponge to soak up Japanese resources, and as a guarantee against an unchallenged Japanese dominion on the mainland which might survive even the reduction of the Home Islands ; at best, as a potential base for offensive operations against the enemy. The British, with only a slight strategic interest in the Chinese theatre, and doubtful of the Generalissimo's capacity to stage an offensive, were content simply with his continued resistance; the Americans, whose more direct strategic concern was supported by a traditional affection, were prepared to foster him in a more active role."[1] This could be done either by improving the Chinese armies or as an alternative by the employment of American tactical air power to harass the Japanese so as to compel them to leave large areas on the mainland. The third mode was to establish an American strategic air force in China to bomb the Japanese islands or their approaches. This last became the most active pursuit in the year 1944; and for all these the indispensable requirement was to increase the volume of American supplies to China, which inevitably had to pass through India. Air transport was the sole mode in the beginning, but General Stilwell had all the time been pressing for the opening of land communications by linking the old Burma Road with India by a direct link road, which was under construction. In his strategy, therefore, emphasis shifted from the mere defence in depth of the airfields in Bengal and north-east India to the reconquest of northern Burma. The British were not primarily interested in either of these, and the recovery of northern Burma to them could be only as a preliminary to the expulsion of the Japanese from the whole of Burma and Malaya ultimately. The Americans had little interest in the return of the old empire to the British; and therefore viewed with dismay any diversion of the Allied resources, naval, air or military, to the British plans of amphibious operations directed against Malaya, Andamans or Sumatra as a step to the recovery of these lands. Meanwhile, the events were moving fast to force a decision as regards an agreed strategy. The expulsion of the Japanese from the Kohima-Imphal sector, and the success of Stilwell's Ledo force in pushing through Kamaing and capturing the airfield of Myitkyina on 17 May 1944 posed a new problem. "To the Americans," in the words of Ehrman, "possession of the airfield and the town, apart from their value to the Ledo Road and its pipe-line, seemed essential to provide a base for an easier route to China than that over the Hump. To the British, it represented a further stage in the extension of the campaign in the north. Similarly, the victory of Imphal imposed the question of the shape of future strategy."[2]

The pressure of these events and the inability of India to serve as a base for a major naval operation in South-East Asia, owing to the near famine conditions and the effects of political movement in the country, led to the surrender of Churchill's plans of attack on Sourabaya, and an agreed directive was issued to Admiral

[1] John Ehrman: *Grand Strategy*, Vol. V, pp. 125-26, H.M.S.O.
[2] Ibid, p. 418.

Mountbatten in June 1944 for operations in his command. The directive was worded as follows:

"To develop, maintain, broaden and protect the air link to China, in order to provide maximum and timely supply of P.O.L. and stores to China in support of Pacific Operations; so far as is consistent with the above, to press advantages against the enemy, by exerting maximum effort, ground and air, particularly during the current monsoon season, and in pressing such advantages, to be prepared to exploit the development of overland communications to China. All these operations must be dictated by the forces at present available or firmly allocated to S.E.A.C." This directive might have solved the immediate problem and offered agreement on the tasks for the monsoon months, but it did not provide an answer either to the aspirations of the British Prime Minister or to the absolute security of the eastern frontiers of India. The declining strength of the Japanese, and their lack of drawing effective reinforcements into Burma might have operated as guarantees against the recurrence of another Kohima, but the Western Allies in their strategic calculations ignored this aspect of India's security in preference for the utilisation of her as merely a base for their own ends. The June directive was a glaring elucidation of this purpose of theirs, for the emphasis was on increased supplies to China by broadening the air link and developing the overland communications. However, the importance of Burma was now recognised and the campaign there in which the Indian armed forces were primarily involved was duly placed on the map of global strategy of the Western Powers.

The June directive was conditioned on one limitation that the operations were to be conducted only with the forces then available in the theatre. Lord Mountbatten interpreted the new orders to mean, in his own words, "that we had to conquer most of Northern Burma, and really it meant that we should have to go and liberate the whole of Burma because I did not feel it was militarily sound to remain poised in mid-Burma without any firm surface line of communication, particularly during the Monsoon". He was not happy with his orders, but he considered them as the basis for further planning with the priorities being indicated. Largely the June directive coincided with Stilwell's programme of the capture of Mogaung-Myitkyina area as a preliminary to the expansion of the air supply programme to China and the intensification of the bombing of Japanese bases as a preliminary to attack on Formosa. The Supreme Commander of South-East Asia favoured the first part of it, but was not prepared for the denudation of the air cover of his theatre. He also fully realised the inevitability of the next step after the capture of Myitkyina which was the recovery of Central Burma and ultimately the whole of Burma, because Myitkyina could not remain an isolated oasis in the midst of Japanese-held territory all around it. Therefore, as soon as, by the end of June, Japanese withdrawal from the plain of Imphal became a reality, and, in July, their forces had been back on the Chindwin or down the Tiddim road, Lord Mountbatten started planning for an offensive after the monsoon, and in the words of Ehrman "could embark with certainty on operations which he had hitherto been unable to accept".[3] His plan envisaged the movement of Stilwell's force from Mogaung-Myitkyina area to the Katha-Bhamo line, and the advance of the IV and XXXIII Corps to the line of the Chindwin, aimed at the clearing of the mountains of northern Burma; or, alternatively, leading the British Indian troops to Kalewa, Ye-U and Shwebo and ultimately to Mandalay, thus exposing Central Burma to Allied exploitation. As an auxiliary to this plan, and aimed mainly at avoiding delay, he put forth the plan of a seaborne and airborne attack on Rangoon, which would have the effect of forcing the Japanese to withdraw to the south thus leaving northern and central Burma to be cleared by the Allied forces without any delay. The capture of Rangoon would be followed by march northwards. These operations demanded more troops and greater resources, which conflicted with the condition imposed by the June directive.

The new plans were submitted to the Chiefs of Staff and prolonged discussions continued on their implications. Meanwhile, the situation was complicated by the revival of Churchill's pet idea of the reconquest of Malaya or Sumatra by naval operations, and his lack of enthusiasm for Mountbatten's plans which did not contemplate any operations outside the limits of Burma. The Prime Minister had an abhorrence for the "laborious reconquest of Burma swamp by swamp", and had set his heart on leaving "the enemy to rot and starve behind us, while we concentrated our resources elsewhere".[4] His emphasis on the tip of Sumatra came in the way of the acceptance of seaborne attack of Rangoon, which he considered as a waste of good resources which might be employed to free South-East Asia. However, on 8 August 1944, the Chiefs of Staff in London agreed on a compromise which gave priority to Burma and relegated 'Culverin' or the recapture of Malaya, to a secondary place, only if German resistance collapsed early or when the necessary forces became available. The new objective was to contain the Japanese in northern Burma and plan for the capture of Rangoon by seeking fresh resources from other quarters. These proposals were communicated to the American Chiefs of Staff. The latter were prepared to accept Lord Mountbatten's proposals as long as they did not affect the full force of the campaign in northern Burma against the Japanese. There-

[3] Ehrman: Vol. V, p. 492.
[4] Ibid, p. 496.

fore, they agreed to the issue of a fresh directive that subject to the European operations not being affected, Lord Mountbatten's plan aimed at the "attainment of line Kalewa-Shwebo-Mogok-Lashio, and exploitation toward Pakokku-Mandalay-Kyaukma" be accepted, and that the plan for the recapture of Rangoon might be initiated in March 1945. This settlement in September 1944 resolved the differences in the outlook of strategy and gave a certain priority and definiteness to the Burma theatre in defeating the Japanese aggression in South-East Asia and on the borders of India.

In the autumn of 1944, the campaign in Burma was fought on three fronts, the Arakan where the XV Indian Corps was moving down to Akyab, the central or Chindwin front where the Fourteenth Army was driving down the hills south of Imphal to the Chindwin, and the northern, where the Northern Combat Area Command was driving down from the Myitkyina area. The September directive envisaged operations (Capital) in four phases for the reconquest of the central plain of Burma; the first to the area Kalewa—Kalemyo, the second to seize Ye-U, the gateway of the Mandalay plain, and exploit the area Ye-U—Shwebo, the third to gain the line Mandalay—Pakokku and the fourth, the 'consolidation of the line reached and exploitation southward'. The Northern Combat Area Command, at the same time, was to move down to Loilem on the eastern flank. These operations were to be followed by 'Dracula', the seaborne attack on Rangoon and the subsequent exploitation northwards.

The delays and difficulties of the European campaign, at times, led to the apprehension that the Burma theatre might be starved of the necessary resources in men and material, and the expeditious execution of the operations to contain the Japanese forces in Burma and destroy them might be severely affected. However, the events took a happy trend, and the courage and resolve of the Indian and British troops in Burma, together with the air superiority which had been acquired in that theatre, led to a speedy collapse of the Japanese resistance. The monsoon did not deter the advance of the forces, and even when the Indian armed units were faced by strong Japanese opposition at places, they held their ground and stayed, supported by air-droppings of supplies, to break the patience of the hostile forces. This succeeded in the end in taking them to Mandalay, and beyond south to Meiktila, which opened to them the rich oil bearing area, the road down the Irrawaddy, and ultimately the gates to Rangoon. Meanwhile 'Dracula' also had been mounted; and there was the race by the northern, western or southern forces to reach the city of Rangoon. The Japanese had offered stiff resistance, but their lines of communication with the homeland had been intercepted, their air power had been destroyed, and their morale had been shaken; and they hurried back to disengage themselves from the British-Indian grip and retreat to Thailand or Malaya, before it was too late.

Burma weakened the Japanese considerably and contributed, though indirectly, to their defeat ultimately. The contribution of the Burma campaign was two-fold, firstly, that it enabled the Americans to bomb the Japanese bases from China and secondly that it held large forces in the south-west which could have otherwise supplemented the home forces and sustained Japanese resistance for a little time more. The success of Indian and British forces in Burma itself was greatly accelerated by the victorious onward drive of the American forces in the South-West Pacific and their heavy air bombing programme. The result of the campaign was to free the Indian frontiers of the danger of alien aggression, which at a time had become a reality. The expulsion of the Japanese from Burma and their surrender ultimately had been hastened by factors outside the purview of this narrative.

BISHESHWAR PRASAD

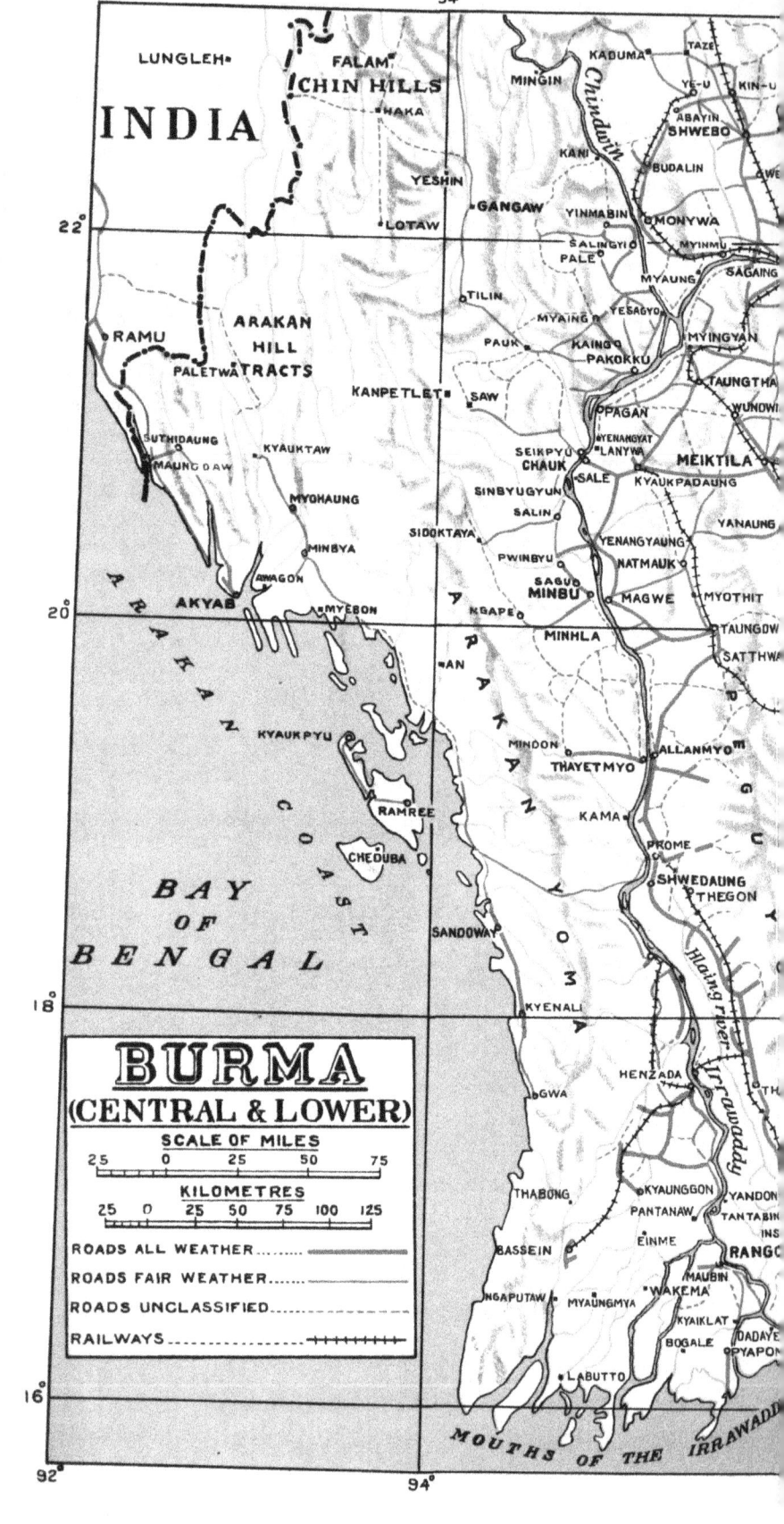

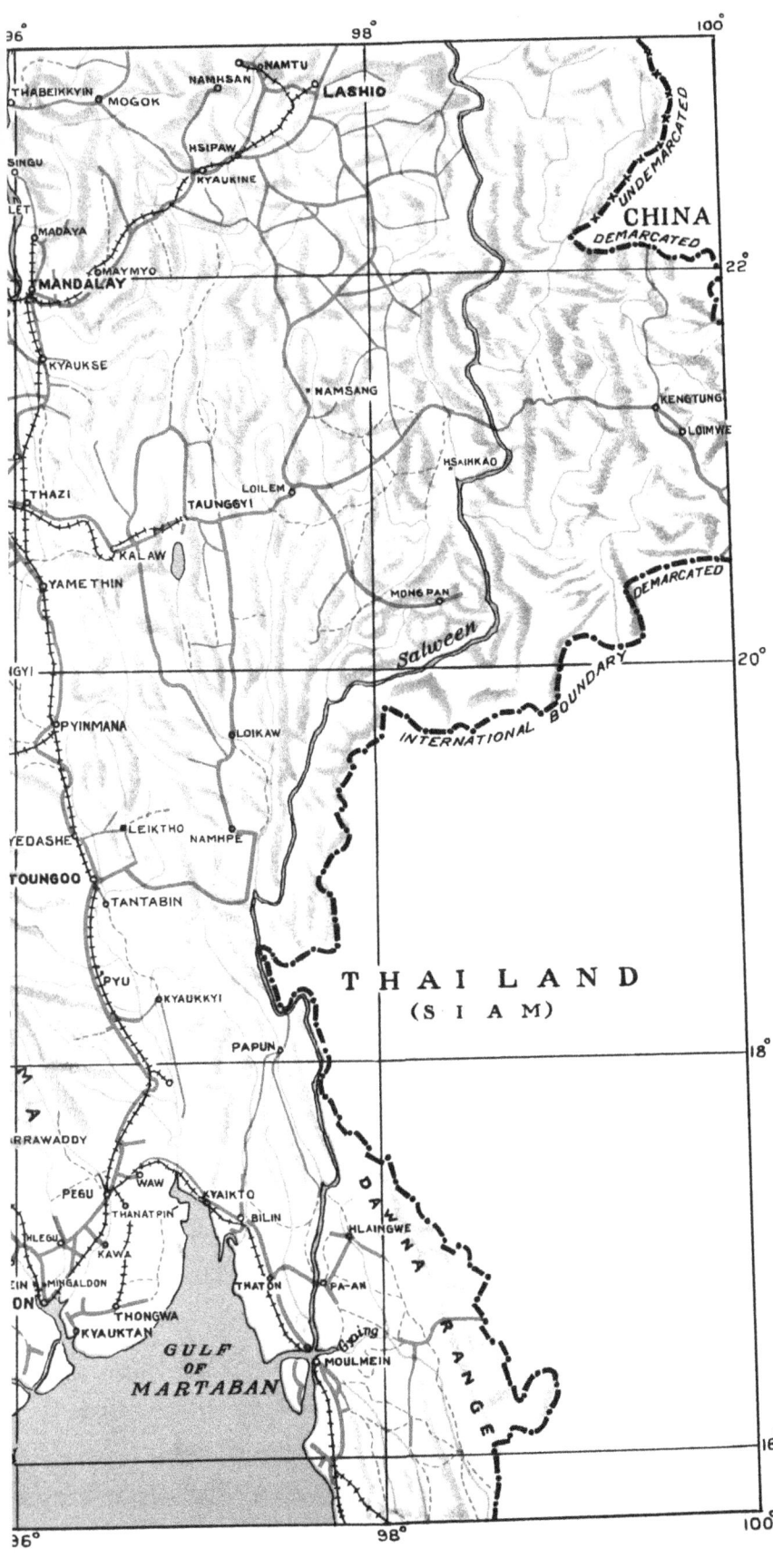

CHAPTER I

Higher Strategy and Plans

THE STRATEGIC SITUATION

In Chapter XV of the first volume, the reopening of the Dimapur-Imphal road has already been described. As shown there, by 22 June 1944 the great Japanese offensive had definitely petered out and the troops of the IV Corps and XXXIII Corps had firmly taken the offensive. The repeated attacks of the Japanese *33rd Division* and *15th Division* in the Bishenpur, Palel and Litan sectors had been held and thrown back, and the attackers had been decimated by continuous fighting and the ravages of hunger and disease. The Allied troops, on the other hand, were ready to advance up to the Chindwin and beyond.

On the other fronts too, the war had been going favourably for the Allies. In Arakan, the XV Corps had made local advances after repelling the Japanese encircling attack against the 7th Indian Division. Amphibious operations had been planned to capture Akyab before the monsoon set in, but removal of the 7th and the 5th Indian Divisions from Arakan to the Central Front and of the 36th British Division to the Northern Combat Area Command had made it impossible to carry them out just then. The Supreme Allied Commander, South-East Asia, had, therefore, ordered the XV Corps to take up monsoon positions and mark time till the season improved.

In accordance with this decision, Buthidaung was evacuated and the XV Corps took up positions on higher and less malarial ground westwards, holding a line from Godusara to the Tunnels and on to Taung Bazar. But on the Northern front, as already related, important advances were recorded by the Allied forces under Lieut.-General Stilwell. During April 1944, the Japanese *18th Division* appeared to stabilise the front north of Kamaing, slowing down the Allied advance to a crawling pace. It had been intended to advance against Myitkyina after capturing or encircling Mogaung, but when the operations had slowed down, an attempt was made against Myitkyina without waiting for the fall of Mogaung. A column of Chinese troops and the American "Galahad Force" secretly crossed over the Kumon range, and captured the airfield outside the city of Myitkyina on 17 May, before the surprised defenders could organise resistance[1]. Artillery and engineer reinforcements were immediately

[1] *Campaign in Burma*, a booklet produced by SEAC.

flown in to the captured airfield and soon there were five all-weather airfields in operation around Myitkyina. But the Japanese troops defending the city put up a stout resistance, keeping at bay the attacking troops. In the meantime, the Special Force, the 3rd Indian Division, had destroyed many Japanese supply dumps and cut the road and railway from Mogaung to Mandalay. As already related in the previous volume, the Special Force in conjunction with the Chinese troops had captured Mogaung on 26 June, while Kamaing fell to the Chinese on 16 June.

The Chinese army from Yunnan had also started advancing towards Lashio in the third week of April. Composed of about 200,000 men and guided by a United States Military Mission attached to it, this Army started crossing the Salween on the night of 10/11 May. On the demand of Generalissimo Chiang Kai-shek, it was arranged to supply four divisions of this army by air from India, and 13 Dakota planes were transferred from the Troops Carrier Command to the 14th United States Army Air Forces for the purpose. But the dogged and fierce resistance of the Japanese garrison of Myitkyina continued. The siege dragged on day after day and week after week, in spite of the terrible pounding of the city by guns firing at the closest range and repeated bombardments from the air. It was not till 3 August 1944, when the siege had lasted 79 days, that Myitkyina fell finally to the Allied troops.

Throughout these bitter battles on the Northern and Central fronts, both the High Commands had played their cards confidently and well. Even in the black days of early April when the Japanese *31st Division* was pressing perilously close to the Assam Railway and Dimapur, the South-East Asia Command had not diverted any unit from the Northern front for defending the railway. Lieut.-General Stilwell had indeed seemed worried and had offered to send back some troops; but that would have inevitably weakened the offensive on the Northern front; hence Lieut.-General Slim, General Officer Commanding-in-Chief, Fourteenth Army, declined the offer[2].

The columns of Special Force, too, were allowed to continue their attacks against the communications of the Japanese *18th Division* facing Lieut.-General Stilwell, instead of being directed to operate westwards, towards the Chindwin, to afford some relief to the hard-pressed Imphal garrison[3]. The Japanese General Mutaguchi, General Officer Commanding-in-Chief, *15th Army*, similarly, tried to

---

[2] General Stilwell, however, assumed responsibility for the defence of his Line of Communication as far west as Nazira—Wakching, and probably sent a few Chinese light tanks to Jorhat. File No. 601/8511/H.

[3] After the war, General Slim has stated that he should have ordered the Special Force to operate westwards against the rear of the Japanese forces attacking Imphal and Kohima, and that this would have produced better results than those obtained by the Special Force operating northwards.

combat the Special Force by means of his Line of Communication troops only, assessing correctly that the decisive battle was being fought around Kohima and Imphal and no diversion of forces from there must be attempted to cope with the Special Force.

DETERMINATION OF FUTURE STRATEGY

In the summer of 1944, once again, the old controversy about the purpose and direction of strategy in the South-East Asia theatre came prominently to the surface. There was, firstly, the view that the best way to defeat Japan was to keep China in the war and use her resources for air offensive against the island empire. The protagonists of this view sincerely believed that all that was necessary was to maintain the air-link to China and to develop the land route northwards, and not waste energy and resources on the reconquest of Burma. On the other hand there was another view, earnestly held, that even for keeping China well supplied, it would be essential to reconquer the whole of Burma, defeat Japanese opposition there, and restore the old Burma Road for maintaining a steady and even outflow of supplies to China. This view laid emphasis on the reoccupation of Burma as a primary step, and for this a two-pronged attack was necessary, one amphibious for the capture of Rangoon and march upwards to free the Burma Road, and the other overland through Assam to strike a mortal blow against the Japanese army in Central Burma. Lieut.-General Stilwell and the American Chiefs of Staff advocated the former approach whereas Lord Mountbatten and the South-East Asia Command held strongly to the other line of action. The British Chiefs of Staff also laid stress on the amphibious strategy and gave priority to the reconquest of Burma as a measure for helping China.

These differences of strategy had long persisted; hence Lord Mountbatten despatched the Axiom Mission, with Maj.-General Wedemeyer at its head, to London and Washington to explain the view-point of the South-East Asia Command and get directions from the Combined Chiefs of Staff.

During its visit to London and Washington in March/April, the Axiom Mission pressed the British view-point for acceptance by the Combined Chiefs of Staff. It favoured the development of the Myitkyina area as a major air base and road terminus, where airfields and supply dumps were to be constructed. From there, petrol, ammunition etc. would be flown over to China for the American bomber squadrons based there, so that they might carry out the strategic bombing of Japan. At the same time, the initiative in Burma was to be retained by continuing attacks against the Japanese, southwards towards Mandalay. The Myitkyina area, vital for both the air route and the land route into China, would be safe from Japanese attacks only if they were kept on the defensive throughout, and the whole of Burma was recaptured. For this, an amphibious assault on Rangoon would be necessary, after which the Japanese would be driven out of Burma and the route to China made safe.

Lieut.-General Stilwell was "not in favour of the amphibious operation, in any case, because it would open another front and would take resources away from the opening of overland communications to China"[4]. Behind this view may have been the suspicion that the British desired the reconquest of Burma due to Imperial interests and considerations of prestige. This view-point was forcefully represented by the independent mission sent at the same time by Lieut.-General Stilwell to Washington without consulting Lord Mountbatten. The American Chiefs of Staff supported Lieut.-General Stilwell's views, saying that the opening of overland communications with China was of great importance. If the Japanese were cleared from the area, the Burma Road could carry much needed supplies to China, even though in limited quantities. Moreover, it would then be possible to build a pipeline alongside the road from Burma to China and thus supply large quantities of fuel required by the United States bombers based there. They did not favour the amphibious operations against Rangoon and declared that all the available American amphibious assault craft were being sent to the Pacific for General MacArthur's attack on the Philippines. The British amphibious craft were still required for war in Europe, so the assault on Rangoon appeared impracticable then.

The Axiom Mission countered these arguments by pointing out the difficulties of maintaining and supplying troops in upper Burma from Assam. The advance till then had been carried out against the grain of the country, along the solitary Ledo Road. If a further advance was desired to link up with the Chinese forces in Yunnan, and the old Burma Road was to be rebuilt, the Ledo Road would have to carry supplies to the advancing armies as well as immense quantities of engineer stores for building the Burma Road. The proposition was impracticable, unless the advancing troops were supplied largely by air, and for this several hundred more transport planes would be required. The other party countered these arguments by expressing their willingness to send the additional planes required. On 25 March 1944, General Arnold, head of the American air force, offered to send four Special Combat Cargo Groups, each containing 100 Dakotas, and also four Air Commandos, the reinforcements to begin arriving in SEAC from July 1944[5]. In effect,

---

[4] Report by the Supreme Allied Commander, South-East Asia to the Combined Chiefs of Staff (or Mountbatten's *Report*), para 223.
[5] *Ibid*, p. 55.

Admiral the Lord Louis Mountbatten of Burma, Supreme Allied Commander, South-East Asia Command

Lieut.-General Sir Oliver Leese
Commander ALFSEA

Lieut.-General (later Field Marshal) Sir William Slim, Commander Fourteenth Army

Lieut.-General
Sir Geoffry Scoones
Commander IV Corps
16 Nov. 43—8 Dec. 44

Lieut.-General
R. A. Wheeler (U.S. Army)
Deputy Supreme Allied
Commander

this offer killed the proposal for the amphibious assault on Rangoon in 1944, and decided the case virtually in favour of Lieut.-General Stilwell's point of view. But Mr. Churchill kept pressing for an amphibious assault against Burma, and even when it was clearly realised that sufficient forces and equipment would not be assembled for retaking Rangoon, he insisted that a minor amphibious operation "of some kind" should be undertaken before the end of 1944.[6]

On 24 March 1944, Lord Mountbatten was asked by the British Joint Chiefs of Staff for his views and comments on the proposal to concentrate on reopening the land route into China. Replying on 14 April, the Supreme Allied Commander reiterated the argument that both the air route and land route into China would be in constant danger from a new Japanese offensive unless the Japanese armies in Burma were decisively defeated, either by a major battle in the Shwebo plain or the recapture of Rangoon from the sea. But, in view of the opposition to his plans, Lord Mountbatten proposed that the new directive about to be issued to him might be so phrased as to leave him a wide discretion, and the aim be defined as the development, broadening and protection of the air-link to China.

During the rest of April and May, signals flashed to and fro between Washington, London, Kandy and Lieut.-General Stilwell's headquarters in the jungle. General Stilwell was also invited to put forward his views, and General Arnold demanded to know how the several hundred extra transport planes promised by him were to be used in South-East Asia Command. General Stilwell again pressed for the reopening of a road from the Myitkyina area into China, and the construction of a pipeline alongside it. Lord Mountbatten pointed out once again the impossibility of using the Ledo Road to carry supplies for the large forces fighting the Japanese in the Shwebo plain, and at the same time to transport along the road thousands of tons of engineer stores required for building the road and the pipeline to China. The land battle in the Shwebo plain was necessary, in any case, to protect Myitkyina through which both the air and the land routes would pass. Many of the requirements of the battle, such as heavy guns and tanks, would inevitably have to come by road. The remaining capacity of the Ledo Road, even when augmented by the air transport promised by General Arnold, would hardly be adequate for reconstructing the road and the pipeline. On the other hand, comparatively much smaller tonnage of stores would be required for developing the Myitkyina area as a major air base and for flying over from there to China the petrol and bombs needed by the American bombers.

[6] *Ibid*, p. 56.

The crucial debate was still continuing when the capture of Myitkyina airfield on 17 May compelled an urgent decision. It was necessary to determine quickly whether the newly captured area should be supplied with stores for building more aerodromes and more houses for an air base, or whether road-construction parties and equipment should be sent there. Faced with the critical decision, the Combined Chiefs of Staff issued a directive to the Supreme Allied Commander, South-East Asia, on 3 June 1944, laying down the following two tasks for the Command:[7]—

> (a) "To develop, maintain, broaden and protect the air link to China, in order to provide the maximum and timely stock of petrol and stores to China in support of Pacific operations.
>
> (b) So far as is consistent with the above, to press advantages against the enemy, by exerting maximum effort, ground and air, particularly during the current monsoon season, and in pressing such advantages, to be prepared to exploit the development of overland communications to China. All these operations must be dictated by the forces at present available, or firmly allocated to South-East Asia Command."

The first part of the directive gave to Lord Mountbatten, as desired, a fair degree of latitude in the actual operations to be undertaken. But the addition of the second part pointed to the inclination of the Combined Chiefs of Staff in favour of General Stilwell's strategy. But it was an important concession that the protection of the airlift was made the first task, and the road-link was to be forged only if circumstances permitted.

THE REORGANISATION OF GROUND COMMAND

Apart from the determination of future strategy, the problem of command set up for ground forces occupied Lord Mountbatten's attention during the summer of 1944.

It had been agreed in the autumn of 1943 that the Chinese Expeditionary Force on entering Burma from Yunnan would be placed under the South-East Asia Command. Since these forces and those under Lieut.-General Stilwell were both working their way to join each other, it was considered advantageous to give him overall command over the entire area and all the troops in it. On 19 May, General Giffard recommended this step to Lord Mountbatten but added that since Lieut.-General Stilwell would then be commanding almost an army, he should be

---
[7] *Ibid*, p. 64.

placed directly under the General Officer Commanding-in-Chief, 11th Army Group, analogous to the position of the General Officer Commanding-in-Chief, Fourteenth Army, Lieut.-General Slim. The next day Lieut.-General Stilwell himself brought up the same point, reminding the Supreme Allied Command that his troops were about to reach Kamaing, and that then he (Stilwell) would be released from the agreement to be subordinate to General Slim and would come under Lord Mountbatten direct. But the latter did not like an arrangement whereby he would have to deal with two independent commanders of land forces, namely General Giffard and Lieut.-General Stilwell. He sought to solve the tangle by making General Giffard the Commander-in-Chief of Allied Land Forces in the theatre, but was dissuaded from that step by his American senior officers, Maj.-General Wheeler and Maj.-General Wedemeyer, who told him that General Stilwell, as Deputy Supreme Allied Commander, considered himself senior to General Giffard and would not accept being placed under him in any case.[8] The subject was taken up in London also by Lieut.-General Pownall, the Chief of Staff to the Supreme Allied Commander, who was sent there on a mission.

Lieut.-General Pownall was instructed to represent the difficulties involved in the Supreme Allied Commander having two independent land force commanders under him, and to press for relieving Lieut.-General Stilwell of some of his numerous posts. But while these representations were being made, on 20 June 1944 General Stilwell's wish was fulfilled, and he was placed parallel to General Giffard—directly under Lord Mountbatten.[9] This arrangement was continued during July, but when in August Lord Mountbatten visited London he pressed strongly for setting up a unified command for the ground forces on an Allied basis. His headquarters was not properly constituted for deciding purely army problems, and he had still to deal with one army commander, General Stilwell, direct and with the other, General Slim, through General Giffard, Commander-in-Chief, 11th Army Group. Hence he insisted on reorganising the command of land forces by taking in some American officers and changing the Headquarters 11th Army Group into Headquarters Allied Land Forces, South-East Asia. The British Chiefs of Staff promised to consider the subject in consultation with their American counterparts, and in the meanwhile Lieut.-General Sir Oliver Leese was tentatively selected as the Commander-in-Chief of the proposed Allied Land Forces Command. But the reorganisation was not carried out while General Stilwell remained in the theatre. In October 1944, however, he was recalled to become the Commanding General, Army Ground Forces in the United States, and his numerous posts were divided up

[8] *Ibid*, p. 62.
[9] *Ibid*, p. 65.

between several officers. On 12 November 1944, Lieut.-General Wheeler succeeded him as the Deputy Supreme Allied Commander while retaining his old post as Principal Administrative Officer, South-East Asia Command. Major-General Wedemeyer, the Deputy Chief of Staff to the Supreme Allied Commander, was promoted to the rank of Lieutenant-General and posted as Commander of the United States Forces in the China theatre and Chief of Staff to the Generalissimo. The India-Burma theatre, which was now separated from the China theatre, was taken over by Lieut.-General Sultan, who also took up the command of the Northern Combat Area Command. In line with these changes, the Headquarters Allied Land Forces, South-East Asia, was created on 12 November 1944, and Lieut.-General Sir Oliver Leese took over the new appointment as its Commander-in-Chief.[10]

REORGANISATION OF THE AIR COMMAND

The defeat of the Japanese offensive against Imphal and Kohima had been greatly facilitated by the constant air strikes against the Japanese troops and their lines of communication. As a matter of fact it would be no exaggeration to say that the Allied victory would not have been possible without the assistance given by the air forces. Still, the Supreme Allied Commander felt that the standard of co-operation between the air forces and the armies was not all that might be desired.[11] Closer co-operation appeared possible after a little reorganisation. Moreover, the air forces in South-East Asia Command were still organised and deployed according to a strategy which was basically defensive, and had been forced on the Allies since the disastrous retreat from Burma in 1942. The collapse of the Japanese offensive in 1944 had opened out new vistas of an Allied offensive on a major scale. In accordance with the new prospects, it was necessary to reorganise and reorientate the air forces in the theatre so that they might change over from a static and defensive role to a mobile and offensive one.

As a preliminary, a memorandum was prepared in the Headquarters South-East Asia Command laying down over again the principles of co-operation between the ground and air forces on the basis of the lessons learnt in the recent campaigns in North Africa. The techniques evolved in the United Kingdom for air support during the invasion of Normandy were also considered and incorporated. In June 1944, this memorandum was approved by the Supreme Allied Commander and was issued to the subordinate army and air

[10] After these changes, South-East Asia Command was organised as shown in the Chart at Appendix 1.
[11] Mountbatten's *Report*, p. 59.

formations for their guidance.[12] At the same time, an Inter-Services Committee was appointed under Air Vice-Marshal Whitworth-Jones to study the problem of air support on the spot in Burma and to make recommendations for improving it. Its work had reference only to the Central front and Arakan, since the Northern Combat Area Command was being run by Lieut.-General Stilwell along different lines suited to American methods and technique.

While the Whitworth-Jones Committee was conducting its investigations, some reorganisation was carried out in June mainly in relation to the air support for the Northern Combat Area Command. On 20 June, the Northern Air Sector Force, which had provided air support to the Northern Combat Area Command, was dissolved and a 10th United States Army·Air Force was set up. This air force assumed responsibility for protecting the Assam airfields, the air-ferry route from there into China and the Myitkyina air base, and for supporting the ground forces in the Northern Combat Area Command. The Troop Carrier Command also was abolished in the same month, and its transport planes were divided between the 10th United States Army Air Force and the Third Tactical Air Force.

The Whitworth-Jones Committee submitted its report in August 1944. Its main recommendations were:[13]

"(a) that 221 and 224 Groups should be organised on a mobile basis, and relieved of the responsibilities of static defence of vital areas such as Calcutta and Chittagong;

(b) that mobile signals and radar equipment adapted to conditions in Burma should be developed and placed at the disposal of the mobile groups;

(c) that the land forces allotted to offensive operations should be closely co-ordinated under an Army headquarters and be relieved as far as possible of preoccupation with administrative responsibilities in back areas;

(d) that an Allied Commander of all land forces in Burma should be appointed;

(e) that the respective headquarters of land and air forces required to operate jointly should be adjacent, so that joint planning and joint control of day-to-day operations could be facilitated; and that the land and air commanders should both be prepared to sacrifice some of their respective interests so as to gain the advantages which a Joint Headquarters would provide."

The report was approved by Lord Mountbatten and became the basis of army-air co-operation in his command. All the recommendations were ordered to be implemented without delay, except item

[12] *Ibid.*
[13] *Ibid*, p. 78.

(*d*), which involved a wider question and was being taken up with the Combined Chiefs of Staff, as already related.

Further reorganisation of the air command in South-East Asia took place in October 1944.[14] This reorganisation affected only the machinery for air supply for the ground forces in the Arakan and the Central front, General Stilwell's Northern Combat Area Command being supported and supplied by the 10th United States Army Air Force independently. Since the dissolution of the Troop Carrier Command in June, the load of air-supply as well as tactical support for the Fourteenth Army had fallen on the Third Tactical Air Force. As the volume of air-supply continued to expand, the Third Tactical Air Force was faced with unduly heavy burdens. The tactical air support of a large army in continuous battle was itself an onerous task requiring single-minded attention. At the same time, the daily supply of the armies on the move, the aerial evacuation of casualties and the organisation of airborne operations had to be undertaken, and this could not be effectively carried out by an organisation consisting of air force officers only. In October 1944, therefore, a joint army and air force organisation was set up at Comilla. There were two distinct components in the new machinery, viz., the Combat Cargo Task Force, and the Combined Army Air Transport Organisation. The Combat Cargo Task Force was manned by both British and American officers, and was headed by Brig.-General Frederick W. Evans, who was made directly responsible to Maj.-General Stratemeyer, Air Commander of the Eastern Air Command. The Combat Cargo Task Force controlled all the American and British transport squadrons available for supporting the 11th Army Group. The Combined Army Air Transport Organisation was placed under Colonel I. A. Dawson who was responsible to General Giffard, and to Lieut.-General Leese on the formation of the Allied Land Forces, South-East Asia. The Combined Army Air Transport Organisation replaced Headquarters Fourteenth Army as the central controlling authority for all details of military organisation behind air supply, and became the clearing house for all demands for supply droppings by air, placed by the ground forces. Since the demands of the armies for air supply almost always exceeded the capacity of the transport fleets, one of the most important functions of the Combined Army Air Transport Organisation came to be the allotment of priorities for the supply drops. Moreover, the organisation was given control over the Rear Airfields Maintenance Organisation also.

With the birth of this new organisation of the Combat Cargo Task Force and the Combined Army Air Transport Organisation, it became possible to disband the Third Tactical Air Force, and to substitute for it a smaller machinery named Headquarters Royal Air

[14] *Ibid*, p. 86.

Force, Bengal/Burma. Air Marshal W. A. Coryton, who had replaced Air Marshal Baldwin as the commander of the Third Tactical Air Force on 15 August 1944, became the Air Officer Commanding, Royal Air Force, Bengal/Burma, and Deputy Air Commander, Eastern Air Command. The administrative and other non-operational functions of the Headquarters Third Tactical Air Force were taken up by the Headquarters Royal Air Force Bengal/Burma. But the 221 and 224 Royal Air Force Groups, which were subordinate formations of the Third Tactical Air Force, were now placed directly under the Eastern Air Command. The two Groups still operated in support of the ground troops on the Imphal front and Arakan as before, and the Headquarters 221 Group at Imphal and the advanced Headquarters 224 Group at Cox's Bazar continued unchanged.

In addition to these important changes, October 1944 saw the formation of a Headquarters Base Air Forces, South-East Asia. In that month, the Air Command South-East Asia had to move down from Delhi to Kandy, hence it became necessary to set up a new machinery to maintain close contacts with the Government of India.[15] The Headquarters Base Air Forces, South-East Asia, Commanded by Air Marshal Sir Leslie Hollinghurst, was placed directly under the Allied Air Commander-in-Chief and was charged with the extensive and intricate negotiations which had to be carried on with the Government of India and the General Headquarters (India) concerning the development of airfields etc., for the air forces. Matters directly concerned with the operations and the higher administrative control of the air forces were still decided by the Headquarters Air Command, South-East Asia.

These extensive reorganisations of the air command in South-East Asia greatly facilitated the subsequent major operations for the reconquest of Burma. The air forces in the theatre were now placed in a position to support a major offensive into Burma without confusion or dislocation.

[15] *Ibid.*

CHAPTER II

The Northern Sector—Allied Offensive and the Recapture of Ukhrul

THE GENERAL SITUATION

The high-level planning and reorganisation described in the last chapter produced no immediate effect on the operations in progress around the Imphal plain. As described below, bitter fighting continued along the whole front for dislodging and destroying the Japanese troops, from the Ukhrul area in the north to the Tiddim road in the south.

By the end of the third week of June 1944, the monsoon had fully set in. Rain fell in sheets from leaden skies, averaging about sixteen inches per month in the Kabaw Valley and the Naga hills around Ukhrul. The tracks were washed away. Portions of the road slid bodily down the slopes and rested at the bottom of the *Khud*. The remainder was turned into a sea of slimy mud over which movement of vehicles was all but impossible. Malaria and dysentery raged in the wet, dripping jungles. Leeches, thin as a thread and hardly visible, dropped down from the trees and bushes on unsuspecting men and animals and fattened on the blood of their victims. To the Allied and the Japanese soldiers alike, it was a grim prospect, fighting nature and the enemy at the same time. The Japanese had already suffered terrible casualties and were depressed by their first major reverse of the war. Their supply and medical arrangements had completely broken down and men were dying in camps and on the roadside like flies. Their only hope was that fighting would die down during monsoon, enabling them to reorganise their shattered formations and obtain reliefs and reinforcements.

But an unpleasant surprise was in store for the Japanese, as the Supreme Allied Commander had ordered the full tempo of war to be maintained even during the monsoon, a radical departure from the existing practice of withdrawing into camps behind the line when bad weather came. His objective was not so much to capture territory as to inflict the maximum casualties on the disorganised Japanese troops, give them no opportunity to re-group and re-form their forces, and to annihilate the *31st Division* which had been badly mauled at Kohima and was then withdrawing precipitately over poor mountain tracks made worse by the monsoon, in the

Lieut.-General
Sir Montagu Stopford
Commander XXXIII Corps

Lieut.-General
Sir Frank Messervy
Commander IV Corps
8 Dec. 44—1 Nov. 45

Air Marshal
Sir John Baldwin
Air Commander
Third Tactical Air Force

Rear-Admiral
B. C. S. Martin
Flag Officer
Force "W"

Lieut.-General
F. I. S. Tuker
Commander IV Corps
14 July 45—18 Aug. 45

Major-General
C. G. G. Nicholson
Commander
2nd British Division

Major-General
G. C. Evans
Commander
7th Indian Division
29 Dec. 44—7 Feb. 46

Major-General
C. C. Fowkes
Commander
11th East African Division

general direction of Ukhrul. Part of the division retreated eastwards from Kohima along the Jessami track, turning south at Tsozipfemai for Ukhrul. Other Japanese parties withdrew down the main Imphal road from Kohima up to Tuphema and then turned eastwards by the Tuphema-Kharasom track. A composite force of two battalions, sadly depleted in strength, had been left behind by Major-General Miyazaki, Commander of the Japanese *31st Division Infantry Group*, to delay the advance of the XXXIII Corps from Kohima towards Imphal. But subsequent to link-up between the two corps at milestone 109, these Japanese troops ultimately slunk back into the hills to the west and east of the road.

On the other sectors of the Central Front, the Japanese were still fighting bitterly to reach Imphal. Their *15th Division* was ranged in a wide arc stretching from the Kohima-Imphal road in the north to the Imphal-Tamu road to the east of Imphal. The division was divided into three main groups. One group, composed of about three battalions, had been holding back the attacks of the 5th Indian Division from Imphal towards Kohima, and had on 22nd June withdrawn into the hills to the east of the road. The second group of about five battalions had been trying to reach Imphal along the Litan road and the Iril river valley. Defeated in its efforts by the 20th Indian Division, this group was still holding on near MS 18 on the Imphal-Ukhrul track and along the bend of the Iril river near Chawai and was deeply entrenched in the hilly country before Ukhrul. On the road Palel-Tamu, two battalions comprising the third group of the Japanese *15th Division* were operating with the *Yamamoto Group* of the *33rd Division*. This force, too, had suffered heavy casualties but was still trying to force its way to Imphal by mounting determined attacks repeatedly with the help of considerable artillery and a few light tanks. Finally, the main strength of the *33rd Division* was still deployed in the southern sector. Consisting of the flower of the Japanese army in Burma, these troops were still attacking furiously in the area of Bishenpur, with the object of breaking through to Imphal. It had received reinforcements of four battalions recently from the *15th Division*, the *53rd Division* and the *54th Division*, and, although the reinforcements too had got depleted by casualties, the *33rd Division* was confident of holding its position for several weeks.

THE ALLIED PLAN

The weakening of Japanese resistance in the northern sector was obvious. The Allied commanders appreciated that if the beaten Japanese units were pursued vigorously, their retreat would be turned into a rout. An immediate advance would encounter far less opposition and produce much smaller casualties than might be involved in an offensive after the Japanese had gained their balance again. Within a few hours of the reopening of the Kohima-Imphal road, therefore, the commander of the XXXIII Corps visited the commander of the IV Corps at Imphal and consultations began immediately for further operations. To consolidate his hold on the newly-opened road and prevent fresh Japanese attacks against it, Lieutenant-General Stopford realised that it would be necessary to clear up the Japanese remnants from the hills bordering the road. At the same time a drive towards Ukhrul was indicated in order to maintain pursuit and inflict maximum losses on the retreating Japanese forces.

The general military situation at the moment was that fierce fighting had been going on in the Litan road sector and Japanese troops, based on Ukhrul, were trying desperately to break through to Imphal. Meanwhile the 20th Indian Division had carried out a double thrust by the 80th and the 100th Indian Infantry Brigades as an approach march to Ukhrul. The 100th Indian Infantry Brigade was still battling near the Saddle (RK 5878) area along the Ukhrul road, but the 80th Indian Infantry Brigade had advanced in a wide sweep and was holding the upper reaches of the Iril river near Chawai. At the same time, the cross-country marches of the 23rd Long Range Penetration Brigade had carried it to the hills immediately north of Ukhrul. 55 Column of the brigade was operating in the area of Kharasom, 60 Column had reached Tusom Khulen and 56 Column was fighting near Somra. Of the brigades of the 2nd British Division, the 4th Infantry Brigade was holding the stretch of the Dimapur-Imphal road from MS 69 to MS 94 with Brigade Headquarters at Karong; the 5th Infantry Brigade was stationed between MS 94 and MS 102 with Brigade Headquarters at MS 101; and the 6th Infantry Brigade was between MS 102 and 109, with its Headquarters at MS 108.[1] The 114th Indian Infantry Brigade of the 7th Indian Division was located at Kohima. The 161st Indian Infantry Brigade, which had originally formed part of the 5th Indian Division, was ordered to move to Imphal. It reverted to the command of the 5th Indian Division and concentrated at Imphal by 26 June 1944.[2] Similarly, the 89th Indian Infantry Brigade was sent up from Imphal and rejoined its parent unit, the 7th Indian Division, on the morning of 27 June.

The plan evolved after consultations between the two Corps Commanders, visualised the continuation of operations to mop up the Japanese remnants near the road, and at the same time provided for operations for the recapture of Ukhrul. The 21st Indian Division, consisting only of the 268th Indian Lorried Infantry Brigade and 45

---

[1] XXXIII Corps Operation Order No. 6 dated 25 June 1944.
[2] 161st Indian Infantry Brigade Movement Order No. 1 dated 24 June 1944.

Cavalry, was allotted the task of maintaining patrols along the track from the Kohima area to Jessami and Kharasom and of protecting the road from Kohima to Maram. The 2nd British Division was ordered to destroy the stray parties of Japanese troops in the hills on both sides of the Kohima-Imphal road from Maram to the boundary with the IV Corps. For the recapture of Ukhrul, five brigades were detailed to make convergent attacks from three directions. The 23rd Long Range Penetration Brigade was to continue its advance along three parallel routes. Most of the columns were to move via Chingjui and Paowi or via Kongai and Longbi Kachui. But two columns were to advance east on Saiyapaw and cut the main line of communication of the Japanese units holding Ukhrul. From the north-west, the 33rd Indian Infantry Brigade (of the 7th Indian Division) was to start from Maram on 27 June and advance on Ukhrul via Oinam and Tallin. The 89th Indian Infantry Brigade was to move from Kangpokpi almost due east to Chawai and Khunthak and attack Ukhrul. The 80th Indian Infantry Brigade (of 20th Indian Division), which had already reached the Chawai area, was to wait there till the arrival of 89th Indian Infantry Brigade, and then to operate in a south-easterly direction in order to threaten the rear of the Japanese forces opposing the 100th Indian Infantry Brigade. As a result of this manoeuvre by 80th Brigade, it was expected that the 100th Brigade would be able to push forward and occupy Finch's Corner (RK 7589) from where a detachment was to be sent forward to hold Gamnon.[3] With all these five Indian brigades closing in on them, the Japanese, it was expected, would be forced to evacuate Ukhrul hurriedly or else would be encircled and annihilated.

Most of the units detailed for the capture of Ukhrul were already under the XXXIII Corps and Headquarters IV Corps was still busy with the battles in the Palel and the Bishenpur sectors, hence the former was made responsible for the intended operation. To secure unity of command, the 20th Indian Division (except the 32nd Brigade) also was placed under Lieut.-General Stopford with effect from 0800 hours on 30 June 1944. The boundary between the two Corps was laid down. At first it ran from Aishan southwards to the bend of the Iril river, then along the river to Wakhong and then westward to Mailbung and Sengmai and onwards to Langga. But from 30 June, they readjusted it to run from Langga eastwards to Khurkhul and Sengmai, thence to the bridge at RK 389683, bending southwards to Imphal Truel, along the Truel to RK 3442 and finally eastwards to Akang Khulen and Meiti. The XXXIII Corps took charge of all operations north of this line.

---

[3] IV Corps Operations, 8 March to 31 July 1944.

MOPPING UP ALONG THE KOHIMA ROAD

After the link-up between the XXXIII Corps and the IV Corps on 22 June there were many stray Japanese parties roaming about in the hills on both sides of the Kohima-Imphal road. These troops belonged to either the *Miyazaki Force* of the *31st Division*, or were elements of the *15th Division*. The *Miyazaki Force* had consisted originally of *1* and *5 Companies* of the *58th Japanese Regiment, 1st Battalion 124th Japanese Regiment* and the *1st Battalion 138th Japanese Regiment* with some artillery and engineer troops, but after the fierce battles around Kohima and along the Imphal road this unit was reduced to only 500 fighting troops. The force from the *15th Japanese Division* had been made up of the *2nd Battalion 60th Japanese Regiment, 3rd Battalion 60th Japanese Regiment* and *3rd Battalion 67th Japanese Regiment*. This force had been reduced to about 750 men only by battle casualties and the ravages of disease during the fighting in April, May, and June.[4] They were no longer a well organised and concentrated formation but were cut up into small roving bands each trying individually to make its way towards Ukhrul.

Operations against these Japanese parties started immediately after the reopening of the road on 22 June 1944. The 21st Indian Division was operating in the northern sector of the road between Maram and Kohima. The units of the 268th Indian Lorried Brigade were stationed along the road and on the jeep tracks to Jessami and Kharasom and started intensive patrolling. But the Japanese had already cleared out from this area. The Indian patrols failed to find any Japanese troops in spite of their extensive patrolling, and consequently consolidated their hold on the area without any incident.

Southwards from Maram, the brigades of the 2nd British Division had been ordered to undertake operations to mop up the stray Japanese parties. On 23 June, the 6th British Brigade, which had been leading the 2nd British Division in the final phase of the thrust down the Imphal road, was concentrated in the area of MS 108 except the 1st Royal Berkshire Regiment, which was then fighting against a Japanese party of about 175 men near Point 5797, two miles east of the road. With the help of artillery fire 1 Royal Berks easily captured Point 5797 on 23 June killing at least 50 of the defending troops. The battalion then opened fire against the village of Thumion Khulen just near the hill which was still occupied by Japanese troops. Early on the morning of 24 June, 1 Royal Welch Fusiliers attacked and occupied Thumion Khulen after slight resistance.[5] The defenders retired hurriedly eastwards in the direction of Aishan

---

[4] Account of Operations of XXXIII Corps, Vol. II. File No. 601/8758/H.
[5] *Ibid.*

leaving their equipment and about a dozen casualties behind them. The next day the villages of Thumion Khongjai and Thumion Khunou had been evacuated by the Japanese. These along with Point 5247, were occupied by the Allied forces without opposition. Continuing their sweeps and patrols, by 29 June, the units of the 6th Brigade visited the villages of Hengjang and Heinoupok and met with no Japanese troops in either locality. The Japanese withdrawal continued and contacts with their parties became more and more infrequent. On 1 July, the 6th Brigade moved to the Maram area and became responsible for the security of the road from MS 80 to MS 91.

Meanwhile the 5th Brigade was operating similarly in the area of MS 100. Changobung was occupied by 1 Worc R who captured a fair amount of arms and equipment. All the Japanese troops encountered in the area were found suffering greatly from the shortage of supplies and the complete lack of medical facilities. Many of them were reduced to skeletons and were described as being "at the end of their tether."[6] Mopping up operations continued until 26 June, when the 5th Brigade started to move down into Imphal for rest. The move was completed by 28 June and from the next day the brigade assumed responsibility for the security of the Kohima-Imphal road from MS 110 to MS 124.

At the same time, the 4th Brigade was carrying out patrols from Karong. These patrols encountered a Japanese position on the ridge north of Chalhang. By 27 June, some of these troops holding a half-dug position covering the track to Chalhang were thrown out. They, however, held on to their bunkers at Chalhang. The next day another strong Japanese position was discovered at Shorbung. The Allied ground troops experienced considerable difficulty in attacking these positions due to the incessant rains which reduced the indifferent tracks into ribbons of mud.[7] Attacks from the air were, therefore, directed against the Shorbung position on 29 and 30 June, but without perceptible effect. The attacking troops were tired after the strenuous battles of the last several weeks, and by 5 July all the units of the 4th Brigade were withdrawn to Kigwema, being replaced by 2 Recce Regiment and 1 Royal Welch Fusiliers of the 6th British Brigade with 10 Field Artillery Regiment in support. This force was named the Dalforce after its commander, Colonel C. Dalby, and took over the charge of operations from MS 91 to MS 110, including the Shorbung area. On 5 July, further air attacks were made against Shorbung by 113 Squadron RAF and direct hits were obtained on the Japanese positions. The next day a company of 1 Royal Welch Fusiliers moving towards Shorbung from the south

[6] *Ibid.*
[7] *Ibid.*

encountered unexpectedly a party of Japanese troops at Hengjang[8], which was eventually occupied. After the second air attack the Japanese evacuated Shorbung and also the villages of Ngatan and Preyatemei from where their presence had been reported by the Naga villagers. On 8 July, therefore, the patrols of Dalforce found all the three villages clear of the Japanese who had been finally pushed out of the area. Its task completed, the Dalforce was then withdrawn and was dispersed on 11 July.[9]

By the end of the first week of July 1944, therefore, mopping up operations along the Kohima-Imphal road were completed. The 2nd British Division was then allowed to take some time for training and rest. The 4th Brigade was then stationed at Kigwema, the 5th Brigade at Imphal and the rest of the division in the area of Maram.

THE RECAPTURE OF UKHRUL

After the reopening of the Kohima-Imphal road, the units of the 7th Indian Division took a few days to concentrate and complete preparations for the arduous march to Ukhrul. During the operations already described, Ukhrul had been used by the Japanese as one of their main supply bases. At this stage—after the opening of the Imphal-Kohima road—the retreating Japanese were naturally looking towards Ukhrul as the line of withdrawal to the Chindwin. The last stage of the battle for defeating the 'invade India' army was therefore to clear the Japanese from Ukhrul. Hence it was decided that while the units of the IV Corps should press against the Japanese along the axis of the Imphal-Ukhrul road, elements of the 7th Indian Division should come down upon Ukhrul from the north. At this time 33rd Indian Infantry Brigade of the 7th Indian Division was ordered to form a column and advance across country to Ukhrul from the north west. The 89th Brigade was in the Imphal area where it had joined forces with the 5th Indian Division and fought actions near Kanglatongbi. It was now ordered to move against Ukhrul from the west. The 23rd Long Range Penetration Brigade was to cover the eastern flank, while the 20th Indian Division was to attack from the south along the road. "It was thus planned to surround Ukhrul by blocking all the escape routes and then attack and kill the enemy who were holding it."[10]

The 7th Indian Division was also made responsible for the protection of the road from Kohima to Maram. However, on 23 June, the 33rd Indian Infantry Brigade and 25th Mountain Regiment (less one battery) took up positions at their starting line between MS 80

---

[8] On 29 June, patrols had visited Hengjang and found no Japanese there.
[9] Account of Operations, XXXIII Corps, *op. cit*.
[10] 7th Division History, 601/8445/H.

and MS 81, near Maram. The next day, Main Headquarters 7th Indian Division also arrived at Maram. The 161st Indian Infantry Brigade was concentrating at the same place preparatory to moving down to Imphal to rejoin the 5th Indian Division. The 114th Indian Infantry Brigade was ordered to assemble its units in the area north of Mao Songsang and then move on to Kohima for rest. It completed its move to Kohima by 2 July 1944, after a major land-slide at MS 51 on the Kohima-Imphal road had been cleared up.[11]

At the same time, the 89th Indian Infantry Brigade was concentrated at Kangpokpi under the orders of the 5th Indian Division. On the morning of 27 June, the 89th Brigade came under the command of the 7th Indian Division and 161st Brigade passed from its control to the 5th Indian Division. The advance of both the brigades was to be carried out by animal transport only, and orders were issued to include in the brigades only those men and mules who were in perfect physical trim.[12] Supplies were to be dropped from the air as required during the march. Landing strips for light aircraft were also to be constructed where convenient, so that Major-General Messervey, the commander of the 7th Indian Division, could visit the forward troops whenever necessary.

The 33rd Indian Infantry Brigade was at first scheduled to begin its advance on 26 June, but reconnaissance on 24 June showed that the Sangu Lok stream (RE 5434) was in spate due to the rains and could not be forded. The start was then postponed for 27 June, and in the meantime two bridges were quickly built over the stream. With the break of dawn on 27 June, both the 33rd Brigade and the 89th Brigade began their advance on Ukhrul from Maram and Kangpokpi areas, respectively. The 33rd Brigade crossed over the Sangu Lok stream by the new bridges, but was delayed in doing so.

The mules, 1400 of them, consumed the whole day in crossing the bridges, and the last animal did not get across until after dark.[13] By midnight of 27/28 June, however, the 33rd Brigade had reached Purul and there camped for the night. The 89th Brigade also experienced similar difficulties with its mules of the Mountain Battery and reached a position about three miles east of Aishan by nightfall. Both the brigades continued their advance on 28 June. 1 Queens remained at Purul, but the remainder of the 33rd Brigade passed through Oinam and reached the vicinity of Pt 7303 (RE 6227). Japanese resistance was still negligible, although a few shots were fired at 1 Burma as it entered Oinam. On 28 June, it was realised that the country ahead was too broken for the mountain artillery to traverse quickly, and, to avoid delaying the whole brigade, the brigade

---

[11] *Ibid.*
[12] War Diary of Headquarters 7th Indian Division, General Staff Branch.
[13] War Diary of Headquarters 33rd Indian Infantry Brigade, General Staff Branch.

commander was told to send back the 25 Mountain Artillery Regiment from Purul.[14] That day the 89th Brigade Headquarters reached RE 556005 just east of Chawai and the leading battalion, 1/11 Sikh, advanced up to the junction of the track and the stream at RK 595998. The King's Own Scottish Borderers was held up by a broken bridge at RE 500018.

The next day, 29 June 1944, the 89th Brigade and 4/8 Gurkha Rifles reached Mollen with one of the Gurkha companies sent forward to Leishan. The King's Own Scottish Borderers moved up from Yangnoi towards Mollen and 1/11 Sikh arrived at Luinem.[15] That day contact was established for the first time with 1 Devon of the 80th Indian Infantry Brigade of the 20th Indian Division near the nulla at RK 589993. The Japanese troops were not in evidence in the area and the Commander 89th Indian Infantry Brigade ordered to push on to Luithar and Lungshong if no considerable resistance was encountered before Ukhrul, in order to block the Japanese retreat from Sangshak. The 33rd Brigade crossed the Iril river higher up that day by means of a wooden bridge built by the sappers. A party of about 400 Japanese troops was reported by the villagers from Wasangphung and Tingshong just west of the Iril river. To attack them early the next morning 1st Burma Regiment was ordered to send two companies in that direction and one platoon of 4/1 Gurkha Rifles was sent to the track junction at RE 7620.[16] On 30 June, the 33rd Brigade received an "air drop" at RE 655215, but the planes were flying too high and too fast with the result that the supplies landed in a very wide area and only one-third of them could be collected.

Consequently, another supply drop effort was arranged for the next day and the advance for that day was postponed. The troops of the 33rd Brigade on 30 June moved forward from Ngamju and closed up on the east bank of the Iril river. The 89th Brigade that day arrived at Luinem where it received supplies dropped from the air. Some supplies were dropped at Leishan also the same day. A patrol of 1/11 Sikh went to Pharung and had a minor skirmish with a Japanese party there.

On 1 July 1944, General Frank Messervey, commander of the 7th Indian Division, informed the 33rd and the 89th Brigades that parties of Japanese rear-guards, four to five hundred strong, were still fighting around Priyatemei, Shorbung and Wasangphung. These rear-guards were likely to pull out soon for Ukhrul and Lungshong. The two brigades, therefore, were instructed to keep a watch on the expected withdrawal and to destroy the retreating Japanese troops

[14] *Ibid.*
[15] War Diary of Headquarters 7th Indian Division.
[16] War Diary of Headquarters 33rd Indian Infantry Brigade.

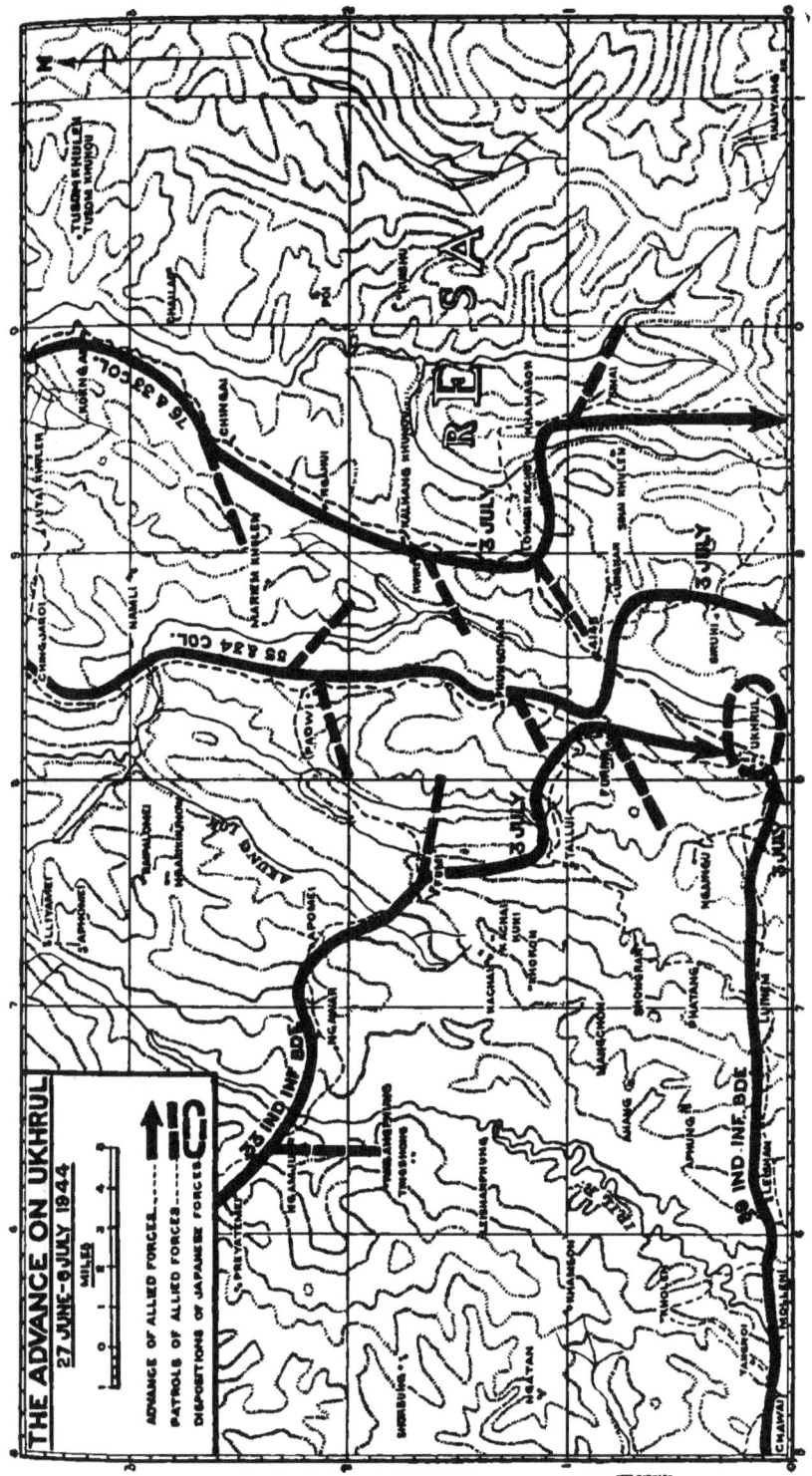

wherever possible.[17] The commander of the 33rd Brigade was authorised to slow down the rate of his advance if he thought it necessary to annihilate the stray parties of Japanese troops who might be in the villages in the area. The supply dropping from the air for the 33rd Brigade on 1 July was successful and the brigade collected enough rations and ammunition to be able to move forward again the next day.

While most of the brigade was busy collecting the supplies, a company of 4/1 Gurkha Rifles was sent forward to Ngawar, but the village was found clear of the Japanese. The 89th Brigade that day sent out patrols to Aphung and Phatang. The Brigade Headquarters and 4/8 Gurkha Rifles were at Luinem (RE 6901) and 2 King's Own Scottish Borderers was at RE 6701.[18] 1/11 Sikh marched off that morning for the final advance on Ukhrul with orders to occupy the hill astride the track at RE 7601, and if possible to get into Ukhrul itself. At 1430 hours on 1 July, the leading company of 1/11 Sikh encountered the first serious resistance from the Japanese defenders who were holding positions on both sides of the track running through a gorge at RE 7601.[19] Stiff fighting took place and two more companies were sent forward to force the passage, but the Japanese positions were sited with the usual skill and the battalion was unable to advance further that day. During the night of 1/2 July, the Japanese again started evacuating their positions but, at 0800 hours on 2 July, they launched a fierce but small-scale attack on 1/11 Sikh in order to cover their withdrawal. In view of this resistance a base was formed at the gorge held by 1 Sikh and 4/8 Gurkha Rifles while 2 King's Own Scottish Borderers remained behind at Luinem. The same day 1 Queen's and 1 Burma of the 33rd Brigade advanced to Apomei. The Brigade Headquarters and 4/1 Gurkha Rifles proceeded to RE 743185 and camped just east of the Akung Lok stream.[20]

On 3 July, the 33rd Brigade concentrated in the area of Tallui and the advance elements of the brigade established contact with 34 Column of the 23rd Long Range Penetration Brigade, one mile west of Khangairam. At the same time two companies of 4/8 Gurkha Rifles burst into Ukhrul from the south taking the Japanese completely by surprise. A third company of the Gurkhas went up to support the two forward companies, but by then the Japanese resistance had stiffened and intensive automatic fire was poured forth on the attacking Gurkha companies from Japanese bunker positions around the track junction to the south of Ukhrul. The next day the

---

[17] War Diary of Headquarters 7th Indian Division.
[18] War Diary of Headquarters 89th Indian Infantry Brigade, File No. 601/354/WD/Pt. 1.
[19] Ibid.
[20] War Diary of Headquarters 33rd Indian Infantry Brigade.

33rd Brigade Headquarters reached Furing and received supply droppings from the air.[21] Arrangements were at the same time completed for the units of the 23rd Brigade to block the tracks leading eastwards, while the 33rd Brigade advanced southwards towards Ukhrul. This arrangement, it was hoped, would trap a large party of about 400 Japanese troops who were still in the valley of the Thoubal river and were trying to retreat eastwards.

The other brigade, the 89th, meanwhile continued its thrust into south Ukhrul. 2 King's Own Scottish Borderers also advanced to the assistance of the companies of 4/8 Gurkha Rifles held up before the Japanese positions, but further progress was not practicable. A few minor positions were captured but the Japanese held on to the hillcrest overlooking the area. Patrolling was carried out by the 89th Brigade units to the south also.

On 5 July, the 33rd Brigade Headquarters and its forward units reached a position on to the main track only two miles north of Ukhrul. Following it up, 1st Burma Regiment took over Furing and 1 Queens reached the area of RE 7515. The general situation remained unchanged. The Japanese held the northern end of Ukhrul and were also strongly entrenched in the fort and in the south-east corner of the town. Their positions were prepared with an excellent tactical eye and they commanded all the tracks approaching the town. As a result the 89th Brigade could make little progress for yet another day. Between 1800 hours and 1900 hours the Japanese fired about thirty rounds from their mountain guns against the Brigade Headquarters and the Allied guns. Their shelling was extremely accurate and they inflicted about twenty casualties on the 89th Brigade, including two killed.[22]

On 6 July the positions remained unchanged and the 33rd Brigade sent out reconnaissance patrols of 4/1 Gurkha Rifles to discover a route passable for mules to Langdang. 4/8 Gurkha Rifles and 2 King's Own Scottish Borderers remained pinned down to the southern portion of the village and the slightest movement on their part was greeted with heavy and accurate fire from Japanese snipers. The next day the 33rd Brigade sent out numerous harassing patrols. A route fit for mules was discovered going round Ukhrul from the east. 4/1 Gurkha Rifles and 1 Burma Regiment in the meantime pushed forward into Ukhrul from the north and occupied positions in the area RE 808018 and RE 813023 respectively.[23]

The 89th Brigade also sent a patrol of 4/8 Gurkha Rifles to try to infiltrate between the Japanese position at RE 804006 and the northern end of Ukhrul. Resistance was again encountered from the

---

[21] *Ibid.*
[22] War Diary of Headquarters 89th Indian Infantry Brigade.
[23] War Diary of Headquarters 33rd Indian Infantry Brigade.

Japanese troops who were occupying buildings in the town and covering its approaches with machine-guns and light automatics. Their strength was estimated at not more than two companies and it was obvious that they were gradually sneaking out to escape eastwards from Ukhrul.

On 8 July, the 33rd Brigade sent 4/1 Gurkha Rifles with some guns on the newly discovered track to by-pass Ukhrul and advance towards Lungshong. The rest of the brigade pressed forward again into Ukhrul. But during the night the Japanese had quietly evacuated the fort and their other positions in the town. At 1210 hours, therefore, 4/8 Gurkha Rifles met 1 Burma of the 33rd Brigade in the centre of the town. During the day the Japanese shelled that area again, and for the last time probably, in order to cover their withdrawal and discourage pursuit. But within a few hours all resistance in Ukhrul had ceased. After the Japanese occupation of over three months, the town had at last been recaptured by the troops of the XXXIII Corps.

OPERATIONS OF THE 23RD BRIGADE

The recapture of Ukhrul would not have been so easy without the simultaneous advance of the 23rd Long Range Penetration Brigade towards the town from the north to attack it from the east. On 22 June 1944, the brigade had reached positions between 25 to 35 miles to the north-east of the town. Its columns had marched over 150 miles through thick jungles and over steep hills under monsoon conditions and using mules for carrying their supplies. Rain had been almost continuous and on several days about six inches of rainfall was recorded. Thunder-clouds veiled the sheer precipices and hung low over the valleys below, adding new hazards to the supply dropping aircraft trying to drop rations and ammunition to the men below. In spite of these difficulties and hazards the advance continued. The 23rd Brigade was moving forward along three roughly parallel routes. On the right axis 34 Column and 55 Column were moving from Gaziphema towards Kharasom. In the centre were the 33 and 76 Columns, moving through the area of Nungphung south towards Ukhrul. On the left axis 56 Column was leading the advance near Somra. Following it were 60 and 88 Columns near Tusom Khulen, and 44 Column brought up the rear on the track from Nungphung to Tusom Khulen.

Continuing its advance the 55 Column had arrived by 25 June at Chingjui and its leading platoon was near Paowi. Behind it, 34 Column was still busy crossing the swollen Laniye river at RE 8546, and the 76 and 33 Columns were moving through the area Nungphung and Chakyang Kuki. On the eastern axis the four columns advancing on Somra were delayed by the Chammu Turel and by the numerous bridges which had been destroyed on the track from Tusom Khulen to Somra by the retreating Japanese. This track lay over a ridge about 8,000 feet high and crossed the frontier into Burma. The Japanese had used it as one of their main lines of communication during the advance, and it was now strewn with corpses of men and animals which gave out a terrible stench in their decomposition. By 26 June, however, 60, 88 and 44 Columns had reached Somra. At the same time 56 Column pushed on further south and reached Fort Keary, the same day. On 27 June, 34 Column completed its crossing of the Laniye river and hurried up behind 55 Column which had by then advanced beyond Paowi and was nearing Phungcham. 55 Column as well as 76 and 33 Columns, advancing slightly to the eastwards, threw numerous patrols in every direction without, however, contacting many Japanese troops. Encouraged by this lack of serious opposition all the columns kept up good pace and by 30 June, had reached the following localities respectively:—

34 Column and 53 Column at	Phungcham
76 Column and 33 Column at	Ngahui and Kongai respectively,
On the left 56 Column at	Saiyapaw
and 60 Column at	Tonghlang, and
88 Column and 44 Column at	Fort Keary.

The next day 34 and 55 Columns established road-blocks at Tallui, Furing and Point 4145 (8508). The tracks leading northwards from Ukhrul were thus completely blocked. 76 Column moved up to Kalhang Khunou and the 33 Column neared Chingai. In the meanwhile the advance had continued on the eastern axis also. Saiyapaw was held by three columns and the leading platoon of 56 Column reached Chammu. This rapid advance blocked the Japanese line of retreat from Ukhrul towards Homalin, and only the southeastern route still remained open for them. As has been related earlier, the 33rd and the 89th Indian Infantry Brigades were by then nearing Ukhrul itself from the north and west respectively, and no serious difficulty was expected in recapturing the town. By 3 July 1944, 34 Column occupied Siruhi and 33 Column entered Ngahui.

Contact was established with the 33rd Brigade of the 7th Indian Division the same day and plans were co-ordinated for an attack on Ukhrul. 76 Column arrived at Longbi Kachui the following day. On 5 and 6 July, 34 and 55 Columns conducted harassing operations against the Japanese garrison in the Ukhrul area and inflicted numerous casualties. The recapture of Ukhrul was considerably helped by these operations. On 8 July, the town fell. By that date 34 Column was closing in on Lungshong. The remainder of the brigade had started to swing round Ukhrul from the east as described below. 76 and 56 Columns were nearing Ongshim, 44 and 88 Columns were at Chammu and 60 Column had reached Chattrik.

REOPENING OF THE UKHRUL ROAD

In the original plan for the recapture of Ukhrul the brigades of the 20th Indian Division were to co-operate tactically with the 89th Indian Infantry Brigade and the 33rd Indian Infantry Brigade in the final assault. It has been related earlier that by 22 June 1944, the 100th Brigade of the 20th Division was held up in the Saddle area (RK 5878) and the 80th Brigade had reached above the bend of the Iril river near Chawai and Mollen. Moreover, the 20th Division had under its command the garrison of Kameng Box (RK 5071), the 153rd Parachute Battalion with a company of Medium Machine-Guns, and these troops were then engaged in mopping up the Japanese forces around Mapao Khunou, west of the Iril river and in the area of Sadang, in the hills within the bend of the river.

The plan involved an advance by the 100th Indian Infantry Brigade from the Saddle area along the Ukhrul road. Accordingly, on 23 June 1944, Headquarters IV Corps ordered Headquarters 20th Indian Division to employ the 80th Indian Infantry Brigade in an outflanking movement southwards from the Khunthak area as soon as the forward units of the 89th Brigade of the 7th Indian Division had reached there, so that the 80th Brigade might threaten the rear of the Japanese units around Litan and thereby facilitate the advance of the 100th Brigade up the Ukhrul road.[24] As a result of this manoeuvre, it was anticipated that the 100th Brigade would be able to advance rapidly from the Saddle towards Ukhrul, and would reach the tactically important road-junction near Finch's Corner (RK 7589), as the brigades of the 7th Indian Division closed in on Ukhrul. It was further planned that on reaching Finch's Corner, one of the brigades of the 20th Division was to go on towards Ukhrul to assist in capturing the town, while the other would swing southwards to cut the main Japanese escape-route from Ukhrul near Gamon.

Opposing the 20th Indian Division was a composite force of the Japanese *15th Division*. This force had originally comprised *1st Battalion 51st Regiment, 3rd Battalion 51st Regiment* and *2nd Battalion 67th Regiment*, supported by two batteries of *21st Field Artillery Regiment*. But it had suffered heavy losses in the operations of April, May and June, and was reduced to about twelve hundred fighting troops only.

To implement the plan, the 80th Indian Infantry Brigade started

---

[24] IV Corps Operation Instruction No. 100 dated 23 June 1944.

moving towards Khunthak on 23 June 1944. The next day, Headquarters 80th Brigade moved up to Yangnoi. Japanese resistance was negligible, and by 26 June, Headquarters 80th Brigade had reached Mollen with the forward units nearing Khunthak. On 27 June, Khunthak was occupied by two companies of 9 Frontier Force Regiment as the 33rd and the 89th Indian Infantry Brigade started their advance from the main Imphal-Kohima road. In the meanwhile, operations had been continuing in the 100th Brigade sector also in a desultory fashion. During the night of 24/25 June, the Sausage hill (RK 5983, held by a company of 14 Frontier Force Rifles of the 100th Brigade, was attacked by a strong Japanese force supported by artillery and mortars, but was repulsed by the garrison with heavy casualties. On 25 June also, the Japanese showed unusual activity in the area and the next evening they attacked Sausage hill again with two companies of troops supported by mountain guns and trench mortars. The defenders, of the strength of a company of 14 Frontier Force Rifles, resisted stoutly but the Japanese stormed the position with desperate valour, using flame-throwers and incendiary grenades.[25] After savage hand-to-hand fighting during which both sides suffered heavy casualties, the defenders were dislodged from their position and Sausage hill passed into the hands of the Japanese again.

By 29 June, headquarters of the 80th Brigade and 3/1 Gurkha Rifles had moved up to Khunthak while 9 Frontier Force Regiment drove out the Japanese from Sirarukhong and occupied the village. Wide patrolling was continued, but little territorial gains were made due to stubborn and strong opposition by the Japanese garrisons at Thawai, Pt. 4241 and the surrounding area.

As related above, on 30 June 1944, the 20th Indian Division (commanded by Major-General D. D. Gracey, CBE, MC,) came under the XXXIII Corps.[26] However, its 32nd Indian Infantry Brigade still remained under the IV Corps, but in lieu of it 152 and 153 Parachute Battalions and a Medium Machine-gun Company of the 50th Parachute Brigade were placed under the command of the 20th Indian Division. Till the end of June, the 100th Indian Infantry Brigade had been fighting near the Saddle with the intention of thrusting forward along the Ukhrul road. The 80th Indian Infantry Brigade had started swinging south towards Litan from the Khunthak area after being relieved by units of the 89th Indian Infantry Brigade. Moreover, the garrison of Kameng Box, commanded since 26 June by Colonel Tarver, had been formed into the Tarforce and comprised 152 and 153 Parachute Batalions, a Medium Machine-gun Company of the 50th Parachute Brigade,

[25] War Diary of Headquarters 20th Indian Division, File No. 601/250/WD/Pt. 11
[26] See page 15 above.

4 Madras less two companies and one company of 1 Devon.[27] This Tarforce was ordered to operate along two divergent routes. The 153 Parachute Battalion less one company, which was named the Sancol, was fighting towards the north-east in the area of Mapao Khunou and the hills within the bend of the Iril river. 152 Parachute Battalion and the Sancol were operating to the south and the south-east in the area of Tangkhul Hundung in order to get poised for striking at the Japanese line of communication running from Ukhrul through Ningthi to Humine. The rest of the Tarforce was holding the area of Nungshigum, Sadang and Tumukhong and in general, backing up the 100th Indian Infantry Brigade.

For a few days more confused and intermittent fighting continued. Patrols of 153 Parachute Battalion reported that the Japanese had evacuated Mapao Khunou on 30 June, and two companies of the battalion were sent up towards Laphurak in pursuit. South of the road, 152 Parachute Battalion encountered a hostile party at Meiring which was dispersed. The same day, the 100th Indian Infantry Brigade threw out ambushing parties on the track between Marou and Sinda. A platoon of 14 Frontier Force Rifles of the 100th Brigade occupied Lower Thawai. The 80th Indian Infantry Brigade ambushed a Japanese convoy which was approaching RK 6291 from the north-east and dispersed it after inflicting casualties. The next day, 1 July 1944, Natjang and Saichang were found clear of the Japanese troops by the patrols of 152 Parachute Battalion. The Japanese attacked the platoon of 14 Frontier Force Rifles at Thawai but were unable to recapture the village as the defenders had received reinforcement.

On the 80th Brigade sector, Khengkot and Shongphel were occupied by 9/12 Frontier Force Regiment and 3/1 Gurkha Rifles, respectively, although the Japanese continued to resist strongly in the area of Shongphel rest-house at RK 6291. The following day contact was established between the 80th Brigade and the 100th Brigade when a patrol of 3/1 Gurkha Rifles met another of 4/10 Gurkha Rifles, near Shongphel[28] On 3 July, Laphurak was found evacuated by the Japanese and northern wing of Tarforce was then ordered to carry out aggressive patrolling and try to join up with the 3/1 Gurkha Rifles in the area of Shongphel. The Headquarters 80th Brigade was then located at Sirarukhong, 3/1 Gurkha Rifles and a company of Frontier Force Rifles were in the Shongphel area and 1 Devon less two companies was moving from Tushar southwards to establish a roadblock across the Ukhrul road at Lammu.

On 4 July, 3/1 Gurkha Rifles of the 80th Brigade was engaged in carrying out a wide encircling movement around the northern

---

[27] War Diary of Headquarters 20th Indian Division.
[28] Ibid.

flank of the Japanese force in Shongphel, and 9 Frontier Force Regiment was moving towards Chepu which commanded the Litan-Ukhrul road from across the Thoubal river. 1 Devon that day reached Lammu, thus establishing a major road-block behind the Japanese troops fighting near the Saddle against the units of the 100th Brigade. On the 100th Brigade sector, the Japanese had evacuated Dongshum but hung on to their positions at Point 4955, Aishan, Chepu and Point 4241. The next day, 5 July, 3/1 Gurkha Rifles continued its advance towards Aishan, but was held up by the Japanese resistance when it was one mile north-east of the village.[29] 1 Devon dug itself in at Lammu and prepared to meet the expected Japanese counter-attacks. At the same time, the Headquarters 20th Indian Division had ordered the 80th Brigade to send a strong force to Sokpao with the task of opening the Ukhrul road from Finch's Corner southwards towards Litan. There were indications that at last the Japanese were ready to pull out of the Litan area. For example, the Tarforce, then in the Yengdoupok area, discovered that the Japanese had evacuated Padhong. In the 100th Brigade sector also the Japanese had evacuated Point 4955, though the next day, on 6 July, 1944 their presence was reported from Point 4241 (RK 5780), Point 3636 (RK 6278) and Thawai.

To impede their retreat, air attacks were delivered on 6 July against a column of about 180 Japanese troops moving with mechanical transport north-east along Ukhrul track at RK 641801. 3/1 Gurkha Rifles was held up north-east of Aishan, but it had started outflanking the Japanese position from the west, in order to hasten their retreat. The Headquarters 80th Brigade and a company of 9 Frontier Force Regiment moved to a position one mile south of Ringui. The rest of 9 Frontier Force Regiment was at that moment chasing the Japanese further south, and entered Chepu almost on their heels. But the retreating force succeeded in escaping towards Sareikhong.

The Japanese hold on the Litan-Ukhrul track was obviously getting shaky. 1 Devon was established securely at Lammu on the road and 9 Frontier Force Regiment was at Chepu commanding the stretch near Litan. During the night of 6/7 July, 4/10 Gurkha Rifles (of 100th Brigade) delivered a surprise attack and started advancing north-east up the Ukhrul road. The Japanese defenders at Point 4241 and on Sausage Hill were taken by surprise, and by the dawn of 7 July, 4/10 Gurkha Rifles had occupied the two spurs dominating the main road at RK 6080 and RK 6180. Subsequent plan was for 3/1 Gurkha Rifles to move up to Aishan and Chepu whereupon 9 Frontier Force Regiment would move down from Chepu and dig in astride the main road. 1 Devon already established at

[29] *Ibid.*

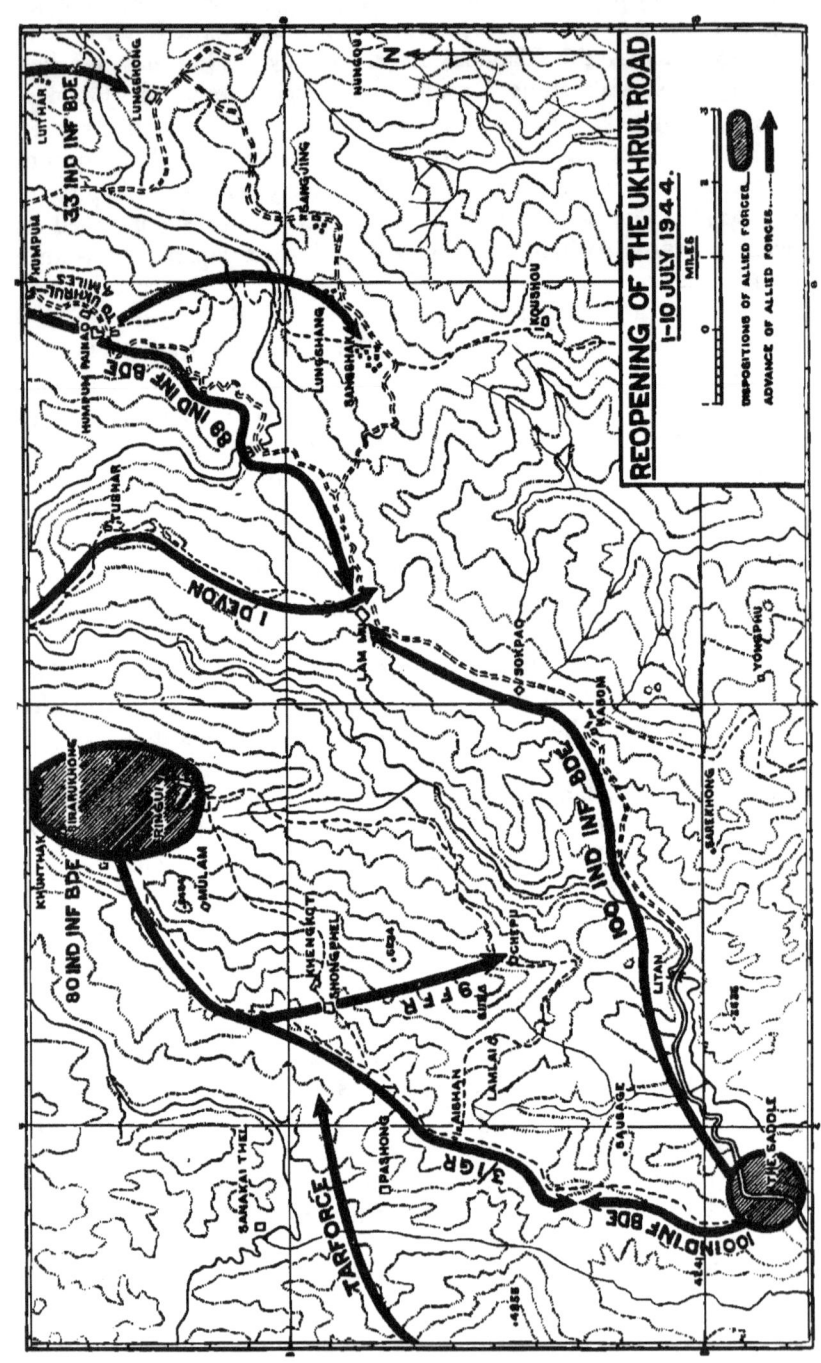

Lammu, was to mop up in the area and then move down south along the road to link up with the advancing troops of the 100th Brigade.[30]

But 9 Frontier Force Regiment was unable to get to the main road due to the strong Japanese resistance. It then continued holding Chepu and used artillery fire to harass and disrupt Japanese convoys moving eastwards along the road. Also 1 Devon started mopping up around Lammu, but during the night of 7/8 July its road-block was attacked heavily by a Japanese column supported by light tanks. Considerable casualties were inflicted on the Japanese convoy, but in the end 1 Devon was forced to evacuate its road-block and some Japanese vehicles and tanks and guns escaped through towards Sangshak. About the same time, another strong Japanese force containing probably the remnants of the Headquarters and *1st* and *3rd Battalions* of the *51st Japanese Regiment* attacked the road-block held by 9 Frontier Force Regiment at Chepu. Fierce fighting went on throughout the day, 8 July, and both sides suffered heavy casualties. But 9 Frontier Force Regiment held to its ground and frustrated all attempts by the Japanese to break through Chepu. Assistance was hurried to it by 3/1 Gurkha Rifles from Aishan and by 4/10 Gurkha Rifles from the main road near Litan. The latter advancing along the main road reached near Litan and its engineers started bridging the Thoubal river.

The heavy Japanese opposition in the 80th Brigade sector led to the revision of operation orders. As described above, 1 Devon had failed to maintain its road-block at Lammu in the face of determined Japanese attacks, and it had become impossible for it to advance down the road from Lammu to Litan.

9 Frontier Force Regiment also had been badly mauled and could not reach the Litan road from Chepu. The 80th Brigade of which these Battalions formed part, was therefore to maintain its road-block at Lammu, clear the track from Saddle to Sirarukhong and mop up in the surrounding area, while the 100th Brigade was ordered to reopen the main road from Litan to Finch's Corner.[31] But the Japanese were already evacuating the entire area. On 9 July, 9 Frontier Force Regiment reassembled in the Chepu area and found that some Japanese had escaped eastwards during the previous night. Then 3/1 Gurkha Rifles occupied Aishan and moved up towards Lamlai and Sausage Hill without difficulty. In the 100th Brigade sector also, 2 Border had taken up the advance and captured Sareikhong. 14 Frontier Force Rifles then passed through 2 Border and reached up to Kasom. 4 Madras of Tarforce followed up the advance and held the high ground overlooking the Litan bridge. 152 Parachute Battalion had by then reached the area of Singkap, Sakok and Lang, thus

[30] *Ibid.*
[31] *Ibid.*

harassing and killing parties of Japanese troops trying to retreat from the main road, towards the south. During the night of 9/10 July, the last of them had by-passed 9 Frontier Force Regiment position at Chepu and succeeded in escaping eastwards. Frontier Force Regiment had proved unable to prevent their escape, but it had forced the retreating troops to discard all guns and heavy equipment and to break up into small parties in order to make good their escape. Moreover, it had inflicted heavy casualties on them. After the escape of the Japanese rear-guards, 4/10 Gurkha Rifles followed them up across the Thoubal river and 9 Frontier Force Regiment started operations to mop up those still remaining on the western bank. On 10 July, 1 Devon at Lammu also was relieved by the leading troops of the 89th Indian Infantry Brigade who were advancing south-westwards along the road from Ukhrul. 14 Frontier Force Rifles of the 100th Brigade also continued its movement eastwards along the road, seizing Kasom and Sokpao in a rapid advance. It linked up with 1 Devon at Lammu and the road was thus reopened right up to Ukhrul on 10 July.

MOPPING UP BEYOND UKHRUL

As related above, the recapture of Ukhrul was completed by 8 July 1944, and two days later the road from Imphal had also been opened again. These successes removed all threat to the Dimapur-Imphal road. Thus the most important task given to the XXXIII Corps after the reopening of Kohima-Imphal road was completed. But the capture of Ukhrul had not decimated the Japanese force as had been expected. Except near the Saddle, the Allied advance had encountered only weak and intermittent opposition. On the other hand, early in July, there were reports of several hundred Japanese troops still fighting far behind the 33rd Indian Infantry Brigade and the 89th Indian Infantry Brigade. About 400 Japanese troops were repelling the attacks of the 2nd British Division in the area Preyatemei and Shorbung. Others held position within the bend of the Iril river, particularly around Pashong and Dongshum. Moreover, about 1200 Japanese troops were estimated to be fighting in the area of the Saddle, Aishan and Thawai.

In order to capture or destroy these Japanese troops, operations had begun even before Ukhrul had fallen. It was obvious that very soon these disorganised Japanese bands would have to flee eastwards. The operations to kill or capture them were planned along the lines of a gigantic shikar drive, with units of the 2nd British Division and the 20th Indian Division acting as beaters to flush and drive the quarry, and the troops of the 23rd Long Range Penetration Brigade, the 33rd Indian Infantry Brigade and Tarforce acting as 'the guns', holding a line right across the Japanese escape-routes. As the quarry retreated before 'the beaters' he would have to pass through the line held by 'the guns' and be destroyed there.

However, there were several escape-routes open to the Japanese. From the Ukhrul area, apart from the tracks leading north and east, which had been previously cut by the 23rd Brigade, there were several tracks leading south-east. One led to Homalin on the Chindwin via Ongshim and Chattrik. Another led to Humine via Lungshong, and Kamjong. A third took off from Sangshak and ran south to Nambashi and the Tamu area via Phalang, Sakok and Meiring. Yet another started from Kasom on the Imphal-Ukhrul road and led towards Sibong via Sinda-Singkap and Tonghlang.

On 2 and 3 July, orders were issued by the XXXIII Corps defining the operations which were to be undertaken after the capture of Ukhrul.[32] The 23rd Brigade was ordered to send 34 and 55 Columns to the Ukhrul area to co-operate with the 89th Indian Infantry Brigade in intercepting and destroying the Japanese troops trying to retreat from the Shorbung area. The rest of the 23rd Brigade was to swing in a wide arc and cut the south-east escape route at Chattrik and Ongshim. Moreover, the 7th Indian Division was at first ordered to send the 33rd Brigade south-west from Ukhrul to Finch's Corner to assist the 20th Indian Division in reopening the Imphal-Ukhrul road, while the 89th Indian Infantry Brigade advanced and took up positions on the Lungshong-Kamjong track and in the area of Leiting and Phalang. But when the 89th Brigade encountered unexpectedly strong resistance in the southern part of Ukhrul, it was allowed to exchange roles with the 33rd Brigade.[33] The latter then marched round Ukhrul by a newly discovered track and proceeded to cut the second and the third Japanese escape-routes mentioned above, and the 89th Brigade held the Ukhrul area with one battalion supported by the two columns of the 23rd Brigade, sending the other two battalions to Finch's Corner and Lammu, as related above. Moreover, while the 80th Brigade and the 100th Brigade of the 20th Indian Division were still trying to reopen the road to Ukhrul, 152 Parachute Battalion of Tarforce was told to operate against the last Japanese escape-route from Kasom southwards, and Sancol was sent to raid the escape-routes far to the south between Kamjong and Humine.

In accordance with these plans, the 33rd Indian Infantry Brigade started moving south on the morning of 9 July 1944. 4/1 Gurkha Rifles led the advance, accompanied by a mountain battery; 1 Queens remained behind at Ukhrul under the command of the 89th Brigade, but the rest of the 33rd Brigade followed the Gurkhas. The brigade spent the night at Luithar (TK 8596) and the next morning

[32] War Diary Headquarters XXXIII Corps, General Staff Branch.
[33] War Diary of Headquarters the 7th Indian Division.

advanced even beyond to establish contact with 1 Devon at Lammu and reopen the road to Ukhrul soon after. The Headquarters 89th Brigade moved to Humpum area. On 11 July patrols of 1/11 Sikh had some success against Japanese stragglers some of whom were captured near Pangsang (RK 7883). Sangjing (RK 8189) and Koushou (RK 7984) were found clear of the Japanese. The 89th Brigade then consolidated its hold on the area occupied, with patrols moving through the hills to prevent any large body of Japanese troops slipping through to the eastward.

The 33rd Brigade also prepared to advance down the track to Kamjong (RK 9870), but the problem of supplies and maintenance presented some difficulty. Supply dropping from the air was not possible, because the hills in the area were perpetually enveloped by clouds and mist. Hence it was decided to use jeeps for supplying the forward units. While waiting for the jeeps to arrive from Imphal, 1 Burma was sent forward on 12 July with three days' supplies on mules. But it came upon a Japanese road-block at RK 907893 north of Maoku, which was covered by one medium machine-gun, two or three light machine-guns, one heavy mortar and one 75-mm gun.[34] An attack launched by 1 Burma on the block failed. Hence, on 13 July, one of its companies started to outflank the road-block and reached MS 20 (RK 9284) on 14 July, after which the road-block was cleared easily, and contact was also established with a patrol of 60 Column from the 23rd Long Range Penetration Brigade.[35] On 16 July, the whole of 1 Burma was established at MS 20. By 18 July its forward troops had reached MS 24½ (RK 9378) with little opposition, and the Tactical Headquarters of the 33rd Brigade was established at MS 23.

But by then the supply problem had become so difficult as to make further advance almost impossible. Jeeps had arrived on 13 July, but they found some difficulty in negotiating even the comparatively fair track near Sangshak. Several got stuck in the mud, and one jeep slid down into the *khud*. On 14 July, the brigade commander inspected the forward track towards Kamjong and found it exceedingly muddy and difficult going, and the senior engineer officer after seeing the track advised strongly against plying jeeps on it. 1 Burma also reported that the route ahead, as well as the track from Apong (RK 8779) to Ningthi (RK 9070), was impassable, even for mules. Meanwhile, three mules of 1 Burma had died mysteriously, and a veterinary officer who went up to see them reported that the dreaded disease "Surra" had broken out among them.[36] On 18 July, finally, reports were received that Kamjong was held by

---

[34] War Diary of Headquarters 33rd Indian Infantry Brigade.
[35] Fifty-five dead Japanese were counted in the area, *Ibid*.
[36] *Ibid*.

a Japanese detachment whose men were fresh, healthy and had new-looking uniform and equipment, indicating that they were part of the small reinforcement sent by the Japanese *15th Army* from Central Burma. In view of all these developments, it appeared hardly possible to reach Kamjong. Some casualties had been inflicted on Japanese stragglers, but the main body had obviously slipped out eastwards through the thick forest and was then nearing the Chindwin and safety. In these circumstances, the 23rd Long Range Penetration Brigade had already started withdrawing, and one of its columns had reached Imphal on 18 July. By 26 July, the entire brigade had withdrawn to Imphal. Hence further offensive operations were given up and the 33rd Brigade also started withdrawing. Tactical Headquarters of the Brigade moved back that day from MS 23 (RK 9382) area. On 20 July, 1 Burma returned to RK 903906, except one company which advanced to milestone 29 without meeting any Japanese opposition. The next day this company pushed on to MS 30, only two miles short of Kamong, before meeting a Japanese road-block and being shelled by a 75-mm gun. No further clash took place, though it remained near MS 30 a few days longer.[37] But Lieutenant-General Stopford had already decided to withdraw the 7th Indian Division to Kohima for much-needed rest and reorganisation. On 22 July, the 89th Brigade began moving back to Kohima via Imphal.[38] The same day, the commander of the 4th Brigade (of the 2nd British Division) which had to take over the defence of the Ukhrul area from the 7th Indian Division, arrived to complete the arrangements for the change-over. The next day, Headquarters 33rd Brigade and 4/1 Gurkha Rifles marched back to Finch's Corner, and on 24 July, the forward company of 1 Burma fell back to MS 23. On 26 July, the 4th British Brigade assumed responsibility for the defence of the Ukhrul area, and two days later the 33rd Brigade reached Zubza near Kohima.[39] The 7th Indian Division was then assembled at Kohima, and entered upon a period of rest, refit and training.

In the meantime, units of the 20th Indian Division and the Tarforce had been engaged in mopping up Japanese remnants in the area between Aishan and Sangshak and in blocking the remaining escape-route running southwards from Sangshak. The Imphal-Ukhrul road had been reopened on 10 July, but there were left many stray bands of Japanese troops on both sides of the road. On 11 July, 4/8 Gurkha Rifles started in pursuit of one of them which had crossed over the Thoubal river and was hiding in the thick jungle between the river and the main Ukhrul road. To prevent

---

[37] *Ibid.*
[38] War Diary of Headquarters 89th Indian Infantry Brigade.
[39] War Diary of Headquarters 7th Indian Division General Staff Branch.

them from escaping eastwards across the road, 14/13 Frontier Force Rifles held positions at Sokpao and 1 Devon at Lammu on the main road.[40] Air attacks were also directed against the escape route, and at Sakok there was a big explosion, as of an ammunition dump blowing up. Further south, the 152 Parachute Battalion of Tarforce continued its harassing patrols. Mopping up continued on 12 and 13 July, 9/12 Frontier Force Regiment establishing a series of blocks to prevent a big Japanese force from doubling back and recrossing to the west bank of the Thoubal river. 4/10 Gurkha Rifles kept up its hot pursuit on the east bank, and on 14 July discovered 30 Japanese at RK 667853 and about 100 at RK 688875. The next day these hide-outs were attacked by the Gurkhas, and 7 Japanese officers and 73 other ranks were killed, the rest dispersing precipitately in all directions.

At the same time, the Sancol (one company of 153 Parachute Battalion) was operating far to the south against the track from Sangshak. It reached the area of Mungba below Kamjong, and killed over fifty-five Japanese troops there.[41] The rest of 153 Parachute Battalion had by this date liquidated the Japanese troops within the bend of the Iril river and was assembling at Chalon before moving down to join Tarforce and Sancol. On 15 July, Headquarters 32nd Brigade, 1 Northamptons and 9/14 Punjab reverted to the command of the 20th Indian Division, at Wangjing. The next day, orders were received for the 80th Brigade and 100th Brigade also to withdraw to the Wangjing area. The 20th Indian Division had been engaged in arduous operations for several months now, and since it was required to play an important part in the further operations planned for the recapture of Tamu, a period of some rest was considered necessary for it.

Operations, however, continued for a few days longer. The 80th Brigade started to move from Aishan towards the Saddle and Wangjing on 16 July, leaving behind 9/12 Frontier Force Regiment (less two companies) to finish mopping up on the west bank of the Thoubal river near Chepu. 4/10 Gurkha Rifles of 100th Brigade operated on the road between Lammu and Sokpao and 152 Parachute Battalion occupied Sakok.[42]

On 18 July, Headquarters 80th Brigade reached Wangjing and Headquarters 100th Brigade moved back to Waithou. The same day, 153 Parachute Battalion (less one company) reached Tangkhul-Hundung on its way forward to join 152 Parachute Battalion. Two days later, Headquarters 20th Division moved back to Thoubal thus completing the disengagement of the division. The defence

---

[40] War Diary of Headquarters 20th Indian Division.
[41] Account of Operations of XXXIII Corps, *op. cit.*
[42] *Ibid.*

of the area south of the road was left to Tarcol, which on 20 July passed under the command of Headquarters 50th Parachute Brigade, to which the two parachute battalions had belonged.[43] The Tarforce continued its operations to inflict the maximum casualties on the Japanese stragglers still trying to retreat southwards by the Sakok track. Minor clashes only were reported for a few days, but on 24 July, 152 Parachute Battalion cleared an important Japanese roadblock at Lang and found thirty Japanese graves in the locality. The 153 Parachute Battalion also harassed and tried to destroy small Japanese parties in the area of Lang—Phaisat.

It was then decided to withdraw the parachute battalions also for a period of rest. The operations were almost concluded and very few Japanese troops were left unaccounted for in the entire area. On 26 July, therefore, the 152 and 153 Parachute Battalions concentrated at Tangkhul Hundung preparatory to withdrawal. Defence of the area was taken over by the 100th Brigade of the 20th Division, and one company 14/13 Frontier Force Rifles was sent up from Sawombung to Tangkhul Hundung to relieve the parachute battalions. By 31 July, the whole of the 50th Parachute Brigade returned to Dimapur *en route* to India.[44]

Between 22 June and 31 July 1944, therefore, the Japanese were hurled back and thrown out of the large area of hills and forests between the Dimapur—Imphal road and the Chindwin river. Ukhrul was recaptured and the main road from there to Imphal was opened again to Allied traffic. In the main, the operations had been a grim game of hide and seek, a gigantic man-hunt in which the units of the Japanese *31st* and *15th Divisions*, broken and fleeing from the battles around Kohima and the Imphal road, were doggedly searched out and killed or captured. The Allied formations inflicted substantial casualties on the retreating and disorganised Japanese bands; the 20th Division, for example, killed 703, wounded 116 and captured 47 Japanese troops.[45] But the main body of Japanese troops had succeeded in escaping from the net, mainly by discarding most of its heavy equipment and slipping out through the thick jungle. It was obvious, however, that they had suffered a terrible defeat, and were back almost at the Chindwin after losing several thousand men. By the end of July 1944, they had been cleared out from the northern sector, and held a salient across the Chindwin only in the Palel sector and southwards.

---

[43] War Diary of Headquarters 20th Indian Division.
[44] Account of Operations of XXXIII Corps.
[45] War Diary of Headquarters 20th Indian Division.

CHAPTER III

Tamu Regained

THE PERIOD OF STALEMATE

In an earlier chapter we have described the fighting in the Palel sector, where, by 22 July 1944, it had reached a virtual stalemate. The *Yamamoto Force* had been held up in the area of Tengnoupal on the main Palel—Tamu road.[1] In the hills to the north of the road, Japanese troops had infiltrated up to Khunbi and RK 5317, to the west of Sibo, with their advance patrols operating only a few miles from Palel. The main Japanese advance was blocked by the massed strength of the 23rd Indian Division comprising the 1st, 37th and 49th Indian Infantry Brigades. The 37th Brigade, with its Headquarters at Shenam, was battling against the *Yamamoto Force* in the Tengnoupal area and along the main road, and was thus bearing the brunt of Japanese attacks in their attempt to break through to Palel. Of the other two brigades, the 1st Brigade had established itself on 23 June in the area of Kakching, from where the track led to Shuganu and the hills south of the main road.[2] Its main task was to defend the road Imphal—Tengnoupal between Thoubal and Scawfell. The 49th Brigade opened its headquarters at Heirok and took up the task of harassing the Japanese troops in the hills to the north of the main road, and preventing any infiltration between the main positions of the 23rd Indian Division on the Palel road and the 20th Indian Division on the Ukhrul road. It has been ordered to hold the post at Sita at all costs, safeguard the line of communication from Heirok via Nungtak and to ensure that no Japanese guns were again located forward to bombard the Palel air-strip.[3]

For about a fortnight after 22 June 1944, no major change occurred in the situation in the Shuganu and Tengnoupal sectors. The former was held by 1/16 Punjab of the 1st Brigade, which carried out aggressive patrolling to harass the Japanese troops in the area and to obtain early information of any attempt on their part to concentrate forces or threaten an advance. Small but fierce patrol clashes took place near Mitlong Khunou in which casualties were inflicted on the Japanese. In the Tengnoupal sector, there were

---

[1] The Yamamoto Force then consisted of 213th Regiment of 33rd Division, 2nd Battalion 51st Regiment and 1st Battalion 60th Regiment of 15th Division, one Independent Anti-Tank Battalion fighting as infantry, and an artillery and engineer component. Account of Operations of XXXIII Corps, *op. cit.*
[2] War Diary of Headquarters 23rd Indian Division, General Staff Branch.
[3] 23rd Indian Division Operation Order No. 20 dated 20 June, 1944.

only some stray artillery duels on a small scale, and a vigilant watch was kept from the observation post at Hambone on Japanese movements. Some traffic was noticed indicating that the Japanese were sending supplies and small reinforcements forward to their units in the Khudei Khunou (RK 5722) area. But neither side attempted any major attack in the sector which remained abnormally quiet.

But in the sector north of the main road, fighting flared up again. Early in June, the Japanese had infiltrated in strength towards Khudei Khunou, leaving the Indian troops holding positions at Sita and Hambone. They occupied Khudei Khunou, Khunbi and Lone Tree Hill, and succeeded in driving a dangerous wedge into the IV Corps defence line which threatened the left flank of the Shenam position, on the one hand, and the front of the key town of Palel, on the other. On 22 June one battalion of Japanese troops was estimated to be in this wedge, distributed as follows:—[4]

Phalbung Spur, excluding Ben Nevis	One Company.
Maibi Khunou—Khudei Khunou	Two Companies.
Langgol—Khunbi	One Company.

Matters came to a head when the Japanese pushed on nearer Palel along the Saibom ridge. On 22 July a roving patrol of 5/6 Rajputana Rifles encountered a Japanese party near Lone Tree Hill, a commanding feature 4500 feet high, overlooking Palel from a distance of only about three miles. This patrol was asked to comb the area, and another patrol of 3/5 Royal Gurkha Rifles of one platoon strength, was also sent there. The next morning these two patrols linked up, when it was discovered that the Japanese were holding the Lone Tree Hill by one full company. At the same time, other Japanese patrols had pushed on further and had clashed with a patrol of Kalibahadur Regiment at Scotts Knob (RK 499199). Orders were at once issued by the General Officer Commanding 23rd Division and the Officer Commanding 37th Brigade to 5/6 Rajputana Rifles to send a whole company to Lone Tree Hill and recapture it with artillery support. Accordingly one company 5/6 Rajputana Rifles and one platoon 3/5 Royal Gurkha Rifles attacked Lone Tree Hill at 1900 hours on 23 June. The attackers reached almost the summit of the hill, but were then held up by a deluge of handgrenades.[5] The fighting continued for a few minutes, but as the defenders continued their fanatical resistance, and as the ammunition carried by the Rajputs began to run low, the attack petered out. On 24 June, the Rajputs discovered that the Japanese positions then extended from Lone Tree Hill to Scotts Knob and they had probably been further reinforced to a strength of three companies during the night. But as the capture of the Lone Tree Hill was of vital

[4] 37th Indian Infantry Brigade Operation Order No. 3 dated 22 June, 1944.
[5] War Diary of Headquarters 37th Indian Brigade.

importance, another attack was mounted on 24 June. At 1500 hours that day, Allied ground-attack planes and light bombers carried out accurate strafing and bombing on Lone Tree Hill. The artillery laid down a "creeping barrage", calculated to cover every inch of the ground and to destroy systematically all Japanese defences. But when the infantry advanced to the attack, it was met once again by a hail of hand-grenades, and the attack failed. On 25 June, therefore, two fresh companies of 5/6 Rajputana Rifles and some mortars and medium machine-guns were despatched by the 37th Brigade as reinforcements. Massed guns opened a terrific barrage on Lone Tree Hill at 1230 hours, and at 1402 hours a vicious air attack was carried out. The Rajputs then stormed their way on to the summit of Lone Tree Hill and captured it by 1515 hours. The Japanese tried to wrest back the position by immediate and savage counter-attacks, resulting in heavy fighting till 1730 hours. But all their counter-attacks were beaten back. During the night of 25/26 June, the Japanese snipers and guns harassed the Rajputs on Lone Tree Hill, and in cold grey dawn attempted another attack.[6] But their efforts bore no fruit. Though both the sides had suffered heavy casualties in this grim fighting for Lone Tree Hill, the position was retained by 5/6 Rajputana Rifles. To signalise its success Lone Tree Hill was renamed Rajput Hill (RK 516190) the same day (26 June).

Meanwhile, operations had continued to eject the Japanese forces from Scotts Knob also. Immediately after the receipt of the first clash in this area between a patrol of Kalibahadur Regiment and the Japanese on 23 June, one company of 4/5 Mahrattas of the 49th Brigade was ordered to seek out the Japanese force and prevent its progress towards Palel. A company of 6/5 Mahrattas was concentrated outside Palel to support the other if necessary, and one troop of 3 Dragoon Guards' tanks was called up near Palel. On the morning of 24 June, the Mahrattas attacked Scotts Knob, which was held by only one company of Japanese troops with 2 medium machine-guns in well-constructed bunkers. The attack was supported by tanks of one troop of 3 Dragoon Guards, but their fire did not reach the Japanese positions, and by 1700 hours the attack had failed. The brigade commander of the 49th Brigade then ordered the Mahrattas to hold RK 488200 to the bitter end, and to send out patrols towards Khunbi. Artillery was also ordered to keep up harassing fire at Scotts Knob throughout the night and the next day, 25 June. As a result, Khudei Khunou was evacuated by the Japanese on 25 June, which was confirmed by reports of the movements of Japanese traffic along the track running south from Maibi Khunou.

[6] *Ibid.*

The next day was also spent in intensive patrol activity and in collecting 6/5 Mahrattas near Palel for an overwhelming attack on Scotts Knob. On 27 June, the hill was attacked simultaneously by two companies of 6/5 Mahrattas and one company of 3/5 Royal Gurkha Rifles. The Gurkhas advanced along the ridge from Rajput Hill and occupied the Knolls lying just east of Scotts Knob. But the Mahrattas' attack against the Knob itself ended in a repulse. However, after an artillery barrage and an air-strike, the two companies of 6/5 Mahrattas dashed forward again. They succeeded in reaching the summit, but were then counter-attacked fiercely by about 300 Japanese behind the main position. The attack failed once again and the Mahrattas withdrew to Bushy Hill and then to RK 495185.

On 28 June, the company of 3/5 Royal Gurkha Rifles continued its slow advance towards Scotts Knob from the east and captured more hillocks. The 49th Brigade that day kept up its extensive patrolling and harassing artillery fire, and sent 4/5 Mahrattas to the Sengmai Turel area to intercept any Japanese troops who might be trying to escape from the Scotts Knob and the surrounding hills. The next morning it reached RK 527233. Other and smaller patrols ranged widely up and down the area, directing the field guns at all localities where any traces of the Japanese was found. Then on 30 June, Scotts Knob was attacked again with powerful support from artillery and the air force. This time the Mahrattas were able to capture the hill without difficulty, and they found there a 70-mm Japanese battalion gun with some ammunition.

The hills to the east and the north of Scotts Knob were also subjected to vigorous patrol activity during the last week of June 1944. From Maibi Khunou and Khunbi the Japanese had penetrated to Langgol also, and on 25 June considerable Japanese movement was noticed in that area. Thereupon the guns of the 49th Indian Infantry Brigade opened fire inflicting some casualties. Meanwhile movement of Japanese traffic was reported from the neighbourhood of Sita also. To counter any threat of Japanese advance northwards from Maibi Khunou on 27 June, Machi and Trim Hill were reinforced by some platoons of 4 Mahrattas and 15 Mountain Battery from Heirok area. The Machi garrison comprised two 3" mortar detachments and one platoon of 4/5 Mahrattas and one medium machine-gun section of 9 Jat. On 28 June, Japanese snipers fired on the Indian observation post at Hambone and were seen in some strength on the Ben Nevis Hill (RK 6116). On 29 June, steps were taken to destroy the parties of Japanese troops which were then expected to retire from the Scotts Knob and Khunbi areas. Two platoons of 3/10 Gurkha Rifles were sent to man a road-block at RK 530211 and 4 Mahrattas established itself at RK 527233.

The latter had a minor brush with a party of Japanese troops coming from the north. By the next day, however, they had withdrawn from Scotts Knob and had apparently succeeded in avoiding the road-blocks. But they still held Langgol and the Phalbung and Saibom areas.

Before withdrawing the Japanese had succeeded in reaching Palel itself in small but determined groups. During the night of 29/30 June one of them made a surprise attack on the Palel bridge. Bitter hand to hand fighting took place, the defenders using their bayonets and the attackers wielding swords. The fanatical attack, however, was beaten back. But in the night of 3/4 July, another Japanese raiding party consisting of one officer and seven other ranks attacked the Palel air-strip (RK 4425). These were all the troops that had been left of a company and were obviously desperate men. Armed with magnetic mines and explosive sticks called the Bangalore Torpedos, they sneaked into the dispersal bays where rows of Hurricanes and Spitfires were parked. Within a few minutes they had succeeded in destroying eight aircraft. To crown their success, they then escaped unscathed in the confusion that followed and before troops could reach there to encircle them. This, however, was the last Japanese triumph in the area. On 5 July, slight advances were made by units of the 49th Brigade in the Khudei Khunou area, and small hill features at RK 5521 and RK 5622 were occupied. Late that night the Japanese suddenly opened fire on the headquarters of 4/5 Mahrattas at Green Hill (RK 560218) in the course of which both the commanding officer and the Adjutant of the battalion were unfortunately killed. The next day, 6 July, a Japanese party of about fifty tried to recapture the hill at RK 5521. But the attack failed and they lost fourteen men killed while one was made a prisoner of war. Intensive patrol activity was continued on 7 July and 6/5 Mahrattas made slight advance in the Khudei Khunou area.

As has been already mentioned, at 0800 hours on 8 July, the 23rd Indian Division passed from the IV Corps to the command of the XXXIII Corps which then became responsible for all operations in the area east of the Manipur river, leaving the other Corps to deal solely with the fighting in the southern sector along the Imphal—Tiddim road.

On 8 July, the 1st Indian Infantry Brigade of the 23rd Indian Division was holding positions in the hills south of the main Imphal—Tamu road. 1 Patiala was just south of the Shenam area while 1/16 Punjab was disposed at Lamlong-Pantha, Point 5401 and Shuganu. 1 Seaforth was stationed at Wangjing except one company which was on the hill at RK 4221. The 37th Indian Infantry Brigade was holding positions along the main road in the Shenam—Tengnoupal area. 3/3 Gurkha Rifles covered the road junction at

Supply mules cross a mountain stream in Imphal area

Looking back from Scraggy to Malta Hill from which the famous feature was attacked by the Gurkhas. In the foreground is the equipment left behind by the Japanese

Aircraft dropping supplies on Tiddim Road

RK 5912 while 3/5 Gurkha Rifles and 3/10 Gurkha Rifles were slightly to the north between Tengnoupal and Phalbung. Further to the north lay the 49th Indian Infantry Brigade. 5/6 Rajputana Rifles was held in reserve near Kakching. 6/5 Mahrattas was in the area of RK 5521 near Khudei Khunou and 4/5 Mahrattas was slightly to the east near Khudei Khulen. Moreover, 2 Hyderabad was holding positions at Sita and along the line of communication leading to it via Nungtak.[7]

For a few days after the taking over of the charge of operations by the XXXIII Corps the usual patrolling and minor engagements continued. On 8 July a Japanese position at Sagang was bombed from the air and shelled by the guns of the 1st Brigade. The 37th Brigade sent out fighting patrols to the Phalbung area. There were a number of ambushes and skirmishes in which four or five Japanese were killed. 6/5 Mahrattas (of the 49th Brigade) continued to probe forward into the Japanese positions in the area of Khudei Khulen. 4/5 Mahrattas at the same time attacked and occupied two small hillocks at RK 529247 and RK 538243. After this the Khunbi area was gradually evacuated by the Japanese. On 9 July, advance was made in the area of Modi (RK 4102) south of the main road. North of the road a company of 3/3 Gurkha Rifles established itself 600 yards to the west of Phalbung village and prepared to ambush Japanese parties moving in the area. The patrols reported the main concentration of Japanese troops at Phalbung, Point 4600 and in the nullah between RK 576192 and Khudei Khunou. However, during the day the Gurkha company succeeded in killing or capturing some men of the hostile force in an ambush, near Hambone.[8] Small gains were also registered in the Khunbi—Khudei Khunou area by the 49th Brigade, and Khunbi Spur was occupied by one company of 4 Mahrattas. On 10 July 1944, a company of 1 Seaforth left the area of Maha Turel (RK 4515) for Shenam and was replaced by one platoon of 5/6 Rajputana Rifles. The guns of the 36th Brigade opened fire at several Japanese parties moving from the direction of Khudei Khunou towards Phalbung. The 6/5 Mahrattas discovered seven Japanese bunkers at RK 563224 but other patrols of 4/5 Mahrattas found little trace of the Japanese and it was realised that probably their retreat was beginning.

On 10 July the Corps Commander warned Major-General Roberts to be prepared for exploiting the imminent Japanese retreat. The Headquarters 23rd Indian Division therefore issued instructions to the 49th and 37th Brigades, for pursuing and harassing any Japanese withdrawal from the hills north of the road. Intensive patrolling was to be carried out in order to obtain early information

[7] Account of Operations of XXXIII Corps.
[8] War Diary of Headquarters 23rd Indian Division.

of any such movement. Since 3/3 Gurkha Rifles was blocking the main track through Phalbung, it was considered likely that the Japanese would use Khudei Khulen Spur as their main escape route. If that happened, the 49th Brigade was to push forward from Sengmai Turel area (RK 5520) and the company at Hambone (RK 6317) would try to ambush the retreating troops and prevent their escape.⁹ The 49th Brigade was to complete its occupation of the Khudei Khunou—Maibi Khunou area and 2 Hyderabad was to defend the Sita position and its line of communication via Nungtak.

The next day, 11 July, Headquarters 1st Brigade opened at Snowdon. The 3/3 Gurkha Rifles of the 37th Brigade continued patrolling in the area, but patrols of the 49th Brigade encountered opposition from some Japanese at RK 561222 near Khudei Khunou. However, a company of 4 Mahrattas occupied a hill at RK 570252 and reported that there were signs of a hurried evacuation of the feature by the Japanese. At the same time, Headquarters 49th Brigade moved up to RK 5222.¹⁰ The entire area of Khudei Khunou and Khudei Khulen was occupied by 4/5 Mahratta on 12 July, the Japanese garrisons having escaped during the night by little known tracks. Meanwhile, 1 Seaforth of the 1st Brigade had moved up to Water Tank Hill (RK 5413), Patiala Ridge (RK 5514), and Assam Ridge (RK 5412), while a platoon detachment occupied the Rajput Hill (RK 5119). On 13 July the Kalibahadur Regiment was ordered to relieve 1/16 Punjab in the area Lamlong—Pantha (RK 3912) and Shuganu, and was placed under command of the 1st Brigade. Subsequently the battalion was to take over the defence of Palel—Shaiba (RK 474172) area. The usual patrol activity continued in the areas of the 37th Brigade and 49th Brigade, but there were few engagements. Rains had recently been heavy and the Sengmai Turel had become a roaring torrent. The nullah west and north west of Khudei Khulen was also in spate restricting movement.

On 14 July again there was only limited patrolling, and fighting was reported mainly from the Phalbung area. A patrol clash took place at Point 4600 (RK 5917) and five Japanese were wounded in another skirmish in the same area. In the 49th Brigade area movement was practically at a standstill due to the flooded Sengmai Turel. There were difficulties even in supplying the "A" Company of 4 Mahrattas with rations at Khudei Khulen. Also, the sappers failed to bridge the torrent, but by the evening D Company of the Mahratta battalion somehow got across the nulla and joined its sister company.¹¹ On 15 July the Japanese administrative area,

---

⁹ Ibid.
¹⁰ War Diary of Headquarters 49th Indian Infantry Brigade, General Staff Branch.
¹¹ Ibid.

south-east of Phalbung (RK 5818) was shelled, and far to the east near Sita, some members of the garrison at Leibi (RK 7113) surrendered. The next day at 1030 hours, 4/5 Mahrattas attacked a position where the Japanese were still holding out to the east of Khudei Khulen. About fifteen of the defenders were killed and the first few bunkers were captured without difficulty, but the main position was hidden by thick jungle and could not be easily captured. During the night of 16/17 July the Japanese in the Phalbung area attempted a counter-attack which was successfully repulsed. On 17 July, Allied guns opened fire on several small parties of Japanese troops in the Phalbung area and near Ben Nevis (RK 6116). At the latter place a small Japanese party was ambushed. At Scraggy (RK 585125) and Maita (RK 577125) 3/3 Gurkha Rifles was relieved and replaced by 3/5 Royal Gurkha Rifles. Phalbung area was shelled again the next day and Japanese positions at RK 591126 were reconnoitred. Other patrols contacted Japanese parties at RK 591124 and at Lynch Hill (RK 589120). There were minor clashes in the area of Crete (RK 597118) and Morgan's Peak (RK 607106) in the sector of the main road also, but the Khudei Khulen area was found clear of the Japanese who apparently had succeeded in escaping eastwards.[12] The 19 July was unusually quiet. One Japanese section was seen at the south end of Phalbung village, and some patrol activity was continued. But the weather had been extremely wet and foggy for the last few days and movement over the hills was exceedingly difficult. Moreover, units of the 23rd Indian Division were then completing their preparations for the major offensive to destroy the *Yamamoto Force* and recapture Tamu. In the event, the reduced scale of fighting during these few days proved to be the proverbial lull before the storm.

THE PLAN OF ATTACK ON TAMU

Gradually troop reinforcements had been sent up to the Palel area. On 8 July 1944, 1st Medium Regiment Royal Artillery was placed under the command of the 23rd Indian Division. On 12 July, one squadron 11 Cavalry and one squadron 140 Royal Armoured Corps also arrived to support this division's operations. 2/4 Bombay Grenadiers was sent up to the area of Nungtak to improve the track from there to Sita. A large number of field guns were concentrated near the front lines, the Hyderabad Battery of the 3rd Indian Field Regiment being moved to the Saibom Ridge (RK 5517), 27 Light Battery 16th Field Regiment to Assam Ridge (RK 5412) and 13 Mountain Battery 28th Mountain Regiment to Patiala

---
[12] War Diary of Headquarters 23rd Indian Division General Staff Branch.

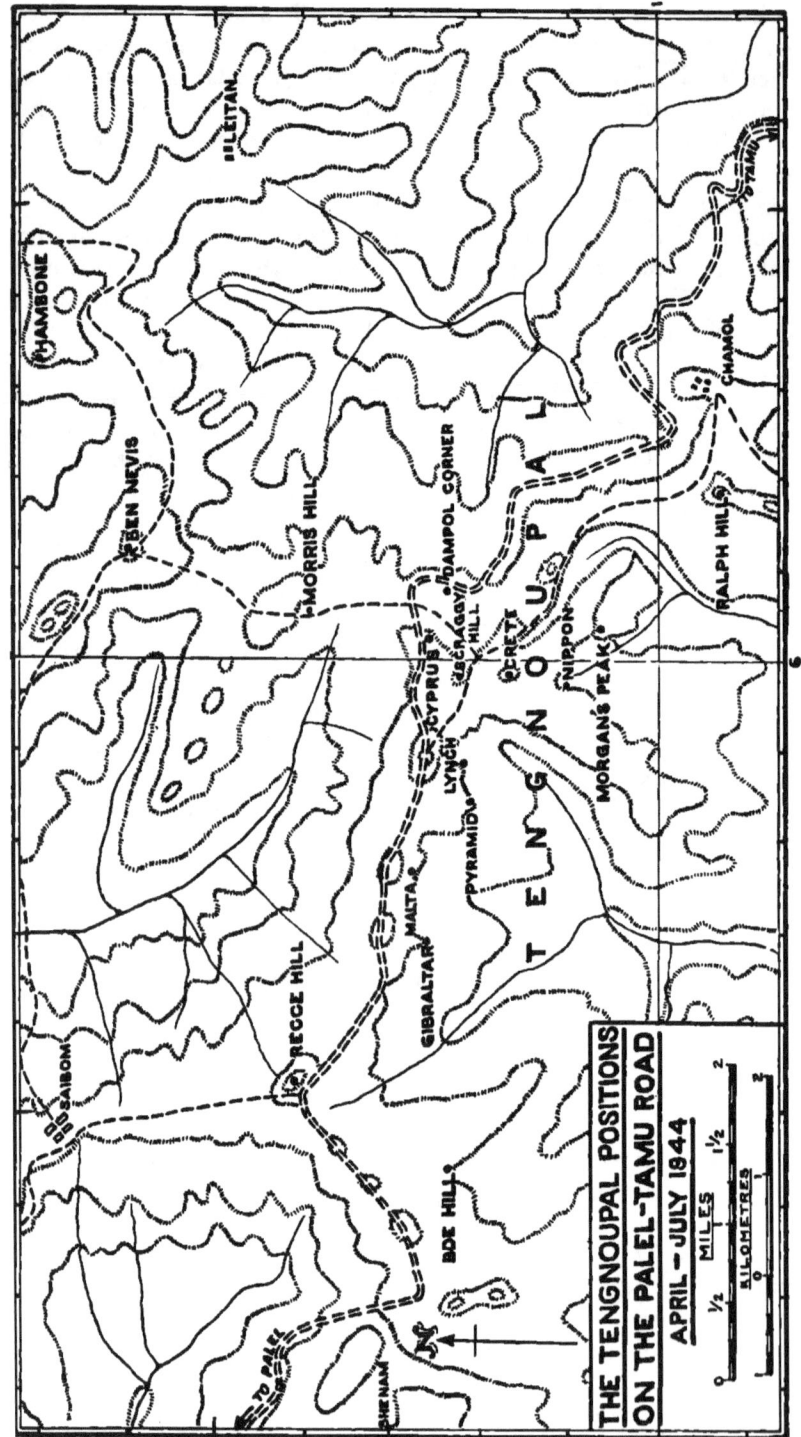

Ridge (RK 5514) on 13 and 14 July. At the same time 19/7 Rajput Heavy Anti-Aircraft Battery (less one troop) arrived for supporting the attack.[13] On 14 July, Lieutenant-General Stopford, the General Officer Commanding XXXIII Corps, ordered the 5th Infantry Brigade of the 2nd British Division and the 268th Indian Infantry Brigade to reinforce the 23rd Indian Division. The 268th Brigade, excepting 17 Rajput but with 2 Hyderabad under its command, was ordered to proceed to the Heirok area (RK 5026) on 16 July, and the 5th Brigade was to concentrate near Palel on 20 July. On 16 July, Headquarters 268th Indian Infantry Brigade and 5/4 Bombay Grenadiers moved to the Heirok area and 208 Field Company further reinforced the engineer units in the sector. The next day, 2 Hyderabad which was holding the forward positions in the area of Sita (RK 5821) and Leibi (RK 7214) was placed under the command of the 268th Brigade. All these movements were carried out with the utmost secrecy in order to achieve complete surprise for the attack. Every advantage was taken of the thick clouds and heavy fog. The guns were handled up to the commanding positions with great difficulty. Dumps of ammunition and rations were collected and all was made ready for the massive assault.

The plan for the attack was issued on 17 July 1944. The intention of the divisional commander was to destroy the two bridges over the Lokchao Stream (RK 7005) and prevent the Japanese *Yamamoto Force* from withdrawing successfully while frontal attacks broke it up and annihilated it. The troops available for the operation were the three brigades of the 23rd Indian Division and the following units[14]:—

    5th British Brigade
    268th Indian Infantry Brigade less one battalion
    B Squadron 149th Royal Armoured Corps of Grant tanks.
    One troop 3 Dragoon Guards of Lee tanks
    A Squadron 11 Cavalry
    Half of one squadron 7 Cavalry
    1 Medium Regiment Royal Artillery
    9th Field Regiment Royal Artillery
    16th Field Regiment Royal Artillery
    19/7 Rajput Heavy Anti-Aircraft Battery (less one troop)
    94th Field Company Royal Engineers
    208th Field Company Royal Engineers
    2nd Engineer Battalion less two companies
    Three companies 10th Engineer Battalion
    One section 442nd Queens Royal Guards company

---
[13] *Ibid.*
[14] *Ibid*; 23rd Indian Division Operation Order No. 22, dated 17 July 1944.

1467 Pioneer Company and
9 Jat Regiment of machine-guns.

For bombing and strafing from the air, 34 Squadron RAF and 113 Squadron RAF equipped with Hurricane bombers were allotted.

The 1st Indian Infantry Brigade was placed on the right flank of the attacking forces. 16 Mountain Battery, 1 Medium Machine-gun Platoon of 9th Jat Regiment and some engineer units were placed under it, which was then given the task of advancing north-eastwards from the Mitlong Khunou (RK 5604) area along the jeep track towards Chamol (RK 6349). It was ordered to deliver a surprise attack on Ralph Hill (RK 617093), hold that area till joined by the other units advancing along the main road and then turn east and seize the area of RK 650087 where the headquarters of the Japanese *Yamamoto Force* was reported to be stationed. The 1 Seaforth was to attack Nippon Hill (RK 599111) frontally under the command of the 37th Brigade and was to rejoin the parent unit as soon as it had advanced and made contact with the 1st Brigade near Ralph Hill. The 37th Indian Infantry Brigade was given the task of capturing Nippon Hill, Crete (RK 599120), Scraggy (RK 597122), Lynch (RK 589122) and Cyprus (RK 603125) hills flanking the main road. As all these hill positions were riddled with Japanese bunkers which had defied attacks during the fighting in April and May, it was obvious that the attack by the 37th Brigade would require overwhelming fire-power to succeed. Therefore, two Medium Machine-gun platoons of 9 Jat, B Squadron, 149th Royal Armoured Corps and 91st Field Company were allotted to it. Moreover, all the field guns of the divisional artillery were placed under the Commander Royal Artillery and detailed to support the attacks launched by the 37th Brigade. After the attack, the 37th Brigade was to thrust down the road to link up with the 1st Brigade.[15] Thereafter one of the brigades was to exploit its advantage in clearing the hilly area of Morris Hill and Ben Nevis while the other would continue the advance down the main road towards Sibong with the assistance of the 5th British Brigade.

The 5th British Brigade was placed immediately behind the 37th Brigade on the main road and it was intended that this brigade would either occupy the areas captured by the 37th Brigade or assist the general attack, as might be necessary. The 49th Brigade was sent round to execute a wide outflanking movement from the left. Proceeding from the Heirok area via Nungtak, Sita and Leibi, it was to get behind the Japanese position and cut off their retreat towards Tamu. Utmost importance was attached to the destruction of the bridges over the Lokchao river; for once these bridges were

---
[15] *Ibid.*

broken the Japanese guns and tanks could not withdraw from the fighting area. If for any reason this operation became impracticable, the 49th Brigade was ordered to establish a strong road-block at 725020 and prevent the escape of the *Yamamoto Force*. Secrecy in movement and boldness in attack were emphasised in the divisional commander's instructions, and detailed reconnaissance, it was laid down, was not to be waited for. Having destroyed the Lokchao bridges or established the road-block, the 49th Brigade was to hold on to its position till the 1st and 37th Brigades advancing down the main road had linked up with it. For the operation, 15 Mountain Battery, 71st Field Company less one platoon and one Medium Machine-Gun platoon of 9 Jat were placed under the command of the 49th Brigade. There was a danger to the left flank of the brigade from Japanese attacks from the Dolaibung area (RK 7418), hence the 268th Indian Infantry Brigade was positioned to counter it. The additional troops allotted to the brigade were 2 Hyderabad, 2 Engineer Battalion less two companies, one platoon 71 Field Company and one company 10 Engineer Battalion.

The task of the 268th Brigade was to protect the line of communication of the 49th Brigade from Japanese attacks, to maintain the Nungtak track in a fit state of repair and protect the 25-pounder guns placed at Hambone (RK 6317). Moreover, it was required to prevent the Japanese, then in the Khudei Khulen area, from escaping eastwards along the Khudei Khulen Spur and to make a threatening advance southwards towards Ben Nevis and down the Leitan Spur (RK 6515). Ben Nevis was to be attacked and captured if held only by a small Japanese garrison. The 268th Brigade operations were not to begin till one day before the main attack so that the Japanese could obtain no previous warning. The guns on Hambone Hill, Saibom Ridge and the other hill positions were placed under the Commander Corps Royal Artillery, XXXIII Corps, and were designed to assist the attack of every brigade as necessary. The brigade commanders were to request for shelling by these guns whenever they encountered stiff resistance in their respective attacks. But it was realized that many of the steep reverse slopes of the hills occupied by the Japanese might not admit of effective bombardment by the field artillery, hence aerial bombing was arranged for . Requests for strafing and bombing from the air were also to be made by the brigade commanders through the Commander Corps Royal Artillery. The air force allotted for the direct tactical support of the attacks was to be in readiness to take advantage of the fleeting fair weather over the targets. The monsoon was then in full fury and inky black clouds hung low over the entire area. But it was expected that with the powerful support of divisional and Corps artillery, the tanks and the air force, the attack would prove successful and the *Yamamoto Force* would be destroyed. The D-Day for the attack had to be postponed twice due to extremely bad weather and the attack was not finally launched till 24 July 1944.

THE THRUST TO SIBONG

While the attacks of the 1st and 37th Brigades were still held up by the continuous rains, on 20 July the 49th Brigade was ordered to commence its outflanking march. The track beyond Nungtak was in a very bad state due to the rains and portions of it were extremely narrow and slippery. Several mules lost their footing and went hurtling down the steep slopes with their precious loads. But the advance continued, and the Brigade Headquarters reached RK 6422 the same day. The 5/6 Rajputana Rifles was leading the advance and had reached Sita by then. The next day the Rajputs marched from Sita to Leibi (RK 716135) and occupied the village without encountering any serious opposition. The remainder of the 49th Brigade and the Brigade Headquarters reached Kampang (RK 7018). On 22 July, 6/5 Mahrattas advanced from Kampang via Leibi to a point only three miles north of Sibong (RK 7204). The next day, Brigade Headquarters and 4/5 Mahrattas also arrived at RK 7205 near Sibong, which was occupied almost without resistance. At 0100 hours on the night of 22/23 July, 5/6 Rajputana Rifles was ordered to move secretly through the jungle and reconnoitre the Lokchao bridges in order to destroy them, if possible. The Rajputs were not detected by the Japanese and spent several hours hiding in the jungle near the bridges. But they found that at least 14 tanks and several guns were defending the vital bridges and so the attack had to be postponed for the next night.

Meanwhile on 23 July, a Japanese reconnaissance patrol blundered into the forward platoon of 6 Mahrattas at Sibong. It withdrew quickly, but the secrecy of the outflanking movement was now gone. The 4 and 6 Mahrattas thereupon proceeded immediately to establish protective positions north-west and south respectively of Sibong. But no major clash took place and Japanese movement was not noticeable. At 2100 hours the same day, 5 Rajputana Rifles moved out again with the intention of blowing up the Lokchao bridges. They returned at 0070 hours the next morning after wandering about the whole night in a fruitless effort to locate the bridges.[16] Torrential rains during the night had added to their

---

[16] War Diary of Headquarters 49th Brigade, General Staff Branch.

hardships and the Sappers particularly were exceedingly tired. It appeared that the demolition of the bridges would not be practicable now. Patrols from 6 Mahrattas were therefore sent out to discover sites for road-blocks on the main Palel—Tamu road in order to prevent the Japanese retreat. The latter had then, however, started reacting vigorously to this threat behind their front lines and continuous attacks were launched, mainly against the positions held by the Rajputs during the night of 24/25 July. All these attacks were repulsed and the Japanese lost a number of men.

On 25 July the 4 and 6 Mahrattas proceeded southwards to cut the main road. A patrol of 4 Mahrattas destroyed four Japanese trucks at RK 700058. The 6 Mahrattas reached the road at RK 720025 and came face to face with a strong Japanese position at RK 718029. In the fighting that ensued, both the parties lost heavily. Nevertheless, the Japanese held on to their positions repulsing the attacks. Consequently the road-block could not be established, but the 49th Brigade covered the Japanese line of communication with fire from medium machine-guns, mortars and artillery, hindering their retreat.

On 26 July, 4/5 Mahrattas established a road-block at RK 729023. It consisted of barrels of tar interspersed with anti-tank mines. It was at once vigorously attacked by the Japanese and the Mahrattas were forced to withdraw about two hundred yards north of the road from where they were in a position to open fire on any traffic passing along the road; nevertheless, some Japanese vehicles managed to escape towards Tamu. At RK 7202 another fierce encounter took place between the Japanese and the Mahrattas. The weather had also cleared up temporarily. Troops had been living soaked to the skin for the past many days and the brief respite from the rain was a welcome relief. By 27 June the Japanese had apparently succeeded in withdrawing a large portion of their troops from the Tengnoupal area. The attacks of the 37th Indian Infantry Brigade and the 1st Indian Infantry Brigade had succeeded and these brigades were driving eastwards to link up with the 49th Brigade. During the day radio telephonic communication was established between the 49th Brigade and the 1st Brigade which were advancing along the main road to form a junction. That evening loud explosions were heard as the Japanese completed their withdrawal and blew up the two Lokchao bridges behind them. The suspension bridge (RK 701058) was also found destroyed when the 6 Mahrattas reached the area of Lokchao bridge (RK 700054), on the morning of 28 July. It found that only men and lightly laden mules could, with difficulty, cross over the Lokchao bridges. The same morning the advancing units of the 1st Brigade reached the other bank of the Lokchao river and contact was established between the two brigades.

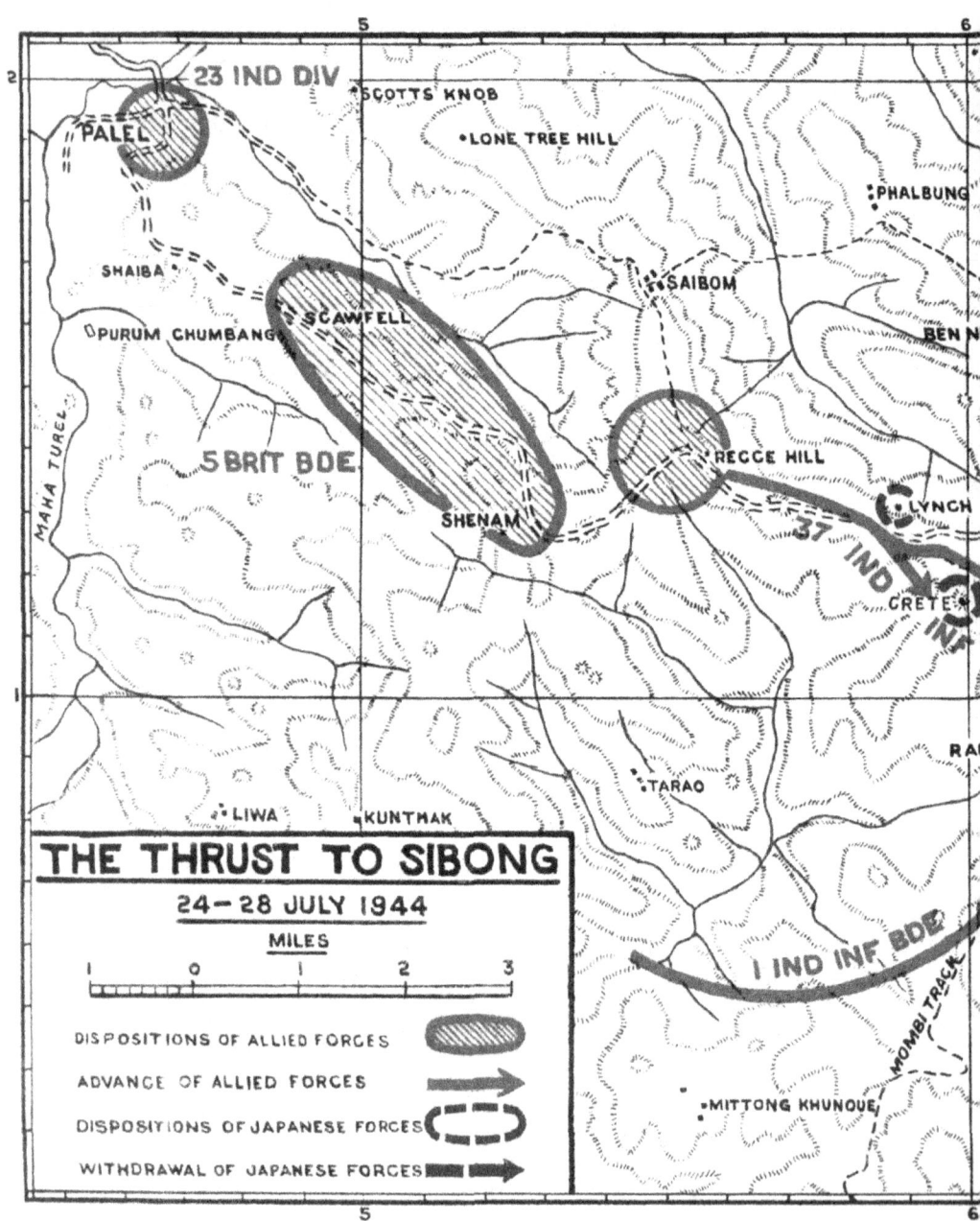

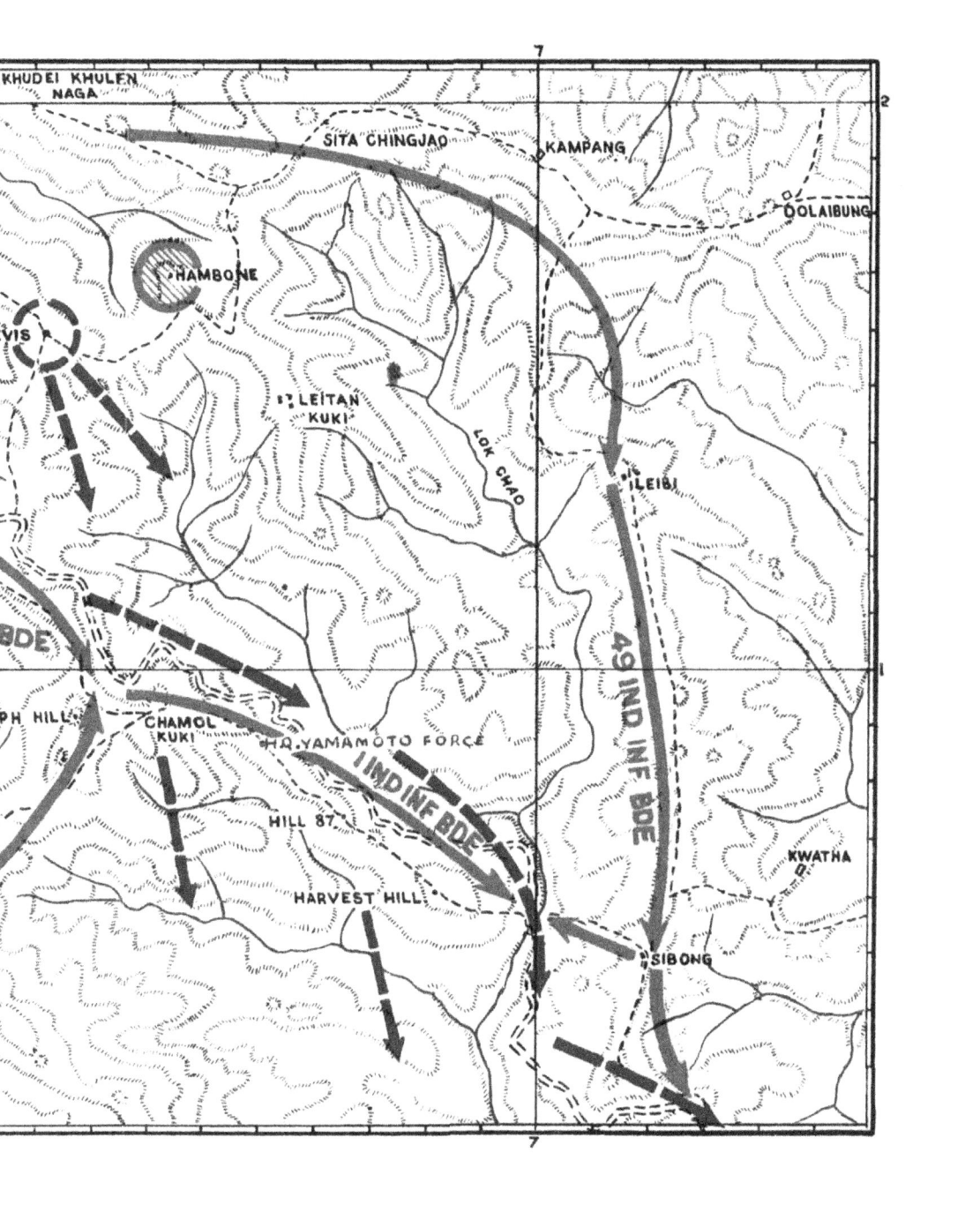

From 20 July to 23 July, intensive patrolling and bombardment of the Japanese positions was carried on from the air and by field guns. Patrols of the 1st Brigade, on 21 July, penetrated the Jap Hill (RK 601104) and Nippon Hill (RK 599111). The former was found unoccupied and on the latter also no movement was detected although there were a number of bunkers there. Other patrols found out from the reports of the local villagers that Dampi (RK 1608) and Saiton Khulen (RK 1615) were still occupied by the Japanese while Sagang (RK 2070) was visited by them frequently for collecting stores and provisions. The village of Kumbi was also found evacuated. On 21 July, patrols of the 37th Brigade also reported that the Japanese strength around Phalbung had increased to over one company during the past two days. Air attacks were made on the Japanese positions on Crete West (RK 598120), and most of the bombs appeared to strike the objectives. Further down the road Allied aircraft tried to bomb the Lokchao bridges, but the Japanese had mounted several anti-aircraft guns of the Bofors type there, and one of the attacking planes was shot down by these guns. The Japanese in their turn had opened fire on the area of Palel airstrip (RK 4525) on the morning of 21 July. Twelve 105-mm shells landed in the area but five of them did not burst and only two Allied personnel were slightly wounded. That day at noon they also shelled Malta (RK 576126), eight shells of 105-mm calibre landing on the positions held by the 37th Brigade. The next day, 22 July, Headquarters 1st Brigade was established at Tarao (RK 5408) and 1/16 Punjab was concentrated there. The patrols of the 37th Brigade visited Scraggy (RK 597122). They found that the hill-top was unoccupied, but there were some Japanese troops cutting wood and digging trenches on the reverse slopes of the hill.[17] Lynch Hill (RK 588123) was also visited by patrols who found it manned by some Japanese troops, and the positions in the Phalbung area were still strongly held. In the hills to the north of the main road, 2/4 Bombay Grenadiers of the 268th Brigade advanced from Sita to Dolaibung and 2 Hyderabad carried out reconnaissance patrols towards Ben Nevis. Ben Nevis Hill was found occupied by about twelve Japanese who opened fire on the Hyderabad patrol near the track junction at RK 749180. On this day the clouds also lifted from the area after several days, thus permitting the Allied guns to complete their 'Registration' on the Japanese positions.

The next day, 23 July, the 1st Brigade completed its preparations for the attack on Ralph Hill from the south. The 16 Mountain Battery joined Headquarters 1st Brigade and 1/16

---

[17] War Diary of Headquarters 37th Indian Infantry Brigade, General Staff Branch.

Punjab at Tarao, and 1 Patiala, accompanied by 1 Platoon of 9 Jat Machine-Guns, and the assault detachments of 68 Field Company, passed through Tarao on their way to the starting line. The Tactical Headquarters of the 37th Brigade opened at Malta at 1630 hours. The platoon of 3/10 Gurkha Rifles at Phalbung was relieved and replaced by 2 Dorset of the 5th British Brigade but the sector remained unusually quiet for the whole day.

The attack on Ralph Hill was scheduled to begin in the early hours of the next morning. For the main attack along the road an armoured column consisting of B Squadron 149th Royal Armoured Corps and some armoured cars from the PAVO formed up on the road between Recce Hill (RK 556140) and Gibraltar. They were ordered to move forward as soon as the Sappers had cleared the road of land mines, and to destroy any Japanese position which the attacking infantry would be unable to capture. As the hour for attack approached, the numerous medium and field guns opened up a terrific barrage against the Japanese positions. The infantry then advanced to the assault in heavy rain and a rolling mist, which hid all movement and smothered the noise of the tanks. By 0830 hours on 24 July, 3/3 Gurkha Rifles had succeeded in capturing Crete West (RK 598120) and Lynch Hill and were advancing against Crete East. It encountered a somewhat stronger resistance at Crete East, but by 1400 hours, that aftrenoon, the feature was securely in Allied hands. 3/5 Royal Gurkha Rifles which had silently assembled just below the Morris Hill (RK 605140) scrambled up and occupied the hill without opposition. On the peak it found evidence of a hurried Japanese retreat, in the course of which considerable equipment had been left behind. Some 105-mm guns, 47-mm anti-tank guns and two Japanese tractors were found abandoned on Morris Hill.[16]

The heaviest fighting, however, took place on Scraggy, where 3/10 Gurkha Rifles had to maintain its attacks for three hours before the Japanese garrison was finally liquidated. Although in the last stages of the attack a few Japanese were seen running away, almost the entire garrison of Scraggy was destroyed by the Gurkhas. At least 48 Japanese dead were counted immediately, and many others were undoubtedly buried in the bunkers and the debris. Moreover two Japanese were taken prisoners. The casualties of 3/10 Gurkhas too were not light, and came to 90 men killed or wounded, mainly from grenade splinters. The attack of 1 Seaforth against Nippon Hill also encountered heavy opposition. There were a number of Japanese bunkers on the reverse slopes of the hill, which for a while held up the attack. But the Indian Engineer Assault parties crept forward and blew up five or six bunkers with 'Wade'

[16] *Ibid.*

charges. The Japanese were caught evidently by surprise, and the Sappers suffered no casualties, while about four men of the other side were killed and buried in the collapse of each bunker.

After the capture of Nippon Hill, 1 Seaforth went on and attacked Morgan's Peak (RK 607105). This Hill was captured without difficulty, and by 1400 hours 1 Seaforth was ready waiting to advance towards Ralph Hill (RK 618093) where 1 Patiala of the 1st Brigade was still held up.

The 1st Brigade had only two battalions for its attack, having left 1 Seaforth under the 37th Brigade for attacking Nippon Hill as mentioned earlier. Of the two available battalions 1/16 Punjab was held back in reserve for a special task while 1 Patiala advanced to the attack. It captured the Ring Contour at RK 612084 on the southern slopes of Ralph Hill without difficulty. But the main Japanese positions on Ralph Hill could not be captured that day.[19] The Japanese opposition was strong, visibility was exceedingly poor and the going very difficult. These factors had also prevented the 1/16 Punjab from attacking the headquarters of the *Yamamoto Force* at RK 650087. It had, however, concentrated secretly at RK 592060 and had intended to launch a right hook against RK 650087 in the hope of capturing the Japanese Headquarters. But the appalling conditions of the track made the advance impossible. The attack of the 268th Brigade against Ben Nevis (RK 611155) scheduled for the day had also failed, though for different reasons. Earlier, patrols had reported only about a dozen Japanese in the area, but when 2 Hyderabad advanced to attack on the morning of the 24th it was counter-attacked by approximately three platoons of Japanese troops. The attack failed and the battalion was forced to withdraw, with the loss of four killed and eight wounded. The 268th Brigade was then ordered to be prepared to attack and capture Ben Nevis as soon as the weather cleared and the 25-pounder guns at Hambone (RK 635163) were able to bombard the hill in support of the attack.

The 1st Indian Infantry Brigade continued its attack the next day, 25 July, and by 1045 hours the whole of Ralph Hill (RK 617092) was occupied. The 1 Patiala then followed up towards Morgan's Peak (RK 607106). It encountered opposition at RK 615102 and was held up, although eight casualties were inflicted on the Japanese defending the position. 1/16 Punjab moving northwards found three Japanese road-blocks just south of the track junction at RK 624092. All these road-blocks were stormed gallantly and seized. The Japanese then destroyed the ammunition stocked there for their 75-mm guns and melted away into the forest. By

---

[19] War Diary of Headquarters 1st Indian Infantry Brigade, General Staff Branch.

1400 hours the headquarters of the three battalions of the 1st Brigade were located as follows[20]:—

1/16 Punjab with Mountain Battery	RK 592060
1 Patiala	RK 612084
1 Seaforth	RK 607106

The 37th Brigade on 25 July cleared up the whole of Morris Hill and Cyprus, counting numerous Japanese dead bodies and collecting abandoned Japanese equipment. A strong Japanese position at RK 602112 was overpowered with the help of tanks. The defenders retreated, leaving behind a British 6-pounder anti-tank gun as a reminder of their early victories. At 1200 hours that day, the Headquarters 37th Brigade was at Malta, 3/3 Gurkha Rifles was holding Cyprus and Crete East (RK 601122), 3/5 Royal Gurkha Rifles was stationed on Morris Hill, Scraggy and Lynch, and 3/10 Gurkha Rifles was on Crete West. The 268th Brigade confined its activity on 25 July to patrolling towards Ben Nevis, and in heroic efforts to keep open the track from Nungtak to Sita (RK 6720). A major landslide carried away a part of the track, and the Sappers had to work the whole night of 25/26 July to restore the breach.

The 25 July had been spent, generally speaking, in consolidating the gains made on the previous day, but another major attack was ordered for 26 July. The General Officer Commanding 23rd Division, ordered the 37th Brigade to open the road up to Ralph Hill with the help of tanks, and send a jeep convoy with supplies to the 1st Brigade. The 268th Brigade was ordered to capture Ben Nevis as soon as possible, while the other brigades continued their operations according to the earlier instructions.[21] But at 0800 hours on 26 July, a big landslide occurred at RK 613111 on the main road, thus blocking the 37th Brigade's tank thrust. After herculean efforts, the road was cleared by 1520 hours the same day, but the tank attack could not take place, and hence the supplies could not reach the 1st Brigade at Ralph Hill (RK 618093). The 268th Brigade also failed to attack Ben Nevis on 26 July. Major-General Roberts then gave positive orders to the 268th Brigade to attack the hill on 27 July, unless it had been evacuated by the Japanese earlier.

Only the 1st Brigade recorded some progress on 26 July. The 1/16 Punjab advanced along the road and reached the track junction at RK 650088. Its advance was contested by several small Japanese parties, but they were easily brushed aside and considerable war material was captured. 1 Patiala also defeated and dispersed a Japanese party near the junction of the main road and the Mombi

---
[20] *Ibid.*
[21] War Diary of Headquarters 23rd Indian Division, General Staff Branch.

track. 1 Seaforth also advanced some distance eastwards along the north of the main road, but was held up by the Japanese fire from RK 637097.

The next morning, 27 July, 1 Seaforth overcame the opposition and pushed on up to Harvest Hill (RK 688060) overlooking the Lokchao bridges. At the same time, 1/16 Punjab advanced towards RK 668072, capturing Gurkha Hill (RK 657080) from the south-east. By 0900, the troops of 1/16 Punjab had reached Hill 87 (RK 665072). Behind it, 1 Patiala recaptured a hill at RK 660075 which it had been forced to abandon earlier. The Headquarters 1st Brigade was moved forward to Hill 87 (RK 665072) and final plans were made for 1 Patiala to push on the next day accompanied by tanks in order to link up with the 49th Brigade at Sibong. More Japanese guns, ammunition and equipment were collected from the areas abandoned by them during the day. The 37th Brigade also found some abondoned Japanese flame-throwers and documents on Morris Hill on 28 July. One wounded Japanese straggler was captured at Dampol Corner (RK 606124) and eight Japanese were killed in a patrol encounter at RK 623136. The same day the 268th Brigade advanced against Ben Nevis as ordered. But the company of 2/19 Hyderabad sent on that mission found Ben Nevis deserted, and so the occupation of the hill was completed the same morning peacefully. The 268th Brigade then linked up with the 37th Brigade near Morris Hill. At Ashang Khulen (RK 8125) also no Japanese defenders were found. Their dogged defence of the hills north of the Tengnoupal position had obviously ended, hence a strong patrol was sent by the 268th Brigade farther afield towards Mintha (RK 9018). Early on the morning of 28 July, 1 Patiala of the 1st Brigade resumed its advance from the main road. Tanks rumbled along to assist it, and helped to overcome quickly a weak Japanese resistance along the road at 0800 hours. Forty minutes later, the column reached the western bank of the Lokchao stream and contact was established with units of the 49th Brigade on the other bank. Responsibility for the defence of the Lokchao bridge area was taken over by the 1st Brigade from the 49th Brigade the same day, and 1/16 Punjab concentrated at Hill 87 (RK 665072) to be ready to move forward. Behind the 1st Brigade the 37th Brigade continued its consolidation of the Tengnoupal area, and spent the day in counting more Japanese dead bodies and sorting out the captured equipment.

The Allied counter-offensive thus opened very successfully, and hurled back the Japanese from Tengnoupal to Sibong in one stroke. Although the failure of the 49th Brigade to prevent a Japanese retreat along the road to Tamu had saved the *Yamamoto Force* from complete annihilation, the threat to Palel was finally removed. The

Japanese were in headlong retreat and the road to Tamu and the Chindwin lay open.

THE FALL OF TAMU

Meanwhile, it had been decided to push on further down the road and recapture Tamu. Apart from the propaganda value of reoccupying that town, it was obviously desirable to keep the Japanese on the run. The *Yamamoto Force* had broken and fled from Tengnoupal. Swift and relentless pursuit of the beaten enemy is universally recognised as the most profitable operation of war. If the Allied troops could dash forward and catch up with the retreating remnants of the *Yamamoto Force*, a decisive victory would be gained west of the Chindwin. Moreover, the recapture of Tamu with its valuable air-strip would provide the advancing army with a good forward base.

Hence on 25 July, immediately after the attacks by the 37th Brigade had succeeded against Scraggy, Crete etc., Lieut.-General Stopford set the 23rd Indian Division the task of capturing the Tamu—Laiching (RK 7999) area and of destroying all the opposing forces there.[22] After this task had been carried out, operations would continue with the object of advancing along the Tamu—Sittaung road and occupying the hilly watershed between the Chindwin and the Mu rivers. This advance would be undertaken either by the 23rd Indian Division, or by the 11th East African Division. The latter had arrived in the Imphal area in the middle of July, and was gradually moving into position behind the 23rd Indian Division. On 20 July 1944, it assumed command of the Nepalese Kalibahadur Regiment and took over the protection of the main Imphal plain. By 25 July its troops started patrolling, and two days later the 25th Brigade Group of the 11th East African Division completed its concentration at Kakching (RK 4224).

Operations had continued after the linking up of the 1st Indian Infantry Brigade with the 49th Indian Infantry Brigade at the Lokchao bridge on 28 July 1944. By that date, the Japanese had cleared out from Sibong and all the territory to the west of it. But patrols of 5/6 Rajputana Rifles had reported that they were still holding positions on Battle Hill (TK 718029), commanding the road from Sibong to Tamu. Their medium guns had opened fire against the 49th Brigade from the Moreh position also on 28 July. But Allied guns quickly laid down a heavy and accurate counter-battery fire and silenced the Japanese guns. The 5/6 Rajputana Rifles then launched an attack on Battle Hill on the same day. The battalion fought its way to a point only 200 yards from the top of Battle Hill. But then

---

[22] Log Sheet No. 104, War Diary of Headquarters XXXIII Indian Corps, General Staff Branch for the month of July 1944.

it was faced with a fire-swept zone. The hill-top was honey-combed with Japanese bunkers, and five medium machine-guns covered the approaches with criss-crossing fire. The Rajputs could not advance further in spite of their best efforts, and had to retire after suffering heavy casualties.

This was the first major stand made by the Japanese after the opening of the 23rd Division's attacks in the Tengnoupal area. These attacks, as described earlier, had shown a general cracking up of Japanese morale, and the men of *Yamamoto Force* had turned and fled from the prepared positions or had been overwhelmed by the attack. The *Yamamoto Force* itself was indeed shattered. It was gradually discovered that the vigorous stand at Battle Hill was made by fresh Japanese troops of the *4th Division*. The first indication of the arrival of these troops was gained when a Japanese prisoner captured near Dampol Corner (RK 606124) was found to belong to *1st Company* of *1st Battalion, 61st Regiment* of *4th Japanese Division*. From later evidence it appeared that Battle Hill was held by *1st* and *3rd Battalions* of *61st Regiment, 4th Japanese Division*. These units were acting as the rear-guard to delay the pursuit by the 23rd Indian Division so that the broken remnants of *Yamamoto Force* might have time enough to escape to the Chindwin.

The 29th day of July was spent in patrolling and finalising plans for the reduction of the Battle Hill. This feature was a steep and rocky peak, and the Japanese were dug in securely and covered the approaches with machine-gun fire. The commander of the 49th Brigade realised that the hill would not be taken without being softened up by furious shelling and aerial bombing. But the wet weather hampered even that. A heavy fog and rolling mist covered the entire area. Twice on 30 July, aircraft took off from Imphal plain to bomb Battle Hill, but by the time they reached their target, the clouds and the fog had closed up again, hiding the cruel, jagged rocks in soft, fleecy vapour. Heavy rains and the resultant floods further damaged the Lokchao bridge and made it impassable for mechanical transport. The guns could not be brought forward due to the swollen Lokchao stream. It was, therefore, decided to place one Field Battery and two medium guns in the Khongkhang (RK 6508) area. These guns, the mountain guns with the 49th Brigade and the medium guns in the Tengnoupal area would bombard Battle Hill in support of the attack. One battalion, 6/5 Mahrattas, was detailed to go round by road and encircle the Japanese strong-point, while the rest of the brigade would attack the hill as soon as preliminary arrangements for artillery support were completed. The next day, 30 July, was spent in these preparations. The mountain guns were carefully sited to bombard the hill from point-blank range, and vigorous patrolling was carried out. By that evening, all preparations were completed, and the attack was scheduled for the next day.

On 31 July, early in the morning, patrols reported that Battle Hill was still under Japanese occupation. Troops then moved forward for the attack. 6/5 Mahrattas started at 0630 hours with orders to go round the flank of the hill and climb it from the south. The rest of the brigade, led by 5/6 Rajputana Rifles surged forward to storm the height frontally. Allied aircraft again took off to lend direct air support to the attack, but had again to return without sighting Battle Hill due to the low clouds. The artillery, however, opened a fierce bombardment with all available guns. High explosive shells from mountain, field and medium guns rained down on the Japanese positions with pin-point accuracy, and the infantry delivered its assault under their cover. Starting at 1240 hours, the attack soon overwhelmed the defenders. The peak was reached without difficulty by 5/6 Rajputana Rifles at 1345 hours, and only two minutes later 6/5 Mahrattas joined it there from the other slope of the hill.[23] Thus fell Battle Hill, and the last serious opposition offered by the Japanese before Tamu was at last overcome. A considerable amount of ammunition and equipment was found in the bunkers and at least 40 dead Japanese were counted.

At the same time, the other brigades under the 23rd Indian Division were pressing on in the wake of the 49th Indian Infantry Brigade. On 31 July, the 5th Brigade took over the positions of the 1st Indian Infantry Brigade on the west bank of the Lokchao river, and the latter was ordered to move up and relieve the 49th Brigade in the Sibong area. The fighting patrol of the 268th Brigade which had left for Mintha early on 27 July, now returned with a very encouraging report. It had reached RK 8919 overlooking Mintha at 1300 hours on 27 July, and had entered the eastern portion of the village, where it found that all the Japanese had retreated from Mintha towards Tamu four days earlier, and only some 75 sick Indian National Army soldiers were left lying in the village, who were removed to safety by the patrol. The low-lying area was largely water-logged. Dead bodies of the Japanese and broken-down vehicles littered the roads. The monsoon and disease were turning the Japanese retreat into a rout.

The Japanese opposition had indeed disintegrated. The area west of Sibong had been swept clear of all their troops, except some parties of starving men who had apparently lost their way in the forests. One such party of three men was wiped out near Lokchao bridge on 1 August 1944. More significant was the surrender of two able-

---

[23] War Diary of Headquarters 49th Indian Infantry Brigade, General Staff Branch; also War Diary of Headquarters 23rd Indian Division, General Staff Branch for the month of July, 1944; Appendix J (a) 63.

bodied Japanese soldiers in the Battle Hill area on 2 August. The 268th Brigade moved up in force to Narum (RK 783232) and Mintha (RK 9118) on 1 August without encountering any opposition. This force was accompanied by a medical officer with medical supplies to evacuate towards Palel the sick and wounded Indian National Army troops from that area. Meanwhile the 49th Brigade had received orders to withdraw to Khongkhang (RK 6508) after the strenuous operations at Sibong. The brigade started withdrawing on 1 August and assembled again at Palel on 3 August. Its place at Sibong was taken over by the 1st Brigade while the 5th Brigade moved forward through the 1st Brigade positions to continue the advance on Tamu. The 37th Brigade remained at Tengnoupal (RK 5912). On 4 August, the 1st Brigade troops advanced and took up positions at Kuntaung (RK 8105) between Mintha and Tamu.

Encountering little opposition, the 5th Brigade reached Moreh on 3 August and entered Tamu the next day. An indescribable scene greeted the victors as they marched into the border town. The streets were deserted. Vehicles and guns littered the squares and courtyards of the quaint little town. The air was heavy with the stench of decomposing bodies. The dead lay everywhere. They sprawled on the streets, lay on the floor in every hut and hamlet, sat at the steering wheels of motionless lorries. Others lay in heaps at the foot of the temples where they had crawled up to die. Then there were the wounded and the sick, with neither medicine nor food, forsaken and uncared, they were too weak even to cry. Some were emaciated beyond belief by starvation so that even a nourishing meal was poison for their withered intestines. More dead than alive, they waited patiently for the mercy of the end. The damp, steamy heat, the slimy mud and the millions of flies completed the picture, so that on 4 August, Tamu bore closer resemblance to hell than to any place on this green earth. When next day the Allied troops set fire to every building that had a corpse in it as the quickest method of cleaning up and disinfecting the town, the picture of Dante's "Inferno" was complete.[24]

INDIAN TROOPS RELIEVED

By the time Tamu had fallen, the 23rd Indian Division had been fighting continuously for over six months. It had met and beaten back the determined Japanese offensive in March 1944 and had held its place throughout the following months of the bitter ding-dong battles for the defence of Imphal. By the middle of July, therefore, the troops were worn-out and sadly in need of a period of rest and

---

[24] War Diary of Headquarters 23rd Indian Division, General Staff Branch, for August 1944.

refitting. Meanwhile the 11th East African Division had begun arriving in the theatre and would soon be available for relieving the 23rd Indian Division. Hence at the beginning of the thrust to Sibong the troops were informed in an Order of the Day that they would be withdrawn from the front line and leave would be opened as soon as the major thrust had been successfully carried out.

Accordingly, the 49th Brigade moved back to Khongkhang area on 1 August and reached Palel on 3 August. The next day, the 25th East African Brigade of the 11th East African Division, which was moving forward under the command of the 23rd Indian Division, was ordered to pass through the 5th British Brigade's positions at Tamu and continue the advance towards Sittaung and down the Kabaw Valley.[25] On 6 August, the 1st Indian Infantry Brigade started concentrating at Palel on its way to Shillong, and the 49th Brigade left finally for Shillong. The same day, the 26th East African Brigade of the 11th East African Division was placed temporarily under the command of the 23rd Indian Division and its advance guards reached the Lokchao bridge area.

At 1200 hours on 7 August 1944, the 23rd Indian Division handed over the charge of operations east of the Lokchao bridge to the 11th East African Division. The next day, the 1st and the 37th Indian Infantry Brigades assembled at Palel while the 5th British Brigade withdrew to the Khonkhang (RK 6508) area and prepared to move out to Kohima. But 1 Patiala of the 1st Brigade and 2/4 Bombay Grenadiers of the 268th Brigade were still at Kuntaung and Mintha respectively, hence it was arranged that they would be relieved by the African units by 12 August. On 10 August, the 26th East African Brigade was handed back by the 23rd Indian Division to the 11th East African Division. The next day, the 5th British Brigade reverted to the command of its parent formation, the 2nd British Division. The Tactical Headquarters 268th Brigade moved back to Heirok and Headquarters 1st Brigade closed down to reopen at Shillong on 13 August. The same day, 11 August, the advance party of divisional headquarters also left for Shillong. On 12 August, the 268th Indian Infantry Brigade assembled at Heirok and was taken over directly under its command by Headquarters XXXIII Corps. Early the next morning, the main Headquarters 23rd Division left Palel for Shillong by road, while the 37th Indian Infantry Brigade began assembling at Palel. At 0800 hours on 16 August, the Headquarters 23rd Indian Division was established at RC 120482 in the Happy Valley of the Shillong hills. On 21 August, the 37th Indian Infantry Brigade completed its move from Palel to the Shillong area. The last Indian troops thus left the

---

[25] 23rd Division Operation Instruction No. 29 dated 4 August.

scene of their travails and exploits along the Palel—Tamu road. The pursuit to Sittaung and down the Kabaw Valley to Kalemyo was left to the fresh troops of the 11th East African Division, while the veterans of the 23rd Indian Division addressed themselves to the pleasanter task of resting their tired limbs and getting ready for future battles.

CHAPTER IV

The Pursuit to Tiddim and Kalemyo

THE STALEMATE CONTINUED

As has been related earlier, by 22 June the momentum of Japanese attack in the southern sector had slackened.[1] But bitter and confused fighting still continued around Bishenpur, with neither side being able to obtain the upper hand. The troops of the Japanese *33rd Division*, who had surged forward in March 1944, were decimated by heavy casualties; but after having received reinforcements in May and early June they were able to resume their attacks. Though they might have lost all real hope of capturing Imphal after the failure of their "last attack" early in June,[2] they continued to fight with determination. Indeed the Japanese had thinned out from the hills north of the Silchar track, but were still holding in strength the positions in the Thinunggei—Ningthoukhong area and at Ingourek (RK 0938) and Mortar Bluff (RK 116441) near milestone 20 on the Silchar track. Of the Allied troops in this sector the 32nd Brigade was engaged in clearing the Japanese positions along the Silchar track; the 63rd Brigade was operating around Khoirok (RK 116448) and the hills north of the Silchar track and the 48th Brigade was holding positions on the main road covering Bishenpur, with its forward elements at Potsangbam and Ningthoukhong.

The broad tactical idea behind the operations of the 17th Indian Infantry Division at that stage of the fighting was to hold the Japanese on the main road by one brigade, and to employ the remaining two brigades to liquidate the Japanese parties which had penetrated through the jungle to the Silchar track and the hills overlooking Buri Bazar. Once these parties were thrown out or annihilated, the division would be able to concentrate all its strength and push forward along the main road towards distant Tiddim.

On 22 June 1944, the 63rd Brigade was ordered to clear up the Khoirok area and drive out or annihilate the remaining Japanese troops there, then move up north and join hands with the Woodforce near Laimaton (RK 1247). The latter, composed of the Headquarters 50th Parachute Brigade, 4/12 Frontier Force Regiment, 1/4 Gurkha Rifles and 7/10 Baluch (less one company which was at

---

[1] See Chapters XII & XIII, *The Reconquest of Burma*, Vol. I.
[2] Special order of the Day dated 2 June 1944 by General Tanaka, General Officer Commanding, Japanese *33rd Division*.

Pt 3351) was at that time advancing on Laimaton from the Loiching (RK 1254) area. By this double enveloping movement, it was expected to destroy all the Japanese forces in the Khoirok area and remove finally the threat to Buri Bazar (RK 245513) and the Headquarters 17th Indian Division. Simultaneously the 32nd Brigade was also ordered to establish firm control over the Youyangtek (RK 074440) area and immediately attack any Japanese concentrations on either side of the Silchar track in that neighbourhood. 7/10 Baluch was also placed under the command of the 32nd Brigade to give it added strength, and one battalion of the brigade was to be kept ready as a mobile striking force to cope with any sudden development.[3] Accordingly, the 32nd Brigade began operating aggressively in the Youyangtek area and sent out numerous patrols in all directions. Several clashes took place with small Japanese parties and casualties were inflicted on them. But the Japanese were gradually withdrawing from the northern hills of their own accord, hence neither the 32nd Brigade nor the 63rd Brigade was involved in any major engagement north of the Silchar track. Heavy fighting took place only when the Indian troops tried to cut off the retreat of the Japanese forces streaming south from across the track.

On 23 June, when one such engagement developed, units of the 63rd Brigade were involved in bitter fighting at Sapper Picquet (RK 1733) at MS 20 on the track. This post changed hands several times in the course of the engagement. But, finally, accurate shelling from the Japanese guns and mortars compelled the Indian troops to withdraw leaving the Picquet to the former. Sporadic fighting continued in the area on 24 June also, without either side gaining any signal success. The next day, the 63rd Brigade received orders to change places with the 48th Brigade and take over the defence of a line running from Pt 2614 (RK 1638) across the main road to Kwa Sipahi village. The 48th Brigade came up to support the 32nd Brigade operations along the Silchar track on 25 June. On 27 June, a detachment of 9/14 Punjab of the 32nd Brigade raided a Japanese position at MS 226 on the track near Tairenpokpi. Other units attacked and occupied Dog Picquet, a small Japanese position at RK 1340 near MS 20, which had, however, to be given up owing to the intense fire from two Japanese 75-mm guns which commanded the hillock. Further west, a company of 3/8 Gurkha Rifles was engaged in minor skirmishes in the thick jungle around Ingourek (RK 0938) on 27 and 28 June.

The sector of the main road around Potsangbam and Ningthoukhong remained quiet in the last week of June. On 22 June, the

---

[3] Operations of IV Corps.

48th Brigade was holding these villages in strength. But the torrential rains of the previous week flooded out the low-lying area. The road was covered with one foot of the muddy gurgling tide, while in the dug-in positions the troops stood in waist-deep water. The main line of communication from Ningthoukhong to Awang Khunou was mainly by boat along the submerged road. The Japanese, moreover, kept up firing at the villages. The prolonged, though intermittent, shelling and the flood involved acute and unnecessary hardship for the troops, hence on 23 June, orders were issued for the 48th Brigade to withdraw to a line from Pt 2614 (RK 1638) to Kwa Sipahi. As this line was too close to Bishenpur, the 48th Brigade was ordered to hold it at all costs if the Japanese attacked. The 1 West Yorks was left at Potsangbam with one company forward at Ningthoukhong in order to give early warning of any hostile advance.[4] But no advance took place, and on 25 June, the 48th Brigade was switched over to the Silchar track area to assist the 32nd Brigade while the 63rd Brigade took over the defence of the main road sector, which remained quiet for the rest of the month.

By 30 June, it was estimated that most of the troops of the Japanese *124th Regiment* that had crossed the Silchar track and entered the hills to the north were either killed or had escaped back across the track. 9/14 Punjab reported that nearly 50 Japanese were left there in the Youyangtek area and even they were split up into small parties. Nevertheless they kept on harassing the Indian troops along the Silchar track, and on 30 June reoccupied positions at MS 26 near Youyangtek. That day, the 17th Indian Division was regrouped and the battalions were allotted as follows:

32nd Brigade	1 Northamptons
	9/14 Punjab
	One Company 3/8 Gurkha Rifles
48th Brigade	7/10 Baluch
	2/5 Royal Gurkha Rifles
	3/8 Gurkha Rifles less one company
63rd Brigade	1st West Yorks
	9 Border
	1/3 Gurkha Rifles
	1/4 Gurkha Rifles
	1/7 Gurkha Rifles
	1/10 Gurkha Rifles
Woodforce	Headquarters 50th Parachute Brigade
	4/12 Frontier Force Regiment

[4] War Diary of Headquarters IV Corps General Staff Branch, for June 1944.

The tasks of the formations were also defined anew. The Woodforce was ordered to hold Pt 3351 (RK 1545), Piffer Hill (RK 1345) and Bungte (RK 1545) and to keep open the main road from Buri Bazar to the suburbs of Bishenpur. The 63rd Brigade was to keep one battalion at Khoirok, north of the Silchar track, while the other five battalions would operate aggressively along the main road from Bishenpur to Ningthoukhong. In other words, it was to hold the left wing of the divisional front, which resolutely faced south and prepared to advance on the road to Tiddim. The centre of the front was occupied by the 48th Brigade, which was ordered to maintain a series of picquets to defend the Silchar track and to hold one and a half battalions in readiness as a mobile striking force. The 32nd Brigade was allotted to right wing, with the task of mopping up in the Youyangtek area and holding Kungpi (RK 0939) and Pt 5846 (RK 1040).

The task of Woodforce was soon completed. The tide of battle was already ebbing from the hills north of the Silchar track. Moreover, the units of the 5th Indian Division had started moving into the area to mop up the remaining groups of Japanese stragglers. On 1 July Tactical Headquarters 123rd Indian Infantry Brigade of the 5th Indian Division moved to Buri Bazar and 1/17 Dogra occupied Laimaran (RK 1851) without opposition. The next day, four platoons of 1/17 Dogra occupied the Saddle (RK 125528), which had already been evacuated by the Japanese. The troops of 3/2 Punjab patrolled to the hills from Wainen (RK 1647). On 3 July, Nunggang was occupied by the Woodforce and Laimaton by 3/2 Punjab. On 4 July, Headquarters 161st Indian Infantry Brigade reached Buri Bazar and 4 Royal West Kents relieved 1/17 Dogra at Laimaton; the latter then sent out patrols up to Loiching (RK 1253) without contacting any Japanese troops. The next day, orders were issued for the 5th Indian Division to take over the defence of the Bishenpur and Silchar track areas in order to free the units of the 17th Division for a major thrust towards Moirang (RK 1824). For the next two days, the troops of the 161st and 123rd Brigades carried out extensive patrolling. But the Japanese had cleared out from that area and no contact was made with them. On 6 July, the Woodforce was disbanded on completing its task and 4/12 Frontier Force Regiment returned to the direct command of the 17th Division. The 161st Brigade occupied without opposition the hills at RK 112409, RK 116411 and RK 127417 on 8 July, and RK 125298, RK 128398, RK 130395 and RK 129395 on 11 July. The only fighting that took place was when the Japanese threw a few shells at RK 120402 on 8 July and Ingkhol the next day. But no one was killed or injured by these shellings. On 12 July 2 Suffolk of the 123rd Brigade occupied RK 128375 against weak Japanese opposition and 1/1 Punjab of the 161st Brigade captured RK 115395 after killing 25 of the defenders.[5] By this date, all the three brigades of the 5th Indian Division had arrived in the Silchar track area and were patrolling extensively. On 9 July, the 161st Brigade had taken over the task previously assigned to the 48th Brigade and on 13 July started relieving the 32nd Brigade also. The 32nd Brigade was then ordered to leave the Bishenpur sector and rejoin its parent unit, the 20th Indian Division. The 48th Brigade, on the other hand, was to undertake another major operation before withdrawing from the front line, viz. the capture of Ningthoukhong and Thinunggei. Plans were also there for the 63rd Brigade to advance south-east from this track to Laimanai, Sadu and Komkeirap, and to exploit the line Point 4612—Phubalowa.

BEGINNING OF THE ADVANCE

Under the plan, the 48th Indian Infantry Brigade was to thrust forward along the main road from the Potsangbam area and capture the villages of Ningthoukhong and Kha Khunou on either side of the road, near MS 21. These villages were to be occupied by 11 July, and then the brigade was to push forward and capture by 15 July Thinunggei village near MS 22. Simultaneously, the 63rd Brigade was to advance south from the Silchar track on Komkeirap, Sadu and Laimanai. After capturing these villages, the 63rd Brigade was to exploit its advantage and move up to a line running from Pt 4612 to Phubalowa village. After concluding this operation, the 17th Indian Division was to be withdrawn from the battle for a period of rest and re-equipment. The division had been constantly fighting since November 1943 and fatigue and casualties were beginning to reduce the fighting efficiency of the units.

Accordingly, the operation started on 11 July 1944. That evening 1/3 Gurkha Rifles was placed under command of the 48th Brigade, the headquarters of which was then located at Potsangbam. On receiving information from patrols that the village of Kha Khunou was held by a very small Japanese garrison, the brigade commander decided to launch an attack immediately without waiting for the usual artillery bombardment. Nonetheless, by 1900 hours on 11 July, the field and medium guns had fired about 3,000 rounds in a concentrated barrage, and one company of 1 West Yorks had moved forward to occupy Kha Khunou. One company of 1/7 Gurkha Rifles was also ordered to be ready to support the West Yorks if necessary and occupy the captured

---

[5] War Diary of Headquarters 5th Indian Division, General Staff Branch for July.

position. The West Yorks found no difficulty in establishing themselves in the eastern fringe of the centre of the village. The company of 1/7 Gurkha Rifles was then ordered to move up from Ningthoukhong village and occupy the northern end of Kha Khunou. But the Gurkhas were delayed by two hours by a party of Japanese troops who were holding a few bunkers at the southern end of Ningthoukhong village. After overcoming this resistance the Gurkhas advanced again towards Kha Khunou. But by then the resistance there had stiffened. The Japanese garrison of Kha Khunou which was larger than expected had taken shelter in the paddy fields just outside the village during the artillery bombardment that preceded the Allied attack. As the bombardment lifted, they swarmed back into the village and reoccupied their positions. When the Gurkhas reached Kha Khunou they found that the company of West Yorks was hard pressed and surrounded on all sides by the Japanese. The Gurkhas, however, established a precarious foothold into the north side of Kha Khunou and hung on for the night. The West Yorks that night repulsed attack after attack in the course of which they destroyed three Japanese tanks.

On 12 July the Japanese bunkers to the south of Ningthoukhong were destroyed systematically by "Lee" tanks and 3.7" mountain guns. It proved to be a very slow process hunting out the determined defenders bunker by bunker, but by the evening only a few of them remained in Japanese occupation. In Kha Khunou, that day, the company of 1/7 Gurkha Rifles tried to move round the west flank of the village and establish contact with the West Yorks, but while the Gurkhas were crossing an open paddy field the Japanese opened heavy fire from 75-mm guns causing havoc in the Gurkha ranks. The company commander was killed and another officer was wounded and the Gurkhas had to withdraw towards Ningthoukhong. West Yorks were also short of rations and supplies, and an air supply drop which was arranged at 1630 hours failed to render relief as most of the supplies dropped fell outside the perimeter, into the Japanese occupied portion of the village. To aggravate their predicament, the Japanese launched a vicious attack against the West Yorks from the west driving them back with heavy casualties. The village of Kha Khunou thus could not be wrested from the Japanese.

At this stage the units of the 48th Indian Infantry Brigade were located as follows[6]:

1/7 Gurkha Rifles ...	Ningthoukhong
Two companies 2/5 Royal Gurkha Rifles	Ningthoukhong
2/5 Royal Gurkha Rifles less two companies	Awang Khunou

[6] War Diary of 48th Light Indian Infantry Brigade.

1 West Yorks less two companies	Awang Khunou
1/3 Gurkha Rifles	Potsangbam
Headquarters 48th Brigade	Potsangbam
One platoon West Yorks	Upokpi
6 Mountain Battery	Upokpi
One company 9 Border	Toupopki
One platoon West Yorks	Toupopki

The next day was spent in shelling by both sides. The 48th Brigade fired another 3,000 shells at Kha Khunou village and the Japanese replied with 155-mm, 105-mm and 75-mm shells against Ningthoukhong, Awang Khunou and Potsangbam. Allied patrols were also active and destroyed some Japanese vehicles on the road from Kha Khunou to Thinunggei. On 14 July, the troops in Ningthoukhong were reinforced by 2/5 Royal Gurkha Rifles and the sappers cleared the road for tanks. The next day the Japanese tried to create confusion in the Ningthoukhong position by sending "jitter parties", but meanwhile the Allied patrols had reported that the Japanese strength in Kha Khunou and Thinunggei was decreasing. During the night of 15/16 July, a terrific artillery barrage was directed against the Kha Khunou village. As the barrage lifted, 2/5 Royal Gurkha Rifles rushed forward and occupied the village without opposition. They found there nine tanks, one 37-mm anti-tank gun, three flame-throwers and considerable quantities of other equipment abandoned by the Japanese. The terrible artillery barrage had destroyed every dwelling in the area and had churned up the ground into a mass of rubble and mud. The remaining Japanese bunkers to the south of Ningthoukhong were also liquidated the same day. When the occupation of Kha Khunou and Ningthoukhong was completed the next day, the 48th Brigade was withdrawn and was replaced by the 63rd Brigade. By 1600 hours on 17 July, Headquarters 48th Brigade was established at RK 340550 near Imphal and the 63rd Brigade took up the pursuit.

The Headquarters 63rd Brigade was then at Bishenpur and the troops were disposed as follows:—

1/7 Gurkha Rifles	Bishenpur
1/3 Gurkha Rifles less one company ...	Awang Khunou
One Company 1/3 Gurkha Rifles	Potsangbam
4/12 Frontier Force Regiment	Ningthoukhong
1/10 Gurkha Rifles	en route to Thinunggei

During the night of 17/18 July, the 63rd Brigade sent out patrols along the road, which reported that by the next morning Phubalowa village would have been evacuated by the Japanese. The village was immediately occupied. Later in the day, the hamlets of Shunu

Sipahi (RK 1628) and Naran Seina were also found clear. The Indian front line thus advanced to MS 25 on 18 July. The 17th Division made its exit in that hour of its triumph. At 1400 on 18 July, the 63rd Brigade was placed under the command of the 5th Indian Division, and the 17th Indian Division handed over to the 5th Division all responsibility for operations on the Bishenpur front.[7] The next day Headquarters 17th Division left that area and was opened at Langthabal (RK 3455) near Imphal. The 63rd Brigade, after spending another four days in the area, during which no major engagement took place, reverted to the command of the 17th Division on 22 July. The 17th Division was ultimately sent to Ranchi for refitting after being in Imphal for a month for rest.

The operations in the Bishenpur sector were left to the 5th Indian Division, and these were proceeding smoothly. By 15 July, the hills north of the Silchar track had been cleared of the Japanese and the 161st Brigade was pushing slowly southwards. On 16 July, 1/1 Punjab reached Sadu and captured two Japanese prisoners there. Behind it, 2 Suffolk of the 123rd Brigade occupied features at RK 119372, RK 121371, and RK 123372 without opposition. The next day, the forward elements of the 161st Brigade reached Laimanai and Youyangtek, seeing only a few Japanese stragglers but a large number of dead bodies near the villages. On 18 July, Headquarters 5th Division moved up from Imphal to Buri Bazar to assume command of the entire operations in the sector. The 123rd Brigade was switched on to the main road, and the 9th Brigade assembled at Buri Bazar (RK 2452) and got ready to pass through the positions of the 123rd Brigade and continue the advance along the main road.

The 2 Suffolk of the 123rd Brigade captured Moirang (RK 1834) on 19 July, and pushed on up to Okshungbung (RK 1623) where it was held up by the Japanese rear-guards with a number of light machine-guns. The Headquarters 123rd Brigade moved up to Shunu Sipahi, and the next day Okshungbung village was occupied without opposition. Much abandoned Japanese equipment was captured there, and 1/17 Dogra placed a company on Pt 4612. The 123rd Brigade was ordered to halt and consolidate its gains, while the 9th Indian Infantry Brigade took up the pursuit the next day. Its target was laid down as MS 38 on the Tiddim road. The West Yorks advanced along the road without meeting any Japanese resistance. The 3/14 Punjab pushed on parallel to the road through the hills to the west of it. The Japanese *33rd Division* had made a clean break-away, and no contact was made with them. The patrol moving east towards the road-junction (RK 1214) was fired on from RK 117137, and another small Japanese party was located at

---

[7] War Diary of Headquarters 17th Indian Division.

Kangwai Kuki (RK 0815). However, hills at RK 1314 and RK 103133 were occupied without opposition by a company of 2 West Yorks and a company of 3/9 Jat respectively.

Continuing the advance on 24 July, the road diversion at RK 114126 was reached, and hills at RK 094124 and RK 101254 were occupied without opposition. But light machine-gun fire was again encountered that day at the road diversion, and there was some shelling at RK 129172 by the Japanese. The next day, resistance stiffened perceptibly. The 3/14 Punjab found a strong Japanese position on the hill at RK 098108, and failed to capture it in the preliminary attack. It then called for air support, and the position was heavily bombed. The same day, 25 July, relatively heavy fighting took place at the road diversion RK 114126 where 2 West Yorks had met with light machine-gun fire the previous day. A troop of tanks of 3rd Dragoon Guards went up and bombarded the position, but in its turn it came under fire from a 75-mm gun which damaged the leading tank. At the same time, a company of 2 West Yorks attacked a position at Pt 3404 (RK 129131) but was repulsed by fire from seven medium machine-guns. The attacks were renewed the next day, when Pt 3404 was captured and 2 West Yorks advanced up to RK 132125. The position at RK 091808 which had been bombed on 25 July was attacked and occupied by a company of 3/14 Punjab. The road diversion was again attacked and was captured by a company of 3/14 Punjab with the help of tanks on that day.

On 27 July, Headquarters 5th Division moved up from Buri Bazar to Moirang and the 123rd Brigade was concentrated at Torbung with orders to occupy defensive positions in the hills on either side of the road.[8] The 9th Brigade also kept up its slow advance. A hill at RK 133114 was captured by the West Yorks against weak opposition, and patrols of 3/14 Punjab and 3/9 Jat penetrated up to RK 111122, RK 100078 and RK 075092. The next day, 2 Suffolk of the 123rd Brigade relieved 2 West Yorks of the 9th Brigade, which thereafter continued to pursue the retreating Japanese force up to MS 70 on the main Tiddim road.

The Japanese resistance had dissolved for the time being, and they were only trying to delay the Allied advance by blowing up bridges on the road. Signs of hasty withdrawal were everywhere, and broken guns, derelict tanks and burnt-out lorries lay abandoned along the road. On 29 July, the 9th Brigade advanced rapidly to Lumka. The 3/9 Jat sent a company west towards Churachandpur. The Jat advance was blocked by approximately a platoon of Japanese troops at the small bridge at RK 077042, but the defenders withdrew promptly when attacked from the air. The 3/9 Jat then

[8] *Ibid.*

continued the advance and entered Churachandpur the same day without opposition. The next morning patrols of 3/9 Jat pushed forward up to RK 072020 without meeting any Japanese troops, but 2 West Yorks was fired upon by light and medium machine-guns from RP 079998 and halted for the night. But the Japanese withdrew again during the night, and the West Yorks resumed its advance on 31 July. It met with only some automatic fire from small rear-guards and sporadic shelling by 75-mm guns. Brushing aside such ineffective resistance, it reached MS 41 (RP 081997) and halted there for the night.

XXXIII CORPS TAKES OVER

At the end of July, the XXXIII Corps relieved the IV Corps of the charge of all operations on the Imphal front. The 17th Indian Division and the 5th Indian Division passed under the command of Lieut.-General Stopford from 1200 hours on 31 July 1944, and Lieut.-General Scoones prepared to move back to India with Headquarters IV Corps. The XXXIII Corps had an impressive strength,[9] and a fortnight later Lieut.-General Stopford assumed command over the Lushai Brigade also, which was operating from bases in the Lungleh-Chaphal area against the Japanese line of communication along the Tiddim-Imphal road.

At the time that the 5th Indian Division passed under the command of the XXXIII Corps, the strategic situation in the theatre was distinctly favourable. The Japanese *15th* and *31st Divisions* had been decisively defeated and their remnants were being pursued towards the Chindwin. Ukhrul had been captured and the neighbouring hills occupied by the 20th Indian Division. The 23rd Indian Division had thrown back the Japanese *Yamamoto Force* from Tengnoupal and the troops were approaching Tamu. The 11th East African Division was moving forward to take over from the 23rd Indian Division and continue the operations in the Kabaw Valley. The 2nd British Division was resting and reorganizing at Maram, except the 4th British Infantry Brigade near Ukhrul and the 5th British Infantry Brigade near Sibong. The 7th Indian Division was resting in the Kohima area and the 17th Indian Division was near Imphal preparatory to its withdrawal to India. The 20th Indian Division had also been withdrawn and was then stationed in the Wangjing-Thoubal area. The 5th Indian Division had started advancing along the Tiddim road and was then near MS 42. The battle for Imphal and Kohima was thus definitely over and it was time to start systematic offensive operations towards the reconquest of Burma.

[9] For Order of Battle XXXIII Corps on 1 August 1944, see Appendix 2.

On 2 August, the XXXIII Corps was given the task of clearing all hostile forces from the area bounded by Tamanthi—Yuwa-MS 126 Tiddim road, and of inflicting the maximum losses on the retreating Japanese troops west of the Chindwin river. On 6 August these tasks were further extended,[10] and Lieut.-General Stopford was then ordered to:
  (a) pursue the Japanese with not less than one infantry brigade group on each one of the following axes:
    (i) Imphal—Tiddim—Kalemyo—Kalewa
    (ii) Tamu—Indainggyi (RU 1675)—Kalewa and
    (iii) Tamu—Sittaung (SL 1086);
  (b) occupy Sittaung and deny use of the Chindwin river to the Japanese;
  (c) seize Kalewa if a favourable opportunity presented itself so that a bridgehead across the Chindwin might be established later on.

Accordingly on 7 August 1944, Lieut.-General Stopford issued operation instructions for the new offensive.[11] The intention was to destroy all remaining Japanese troops on the west bank of the Chindwin river from Tamanthi to Kalewa and to secure the important crossings over the Myittha and Chindwin rivers at Kalemyo and Kalewa, respectively. For this purpose the 23rd Indian Division was to be relieved by the 11th East African Division which was ordered to secure Sittaung and the track Ya-Nan—Sittaung with one infantry brigade group. After occupying Sittaung, the 11th East African Division was to establish approximately one company each at Kuntaung and Mintha to protect the northern flank of the Tamu—Sittaung road. Finally it was to advance down the Kabaw Valley and secure Kalemyo. Due to the difficulties of maintaining ground lines of supply in the Kabaw Valley, during the monsoon, only one infantry brigade group was to undertake the advance towards Kalemyo. The 3rd Brigade of the 11th East African Division was to be kept on the Palel—Tamu road pending further orders from the Headquarters XXXIII Corps. The 20th, 7th and 17th Indian Divisions were ordered to patrol intensively and destroy all Japanese troops still remaining within the respective divisional boundaries. The advance towards Tiddim was entrusted to the 5th Indian Division, which was ordered to move at the maximum speed in order to catch up with the retreating Japanese *33rd Division* and destroy it. The Lushai Brigade was to co-operate with the 5th Indian Division by harassing and disrupting the retreat of the Japanese troops towards Tiddim. Kalemyo was laid down as the grand objective of this thrust and the divisional commander was to

---
[10] Account of Operations of XXXIII Indian Corps.
[11] XXXIII Indian Corps Operation Instruction No. 14 dated 7 August 1944.

prepare plans for capturing Kalewa also with the help of the 11th East African Division. After the capture of Kalemyo and Kalewa, troops of the XXXIII Corps would be poised and readied for jumping across the Chindwin and undertaking further major operations for the reoccupation of the entire North Burma.

PURSUIT TO THE BURMA BORDER

These instructions, however, did not introduce any change in the operations then being undertaken by the 5th Indian Division. As already related, by 31 July the forward elements of the division had reached milestone 41 on the Imphal—Tiddim road. On 1 August, the advance was taken up and 2 West Yorks moved up another three miles. At MS 44, however, it encountered fire from 75-mm battalion guns and light machine-guns. Allied guns and aircraft attacked the Japanese gun positions but the advance was halted for the day. A Company of 3 Jat occupied Point 4511 (RO 0498) to the west of the road without opposition. The same day two companies of 3/14 Punjab moved off to the east with the object of crossing the Khuga river and cutting the road behind the Japanese at MS 50. The next day, the opposition at MS 44 was overcome and 2 West Yorks reached MS 45 where it was again subject to machine-gun fire. The Punjabis captured two medium machine-guns, three light machine-guns and considerable ammunition at RP 0799. The B Company of 3 Jat struck through the hills and descended on the road at MS 43.5 but the Japanese kept up their retreat, and, on 3 August, 3/14 Punjab approached MS 48 encountering no opposition. The advance continued and MS 50 was reached the next day. At 1800 hours on 4 August, 1 Royal Jat, then operating under the Lushai Brigade in the area of the Tiddim road north of MS 70, was placed under the command of the 5th Indian Division. The Headquarters 9th Brigade moved up to MS 46. Although no Japanese troops were contacted, there was evidence everywhere of their desperate plight and hurried retreat. Near MS 48, for example, were found two Japanese vehicles with their drivers sitting in them, dead.

With the break of dawn on 5 August, 3/14 Punjab pushed on but was soon held up by fire from a Japanese position at RP 0389. It was immediately subjected to heavy air attack and artillery bombardment, but when 3/14 Punjab moved up again to the attack, it found that the Japanese were well dug-in, in carefully sited positions, and the attack did not succeed. One company of 3/9 Jat was then despatched to establish a road-block behind the position in the area of MS 54. This company reached MS 54 the following morning. At 1000 hours that day the Japanese position was again bombed and strafed, but the Japanese hung on. A second company of 3/9 Jat was then sent round to establish another road-block. On the morning of 7 August, 3/14 Punjab advanced again and found that the defenders had slipped away form their position during the night. The Japanese made no attempt to break through the road-blocks behind them, but escaped by entering the surrounding jungle to the west of the road. 3/14 Punjab then moved up and reached MS 51, capturing a medium tank, a 37-mm anti-tank gun and a 75-mm gun along its advance. More Japanese equipment was dug out from the Churachandpur area including five 75-mm guns and large quantities of mines, shells and rifle ammunition. A wounded Japanese was captured near MS 48. He was identified as belonging to *8th Company* of the *154th Regiment* of the *54th Division* and stated that a Battalion of his regiment was acting as the rear-guard for the troops of *33rd Division* and their intention was to withdraw slowly at the rate of two to three miles a day towards Tiddim.

On 8 August, the advancing troops of the 9th Indian Infantry Brigade reached MS 55½, where resistance was encountered from a Japanese position at PP 0182. Two companies of 3/9 Jat then dug themselves in, in front of the Japanese position, and prepared to attack it the next morning. Patrols found no signs of the Japanese in the other villages in the area, including Boughal. Units of the 123rd Brigade also were engaged during that week in wide patrolling all around Churachandpur. All the villages in the neighbourhood were visited, and the patrols penetrated as far east as Monglen and Mongbung, but no Japanese troops were found anywhere. During the night of 8/9 August, the defenders retreated once again from their position at RP 0182, and the next day the advance reached MS 57 without opposition. That day the Headquarters 9th Indian Infantry Brigade moved up to MS 54, and on the next day, 10 August, the main headquarters of the 5th Indian Division was established at RK 0804 near Churachandpur. By then 3/9 Jat leading the advance had reached MS 58, with its forward platoon another four furlongs down the road. Resistance there was none, except for some sniping.

On 11 August, 2 West Yorks took over the vanguard position from 3/9 Jat and continued the advance. Some resistance was encountered from a Japanese position at RO 979788, but it was quickly overcome with the assistance of tanks. One platoon was left to consolidate the captured position, while the rest of the battalion took up the advance again and reached RO 975776 near MS 60 without opposition. The next day, MS 61 was passed, but beyond that a road-block of fallen trees was discovered lying across the road. Clearing this road-block and taking in their stride several demolitions and large craters, the forward troops reached MS 63 the same day.

But on 13 August the Japanese resistance stiffened again. On 11 August, a company of the West Yorks advancing along a rough track towards Hengtam village had observed some Japanese activity near MS 64 on the road. When the main advance reached that position two days later, the defenders opened fire with light machine-guns from the bridge at RO 960728. To avoid unnecessary casualties in an infantry attack, tanks were called forward. While the tanks pulverised the Japanese position, a company of the West Yorks carried out an outflanking movement from the east and occupied the road behind the defenders. The position was captured the same day. The next day, 14 August, a hill at RO 965716 was occupied. But the Japanese were holding the reverse slope of the hill with a considerable force and they opened fire on the West Yorks with light and medium machine-guns. A 75-mm gun also shelled the attackers from the area of MS 66. Tanks were immediately called up to assist the West Yorks, but were held up by a large demolition that had destroyed the road at RO 967716. The sappers thereupon went forward to assist the tanks. But they found great difficulty in putting into position their 'scissors bridge', and the advance was temporarily held up.

The next morning, 15 August, the bridging over of the demolition was completed.[12] The tanks immediately rolled forward over the bridge. One platoon of the West Yorks spear-headed by a tank soon reached MS 65½. A company of 3/14 Punjab then took over the lead and pushed ahead. A few shells were fired at it by a Japanese gun from MS 67, and some Japanese snipers also tried to delay the advance. But by the afternoon, the company of 3/14 Punjab had reached very near MS 67.

On 15 August at 1200 hours, the Lushai Brigade was also placed under the command of the 5th Indian Division, and reported brisk Japanese traffic on the road near MS 70. Most of the movement was southwards, and the Lushai Brigade was trying to hamper and harass the retreating Japanese troops. The next day the foremost company of 3/14 Punjab advancing with the help of tanks reached MS 70 and linked up with 1 Royal Jat of the Lushai Brigade. There were no Japanese troops left in the area and the advance was not contested. The same day, Headquarters 161st Indian Infantry Brigade moved up from Bishenpur to MS 54. Headquarters 5th Indian Division moved up from RK 0804 to MS 49, on 17 August. The forward troops, viz., a company of 3/14 Punjab, were then at MS 72½ and were facing a strong Japanese position at MS 73. But when the Japanese were subjected to intense fire from medium machine-guns and tanks, they fled from the position leaving

---

[12] War Diary of Headquarters 5th Indian Infantry Division, General Staff Branch.

behind a 70-mm battalion gun. The position at MS 73 was then occupied.

But the next day, 18 August, the advance was barred by an unusually strong defensive position at RO 951608 (MS 73½). This position was well sited and covered with automatic fire a bridge at RO 951611 which had been blown up. About 40-50 Japanese troops armed with light and medium machine-guns and grenade dischargers held the position and appeared determined to hold up the advance. Allied guns opened a fierce barrage and aircraft bombed the position twice. But the defenders were neither destroyed nor dislodged. They hung on to their bunkers the next day also, in spite of more artillery bombardment. Meanwhile, 1 Royal Jat was at Khuaivum and had sent forward one company to intercept traffic along the road at MS 77. However, during the night of 19/20 August, the Japanese evacuated quietly their position at RO 951608 and rejoined their retreating comrades. The next morning a company of 3/9 Jat moved up without opposition and reached MS 75 just inside the Burmese boundary. MS 78 was gained on 21 August and 3/9 Jat established contact then with the main force of 1 Royal Jat. A damaged bridge at RO 942563 was repaired with a 'scissors bridge' and the forward patrols of 3/9 Jat reached MS 82, the same day. The Japanese had succeeded again in breaking away cleanly and no contact was made with their rear-guard on 21 August. Patrols of 'V' Force Irregulars visited the villages of Vanglai and Phaisat in the hills to the east of the road, but found no Japanese troops in the area. On 22 August, patrols of 3/9 Jat pushed on to MS 83 without opposition, and were joined there later in the day by one company of 2 West Yorks. Considerable Japanese movement was reported by the 8 Frontier Force Rifles of Lushai Brigade from the area of MS 84-85, and three companies of the battalion moved up that day from Vaivet to Zampi.

The advance of the 9th Brigade was made at an average speed of two miles per day and the losses in killed and wounded were negligible (nine killed and eighty-five wounded). But the brigade had to move through constant heavy rain which turned the mountain tracks into thick mud and accounted for considerable sickness. The brigade had succeeded in capturing valuable Japanese equipment which included 11 tanks, 15 guns and over 200 mechanical transport.

PURSUIT TO THE MANIPUR RIVER

The advancing units of 9th Brigade of the 5th Indian Division had crossed the border and gained a footing inside the Burmese territory. The task given to the 9th Brigade was thus completed and the 161st Indian Infantry Brigade was sent forward to relieve it and act as the spear-head of the advance.

On 23 August, therefore, the 161st Indian Infanry Brigade

passed through the lines of the 9th Brigade and took up the advance. It reached near MS 84 before encountering opposition from the Japanese rear-guard which fired a few shells, judged to be of 105-mm calibre. The Japanese position was located at RO 960478, and the advance was halted for the day in front of it. The 9th Brigade meanwhile had started consolidating its position around MS 82; the 123rd Brigade was still in the area of MS 32 where the hills closed up around the Imphal plain.

On 24 August, the Japanese position at RO 960478 was found abandoned. Advancing beyond it, a company of 1/1 Punjab of the 161st Brigade reached MS 86. It was halted there by another Japanese position on Point 3903 (RO 974470). The 8 Frontier Force Rifles of the Lushai Brigade was by then securely based on Zampi and was raiding the Japanese traffic on the road between MS 100 and MS 109.

The next day fighting flared up momentarily when a platoon of 1/1 Punjab blundered into another Japanese position at RO 983464. The Japanese suddenly counter-attacked the Punjab platoon and forced it to withdraw. The Allied guns then opened up against the position and a patrol moved round to the north to outflank it. This patrol had a minor skirmish in the course of which a few casualties were inflicted on the Japanese, and they were scattered. Meanwhile, the Royal West Kent was moving through the hills to the east with the intention of cutting the road at MS 90 behind the Japanese position. By the afternoon of 25 August, it had reached RP 0049 without opposition. The next day, patrols of the Royal West Kent reported the presence of Japanese troops from Khuadam and a secure position was established by the battalion at RO 994456. The Japanese position at RO 983464 was again bombarded heavily that day and the next day, and troops were sent round in outflanking movements, but the defenders hung on. Another Japanese position was discovered by the Royal West Kent at RO 906455 and was surrounded lightly by two platoons. But the resistance continued and the Japanese inflicted a few casualties by shelling the area of MS 86 with a 75-mm. gun. Allied aircraft went up to destroy the gun, but could not detect it in the forest covered area. But during the night of 27/28 August, the Japanese evacuated their positions at RO 983464 and RO 906455 and abandoned Khuadam village also. The troops of the 161st Brigade occupied all these points and advanced up to MS 90½ without meeting any further opposition.

The Lushai Brigade, menwhile, was continuing its harassing operations against the Japanese escape-route. The 8 Frontier Force Rifles raided the area of MS 109, and 7/14 Punjab repulsed with heavy losses a Japanese attempt to cross the Manipur river at RP 110018. That stretch of the Tiddim road ran close alongside the Manipur river, and the Punjabis used to open murderous fire from the west bank of the river at Japanese convoys along the road. Irregular levies operating under the Lushai Brigade ambushed Japanese troops in the area of Lungpi also and inflicted casualties.

On 28 August, a Japanese position at RO 994416 was captured after minor fighting by 4 Royal West Kent, but then another Japanese position was discovered at Point 5860 (RO 986405). The field guns opened a harassing fire against this position, while the infantry prepared to capture it the next day. Then on 30 August, the Royal West Kent moved round the Japanese position on Point 5860 and occupied a small hill to the east of it at RO 984403. The same day, 4/7 Rajput started advancing on the Seitual track with the intention of outflanking from the east the Japanese positions on the main road and reaching MS 100. The Rajputs moved fast, and by nightfall reached Point 5320 (RP 0235) just north of Seitual village. Reports from the Lushai Brigade and the 'V' Force continued to pour in saying that the Japanese were still withdrawing along the road and had evacuated the villages of Haipi, Gampum and Buangmual.

On the last day of August 1944, 4/7 Rajput passed Seitual village and encountered a small party of Japanese troops a few furlongs south of it. A brisk and brief action followed, and the Japanese soon broke and ran away in all directions. But their position on point 5860 continued to hold on. It was subsequently surrounded on all sides. The A Company of the Royal West Kent was to the north-west, the D Company to the north-east and the C Company to the south. Allied guns kept blasting away at the position. But the garrison, estimated at one company in strength, held on to its bunkers. On 1 September, however, Point 5860 was attacked by two companies of 4 Royal West Kent with full artillery support. By 1200 hours the peak was occupied. The few Japanese survivors tried to retreat southwards, but were caught in an ambush by B Company and were completely wiped out. The Allied advance was then resumed along the main road and MS 98 was reached the same evening. 4/7 Rajput, meanwhile, had a sharp engagement with a band of Japanese troops south of Seitual, who attacked thrice with vigour, but fled when all their attacks had been repulsed.

The next day, 2 September, Headquarters 161st Brigade moved forward to MS 96. The 1/1 Punjab passed through the positions held by the Royal West Kent and took up the advance. Weak resistance was encountered from a rear-guard of 15-20 Japanese troops, who fired a few bursts from their light machine-guns and then retreated from one hillock to another. A Japanese gun firing from the neighbourhood of MS 102 also tried to harass the advancing Punjabis, but could inflict neither casualties nor damage. The Royal Air Force continued flying "close support missions" whenever operations required them and the weather permitted. Moreover, it dropped delayed action bombs with time-fuzes set to explode from 6 to 12 hours later at the crossing of the Manipur river near MS 126, so as to disorganize and delay the Japanese crossing of the river at night. Further south, 7/14 Punjab of the Lushai Brigade ambushed the retreating Japanese troops at RP 110010 and killed 27 of them.

On 3 September 1944, the leading troops of 1/1 Punjab reached a point three furlongs beyond MS 103. On the eastern track via Seitual, 4/7 Rajput had advanced to RP 012373 where it found the way barred by a company of Japanese troops in a prepared position.[13]

On 4 September, 1/1 Punjab reached MS 105 in the morning without meeting any opposition. Patrols were sent from MS 102 south-east towards MS 110 and from RO 996298 near MS 105 down the spur towards MS 109. In the meanwhile, 4/7 Rajput found that the Japanese had fled from their position at RP 012373 and immediately pushed forward. It met a party of 15 Japanese troops armed with light machine-guns at RP 015327 and attacked vigorously. The position was carried by assault and the defenders lost one killed and seven wounded. The troops of the 161st Indian Infantry Brigade were soon closing in from several directions on the big depot area and maintenance base at MS 109. The Japanese resistance was negligible and the day was still young. All the troops, therefore, pressed forward eagerly. 1/1 Punjab entered the MS 109 area within a few hours and went on up to MS 110. A company of 4/7 Rajput reached the place soon after and linked up with 1/1 Punjab. Thirty-two derelict vehicles, one damaged gun-tractor and fair quantities of ammunition and supplies were found in the depot area and along the road leading to it. But the installations and buildings had been completely destroyed. The Kaphi Lui stream was swollen by the rains and roared down its course like a torrent. The old bridge across it was wrecked, but a patrol of 1/1 Punjab somehow scrambled across and prepared to push forward again the next morning.

The next day, 5 September, 1/1 Punjab and 4/7 Rajput resumed the advance. The former was fired on when it was nearing MS 112, while the latter encountered resistance one mile further up. Two Japanese prisoners were taken and the forward units halted for the night near MS 113. Along the road behind them, more war-booty was collected, including a 105-mm gun and four Japanese medium machine-guns in working order. Meanwhile, the Japanese resistance

---

[13] At the Headquarters of the 5th Indian Division the same day, Major-General Evans, the General Officer Commanding fell ill and had to be sent off to the 41 Indian General Hospital at Imphal. Brigadier Mansergh O.B.E., M.C., the Commander Royal Artillery of 5th Indian Division, was recalled immediately from leave and took up the command of the 5th Division for ten days till on 13 September Major-General C. G. G. Nicholson, C.B.E., D.S.O., M.C., was appointed as the officiating commander of the division.

was stiffening again and sharp fighting took place on 6 September. 4/7 Rajput found itself faced with a strong hostile position at RP 029269 when it began its advance that morning. The forward position was made up of several bunkers and was held by one platoon armed with three light machine-guns. About 75 yards behind it was another position containing two light machine-guns and a grenade discharger and held by another platoon of Japanese troops. While a company of 4/7 Rajput tackled the obstacle frontally, a platoon was sent round via the Sakawng village. This left hook reached the Japanese position from the north-east and delivered a gallant attack. The occupants of at least two bunkers in the main position were either killed or wounded by the platoon of 4/7 Rajput, but the Japanese in the supporting position opened withering fire on the Rajputs, killing four and wounding another sixteen. The platoon was pinned down by the murderous fire, but a company of the Rajputs immediately advanced and relieved it, returning again with the platoon and all the casualties.

The next morning, 4/7 Rajput advanced again and faced resistance from a position at RP 046257. The advance was halted and two companies took up positions between the road and a hill at RP 45361. Other units reached the area of MS 115½ (RP 039269) along the road, and patrols penetrated as far as RP 049259 without meeting any Japanese troops. But the artillery was active on both sides. A Japanese gun fired from the neighbourhood of Mualkawi; Allied guns opened up in reply. During the night of 8/9 September, the Japanese evacuated their position at RP 046257. When morning came, the Rajputs resumed their relentless advance. A party of Japanese troops with two light machine-guns tried to halt it at RP 057262, but withdrew when outflanked by the Rajputs. Another minor brush took place between MS 115½ and RP 063256 when a company of the Rajputs suddenly came upon a group of six Japanese troops, who at once took to their heels, leaving behind a light machine-gun and some equipment. By the afternoon, MS 117 was reached, with a standing patrol as far forward as a point two furlongs beyond MS 118.

The next day, 10 September, the main force of 4/7 Rajput joined up with the standing patrol beyond MS 118 without meeting any opposition, and the advance was continued further. Some opposition was however encountered at Mualkawi village but the Japanese withdrew when the guns began to bombard the village. The Rajputs occupied it at 1500 hours and then pushed on to a point only two furlongs short of MS 120. Japanese guns were not in evidence that day, but the Allied artillery had started shelling the MS 126 area where the road crossed the swollen Manipur river.

On 11 September, Headquarters 5th Indian Division moved

forward to MS 100 to be in closer touch with the forward troops, who started moving from the position held overnight, and 4 Royal West Kent passed through 4/7 Rajput to continue the advance. But it was held up by strong Japanese defensive positions on Point 60_{27} (RP 0824) at RP 078738 and at RP 072226, covering the road. In consequence, 4 Royal West Kent was unable to advance beyond MS 120 that day. Preparations were, however, made to reduce the positions systematically the next day. The position at RP 072226 was shelled by guns and bombed from the air on 12 September, but the defenders were not dislodged. As a result, no advance was registered and the day was spent only in sullen artillery duels. The Allied guns bombarded the Japanese positions with unknown result and the Japanese replied with two 105-mm guns.

But the next day, 13 September, good progress was made along the road. A patrol of 4 Royal West Kent found Point 60_{27} evacuated by the Japanese, and one of its companies occupied the position at RP 072226 without opposition. The area of MS 121 was occupied, and thus the troops of the 161st Indian Infantry Brigade obtained a clear view of the river crossing at MS 126. But the Japanese had already retreated across the river, and none of them was found by the pursuers even the next day. On 14 September, a company of 1/1 Punjab came up and reached down to the Manipur river along a side track, forming a secure box at RP 085212. The rest of the battalion reached RP 095212, and patrolled forward to the river crossing near MS 126. 4 Royal West Kent then moved in two columns, one advancing along the road and the other across the hills to the east of it, descending on the road at MS $122\frac{1}{2}$. Later the battalion occupied positions near MS 124. In all these movements, and during the whole day, no Japanese opposition was met with.

By the evening of 14 September, the units of the 161st Indian Infantry Brigade were lined up along the banks of the Manipur river, which was in full flood and presented an awe-inspiring sight. The waters roared down at a speed of about 12 miles an hour, carrying broken trees and dashing against giant boulders in clouds of white spray. The bridge had been broken long ago, and the river offered a formidable military obstacle. But the commander of the 5th Indian Division had considered the problem well in time, and a tactically brilliant solution was already being applied.

THE OUTFLANKING MARCH BY 123RD BRIGADE

As early as the third week of August 1944, the General Officer Commanding, 5th Indian Division, was contemplating the forcing of the crossing of the Manipur river by a left hook. The roaring torrent was a major physical obstacle, and Japanese opposition would make the crossing a hazardous operation. The Japanese during their thrust in March had solved the same problem by a left hook that cut the road at MS 109. Major-General Evans decided to employ this manoeuvre against its authors. With the approval of Lieutenant-General Stopford, he decided to use the 123rd Indian Infantry Brigade as the left hook and to send it round via Imphal and Shuganu, a village situated at the south-eastern end of the Manipur plain and on the east bank of the Manipur river. It was hemmed in by rugged hills from three sides, and a rough track led southwards parallel to the river and over the hills. Passing through Mombi (RP 3580) and Lenikot, the track continued southwards and finally linked up with the main Imphal—Tiddim road in the area of MS 127 and Tonzang. The distance from Shuganu to the objective was over 70 miles.

The Headquarters 123rd Indian Infantry Brigade was then located at RK 105153 near MS 32 on the Imphal—Tiddim road. On 28 August the brigade was informed of the intended move. On 30 August the Brigade Major left the brigade headquarters for Shuganu in order to reconnoitre the area and make arrangements for the arrival of the brigade. The next day, the 5th Indian Division's Operation Instruction dated 29 August reached the brigade.[14] It was based on the information that the Japanese facing the 161st Indian Infantry Brigade were the remnants of the *214th Regiment*, *215th Regiment* and *154th Regiment*, and were expected to withdraw to Kalemyo after acting as the rear-guard up to the Manipur river crossing. On the east bank of the river were other Japanese troops who were sure to defend the crossing and hold up the advance for many days. To turn these hostile positions on the east bank of the river, the 123rd Brigade was ordered to go round via Imphal, Shuganu, Chakpi Karong, Lenikot, Khuangkhan and Lungtak and occupy the hills to the south-east of Tongzang. Then the brigade was to attack and destroy the Japanese force between the Manipur river-crossing, Tuitum and Tonzang, and pursue the beaten force up to Tiddim. This bold left hook was itself open to a flank attack from the Japanese in the Kabaw Valley. But conditions then existing made that a negligible risk. The hills between the Manipur river and the Kabaw Valley were almost impassable during the monsoon, and the Japanese in the Kabaw Valley were themselves fighting defensively against the advance of the 11th East African Division. That division had started from Tamu towards Kalemyo and had by then reached Minthami.

[14] 5th Indian Division Operation Instruction No. 92 dated 29 August 1944: War Diary of Headquarters 123rd Indian Infantry Brigade, General Staff Branch, for August 1944.

For the operation, the following additional units were placed under command of the 123rd Brigade:—

> One company 2/1 Punjab
> 11 Battery 24 Indian Mountain Regiment
> 74 Field Company Indian Engineers
> 45 Indian Field Ambulance
> A mule company, a detachment of V Force, interpreters, porters, etc.

Air support was made available for the brigade, and for additional fire-power it was arranged that the field guns with the 161st Brigade on the west bank of the river would support the 123rd Brigade as necessary. Beyond Shuganu the track was not motorable, so the brigade was to be maintained in the field by supplies dropped from the air.

Accordingly, on 1 September, 3/2 Punjab of the 123rd Brigade was carried in mechanical transport to Shuganu. It was joined there the next day by the Dogras and the Brigade Headquarters. The 2 Suffolk, the third battalion of the 123rd Brigade, was exchanged for 2/1 Punjab, which assembled at Shuganu in the afternoon of 5 September. The 123rd Brigade was then ready for its southward march over the hills.

For the intended operation the brigade was divided into four columns. They were named W, X, Y and Z Columns and were composed as follows[15]:

W Column	I Company 3/2 Punjab
	I Mortar detachment 3/2 Punjab
	Detachment Brigade Signals
	One platoon V Force
	A strong reconnaissance party and fifty porters
	Royal Engineer Reconnaissance Party.
X Column	3/2 Punjab minus one company and the mortar detachment
	One section 11 Mountain Battery
	74 Field Company Indian Engineers
	Tactical Brigade Headquarters
	Deatchment Brigade Signal Section and "Eureka" Beacon
	Tactical Headquarters Royal Artillery
	One platoon of Defence Company 2/1 Punjab
	One platoon Chin Levies

[15] 123rd Indian Infantry Brigade Operation Instruction No. 83 dated 3 September 1944.

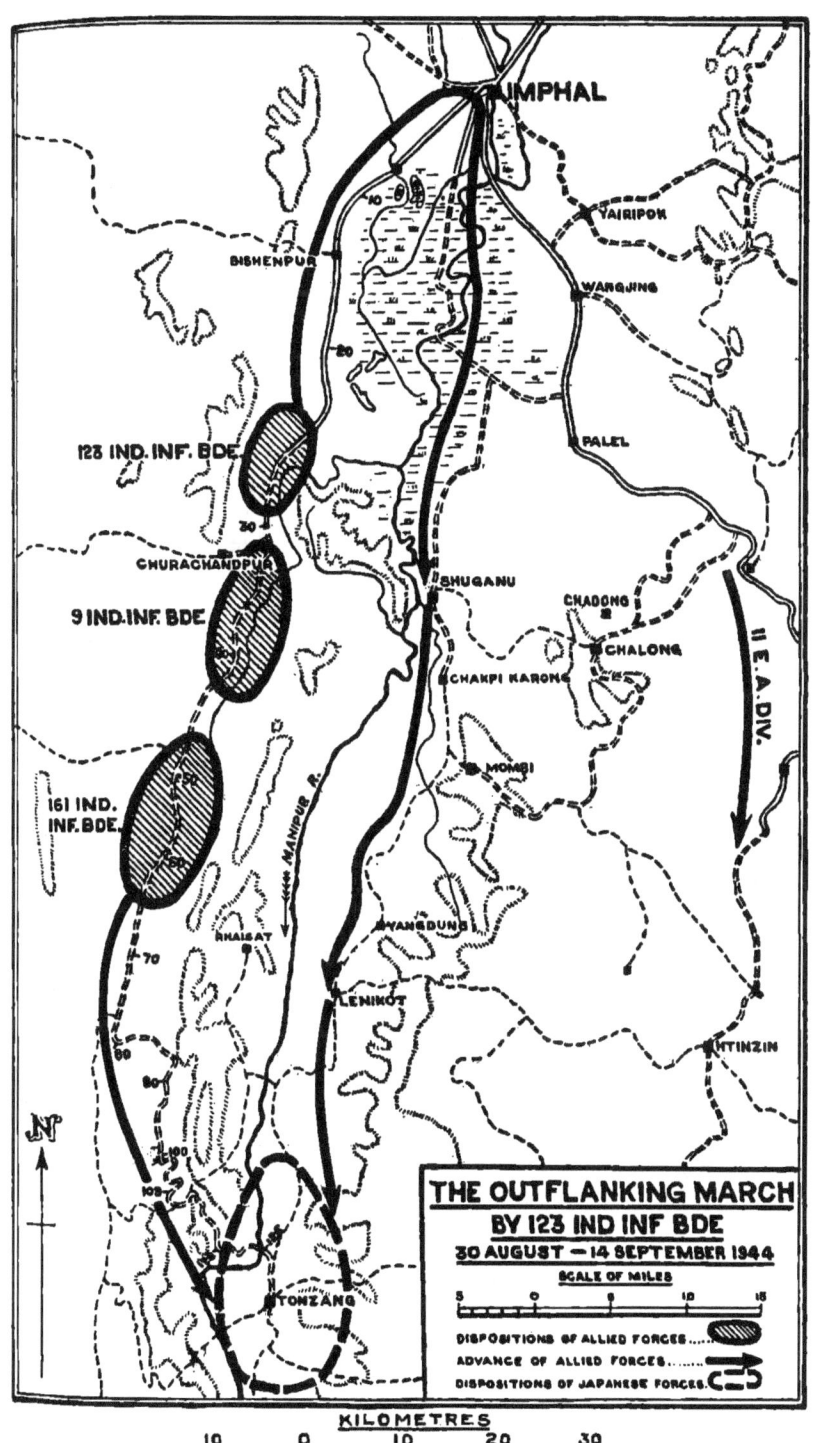

Y Column	A detachment V Force
	A detachment field ambulance, interpreters, guides and fifty porters.
	Troops 1 Dogra
	11 Mountain Battery less one section
	Main Headquarters 123rd Brigade
	Brigade Signal Section minus three detachments
	Defence Company 2/1 Punjab minus one platoon
	Field Ambulance less detachments
	A detachment of V Force
	Reconnaissance parties and 100 porters.
Z Column	2/1 Punjab less one company
	A detachment of Brigade Signal Section
	A detachment of V Force
	A detachment of Field Ambulance and 50 porters.

The advance was to begin from Chakpi Karong about 4 September and was to be led by the W Column. The X Column was to follow the W Column one stage behind. The Y Column was to keep one stage behind the X Column and the Z Column was to bring up the rear. According to the provisional moves planned, the W Column was to reach Anlang on 11 September, and by 14 September the rest of the force was scheduled to concentrate immediately to the north of it. Elaborate security precautions were laid down for the troops in order to achieve maximum surprise.

On 5 September, the W Column reached Mombi while the X Column established itself at Chakpi Karong. That day supplies were dropped from the air at Chakpi Karong. The next day, the X Column moved from there to Mombi and the W Column reached Point 5128 from Mombi. The Y Column moved up from Shuganu to Chakpi Karong accompanied by the main Brigade Headquarters. On 7 September, the whole brigade was strung out to its full length from Chakpi Karong to Yangdung. The W Column was at Yangdung, the X Column at Point 5128, the Y Column was at Mombi and the Z Column at Chakpi Karong. The Tactical Headquarters 123rd Brigade reached Mombi from Chakpi Karong. The next day the W Column arrived at Khuangkhan and the rest of the columns also moved up one stage onwards. On 9 September the W Column was joined at Khuangkhan by the X Column and the Tactical Headquarters of the brigade. No resistance had been encountered so far but the physical difficulties of the march were formidable. Every little stream was a torrent and the engineers were kept busy every day repairing broken bridges or improvising other methods of crossing them. The Royal Air Force had dropped supplies every day for the advancing troops except on 9 September when the planes could not find the dropping zone owing to violent storms. On 10 September the W Column moved from Khuangkhan. The next day the W and X Columns composed of troops of 3/2 Punjab joined each other at Anlang and the Z Column of 2/1 Punjab joined the Brigade Headquarters at Khuangkhan. On 12 September, the Brigade Headquarters reached Anlang. There was still no evidence of the Japanese troops in the area and 3/2 Punjab sent patrols up to Gelmual village. The next day, 13 September, all the columns were assembled in the Anlang area, the approach march was successfully completed and offensive moves were immediately taken in hand against the Japanese force at MS 127, Tonzang.

MANIPUR RIVER CROSSING

On 14 September, Point 5801 (RP 1620) was occupied without opposition by 3/2 Punjab. But its B Company which was approaching the hill from the east came under heavy fire from Japanese machine-guns and had to withdraw after losing six wounded and eight killed, including the commander of the leading platoon and the company commander. Elsewhere there was no contact with the Japanese troops, and the patrols found the village of Kianglam also clear of the Japanese. That day, the Brigade Headquarters and 1/17 Dogra remained near Gelmual and 2/1 Punjab at Anlang.

By the evening, the 161st Indian Infantry Brigade had reached the west bank of the Manipur river. But the next day, 15 September 1944, no contact was established between the two brigades due to the difficulty of crossing the stream. Both the brigades spent the day in consolidating their gains, and the 123rd Brigade sent out strong patrols towards Phaitu and Khamzang. On 16 September, a company of 4 Royal West Kent of the 161st Brigade somehow managed to struggle across the river at RP 1221 and to contact the troops of 3/2 Punjab on the east bank. But the frantic efforts of the engineers to bridge the river failed again, and the rest of the 161st Brigade remained on the west bank. Belatedly, the Japanese shelled RP 1221 where the 4 Royal West Kent had been ferried across. The shelling was ineffective, but the fury of the swollen river continued to baffle the Allied troops for several days. The engineers failed in their attempts to bridge the stream. The efforts of 1/1 Punjab to cross the river lower down also failed, and they came back to the spot where 4 Royal West Kent had got across. But on the east bank, units of the 123rd Brigade further consolidated their position, the 1/17 Dogra occupying Point 6535 and 3/2 Punjab entering Tuitum, while 2/1 Punjab moved up towards Salzang on 17 September.

By then the Japanese had cleared out from the hills between the river crossing and Tuitum and were holding positions around Tonzang. A patrol clash took place at the track junction at RP 123165 just north of Tonzang on 18 September. A party of Japanese troops with light machine-guns was located there, with more Japanese troops in the village itself. The Royal Air Force was requested to bomb and strafe Tonzang, but the low clouds made the task impossible. Further to the south-east, the patrols of 1/17 Dogra continued probing forward towards the Phaisi Lui stream just south of Salzang.

The next day, 19 September, patrols of 2/1 Punjab, carried out offensive probes in the same area, and two Japanese positions were pin-pointed in the Tonzang area. One was located at RP 128137 and contained two 105-mm guns, and sixty men. The other was at RP 115124 and was held by 40 men. Japanese guns from this area exchanged fire with the Allied guns.

On 20 September, the Japanese were still holding their positions at RP 126163 and RP 128137 and a new position was discovered at RP 131135. Shelling and patrols inflicted many casualties on them in this area and it was also discovered that fresh Japanese troops had arrived in the Tiddim sector.

During the night of 20-21 September, much Japanese movement was heard near Tonzang, and the next day it was discovered that the defenders had evacuated Tonzang and the area to the north of it. Tonzang was then occupied without resistance by 3/2 Punjab. The patrols of 2/1 Punjab were meanwhile ranging far to the south, up to Mongken. On the west bank of the river, Headquarters 9th Indian Infantry Brigade moved up to MS 109 that day.

The next day, 22 September, Headquarters 123rd Brigade moved up to Tonzang. One company of 2/1 Punjab carried out patrols to the east of Lungtak. The 3/2 Punjab advanced to MS 142 (RP 1006) on the main road, while 1/17 Dogra combed the low-lying strip of land along the Manipur river. On the west bank, the 161st Brigade was still concentrated at the river-crossing, and the ferrying of troops to the east bank had been stopped the previous day owing to increased speed and force of the current. 4 Royal West Kent, which had already reached the east bank, was near MS 133 (RP 1218) and was patrolling towards Mukwe Vum (RP 0817).

On 23 September, the advance continued. The Headquarters 123rd Brigade moved up to RP 114121 and 1 Dogra reassembled at RP 117115. 3/2 Punjab advanced another mile down the road and reached points between MS 143 and MS 144 (RP 1003). The patrols of 2/1 Punjab reached up to Haimual brushing aside a small party of Japanese troops on the way.

On this day, the 5th Indian Division had found a new com-

General view of the "Chocolate Staircase" showing some of its 39 hairpin bends

Vehicles move along the muddy Tiddim Road

Troops of 4th J & K Infantry move up to consolidate the newly won position on the Kennedy Peak

mander, Maj-Gen. Warren, D.S.O., O.B.E. who had succeeded Maj-Gen. Evans. Lt-Gen. Stopford, the General Officer Commanding XXXIII Corps, had also arrived at the front a day earlier. The future tasks for the 5th Indian Division were finalised and a plan of operations was issued. The capture of Kalemyo remained the final objective. The operations for gaining it were divided into three phases. In the first phase, which was to begin at once, the 123rd Indian Infantry Brigade was to advance southwards on a broad front and occupy the road from Tiddim to the Vital Corner (RU 205845).[16] The rest of the division was to assemble on the east bank of the river. All those who were not completely fit, and all second-line vehicles etc., were to return immediately to Imphal, for all casualties would have to remain with the division till a line of communication was again opened. After their return, the Imphal-Tiddim road would not be maintained, and the division would be dependent entirely on air supply. In normal circumstances, transport planes allotted for the division would be able to supply the troops with full rations and either patrol or ammunition, but not both. Instructions were given, therefore, to use artillery ammunition, particularly 25-pounder shells, as sparingly as possible, and to employ mules as much as possible in order to conserve petrol.

The artillery units ordered to accompany the division in its advance were one field regiment, 24 Mountain Regiment minus two batteries, and 56 Anti-Tank Regiment, which was to leave its guns and mortars behind and act as the Divisional Headquarters' Battalion. The only tanks taken forward were one half squadron of 3 DG; they and the guns were normally to support the advance of the leading brigade. In the first stage, while the 123rd Brigade advanced southwards, the other two brigades were to remain just behind it, and maintain a firm base for the division in the area between the river-crossing and Tonzang.

By the evening of 23 September, 1/17 Dogra had reached MS 143 (RP 10005) without encountering serious opposition. On the following morning, mountain artillery engaged and dispersed a party of fifty Japanese in the area of MS 144. 2/1 Punjab was moving south, parallel to the main axis, on the track through Ngamngai and 3/2 Punjab reached MS 145 along the main road. During the day patrol activity was continued, and some Japanese troops were seen, but they were all trying to get away and no engagements took place. But a Japanese camp was reported near MS 150 and was bombed by 23 Hurribombers. On 25 September, the advance was continued further. The Divisional Headquarters crossed the Manipur river and, at 1800 hours, opened at RP 1221. The 161st

[16] 5th Indian Division Operation Order No. 1/S dated 23 September 1944. See also amendment No. 1 dated 26 September.

Brigade moved up to RP 1117. 2/1 Punjab reached Ngamngai and sent a company towards Singhum Vum. 1/17 Dogra fought its way forward to MS 146 before being halted by a strong Japanese position. On the following day, it advanced a little further and met opposition in the area between MS 146 and 147 around RP 1101.

Two companies started to make an encircling movement round the Japanese positions, and occupied Mongken, whilst artillery opened fire. 2/1 Punjab reached Bumzang and sent patrols to the villages at RU 1896 and RU 2195 near Kahgen, both of which were found to be clear of the hostile troops. 3/2 Punjab concentrated at MS 145, and the Headquarters 123rd Brigade advanced to MS 143. 1/17 Dorgra remained in the area MS 146-147 on 27 September, whilst its two companies continued preparations to attack the Japanese positions from the flank and the rear. 3/2 Punjab concentrated that day at Bumzang, and 2/1 Punjab reached Kahgen village. By the following morning the leading company of 1/17 Dogra had reached Khuadai, thus outflanking the Japanese position from the east. But the Japanese had evacuated their positions at RP 1100 during the night. 1/17 Dogra thereupon continued to advance on the main axis and reached MS 148 without further opposition. The 123rd Brigade was advancing on a wide front, with 1/17 Dogra on the right, 3/2 Punjab in the centre advancing on Haupi, and 2/1 Punjab on the left at Kahgen.

On 29 September, the patrols of 1/17 Dogra crossed the Beltang Lui at RU 1294 and encountered some eighty Japanese troops, armed with medium machine-guns, light machine-guns and mortars, on the high ground overlooking the river. 3/2 Punjab in the centre clashed with a party of the Japanese troops at Hapui and 2/1 Punjab met another party of the Japanese troops beyond Kahgen. The next day it encountered a Japanese position in the area of Sialam Vum (RP 2298) held by approximately one company of Japanese troops armed with medium machine-guns and mortars. The position was attacked, and many casualties were inflicted on the defenders. But the attack was repulsed. Further west, a company of 1/17 Dogra crossed the Beltang Lui stream at RU 118944, but was held up by the strong Japanese positions at RU 114944 and RU 114940. Other troops of 1/17 Dogra advanced along the road and reached RU 092975, where they found the bridge over the Beltang Lui blown up.

THE FALL OF TIDDIM

By the end of September 1944, the 5th Indian Infantry Division was entering the last lap of its long road to Tiddim. So far its main advance had been alongside the Manipur river which flowed through a narrow valley flanked on either side by hills. Before describing the subsequent operations it would be useful to recapitulate the main topographical features of the Tiddim area. After its junction with the Beltang Lui, the Manipur river turned and flowed west for a few miles before resuming its southward course. Within the bend of the river was the high tableland on which lay Tiddim. From the valley of the Manipur river the road climbed up to Tiddim by a series of hair-pin bends; this portion of the road was known by the name of the 'Chocolate Staircase'. Beyond Tiddim, the road ran due east up to 'Vital Corner' and then swung southwards again to reach Kennedy Peak and Fort White. Beyond these places, the main road turned east to enter Kalemyo, while a branch road continued south to Falam and Haka.

Operations against the Tiddim-Falam area were being undertaken jointly by the 5th Indian Infantry Division and the Lushai Brigade. The former was advancing southwards against Tiddim on a broad front extending from the 'Chocolate Staircase' in the west to Kahgen and 'Vital Corner' in the east. The Lushai Brigade was operating against the left flank and rear of the Japanese defenders on an even broader front from Tiddim to Falam.

In the main 5th Indian Division sector, no advance could be made for several days. On 1 October, 1/17 Dogra maintained patrols on the road between MS 149 and MS 150. Attempts were made to cross the Beltang Lui at RU 1096, but had to be abandoned owing to the swift and powerful current and the depth of the river. However, other units of the division operating further to the east made good progress. 3/2 Punjab entered Haupi without resistance. Patrols moving through the jungle east of Ngennung reached Valvum feature and occupied the village of Valvum after a minor resistance. But some other patrols located about two Japanese platoons in Ngennung and 2/1 Punjab maintained contact with the defenders who were found to be holding the Sialam Vum ridge in some strength. On the following day, 3/2 Punjab found a strong Japanese position on the high ground at RU 147864, south-east of Valvum, and estimated that more than 30 Japanese were defending the Ngennung village. Meanwhile 1/1 Punjab, of the 161st Brigade, had commenced to move from the main road at RP 1008 on its way to Dolluang further to the east.

Along the main Tiddim road, sharp fighting took place on 2 October.[17] Strong Japanese positions were discovered at RU 087976 and RU 082974 just south of the Beltang Lui and at the foot of the 'Chocolate Staircase'. In the seven miles stretch of the 'Chocolate Staircase' the road climbed 3,000 feet at an average gradient of 1 in 12. There were no less than 38 hair-pin bends within that stretch.

[17] Orders had been received for the withdrawal to India of 3/14 Punjab of the 9th Brigade, and on 2 October the battalion left for Imphal.

The surface of the road was reduced to ankle-deep mud by the traffic and the monsoon. For the infantry it was a heart-breaking climb, loaded as they were with their full battle-kit. For the vehicles, it was a gruelling test of their mechanism and their drivers, and not a few failed and paid the penalty by hurtling down the steep slopes into the *khud*.

The Japanese position at RU 087976 at the foot of the 'Chocolate Staircase' was attacked by C Company of 1/17 Dogra with the support of mortars and 25-pounder guns. Casualties were inflicted on the defenders, but the position was well sited and protected by machine-guns, and the attack failed. About half of the company was then withdrawn across the Beltang Lui to MS 149. But the stream was very swift and deep, and one man was drowned during this crossing, so the remainder of the company was allowed to remain on the southern bank. The position might have become serious if the Japanese had counter-attacked. But another move was already afoot which restored the situation. On 1 October, two companies of 1/17 Dogra had started from Khuadai southwards. They climbed to the top of the hill by little known goat tracks, and on 3 October they cut the main road at MS 158 (RU 0793) at the top of the 'Staircase', where the road levelled out again to run along the spur to Tiddim. So, by capturing MS 158, 1/17 Dogra largely removed the danger and delay of a strenuous climb up the steep slopes from the Beltang Lui. The Japanese defences at the foot of the 'Chocolate Staircase' were completely outflanked, with the road cut behind them.

Consequently, on 4 October, 1/17 Dogra found the Japanese position at RU 807976 evacuated by the defenders. But the Beltang Lui was still running high, blocking all movement. The advance along the main road, therefore, remained halted, but further progress was made by the centre and left wing of the division. Patrols of 3/2 Punjab reported some Japanese troops at Teklui and dug-in positions at Ngennung, and both these places were later bombed and strafed. 2/1 Punjab continued to probe the Japanese defences in the Sialam Vum area.

As a result of the air attacks, Ngennung was found to be clear on the next day, 5 October. A patrol of 3/2 Punjab pushed on to Leilom but found the Japanese troops established there in considerable strength. Other defensive positions were located on the slopes north and south of Sezang and at RU 145864. In the Sialam Vum area a fighting patrol of 2/1 Punjab inflicted nearly thirty casualties on the Japanese without loss to itself. A hostile patrol approached the battalion's positions in this area but was driven off. Along the main road that day the Japanese troops shelled the positions at MS 158 held by two companies of 1/17 Dogra. But the Japanese were thinning out from the Tiddim area, and during the day patrols from the Beltang Lui had established contact with the MS 158 position. 6 September was a surprisingly clear day. Patrolling continued, but no major clash took place. The Royal Air Force, however, was on its wings the whole day, bombing the positions at Valvum and Dimlo, the gun positions at MS 160 and the Japanese traffic along the road. By the evening of 7 October, the road up to MS 158 was completely clear. The formidable obstacle of the 'Chocolate Staircase' was surmounted at last. During the following night, much movement south from Tiddim was observed, and known Japanese positions were harassed by the artillery.

On 8 October, 3/2 Punjab found the Japanese positions northeast of Tiddim, on the feature at RU 147863 and Point 5955, abandoned. The latter was immediately occupied. A Japanese patrol later approached the Indian positions on Point 5955, was fired upon and lost four killed. Following an air-strike, 2/1 Punjab attacked Japanese position in the Sialam Vum area at RU 211883. But it was found to be a heavily wired bunker position, and, although casualties were inflicted on them, the defenders remained in possession of the feature. In the evening, 1/1 Punjab made contact with the Japanese positions held by about one hundred and fifty of them in the Dolluang area further to the east. On the main road, 1/17 Dogra remained held up in the area of MS 158. During the night of 8/9 October, a party of about sixty Japanese again approached 3/2 Punjab's positions on Point 5955 and endeavoured to encircle them, but was forced to withdraw, when greeted with heavy fire.

On the following morning, 9 October, a patrol of 1/17 Dogra occupied the spur at RU 087911, but the main body of the battalion remained at MS 158. Another patrol reported that the high ground at RU 083907 was clear of the Japanese. During the night of 9/10 October, about 60 Japanese attacked Point 5955 (RU 1686). The position was held only by a platoon of 3/2 Punjab, but the attack was beaten back with heavy losses to the attackers. The slow, inch by inch advance continued. On 10 October, 3/2 Punjab sent out patrols to encircle Japanese parties on the track between Point 5955 and MS 11 Fort White road. A patrol of 2/1 Punjab by-passed the Japanese positions on the Sialam Vum ridge and reached the spur at RU 212867 without encountering any opposition. Several parties of Japanese troops were seen in the area of Vital Corner, who were shelled and dispersed. At 1130 hours on the following morning at least one company of Japanese troops attacked the Allied positions at RU 213883 and forced 2/1 Punjab to make a slight withdrawal from the track behind the Japanese position. The leading elements of 1/17 Dogra, advancing on the main axis, reached the area of RU 085914 without contact but, later in the day, ten bunker positions were located on Point 5753 (RU 0890) by the patrols moving via Laile west of the road. These were immediately bombed and strafed by the Royal Air Force but 1/17 Dogra was unable to continue the advance.

At 1030 hours on 12 October, the Japanese attacked 1/17 Dogra's position at RU 0790, but were repulsed. By then, some tanks had managed to climb up the difficult 'Chocolate Staircase' and 1/17 Dogra, with the support of these tanks of 3 DG and under cover of artillery bombardment and air-strikes, made an attack along the road towards Point 5753. The attack proved only a partial success. Two tanks had their tracks blown off by mines and, during the subsequent withdrawal, another was knocked out by a 75-mm gun. However, two companies of 1/17 Dogra managed to establish themselves in the spur at RU 088921 in the vicinity of MS 159. A little to the east, a further Japanese attack was put in by about 90 men, with artillery support, on 3/2 Punjab's positions at Point 5955, but was repulsed with heavy losses to the attackers. Patrols of 2/1 Punjab found the area of the Sialam Vum ridge at RU 215876 to be clear, but the Japanese had occupied the spur at RU 212867.

By then the Japanese position at Tiddim had become precarious. The units of the 5th Indian Division had been doggedly pressing forward on a broad front. 1/17 Dogra on the right wing of the division was knocking at the gates of Tiddim; 3/2 Punjab and 2/1 Punjab were inching forward in the centre against Valvum and Vital Corner whose capture would have cut the main line of communication behind Tiddim; and 1/1 Punjab was operating on the extreme left flank of the division against Dolluang further to the east. Tiddim could not be safely held very much longer. It was not surprising, therefore that there were numerous reports of heavy Japanese traffic from Tiddim area towards Kalemyo. But on 13 October also resistance continued to be stubborn. Japanese guns were active the whole day. One platoon of 2/1 Punjab by-passed the defences on the spur at RU 2186 and moved to reconnoitre Vital Corner. Along the main road, minor patrol clashes and artillery exchanges took place. The engineers working with 1/17 Dogra spent the day in clearing the anti-tank mines from the road filling big craters which hampered the progress of tanks. On 14 October, patrols of 1/17 Dogra found Point 5753 still held by the Japanese troops. 1/1 Punjab of the 161st Brigade at Tuibel was attacked by some twenty-five Japanese, who were supported by one bren gun and two medium machine-guns. The attack was thrown back and casualties were inflicted on the Japanese. The next day, 15 October, 1/1 Punjab scored another success in an ambush at RU 308843. At the other end of the sector, 1/17 Dogra found RU 085911 evacuated by the Japanese, though Point 5753 was still occupied.

For the past several days, the Royal Air Force had been working at a pitch of intense activity, bombing and strafing along the entire sector. On 16 October two squadrons of Hurribombers strafed hostile positions in support of 3/2 Punjab. The Japanese artillery was also active, and killed six men of 2/1 Punjab in the Valvum area. Wide and intensive patrolling was carried out by all the battalions of the 123rd Brigade, but no major development took place during the day. At last, on 17 October, 1/17 Dogra found Point 5753 clear and resumed the advance along the road. One company of the battalion moved south-west from Teklui. The patrols entered Tiddim the same day and found that it had been evacuated by the Japanese troops. The day that Tiddim fell, far to the south the Lushai Brigade entered Falam without resistance. The troops of the Lushai Brigade had in fact played an important role in the recapture of Tiddim, and it is necessary to review their operations before continuing the story of the main advance.

Levies and Scouts of the Lushai Brigade had crossed the Manipur river about the middle of September and some five hundred of them were then operating from the hills around Mualbem towards the main road Tiddim—Fort White. Clashes were occurring with the Japanese troops as far east as Ngalzang. To the south a Japanese column was ambushed near RU 1939. These clashes went generally in favour of the Lushai Brigade which retained the initiative, and the Japanese suffered casualties and loss of arms and equipment. Further south, 1 Bihar was advancing on Haka.

As already mentioned, the advance of the 5th Indian Division from the Manipur river-crossing to the foot of the 'Chocolate Staircase' had been greatly helped by the raids of 7/14 Punjab of the Lushai Brigade from across the Manipur river. On the advance of the 123rd Brigade reaching MS 150 the raiding operations of 7/14 Punjab were to come to an end. Accordingly, on 27 September Major-General Warren, G.O.C. 5th Indian Infantry Division, authorised the temporary withdrawal of the battalion for a short rest. The following new tasks were then allotted to the Lushai Brigade:

(a) to protect the right flank of the 5th Indian Division in its advance to Kalemyo;
(b) to capture Haka and Falam;
(c) to collect information about Japanese strengths and intentions in the general area of the valley of the Myittha river, lying south of Kalemyo and west of the Chindwin.

To carry out these tasks, units of the Lushai Brigade took up positions in a long line running south from the Tiddim area. Tactical Headquarters and 1 Royal Jat moved south and reached Heilei on 4 October. All the tracks going south from Tiddim were cut during the first week of October. Lushai patrols skilfully probed into the Japanese positions around Tiddim, and one of them pierced right through them and made contact with troops of the 3/2 Punjab, south-east of Tiddim. Other patrols raided Phaileng and ambushed Japanese troops near Bamboo Camp, inflicting many casualties. On 10 October, they had another major success when they killed 12 Japanese troops near Pine Tree Camp (RU 1850) on the Fort White-Falam road. By that time, the units of the brigade were located as follows[18]:

> Tactical Brigade Headquarters and 1 Royal Jat, less two companies, at Heilei, two companies 1 Royal Jat *en route* Kiau.
> 7/14 Punjab, less one company, resting at Champhai, one company (under command 1 Bihar) at Ramkhlau.
> 1 Bihar moving towards Haka and Falam.
> Lushai Scouts area Vangte—Mualbem.
> Shaws levies, area Tsawngthu—Lunghrawh—Zuitu—Zamaul.
> Falam Levies, area Dihai—Khuangli—Lungpi—Mangkheng.
> Haka Levies, area Klangklang—Kuhchah—Kokhua.

In the following week, the Lushai Brigade probed steadily eastwards along a broad front. Its operations had helped the 5th Indian Division by threatening the line of communication of the Japanese at Tiddim. The mounting pressure and fierce attacks of the units of the 5th Indian Division in turn helped the operations of the Lushai Brigade. The Japanese were pulling out of the entire area, and troops of the Lushai Brigade entered Falam without opposition on 17 October, as already mentioned. Two days later Haka also fell in their hands. The Lushai hills were thus cleared of the Japanese invaders.

PURSUIT TO KALEMYO

Tiddim had fallen. By then the overall strategic picture was gloomy indeed for the Japanese. In Europe, the war against their ally, Germany, was entering the last phase. Paris and Rome had fallen to the Anglo-American armies, which had approached the frontier of Germany itself from the west. The Red Army was grinding forward relentlessly from the east. It had knocked out of the war Rumania and Bulgaria, had linked up with Marshal Tito's guerillas in Yugoslavia and was knocking at the gates of Czechoslovakia. Japan's own position was not much better. Although her large armies were still intact and in possession of the rich lands of south-east Asia, the air forces and fleets were being decimated. In the Pacific, the converging drives of Admiral Chester Nimitz and General Douglas MacArthur were about to meet on the Philippines. In Burma itself, Myitkyina had at last fallen to General Stilwell in

---

[18] Account of Operations, XXXIII Corps.

August, and Bhamo was threatened. The XV Indian Corps in the Arakan had taken the offensive once again and was preparing to attack Akyab with irresistible force. North of the Arakan, the Lushai Brigade had captured Haka and Falam and was advancing into the Myittha Valley to isolate Kalemyo from the south, while the 11th East African Division came down on the town through the Kabaw Valley. The Japanese troops opposing the advance of the 5th Indian Division had therefore to look over both their shoulders to avoid being outflanked from the north as well as the south. The tide of the war had indeed turned against them as they fell back from Tiddim towards Fort White and Kalemyo.

On 18 October, 1/17 Dogra advanced from Tiddim and encountered Japanese positions two miles south of the town on the hills at RU 081856 and RU 987850. The positions were immediately attacked by Hurribombers, although low clouds hampered flying. A patrol of 3/2 Punjab went towards the Japanese position at RU 175848 and a patrol from 2/1 Punjab found Japanese bunkers at RU 2089. The next day, 1 Dogra occupied the positions at RU 081856 and RU 087850, and combed the area around Leilom. It then moved forward to MS 3 without opposition. During the day Hurribombers attacked the Japanese positions in the area just east of Tiddim while Mitchell (B 25) bombers of the USAAF dropped bombs on Kennedy Peak and Vital Corner.

On 20 October, 1/17 Dogra occupied several small features and patrolled east as far as MS 6 without opposition. One company of 3/2 Punjab moved through the jungle and descended on the road near MS 10, establishing a road-block there. Intensive patrolling continued which showed that the Japanese were pulling out slowly and methodically towards Vital Corner. They were then holding a small position at RU 180850, as also Point 6680 and the high ground at MS 11 (RU 1884). To the east, they had a strong position at RU 213877 on the Sialam Vum ridge, defended by a breast-high pallisade of logs and numerous medium machine-guns and light automatics. A platoon of 2/1 Punjab tried to capture it by a surprise assault, but had to fall back when greeted by heavy machine-gun fire. The next day, 21 October, 1/17 Dogra inched forward up to RU 1283, before being held up again by a defensive position on Point 7162. In the rest of the sector there was no progress, but a record number of bomber sorties were flown on the divisional front that day. Mitchell bombers repeated their attacks on Vital Corner and Kennedy Peak, and Hurribombers concentrated on Japanese positions on the track leading south from Sialam Vum towards Vital Corner. The same day, Divisional Headquarters moved up to MS 154 and detailed orders were issued for continuing the advance. The general situation appeared propitious for pushing on, for the

Japanese were showing signs of fatigue from the long, gruelling retreat, and "11 E.A. Division and Lushai Brigade operations are making him look over both shoulders".

The objective of the coming push was laid down as RU 253702 just south of Fort White, and at the junction of the jeep tracks from Kalemyo and from Falam.[19] The 123rd Brigade was to complete the occupation of the Vital Corner area and then with two battalions keep a firm base for the division in the area bounded by Tiddim–Mualbem, Vital Corner and Khum Vum. The third battalion of the 123rd Brigade was to block the track leading east from Kennedy Peak at Tuisau so that the defenders of Kennedy Peak might not escape by that route.

The 9th Indian Infantry Brigade was ordered to advance along the road from Vital Corner to a point just short of Point 8225 at RU 2274. The task allotted to the 161st Indian Infantry Brigade was more complicated. It was told to send one battalion in a left hook via Pimpi and Vaona to cut the road at Point 8225. The 9th Brigade advancing south would link up with this battalion at Point 8225, and the battalion itself would operate southwards towards Fort White. The rest of the 161st Brigade would move via Tiddim-Mualbem and reach the Fort White—Falam road at Point 7710 in a wide right hook. From Point 7710 the force would move north up the track and cut the Fort White—Kalemyo road at RU 2569 near Point 7365. Keeping a firm hold on Point 7365, it would then move towards Fort White and link up with the lone battalion of the brigade advancing down from Point 8225. The tanks of 3 Dragoon Guards were allotted to support the advance along the road, as also the 28th Field Regiment.

To carry out the first part of the new plan, efforts were made by the 123rd Brigade to advance up to Vital Corner, a position of great natural strength, with deep bunkers in the rocky face of a steep precipice. On 22 October, 1/17 Dogra made contact with 3/2 Punjab in the area of MS 8.[20] Patrols of 1/1 Punjab reported Point 3971, south of Dolluang, unoccupied, but the Japanese were still holding the high ground commanding the tracks at RU 3378 and Bhopi Vum. A weak Japanese position was also found at RU 2983 but 1/1 Punjab made short work of it by a surprise attack. The next day, 23 October, about twenty Japanese troops holding a small position at RU 181893 sniped at men of 3/2 Punjab in the area of MS 11. They continued to hold their position on Sialam Vum, and Hurribombers had again to bomb and strafe the area in support of

---

[19] 5th Indian Division Operation Order No. 26 dated 21 October 1944.
[20] Between Imphal and Tiddim, the milestone figures refer to the distance from Imphal, e.g. MS 126 at the Manipur river crossing was 126 miles from Imphal. Between Tiddim and Kalemyo the figures refer to the distance from Tiddim, e.g. MS 8 was 8 miles from Tiddim on the road to Kalemyo.

2/1 Punjab. On 24 October the fighting continued in the same dogged, unspectacular manner and one company of 2/1 Punjab moved to establish a block in the area of Point 6138, on the track leading south-east from Sialam Vum. Guns were active on both sides, firing sullenly through the mist at invisible targets.

The next day, 25 October, saw one of the outstanding examples of valour and deathless courage. Troops of 1/17 Dogra, 3/2 Punjab and 2/1 Punjab were patrolling the area round Vital Corner. They discovered three Japanese positions, at RU 186839, at RU 205858 and at RU 213883. These positions were immediately attacked by planes with rockets and machine-guns. Following the air-strike, D Company of 2/1 Punjab was ordered to assault the position at RU 213883. Two platoons of the battalion moved up, to deliver the main attack from the north-east, while one platoon, led by a Jemadar named Ram Swarup Singh, was sent round to stage a diversionary attack from the south-west. The main attack was held up at the stout pallisade, 4 feet high, that surrounded the Japanese position. But Jemadar Ram Swarup Singh stormed the position with a handful of his men. His platoon met a withering machine-gun fire, but it broke through the pallisade and captured several of the trenches inside. By sheer courage and dash, the diversionary attack was thus converted into the real assault. Their leader was shot through both the legs, but the Punjabis continued fighting with desperate valour. The Japanese defenders totalled about sixty and outnumbered the platoon attacking them. They soon launched vicious counter-attacks. In the bitter hand to hand fighting that followed, the trenches changed hand twice. In spite of his serious wounds Jemadar Ram Swarup Singh continued hurling grenades and exhorting his men to press forward. But in the end the valiant Jemadar was killed, and his platoon had to fall back. As a fitting recognition of his valour, Jemader Ram Swarup Singh was given the posthumous award of the Victoria Cross for his inspiring leadership and courage.

In the days following, the deadly game of hide and seek, patrols and ambushes, continued between the Japanese and Indian troops. On 26 October, 1/1 Punjab inflicted several casualties on the Japanese by setting up an ambush at RU 3582 on the track going south from Dolluang. The next day, 3/2 Punjab had a number of patrol clashes and minor skirmishes with the Japanese near Vital Corner. The day after that, on 28 October, the same battalion attacked a Japanese position at RU 187839, but failed to capture it. Allied planes were active, all these days, strafing and bombing the well hidden bunkers that were holding up the Indian troops.

Meanwhile the 9th Brigade had been closing up behind the 123rd Brigade. By 29 October, 4 Jammu and Kashmir Infantry which had recently joined the brigade, was at MS 4, and 3/9 Jat a few miles further on in the neighbourhood of Dimlo—Suangpi. A platoon of 1/17 Dogra formed a base just south of Suangpi, and, employing hit and run tactics, commenced to harass the Japanese near MS 16.[21] Patrols sent out by 1/1 Punjab towards Dolluang and by 1/17 Dogra along the main road kept probing at the Japanese position. A strong Japanese position was discovered near MS 18 (RU 2079), held by about one company of troops, and was fired on with rifles and light machine-guns. Behind these probing attacks 3/2 Punjab inched forward along the main road, capturing MS 11 against slight opposition. The main Headquarters 5th Division also moved up to MS 4 on 30 October.

On 31 October, 3/2 Punjab continued patrolling widely and made contact with large defensive positions covering Vital Corner. At the same time, patrols of 3/9 Jat searched the ridge overlooking the road between MS 19—21 but found no Japanese troops. On 1 November, the patrols of 2/1 Punjab ambushed some Japanese troops at RU 255819 at the track junction east of Kennedy Peak.

By 2 November 1944, all was ready for the major thrust planned a week ago. The units of the 123rd Brigade had completed their detailed reconnaissance of the Japanese positions on the Sialam Vum and the Vital Corner ridge. All the weaker supporting positions had been captured or neutralised, thus exposing the main bulwarks of the defenders. Behind the 123rd Brigade, the 9th Indian Infantry Brigade and 161st Indian Infantry Brigade had closed up. The units of the 161st Brigade were poised ready for the intended double hook. By 31 October, 1/1 Punjab of the 161st Brigade had reached RU 3284, with two companies detached on the track, one at RU 3083 and the other at RU 3583. The rest of the brigade assembled near Mualbem preparatory to the march on Point 7710. The D-Day for the assault on Vital Corner was fixed as 2 November 1944. For several days previous to this, practically every available gun had been shelling and bombarding the positions selected for the attack. To further soften up the defences, the full fury of the Allied air forces was directed on them. On 31 October, the Royal Air Force alone sent 72 bombing and strafing missions over the area. The next day, 44 Hurribombers delivered accurate attacks in the Vital Corner—Sialam Vum area, and Mitchell (B 25) aircraft of the United States Army Air Force rained down bombs on the Kennedy Peak.

The attack opened before dawn on 2 November. A company of 2/1 Punjab blocked the Japanese escape route running from RU 213883 to Tuisau, and another party was in position on the track to the south-east. The main Japanese position at RU 213883 was blitzed by an intensive air attack by one squadron of Hurribombers. The 2/1 Punjab then occupied the formidable stronghold on Sialam

[21] See foot-note 20, p. 98.

Vum almost without opposition. In the words of the War Diary, "The whole position was indescribably destroyed by very excellent bombing of Royal Air Force. Numerous collapsed bunkers with signs of dead bodies underneath"[22] Another position at RU 252815 held by 12 defenders was captured by a platoon. 3/2 Punjab also had substantial successes in the Vital Corner area. Heavy fire was opened on the area from massed guns and mortars, and four squadrons of bombers blasted the positions. The main strength of the battalion maintained pressure on the defenders near MS 13, while A Company climbed up the nulla on the left and occupied MS 14 (RU 2084). The same afternoon, another company came up via the nulla and took up positions about 1000 yards north of Vital Corner, viz. between the main road and the 2/1 Punjab on Sialam Vum hill. Brisk firing and sniping went on the whole day around Vital Corner, and A Company had to repel a fierce counter-attack in the evening.

But the next day, 3 November, the entire area of Vital Corner and Sialam Vum was cleared of the Japanese. The patrols of 2/1 Punjab worked their way down from Sialam Vum and contacted 3/2 Punjab north of MS 14, and the main force of 3/2 Punjab pushed forward from MS 12 and cleared the road up to MS 14. By the morning of 3 November, therefore, the task of the 123rd Brigade was completed. The same day, the Jammu and Kashmir Infantry battalion of the 9th Brigade assembled between MS 14 and MS 15 to continue the thrust to Kennedy Peak and beyond. But Kennedy Peak also fell to the share of the 123rd Brigade when at 0900 hours on 4 November, the company of 2/1 Punjab advancing westwards along the track from Tuisau occupied the hill without opposition. There were no Japanese troops left north of Kennedy Peak. Its mission accomplished, the 123rd Brigade sat back and allowed the units of the 9th Brigade to take up the pursuit.

The 9th and the 161st Indian Infantry Brigades had already got into stride. As early as 2 November, two companies of 3/9 Jat had advanced to Thangnuai and sent out patrol towards MS 20 which lay about four miles south of Kennedy Peak. So, when 3/9 Jat blocked the road at MS 19 the next morning (3 November), the escape route of the defenders in the Kennedy Peak area was again cut. Most of them had already left the area, but a party of about 30, coming from the north, was met by patrols of 3/9 Jat and dispersed with some loss. Some Japanese guns were reported to be near MS 18, and were attacked during the day by Hurribombers. Other fighter-bombers attacked a Japanese position at RU 3784 which was holding up 1/1 Punjab of the 161st Brigade, while B25s turned their attention from Kennedy Peak to Point 8225.

[22] War Diary of 2/1 Punjab for November 1944.

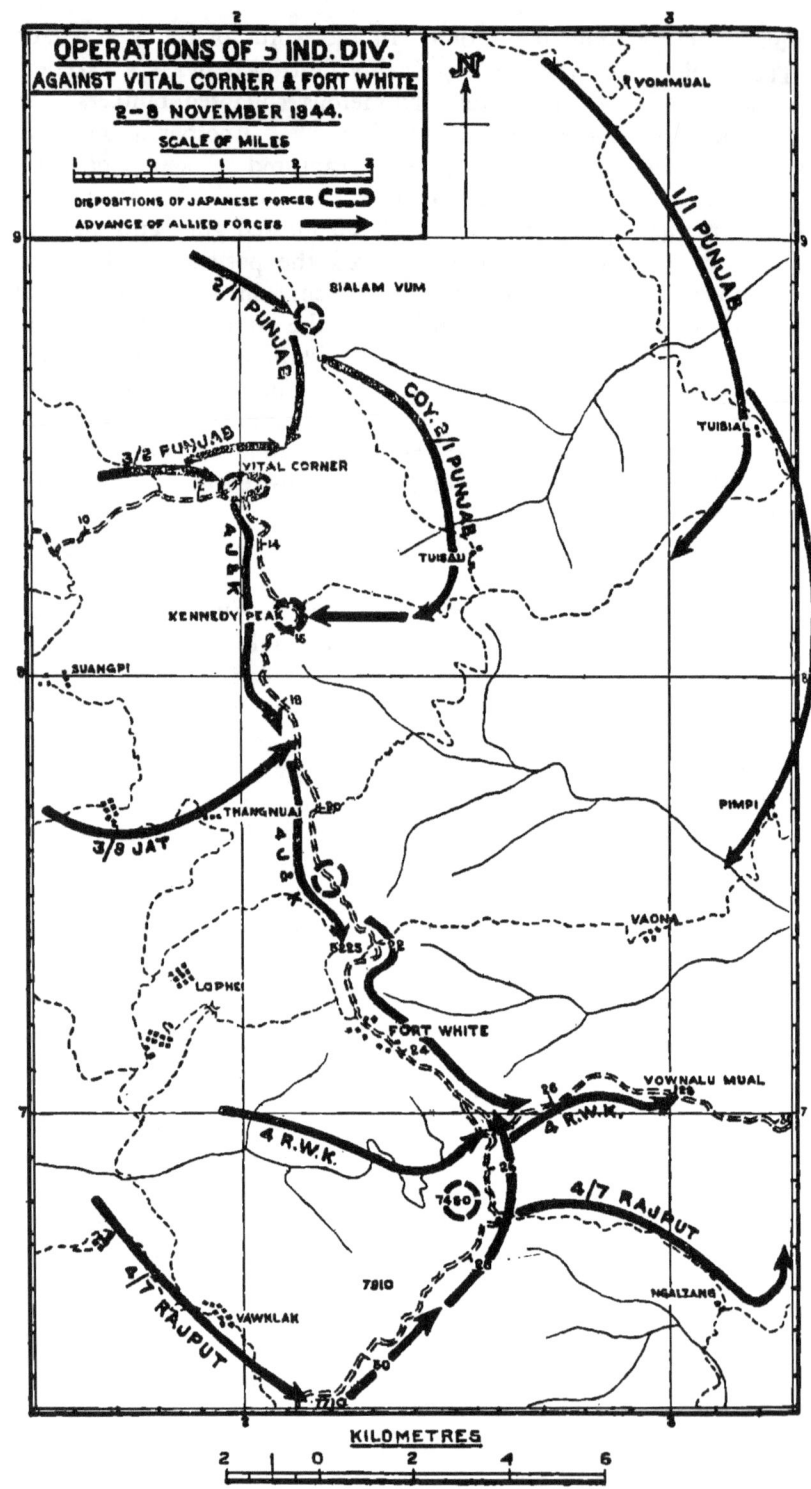

On the next day, 4 November, the 9th Brigade cleared the road up to MS 19. Some resistance was encountered, but 3/9 Jat moving north from MS 19 and 4 Jammu and Kashmir Infantry supported by the tanks of 3 Dragoon Guards moving south from Kennedy Peak quickly linked up. The main force halted for the night near MS 19, but patrols pushed on up to MS 21 and reported a strong defensive position at RU 217754.

Meanwhile, the 161st Brigade also was progressing satisfactorily. On 1 November, the approach march was completed and Point 7710, (RU 2163), on the track from Fort White to Falam, was occupied by 4/7 Rajput. The next day, the Rajputs wheeled north and reached Point 7901 (RU 2365). On 3 November, while the 123rd Brigade was clearing up Vital Corner, the 161st Brigade reached Point 7480 (RU 2567) and encountered serious opposition for the first time. The forward patrols of 4/7 Rajput sprang on the defenders at Point 7480 without warning, and succeeded in inflicting 10 casualties without loss to themselves. But then the defence got set and for several days frustrated all attempts to occupy the hill. The isolated battalion of the 161st Brigade, 1/1 Punjab, was also held up on the track from Point 8225 to Dolluang (RU 3683).

The initial momentum of the attack was spent by 4 November. On 5 November, a company of 4 Jammu and Kashmir attacked the Japanese position at RU 217754 with the support of guns, tanks and planes. But the attack was repulsed. In the afternoon, two squadrons of Hurribombers again subjected the position to accurate bombing, but with no tangible result. The 161st Brigade also registered no progress during the day, and contented itself by vigorous patrolling around Point 7480. On 6 November, the 161st Brigade remained halted before Point 7480, but the 9th Brigade found RU 217754 abandoned by the Japanese. It was promptly occupied and advance continued. Patrols penetrated up to Point 8225 (RU 2274) and saw no signs of the defenders being there. But when the main force moved forward to occupy the commanding feature, heavy fire was opened on it by light machine-guns and grenade dischargers. The Japanese had evidently remained hidden on the peak and had evaded the search by the patrol sent earlier. As a result, the attack on Point 8225 was repulsed and the leading company of 4 Jammu and Kashmir was still 800 yards to the north of the peak when night came. But the defenders had not yet exhausted their resources. During the night, 75-mm guns began shelling 4 Jammu and Kashmir, and the Japanese launched a fierce counter-attack. Confused fighting continued during most of the night. The Japanese were repulsed, but the dawn of 7 November found the battalion back at RU 217754. During the day, however, Point 8225 was again reported clear, and this time was occupied without resistance. 4 Jammu and Kashmir consolidated the position gained, while 3/9 Jat passed through and continued the advance.

The 161st Brigade also had major success that day when it occupied Point 7480. Earlier, 4 Royal West Kent was held up by the Japanese positions at Point 7758 (RU 2371), just south of Fort White. 4/7 Rajput had established itself on the high ground at RU 2365, and had sent two companies to block the junction of the main roads at RU 2570 near MS 25. Further north, 1/1 Punjab was on the track leading east from Point 8225, but the Japanese still occupied Lesan Mual, Point 5151 (RU 3378) and Bhopi Vum. On 7 November, however, Point 7480 was stormed by 4 Royal West Kent and captured after a sharp fight.

The Hurribombers were then directed further afield, bombing Fort White and No. 3 Stockade (RU 3569). A landing strip for light planes was constructed at Saizang. Designed primarily to evacuate casualties from the area, it came into operation by the first week of November. Quantities of equipment and supplies were unearthed as the clearing up of Vital Corner, Kennedy Peak and Sialam Vum areas continued. The Lushai Brigade was also continuing its operations further south. The brigade headquarters and Lushai Scouts were near Haitar and 1 Royal Jat at Hata. The Levies were also pressing forward and had captured Theizang just south of No. 3 Stockade.

On 8 November, two companies of 4/7 Rajput reached the road at MS 25 (RU 2570). While one company established a road-block the other pushed east towards No. 3 Stockade. The rest of the battalion also moved towards No. 3 Stockade via Ngalzang, and 4 Royal West Kent also pressed on from Point 7480 and reached the road. To the north, one company of 4 Jammu and Kashmir entered Fort White at the same time. No defenders were found there, so the column pushed on and made contact with the company of 4/7 Rajput at MS 25. In the afternoon, 4 Royal West Kent advanced further east along the road till it was halted by another Japanese position at Vownalu Mual. 1/1 Punjab had by then cut all the tracks leading east from the position at Point 8225.

By the evening of 8 November, therefore, the main road was cleared up to Vownalu Mual. The 161st Brigade was in the lead, and on 9 November, 4 Royal West Kent overcame the opposition at Vownalu Mual and then pushed on. It was next held up by light machine-guns and medium machine-guns on both sides of the road when it reached MS 31 (RU332698), one mile west of No. 3 Stockade. Meanwhile two companies of 4/7 Rajput, moving via Ngalzang, reached the main road and established a block at RU 3768, two miles behind the Stockade. On the following day, 1/1 Punjab at last reported the Lesan Mual—Dolluang area clear of Japanese troops, although Bhopi Vum was still held by them. Divisional Headquarters moved forward to MS 24½ near Fort White. But the advance remained held up before No. 3 Stockade. 4 Royal West Kent at MS 31 and 4/7 Rajput at MS 34 spent the day in active patrolling and preparations for resuming the advance on the morrow.

The advance was resumed on 11 November. 4 Royal West Kent cleared the defences from the area RU 3369 and advanced without opposition up to and through No. 3 Stockade. It soon reached MS 34 and linked up with 4/7 Rajput there. The latter in its turn had already advanced eastwards along the road and No. 2 Stockade (RU 395700) was soon occupied by the Rajputs. And later the same day, patrols of 1/1 Punjab advancing down from Pimpi joined them there.

The defenders evidently had been taken by surprise by the strength and boldness of the outflanking movement by the 161st Brigade with the result that the potentially strong defensive position at Fort White was captured and the road cleared to No. 2 Stockade, a hilly stretch of 15 miles, in a matter of five days.

Meanwhile the Lushai Brigade had been moving east into the Myittha Valley according to plan and without serious opposition. On 11 November, 1 Royal Jat had arrived at 'Yeshin Camp' at RZ 4995, and 7/14 Punjab had commenced to move to the same area. 1 Bihar was in area of PD 2427 and the Haka Levies were moving on Gangaw. The Falam Levies were already operating in the general area Webula—Natchaung—Sihaung Myauk. To the east, the vanguard of the 11th East African Division was only about five miles from Kalemyo, which was the goal of the 5th Indian Division too, so an exciting finish was expected to the race for the town.

On 12 November, 1/1 Punjab encountered opposition immediately beyond No. 2 Stockade. The battalion at once began outflanking the position. One of its companies cut the road at MS 40 (RU 4469) and another moved off with the object of occupying the village of Siyin during the night. Meanwhile, 4/7 Rajput moved southeast to cut the Kalemyo—Gangaw road near Thazi, about three miles south of Kalemyo. 4 Royal West Kent concentrated near No. 3 Stockade. The Japanese position to the east of No. 2 Stockade was not cleared until the evening of 14 November, and consequently no progress was made by the main body of the division. But, the leading troops of 4/7 Rajput reached Thazi and, continuing north, at 1730 hours on 13 November 1944 made contact with a patrol of African troops of the 11th East African Division. The patrol belonged to 11 KAR of the 25th Brigade of the 11th East African Division, and was met at RU 5666 just south of the town. Soon after, the two

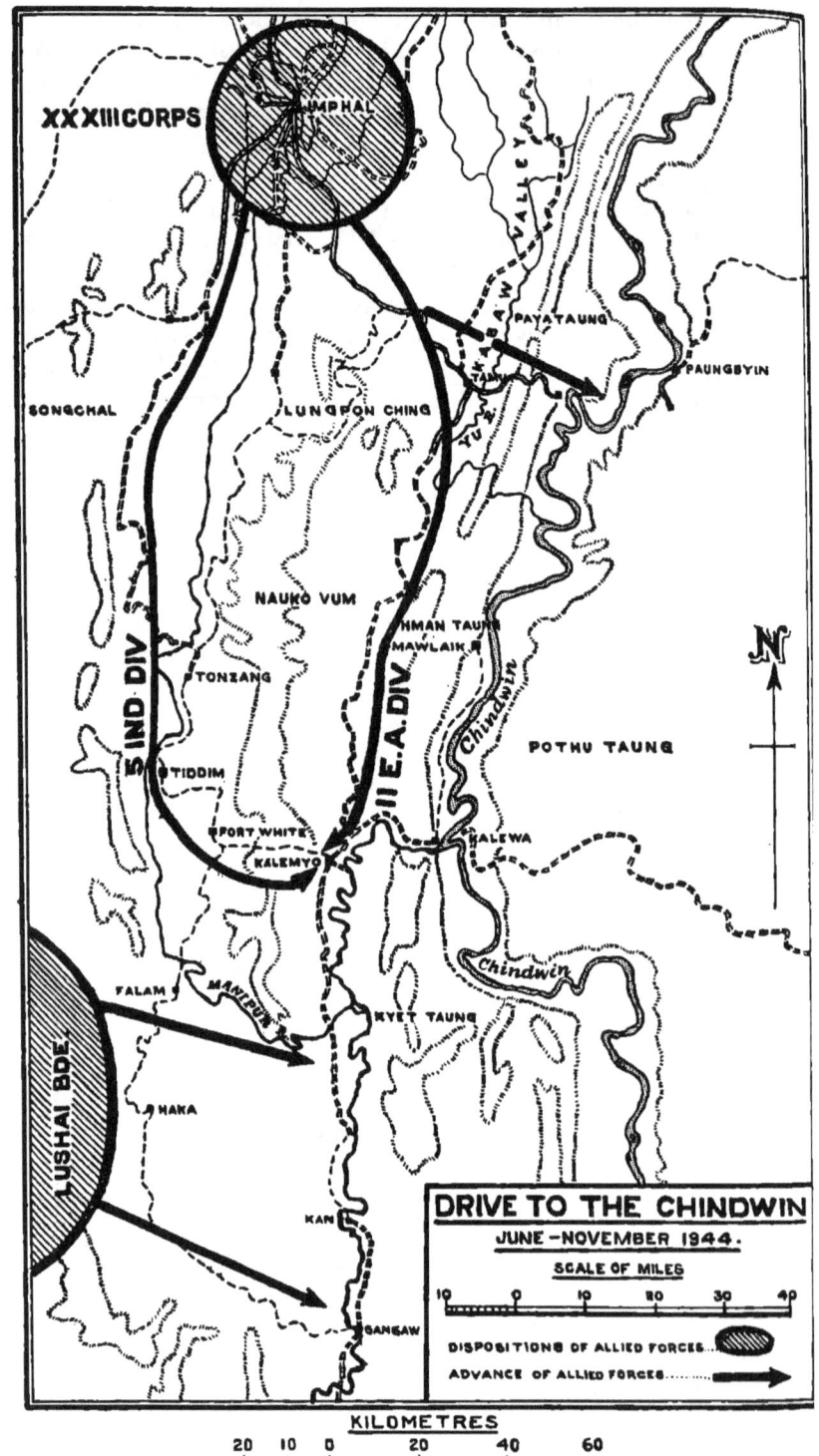

patrols entered Kalemyo together. The town looked deserted; the Japanese defenders had already evacuated it.

With the linking up of the 5th Indian Division and the 11th East African Division, the two gigantic arms of the pincer closed on the Japanese to the west of the Chindwin. The Japanese *33rd Division* had indeed lived up to its reputation as the best formation in the theatre, and had retired slowly and methodically without being encircled or annihilated. But it had been a long retreat from Bishenpur to Kalemyo. To the north and south of Kalemyo too, the picture was the same. The Lushai Brigade was operating to the south and closing in on Gangaw. To the north, the 11th East African Division had retaken the whole of the Kabaw Valley and was approaching Kalewa on the Chindwin. Thus, after suffering staggering losses in men and material and a major defeat, the Japanese armies were back on the line of the Chindwin from where they had launched their bold offensive in March. With the failure of that offensive they were now too weak even to stem the advance of the Allied armies that were pressing on from every side. In Arakan, the XV Corps was poised ready to swoop down on Akyab. In Northern Burma, the Chinese and American forces and the 36th British Division were advancing south towards the central plain in three major prongs. Bhamo was surrounded, and the 36th British Division was approaching Indaw. The Japanese facing this thrust from the north had at the same time to look to their left flank, where the XXXIII Corps was ranged along the Chindwin from Homalin to Kalewa. Major operations, in fact, were already in hand for the crossing of the Chindwin and the drive to the Central Burma plain.

CHAPTER V

Allied Plans—November 1944

In the preceding chapters the story of how the Japanese, after having been driven out of the Indian soil, were pursued by the Allied troops during the monsoon has been narrated. At the end of the monsoon of 1944 the retreating forces were facing the peril of being destroyed by powerful Allied armies which were then moving from the north as well as from the Tiddim side. The aim of these armies was to cross the Chindwin and give battle to the Japanese in the plains of Central Burma.

The strategic situation in November 1944 was that, firstly, the Chinese troops had assumed an offensive for the second time in the north.[1] They were advancing from Myitkyina towards Bhamo and were even developing a distant threat to Mandalay. Secondly, the British 36th Division had driven out the Japanese from the railway corridor and was threatening their bases at Katha and Indaw. Thirdly, the Fourteenth Army from Tiddim was rapidly forging ahead towards the confluence of the rivers Chindwin and Irrawaddy, and was preparing to cross into Central Burma. The Allied power in guns and aircraft was fast increasing and one Japanese army, badly mauled, had retired behind the Irrawaddy to lick its wounds. The stage was thus practically set for the complete reconquest of Burma. Certain plans for this purpose had been finalised by the South-East Asia Command after prolonged discussion and consideration, and some reorganisation of the commands of the land forces was also contemplated. Before a detailed account of the actual operations is given, it is necessary to describe briefly the reorganisation of the commands that took place at this time (November 1944) and the strategic plans of the South-East Asia Command for a complete reconquest of Burma.

REORGANISATION OF COMMAND

For some time the Supreme Allied Commander had been pressing for a reorganisation of the command of Allied land forces in South-East Asia and China-Burma-India theatre. In his own words:

"I had on several occasions pointed out to General Stilwell that it seemed humanly impossible for one man to carry out

---
[1] Their first was the advance to Myitkyina.

tasks which demanded his presence at Kandy, Delhi, the N.C.A.C. front and Chungking—places more than a thousand miles apart from each other—and in May I had finally informed him that I was raising this matter with General Marshall, through the Chief of the Imperial General Staff. My Chief of Staff had, on my instructions, suggested to the C.I.G.S., when urging the appointment of a Commander-in-Chief of the Allied land forces, that the U.S. Command should be divided to fit the theatre boundaries, so that General Stilwell would be free to concentrate on the China theatre, of which his knowledge was unrivalled.²"

Consequently, a decision was taken to divide the China-Burma-India theatre into two zones: the China theatre and the India-Burma theatre. General Stilwell had been recalled to Washington in October 1944 to take up the post of Commanding General, Army Ground Forces in the United States. He was succeeded in his various posts by three men: Lieut-General Wheeler as Deputy Supreme Allied Commander, South-East Asia; Lieut-General Wedemeyer as Commander United States Forces in the China theatre and Chief of Staff to the Generalissimo; and Lieut-General Sultan as commander of the NCAC and the newly formed India-Burma Theatre Command.

On 11 November 1944, Lieut-General Sir Oliver Leese, Bt. K.C.B. C.B.E. D.S.O. who had relinquished command of the Eighth Army a short while ago, succeeded General Giffard as Commander-in-Chief of the 11th Army Group, which now comprised the Fourteenth Army, XV Indian Corps and a large Line of Communication Command.³ In addition, General Leese was given the newly created post of Commander-in-Chief, Allied Land Forces in South-East Asia (ALF SEA) which included NCAC. In line and in reserve, General Leese controlled some twenty Allied divisions. The following were under his direct command:

(a) The Fourteenth Army: This was commanded by Lieut General Sir William Slim and comprised the IV Corps and XXXIII Corps only. In view of the operations in Central Burma, it had been relieved of responsibility for Arakan.

(b) The XV Indian Corps: Commanded by Lieut-General Sir A. F. P. Christison, was separated from the

---

² Mountbatten's *Report* para 266. See also pp. 139-41 of *Reconquest of Burma*, Vol. I.

³ Shortly after this, there was a significant change in the post of the Allied Air Commander-in-Chief also, when Air Marshal Sir Keith Park, of Battle of Britain and Malta fame, took over from Air Chief Marshal Sir Richard Pierse. Sir Richard was to have been relieved by Sir Trafford Leigh-Mallory but the latter met his death in an air crash while on his way out to South-East Asia.

Fourteenth Army on 16 November 1944 and came under the 11th Army Group which was now known as Allied Land Forces South-East Asia.

(c) The Line of Communication Command: Originally suggested by General Giffard, it had just then been formed at Comilla to relieve Lieut-General Slim of administrative responsibilities in the rear areas and to enable him to concentrate entirely on the operations. This command was under Major-General G. W. Symes, and consisted of the 202nd Line of Communication Area and four sub-areas. It thus included a very large number of line of communication units. It was intended that "the rear boundaries of the Fourteenth Army and the XV Corps would be adjusted as the progress of operations allowed, in order to free them from rearward responsibilities."[4]

(d) The 36th British Division.

(e) The Ceylon Army Command (Lieut-General H. E. de R. Wetherall): It consisted of a few locally enlisted battalions and base units, and also various small garrisons in the Indian Ocean islands, e.g. Addu Atoll and Diego Garcia.

In addition, there were certain forces in India which, though not under his command, were assigned to Lieut-General Leese for his future operations. These were: the Special Force (3rd Indian Division), made up of the 14th, 16th and 23rd Infantry Brigades, the 77th and 111th Indian Infantry Brigades and the 3rd West African Infantry Brigade, which, together, formed six Long Range Penetration Groups, and the 50th Parachute Brigade, two tank regiments and certain other small units.

"Lieut-General Leese also exercised operational control through Lieut.-General Sultan, over the American, Chinese and British forces in N.C.A.C.; and over any part of the Chinese Expeditionary Force from Yunnan crossing the border from China into Burma. So that a separate commander of Allied Land Forces in Burma should not be necessary, Lieut-General Leese undertook to fulfil his function in addition to that of Commander-in-Chief, A.L.F.S.E.A.; he therefore was called on to function at two levels; on one of which he worked at the level of the Commander-in-Chief Eastern Fleet, and the Allied Air Commander-in-Chief—while on the other he worked at the level of Major-General Stratemeyer, the Allied Air Commander for Burma."[5]

As the Commander-in-Chief, Allied Land Forces South-East

---

[4] Leese's *Despatch*, para 5.
[5] Mountbatten's *Report* para 269. The Eastern Fleet was later renamed East Indies Fleet.

Asia, Lieut-General Leese had his headquarters at Kandy in Ceylon where also the Supreme Commander and the Air Commander-in-Chief were located. As the Allied Commander-in-Chief for the Burma Campaign, his headquarters moved from Delhi to Barrackpore near Calcutta where they opened on 1 December 1944.[6] Why he chose to have his headquarters in Barrackpore can well be described in his own words:

> "It was not, however, possible for me to exercise command from Kandy of an Army group which was actively engaged on three widely sparated fronts, the XV Corps in Arakan, the Fourteenth Army in the Chin Hills, West of the Chindwin River, and the British/Chinese/American forces comprising the American 'Northern Combat Area Command' in Northern Burma. Even from Barrackpore I was to find that it took me 1,500 miles flying to visit the three fronts. Despite therefore the disadvantages of being separated by so great a distance from the Headquarters of the Supreme Allied Commander and from those of his two other Commanders-in-Chief, it was necessary for me to base myself on my Advanced Headquarters at Barrackpore, which was in fact by far the larger echelon, where all the day to day executive business of the headquarters was carried on. Actually Barrackpore had certain other advantages. First, Headquarters, Eastern Air Command, were located only a mile or two down the Hooghli. I was thus enabled to maintain that close touch with General Stratemeyer, which was essential to our joint operations, while the battle for Burma was in progress. Secondly, I was in a good position to visit Delhi, the Headquarters of the India Base through which all my supplies and personnel had to pass. And, lastly, I was well placed to visit formations training under General Headquarters, India, which had been allocated to my future operations, and in particular those at the Combined Training Centres at Cocanada and near Bombay."

MILITARY POSITION

As described in the previous chapter, in February and March 1944 the XV Corps, at that time a part of the Fourteenth Army, had decisively beaten the Japanese in Arakan. This was followed by the Fourteenth Army's outstanding victory in the Kohima—Imphal battle in May and July, thereby shattering the Japanese dream of 'marching to Delhi'. As the Japanese withdrew, the Allied forces pursued them relentlessly, notwithstanding the monsoon. No respite

[6] Headquarters Eastern Air Command had already moved to Barrackpore a few months earlier.

was given and the Japanese suffered enormous casualties during the rainy season from privation, exposure and starvation. "This was largely due to the tenacity of the 5th Indian Division and of the 11th East African Division who refused to be daunted by appalling conditions of weather and terrain."[7] The problem with which the Fourteenth Army was therefore faced was, how to maintain the impetus of the advance, and to deny the Japanese time to reorganise and stabilise a front. In short the problem was to retain the initiative, with the line of communication increasing rapidly, and to bring the Japanese to battle on a suitable ground. Lieut-General Slim believed that they would fight on the Shwebo plain, and so he based all his plans on that assumption.

STRATEGIC PLANS OF THE ALLIES

During the monsoon when the Japanese were withdrawing from Imphal and Kohima area and were crossing to the east of the river Chindwin, the Allies had under consideration various plans for the total reconquest of Burma. These plans were formulated and discussed at the headquarters of the Supreme Allied Commander during June-July 1944, and certain decisions were taken with the approval of the authorities in London and Washington.[8] Originally there were four plans—three suggested by the South-East Asia Command and one by General Stilwell.

The three plans produced by the Supreme Allied Commander's War Staff in close touch with the Commanders-in-Chief's Planners were called 'X', 'Y', and 'Z'. These were, no doubt, for operations to be undertaken during the dry season of 1944-45, but it was necessary, during the monsoon months to arrive at a basis upon which recommendations might be signalled to the Combined Chiefs of Staff and additional resources demanded for carrying out the approved plan.

Plan 'X'

Plan 'X' envisaged an overland advance by NCAC forces, supported by the 10th USAAF from the Mogaung—Myitkyina area to Katha and Bhamo with the ultimate object of advancing on Mandalay. This would be co-ordinated with an advance by the IV and XXXIII Corps supported by the 221st Group, Royal Air Force, from Imphal to the Chindwin; and with an airborne opera-

---

[7] Leese's *Despatch*, para 20
[8] The Chiefs of Staff in London, influenced by the American view, had laid down a modest objective of developing overland route to China for supplying that country with oil and other stores for the war in the Pacific. But this was before the extent of Japanese defeat at Imphal had been properly appreciated. Slim: *Defeat into Victory*, p. 373-4.

Major-General T. W. Rees
Commander 19th Indian Division

Brigadier P. C. Marindin
Commander Lushai Brigade

tion against the Wuntho area. By these operations it was proposed to occupy northern Burma down to a line Kalewa—Lashio.

This plan had the advantage of accomplishing the objective of protecting the air ferry route and opening the land communications to China. But it had certain disadvantages also. For one thing, plan 'X' tended to concentrate forces in the vicinity of Bhamo, which in effect might imply a threat to the security of the Imphal plain— the key to the defence of Bengal and Assam. The Japanese could undertake an advance in strength from the area south of Imphal against the Allied forces in the Imphal—Kohima area even if it might result in huge losses to them. To prevent this, a very strong garrison would have to be maintained in the Imphal plain. Another disadvantage was that an all-weather road from Tamu to Wuntho would have to be constructed involving considerable waste of time. And then if plan 'X' took up the whole of the dry season of 1944-45, it would mean that the advance on Mandalay and the eventual reconquest of the whole of Burma would have to be postponed to the dry season of 1944-45. It was also estimated that requirements of transport aircraft for plan 'X' were larger than for the alternative plans. This plan was therefore not favoured as being too conservative and time-consuming and not being sufficiently ambitious.

Plan 'Y'

Plan 'Y' envisaged an offensive across the Chindwin by the IV and XXXIII Corps, supported by 221st Group Royal Air Force, so as to deploy the heavy Allied armour against the Japanese in the Ye-U—Shwebo area, and subsequently to exploit to Mandalay. Airborne troops were to seize Kalewa, and a second landing was to be made at the entrance to the Mandalay plain; while NCAC troops and the Yunnan Force, supported by the 10th and 14th USAAF respectively, were to undertake a complementary advance southward.

This plan was considered to be the best of all the plans if the operations in the dry season were to be a logical sequence to the battles which were in progress during the monsoon. The aim was to bring the Japanese to battle in an area where the Allies might do them the greatest damage. Such an area was the Shwebo plain to which Allied armour might be pushed quickly in pursuance of plan 'Y'. But, of course, for this purpose the capture of Kalewa-Kalemyo was essential, which was to be the first phase of the operations. This initial success might be followed by exploitation towards the area Ye-U—Shwebo which would bring the Japanese to battle. The second phase of exploitation would naturally be directed towards Mandalay from where an advance further south towards Rangoon would be made. This would provide an "anvil" for the eventual invasion of Burma from the Rangoon end, since it might be impracticable to clear the whole of Burma from the north alone.

Plan 'Y' which later came to be known as operation 'Capital' had only one drawback, namely the possibility that a break-through in the Kalemyo-Kalewa area might be delayed. This, however, would be overcome with the help of the air superiority which the Allies were building up at that time. As far as the Imphal plain was concerned, this plan was based on the premise that, simultaneously with the execution of operations under 'Capital', containing operations would be undertaken in Arakan, possibly including an amphibious hook on the Arakan coast.

One of the features of this plan was that it involved the maintenance of forces at the end of long lines of communication. The limiting factors in this respect were the engineer resources involved, the provision of sufficient motor transport and drivers, and, during the advance from the Chindwin to Ye-U, the necessity of widening the road to a two-way standard at the same time as it was being used for supplying the advancing forces. All these difficulties were, however, overbalanced by the idea that 'Capital' was likely to yield quicker results. After many discussions with his Commanders-in-Chief and other advisers, Lord Louis Mountbatten finally recommended this plan.[9]

It was estimated that apart from forces in the NCAC area, Plan 'Y' would require the use of seven divisions including one *ad hoc* airborne division and one 'tired' division which would be progressing against the Japanese on the Tiddim road. In addition to these seven divisions there would be one garrison division in the Imphal area.

While submitting the plan to the Combined Chiefs of Staff, the Supreme Allied Commander thought that "for 'Capital' the air resources already in, or tentatively allocated to, the theatre were almost sufficient; nevertheless we should also need the third Combat Cargo Group and the second Air Commando."[10]

Plan 'Z'

The third plan, which was later given the code-name 'Dracula' was directed at the invasion of Rangoon by air and sea. The capture of Rangoon had been the subject of examination in detail even in the middle of 1943 when it was considered a hazardous operation because of lack of air superiority and airborne troops.[11] The Allies had both these now (July 44), and the Supreme Allied Commander, himself belonging to the Royal Navy, was keen on an amphibious

---
[9] Minutes of the Supreme Allied Commander's meeting, file F 134.
[10] Mountbatten's *Report*, para 224.
[11] JPS Paper 100-A and other Joint Planning Staff reports.

operation. From the strategic point of view the capture of Rangoon seemed most attractive as it would cut the Japanese lines of communication at their base, and would provide sea communications for Burma. On purely military grounds, therefore, it was preferable to an overland advance from the north. On the other hand, in order to quickly clear Mogaung and Myitkyina, secure the air ferry route, and to open up a land communication route to China, an operation from the north alone seemed capable of achieving the object. But the danger in the northern advance lay in getting held up, thus deferring the operations in the south of Burma for at least one year. A combination of plans 'Y' and 'Z' therefore seemed best calculated to meet the situation. But it was doubtful whether resources required for both would be made available at the same time. The Allied Air Commander-in-Chief, Sir Richard Peirse estimated that plan 'Z' would require more aircraft than plan 'Y', but after the peak period during the fly-in of the air-transported divisions to the Rangoon area, the requirements would fall considerably. After the assault on Rangoon the aircraft could be released for other theatres of operation. In addition he felt that the Allies would be in a far better position to annihilate the Japanese forces in south Burma because of the advantages of terrain.[12]

Although there seemed to be a general agreement as to the strategic value of an amphibious assault on Rangoon, doubts were expressed as to its practicability. Major-General Sultan[13] thought that the capture of Rangoon was incompatible with the directive under which the South-East Asia Command was then conducting operations. His reference obviously was to the opening up of land communications to China. He thought that "fundamentally the American effort in this theatre had been for the purpose of furnishing assistance to China and keeping China in the war as a means of carrying on the Allied attack against Japan."[14] The Supreme Allied Commander however did not agree with this view. For one thing, he thought that opening up of a land route to China through north Burma would be superfluous if a port in China was captured earlier by the Pacific forces. Secondly, he pointed out that the capacity of the road from north Burma would be fully used in feeding the liberated civil population, thus reducing the supplies which might get through to China. This would not be the case if Rangoon was captured and a line of communication opened up by

---

[12] See Minutes of the Supreme Allied Commander's meeting of 20 July 1944. It was estimated that plan 'Y' would require the allocation of the Third Combat Cargo Group and plan 'X' would require the Fourth Combat Cargo Group as well. Plan 'Z' also would require the Fourth Combat Cargo Group but the aircraft could be released after the initial assault for operations elsewhere.
[13] Deputy Theatre Commander, CBI.
[14] Minutes of the Supreme Allied Commander's meeting of 20 July 1944, *op. cit.*

sea. Moreover there was uncertainty about the attitude of the Generalissimo. It was known that he was keen on an amphibious attack but not at the expense of other operations in Burma. Certain resources had been allocated to the South-East Asia Command at Sextant of which the Generalissimo had been informed. He however had no knowledge that some of these resources had later been withdrawn or allocations cancelled. 'Dracula' could therefore be mounted only at the expense, to some extent, of land operations in the north. It was doubtful how he would view the capture of Rangoon at the expense of operations in north and central Burma, especially with regard to the Mandalay area and the support in north Burma to his Yunnan force.

Nevertheless, the Supreme Allied Commander thought that plan 'Z' might prove to be the quickest method of achieving the reconquest of Burma, depending upon the Japanese reaction to the cutting of their lines of communication at the base.

Fourth Plan

The fourth plan was produced by Lieut.-General Stilwell as an alternative to plans 'X' and 'Y'. He was not in favour of the amphibious operation in any case, because it would open another front and would take resources away from the opening of overland communications to China. His plan therefore was that the IV and XXXIII Corps should advance towards the Shwebo—Mandalay area, while NCAC forces, profiting by this diversion, would occupy Bhamo and launch an airborne operation to capture Lashio.[15]

This plan, somewhat similar to plan 'X', did not find favour because, firstly, the distances involved were immense; secondly, the advance of NCAC and the Fourteenth Army would be on divergent lines, instead of being complementary to each other, and thirdly, it did not envisage the eventual conquest of the whole of Burma. Moreover, other objections on which plan 'X' had been rejected, also applied to this.

Lieut-General Slim, the Fourteenth Army Commander, favoured Plan 'Y' for various reasons. Firstly, the major part in this plan was to be performed by his Army; but apart from this he believed that it offered "the best prospect of making the Japanese fight a battle with their main forces on ground favourable to us."[16] And secondly, he had an unofficial private Fourteenth Army plan, called 'Sob', for the capture of Rangoon which was similar, in all essentials, to plan 'Y'.[17]

[15] Mountbatten's *Report,* para 223.
[16] Slim: *Defeat into Victory,* p. 374.
[17] *Ibid,* pp. 374-6.

After considering all the four plans and assessing their advantages and disadvantages, the Supreme Allied Commander decided to recommend plan 'Y' (Capital), and also 'Z' (Dracula) for consideration by the Chiefs of staff with an appreciation of their relative merits. The appreciation made the following points[18]:—

"(a) both plans ultimately committed us to the reconquest of Burma;

(b) 'Capital' complied most closely with my directive, and was likely to result in the reconquest of Northern and Central Burma. But it involved an overland advance from the north, with all its attendant difficulties of supply and maintenance; and if the land campaign did not go well, we might be compelled to postpone the attack on Rangoon until the following inter-monsoon period. 'Dracula', on the other hand, would allow us to exploit our command of the sea and undertake the reconquest of Burma with good sea communications established; it might also induce the enemy to withdraw his main forces to the south, which would help our forces in Northern Burma to open the road to China;

(c) for 'Capital' the air resources already in, or tentatively allocated to, the theatre, were almost sufficient; nevertheless, we should also need the third Combat Cargo Group and the second Air Commando. 'Dracula', on the other hand, would require, in addition to both of these, the fourth Combat Cargo Group, which could, however, be released soon after the initial fly-in to Rangoon. It would also require additional naval and amphibious forces, and almost certainly two more divisions; though at a pinch either operation could just be carried out with the military forces already at our disposal. Detailed plans had already been submitted to justify the use of the additional aircraft, which could all be provided from the air resources which General Arnold had offered us.

(d) 'Capital' appeared likely to yield the quicker results, but it would be necessary to know before the 1st September which of these two operations we were to prepare for; so that all plans for the offensive could be carried out according to programme, and the Japanese prevented from taking the initiative themselves after the monsoon."

These plans were telegraphed to the Chiefs of Staff on 23 July and Lord Mountbatten himself left for London on 1 August to discuss these and other matters after handing over command of the

---

[18] Mountbatten's *Report*, para 224.

theatre to General Stilwell for the period of his absence. In London, the Chief of Staff, while considering "some form of major land operations in Northern and Central Burma essential," agreed with Lord Mountbatten that "even if all phases of 'Capital' were carried out, it would be necessary to undertake the amphibious operation as soon as possible. Since it was clear, however, that both the overland advance and the amphibious operation could not be carried out in full, it was impossible to set a target date, or decide the scale of the amphibious operation, until we knew to what extent the Americans would agree to a curtailment of the overland advance."[19]

It was in order to acquaint the Americans fully with the reasons which had led Lord Mountbatten to consider an amphibious operation necessary, and to ascertain their views, that in August 1944 he sent Major-General Wedemeyer a second time to Washington.[20] Wedemeyer found that the Joint Chiefs of Staff, though eager that the land operations in pursuance of 'Capital' should be pressed to the utmost, were not altogether averse to an amphibious attack on Rangoon "as a complement to the northern advance."[21] In fact, they stated on 1 September that if German resistance collapsed, making it possible for resources to be allocated for 'Vanguard' (the earlier name for 'Dracula'), the plan might be initiated in mid-March 1945, provided always that nothing should jeopardise the execution of Phase I and II of 'Capital'.[22]

At the second Quebec Conference (Octagon) held shortly afterwards, these plans were considered and approved, and a fresh directive was issued to Admiral Mountbatten on 16 September, superseding that of 3 June.[23] The monsoon was due to end in October, and the South-East Asia Command therefore immediately began making plans for both 'Capital' and 'Dracula'.

[19] Mountbatten's *Report*, para. 228.
[20] The first time he had been sent in February at the head of the "Axiom" Mission. See Volume I, p. 147.
[21] *Grand Strategy*, Vol. V, p. 502.
[22] *Ibid.* p. 503.
[23] *Directive of 3 June*:
"To develop, maintain, broaden and protect the air-link to China, in order to provide maximum and timely supply of POL and stores to China in support of Pacific operations; so far as is consistent with the above to press advantages against the enemy by exercising maximum effort ground and air, particularly during the current monsoon season, and in stressing such advantages, to be prepared to exploit the development of overland communications to China. All these operations must be dictated by the forces at present available or firmly allocated to SEAC".
Directive of 16 September:
"1. Your primary object is the recapture of all Burma at the earliest date. Operations to achieve this object must not, however, prejudice the security of the existing air supply route to China, including the air staging post at Myitkyina, adequate protection of which is essential throughout.
"2. The following are approved operations:
(a) The stages of operation 'Capital' (formerly 'Champion') necessary to the security of the air route; and the attainment of overland communications with China;

Contd. next page bottom

It was hoped that with the surrender of Germany, which was expected in October, resources from the European theatre would be available to launch both 'Capital' and 'Dracula', the date for 'Dracula' being fixed in early March 1945. The expectation was soon belied and in the beginning of October it was clear that on account of Von Rundstedt's unexpected stiff opposition the promised resources in men and material from the European theatre would not be available. Lord Mountbatten was informed of this by Mr. Churchill at Cairo in the middle of October and the target date for 'Dracula' was therefore postponed to the post-monsoon period of 1945.

When it was known that operation 'Dracula' would not take place in the spring of 1945, a very much smaller amphibious operation was planned for Arakan. This was known as operation 'Romulus', and its object was to release certain forces from the Arakan area, where four Allied divisions were locked up as a provision against a possible Japanese advance up the Kaladan Valley. This threat would be liquidated by the capture of Akyab, Myebon and Minbya by an amphibious operation after which considerable troops might be released for operations elsewhere in Burma.

This then was the strategic situation in Burma in the beginning of November 1944. Operation 'Capital' was to be implemented—in fact its first phase had already begun; operation 'Dracula' was postponed till after the monsoon of 1945; and operation 'Romulus' was to take place on the Arakan coast in the beginning of 1945.

ORDER OF BATTLE

Allied Troops

Formations in the Assam—Burma theatre in mid-November comprised the following: XV Indian Corps (Lieut-General Sir A. P. F. Christison) in Arakan consisted of the 25th Indian Division (Major-General G. N. Wood) and 26th Indian Division (Major-General C. E. N. Lomax), 81st and 82nd West African Divisions, 50th Indian Tank Brigade and 3rd Commando Brigade.

The Fourteenth Army (Lieut-General Sir William Slim) in the Chin Hills, west of the Chindwin river, comprised the IV and XXXIII Corps and the 255th Indian Tank Brigade. The IV Corps (Lieut-General Sir G. A. P. Scoones) consisted of the 7th Indian Division

(b) Operation 'Dracula' (formerly 'Vanguard'). The Combined Chiefs of Staff attach the greatest importance to the vigorous prosecution of operation 'Capital' and to the execution of operation 'Dracula' before the monsoon in 1945, with a target date of the 15th March.
"3. If 'Dracula' has to be postponed until after the monsoon of 1945, you will continue to exploit operation 'Capital' so far as may be possible without prejudice to preparations for the execution of Operation 'Dracula' in November 1945."

(Major-General F. W. Messervy), 19th Indian Division (Major-General T. W. Rees) and 23rd Indian Division (Major-General O. L. Roberts). This last division was in the process of withdrawing to India. XXXIII Indian Corps (Lieut-General Sir Montagu Stopford) had the 2nd British Division, 5th Indian Division (Major-General D. F. W. Warren), 20th Indian Division (Major-General D. D. Gracey), 11th East African Division, the Lushai Brigade, 268th Indian (Lorried) Brigade, and 254th Indian Tank Brigade.

NCAC (Lieut.-General Dan. I. Sultan) consisted of the First and Sixth Chinese Armies, 5332nd United States ("Mars") Brigade, one Chinese Tank Brigade and the 36th (British) Division of two brigades. The Chinese divisions were the 30th, 38th and 50th Divisions in the First Army and the 14th and 22nd Divisions in the Sixth Army. The Mars Brigade was practically equivalent to an American Light Division. It had two American regiments, one cavalry and one infantry, and one Chinese regiment.

Japanese Troops

The *28th Japanese Army*, comprising the *54th* and *55th Divisions* and the newly raised *72nd Independent Mixed Brigade*, was distributed between Maungdaw and Bassein in the coastal sector of Arakan. Facing the Fourteenth Army were three Japanese divisions of the *Fifteenth Army*, the *15th*, *31st* and *33rd*, much reduced in strength but in the process of receiving fresh drafts. Of these the *15th* was based on the Wuntho—Pinlebu area, the *31st* was east of the Chindwin, and the *33rd* was in the *Fifteenth Army* reserve in the Ye-U area. Another division of this Army, the *53rd Division*, was in the Naba—Katha area. The *14th Tank Regiment* which had suffered heavily in the retreat was believed to be refitting in the Shwebo area.

Disposed between Bhamo and the Salween river, the *56th*, *2nd* and *18th Divisions* faced the NCAC and the Chinese Expeditionary Force. The Japanese Burma Area Army Reserve consisted of the *49th Division* in the Pegu area. The *2nd Division* at this time facing the NCAC was also to return to the Reserve. The *72nd Independent Mixed Brigade* was at Moulmein.

The Japanese also had for their support two Indian National Army divisions, each about 6,000 strong, and seven battalions of the Burma National Army.[24] In addition to these, administrative units deployed against Major-General Wingate's brigades earlier in the year had proved themselves to be a factor which could not be ignored. They were relied on to fight at least defensively with the usual Japanese desperation. The Indian National Army and the

---

[24] The Burma National Army was organised by the Japanese under Aung San, a Burman, who had earlier been given military training in Japan.

Burma National Army forces had, in the opinion of the Allied commanders, "poor fighting value, but were apt considerably to confuse the battlefield by their similarity to our own Indian troops."[25]

Thus, to summarise, the total Japanese strength in November 1944, in Burma was:
Ten Japanese divisions and two independent brigades
Some 100,000 Japanese Line of Communication troops
One tank regiment
Two Indian National Army divisions
Seven battalions of the Burma National Army.

JAPANESE STRATEGY

After their defeat in the Imphal—Kohima area the Japanese *Fifteenth Army* was ordered by the *Burma Area Army*, on or about 10 July, to "withdraw to the line of the Jupi mountain range, Mawlaik and Tiddim, and to abandon the Imphal Operations."[26] In pursuance of this policy this army had issued separate instructions to each division outlining the plan of withdrawal, the first stage of which was naturally to the Chindwin river, Yazagyo and Tiddim. According to this plan the *33rd Division* was to assemble near Sittaung to cover the retreat, *15th Division* was to withdraw to the neighbourhood of Thaungdut via Humine, *Yamamoto Force* to Mawlaik via Sittaung and the Mu river leaving one portion of the Force to occupy Yazagyo to cover the retreat, while the *33rd Division* was to withdraw to the area of Tiddim and Tongzang. The 1st Indian National Army Division was to retreat towards Kalewa.

In accordance with the above plan the retreat began by the end of July and all the divisions reached, more or less, the line of the river Chindwin by 15 August. About that date instructions for the second phase of the retreat were issued to the various divisions on the river Chindwin, according to which the *15th Division* was ordered to retreat to the Wuntho area and the *31st Division* to the Mandalay area while the *33rd Division* was to take up positions at Mawlaik, Kalewa and Tongzang.

The miserable conditions, the losses in men and material and the hardships suffered by the Japanese troops during these two phases of withdrawal need not be repeated here. Suffice it to say that by 15 September the *15th* and *31st Divisions* had assembled in the areas assigned to them in this phase, while the *33rd Division*

---

[25] Slim: *Campaign of the Fourteenth Army, 1944-45*, p. 3.
[26] SEATIC Historical Bulletin No. 240 being translation of essays produced by Lieut.-Colonel Fujiwara Iwaichi on various topics, File 601/7531/H. For views of other Japanese commanders see Appendix 1 being extracts from interrogation reports.

continued to fight rear-guard actions with the 5th Indian and the 11th East African Divisions. By that date the effective strength of the Japanese troops employed in the Imphal operations had been reduced from 80,000 to about 30,000.[27]

Meanwhile Lieut-General Mutaguchi, General Officer Commanding-in-Chief *15th Army*, had been dismissed and Lieut-General Katamura appointed in his place. The new commander's view was that before he could reorganise the army and restore discipline and morale, all equipment, military supplies and casualties should be removed south and east of the Irrawaddy river and an entrenched position on a new line established.

The area from which the *15th Army* was to withdraw was the Shwebo plain which the powerful mechanised units and air units of the British-Indian army could attack at will. The distance was 400 kilometers including a crossing of the Irrawaddy river. For these reasons, it was absolutely necessary to cover the fact of the withdrawal. Using *31st Division* it was decided to hold the Kawlin, Mogok, Shwebo and Monywa highlands as a line to form a rallying point for the main strength of the army. Further, using this position, the Japanese tried to make it seem as if they were going to make a stand on the Shwebo position. Closely watching the movements of the British-Indian army from this position, a delayed withdrawal would be made to the new defensive position along the Irrawaddy river.

By securing bridgeheads at Sagaing, Minbu, Monywa and Pakokku, the Japanese army intended to disperse the strength of the British-Indian army on both sides of the Irrwaddy river and also make it appear as though the Japanese army was prepared at any time to launch a direct attack against them. The creation of this rallying point, the formation of a line along the Irrawaddy and the withdrawal of military supplies and patients to the rear was falsely published to the local population as measures against British paratroops. Furthermore, the Burmese were ordered to construct defences around their villages as preparations against the possibility of paratroop attacks.

On 5 October, the *53rd Division* which had been operating in the neighbourhood of Katha and Pinwe along Myitkyina railway was also placed under the command of the *15th Army*, which now had the *53rd Division* and remnants of the *15th*, *31st* and *33rd* divisions under it.

By this time the Japanese had recalled Kawabe who was succeeded by General Kimura, a more energetic person. This commander planned for the third and final phase of the retreat. During October

[27] *Ibid.*

and November preparations were to be completed for an orderly and systematic retreat—the retreat itself to begin in December and the final positions to be taken up by the middle of January 1945. In order to ensure that the Allies remained ignorant of the Japanese intentions, false rumours were to be spread to the effect that the construction of defence positions in the rear was merely a precaution against the expected landings of British and Indian airborne troops. Thereafter the various divisions were to take up the defensive positions on both banks of the Irrawaddy river. The *15th, 31st* and *33rd* Divisions were to form the first-line troops, while the *53rd Division* was to be used for the counter-attack. They were to wait for the British-Indian force and launch an attack along the Irrawaddy river. The *15th Army* expected to receive help from the *2nd Division* which was being assembled in the Pegu-Toungoo Area. The *15th Division* was to occupy the heights to the north-east of Mandalay and the bridgehead in the neighbourhood of Singu. The *31st Division* was to occupy the Sagaing bridgehead, the neighbourhood of Myinmu, and the plateau of the southern banks of the Irrawaddy. The *33rd Division* was to occupy Myingyan and the neighbourhood of Pakokku and was to establish connection with the *31st Division*. An advance unit was to occupy the neighbourhood of Monywa. The Indian National Army was to establish liaison with the *33rd Division* and was to occupy the neighbourhood of Pagan. The *53rd Division* was to assemble in the important area around Meiktila. The main force of the artillery of the *15th Division* was to be used on the front assigned to the *31st Division*.

When these dispositions had been completed, namely the heights to the north-east of Mandalay, the Sagaing bridgehead, the area around Mandalay, the plateau in the neighbourhood of Myinmu, and the Pakokku bridgehead had been occupied, these were to be used as bases for an attack against the Allies, utilising the barrier of the Irrawaddy. A decisive engagement was to be fought between the whole strength of the *15th Army* and the Allied forces, on the Myinmu front.[28]

Besides, the *28th Army* (*54th* and *55th Divisions*) was assigned to coastal defence. Distributed between Maungdaw and Bassein, it was intended to repulse attacks in Arakan, on the Irrawaddy Delta and Rangoon. It was also to secure Yenangyaung. The *24th Independent Mixed Brigade* was to protect Tenasserim, and the *33rd Army* faced NCAC with the task of securing the lines Mongmit—Hsenwi and Monglang—Lashio, while aiming at severing and obstructing communication between India and China. Their main object at this time was to secure their hold on south Burma at least, and

---

[28] SEATIC Historical Bulletin, No. 240, *op. cit.*

for this purpose they hoped at any rate to retain in their hands the general line Taungup—Yenangyaung—Mongmit—Lashio. Their aim was to crush the oncoming opponents, while holding the western face of south Burma and cutting the India—China route.

STRATEGIC TASKS OF ALLIED FORCES

In the beginning of November 1944, overall objects of the Allied operations in Burma during the coming dry season were defined as under:—

> "Allied forces in South-East Asia Command will conduct concerted offensive operations with the object of destroying or expelling all Japanese forces in Burma at the earliest date. Operations to achieve this object must NOT, however, prejudice the security of the existing air supply route to China, including the air staging port at Myitkyina, and the opening of overland communications."[29]

This implied that General Sir Oliver Leese's tasks were:

(a) to destroy or expel the Japanese from Burma, without interfering with the protection and opening of the Burma road,

(b) to protect the air route to China, and

(c) to protect the airfields at Myitkyina.

It was clear that these protective tasks would be accomplished by inflicting a decisive defeat in battle on the main Japanese forces in Burma.

In order to achieve this object, the various Allied formations were assigned their respective tasks.

XV Corps

The XV Indian Corps in Arakan had two overall tasks. Firstly, it was required to dispel the remaining Japanese threat in that sector by a limited offensive to clear the Arakan down to the line Akyab—Minbya, as early as possible. This offensive, if successful, was expected to relieve two divisions to replace reserves, certain administrative and engineer units for the contemplated pre-monsoon amphibious operations and the 3rd Special Service Brigade. Secondly, XV Indian Corps was to secure a base for mounting the operation 'Dracula'. To perform this dual role the Corps was to advance by land down the Mayu Peninsula and the Kalapanzin and Kaladan Valleys with the object of clearing the area north of the general line Foul Point—Kudaung Island—Minbya. This advance was to begin as soon as possible. An amphibious assault on Akyab Island

---

[29] 11th Army Group Operation Instruction No. 11 dated 9 November, 1944.

(operation 'Romulus') was to be launched as early as possible in 1945, with the aim of clearing the island by the end of January 1945. The area north of the line Akyab—Minbya was to be consolidated, but the consent of the Supreme Allied Commander would be required to exploit south of Myebon.[30]

The tasks assigned to the XV Indian Corps in Arakan were subsidiary to the main offensive of the Fourteenth Army in so far as the aim was to (i) capture air bases in Arakan from which to supply the Fourteenth Army in its advance on Rangoon, and (ii) release the forces locked up in Arakan for operations, land or amphibious, elsewhere in Burma, and establish a base for mounting 'Dracula' against Rangoon. Operation 'Romulus' was the outcome of this policy.

As the strategy and operations of the XV Indian Corps in Arakan have been fully described in another volume, entitled *Arakan Operations*, it is not necessary to detail them here.[31] It will suffice to say that these operations from November to February were more than successful and air bases were established at Akyab, Ramree and other places in Arakan for supplying the Fourteenth Army in its rapid advance through central Burma. In the words of Lieut-General Leese: "the Japanese had been driven out of Arakan. The air bases, which enabled the Fourteenth Army to continue its rapid advance, had been secured. The Japanese *54th Division* and the *Sakurai Detached Force* of the *55th Division* had been largely destroyed. The balance of the *55th Division*, already seriously depleted by our 1944 offensive was kept deployed on the coast until too late to offer any serious resistance to the Fourteenth Army."[32]

Northern Combat Area Command

The NCAC had the task of recapturing and securing the trace of the Burma Road and its junction with the new road from Ledo, and to hold the Myitkyina air bases. It was to conform with the phases of 'Capital' in its advance on Lashio.

Fourteenth Army

The main task of destroying the Japanese forces was however assigned to the Fourteenth Army in accordance with operation 'Capital'. It was felt that clearing the Japanese from central Burma was essential for ensuring permanent security of the Burma Road and for developing airfields in north Burma. Moreover, an advance down south through central Burma was designed to provide an

---

[30] *Ibid.*
[31] See Volume on *Arakan Operations* (CIS Historical Section, New Delhi).
[32] Leese's *Despatch*, para. 211.

'anvil' for the 'hammer' to come through Rangoon. This operation was divided into three phases as under[33]: —

> Phase 1—the seizure of Kalewa and Kalemyo, while the forces of NCAC advanced to a line Hopin—Nalong;
>
> Phase 2—an overland and airborne assault against the Ye-U area, which aimed at securing Burma down to a line Kalewa—Ye-U—Shewebo by mid-March, while the forces of NCAC made a complementary advance to a line Thabeikkyin-Mogok-Mongmit-Lashio;
>
> Phase 3—the securing of Burma down to a line Mandalay-Pakokku, while the forces of NCAC advanced to a line Maymyo-Lashio.

Phase 1 of 'Capital' was already under way at this time, November 1944, and the forces employed were being maintained from the existing Palel Advance Base.[34]

The position on various fronts was as follows[35]: —

> (i) In the XV Corps area in Arakan the 81st West African Division had reached the outskirts of Paletwa in its advance down the Kaladan. The leading brigade of the 82nd West African Division had arrived in Arakan.
>
> (ii) In the Chin Hills and Chindwin area of the XXXIII Corps, a brigade of the 5th Indian Division had captured Kennedy Peak on 5 November. Fort White had been encircled by troops of this division and the Japanese were forced to evacuate their positions. No. 3 Stockade was taken on 10 November and No. 2 Stockade fell on 11 November. Troops of the 11th East African Division which had been advancing down the Kabaw Valley were about to link up with those of the 5th Indian Division.[36]
>
> (iii) In the northern area, the 36th British Division had almost reached Pinwe, six miles north of the important junction of Naba, and the 38th Chinese Division had occupied Myothit, 16 miles north-east of Bhamo, without much opposition. Lungling had also fallen to the Chinese Expeditionary Force on 3 November. The troops in this area were thus within measurable distance of achieving one of their main objects—the reopening of land communications with China.

---

[33] Mountbatten's *Report*, para. 250.
[34] Minutes of SACSEA meeting, File F. 218.
[35] Based on General Sir G. J. Giffard's *Despatch*.
[36] The link-up was achieved on 13 November.

CHAPTER VI

Fourteenth Army Crosses the Chindwin
(November-December 1944)

As described in the preceding chapter, 'Capital' was the only plan to be implemented at this stage. 'Dracula' had been postponed till after the monsoon of 1945 and operation 'Romulus' was to take place on the Arakan coast in the beginning of 1945. In fact, the Fourteenth Army under Lieut-General Slim had already started operations in pursuance of the first phase of Capital, namely the capture of Kalewa and Kalemyo.

Since the re-organisation of the Army Command described earlier, the Fourteenth Army had consisted of only the IV and the XXXIII Corps, and these two formations were now to be employed for the main purpose of destroying the Japanese main forces in central Burma. To attain this object the ideal terrain was the Shwebo plain which provided favourable ground for manoeuvre and use of mechanised forces. It had also the further advantage of having the formidable obstacle of the loop of the rivers Chindwin and Irrawaddy behind it. The plan was to concentrate both the Corps in this loop and force a battle on the Japanese. According to the instructions given on 1 October 1944, the XXXIII Corps was to cross the Chindwin in the Kalewa area and advance on Ye-U.[1] The IV Corps was to concentrate in the Imphal area and then to seize air-strips in the Ye-U—Shwebo area or to fly into them after they had been seized by the XXXIII Corps. The 255th Tank Brigade was then to join the IV Corps through the other Corps. The Lushai Brigade and the 28th East African Brigade were to protect the flank and line of communication of the XXXIII Corps on the west bank of the Chindwin, south of Kalemyo.[2] In view of the reduction in the air-lift available, Lt-Gen. Slim was forced to modify the plan: instead of flying in, it was decided to move in one division of IV Corps into the Shwebo plain by routes which crossed the Chindwin considerably to the north of Kalewa in the Sittaung area. This would help in effecting a junction with the right flank of NCAC which was pushing steadily south down the railway towards Katha and would also release some air-lift for maintenance.

---

[1] See also XXXIII Corps Operation Order No. 9. 10 November 1944:—"XXXIII Corps will, with all possible speed, secure a bridgehead across the river Chindwin at Kalewa and will advance east . . . .".
[2] XXXIII Corps Operation Instruction No. 20 of 6 October 1944.

IV CORPS

On 1 August, Headquarters IV Corps had left Imphal for Ranchi for a brief period of rest and training for mobile operations. Towards the end of October, it returned from India and reopened near Imphal on 1 November 1944, with the 19th Indian Division under command, and to that the 268th Indian Infantry Brigade was added shortly afterwards.

The general situation was that the Japanese were everywhere on the defensive. As described in the previous chapter, they were actually engaged in a withdrawal to the Irrawaddy to take up final positions by January 1945 for holding central and southern Burma. Facing the Fourteenth Army at the beginning of November was the Japanese *15th Army* consisting of the remnants of the *15th, 31st* and *33rd Divisions.* On 5 October, the *53rd Division* which had been operating along the Myitkyina railway had also been placed under the command of the *15th Army.*[3] According to the Japanese own account, the *15th Army* "checking the English advance was concentrating its main forces near Mandalay, Meiktila, Kyaukpadaung and Pakokku and was preparing for the next operation. A powerful portion of the Army was to prepare the district around Sagaing, Pakokku and the right bank of the Irrawaddy to check the English troops advancing in that direction."[4]

According to the information with the Allies, the *15th Army* units facing the Fourteenth Army at the beginning of November were disposed as under[5]:—The Japanese *33rd Division* was withdrawing the bulk of its strength across the Chindwin in the face of the 11th East African Division's advance on Kalewa and was expected to fight delaying actions. The balance of this Japanese division had already retreated south from Kalemyo. The *15th Division* had already withdrawn east of the Chindwin and was based on Pinlebu and Wuntho. The *31st Division* had suffered most heavily in the abortive invasion of India and had consequently withdrawn from combat. It was believed to be in the *15th Army* reserve with the bulk of its forces in the Shwebo plain. The *14th Tank Regiment*, which had also suffered heavily at Imphal, was not facing the Fourteenth Army and was supposed to have withdrawn to the Mandalay area for refitting. The *53rd Division* was the only other firmly identified Japanese force which was close enough to influence the Fourteenth Army operations and was in the railway corridor north of Indaw and Katha, retreating southwards in face

---
[3] SEATIC Historical Bulletin No. 240.
[4] *Japanese account of their operations in Burma*, p. 28.
[5] Operations, IV Corps.

of the advance of the 36th British Division,[6] and finding itself too weak to resist the pressure from the north.[7]

The Dagger Division appears on the scene

The IV Corps was ordered to seize Pinlebu with at least one brigade group, and to reconnoitre routes from the Chindwin eastward to the railway corridor with a view to moving a larger force on this axis. The Corps' choice for this task fell upon the 19th Indian Division, popularly known as the "Dagger Division" from the sign on its divisional emblem.[8] This division was making its first appearance on the Burma front, having been stationed in India since the time it was raised in 1941. Thus it had had the longest period of training of any division in the Fourteenth Army. The idea of sending this force to Pinlebu, and from there to Indaw, was that it should take over Burma's main railway line from the 36th British Division, thus freeing the latter to concentrate on helping the Chinese and American Mars Task Force (under General Sultan's command) to clear the Burma Road and reopen land communications between India and China.

On 9 November, the 19th Indian Division received orders[9] to

(a) capture Pinlebu by an overland advance and from there operate eastwards by patrolling in the direction of Indaw-Katha, and establish contact with NCAC, as also towards the rail-road in the area of Wuntho-Indaw;

(b) reconstruct as early as possible, but not later than 15 December, the following roads to a one-way fair-weather standard:
   (i) Tamu-Thanan-Tonhe;
   (ii) Tamu-Sittaung;

(c) reconnoitre and develop air-strips;

(d) develop brigade group camp sites.

The ultimate intention was to concentrate the IV Corps in the area Ye-U—Shwebo as early as possible but not later than 15 February.

The force to be employed initially was the 62nd Indian Infantry Brigade Group which was to cross the Chindwin not later than 20 November. After crossing the Chindwin it was to operate as a Long

---

[6] The 36th British Division had taken over the Railway Corridor from the Chindits and was advancing in two columns from Mogaung. Its object was to clear Burma Road and establish a land-link with China.

[7] Japanese forces further south (not facing Fourteenth Army) in Burma were:— *28th Army* defending the Taungup area, the territories from the Arakan Yomas to the Irrawaddy Delta, Rangoon area and the oilfields at Yenangyaung. *49th Division* (less two regiments) was located near Toungoo and Pegu. *The Japanese Account of their Operations in Burma*, p. 28.

[8] The division had 62nd, 64th and 98th Indian Infantry Brigades under it and was commanded by Major-General R. W. Rees.

[9] 19th Indian Division Operation Instruction No. 1. 9 November 1944.

Range Penetration Group and to be supplied by air throughout the operations. From Pinlebu it was to patrol to the Indaw-Katha area and establish contact with the 36th British Division moving south along the railway corridor and to the rail-road in the area Wuntho-Indaw. Routes were to be explored with a view to judging their practicability for use later by a larger force including medium tanks. Information was to be gathered regarding suitable sites for Dakota air-strips between the Chindwin and Pinlebu. One battalion (1/6 Gurkha Rifles) of the 64th Indian Infantry Brigade was to cross the Chindwin after the 62nd Brigade Group and was to provide flank protection on the left and to prevent hostile interference with the brigade's movements, from routes leading north and north-east from Paungbyin. The rest of the 64th Indian Infantry Brigade was to concentrate on improving Tamu-Sittaung Road.[10] On the right flank of the 62nd Indian Infantry Brigade was the 268th Indian Infantry Brigade[11] which was to come under the command of the IV Corps on 11 November.[12] One battalion from the 98th Brigade was ordered to cross at Tonhe and patrol eastwards.[13]

268th Brigade and 2 V Operations V Force

Meanwhile, on 11 November, the 268th Indian Infantry Brigade (Brigadier G. M. Dyer O.B.E.) and 2 V Operations V Force, had also come under the command of the IV Corps. The brigade comprised 4 Madras, 1 Chamar, 1 Assam, Mahindra Dal and Kalibahadur Regiment, besides 2 Baroda which came under its command on 14 November. It had crossed the Chindwin and had been carrying out active patrolling in Kongyi, Ta-nga, Nanbon, Auktaung, Wetkauk, Naungphalan and Napan areas during October. On assuming its new role, the force was assigned the following tasks:

    (*a*) To capture Maingnyaung with the intention of misleading the Japanese in the initial stages by a move on as broad a front as possible and of protecting the southern flank of the 62nd Indian Infantry Brigade, and, after co-ordinating its movement with the advance of the 62nd Indian Infantry Brigade, it was to send columns east and south-east from Maingnyaung with the object of seizing the crossings over the escarpment leading to Yeshin-Thaiktaw-Chaungzauk.

    (*b*) 2 V Operations was ordered to operate in a sector bounded by the track Humine-Tilawng on the south and Homalin-Uyu river on the north, with patrols east of the Chindwin

---

[10] War Diary 64th Indian Infantry Brigade, 8 November 1944.
[11] War Diary 62nd Indian Infantry Brigade, November 1944.
[12] 19th Division Operation Instruction No. 1, 9 November 1944.
[13] 19th Division Operation Instruction No. 3, 17 November 1944. Also XXXIII Corps Operation Order No. 9 of 10 November 1944.

with particular reference to the area of Metkalet. Contact was also to be established with the American guerilla groups working in the area under Colonel Pears.

Deployment of 19th Indian Division and 268th Brigade

By 12 November, the 62nd Indian Infantry Brigade Group and 1/6 Gurkha Rifles were concentrated at milestone 8 on the Tamu-Sittaung track. All available engineer resources were being used on this track and on the road Tamu-Thanan-Tonhe, to make them serviceable. Also Headquarters 268th Indian Infantry Brigade moved to Hlezeik on 13 November and gradually the force began to move down into the areas Ta-nga-Yuwa, developing the track Hlezeik-Ahlaw-Tilaung-Kyaukchaw-Yuwa as they went.

62ND BRIGADE CROSSES CHINDWIN

Meanwhile the 62nd Indian Infantry Brigade had been ordered to cross the Chindwin at Sittaung, as an independent task force on long-range penetration job and capture Pinlebu. The Divisional Operation Instruction of 9 November 1944, had defined its tasks; but one week later, on 16 November, Major General Rees further amplified them.[14] He emphasised the fact that the Allies were on the offensive and this principle should govern all planning and execution thereof. This required seizing the initiative and maintaining it, from the outset. To gain ascendancy it was vital that all opportunities of liquidating hostile detachments should be availed of and carefully planned offensive action should be undertaken. This might involve night movement and "maximum measures to deceive and neutralise Japanese agents and spies." This offensive had been made feasible by the then situation of the Japanese forces and the non-dependence of the brigade on land lines of communication owing to the use of air supply. The Japanese had only 'reconnaissance elements forward at the moment, though they might appear to present the show of greater strength.' Lieut-General Rees also suspected that the Japanese would attempt to delay the advance of the 19th Indian Division by undertaking a series of actions as far west as possible and would adopt their customary offensive tactics. Hence the need was for preventing the Japanese from initiating such operations, and the 19th Indian Division to get as far eastward of the Chindwin as possible. Such advance must be on a 'broad front, getting forward, round and behind the Japanese wherever possible'.

On the morning of 18 November, the 62nd Indian Infantry Brigade started crossing the Chindwin on rafts. The outboard motors caused a lot of trouble "through their temperamental habits

---

[14] 19th Indian Division Operation Instruction No. 2, 16 November 1944.

with regard to starting".[15] Every river-crossing expedient, known and unknown, was used[16] and by 19 November the complete brigade was across without incident. Men, jeeps, mules, trailers, stores and rations—in fact everything was ferried across by the divisional engineers.[17] The route to be followed east of the Chindwin was Nanbon—Wayongon—Pinlebu. Further north, 4/4 Gurkha Rifles of the 98th Indian Infantry Brigade was concentrated at Thanan with one company already on the banks of the Chindwin at Tonhe, while 4/4 Bombay Grenadiers, of 255th Tank Brigade, temporarily under the command of the 19th Indian Division, had established a firm base across the river at Naungtaw.

Plan Modified

Reports sent by both ground and air reconnaissance regarding the routes were so favourable that on 20 November, the original plan was extended and instructions were issued for the employment of the whole of the 19th Indian Division for the capture of Pinlebu. This operation was to be co-ordinated with the advance of a brigade group of four battalions from the 20th Indian Division under the XXXIII Indian Corps, which was scheduled to cross the Chindwin during the first week of December and move along the axis Lawtha—Pyingaing. Prior to the advance on Pinlebu and during the concentration of the 19th Indian Division the whole area up to the general line Lawtha—Maingnyaung—Nanbon—Paungbyin—Indauktha—Tonhe was cleared to provide a firm bridgehead and base. The ultimate intention was to move one brigade on the southern route on pack, with another brigade on mechanical transport on the northern route Wetkauk—Sinlamaung. The third brigade after fulfilling a protective role in the bridgehead area was to move subsequently on the northern route to Pinlebu. It was hoped to use medium tanks on the northern route and work was started to bring the road Thanan—Tonhe up to that standard. After capturing Pinlebu contact was to be made with the 36th Division in the area of Banmauk.

The 268th Indian Infantry Brigade was to co-operate in the advance by a swift move to hold the passes on the escarpment already referred to. The 64th Indian Infantry Brigade, less a battalion, was ordered to cross at Sittaung and move to Mauksapha—Paungbyin—Wetkauk. Thus, by the end of November, the whole of the 19th Indian Division was on its way across the river.

On 5 December, reliable reports showed that all Japanese troops had been withdrawn from Pinbon and from the pass through the

---
[15] 19th Indian Division Engineers History (601/744/H).
[16] War Diary 62nd Indian Infantry Brigade.
[17] 19th Indian Division Engineers History, *op. cit.*

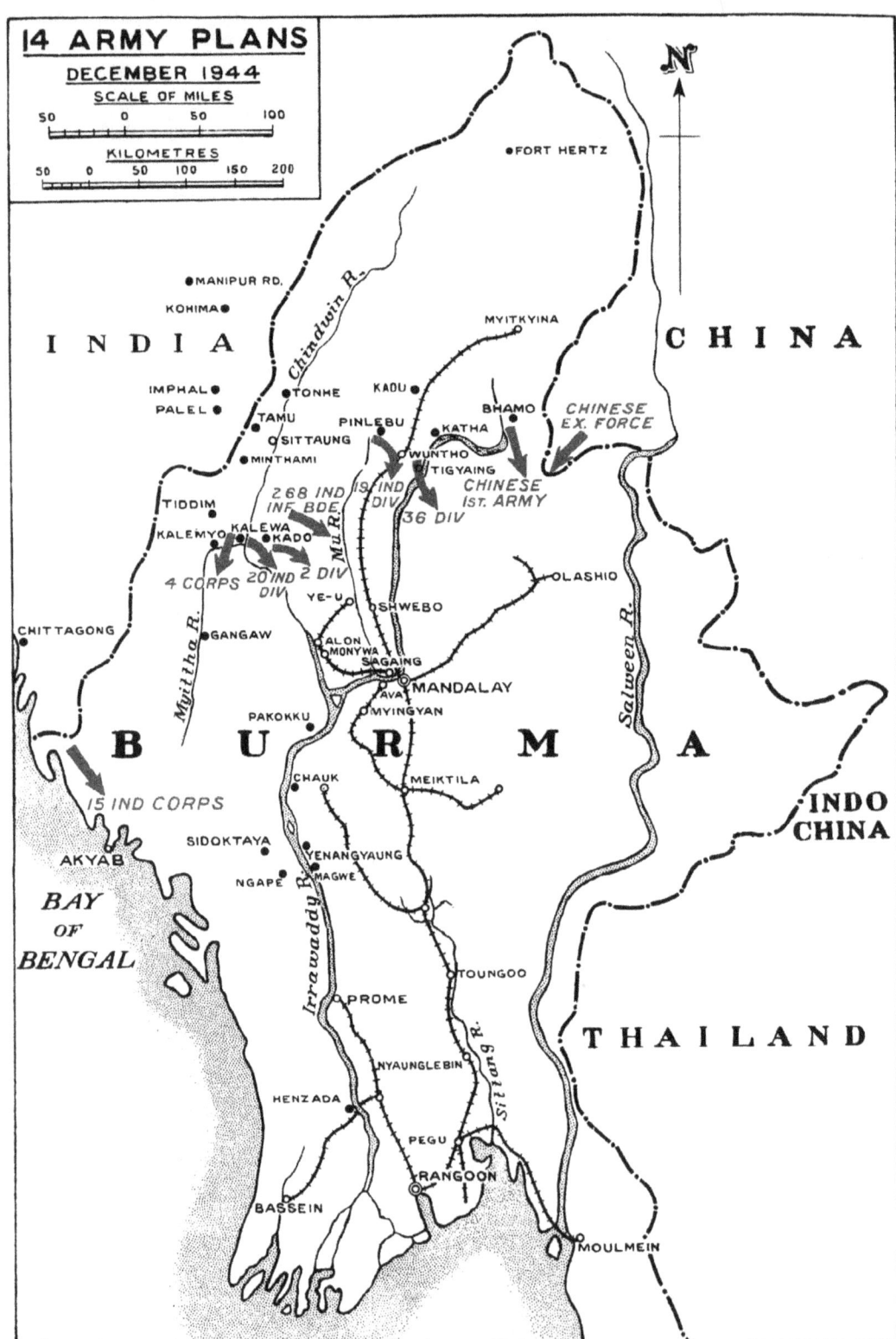

Zibyutaung Range at SG 1037. There were also indications of a further re-positioning southward of the Japanese *15th Division* at least as far as Wayontha. In view of this, the advance of the whole of the 19th Indian Division was accelerated, and it was ordered on 9 December to move as rapidly as possible, to seize Pinlebu—Pinbon as its first objective, and then move on to Kawlin—Wuntho—Rail Indaw for establishing contact with the 36th Division. The main axis of advance was to be the road Wetkauk—Sinlamaung—Pinbon, with the 62nd Indian Infantry Brigade Group continuing on its original axis.[18]

THE ADVANCE ON PINLEBU

We may now narrate the operations of the 19th Indian Division from the time it was commissioned to capture Pinlebu.

On the 62nd Indian Infantry Brigade front, all units stayed one night at Thazi on the east bank of the Chindwin after crossing the stream. On 19 November, 4/6 Gurkha Rifles followed by 3/6 Rajputana Rifles moved through Gwengu to take up positions preliminary to the advance of the brigade group; 4/6 Gurkha Rifles moved to Ontha and 3 Rajputana Rifles to Nanbon area.[19] It was to the south-east of Nanbon that 3 Rajputana Rifles had its first clash with the Japanese. Nanbon was occupied on 22 November without opposition.[20] On the same day a Japanese bunker position was discovered south of Pahe and the first air-strike was demanded by 3 Rajputana Rifles against that position. The air-strike was very successful and when patrols visited the site on 23 November they found that only one bomb had fallen outside the target area. An unknown number of bodies were found beneath the smashed bunker debris.[21]

Several clashes occurred with the Japanese during the next few days in one of which 30 Japanese were killed north-east of Pahe at SL 3870. Meanwhile, a light-aircraft strip was constructed at Nanbon from which the first Allied casualties were successfully evacuated by air on 26 November.[22]

On the morning of 24 November, a fighting patrol comprising one platoon of C Company of 3/6 Rajputana Rifles proceeded to investigate the reports of the existence of a Japanese position at Pahe. It reached Nankan Chaung in the afternoon and came upon a party of Japanese troops bathing in the chaung. The latter taken by surprise took to their heels and were engaged immediately with light machine-guns. The survivors withdrew up the slopes of the

---
[18] Operations IV Corps, October 1944—May 1945, paras 12, 18.
[19] War Diary, 62nd Brigade Group, November 1944.
[20] Operations IV Corps, October 1944—May 1945, paras 12-18.
[21] War Diary, 62nd Infantry Brigade, 22/23 November 1944.
[22] *Ibid.*

chaung to their position. The patrol then located the Japanese position but came under extremely heavy fire and was withdrawn with difficulty. On 27 November, two companies of 3/6 Rajputana Rifles cleared Nankan and considerable advance had been made along the rest of the front. The 268th Indian Infantry Brigade was concentrating in the area Yuwa—Pantha with elements still in Maingnyaung. 1/6 Gurkha Rifles of the 64th Indian Infantry Brigade had crossed the Chindwin on 21 November and had moved from the bridgehead at Sittaung to Auktaung. The 4/4 Gurkha Rifles of the 98th Indian Infantry Brigade, whose remaining troops in conjunction with 5/10 Baluch were working on the road from Thanân—Tonhe, had crossed the Chindwin at Nanthanyit and was established at Naungtaw on the east bank. The only opposition these troops encountered, except in the Pahe engagement, was from the Japanese stragglers.[23]

Meanwhile the 2nd Battalion of the Welch Regiment (referred to as 2 Welch) originally kept in the rear, pushed up to Paungbyin and occupied it without opposition. From here it moved towards the Mu Chaung, a very fast flowing tributary of the Chindwin, which was crossed with some difficulty.[24] By 3 December, two companies of 2 Welch along with the Brigade Headquarters, Field Ambulance and a section of 65 Field Company were at Ontha where orders were received on 4 December for the 62nd Indian Infantry Brigade Group to concentrate Wayongon before moving on Pinlebu, with all possible speed.[25]

By 5 December, the 64th Indian Infantry Brigade, with 4/4 Gurkha Rifles under command, was in the area Wetkauk—Le-u. 1/6 Gurkha Rifles which had reverted to the command of the 64th Indian Infantry Brigade on 3 December reached Sinlamaung on the 10th and moved rapidly towards Pinbon.

3/6 Rajputana Rifles continued its advance along the track from Nanbon and by 5 December had reached Nanaung with patrols forward to Kanti. Meanwhile the rest of the brigade was advancing from Ontha eastward and had patrolled as far as Point 2210 (SL 6879) on 6 December. On the following day, however, two companies of 4/6 Gurkha Rifles met determined opposition from a small party of Japanese troops, about 15 in number, well dug in on Point 2210. The position was cleared on 9 December, and the Japanese rear-guards finding themselves outflanked by 3/6 Rajputana Rifles to the south, withdrew east of Wayongon. 3/6 Rajputana Rifles had by that time reached south of Wayongon, not far from Thazi, where the two columns were to meet. They had traversed

[23] Operations IV Corps, paras 12-18.
[24] War History, 2 Welch File 601/7500/H.
[25] Operation Instruction No. 5 of 62nd Brigade, dated 4.12.44.

a very difficult terrain and over the whole of their route the Japanese had been fighting delaying actions. On 11 December they fell into an ambush. While the column was winding its way along the Nankamu Chaung it met with an outburst of fire from a well-sited Japanese position covering its approach. The column with difficulty climbed the steep jungle-clad slopes to the chaung bank but not before it had suffered loss of 3 killed and 4 wounded. Wayongon was entered by 3/6 Rajputana Rifles on 11 December. The same day the Brigade Headquarters, 2 Welch (less two companies) and 4/6 Gurkha Rifles (less 2 companies) arrived at Kaingshe. On the 12th, 3 Rajputana Rifles drove the Japanese from position SL 7937—SL 8573 after inflicting some casualties. The next day in a further encounter with two Japanese platoons on the escarpment south-west of Pinlebu, the unit inflicted some more casualties.

The advance in the afternoon of 13 December lay along a track which ran across a large chaung. The track went steeply down to the level of the water and then rose as steeply up to the summit of the last range of hills before dropping into the Mu Valley. The leading section had reached the bottom of the slope when it came under fire from the far side. The Japanese were established on a feature which was known as Easter Hill. For securing control of the chaung it was found necessary to seize a small hill immediately in front on the far side. A platoon of A Company of 3/6 Rajputana Rifles executed a left hook and reached its objective but found it completely dominated by the Easter Hill. The Japanese immediately attacked with a platoon with bayonets but this charge was broken up by grenades. The Japanese had also sent another party round the battalion's left, and it was feared that if it succeeded in seizing the high ground on the nearside behind the battalion, the Rajputana Rifles would be sandwiched in the chaung. The battalion therefore took up a position on this high hill and the platoon on the far side retired to it. During the night, B Company crossed the chaung and jittered the Japanese position all night. The next day D Company seized a feature beyond and a little higher than the position occupied the previous day and remained in contact all day and night. In the meantime, the brigade commander had, in view of the opposition encountered by the Rajputana Rifles, sent 2 Welch that night to form a hook and get behind the Japanese at SL 866726, but unfortunately it lost direction and arrived at SL 858724 instead, thus allowing the Japanese, whose strength was estimated at two companies, to make their escape.

Fresh Japanese troops were encountered in this area (east of Wayongon) with brand new clothing and equipment. These troops fought well but were generally content to withdraw.[26] In the meantime, the 98th Indian Infantry Brigade was relieved on the Thanan—Tonhe track by the 114th Indian Infantry Brigade of the 7th Indian Division on 11 December, so that the former could follow up the rapid advance of the 64th Indian Infantry Brigade on the northern route Wetkauk—Sinlamaung—Pinbon—Banmauk. On 13 December the Allied troops were reported to be in Naungkan and Napin, and by noon that day a jeep patrol of 1/6 Gurkha Rifles of the 64th Indian Infantry Brigade had reached within 10 miles of Pinbon without any contact with the Japanese. "The troops worked splendidly on the road, improving it as they went, showing the same enthusiasm as they had done on the building of the Thanan—Tonhe road, where everyone led by the Divisional Headquarters staff was made available".[27]

Pinlebu Captured

1/6 Gurkha Rifles entered Pinbon on 15 December and moving towards Indaw established contact with the Chinese forces. Meanwhile, the 62nd Indian Infantry Brigade had started on 15 December for its final march to Pinlebu, with 2 Welch leading. The Mu river was crossed by the latter at Pintha and by the rest of the brigade at Ingon. Passing through various villages, A Company of 2 Welch finally entered Pinlebu at 1300 hours on 13 December only to find that the Japanese had left the place the previous day.[28] The rest of the brigade entered Pinlebu from the Ingon side to the west. Thus the first objective had been gained,[29] and further detailed orders were necessary for the accomplishment of the second objective, the seizure of Kawlin and Wuntho and contact with the 36th Division at Rail Indaw.[30]

SITUATION AFTER THE CAPTURE OF PINLEBU

In the third week of December, the general retreat of the Japanese continued unabated. They were prone to adopt delaying tactics but had always shown a fear of encirclement and had withdrawn when threatened with encircling moves. On the western flank, opposite the 2nd Division and the 20th Indian Division, they were withdrawing south-east along the main route from Kalewa towards Ye-U and Shwebo. Down the Mu Valley the Japanese *15th Division* was withdrawing swiftly. Some of these troops were those

---

[26] War Diary, 19th Division, 13 December 1944.
[27] Operations IV Corps, para 24.
[28] War History 2 Welch, File 7500.
[29] The Army Commander and Commander IV Corps sent messages of congratulation to 19th Division on its performance. (Appendix D to 19th Division War Diary for December).
[30] Operations IV Corps, para 25.

who had been driven back by the 62nd Indian Infantry Brigade of the 19th Indian Division during its successful drive to Pinlebu and others who had withdrawn hastily south via Pinlebu to avoid being cut off by the rapid advance of the 19th Indian Division.

On the 19th Indian Division's immediate front, the direction of Japanese withdrawal was generally south, parallel to the railway and the river Irrawaddy. It appeared from local reports that some Japanese troops were also moving east with a view to crossing the river Irrawaddy by country boats. These were all men of the *15th Division*. The 19th Indian Division (all the three brigades) was in hot pursuit of the precipitately retreating Japanese troops. The exact axis of withdrawal of the *53rd Division* was uncertain but a considerable portion was known to be moving down the Kunbaung Valley to Tigyaing where it might cross the Irrawaddy. Other sources, however, indicated that part of the *53rd Division* might be withdrawing on Shwebo.[31]

On 15 December, the 36th Division was holding Pinwe—Naba —Katha—Rail Indaw. The 72nd Brigade was crossing the Irrawaddy at Katha prior to moving south-east. The rest of the division was to move south from Rail Indaw down the Kunbaung Valley and cross at Tigyaing as soon as possible after 20 December. On this front the Japanese had certainly retreated south-east across the Irrawaddy.

The Plan of Operations

The next phase of the plan of operations subsequent to the capture of Pinlebu was defined as follows[32]:—

(a) 19th Indian Division:
  (i) To move one brigade group (64th Indian Infantry Brigade) to Nankan, thence south to Kokkogon, with the primary object of clearing the area of the Meza bridge. At least one battalion was to move via Rail Indaw to make physical contact with the 36th Division.
  (ii) To move the 62nd Indian Infantry Brigade to capture Wuntho and Kawlin, and thence south down the axis of the railway, to be followed by the 98th Indian Infantry Brigade which was to reach here by the quickest possible route.

(b) 268th Indian Infantry Brigade:
  After establishing a block at Yeshin to be prepared to move south, in conjunction with the 19th Indian Division, west of the Mu river. It was, however, found

---

[31] Operations IV Corps, Oct. 44—May 45, para 26.
[32] *Ibid*, para 28. See also IV Corps Operation Instruction No. 115 of 15 December 1944.

impossible from the supply point of view to maintain more than two battalions in this area and the plan was modified accordingly.

(c) 2 V Operations:
To concentrate at Pinbon for operations on the east flank of the 19th Indian Division south of Tigyaing.[33]

After the capture of Pinlebu on 16 December, the advance of the 62nd Indian Infantry Brigade continued without incident. Wuntho was occupied on 19 December and Kawlin on 20 December.[34]

The 64th Indian Infantry Brigade entered Banmauk unopposed and a patrol pressed on to Rail Indaw where it made contact with the troops of the 36th Division on 16 December, thus establishing a more or less continuous Allied front from India to the Chinese border. The 98th Indian Infantry Brigade was following close upon the 64th Indian Infantry Brigade and had moved east from Sinlamaung late on 15 December.

After firm contact had been made with the 36th Division in the Meza area, the 64th Indian Infantry Brigade, with 2 Worcestershire Regiment leading, turned south from Banmauk. Nankan was occupied after slight opposition on 19 December, and on 21 December most of the brigade was concentrated in that area. By an equally swift advance the 98th Indian Infantry Brigade reached Kawlin on 21 December via Maungkan and Pinlebu.

Various small engagements took place in the Kawlin area and some prisoners were taken. But the Japanese avoided contact as far as possible.[35] On 21 December, a column of 2 Welch made contact with a Japanese force estimated at one platoon in the area of milestone 14, near Kyaukpintha. But again they quickly slipped away at night before they could be surrounded on account of the failure of the forward British troops to maintain contact during the night by vigorous patrolling. The pursuit continued and contact was regained south-west of Kokkogon by the 98th Indian Infantry Brigade on the evening of 22 December, but no decisive action was fought. The advance continued against very slight opposition both on the railway and on the road Kokkogon—Letpanda—Baw, with sweeps along all the connecting roads. By 23 December, the leading elements had been pushed as far as 30 miles south of Kawlin into and east of Kyaikthin.

By 19 December two battalions of the 268th Indian Infantry Brigade (4 Madras and Mahindra Dal) had crossed the escarpment and occupied Yeshin and Megin. The brigade's task was to patrol

---
[33] Meanwhile the 7th Indian Division was to follow 19th Indian Division to Pinlebu and improve the road to tank-transporter standard. See IV Corps. Op. Instn. No. 115, *op. cit.*
[34] Operations IV Corps, *op. cit.*, para 29.
[35] *Ibid.*, paras 31-35.

widely in the area of the Mu river and maintain contract with the 19th and 20th Indian Divisions. 4 Madras took the lead and arrived at Thetkegyin on the 24th, at Leiksindaung on the 28th and Kyigon on the 30th. Mahindra Dal followed and reached Kyigon on the 31st. The same day a patrol established contact with the troops of the 19th Indian Division.

At 0700 hours on 26 December, the 19th Indian Division,[36] 268th Indian Infantry Brigade and 2 V Operations passed to the command of XXXIII Corps. At this point the leading troops of the 19th Indian Division were located on the line Kanbalu—Sadwingyi—Baw.

It had been intended that the 7th Indian Division should follow up the 19th Indian Division across the Chindwin and move via Pinlebu to the Ye-U—Shwebo area. On 28 November, this division issued order for the 114th Indian Infantry Brigade Group together with a proportion of divisional troops to concentrate in the Kabaw Valley by 25 December. Owing to the rapid advance of the 19th Indian Division and the necessity for relieving the 98th Indian Infantry Brigade Group engaged on constructing the road Thanan—Tonhe, the move forward of the 114th Indian Infantry Brigade was accelerated, and on 11 December responsibility for the sector Thanan—Tonhe passed from the 98th Indian Infantry Brigade to the 114th Indian Infantry Brigade. This responsibility was shortly afterwards extended to include everything west of the river Chindwin.[37]

At this juncture, the 19th Division instructed its troops to continue the pursuit "with all the dash, speed and determined endurance we are capable of". The men were told to realise the fact that the Japanese were on the run, "and if we can keep driving after him, it will prevent his getting reorganised and dug in and so save us many casualties. Risks will be taken freely and without hesitation".[38]

Movements in pursuance of these instructions were already going on and were continued, which will be described in the next Chapter. Lieut-General Slim had formulated a new plan of operations at this stage (middle of December), under which the 19th Indian Division was placed under the command of the XXXIII Indian Corps.

However, before we turn to XXXIII Corps operations during the same period (November-December 1944) it will be appropriate to assess the achievements of the 19th Indian Division. In five weeks this division, a new and untried formation, had advanced nearly 250 miles over some of the most difficult country imaginable, and had

---
[36] See Operation Instruction No. 12 of 24 December.
[37] Operations IV Corps, para 36.
[38] 19th Indian Division Operation Instruction No. 12.

completed the first phase of its operations. The following two examples, out of many, show the dashing spirit of the troops which marked this astonishing march.[39]

One Gurkha battalion covered 31 miles over mountainous tracks in 16 hours; 2 Worcestershire Regiment made a forced march of incredible swiftness from Banmauk to Nankan. Communications became stretched to breaking point by the speed of the advance and in their eagerness the Allied troops were more often than not far beyond their scheduled dropping zones at the appointed time. Contact was kept by means of liaison officers in light planes landing wherever a halt of sufficient time was made to allow a strip to be constructed. Admittedly the opposition met with was scattered and at places almost negligible, but wherever it was offered, it was offered with typical Japanese desperation. The 19th Indian Division had, however, waited long enough for a chance to get at the Japanese and now that it had got it, its determination to overcome all physical difficulties became more fixed.

XXXIII CORPS

After the failure of the Manipur offensive, the Japanese had intended to hold a bridgehead west of the Chindwin and organise the remainder of their battered army east of the river for a future offensive. The weight and speed of the Allied operations during the monsoon, had, however, upset the Japanese calculations and they had to cut down their original plan. Their new plan seemed to be restricted to delaying the Allied advance as long as possible.

By the middle of November, the bulk of the Japanese *15th Army* had been driven back across the Chindwin and whatever force remained west of the river was in the area Kalemyo—Kalewa and down in the Myittha Valley. The responsibility for dealing with the Japanese forces in this area was assigned to the XXXIII Indian Corps, to whose operations we may now turn.

On 1 October, this Corps had been allotted the following tasks[40]:

    (a) to capture the area Kalemyo—Kalewa,
    (b) to establish a bridgehead over the river Chindwin at Kalewa,
    (c) to advance astride the road Kalewa—Pyingaing—Ye-U as quickly as possible and to capture Ye-U.

---

[39] Operations IV Corps, para 37.
[40] For these operations, the Corps had the following formations under command:—2nd British Division, 5th Indian Division, 11th (East African) Division, 20th Indian Division, Lushai Brigade and 254th Indian Tank Brigade.

Importance of Kalemyo—Kalewa

From the military point of view Kalemyo—Kalewa area was, perhaps, the most important zone on the upper Chindwin front. This was so because it was roughly half-way between the Imphal plain and the Shwebo plain and lying on the axis of the shortest route between these two plains. If the Japanese lost the area Kalemyo—Kalewa, they would lose not only their last chance of holding a worthwhile foothold west of the Chindwin, but would also open the "Gateway to northern Burma" to the swiftly moving Allied troops, at the beginning of the dry season.

Diversion of aircraft to China

Here it may be noted that, according to the original plan of 'Capital', Kalewa was to be seized by airborne troops, whilst a second landing was to be made at the entrance to the Mandalay plain. But soon after, Lieut-General Slim had come to the conclusion that to use available aircraft for maintenance would pay him better than to use them for taking Kalewa by air. The airborne part of 'Capital' was therefore cancelled. Another reason for this step was the diversion of some air force squadrons to China. Lieut-General Wedemeyer, the Chief of Staff to the Generalissimo in China, discovered that during the last five months the Japanese had advanced 500 miles from Yochow to Liuchow, from where they were threatening either Chungking or Kunming (the 'Hump' terminal). He feared that the fall of either of these would probably throw China out of the war. Hence he requested the Supreme Allied Commander to send him a few squadrons of fighters and bombers in addition to the two Chinese divisions. This was conceded; and consequently sufficient force could not be transported by air to Kalewa, but had to be moved by road as in the case of Shwebo.[41] In the event, this decrease in American supply aircraft caused a delay of three weeks in the build-up for crossing the Irrawaddy.

XXXIII Corps Plans

To achieve the tasks assigned to it in October 1944, the XXXIII Corps plan was to capture Kalemyo-Kalewa area, establish a bridgehead over the river Chindwin at Kalewa and then to concentrate the rest of the Corps forward, preparatory to an advance east on a wide front. Orders to this effect were issued on 10 November 1944.

To achieve the first of the above objects two divisions were converging in October-November 1944, on the Kalemyo—Kalewa area— the 5th Indian Division from the west along the axis Fort White-

---

[41] See page 127.

Kalemyo and the 11th East African Division from the north along road Tamu—Kalemyo and along both banks of the Chindwin from Mawlaik, with the ultimate objective of capturing Kalewa. Further, the Lushai Brigade, under the command of the 5th Indian Division, protected the right flank of the division and was thus operating in pursuance of the directive to move into the Myittha Valley and establish a road-block on the road Gangaw—Kalemyo, in the vicinity of Gangaw.[42] On the occupation of Kalemyo area, the Lushai Brigade was to dominate the area Chaungwa—Mingin—Kani—Gangaw. The purpose of this role was to compel the Japanese east of the Chindwin to look for any further Allied activities on a wide front. This impression was to be further strengthened by the "spreading of calculated rumours" to that effect.[43] We shall now discuss the operations of these three units separately to see how each accomplished its task.

5th Indian Division, November 1944

The exploits of the 5th Indian Division during the monsoon of 1944 have already been described in an earlier chapter. The climax of its gruelling advance during these long months through mud and rain and forest had been the capture of Tiddim on 17 October. But this was by no means the end of its campaign. Some 13 miles from Tiddim lay the Vital Corner through which ran a route to Kennedy Peak which was the next objective. After some brilliant manœuvring, 3/2 Punjab had got behind the Japanese positions at Vital Corner by 1 November and attacked them from the south. By 3 November, the Japanese resistance was completely broken and all commanding features in the area, including Vital Corner, were occupied by the Allied troops. Kennedy Peak was occupied next day (4 November) by the 4th Jammu and Kashmir Infantry.[44] From this date a new stage may be said to have begun in the operations conducted by the 5th Indian Division. The road to Kalemyo seemed dry, the monsoon was over and the brilliant sunshine diffused warmth and cheer among the troops. A long and hard campaign lay ahead but it was through a different country and under different climatic conditions.

Advance towards Kalemyo was immediately begun and contact with the Japanese was made at milestone 21 on the Kalemyo road, on 5 November. Opposition from milestone 21 onwards was stubborn but was overcome following successful air-strikes by Hurribombers; and Elephant Hill, and finally Fort White were occupied by 8 November. Good progress was also made on 9

---

[42] XXXIII Corps Operation Instruction No. 20, 6-10-44. See Appendix 6.
[43] *Ibid.*
[44] War Diary Headquarters, XXXIII Corps, GS Branch.

November when, on the 161st Indian Infantry Brigade front, 4 Royal West Kent reached milestone 31 on the Kalemyo road and made contact with a Japanese force, within one mile of No. 3 Stockade. Two companies of 4/7 Rajput reached the main road and established a block in the area of milestones 34/35 between No. 2 and 3 Stockades.[45] By 11 November, No. 2 and 3 Stockades were captured, though some Japanese continued to hold on to the east of No 2 Stockade. This held up the advance of the main body of the 123rd Indian Infantry Brigade, but 1/1 Punjab by-passed it and pushed on to the east.[46] Meanwhile, 4/7 Rajput entered Thazi (13 November) and its patrols made contact with the East African Askaris (11 KAR), west of Kalemyo, and entered the village. The object of the two-pronged drive down the Tiddim road and the Kabaw Valley was thus achieved.

The condition of Kalemyo is described thus by Anthony Brett-James:[47]—

> "Kalemyo was a ruined township. The Burmese had fled from crumbling walls to villages that were safe within the jungle, and the few Indian shopkeepers and money-lenders had gone the same way. Now the town lay deserted by its former inhabitants, and only nature grew apace among the ruins. The roads were overgrown with weeds. Trees and creepers stretched up to the broken windows, and the splintered balconies were vanishing beneath tall undergrowth. And this same undergrowth concealed the roofs that had fallen down, and the rubble caused by bomb and shell. A moat, now derelict and thick with weeds, surrounded this town, which had become like this during the two years since the Japanese first came inside its walls."

The fall of Kalemyo was followed by the capture of Taung-u on 15 November, and Pyinthazeik on 16 November, and active patrolling in the surrounding area. Meanwhile the sappers were constructing an outstrip and as soon as it was ready the 5th Indian Division was flown out to Imphal, in accordance with the Operation Order No. 10 of XXXIII Corps, at the end of November, for a well-earned rest.[48] It had fought continuously for more than a year through all kinds of weather and had inflicted considerable casualties on the Japanese. It had marched through difficult country, many men had to fight against serious illness, but in the end it had come through the ordeals.

[45] *Ibid.*
[46] *Ibid.*
[47] *The Ball of Fire,* p. 389.
[48] This was in accordance with Fourteenth Army Operation Instruction No. 77 of 12 November 1944.

The Lushai Brigade

During all this time, the Lushai Brigade was moving on the right flank of the 5th Indian Division in order to establish a block on the Gangaw-Kalemyo road. This brigade had been formed in March 1944 and initially was assigned the role of halting an apprehended Japanese thrust against India through Haka and Lungleh to Silchar or Chittagong. For about three months after its formation, it had operated in the Haka and Falam areas doing very useful work, mostly of a "watching" nature. But, from July onwards, the brigade had been assigned a new role by the Fourteenth Army. The Japanese were withdrawing from the Imphal and Kohima area and were using the Tiddim road as their line of retreat. The Lushai Brigade was ordered at the end of June to 'dislocate the Tiddim road as a Japanese line of communication.' The 5th Indian Division had also received orders to advance down the road. The Lushai attack was to coincide with it. The duty of the brigade was to establish three battalions in secure bases within striking distance of the road.[49] From these bases attacks were to be made on the road at night as the Japanese had stopped using the road during the day on account of Allied air activity. This plan worked very well during July, August and September. While certain units of the brigade were employed on this task, other units captured Haka and Falam by the third week of October. During all these operations, the brigade had been supplied from the air.

The Lushai Brigade spent a few days (21 October to 3 November) at Falam and Haka concentrating and reorganising, when it received orders to continue the advance down the Myittha Valley. It was also decided, as a part of its deception plan, to "make itself as conspicuous as possible and simulate a large force, in order to give the Japs the impression that the thrust was a major and not a subsidiary one."[50]

The plan adopted was that the Brigade Headquarters, Assam Rifles, Lushai Scouts, 1/9 Jat and 7/14 Punjab Regiment were to form a firm base at Yeshin and clear the valley eastwards up to the river Chindwin, southwards to Myintha and north to Kinyan Myauk. The Falam levies were to move northwards and after clearing the area around Natchaung and Sihaung Myauk were to move east towards the Chindwin. The Bihar and 8 V Operations were to form a secure base and operate in the Kan area. The Haka Levies were to operate in a harassing role in the valley between Gangaw and Tilin. Thus, the overall plan of the Lushai Brigade for this period (November-December) was to operate in four

---

[49] Lushai Brigade Operation Instruction No. 4, 7 July 1944.
[50] Brigadier P. C. Marindin's account (MSS), File 4576.

different columns as described above, and then finally to concentrate for an attack against Gangaw.

Good progress was made by the first column from the start. By 11 November, 1 Royal Jat was within 8 miles of Myintha, which was found to have been evacuated on 15 November. It was clear that no Japanese troops remained in the valley between Yeshin and Myintha. The Lushai Scouts, 5 V Operations and Assam Rifles were therefore sent to clear the country eastwards up to the Chindwin. They accomplished this task by the end of November against very slight resistance and then proceeded south.

Similarly the Falam Levies also accomplished their task easily and reached the Chindwin on 17 November after clearing Natchaung area. After patrolling for a few days, without meeting any opposition, 1 Bihar decided to cross the river and move on Kan. The river was successfully crossed on the night of 26/27 November, but as the battalion moved southwards along the east bank of the river, strong opposition was encountered. Fighting continued during the afternoon of 27 November and finally 1 Bihar withdrew to the west bank leaving a company to hold the crossing site at Thagaung. Next day patrols of this company reached Kan and found that the Japanese had withdrawn. Kan was thus captured unexpectedly, though the Japanese had set fire, before withdrawing, to the various dumps containing considerable quantities of food, clothing and ammunition.

Similarly, the fourth column (Haka Levies) also met with success. Operating on a wide front this column reached the Gangaw-Tilin area about the same time as 1 Bihar. There were many clashes in which both sides suffered casualties, but on the whole the Japanese suffered more.

Thus during the operations in November, "the Myittha Valley had been cleared to within striking distance of Gangaw and also east of the Chindwin, to Mingin".[51] It was clear that the Japanese aim at this stage, in that area, was to fight rear-guard actions in order to evacuate stores, and to resist only at Gangaw for the attack on which the stage was set.

The operations of the Lushai Brigade, during December 1944 and January 1945, leading to the fall and capture of Gangaw will be described in the next chapter.

11TH EAST AFRICAN DIVISION OPERATIONS, NOVEMBER-DECEMBER

Capture of Kalewa

It may be recalled that on 1 October 1944, the XXXIII Corps had been given three tasks, namely to capture the area Kalemyo-Kalewa,

[51] File 4576.

establish a bridgehead at Kalewa, and then to advance towards Ye-U. Kalemyo had been captured by the 5th Indian Division on 13 November, as already described in an earlier chapter. The 11th East African Division had moved simultaneously with the 5th Indian Division; while the latter had moved from the west along the axis Fort White—Kalemyo, the former had moved from the north along the road Tamu—Kalemyo, and along both banks of the Chindwin from Mawlaik with the ultimate object of capturing Kalewa.[52]

Following the capture of Kalemyo on 13 November, the 25th and 26th Brigades of the 11th East African Division were ordered to clear the triangle Indainggyi—Kyigon—Hpaungzeik.[53] The 25th Brigade had under it the 11th, 26th and 34th Battalions, while the 26th Brigade had the 22nd, 36th and the 44th Battalions of the King's African Rifles. The movement to clear the triangle mentioned above began immediately and on 20 November Indainggyi was occupied by the 26th Brigade. On the same day the 25th Brigade was ordered to advance on Kalewa on the axis of the main road and the 'telegraph track'. Stiff opposition was encountered from Japanese positions but with the assistance of Hurribombers this was overcome. On 21 November, 11 King's African Rifles of the 25th Brigade supported by one troop of 7 Cavalry secured Kyigon. 11 King's African Rifles pushed on the axis of the road and occupied Yenatha on the 24th. A Japanese strong position east of Chaunggyin at RU 733692 prevented, for some time, any advance along the Kelewa road but on 29 November after twenty-four Hurribombers had strafed this main Japanese position, they withdrew.[54] On 30 November, 26 King's African Rifles, supported by one troop 7 Cavalry, resumed the advance and occupied Thitchauk on 1 December. On 2 December, the advance was continued and after overcoming slight opposition, the leading troops entered Kalewa about noon and found the village deserted. The Japanese had, however, managed to remove all their supplies from the place. After the fall of Indainggyi to the East Africans, the Japanese had been engaged in carrying out a clever withdrawal while holding up the Africans long enough to remove the bulk of their stores from the various dumps.[55]

In the meanwhile the 21st Brigade of the 11th East African Division was driving south towards Kalewa from Mawlaik along both the banks of the Chindwin. Opposing it was the Japanese *213th Regiment*, with an estimated strength of approximately 340.

---

[52] 11th (East African) Division Operation Instruction No. 8, 12 November 1944.
[53] 11th (East African) Division Operation Instruction No. 10, 16 November 1944.
[54] 11th (East African) Division, Daily Intelligence Summary No. 112.
[55] 11th (East African) Division, Daily Intelligence Summary No. 115.

On the west bank, 2 King's African Rifles occupied Paluzawa on 18 November. 1 NRR then passed through and continued the advance. After overcoming resistance at RU 8289 it occupied a village at RU 3283 on 23 November.

On the east bank of the Chindwin 5 King's African Rifles patrolled the area of Ywatha and engaged a small party of the Japanese to the south of the village in the area of RU 8589. On 20 November, 5 King's African Rifles made contact with some twenty Japanese troops holding the line of the Masein Chaung in the area of RU 8691.

Whilst these operations were in progress the main body of the 11th East African Division had entered the Myittha gorge and had commenced the last stage of its advance on Kalewa. Major-General Fowkes, the divisional commander, had, accordingly, given instructions for the 21st Brigade (less 1 NRR) to cross the river Chindwin on reaching the area of Masein, operate on a broad front and thereby outflank any Japanese positions on the high ground opposite Kalewa. The plan was that 1 NRR was to remain on the west bank and move south to Kalewa on a jeep basis, while the remainder of the brigade would move on a two-battalion front down the east bank. It was also intended that 2 King's African Rifles would move ahead to Kyawdaw area. The 4 King's African Rifles would provide protection for the remainder of the force while they closed up. This battalion would then, in turn, relieve the 5 King's African Rifles and continue moving south by the Gonga track.

By 24 November, the 5 King's African Rifles was established in the general line RU 857833—Kazet (RU 8884). About one hundred Japanese troops located at RU 892842 were attacked by two squadrons of Hurribombers and the position was evacuated by them on the 25th. Another position at RU 896844 was also evacuated the same day following an attack by twelve Hurribombers. The 2 King's African Rifles had in the meantime come up and by the evening of 26 November, the 5 King's African Rifles and the 2 King's African Rifles were established on the line Singaung—Balet Chaung—Kanuni Chaung, RU 9382. The 4 King's African Rifles was concentrated at Kongyi.

On 27 November the forward troops of the 5 King's African Rifles were attacked from the direction of RU 8980 but the attack was repulsed. The Japanese position on the hills south of Singaung was fairly extensive and strongly held. In order that the 4 King's African Rifles might be in the best position to help, if necessary, and also to get astride the Japanese line of communication and threaten their rear, it was ordered to be established on the high ground south of Point 692 by the evening of 28 November. After several skirmishes the line was established. On the 28th, the Japanese position was bombed and strafed by twelve Hurribombers, and the 5 King's African Rifles captured it on the 29th and made contact with the 4 King's African Rifles to the south.

Meanwhile, the 2 King's African Rifles had occupied Zidaw on the 27th. Patrols of this battalion visited Thingan on the 28th and Hmangon on the 29th and found them clear.

On 29 November, the 21st Brigade regrouped with 4 King's African Rifles on the right, 2 King's African Rifles on the left and 5 King's African Rifles in reserve. The 4 King's African Rifles had encountered some opposition but by the evening of 29 November, it had established the line Point 831 (8877)—Gonga. One company in particular had sustained casualties in an action against two sections of the Japanese troops dug in on top of a steep-sided 'pimple'. After some bitter fighting it succeeded in driving the defenders off. In the 2 King's African Rifles area also a patrol sent to Kanni encountered some Japanese opposition. On the 30th 2 King's African Rifles fought throughout the day with some Japanese troops south of Hmangon on the ridge at 917777. On 1 December, three squadrons of Hurribombers bombed and strafed the position but could not dislodge the Japanese. The same day a company of 2 King's African Rifles occupied the area RU 9982 following a Japanese withdrawal. The 4 King's African Rifles also had pushed on south. The Japanese held some positions in the Gonga area. On 2 December two squadrons of Hurribombers attacked these positions at RU 884770, in support of the 4 King's African Rifles.

On the west bank of the river, 1 NRR maintained contact with the Japanese troops and by 29 November was established on the line RU 816785—RU 836781—RU 8578. Some thirty Japanese were at RU 8277 which was bombed and strafed during the day by eighteen Hurribombers. The Japanese were evidently pulling out and on 1 December, 1 NRR reached RU 8171 and Tonnan without opposition. The next day, 2 December, they made contact with the troops of the 25th Brigade (11th East African Division) who had entered Kalewa that day at 1327 hours. There is no doubt that the threat imposed by the 21st Brigade had induced the Japanese to leave Kalewa and had helped the 25th Brigade to capture Kalewa so easily.[56]

Establishment of the Bridgehead

Earlier, Major-General Fowkes had been ordered by the XXXIII Corps to establish a bridgehead over the river Chindwin, as

---

[56] Kalewa had fallen to 26 KAR and four tanks of 7 Cavalry who, while moving against the place, had been given a Union Jack in anticipation of the successful attack and ultimate capture of Kalewa. WD 25th (EA) Brigade, 2 Dec. 1944.

soon as possible, with the object of making secure the crossing place and the forward movement of the 2nd Division against Japanese interference by infantry, tanks or artillery. He was further instructed that the foremost defended locations to cover the bridgehead would include the general line Zayatkon—Kywe—Thanbaya—Point 826—Chaungzon—Point 993—Point 752—Gonga—Kywenan.

Major-General Fowke's appreciation was that although the Japanese had surrendered Kalewa and the west bank of the river Chindwin in that vicinity, without much opposition, and some African troops had been operating on the east bank, it was probable that they would resist any attempt on the part of the Allies to form a bridgehead east of the river. He did not anticipate that this resistance would be in any great strength but it was likely to take the form of numerous strong positions held by only a small number of troops. Accordingly he laid down the following plan of action for his African division:

(a) 21st Brigade to continue operations on the axis Thingan—Mutaik.

(b) 25th Brigade to secure a bridgehead across the river north of Kalewa on the night 3/4 December.

(c) 26th Brigade to pass through the bridgehead and seize all tactical features within the range of arillery established on the west bank of the river and, subsequently, to advance on Shwegyin and Mutaik in order to effect a junction with the 21st Brigade.

Crossing the Chindwin

On 3 December, divisional headquarters opened in the area Waye Chaung at RU 759687. The 25th Brigade was disposed in the area Kalewa and on the axis of the road, as far west as Chaunggyin. The 26th Brigade, less certain detachments, was in the Natkyigon area. During the day a single Japanese gun fired a few rounds into the Kalewa area and on to the landing strip south of the Myittha river at RU 8267.[57] One company of 26 King's African Rifles operating in the latter area reported that the villages of Shan Dat (RU 8068) and Obinzu (RU 8268) and the surrounding foothills were clear of the Japanese. On the east bank of the river Chindwin, it was apparent from the almost fanatical resistance being put up by the Japanese against the 21st Brigade that they intended to hold their line at all costs. The 4 King's African Rifles, therefore, outflanked the Japanese position south of Point 831 and established one company at RU 883757 and a second one at RU 891758. This forced the Japanese to pull out from their

[57] War Diary, XXXIII Corps, 3 December 1944.

position south of Point 831. The 2 King's African Rifles continued to meet stubborn resistance in the area of the high ground south of Hmangon and the Japanese in this area were attacked by twenty-four aircraft. However, one company of 2 King's African Rifles reached the area of RU 924773, and patrols into Thingan again found the village clear. Meanwhile, the 5 King's African Rifles less one company had proceeded to the feature, Point 752, and finding that it had been evacuated by the Japanese it was ordered to occupy the portion as quickly as possible. It was hoped that its presence well in the rear of the forward line of the Japanese would force them to divert some of their troops from the positions opposing 2 King's African Rifles and 4 King's African Rifles.

During the night of 3/4 December, deception devices were floated down the river Chindwin and these brought forth very satisfactory response from the Japanese who ran along the bank firing at them.[58] While they were thus engaged, 34 King's African Rifles of the 25th Brigade started crossing the river at Kalewa, during the night, at approximately 0230 hours They had selected two crossing places which were named Dover and Folkstone. The first flight from both beach-heads was swept away downstream about 300 yards, and it became necessary—at the expense of silence —to fit outboard motors. Thereafter, the crossing continued in boats fitted with outboard motors.[59] It was a slow process and the Japanese must have heard the noise, but there was no opposition, probably because the mist prevented any observation of these crossings. In the morning of 4 December, when the mist lifted, the Japanese shelled the crossing places, but, by that time, all the troops had crossed the stream. During the morning a patrol of the strength of a platoon surprised some Japanese troops while bathing in a chaung at RU 843704 and drove them back into the hills. Two companies of 34 King's African Rifles then advanced from the bridgehead, secured the bridge at RU 845701 and continued to probe forward. They encountered Japanese positions at RU 846702 and astride the road at RU 845704. After artillery and mortar concentrations, this African force dislodged the Japanese and then established a road-block at RU 842698. Later in the day other Japanese positions were similarly encountered at RU 853698 and 853701, covering the road to the east of the Paung Chaung. Meanwhile patrols operating south of the Myittha river investigated Point 1108 (RU 8364) and Point 1063 (RU 8366), and found that there were no Japanese troops there. Good progress was made during the day on the 21st Brigade front also, although the Japanese continued to resist fiercely south of Hmangon. The leading companies of 4

[58] War Diary, XXXIII Corps, 4 December 1944.
[59] WD, 25th (EA) Brigade, 4 December 1944.

Major-General
F. W. Festing
Commander
36th British Division

Major (later Major-General) Sarda Nand Singh of 5th Indian Division and Major E. Wilson V.C., of East African Division meet at Kalemyo to mark the closing of the pincers

Major-General
D. D. Gracey
Commander
20th Indian Division

Gurkhas advance cautiously in outskirts of a village during Fourteenth Army advance prior to crossing the Irrawaddy river

King's African Rifles reached the area RU 883757 and 892751 and then encountered resistance on the line RU 882746—895732. Two squadrons of Hurribombers attacked the hostile positions at RU 913779 and 916777 in support of 2 King's African Rifles. The remaining platoon of this battalion was withdrawn from the Yashe area. 5 King's African Rifles pushed south and occupied Point 752 without opposition.

Further Crossings

At midnight of 4/5 December, the 26th Brigade started to cross the Chindwin with orders to pass the leading battalion through 34 King's African Rifles positions and clear the Japanese positions astride the road on the east bank of the Paung Chaung. Except for some inaccurate shell fire, there was no opposition by the Japanese, and the crossings continued unimpeded into the bridgehead which was by now finally established by 34 King's African Rifles. One company of 1 NRR also crossed and moved to the area RU 834703. The Japanese made no attempt to interfere with the crossing, apart from putting down badly directed shell fire at irregular intervals. The leading company of 34 King's African Rifles then proceeded to clear the main road as far as RU 847703, although small hostile parties continued to be active in the thick jungle to the south of the road in this area. The Japanese positions on the east bank of the Paung Chaung were bombed and strafed by Hurribombers. Little progress was made by 4 King's African Rifles but 2 King's African Rifles attacked and drove the Japanese out of their positions south of Hmangon on the night of 4 December. The Japanese troops facing 4 King's African Rifles were holding a line approximately 2000 yards wide and the country was so precipitous that encircling movements were practically impossible. It was then decided that the main force would carry out an encircling movement to the area of the Ingon Chaung. In order to counter hostile artillery fire a force from the special boat section landed at RU 852735 at 2230 hours on 5 December, with the object of working south from this point, along the ridge, through Point 951 (RU 8472) and clearing any Observation Post which might be met with. Point 951 was reached at 0330 hours on 6 December, and no Japanese were seen there. The patrol moved south down the ridge without opposition.

Advance held up

By the morning of 6 December, two battalions of the 26th Brigade had crossed to the east bank of the Chindwin but their advance was held up for several days by determined opposition, and the bridgehead area could not be extended. The brigade headquarters crossed to the area RU 839695 and assumed command of all troops in the bridgehead.[60] Despite the heavy air attacks of the previous day the Japanese continued to hold their positions on the east bank of Paung Chaung. Meanwhile other Japanese positions had been located on the high ground at RU 844708 and 844712 which also continued to resist liquidation. 4 King's African Rifles continued to engage the Japanese in the area RU 8812746 and located some other hostile positions at RU 888747 and 895732. 5 King's African Rifles also located a large number of Japanese troops on the track south west of Point 752. They were subjected to an attack by two squadrons of Hurribombers whilst two companies of 5 King's African Rifles established a block in their rear. 2 King's African Rifles then pushed on south in the area south-west of Thingan.

On the following day 44 King's African Rifles with one platoon of medium machine-guns and a battery of mountain artillery crossed the Myittha river to the area of Onbinzu. The patrols of 26 King's African Rifles into the hills west of the Chindwin river encountered no opposition. Two companies of 1 NRR moved up the river in Dukws to Singaung to rejoin the 21st Brigade. In the bridgehead area the 26th Brigade was held up by the Japanese holding Point 750 and little progress was made.[61] The 21st Brigade, however, continued to push south. One company of 4 King's African Rifles descended down the cliff in the area RU 8875 by ropes and then succeeded in reaching the Paung Chaung, RU 862710, where it took up positions in the rear of the Japanese troops who were holding up the advance of the 26th Brigade. The remainder of the battalion stayed in its original positions. The brigade headquarters with 2 King's African Rifles less two companies and 5 King's African Rifles less two companies concentrated at the Ingon Chaung in the area RU 918710. The company of 2 King's African Rifles in the Hmangon area brought the Japanese troops on the ridge to battle, killed twelve of them and pushed on south to rejoin its battalion. One company of 2 King's African Rifles remained in contact with the Japanese south-west of Thingan. The patrols of 5 King's African Rifles found Point 626, Point 807 and Point 933 clear of the Japanese. Other patrols were despatched to Ingon and to the main road in the area RU 9466 to harass the Japanese and to lay mines. Meanwhile, tactical divisional headquarters had moved into Kalewa.

On 8 December, the Japanese troops facing the 26th Brigade, except for some isolated parties, withdrew south of the Paung Chaung. 22 King's African Rifles passed through 34 King's African Rifles

---

[60] XXXIII Corps War Diary, 6.12.44. The force across the river now included 22 King's African Rifles, 34 KAR, two companies of 1 NRR and a company of 5 King's African Rifles in addition to the 21st Brigade.
[61] 26th (EA) Bde Op. Instn. No. 51, dated 7 December 1944.

and occupied the Japanese positions on the high ground at RU 8470 which had been previously evacuated. They also made contact with 4 King's African Rifles in the chaung itself. The leading company, however, was unable to progress beyond the Paung Chaung. Thirty Japanese troops seen digging at Shwegyin on the high ground RU 874632, were successfully engaged by artillery. Meanwhile 13 King's African Rifles moved to the area of Kaing Shwedaung and 1 NRR less two companies crossed to Kaing. 5 King's African Rifles encountered some fifty Japanese troops in the area of the Ingon Chaung at RU 905706 and casualties were suffered on both sides. Eleven Hurribombers later attacked this area. A patrol to Ingon reported approximately one hundred Japanese troops in that area. A fighting patrol of 5 King's African Rifles established a base at RU 951694 preparatory to commencing harassing operations against the Japanese movement on the road in the area of Chaungzon. Meanwhile, to the north, 2 King's African Rifles and 4 King's African Rifles continued to meet opposition south of Thingan and in the hills to the west. A 'V' Force patrol reported that the area Yashe—Kanni—Letpannginaung was clear.

On the following day patrols of the 25th Brigade, who had been operating along the telegraph track from the Labin Chaung to Point 323 (RU 3662), reported the area to be clear of the Japanese troops and the route almost impassable for fully equipped infantry. In the bridgehead there were indications that the Japanese were withdrawing to Shwegyin. The 26th Brigade advance towards Shwegyin was continued on 9 December and the forward troops were within three miles of the place. Little opposition was encountered but the advance was slowed down by mines on the road and trees lying across it. Twenty Japanese troops were seen moving south along the road between Kongyi and Shwegyin by the artillery observation post, on the west bank of the river Chindwin, and were shelled. A force consisting of 1 NRR less two companies and one company of 5 King's African Rifles moved up the Paung Chaung to rejoin the 21st Brigade. After heavy and accurate air-strikes the Japanese in the area of the Ingon Chaung at RU 905706 withdrew, but at 1745 hours hostile artillery shelled troops of 5 King's African Rifles to the north-east and was engaged by the Allied mountain artillery.

On 10 December, 22 King's African Rifles encountered only small hostile parties. On the axis of the main road the forward troops began to harass Japanese rear-guards in the area of Kongyi, and on the track they reached RU 867675. 4 King's African Rifles cleared the Japanese from their positions in the hills west of the Gonga Chaung. The battalion then redisposed itself between Point 752 and 1 NRR, less two companies who were established at RU 882718. Two companies of 1 NRR moved to Point 626; and Headquarters

21st Brigade and 5 King's African Rifles, less one company, concentrated at RU 922677. A patrol to Chaungzon located a Japanese camp on the south bank of the Ingyingaing Chaung at RU 964692. An air observation post conducted a very successful shoot on this camp, into which heavy anti-aircraft artillery fired fifty-eight rounds. Many Japanese were caught in the open and a basha, believed to contain ammuntition, was destroyed. It is of interest to note here that by this time (1530 hours) Indian sappers had achieved the feat of erecting across the Chindwin a thousand-foot Bailey pontoon bridge in a remarkably short time of 36 hours. During the night Japanese jitter parties, active against the forward position of 22 King's African Rifles, were engaged by defensive fire. 4 King's African Rifles, moving rapidly south cut the main road in the area of Mutaik and 2 King's African Rifles cut it in the area of RU 920660. 5 King's African Rifles then moved to cut the road further to the east.

On 11 December, 13 King's African Rifles passed through 22 King's African Rifles, but was held up 500 yards north of Shwegyin by hostile positions which covered the main road and were protected by a sniper screen on the west flank. One company, making a left hook, was led into an ambush by a Burman, who had offered to act as a guide. One Askari was killed and one wounded. A small patrol reached the mouth of the Shwegyin Chaung without opposition and engaged numerous boats evacuating Japanese troops. Artillery also engaged this target and at least one boat was sunk. 44 King's African Rifles reverted to the command of the 26th Brigade and returned to Kalewa preparatory to crossing into the bridgehead. In the 21st Brigade area 2 King's African Rifles had established itself astride the main road by 0600 hours on 11 December. Later in the day, a company of this battalion established itself in the area of RU 929660, engaged twenty Japanese troops, and forced them to withdraw. A patrol from this company then made contact with a patrol of 4 King's African Rifles on the main road at RU 910661. 4 King's African Rifles less one company was established 1000 yards north of Mutaik.

At 0300 hours on 12 December the main divisional headquarters opened at Kalewa. At 0935 hours five Japanese aircraft (Oscars) bombed the Bailey pontoon bridge at Kalewa. The damage caused was negligible. Anti-aircraft fire shot down two of the attacking aircraft and damaged another. The main advance of 13 King's African Rifles was still held up by the Japanese on the ridge north of Shwegyin, but a patrol succeeded in entering the village and drew fire from RU 880642 and from the high ground south of the Shwegyin Chaung. The resistance by the Japanese in the Shwegyin area necessitated the diversion of 4 King's African Rifles to the west to exert pressure on the strong hostile positions which were holding up the advance of the division. 4 King's African Rifles less one company moved from Mutaik to establish contact with the 26th Brigade and by the evening established itself south of the Shwegyin Chaung after a short encounter on the road below Mutaik. 2 King's African Rifles started to clear the road east of the 95 grid line, and 5 King's African Rifles to mop up west of the grid line. One company of 5 King's African Rifles established itself in the hills above Chaungzon and a patrol to the east found a Japanese camp and some activity at SQ 010675. Small parties of the Japanese troops remained active in the areas of Mutaik and Ingon. At 1930 hours one company of 44 King's African Rifles left Kalewa in Dukws for Kyauktan and during the night the rest of the battalion crossed into the southern end of the bridgehead. The Japanese evacuated their positions on the ridge north of Shwegyin and some fifty Japanese also withdrew from the Mutaik area.

On 13 December, one company of 25 King's African Rifles was withdrawn from the south of the Myittha river to Kalewa, and a Dukw-borne patrol of 11 King's African Rifles moved down the Chindwin to Kywenan where no Japanese troops were seen. South of Shwegyin the company of 44 King's African Rifles found Saingthe clear. 13 King's African Rifles found Shwegyin clear, although one company was, for a time, held up by hostile positions at RU 875632, which covered the road at the Shwegyin Gorge. One company of 1 NRR relieved one company of 4 King's African Rifles of the task of clearing the Mutaik/Ingon area. Patrols to the latter village and to Point 933 saw no Japanese troops there. 4 King's African Rifles occupied the high ground overlooking the Chindwin south of the road and drove off twenty Japanese troops from RU 919661 with casualties, and engaged others seen digging in at RU 906680. By the evening, 21st and 26th Brigades were firmly linked up and commenced to clear the area east and north-east of Shwegyin and the tracks to south and south-east.

On 14 December, 44 King's African Rifles, less one company, concentrated at RU 892653. The company in the Kyauktan area moved south-west of Kywe and sent patrols north towards Thanbaya to meet the patrols moving there from the north. Elements of 13 King's African Rifles moved south from Shwegyin towards Kyauktan. Japanese snipers also continued to be active between Shwegyin and Siswe. The situation on the Shwegyin front had improved considerably by the evening of the 13th and permission had been given by the Divisional Headquarters for 4 King's African Rifles to be employed to the east on 14 December. 4 King's African Rifles accordingly concentrated in the area RU 920660 and 5 King's African Rifles moved east towards Chaunggon along a track to the north of the road. Artillery again shelled a camp in this area and inflicted much damage and several casualties on the Japanese. To the north a 'V' Force patrol reported having seen no Japanese troops at Gonga, Hmangon, Aingbalu and Myothit—Tawgan, and other villages in the area were also found to be clear.

On the following day operations to clear the area north and south of the main road were continued by 2 and 5 King's African Rifles. Contact was made with the Japanese positions astride the road to the west of Chaungzon, but as the divisional artillery was available to give support there, they did not offer the resistance that had always been experienced before. A patrol of 44 King's African Rifles confirmed a local report that Thanbaya was clear of the Japanese. Meanwhile the 2nd British Division had commenced to pass into the bridgehead area.[62] On 16 December, 5 King's African Rifles cleared the opposition at Chaungzon and the leading troops pushed another two and a half miles farther east without opposition.

The securing of the Chaungzon area may be said to have marked the establishment of the bridgehead, and completion of the task assigned to the 21st Brigade,[63] although parties of the Japanese troops were still active in the area to the north of the main road. The 26th Brigade continued searching the area and mopping up whilst the remainder of the African division moved to a concentration area about Indainggyi—Indainggale and the 2nd British Division moved into the bridgehead to relieve it.

Thus during the ten days fighting (from 6 to 16 December) a semi-circular area, extending from a point six miles north-east of Kalewa to Shwegyin, five miles to the south-east, was cleared. The East Africans who had acted as the leading division of the XXXIII Corps were now to be withdrawn on being relieved by the 2nd British Division. The withdrawal was completed by the end of December.

20th Indian Division

In the overall strategy for phase 1 of 'Capital', crossing of the river Chindwin had been planned at various places. Two of these had been made, one by the 19th Indian Division at Sittaung, and the other by the 11th East African Division at Kalewa. The third crossing was to be made by the 20th Indian Division at Mawlaik, about 30 miles to the north of Kalewa.

---

[62] The task of the 2nd British Division at this stage was to pass through the Kalewa bridge and exploit eastwards.

[63] The brigade was then ordered to move to the divisional rest area. WD 21st (EA) Bde., Dec. 1944.

Under the orders issued on 10 November, the task of the 20th Indian Division was to provide one infantry brigade group of four battalions on an animal transport basis to operate east from Mawlaik on the axis Chingyaung—Pyingaung. The rest of the division was to concentrate in the Htinzin area in Corps reserve and to be prepared to move one infantry brigade to the Kalemyo area in relief of the 5th Indian Division. Its plan to carry out the above tasks was as follows:

(a) The 32nd Indian Infantry Brigade Group to move by march route via Shuganu—Mombi—Khampat and complete its concentration in the area Sunle.

(b) The 80th Indian Infantry Brigade to be prepared to move to the area Kalemyo in relief of the 9th Indian Infantry Brigade of the 5th Indian Division.

(c) The rest of the division to be prepared to move to the area Htinzin by mechanical transport.

How the various units of the division accomplished these tasks does not require a detailed description as there was practically no contact with the Japanese. Briefly, the following movements took place.

On 22 November, the leading battalion (1 Northamptons) of the 32nd Indian Infantry Brigade started its march to Mawlaik while the rest of it followed during the next three days. On 24 November, a party of two officers and eighty other ranks of 3/8 Gurkha Rifles overtook them in mechanical transport and then moved by march route in advance of the main body of the brigade in order to relieve 1 Assam and start patrolling acrosss the Chindwin. The brigade completed concentration at Mawlaik by 3 December. On the same day a plan was chalked out for the whole brigade to move on the axis of the Pondaung Chaung to the area of Kyaunggyigon. On arrival there it was to clear any hostile positions remaining in the area Indaw—Gas Spring and to move at least one battalion to the area Chingyaung to establish a patrol base. Accordingly 1 Northamptons commenced crossing the river Chindwin to the north of Mawlaik, the rest of the Brigade followed and completed the crossings on 8 December and was established on the east bank of the river. "The passage was made by rafting, and 5065 men, 1456 mules and 30 tons of equipment were put across this formidable obstacle in 100 hours for the loss of one mule."[64] The brigade had moved at an average speed of 2 miles per hour along the sandy bed of the Pondaung Chaung and had marched knee-deep in water. No contact with the Japanese had been made apart from a clash with a party of seven of them at Kyaunggyigon, but they too fled before proper contact was established. By 16 December,

---

[64] Leese's *Dispatch*, para 34.

1 Northamptons had moved to the area SQ 4093 and the rest of the brigade had arrived at Chingyaung.

Meanwhile, on 15 November, 1 Devon and 3/1 Gurkha Rifles of the 80th Indian Infantry Brigade had moved to the area Khampat for road maintenance. 9 Frontier Force Regiment and Brigade Headquarters joined them on 19 November. Troops already located in the area were put under the responsibility of the 20th Indian Division from 20 November, and the troops of 1 Assam were also placed under its command pending relief by two infantry companies of the division.

On 2 December, the 80th Indian Infantry Brigade relieved the 9th Indian Infantry Brigade and came under the direct command of Headquarters XXXIII Corps. The tasks allotted to the brigade were:

    (a) To remain concentrated in the Corps reserve and be responsible for the protection of airfields, (existing or under construction).

    (b) To patrol to the east bank of the Myittha river, south to maintain contact with the Lushai Brigade and north to the line Segyi Chaung to Neyinzaya Chaung.

Operations of the 2nd Division—21 November to 16 December

In the beginning of November, the 2nd British Division was in Kohima area. The part to be played by this division in this phase of the operations was to concentrate in the Yazagyo area and then pass through the bridgehead at Kalewa, and from there exploit eastwards.

Accordingly on 21 November, the leading brigade of the division began its move from Maram to Yazagyo. By 7 December the whole division was concentrated in the Yazagyo area. On the next day, the 6th Infantry Brigade was ordered to be ready on 24 hours' notice to move across the river Chindwin into the 11th East African Division's bridgehead. It began to move on 12 December and completed concentration in the Mutaik area on 17 December, preparatory to the advance of XXXIII Corps forward into the plains of Burma.

Conclusion

Thus by the middle of December 1944, the Chindwin had been crossed at three places, at Sittaung by the 19th Indian Division, at Kalewa by the 11th East African Division, and at Mawlaik by the 20th Indian Division. Phase 1 of 'Capital' had been completed, and forces of the Fourteenth Army were poised for the next phase which was to bring the main Japanese strength to battle in central Burma and defeat it. The decision to fight in the rainy season had been completely justified by results, as the British-Indian forces were, at the beginning of the dry season, placed in the plains of Burma. The Japanese *Fifteenth Army* had had no respite during all these months, having been relentlessly pursued, and was therefore still not reorganised after its defeats in Imphal and Kohima.

CHAPTER VII

The IV Corps Advance to the Irrawaddy

THE JAPANESE WITHDRAW BEHIND THE IRRAWADDY

The middle of December 1944 had seen the leading formations of the Fourteenth Army across the Chindwin, where many bridgeheads had been established and some air-strips constructed or repaired. The Allied strategy for bringing the Japanese to battle on the Shwebo plain seemed to be fast developing. The troops, having left the jungle behind, were adapting themselves to the tactics of mobile warfare suited to the flat open country and low hills of central Burma. While these schemes were maturing according to plan, the Japanese had their own ideas of frustrating the Allied expectations. Their plan was simple: they just decided not to fight in the Shwebo plain.

Early in December signs were visible that the Japanese, contrary to the appreciation of the South-East Asia Command, did not propose to make a stand in the Shwebo plain and were withdrawing across the Irrawaddy. This became evident only in December, when considerable Japanese forces had already withdrawn behind that river but the withdrawal had been decided upon as early as September and had begun in October.[1] The first phase of the withdrawal was of course to the east of the Chindwin for reorganisation. Since the Allied armies were in hot pursuit, it was decided that the reorganisation would take place only after all stores, equipment and casualties etc. had been removed to the south and east of the Irrawaddy. It was also feared by the Japanese that the Allies would be able to attack them at will in the Shwebo plain. In order to cover the fact of the withdrawal to the left bank of the Irrawaddy, the *31st Division* was to hold the Kawlin highlands and the Mogok, Shwebo and Monywa area as a line to form the rallying point for the main strength of the army. They decided to give the impression that they were going to make a stand on the Shwebo plain. While closely watching the movements of the British-Indian army from this position, a delayed withdrawal was to be made to the new defensive positions along the Irrawaddy river, particularly on the left bank. And this course of action had been decided upon in September.[2]

---

[1] Subsequent interrogation of prisoners and examinations of Japanese documents confirm this. Mountbatten's *Report*, para 310.

[2] See SEATIC Historical Bulletin No. 240, being translation of essays produced by Lieut.-Colonel Fujiwara Iwaichi on various topics. Historical Section File No. 7531.

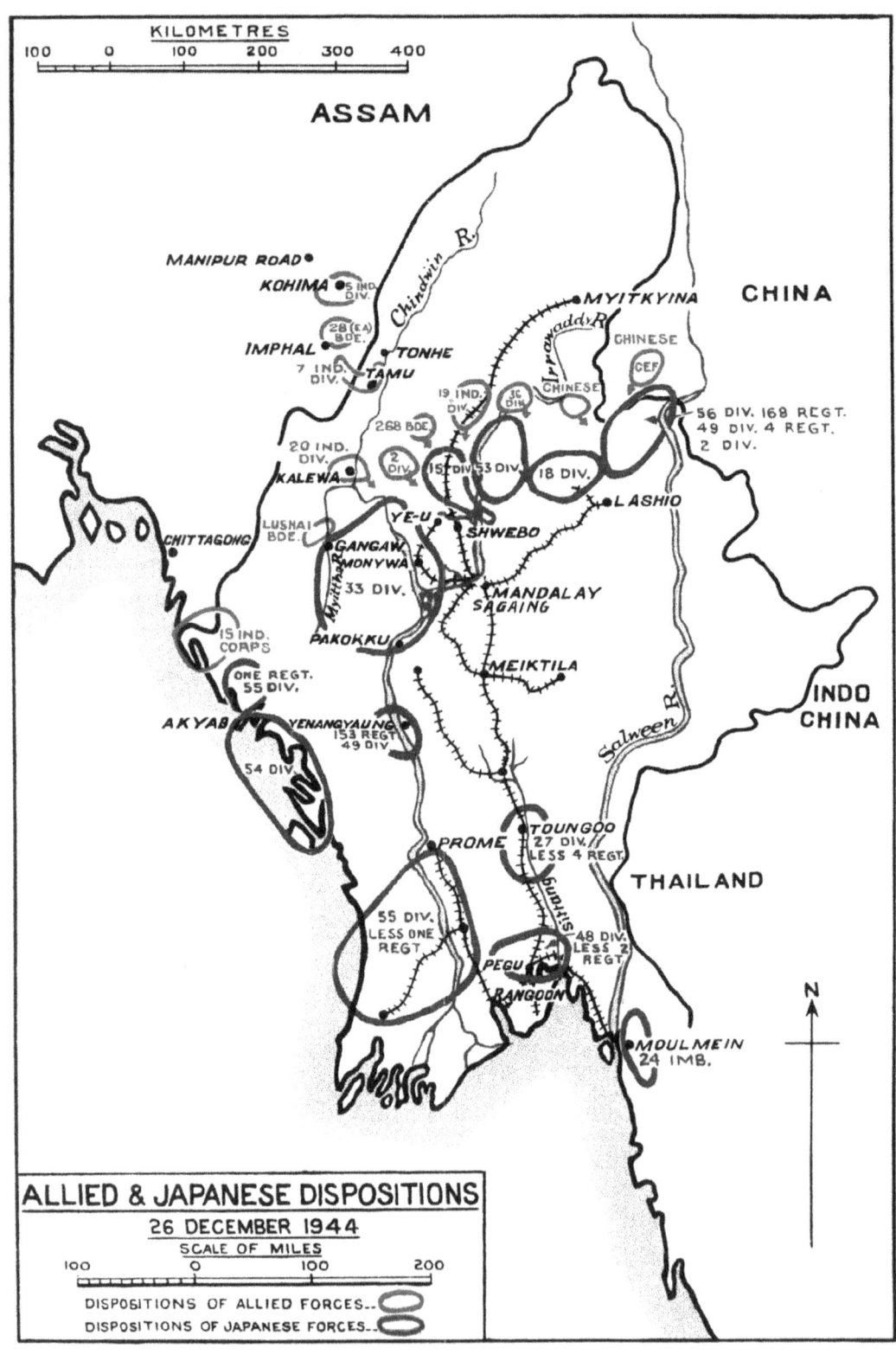

It was a brilliant manoeuvre and Lieut-General Slim, who firmly believed that the Japanese would fight in the Shwebo plain, has aptly recognised its value when he writes:[3] "In this he (enemy) was wise—wiser than the Germans in similar circumstance on the west of the Rhine. Kimura was showing a greater sense of realities than his predecessor, Kawabe, had at Imphal." As a result of this move the plan of concentrating the whole of the Fourteenth Army about Shwebo had to be abandoned and a modified plan for the third phase of 'Capital' was devised. Before, however, we consider the new Allied plan, it will be appropriate to review the situation of the Japanese forces about the middle of December, 1944.

Japanese Positions, December 1944.

As a result of the NCAC advance in the north and the pressure exerted by the Fourteenth Army over a broad front, the Japanese were continuously readjusting their positions. In the *15th Army* sector in the north, the *53rd Division* was then crossing the Irrawaddy and taking up positions east of the river. The *15th Division* likewise was withdrawing to the Mandalay area. The *31st Division*, after withdrawing from the Ye-U area, was disposed in a strong bridgehead west of the river, based on the natural bastion of the Sagaing hills. The *33rd Division*, which was made responsible for the defence of the river line, was disposed on a line running west-south-west from Myinmu to Pauk in continuation of the line to be held by the *31st Division*. And at Pauk, the *15th Army* which controlled all these divisions, linked up with the *28th Army* which was entrusted with the task of holding the Irrawaddy Valley. This latter army was then building up a strong force in the Yenangyaung oilfields area, which comprised one independent mixed brigade (*72nd Mixed Brigade*) of four battalions, one regiment of the *49th Division* brought up from south Burma and a considerable force of Indian National Army troops.[4] "By January 1945 the estimated overall strength of the Japanese in Burma was 175,000."[5]

The new positions which the Japanese then occupied implied that they had virtually lost the battle for the dry belt of central Burma. The line of the escarpment running through Pinlebu and Pyingaung represented the last opportunity that they had of compelling the Allies to fight on a narrow front and on something approaching level terms.[6] To compensate for the drawback of losing the dry belt, the Japanese had the advantage of having disposed two divisions (*53rd* and *15th*) in depth, east of the Irrawaddy, protecting Mandalay from

---

[3] Slim: *Campaign of the Fourteenth Army*, p. 8.
[4] Leese's *Despatch*, para 56.
[5] Roy McKelvie: *The War in Burma*, p. 236.
[6] Leese's *Despatch*, para 57.

the north, with their left flank protected by the river. They had the further advantage of occupying the dominating Sagaing hills position, which had been carefully prepared. From this vantage point they could not only counter-attack the forces of the Fourteenth Army as they approached the Irrawaddy, but also occupy the only high ground on the west bank and thereby prevent any hostile observation across the river.

The Japanese had good reasons for not fighting seriously for the Shwebo plain. The speed of the Foruteenth Army in moving considerable forces across the Chindwin had an element of strategical surprise for them. And though the Allies were not aware of it at the moment, some of the Japanese formations had been badly damaged by their defeats at Imphal and Kohima, and had no respite during the monsoon. Nor was it feasible to bring up reserves from the south quickly to reinforce or replace the tired and battered troops. In the circumstances, the Japanese plan to fight to the east of the Irrawaddy and to protect Mandalay and then gain time to re-equip and reorganise was perhaps the most practicable. And this naturally upset the plans of Lieut-General Slim, who wrote, "one of the three[7] main foundations on which I had built my plan—that the Japanese would stand and fight for the Shwebo plain—had crumbled under me. Their covering forces were wriggling out of the river loop and their main forces were grouping in defensive positions in depth behind one of the world's greatest rivers. If I continued with my plan to concentrate the whole army about Shwebo, I should have no alternative to a direct frontal assault on superior forces across this great obstacle. My object remained the same—the destruction of the enemy's main forces—but I was not likely to achieve it that way. An adjustment in plan was indicated. Luckily it was not too late to retrieve my mistake."[8] And that he did by putting an alternative plan into action which he had in his mind for sometime.[9]

THE NEW PLAN

Lieut-General Slim decided that if the Japanese did not wish to fight in the Shewebo plain, the Allies should cross the Irrawaddy and fight the major battle in the plains around Mandalay, and in the low hills around Meiktila. The object was the same, namely the destruc-

---

[7] The three assumptions on which Lieut. General Slim's plan was based were:—
  (i) That a definite figure for air and road lift will be available;
  (ii) That other Allied forces in Burma could contain some four and two-thirds enemy division;
  (iii) That the enemy intended to fight with his main forces north and west of the Irrawaddy.
Slim: *Campaign of the Fourteenth Army.*
[8] Slim: *Campaign of the Fourteenth Army*, p. 8.
[9] Leese's *Despatch*, para 60.

tion of the Japanese forces in central Burma, but the difficulties of achieving it had increased. The masterly withdrawal of General Kimura's forces to the east of the Irrawaddy, which now they held in strength, made it necessary for the Fourteenth Army to cross another great river. Since any single crossing was bound to be strongly opposed, Lieut-General Slim decided to have many crossings. This would keep the Japanese guessing as to where the main crossing might be made, and where the real assault in strength would be mounted. Since the main crossing was to come at some point on the river Irrawaddy below Mandalay, another sufficiently strong crossing was considered necessary to the north of Mandalay to draw the main Japanese forces.

The essence of the new plan was to strike the hostile force in its rear. This could be done only by a regrouping and redirection of the two Corps in order to get a force to the south of the Japanese concentration along the river, while another force should attack from the north. The XXXIII Corps consisting of the 2nd British Division, the 19th[10] and 20th Indian Divisions, 268th Indian Lorried Brigade and 254th Indian Tank Brigade, was to keep on to its objectives, Shwebo, Monywa and Mandalay, thus holding the Japanese by a frontal attack. The IV Corps was to be switched over from the left flank of the Fourteenth Army to the right flank and was to advance with all speed down the Gangaw Valley, cross the Irrawaddy somewhere in the Pakokku area early in February and capture Meiktila, an important strategic road and rail centre on the Japanese line of communication from Rangoon to Mandalay, for which they were certain to fight. It was then to act as the "anvil", on which the XXXIII Corps as the "hammer" would drive south and destroy the major part of Japanese forces in central Burma. This switching over of the IV Corps from the left to the right flank of the XXXIII Corps and the subsequent advance by the IV Corps over a long distance to Pakokku were to be effected in secrecy. Elaborate deception measures were to be adopted to keep the march of the IV Corps a complete secret from the Japanese.[11] These deception measures are described in detail later while narrating the IV Corps operations on page 171.

Before the attack on Meiktila by the IV Corps, XXXIII Indian Corps was to capture a bridgehead across the Irrawaddy to the north of Mandalay to mislead the Japanese into the belief that the main blow against their *15th Army* was to come from that side. After capturing Meiktila and Mandalay, both Corps were to exploit south,

---

[10] This Indian Division was put under command of XXXIII Corps on 26 December 1944. 268th Indian Infantry Brigade also came under command of XXXIII Corps at about the same time.
[11] Operations IV Corps.

capture a seaport in southern Burma and open sea communications before the next monsoon.

Risks of the plan

The new plan was full of administrative risks but there was no other alternative to it and hence it was pushed through. The boldness of the plan is clear from the fact that the IV Corps had to move down the Gangaw Valley for about 320 miles in secrecy, making its own roads, and then, at the end of this long march, it had to seize Meiktila and its airfields by a surprise and sudden armoured assault. All the administrative planning had to be completed in less than two months, at a time when the air transport situation was none too bright. This was due to the fact that on 10 December the Supreme Allied Commander had to fly two Chinese divisions from the NCAC front to China at the request of Marshal Chiang Kai-shek, as well as three combat cargo squadrons (75 aircraft) which were allotted for the Fourteenth Army's day-to-day maintenance. In addition, two Air Commando troop-carrier squadrons had to be diverted temporarily to the China run. This diversion of the air-lift was put into effect so swiftly and suddenly by the Eastern Air Command that the Fourteenth Army did not even get a warning of it before the move began.

This sudden and unexpected reduction in transport aircraft had two serious effects on the Fourteenth Army operations. Firstly, the removal of two Chinese divisions checked Lieut-General Sultan's advance and thereby released Japanese forces for concentration against Lieut-General Slim. This meant that the Fourteenth Army would be attacking numerically stronger forces, but its commander decided to take the risk as he believed in the spirit and high fighting value of his troops.[12] Secondly, and this was more serious, the loss of seventy-five Dakotas worsened the already difficult administrative problem.

The circumstances leading to this "depredation" of the resources of the South-East Asia Command, and its effects are described by the Supreme Allied Commander in these words:[13]

> "When General Wedemeyer arrived in Chungking he discovered that over a period of five months the Japanese had advanced 500 miles from Yochow to Liuchow, and that having got to Liuchow they were threatening either the capital—Chungking, or the vital "Hump" terminal—Kunming, the fall of either of which would have been so disastrous as probably to throw

---

[12] Slim: *Defeat into Victory*, p. 382.
[13] *The Strategy of the South-East Asia Campaign*: being a lecture delivered by Admiral the Earl Mountbatten of Burma to the Royal United Service Institute on 9 Oct., 1946.

China out of the War. General Wedemeyer immediately telegraphed to me asking me to send him two Chinese divisions, three combat cargo squadrons, two troops-carrier squadronts of the Air Commandos and some heavy bombers. He repeated this demand simultaneously to the Combined Chiefs of Staff. Although the loss of these forces could not fail to have a very serious effect on my own operations, I realized that my own operations were in fact directed towards helping China and they would all be in vain if China was forced out of the War. I, therefore, immediately agreed and gave orders for the moves to start. I must confess that I also hoped that by this quick display of generosity I might be spared further depredations.

"The first effect of these moves was to cause the cancellation of the airborne part of 'Capital'. The second effect was to slow up the whole of both Fourteenth Army and NCAC for lack of aircraft. The third effect was to upset General Sultan's military plans by the withdrawal of a large proportion of his land forces. However, it was not the first time that our theatre had to suffer through lack of priority."

Lieut-General Slim calculated, rightly as events turned out, that his operations would be retarded by two to three weeks.[14] The crossing of the Irrawaddy lower down was possible only fourteen days later than anticipated, mainly on account of the lack of aircraft. This had the inevitable effect of making the 19th Indian Division, which had crossed the Irrawaddy north of Mandalay, hang on to its bridgehead for 14 days longer than was necessary against a greater concentration of the hostile force. This involved the Indian division in bitter fighting resulting in severe casualties. Not that the 19th Indian Division gave up any of its positions; it hung on despite several attempts to dislodge it. But of this later.

Since no aircraft were available, all operations had to be overland and the rivers crossed in boats. Since the roads were bad, water transport on the Chindwin—from Kalewa to Myingyan—had also to be used. And since the railways had been damaged by Allied bombing, arrangements were made to concentrate railway operating, construction and maintenance companies at Dimapur from where they might be sent when required. Plans to get rolling stock and engines from India were made, and of course plans to build and repair air-strips, as quickly as possible, in the wake of the advancing armies were finalised. And all these administrative tasks were to be completed within two months.

---

[14] Slim: *Defeat into Victory*, p. 396.

PROGRESS OF THE NEW PLAN

The reasons for an alteration in the Fourteenth Army plan have just been explained. The main reason was that the Japanese were retreating everywhere and had no intention of fighting in the Shwebo plain. Reports emanating from the Burmese villagers showed that they contemplated a withdrawal south of Mandalay, and even Rangoon was mentioned as their destination. To meet this situation and in order to bring the Japanese to decisive battle in central Burma, Lieut-General Slim had decided on a fundamental regrouping of the Fourteenth Army. As has been related earlier, the XXXIII Corps was to continue with its objectives as Shwebo, Monywa and Mandalay, with a target date for Mandalay of 28 February. The 19th Indian Division, transferred to this Corps under the regrouping plan, crossed the Irrawaddy to threaten Mandalay from the north. It was hoped that this manoeuvre would draw large Japanese forces towards Mandalay, thereby enabling IV Corps to carry out its secret march towards Pakokku.

According to the plan, the IV Corps was to be switched over to the right flank of the XXXIII Corps, to advance with all speed down the Kabaw and Myittha Valleys towards Pakokku, cross the Irrawaddy early in February, "and, without pause strike violently with armoured and airborne forces at Meiktila," an important strategic road and rail centre on the Japanese lines of communication from Rangoon to Mandalay, and then act as the 'anvil' on which the XXXIII Corps as the 'hammer' would drive south and destroy the bulk of the Japanese forces in central Burma. By cutting their line of communication at Meiktila a main frontal attack across the Irrawaddy would be avoided, the escape route cut, and the Japanese would be forced to give the major battle which the Fourteenth Army commander desired.[15]

Lieut-General Slim's plan truly laid the foundation for the complete destruction of the Japanese army in Burma. It was a bold plan, relying for its fulfilment on secrecy, on speed, and on taking great administrative risks. Planning and execution had to be completed in a short time, and in order that it might have the best chance of succeeding, the administrative resources on land and in the air were strained to the utmost. The move from Tamu to Pakokku, of the IV Corps alone, involved the transportation of two full infantry divisions and a tank brigade over 328 miles of rough road, "which in rain was impassable mud and in dry weather almost impassable dust."[16] During the move, the Corps had to be supplied and the casualties evacuated by air. This would necessitate the construction

---

[15] Slim: *Defeat into Victory*, p. 394.
[16] Slim: *Defeat into Victory*, p. 397.

of many airfields and the repair of Japanese airfields when captured, for heavy transport aircraft as well as for fighters to provide essential cover. But the air supply was considered adequate only for the forward formations, and all other means of transport—road, rail and water—had therefore to be pressed into service for supplying the rear formations.

On account of shortage of time and resources, the idea of constructing all-weather roads was abandoned except for the stretch between Tamu and Kalewa. It was feared that the Burma railways would have been badly damaged by Allied bombings and Japanese demolitions; but it was hoped that, since the Japanese had been working these railways, the Fourteenth Army should also be able to bring into operation sectors of the line that fell into its hands as it advanced towards Meiktila. In addition, use was made of water transport also. In the beginning there were no boats, all shipping on the Chindwin having been sunk in 1942 during the Allied retreat, and later by air attacks. But the ingenious engineers of the Fourteenth Army, helped by Inland Water Transport Companies from India, soon began to produce large numbers of boats and Kalewa again became an important river port. "The boats," writes General Slim, "were not graceful craft; they looked like Noah's Arks without the houses, but they floated and carried ten tons each. Three of these, lashed together and decked, made a very serviceable raft that would carry anything up to a Sherman tank."[17] Thus in addition to supply by air, road and railway, the water link was expected to serve the IV Corps from Kalewa to Myingyan, a distance of about 200 miles, when the rainy season began in May.

As has been mentioned eariler, the IV Corps handed over the command of the 19th Indian Division, 268th Indian Lorried Brigade and 2 V Operations (a unit of 'V' force) to its sister Corps on 26 December. After the regrouping the former retained the 7th Indian Division under command and took over the following formations:

    255th Indian Tank Brigade Group
    11 Cavalry (PAVO)
    28th East African Brigade Group
    Lushai Brigade
    'B' Group V Force
    457 Forward Airfield Engineers.

In addition, the 17th Indian Division (Major-General T. D. Cowan, C.B., D.S.O., M.C.), which was then being reorganised at Ranchi in India as a standard division, after its strenuous battles in Imphal, was also provisionally allotted to it. This division was to be

[17] Ibid, p. 399.

available after it had completed its reorganisation and was to be moved in either by air or up the Assam line of communication. The distance involved from Dimapur railhead to the Irrawaddy at Pakokku, was nearly 500 miles, much of it on a one-way road.

The above redistribution left the 5th Indian Division, which had been withdrawn to rest in the Kohima area, as army reserve. The organisation of the 5th and 17th Indian Divisions was being changed; in each of these, two brigade groups were being fully motorised, and one brigade group made air-transportable.

Reference has been made to the inhospitability of the route which the IV Corps had to follow for 328 miles from Tamu to Pakokku. The first 110 miles were already in use as the main artery of the XXXIII Indian Corps whose traffic had covered the surface with deep dust. Beyond Kalemyo it was an indifferent, one-way and fair-weather road which required re-bridging throughout its length to take the weight of heavy vehicles. The road wound through very close and easily defensible country, especially in the narrow 30-miles hill section over the Pondaung range between Tilin and Pauk. Not until Pauk, 48 miles before Pakokku, was there any hope of deploying armour on any but a narrow front. From Pauk it was still 120 miles to Meiktila, and the wide Irrawaddy lay in between.

The Lushai Brigade was deployed alone at the end of December on the new axis of advance of the IV Corps, and was in contact with the Japanese *33rd Division* just north of Gangaw in the Myittha Valley, 110 miles south of Kalemyo. This brigade had advanced far and fast through the Chin Hill and was already tiring. It had no artillery and up to that moment it had really acted only as a light flank-guard for the advance of the XXXIII Corps across the Chindwin.

The rest of the IV Corps was still far distant from the battlefield. The 7th Indian Division was still stretched beween Imphal and Tonhe, 60 miles north of Tamu on the Chindwin.[18] The 28th East African Brigade was concentrating in Imphal but possessed proportionately more motor vehicles than the 7th Indian Division. The

---

[18] It was originally intended that the 7th Indian Division would concentrate in the Kabaw Valley prior to following in the wake of the 19th Indian Division. Since November, 114th Brigade, 136th Field Regiment and much of the Divisional Engineers had moved down from Tamu with orders to construct a motorable road to the Chindwin at Tonhe. The detachment built camps in the teak jungles and the sappers aided by all possible troops began transforming the dense jungles into a motorable highway, which however was never used for the purpose for which it was originally intended. Within the month the road was being used by more and more motor transport and by the middle of December tank transporters were able to travel from Tamu up to the Chindwin river, a distance of 60 miles. It was when the divisional engineers had just finished constructing ferries to cross the Chindwin and got them into operation, that orders were received for the move of the 7th Indian Division elsewhere. File No. 601/8445/H.

Tank Brigade and the 11 Cavalry were also in the Imphal plain. There was not a day to be lost and much improvisation had to be effected if the Corps was to reach its objectives, the Irrawaddy and Meiktila, in time.

IV Corps Plan

The first need was to help the Lushai Brigade to thrust far and fast towards Pauk. A British battery of 25-pounders and some additional engineers (62 Indian Field Company) were sent off on 23 December from the 7th Indian Division to support the Lushai Brigade. Its task was to reach Pauk if it could, before being relieved in the van, but it was realised that this might well be beyond its power if serious opposition were encountered. In order to deceive the Japanese the 28th East African Brigade was ordered to move south with all speed to back up the Lushai Brigade and relieve it in the lead as soon as necessary. The Fourteenth Army Commander hoped that when the Japanese saw the East African Brigade, they would mistake it for the 11th East African Division, which they knew was part of the XXXIII Corps.

Simultaneously, the divisional engineers of the 7th Indian Division were sent forward to make the road fit for transporting guns to the Lushai Brigade by 28 December. The route from Tamu to Gangaw looked long and tortuous on the map but on the ground it was far worse. Of the 180 miles from Tamu, the first 90 traversed an average road, the next 60 made a jeep track, and the last 30 miles passed over a track which in places was really fit only for mules. On the way lay the 200-feet wide Manipur river. One sapper company got itself and all its equipment across by constructing rafts out of large patrol drums. This company then pushed on, working from dawn to dusk on improving the road ahead. Thanks to the stout efforts of these Indian sappers the guns went into position with the Lushai Brigade by 27 December.

It was Lieut-General Messervy's appreciation that, as the main axis of Corps' advance was dependent on the only available road, speed and deception were the two main factors essential for the surprise on which success depended. He issued a provisional general outline of operations with separate directives to all the formations under the Corps to plan their individual operations.

The whole operation up to and including the capture of Meiktila was to be termed 'Multivite'.[19] It was divided into four phases. (1) *"Vitamin 'A'."* The capture of Pakokku by the 7th Indian Division after passing through the Lushai Brigade and an advance towards Seikpyu and Yenangyaung. (2) *"Vitamin 'B'."* The establishment

---

[19] Operations IV Corps, para 46. See also IV Corps Op. Instruction No. 125.

by the 7th Indian Division of a Corps bridgehead over the Irrawaddy in the Pakokku—Pagan area; the target date being fixed as mid-February. (3) *"Vitamin 'C'."* The concentration of the Corps including the 17th Indian Division, the Tank Brigade and the Corps artillery on the east bank of the Irrawaddy. (4) *"Vitamin 'D'"*. A lightning overland thrust, assisted, if possible, by an airborne operation to seize the Meiktila—Thazi area. The target date for this was to be as soon as possible after mid-February. It was to be followed by the liquidation of any Japanese forces which might still be to the south and south-west of Mandalay.

COMMANDER IV CORPS APPRECIATION

Lieut-General Sir Frank Messervy, commander of the IV Corps realised that the success of his plan depended on a combination of deception and speed. In his appreciation of the situation on 19 January 1945, he wrote, "surprise must be attained by speed and deception", and "there is only one way of achieving the necessary speed." His view was that "both air and mechanical transport must be employed to the maximum available extent to concentrate the Corps forward", for once its presence was detected the element of deception would cease to operate. The essence of the plan therefore was a quick concentration in the Pakokku area and a lightning thrust to Meiktila. Accordingly, in the middle of January, he recommended that the 17th Indian Division should be put on mechanical and air transport basis. "There is no place for mules in such a technique," he wrote. According to him, airborne and air transported operations could help in the following main aspects:[20]

"(a) Concentration forward of such elements of 17th Division as cannot be moved in mechanical transport.

(b) A glider-borne operation to speed up the establishment of a bridgehead over the river Irrawaddy.

(c) Transportation of bridging material both in transport aircraft to Pakokku airfield and in gliders to the bridging site.

(d) To build up 17th Division in the Meiktila area by air transport of the non-mechanised portion of the Division."

Lieut-General Silm agreed with Lieut-General Messervy and all necessary steps were taken to implement the scheme.

An estimate of the fastest timings made at this stage was:[21]

"7th Indian Division to seize Pauk area up to the easternmost crossing of the Yaw Chaung by 1 February.

---

[20] See Appendix E of Operations IV Corps for Lieut.-General Messervy's appreciation of 19 January 1945. See Appendix 10.
[21] *Ibid.*

7th Indian Division to have seized bridgehead over river Irrawaddy—probably in the Nyaungu area, by 15 February.

7th Indian Division to have crossed Irrawaddy less one Brigade by 18 February and to have enlarged bridgehead by 19 February.

17th Division to start crossing mechanised force and Tank Brigade less one regiment on 19 February and to concentrate east of Irrawaddy by 22 February.

The drive on Meiktila—80 miles—to start by 23 February and to reach Meiktila area by 25 February."

As things turned out this provisional plan remained virtually unaltered and the timings proved remarkably accurate.[22] The plan varied only in two main respects. First, the relief of Lushai Brigade in the van of the advance down the Myittha Valley occurred somewhat earlier than the plan envisaged, and secondly, in the last phase only the 17th Indian Division was used for Vitamin 'D', instead of both the 7th and 17th Indian Divisions converging beyond the Irrawaddy against Meiktila.

DECEPTION PLAN[23]

In order to help deception and avoid discovery by the Japanese of its major regrouping and change of plan, the Fourteenth Army put into operation a very elaborate scheme of deception by false signals purporting to show the continued presence of the IV Corps on the north flank of the other Corps. This involved leaving a full-blown dummy Corps headquarters north of Tamu, passing normal live traffic, and also in advancing south for as long as possible in complete wireless silence despite the great difficulties involved. Even the British Broadcasting Corporation was enlisted to help in strengthening the impression that the 19th Indian Division was still the spear-head to the IV Corps.

Throughout 'Multivite', great attention was paid to a very detailed deception plan named 'Cloak' which was aimed, once the Japanese became aware of a sizeable Allied force heading for Pakokku, at "selling" the Yenangyaung oilfield as the main Corps objective rather than Meiktila. The advance of the IV Corps was to be led by the 28th East African Brigade to give the impression that the 11th East African Division was again in the line under command of the XXXIII Corps, and that the IV Corps was still operating north of Mandalay. The separation of the 19th Indian Division from the IV Corps, and its presence north of Mandalay, was another measure calculated to strengthen that impression.

[22] Operations IV Corps, para 47.
[23] *Ibid* paras 47-49. See also IV Corps Op. No. 124.

Feint crossings, inquiries from local people regarding boats, strength of current etc. at wrong places, 'losing' maps indicating false objectives and many similar devices were employed to deceive the Japanese.[24]

REDEPLOYMENT OF IV CORPS

The IV Corps began its redeployment at once. The plan was that the 28th East African Brigade would lead the advance, followed by the 7th Indian Division. The whole of the division was to concentrate in the Gangaw Valley and advance on Pakokku via Tilin and Pauk. Pakokku was to be captured and a suitable crossing point on the Irrawaddy selected.[25] The left flank of the 7th Indian Division, during its advance, was to be protected by the Falam Levies and the Lushai Scouts. The 7/2 Punjab Regiment[26] was given the task of operating on the extreme left flank of the division and of advancing southwards along the west bank of the river Chindwin, towards Pakokku.

7th Indian Division Move Begins

First of all the sappers and engineers of the 7th Indian Division, working on the Thanan-Tonhe road, were withdrawn and ordered to proceed towards Gangaw and make the road fit for the transit of 25-pounder guns. The rest of the division then moved from Kohima during the latter part of December, and concentrated at Tamu. From there it began moving on 28 December, some marching and some ferrying in mechanical transport. During the early part of January the division was spread out over an area Kan-Manipur river-Tamu-Kohima.[27]

The condition of the road from Tamu southwards was appalling. It was badly cut up by very heavy mechanical transport movement and in places the dust was over two feet deep. Even the slowest moving vehicle raised clouds of dust, sometimes reducing visibility to a few yards. The once green jungle soon became covered with dirty, reddish coating of dust and the monotony of driving a hundred miles on such a route had to be experienced to be believed. Along the roadside there were many indications of the destruction of the Japanese forces which had only recently been attacking Imphal and Kohima. The jungle contained many hundreds of abandoned

---

[24] For details of 'Cloak' see Appendix 11.
[25] At this time (end of December) it was not certain whether the crossing would be made at Pakokku, Nyaungu or Chauk.
[26] 7th Indian Division Reconnaissance Regiment.
[27] The following distances should be noted:—
    Kohima—Tamu   200 miles
    Tamu—Kan   150 „
    Kan—Pakokku   165 „

Japanese transport vehicles and it was estimated that in the area of Tamu alone there were well over a thousand such vehicles.

The road from Kalemyo to Pakokku was of primary importance for a successful implementation of the plan. All engineer resources of the Corps were therefore employed to make this road fit for transporting tanks by 31 January.

Lushai Brigade at Gangaw, December-January

While the concentration of the 7th Indian Division and the 28th East African Brigade was proceeding south of Tamu, the Lushai Brigade was already in contact with the Japanese and was continuing its operations in the Gangaw area against their rear-guard.[28] This brigade was accustomed to acting dispersed, but in the operations before Gangaw it was, for the first time, more or less concentrated. It was very much under strength and nearly 1000 of its men were operating on the front from Tilin to the Chindwin. Two of its battalions, five platoons of Assam Rifles, some Levies and later the Chin Hills Batttalion, actually took part in the operations for the capture of Gangaw. Out in the mountainous country between the Gangaw road and the Chindwin other irregular forces, called the Falam Levies and the Lushai Scouts, were operating, from whom much useful information was gleaned. South of Gangaw the Haka Levies[29] were harrying the Japanese line of communication as far as Tilin with some success. There were estimated to be about 250 Japanese in the Gangaw area with another 200 at Tilin and 200 at Kyin.[30] This Japanese position, like their positions elsewhere, was very well sited and a hard nut to crack, but it was believed that their men had lost the offensive spirit.

MYAUKKON

North of Gangaw at a distance of about one mile across the open lay Myaukkon, the key to the defended area of Gangaw, standing on a bluff overlooking the river. There was a belt of open paddy land, about a quarter of a mile north and east of Myaukkon, which merged into thick jungle. The river made impracticable an attack from the

---

[28] The brigade consisted of Lushai Scouts, the Falam & Haka Levies, 1 Assam Rifles and the Chin Hills Battalion. See File No. 601/4576/H.

[29] Irregulars with the Lushai Brigade comprised: Western Chin Levies, under Lieut-Colonel Oates, a mixture of regular soldiers and local irregulars, divided into two zones, Haka and Falam, each zone containing a number of sectors, each sector, having two British officers. Transport: 6 mules and 40 elephants. Weapons: rifles, light machin-guns and 2" mortars.

Lushai Scouts under Major Longbottom, MC, BS, comprised two companies of 150 men each and were organised similarly to the Western Chin Levies.

[30] Brigadier Marindin, however, points the figures at 400 and 500 for Gangaw and Tilin. ('History of the Lushai Independent Brigade Group' (Mss) Historical Section File 4576). See also 'Operations IV Corps', para 52.

west. East of the small plain stretching round to the hills south of Gangaw lay a very thick, hilly, and at this time of the year, waterless jungle, in which the difficulties of water supply made operations difficult. As a preliminary to the advance of the 7th Indian Division, the Lushai Brigade was asked to capture this strong-point and then Gangaw.

Myaukkon, a very strong natural position, well dug in, was held by a fluctuating garrison of between 30 and 70 Japanese troops. In view of its natural strength it defied attack for a long period. In addition to Myaukkon, the Japanese had defended localities in west and east Gangaw and another at Pya, just to the south. The supporting weapons were positioned at this last place. The remainder of the Japanese force was strongly dug in at Lema, and was operating offensively to keep open the route for the evacuation of stores. A pack track ran east from Gangaw through Pyitma to Lema and thence some twenty-five miles south-east to Kyaw, where the Japanese had a large dump. It was believed that the Japanese had stationed their forces at Lema to cover the removal of stores from the dump. Attempts were made to block this with Levies but water difficulties made it impossible to operate in this area except for patrols. The Lushai Brigade had previously no artillery, but a field regiment of 25-pounders had recently arrived.[31]

Plan for Attack

The general plan of attack on Gangaw was as follows: The 1st Bihar Regiment from Thagaung with four platoons of the 1st Assam Rifles under command was to move through the hills via Kunze and establish itself at Lema. The 1/9 Jat was to advance on Gangaw from the north. The Levies, about one hundred, already in the west Gangaw area, were to block the southern exits from Gangaw. At this time the absence of a third battalion in the Lushai Brigade began to be keenly felt. The Jats, badly afflicted by an epidemic of scrub typhus in November, were reduced to a total of 550 all ranks. The Bihar Regiment had a better strength of 650 men. All were very tired, and the force was really quite inadequate to hold such a large perimeter, guard its firm bases and installations, and adopt the very aggressive attitude which circumstances obviously demanded.

It was felt, however, that the Japanese were also tired and were on the defensive and chances must be taken. The above plan was the only practicable one, and similar plans had previoulsy been successful at Haka and Falam. Though eventually it proved successful, it was, nonetheless, felt that a great risk was being taken. The country was much more favourable for Japanese movement than the

---

[31] Marindin's Account, *op. cit.*

Chin Hills had been, and if the Japanese had shown an offensive spirit the Lushais would have been rapidly forced back on the defensive, and the Bihar Regiment might have got into a real jam. In addition to the Japanese forces at Tilin, which, if properly handled, could have swept the Levies aside and come in on the Lushais' western rear sandwiching them up against Gangaw, there was also the possibility of reinforcements arriving from Kyaw and catching the Bihar Regiment at Lema in the same way.[32]

Attack Begins

On 8 December 1944, the Lushai Brigade began its operations against the Japanese defences. On that day the Jats moved south down the west bank via Mauk and Kyundat pushing a company across to the east bank at Myinza. This company on the east bank met with some very minor opposition and by the 10th the Jat battalion, less one company at Yazi, was concentrated at the Zahaw Chaung. On 11 December, the company at Yazi, east of the river, made a testing attack on Myaukkon, supported by mortars from the west bank. The immediate objective, besides testing the Japanese reactions, was to gain a foothold, if possible, on the bluff. The foot of the bluff was fairly heavily wooded with a concealed nulla running down to the river. The attack reached the edge of the nulla, successfully killing a few Japanese in the process, but the farther bank was heavily fox-holed and strong opposition was encountered; hence the attack was called off to prevent unnecessary loss of life. On 12 December, the Jats moved east of the river and established their reserved base at Yazi, about 1½ miles from Myaukkon, in the jungle. The Bihar Regiment which had started to move at about the same time as the Jats, had still not reached Lema and the only other troops in position were the 100 Levies to the west of Gangaw area. It was obvious, therefore, that the Japanese must be contained in their area by vigorous offensive action to keep them to the east bank and prevent them from infiltrating to the west bank with the idea of driving a wedge into what was intended to be the centre of the Allied position. Hence, on 14 and 15 December the Jats made demonstrations in force against the Myaukkon position to test the defences, and exploit if success was obtained. This operation showed that the position was too strong to be taken without heavy casualties, unless supported by heavier weight of metal than available at the moment. The Jats were, therefore, ordered to undertake a vigorous programme of day and night 'jitter' patrolling till reinforcements arrived. The brigade headquarters and reserve troops arrived on 16 December.

By this time, 1 Bihar, with four platoons of the Assam Rifles

---

[32] Marindin's Account, *op. cit.*, pp. 19-20.

under command, had reached Lema and had begun to probe towards Gangaw. Although only ten miles from the brigade headquarters as the crow flies, 1 Bihar was two days' walk out of personal contact with the headquarters. The brigade commander (Brigadier P. C. Marindin, D.S.O., M.C.), with his reserve of merely one platoon each of the 1st Assam Rifles and the Lushai Scouts, set up his headquarters in a strong position on the hills overlooking the Zahaw Chaung, and the work on a light air-strip began. It may be remraked here that, in November, 7/14 Punjab had left the Lushai Brigade to join the 5th Indian Division. Consequently, the brigade reserve was not completed until the Chin Hills Battalion arrived on 23 December.

While the main body was endeavouring to drive the Japanese from Gangaw, the rest of the brigade was operating on the flanks. In the hills west of the Myittha Valley, the Haka Levies with four platoons of the 1st Assam Rifles were harassing the Japanese between Gangaw and Tilin; and the Lushai Scouts and Falam Levies were clearing small hostile parties between the Myittha river and the Chindwin.

On 17 December, an air-strike was obtained on Myaukkon, but the follow-up by infantry proved that the defences had not been adequately softened. On the 18th, the Jats tried again and a company obtained a footing on the bluff after suffering some casualties, but as it was clear that no further progress could be made without heavy casualties, the attack was called off and the Jats resumed their 'jitter' patrolling. Information was then received that the Lushai Brigade had passed from the XXXIII Corps to IV Corps and that the thrust down the Myittha Valley had changed into a major operation. This was the position on 23 December, when the brigade received orders to clear the Gangaw area as quickly as possible to open the way for the advance of the IV Corps to Pakokku, and itself to advance to Pauk before being relieved in the van. The brigade was given a field regiment from the 7th Indian Division and was promised really strong air support.

Three singularly important events then occurred. The first was that on 23 December the Chin Hills Battalion relieved the Jats at Yazi. The latter, very tired by this time, came into the reserve at Zahaw and took over the duties of the Assam Rifles and Lushai Scouts detachments which were sent to reinforce the Levies in the western Gangaw area. The second was that on the 24th, the field artillery[33] arrived after an extremely rapid march over some most difficult country. They tucked up their guns near the brigade headquarters protected by a company of the Jats with an observation post

---

[33] 347th Field Battery RA.

A section of well armed Chin Levies with one of their trophies—a Japanese flag

Budalin in flames being attacked

Jat machine-gunners support the advance of 14th Punjabis to Monywa

4/10 Gurkha attack a burning Burmese village

on the hill above. One very interesting consequence of their arrival was a change in the attitude of the local population. Though the Lushai Brigade had been in the valley for nearly two months, the local inhabitants had remained passive and had never volunteered any help beyond what was demanded. Information was very hard to obtain. This attitude might have been a reaction to the effects of the first Wingate expedition, and they probably thought that the Allies were just on a strong raid. When, however, they saw artillery they decided that the attackers had come to stay. Information poured in and two Allied prisoners, a Chin and an Indian Sapper held in Myaukkon, were smuggled across. The third and most important occurrence on 24 December was the arrival of Lieut-General Messervy on the air-strip just then completed. He had come to see things for himself and to concert arrangements for blasting the Japanese out of the Gangaw defile and clearing the road for the rapid progress of the Corps.

BATTLE FOR MYAUKKON

In view of the strong defences at Myaukkon a definite daily softening-up programme of air-strikes was arranged, followed by night patrols to ascertain the effects. The attack, if the Japanese had not withdrawn before, was to take place on 1 January under the support of the field regiment and minor 'earthquake' air raids. Meanwhile the Biharis had been having a hard time at Lema. The Japanese had reacted very strongly to their presence in the area and become aggressive. They took up a strong position directly opposite, and, in addition to two attacks, did all in their power to contain the Biharis by sniping and a harassing fire. In spite of these difficulties the Biharis contrived to remain mobile, and after some difficulty in fully establishing themselves, contrived to get ambush parties on the Japanese evacuation route, and penetrated as far as Pyitma. Clashes were a daily occurrence with varying results, the balance tilting in favour of the Biharis. On one occasion a Bihar company surprised a party of seventy Japanese coming up the bed of a chaung and inflicted casualties.

The air-strikes continued with the loss of two planes from ground fire but the night patrols invariably found the position as strongly held as ever. Day patrolling was also tried to see if the Japanese were evacuating during the day owing to air action but the position was found held by day and night. On the night of 21/22 December, a Jat patrol in the area of Myaukkon found that the Japanese positions were strongly booby-trapped.[34] Meanwhile, in the southern

[34] Sitrep up to 1800 hours, 22 December, Lushai Brigade. War Diary, December, Appendix H.

sector, the Haka Levies occupied Tilin at 0500 hours on 25 December, where 30 Japanese troops were encountered, who, however, withdrew eastwards.[35]

Attack Postponed

A minor "earthquake" air raid on Myaukkon was scheduled for 30 December but as the air force refused to agree to the suggestion of the ground troops to change the start line, it was postponed and did not take place till 10 January. The commander of the IV Corps justifiably chafed at this delay to the onward move of his Corps. But the delay had this merit that it enabled the administrative services to catch up on the combatant troops who were overrunning supply.

On the night of 31 December/1 January, the Levies and Assam Rifles in the west Gangaw area, who had been ordered to make a strong diversion to chime in with the first January attack, charged and cleared west Gangaw, the Assam Rifles showing particular dash. The Japanese reacted most strongly with artillery, mortar and machine-gun fire from the east bank, and the attack did not succeed. For the next few days there was no remarkable incident, and 10 January was chosen as the date for launching a fresh attack.

The plan was that Chin Hills Battalion would attack and capture Myaukkon from the north under cover of an 'earthquake minor'. The Bihar Regiment would advance via Pyitma on to east Gangaw, and the Western Chin Levies and Assam Rifles would attack and capture Pya.

Final Attack

The attack finally went in on 10 January and was a complete success. The air-strike was carried out in the presence of a most distinguished gallery of spectators, including Lieut-Generals Slim, Messervy and Sultan. This was due to the fact that the 'earthquake minor' was being tried out for the first time in the Fourteenth Army.

In the morning, there was a heavy ground mist and everybody was wondering whether the attack would take place. After 1100 hours, however, it began to clear and the attack commenced at 1400 hours. Everything went like clockwork and the Japanese scuttled away after a brief fight. Their nerves were completely shattered by the effect of bombing by four squadrons of medium bombers (B 25s), three squadrons of Hurribombers and one of Thunderbolts. After these planes had accurately bombed the six pin-pointed positions, the Chin Hills Battalion went in and captured and consolidated the Myaukkon position for the loss of only two wounded. The Japanese had left precipitately and none was killed by bombing, the five found

---

[35] Sitrep 27 December, Lushai Brigade War Diary.

later on the ground having been killed by bayonets of the Chin Hills Battalion. By nightfall, Myaukkon was safely consolidated and patrols were probing west Gangaw. Pya was captured by the Levies at the same time.

The attack by the Biharis on east Gangaw was not productive of any tangible results, being somewhat delayed by unforeseen circumstances. The demonstration, however, undoubtedly had its effect. On the night of 10 January, the Japanese withdrew from Gangaw, by-passing the Biharis through the jungle down to the positions on the Lema track. The Gangaw area was thus finally cleared of the Japanese by 11 January.

A change in the role of Lushai Brigade had been made a few days previously. It was, by then, with the exception of the Chin Hills Battalion, very tired and under strength, and Japanese resistance between Tilin and Pakokku was again building up to a greater degree than had been previously anticipated. The Corps Commander decided, therefore, that the fresh 28th East African Brigade should take over on the fall of Gangaw, and continue the advance, using the name, style, and codes of the Lushai Brigade to continue the deception. The Chin Hills and the Lushai Scouts were to pass to the 7th Indian Division and the Levies were to be withdrawn on the fall of Tilin. This came into effect on 12 January and the brigade commenced its withdrawal to Kan.

Falam Levy Column and Lushai Scouts

While the Gangaw operations were going on, the rest of the brigade front was not quiet. In December, the 20th Indian Division had taken on the responsibility for safeguarding the Chindwin, operating from the east bank. The Lushai troops therefore withdrew from that area and commenced moving south inland clearing up small parties of the Japanese. On the 23rd they were ordered to join up and move on Kani. They were still in the process of doing so when the Lushai Brigade was withdrawn and they passed under the command of the 7th Indian Division.

Haka Levy Column

A word must be said here about the Haka Levy Column, a small force of about 300 irregulars. They did excellent service in containing the Japanese forces (about 5 to 7 hundred strong) in Tilin area. The Japanese who believed the Hakas to be in much greater strength tried to exterminate them but failed completely.

On 15 December, a party of Levies was strongly attacked at Nyaunggan while receiving an air-drop. As the planes continued the drop, the Levies had a hard task in stalling the Japanese off and at the same time collecting their stores. This, however, was successfully accomplished. But they were forced to withdraw to Aigama. The Japanese followed up, and on the night of 17/18 December made a determined night attack on the Levy camp. This was beaten off with some difficulty, with casualties on both sides. The Levies then withdrew to the west bank.

On Christmas Day, a party of Levies attacked Tilin to confirm or disprove a report that the Japanese were evacuating. On finding it evacuated they occupied it. Some other clashes occurred in the new year but the Levies beat off the attacks.

This concludes the story of the active operations of the Lushai Brigade. On 12 January, the 28th East African Brigade took up its place as advance guard, while the fresh Chin Hills Battalion and all the irregulars passed under the command of the 7th Indian Division. The remainder of the Lushai Brigade, including some Indian units, returned to India for a well-earned rest, after completing Kan air-strip.[36]

FORWARD CONCENTRATION OF THE 28TH EAST AFRICAN BRIGADE AND THE 7TH INDIAN DIVISION

The 28th East African Brigade and the 7th Indian Division moved to the Gangaw area by a combination of ferrying, by transport and by march route. The former began its move forward from Minthami on 29 December and by the evening of the next day, the brigade less one battalion was concentrated at its first staging area, the Manipur river crossing RU 52. By 4 January the whole brigade was concentrated at Myintha, 30 miles north of Gangaw. Heavy rain prevented immediate advance further but the headquarters and a battalion reached Gangaw air-strip on 8 January, the relief of the Lushai Brigade began then and the advance from Gangaw onwards was taken over by the East Africans, followed by the 7th Indian Division.

The order of march of the 7th Indian Division was:—
114th Indian Infantry Brigade Group
7/2 Punjab
Division Headquarters

---

[36] The units which returned to India were:—
Headquarters Lushai Brigade
1 Jat
1 Bihar
1 Assam Rifles (Civil Armed Forces)
231st and 232nd Indian Cipher Sub-Sections.
5th Indian Animal Transport Company
35th Indian Animal Transport Company
1616th Company Porter Corps
Lushai and Chin Porter Corps.
For a fuller account of the Lushais see Brigadier Marindin's Account is File No. 4576.

89th Indian Infantry Brigade
33rd Indian Infantry Brigade
Division Troops.

Artillery moved separately in its own transport. Staging areas were fixed at Manipur river crossing and Kan. As has been described earlier, the move began on 28 December. By 4 January the leading battalion was at Kan. Gradually the rest of the division moved up as road conditions and transport permitted, so that by 17 January the division, less one brigade, was in Kan while the 114th Indian Infantry Brigade had reached Gangaw area. Periodic rains seriously hampered movement on the Kabaw Valley road and turned the dust into deep mud. The whole move of the division from Kohima to Gangaw was a most complicated affair, and gave the "Q" services many nightmares. Nevertheless, thanks to the adaptability of all units and hard work of 'Q' staff and the transport companies of the Royal Indian Army Service Corps, the move was accomplished with very few serious hitches.

7/2 Punjab as Flank Guard.[37]

On 31 December, in order to cover the gap between the Corps axis and the river Chindwin, 7/2 Punjab, the reconnaissance battalion of the 7th Indian Division was ordered to act on the extreme left of the IV Corps axis. The area allotted to it was east of the Taungdwin Chaung to Thitkaungdi-Kuzeik-Chinbyit-Kabyu with the river Chindwin as the eastern boundary. The operation was to be conducted on all-pack basis with the help of 270 mules.

The mission involved 7/2 Punjab in a long cross country march which carried it down to Pakokku along a distance of over 250 miles. The battalion bore everything on the man or on mule-back, but it was supplied entirely by air. As it marched, the battalion built small temporary air-strips on which light aircrift could land. These served for the evacuation of the sick and the wounded. The going was extremely hard, as the track broke down in many places owing to heavy rainfall, especially in the early stages of the march.

Moving east from Kokko on 4 January, the leading company reached Kyawywa. From there, progress was faster and the major portion of the force reached Sitlingyaung by 10 January. On 12 January, when it arrived within a day's march of a small column of the 20th Indian Division at Kani on the Chindwin, the battalion came once more under the command of its parent division. From this point, 7/2 Punjab continued to advance on Pakokku, entirely cut off from the rest of the division and the Corps. Although it never fought any pitched battles, its patrols had many successful encounters with scattered hostile parties.

[37] Draft of "7th Indian Division History". 601/8445/H.

Meanwhile, the long-awaited "earthquake" air-strike had taken place and Myaukkon was occupied on 10 January as already described. So at mid-day on 12 January, the 7th Indian Division took over operational control in the Gangaw area, taking under its command:—

28th East African Group
Chin Hills Battalion
Lushai Scouts
Western Chin Levies (Falam & Haka).

7TH INDIAN DIVISION TASKS

The 7th Indian Division was assigned the task of pushing on vigorously to secure a bridgehead over the Irrawaddy somewhere in the Pakokku area through which the 17th Indian Division would pass. From air photographs, Nyaungu appeared to offer the best possibilities since approaches elsewhere were for the most part unsuitable.

The division's immediate task was to cut off and encircle as many Japanese forces as possible and to form mobile columns to carry out the pursuit to the Irrawaddy and prevent them crossing it without opposition.[38] It was necessary to secure the Pauk area up to and inclusive of the easternmost crossing of the Yaw Chaung as rapidly as possible, and not later than 1 February. This was so to enable an air-strip to be constructed and to build up administrative resources there for the move of the IV Corps Forward Maintenance Area from Kan. Finally, it was important to confirm "as unobtrusively as possible" that Nyaungu was the most suitable crossing place for the Corps,[39] seize a bridgehead there for the passage of the 17th Indian Division in its advance on Meiktila. The date for the establishment of the bridgehead was, if possible, to be not later than 15 February.[40] The 17th Indian Division had moved back into Assam from India and was reorganising on an all mechanical and air-transport basis, and was scheduled to concentrate at Pauk by 23 February.[41]

7th Indian Division Plan

The plan for the advance of the 7th Indian Division, as outlined in an Operation Instruction issued on 7 January, was that the 28th East African Brigade was to clear up the Gangaw area, including Lema and Pya and then continue the advance along the axis of the main road, and the 89th Indian Infantry Brigade was to carry out a deep encircling movement east of the road on a mule or mule-

---

[38] IV Corps Op. Instn. No. 120. See also draft of "7th Indian Division History" 601/2445/H.
[39] Ibid.
[40] IV Corps Op. Instn. No. 122.
[41] Ibid.

and-jeep basis with the Chin Hills Battalion moving ahead to establish a firm base in the area Kyaw PJ 56. The 114th Indian Infantry Brigade was to follow up the African Brigade and to carry out short encircling hooks as necessary. It was unlikely that the Japanese, on this front, whose strength was estimated at not more than five battalions, would offer any major resistance until the Irrawaddy was reached, though they might offer a stubborn rear-guard action on the Pondaung range between Tilin and Pauk.

Advance to Tilin

In the Gangaw area, the 28th East African Brigade assumed charge after completing the relief of the Lushai Brigade, and had its first clash with a Japanese platoon four miles east of Gangaw. The Japanese, however, were withdrawing from the area. Lema was found clear on 13 January, and Pyitma on the 14th, though all the tracks in this area were mined and booby-trapped. The brigade continued its advance south both from Lema and along the main road, while the 114th Indian Infantry Brigade and Headquarters 7th Indian Division moved in bounds behind it. The African brigade met no opposition on the way till the night of 20/21 January, when patrols to Ponna contacted a small Japanese position and captured it the next morning. On 23 January, Tilin was reached and captured by 46 KAR when a position guarding the entrance to it had been liquidated. Japanese opposition up to the capture of Tilin had taken the form merely of numerous obstructions on the cart track by which the East Africans were marching, particularly from trees felled across it. After Tilin, however, the opposition came from small but determined rear-guards. On 24 January, advance towards Pauk was resumed, 7 KAR along the road and 71 KAR across the country, parallel to the main axis. No opposition was met on the way and the brigade reached Yebyu where it made contact with the 89th Indian Infantry Brigade, another formation of the 7th Indian Division, on 26 January.

Encircling Movement by the 89th Brigade

In order to hasten the move to Pauk it was decided to cut the line of communication of the Japanese at Yebyu between Tilin and Pauk, in the hope that this manoeuvre would cut off a large number of them. Accordingly, the 89th Indian Infantry Brigade dumped all but its essential kit and set off, on 19 January, to conduct a deep encircling movement by penetrating the country eastwards between the Gangaw Valley and the Chindwin. The Lushai Scouts and Chin Hills Battalion formed the flank to the left, while 7/2 Punjab extended it yet further eastwards.

The 89th Indian Infantry Brigade marched very light. Relying on air supply, it took only mountain artillery and pack transport. Wireless was its only touch with the outside world. Sick and wounded were carried within the brigade. Only with the novel aid of air supply did a whole brigade possibly traverse one hundred and eighty miles of difficult country without an unwieldy mass of animals. For this flanking operation, which was expected to take about nine days, two columns were formed. Column A consisted of 4/8 Gurkha Rifles, 23 Mountain Battery and one platoon of 62 Field Company. Column B was formed of 1/11 Sikh, 2 KOSB and the rest of the brigade.

Column A, having set out on 19 January, was followed by Column B the next day. The ground presented considerable difficulties as the track was very rough and ill defined. Otherwise the march was uneventful and no opposition was encountered on the way. Although the brigade reached the main road at Yebyu two days earlier than the date set for it, it was just too late to cut off any Japanese troops, who seemed to have retired faster than expected. Nevertheless, this masterly move to threaten their rear had one desirable effect. By hastening their withdrawal, it prevented the Japanese from carrying out demolitions which would have seriously delayed the advance.

89th Brigade in the Van

By this time, it had been decided that the main divisional crossing by the 7th Indian Division would be at Nyaungu with a subsidiary crossing at Pakokku, north-east of Nyaungu, if possible. In order to conceal this move from the Japanese, it was decided that the East African Brigade should move towards Chauk on the Irrawaddy, 18 miles to the south of Nyaungu, to give the impression that a crossing was going to be staged there. It was also to create the impression that the whole of the East African Division was moving towards that objective. Meanwhile, the 89th Indian Infantry Brigade was to form the vanguard of the advance to Pauk from where it would move south-east towards the real crossing point.

Consequently, the 89th Indian Infantry Brigade was ordered on 26 January to capture Pauk and patrol vigorously towards Thamadaw. This was followed by Operation Instruction No. 69 of 26 January 1945, which laid down that the 7th Indian Division would capture the general line Sulegon—Point 875—Thanat Binzin. The Africans would arrive at Yagyibyin and from there move towards Seikpyu. The 114th Indian Infantry Brigade would concentrate at Thamadaw and be prepared with mobile columns to clear the Japanese from the west bank of the Irrawaddy between Pauktaw and Pakokku.[42]

[42]33rd Indian Infantry Brigade was left at Zahaw where it was getting training in river crossing.

7/2 Punjab would operate up to the west bank of the Irrawaddy in the area Yesagyo—Myaing. Air-strips were to be built by the African brigade at Chaung-U, south-east of Pauk, and by the 89th Indian Infantry Brigade in the Sinthe area.

Pauk Captured—28 January

Accordingly, on 26 January the 89th Indian Infantry Brigade began to move south from Yebyu. On 27 January, 1/11 Sikh came up against a Japanese position at PJ 7307. This was overcome and the Sikhs occupied Pauk the next day after an artillery concentration, three days ahead of schedule. The high ground east of Pauk was also occupied.[43] By 29 January, Pyinchaung had been occupied and this enabled work on the new Corps forward maintenance area at Sinthe to be started. Sinthe was the intended air-head for the crossing of the Irrawaddy. By 31 January the 89th Indian Infantry Brigade had concentrated in the Ondaw area and started patrolling forward. Fighting during this period was not intense and the Japanese seemed to be staging merely rear-guard delaying and harassing actions.

Meanwhile, 7/2 Punjab after occupying Kani on the Chindwin had continued its advance south without opposition, and by the end of January was in the area of Lingadaw. During this time, the 33rd Indian Infantry Brigade had remained in the Zahaw area near Gangaw training in watermanship as it had been chosen as the assault brigade for the crossing of the Irrawaddy. The 114th Indian Infantry Brigade had concentrated at Tilin and moved up the main road less one battalion, reaching Thamadaw by 31 January. By a fortunate coincidence, 4/14 Punjab, one of its battalions, had been left behind in the neighbourhood of Tilin, for after the East Africans had passed Tilin, the Japanese attacked the Falam Levies, who were still operating on the right of the division near Lessaw, and 4/14 Punjab had to rush to the assistance of the Levies. The battalion had orders to destroy all Japanese troops in the Lessaw area. It repulsed an attack on Kyi on the night of 29/30 January, and helped to restore the situation. Later, on the arrival of Westcol, supporting troops formed from the Chin Hills Battalion, 4/14 Punjab was withdrawn to join its brigade at Thamadaw, where the 114th Indian Infantry Brigade was preparing to take over the advance on Pakokku from the 89th Indian Infantry Brigade, and to clear the west bank of the Irrawaddy between Myitche and Pakokku.[44]

The situation at the beginning of February was that the 89th Indian Infantry Brigade was occupying the high ground east of Pauk, the 114th Indian Infantry Brigade had concentrated in

[43] Outline History of 1 Sikh Regiment (1946) in World War II. 601/7630/H.
[44] File No. 2445.

Thamadaw by 2 February preparatory to advance on Pakokku, and the Chin Hills Battalion with Westcol was to advance towards Yenangyaung on 1 February. The East African Brigade also was preparing to advance south on 3 February to capture Seikpyu and the 33rd Indian Infantry Brigade was still in training at Zahaw.

Towards Yenangyaung

Early in February, therefore, two movements started in a southerly direction from the main road between Tilin and Pauk. Both these manoeuvres aimed at engaging the attention of the Japanese some distance away from the proposed point of crossing the Irrawaddy. First of all, Westcol, which was formed from the Chin Hills Battalion and Lushai Scouts, set out from Yedu, on 1 February, to advance on the axis Saw—Sidoktaya—Ngape towards Yenangyaung. Its task was first to drive back opposition and develop a threat to Yenangyaung and Magwe, spreading exaggerated reports of its strength in order to hold the Japanese forces in the Yenangyaung area while the IV Corps crossed the Irrawaddy further north. Secondly, to implement this plan of deception, the 28th East African Brigade with a troop of armoured cars wheeled south from the Pauk—Pakokku road, on 3 February, with the object of capturing Seikpyu. Deception measures were adopted in earnest to make the Japanese believe that the brigade was merely the forward element of a whole division, the 11th East African Division, which was going to cross the Irrawaddy somewhere near Chauk. False signs were worn on the uniforms, faked dust-clouds were raised to give the impression of large troop movements and fireworks were let off to imitate machine-gun fire.

CAPTURE OF SEIKPYU

The East African Brigade advanced south down both the arms of the Yaw Chaung in two columns—Dimcol and Milcol. Milcol on the western axis met opposition at Chaungwa on the first day, but succeeded in capturing the position. The Japanese counter-attacked but were repulsed, at least sixteen of them being definitely killed. Milcol reached Taunggyo on 4 February and Paing on the 6th, meeting no further opposition. Dimcol on the eastern axis moved via Letse and reached Gwebin on 6 February. On 7 February, 46 KAR reached within 3 miles of Seikpyu, an area bristling with Japanese positions, some very elaborately defended. One position was found to contain fifty fox-holes and twenty bunkers. From these positions the Japanese offered determined resistance which made their repulse no easy task.

On 8 February, 46 KAR captured some of the forward defensive points and drove the Japanese back to their main positions. During the night of 9/10 February, they made a counter-attack which was, however, repulsed. In the meantime Milcol which had concentrated in Kazunma area on 9 February joined the other group in Seikpyu area and the brigade again became complete. A concerted attack was then delivered on this area on 10 February, but the success was not 'marked. An attack on a Japanese location in Ywathit was driven back by mortar and medium machine-gun fire. One company of 7 KAR, however, succeeded in overcoming opposition in north-west Seikpyu and invested positions immediately to the north, while 46 KAR was in contact with the Japanese further north, who continued their resistance from strong-points in the court area and the inspection bungalow. On 11 February, they tried to break out from the court to the south. They were opposed by heavy fire and the fighting here continued all day, the Japanese estimated at 70 using extensive mortar and grenade discharger fire from bunker positions. On 12 February, however, the court and pagoda positions were captured by a company of 7 KAR, and by 1300 hours the inspection bungalow had also fallen and the whole of Seikpyu was occupied. Lanywa, another defended place near Seikpyu, was found to be strongly held with signs of reinforcement ferrying over from Chauk on the opposite bank.

On the 13th, a 25-pounder battery, on loan from the 7th Indian Division, fired concentrations into the oilfield town of Chauk, and this had the desired effect. The Japanese brought in troops from elsewhere to meet what they considered to be a full-scale assault. They counter-attacked vigorously on 15 February and continued to do so for the next nine days. But the effective firing by the guns saved some ugly situations. On 24 February, a battery of the 2nd Indian Field Regiment of Corps artillery relieved the gunners who rejoined their parent unit in the 7th Indian Division to whose operations we may now turn.

CLEARING OF THE WEST BANK BY THE 7TH INDIAN DIVISION

Capture of Kanhla

Meanwhile, the 89th Indian Infantry Brigade had also resumed its advance along the road to Pakokku. Ledaing was occupied unopposed, and after minor clashes with the Japanese, Kandaw was also occupied on 3 February. Some patrols of this brigade working north of the main road, linked up with 7/2 Punjab, south of Myaing, which had been captured by it that day. Meanwhile 1/11 Sikh had moved south, down the Yaw Chaung, and explored a little used track that led to Myitche, on the river bank opposite Pagan, the ancient Burmese royal capital. The Japanese left the track uncovered and Myitche was found undefended. On 5 February, the Sikhs occupied the town.

The 114th Indian Infantry Brigade, which 4/14 Punjab had rejoined, passed through the 89th Indian Infantry Brigade to lead the advance on Pakokku, which it was ordered to capture with the utmost speed and establish contact as soon as possible with 7/2 Punjab, then operating in the area of Myaing, and to clear the west bank of the Irrawaddy not later than 10 February. The brigade was to carry out reconnaissance on the east in the Pakokku area and be prepared to cross the river if the east bank was not held by the Japanese.

On 3 February, 4/5 Royal Gurkha Rifles of the 114th Indian Infantry Brigade, with one troop of 116 RAC in support, was given the task of capturing Pakokku. They established themselves at Ngapaunggan on 4 February. Resistance stiffened as they approached Kanhla, 7 miles west of Pakokku.

Kanhla cross-roads—the immediate objective of 4/5 Royal Gurkha Rifles at this time—were of vital importance as it was here that the road to Myitche led off. That is why the divisional commander had fixed a date by which the cross-roads had to be taken. To the immediate east of this point was a dominating feature on which the Japanese had built strong positions which were manned by the *3rd Battalion* of the *214th Regiment*. There were other defensive positions also which, it was feared, would put up determined resistance.

Early on 5 February, C Company of 4/5 Royal Gurkha Rifles concentrated in the area of the 'two pagodas' at PP 316897. The same day A and D Companies began a lengthy left-hook movement on Kanhla. There was sporadic Japanese shelling during this advance and one outpost was met and dealt with effectively by a platoon of A Company. By 1630 hours more intensive shelling and some automatic fire was encountered. The Japanese main defences had been located on the bluff east of the cross-roads, 200 yards to the south-east of the area reached, and contained at least one company, 3 medium machine-guns, 3 light machine-guns and one gun. A Company was ordered to move round to the left and assault from the north-east while tactical headquarters and D Company were to assault from the west. A Company was completely pinned down at PP 344900. D Company assaulted at 1740 hours, and swept aside the stubborn Japanese resistance and took more than half of the position, killing at least 20 and destroying some of the medium machine-guns. The attack had almost succeeded but, by this time, their ammunition was very nearly exhausted, and so both the companies were withdrawn to the 'two pagoda' area under cover of darkness.

On 6 February an air-strike was put in on several of the Japanese bunkers located in Kanhla area, but there was little success. Hence another strike was directed on a gun position at PP 362901 which was also unsuccessful. On 7 February, the battalion less B and D Companies withdrew, being relieved by 4/1 Gurkha Rifles.

The Japanese were still holding Kanhla area and a plan was drawn up for a co-ordinated attack by air, tanks and artillery on their positions on 10 February. The air-strike failed to take place but the ground attack was not deferred on that account. C Company moved forward on tanks from the north at 0645 hours but it was held up at PP 341906. A Company then moved east to 397903 and from there due south till almost on the road, and moved in on the position from the east. C Company came in from the north-east. The attack proved sucessful, though D Company coming from the west had difficulty in annihilating the snipers. Japanese casualties were 51 dead. Many others were shot up by tanks and by 4/14 Punjab as they fled south of the road.[45] One 75-mm gun, one medium machine-gun, and one light machine-gun were also captured.

During the night there were six Japanese counter-attacks on the battalion positions but all of them proved unsuccessful as were further attempts on the night of 11/12 February. The battalion then started clearing the area between Kanhla and Pakokku which was done gradually. 1/11 Sikh was already established south of Myitche on the west bank of the river opposite to Pagan.

Thus, while the East Africans attempted to divert the Japanese in the south and the 114th Indian Infantry Brigade contained them in the Pakokku area, the west bank of the Irrawaddy was clear of all opposition from five miles south of Myitche to the western outskirts of Pakokku. Myitche, in sight of the countless and beautiful pagodas on the opposite bank, many dating back to the 11th and 12th centuries, became the scene of feverish activity as Indian troops and their British comrades built up all their requirements for assaulting the far bank.

Meanwhile, 4/14 Punjab advancing along the line of the Irrawaddy overcame stiff resistance in the outskirts of Pakokku. A converging movement was made on the town by 4/5 Royal Gurkha Rifles along the axis of the main road, 4/14 Punjab along the line of the river bank and 7/2 Punjab from the north-west. This resulted in the final capture of the town of Pakokku.

---

[45] Fierce fighting, involving 4/5 Royal Gurkha Rifles and a squadron of Sherman tanks from the 116th Royal Armoured Corps (Gordon Highlanders), took place at Kanhla cross-roads where the road to Myitche took off. After VJ Day a Japanese officer stated that of the rear party of seventy men left to defend Kanhla to the last, sixty-nine were reported to have been killed after the 114th Brigade attacked.

With the vital cross-roads captured, Pakokku in Allied hands and a large number of Japanese killed, they must have begun to suspect that the crossing of the Irrawaddy was going to be attempted in the Pakokku area.[46]

255TH INDIAN TANK BRIGADE'S 400 MILES MARCH

Meanwhile the 255th Indian Tank Brigade had moved down from Imphal to Tamu to follow the 7th Indian Division towards Pakokku. The whole move from Imphal to the Irrawaddy, a distance of 400 miles, spread itself over eight weeks because of the state of the road and the scarcity of transport. No. 590 Tank Transporter Company, the RIASC company which shuttled the tanks all the way, worked extremely hard under truly terrible conditions. In one stretch south of Gangaw tanks had to be off-loaded no less than seventeen times. Sometimes the tanks even had to be used to tow the empty transporters.[47]

According to the account by Probyn's Horse (5 Horse) the going was really too rough for transporters.[48] The original intention of moving all tanks on these vehicles, anyhow as far as Kan, was practically abandoned owing to rain which, though spasmodic, was heavy. The Royal Deccan Horse tanks, for instance, averaged 200 miles on their own tracks before reaching the Irrawaddy. The heavy going and hundreds of bends on the mountain road necessitated much work in low gear and frequent 'pulling on the sticks'. Hardly a tank completed the journey that did not have to have new bogies fitted, or its idlers and sprockets welded. It is no wonder that men of the Indian Electrical and Mechanical Engineers' Corps in brigade workshops and regimental Light Aid Detachments frequently worked all night to get tanks ready for the road by the morning. Nor were their difficulties lightened by the fact that every spare part had to be flown in by air.

The 4th Indian Grenadiers endured a dusty and arduous ride on top of the tanks, a severe tax on the men. Companies harboured at night with regimental groups at each successive brigade harbour. In each it was possible to devote time to training, to study future battle tactics and despatch platoons on distant patrols.

17TH INDIAN DIVISION MOVES SOUTH

The 17th Indian Division, which was to pass through the 7th Indian Division's bridgehead for its dash to Meiktila, reached

---
[46] The actual crossings are described in Chapter X.
[47] Operations IV Corps, Oct. 44 to May 45, p. 39.
[48] *Operations in Burma by Probyn's Horse Feb.-April 1945.* (Oxford Printing Works, New Delhi).

Imphal from Ranchi during January. It then hurriedly reorganised as a mechanical force. The 99th Indian Infantry Brigade, being chosen for the airborne operations, concentrated at Palel in readiness for flying to Meiktila. The 48th and 63rd Indian Infantry Brigades and the rest of the division made themselves fully motorised. This they did by leaving their mules behind, reshuffling transport among themselves and absorbing the transport which was stripped for them off the 5th Indian and the 11th East African Divisions. These brigades and the two regimental groups of the 255th Indian Tank Brigade with whom they were to be affiliated in the field joined together in making plans for their future co-operation in battle. Finally, the 17th Indian Division and the 255th Indian Tank Brigade, except the airborne brigade waiting at Palel, succeeded in concentrating between Pauk and the Irrawaddy by 18 February, five days after the 7th Indian Division had begun to cross.[49] The 17th Indian Division had accomplished the move by ferrying with barely more than its own transport.

JAPANESE FORCES IN MYITTHA VALLEY

The Japanese who opposed the IV Corps in the Myittha Valley appear to have been the rear elements of the *215th Regiment* of the *33rd Division*, which was still too weak to offer any serious resistance. They had been driven south from Gangaw as the Allies advanced, and an identity disc captured by Levies near Tilin on 19 January provided the first identification in Burma of the *153rd Regiment* of the *49th Division*. Subsequent identifications and details obtained from the prisoners and captured documents showed that the Japanese had brought this regiment up from South Burma and positioned it west of the Irrawaddy, to hold a sector stretching from the Chin Hills to the Irrawaddy.

Evidence was also obtained, at much the same time, of the presence of an unidentified formation in the area of Yenangyaung. This formation was eventually identified as *72nd IMB*, which had been rather hastily formed from *1st* and *3rd Battalions, 61st Regiment*, and from the two battalions of *34th IMB* which had formerly been in the railway corridor under the command of the *53rd Infantry Division*. "The Commander of *72nd IMB* turned out to be none other than our old friend Major-General Yamamoto, formerly commander of the *33rd Infantry Division*, who had led the enemy forces which attempted to enter the Imphal plain via the Tamu road."[50]

The available evidence on the Japanese side is very slender, but it appears that they failed to see through the magnitude of the

---

[49] Operations IV Corps, Oct. 44—May 45, p. 12.
[50] *Ibid*; para 72.

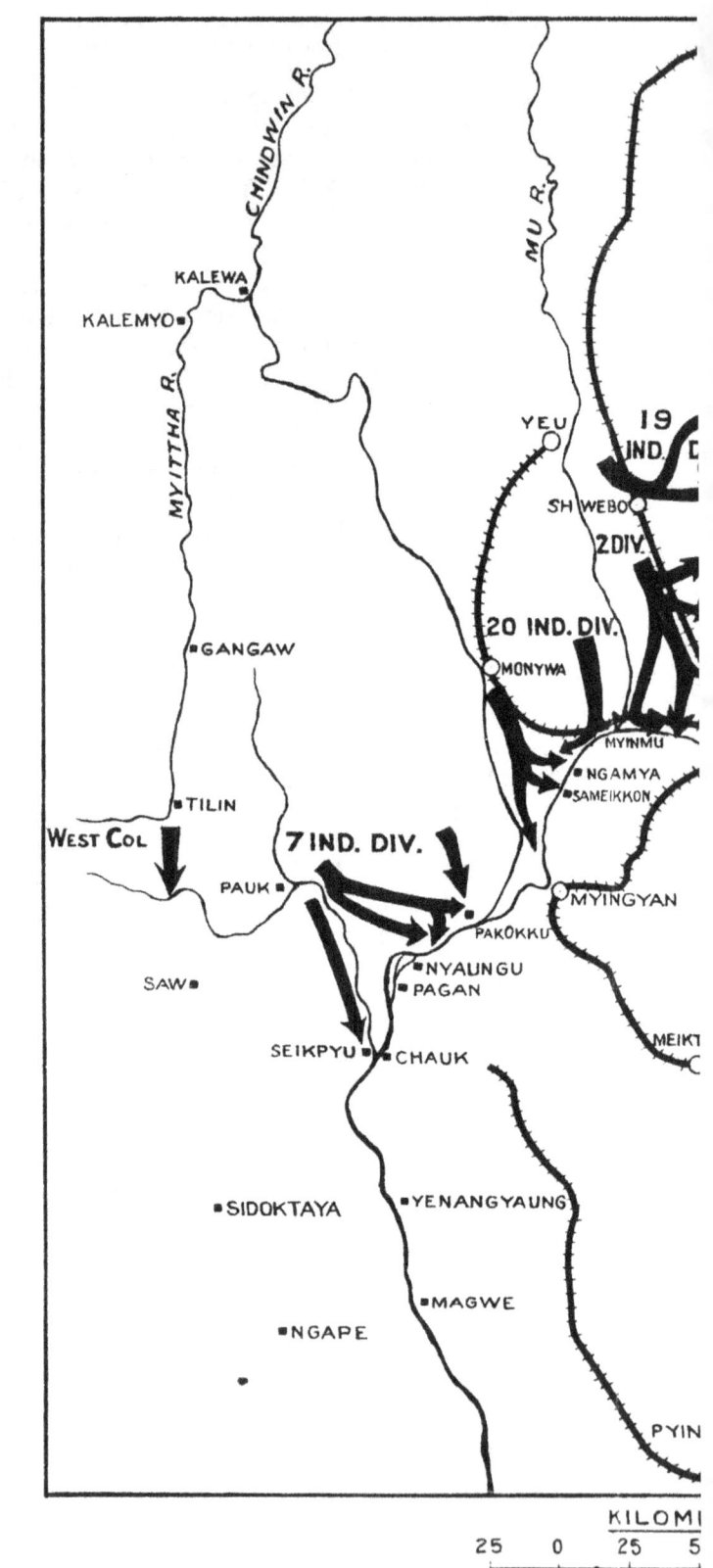

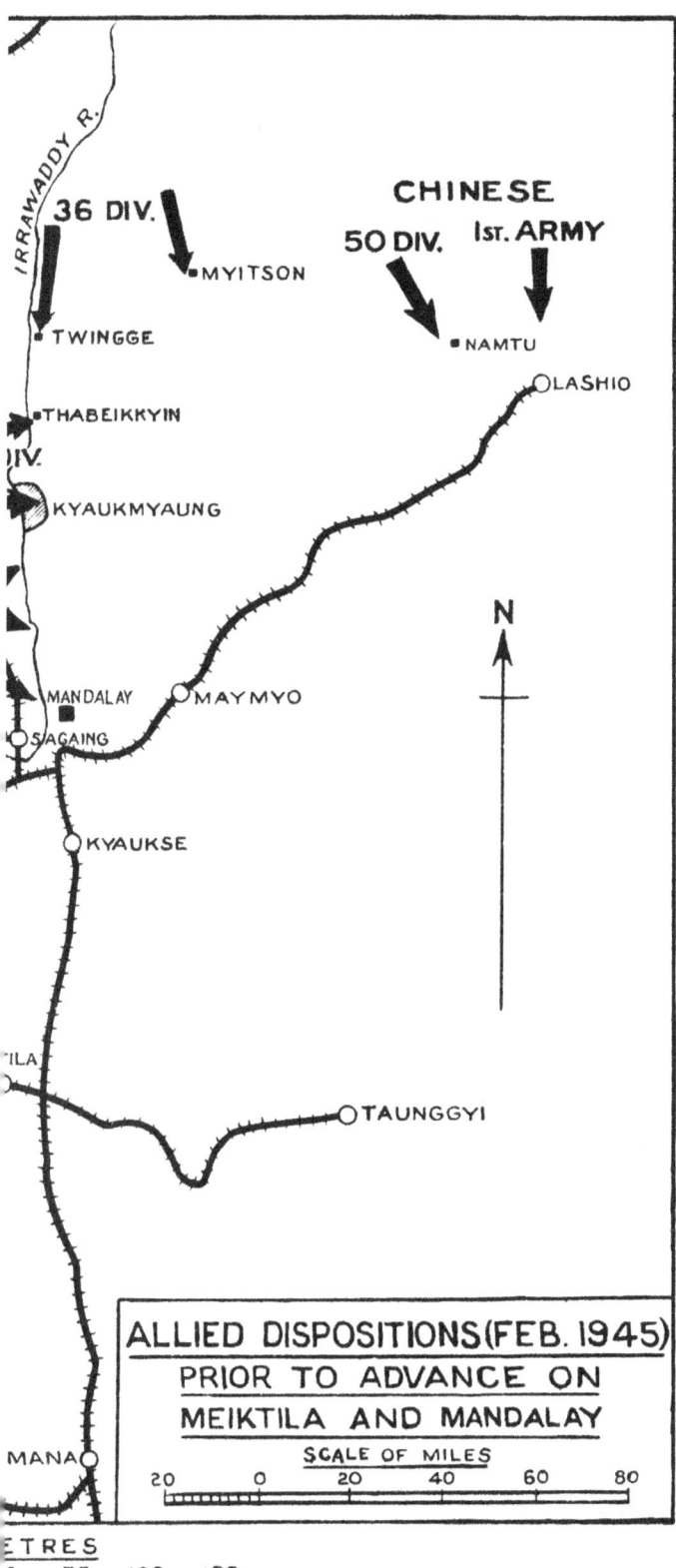

threat developing against them, or the possibility of the IV Corps forcing a bridgehead at Nyaungu. This was admitted by General Kimura later in his interrogation when he said, "I did not consider 7th Division's crossing at Nyaungu to be a serious threat to our position. My staff appreciated it as a feint but realised their error later."[51] That is why the Japanese rear parties on this front offered resistance that was merely sporadic. They must have had orders to retire when strongly attacked. Otherwise they might have easily caused more delay to the advance of the IV Corps, confined as it was to a defile astride a narrow and indifferent road on which much engineer work was necessary.

Thus by the second week of February, the IV Corps had reached its first objective and was ready to force a passage of the mighty Irrawaddy. It would be easier to follow the course of events if we continue with the plans for putting the 7th Indian Division across the Irrawaddy; but during January and February three other divisions, two of them Indian, were pressing on with an identical object further north, and one of these, the 19th Indian Division, forced its passage a month ahead of the others. The next chapter will therefore deal with the advance of these three divisions of the XXXIII Corps towards the Irrawaddy.

---

[51] SEATIC Bulletin No. 242, p. 58, Item No. 2273.

CHAPTER VIII

XXXIII Corps Advance to the Irrawaddy

As mentioned in the previous chapter, the new plan of the Fourteenth Army had envisaged the transfer of the IV Corps from the left to the extreme right flanks for a secret march from the Gangaw Valley down south for a decisive strike at Meiktila in the rear of the Japanese forces. This change of plan, however, did not affect the XXXIII Corps to any great extent, and its tasks, redefined on 19 December, remained practically the same as before. These were:

(1) To capture and construct airfields in the Ye-U—Shwebo area.
(2) To capture Monywa and construct airfields there.
(3) To cross the Irrawaddy, capture Mandalay, and be prepared for a further advance southwards.[1]

On 20 December 1944, the Corps Commander held a conference with his formation commanders, and their tasks were defined as follows[2]:

(a) The 2nd Division was to continue its advance on the main axis, and capture the area Ye-U—Shwebo, as rapidly as possible, preparatory to a southward advance on Mandalay.
(b) The 19th Indian Division would continue to advance on its existing axis, the railway Kawlin—Kanbalu—Shwebo. Its object was to capture Shwebo and thereafter to cross the Irrawaddy river near Thabeikkyin and then operate against Mandalay.
(c) The 20th Indian Division on the right was to advance south-east on axis Chindwin river and track Pyingaing—Palusawa—Songon—Budalin. Its object was to capture Monywa and then to cross the Irrawaddy and operate against Mandalay from the south-east.
(d) The 268th Indian Infantry Brigade was ordered to move down the Mu river and to make patrol contacts with the 2nd Division and the 19th Indian Division.

It was considered important that the 2nd British and the 19th Indian Divisions must capture intact the canal works at Kabo weir.

---

[1] XXXIII Corps OO No. 11.
[2] Minutes of a conference held by the Corps Commander with his Divisional Commanders at Corps Headquarters. See Appendix D to XXXIII Corps War Diary, December 1944.

It was even more important to advance quickly and seize air-strips. The rear services could not maintain a Corps of three-and-one-third divisions and an armoured brigade along a line of communication which either ran through mountains or had a bull-dozed surface. Hence airfields must be seized or built in the Shwebo plain. A forward air-strip would afford more fighter cover to the Allied troops and save advancing forces from harassment by the depleted Japanese air force.

The activities in pursuance of these instructions can be divided into two phases. In the first, lasting up to the first week of January 1945, the 19th Indian and the 2nd British Divisions captured and cleared Ye-U and Shwebo, and the 20th Indian Division invested and later captured Budalin, preliminary to the capture of Monywa. In the second, up to the second week of February 1945, the 20th Indian and the 2nd British Divisions completely cleared the area of the Shwebo plain right up to the confluence of the Irrawaddy and the Chindwin, captured Monywa and got ready to cross the Irrawaddy, while the 19th Indian Division actually crossed that river and established bridgeheads on its east bank north of Mandalay. Operations in the first phase are described in this chapter, while those in the second phase form the subject matter of the next.

JAPANESE DISPOSITIONS IN MID-DECEMBER 1944

After the Allied forces had crossed the Chindwin river and established bridgeheads there, the Japanese High Command had, it seemed, accepted the necessity of at least a partial withdrawal in north-east Burma, and it was later known that they had decided to yield considerable territory with the object of forming a defensive line, probably running across Lashio—Mandalay—Pakokku. This line, however, they intended to hold at least until the arrival of the 1945 monsoon, and the XXXIII Corps expected that the withdrawal would only take place when forced by the Allied troops, and then only after stiff resistance and delaying rear-guard actions.

The Japanese forces which were opposed to the XXXIII Corps were commanded by the *15th Army*, and consisted of the *15th*, *31st* and *53rd Divisions*. Of these the *15th Division* had been re-formed after its virtual disintegration during the Manipur operations and numbered approximately 7000 men. The *31st Division* was also in the process of re-forming after the equally severe handling it had received at the same time and was estimated to be 10,000 strong. The *53rd Division*, which had borne the entire brunt of the well-executed withdrawal from Imphal, was still in contact with the troops of the 2nd Division and the 20th Indian Division, but numbered no more than 4000 effectives.[3]

These forces were obviously insufficient to meet the double threat presented by the XXXIII Corps bridgehead at Kalewa and the 19th Indian Division bridgehead at Thaungdut/Sittaung. The Japanese *15th Division* in the north faced the 19th Indian Division, and *33rd Division* in the south faced the XXXIII Corps. The *31st Division* remained in reserve in the Shwebo plain prepared to act on either axis.[4]

By the middle of December it was clear that the 11th East African Division's bridgehead was secure against all but raiding parties. On the main Shwegyin—Ye-U road contact had been temporarily lost with those elements of the *33rd Division* which had formed the final defence of Kalewa. These elements which included the *214th Regiment* and *1st* and *2nd Battalions* of *215th Regiment*, together with other miscellaneous troops, and could muster at the most some 3000 men, had regrouped in the Shwegyin area after conducting their masterly retreat down the Tiddim road. It was believed, however, rightly as events later proved—that the majority of these troops had been withdrawn down the river axis to the area of Monywa.

The *Yamamoto Detached Force* was still active north of the main Shwegyin—Ye-U road. After conducting the final withdrawal down the east bank of the Chindwin above Kalewa, this force still numbered nearly 1000 men and was made up of the *213th Regiment* and *2nd Battalion* of *124th Regiment* of the *31st Division*. For several days during the last week of December 1944, it remained in the general area of the Kanni Chaung and as far north as Indaw as a potential threat to the flank of the 2nd Division. Eventually, however, it withdrew along the axis of the main road.

Originally it was expected that the Japanese would make a stand in the area of Pyingaing. But the withdrawal of the bulk of the *33rd Division* rendered this impossible, and also made the appearance of part of the *31st Division*—the last Japanese reserve—imperative on this axis. The force chosen for this role was the *124th Regiment*, which did, in fact, provide stubborn opposition at Wainggyo and Ye-U. This regiment numbered in all 1500 men and was unable to do more than temporarily delay the advance of the 2nd Division.

2ND DIVISION ADVANCES INTO THE SHWEBO PLAIN

By the evening of 15 December, the 11th East African Division had reported that the Chindwin bridgehead area was free from any

---
[3] XXXIII Corps Account of Operations Vol. 3, p. 4.
[4] *Ibid.*

organised Japanese resistance, and the following morning tactical headquarters of the 2nd Division opened at Shwegyin. The 6th Brigade had already left the divisional concentration area at Yazagyo and was concentrating at Kalewa, prior to crossing the Chindwin. On 17 December, Brigade Tactical Headquarters, 2 DLI and 1 RWF had arrived at Mutaik.[5]

Advance to Pyingaing

On 18 December, the 2nd Division Operation Instruction No. 6 laid down the capture of Pyingaing Myauk as the main task of the division; the 6th Infantry Brigade consisting of 1 RWF, 2 DLI and 1 Royal Berks with the support of one squadron 2 Recce Regiment RAC and ancillary troops was to take up the advance.

On the same day, the 11th East African Division was ordered by the Corps Commander to continue active patrolling until the 2nd Division passed through and took over the advance. In particular, the African division was to clear Kanni Chaung area, from which persistent local reports of Japanese concentrations of not more than 200 had been received. This was carried out and two companies of 13 KAR were despatched to the area. On arrival there, they were to continue down the chaung to the main road. The 2nd Division passed through the 11th East African Division positions on 19 December[6] and by 24 December the latter withdrew from the east bank of the Chindwin. The Kanni Chaung area was now clear, and in its advance nearly 3½ miles east of Chaungzon, the 11th East African Division had cleared the road of mines and felled-trees left by the Japanese to hinder the Allied advance.

The 2nd Division advanced rapidly along the road from Kalewa towards Pyingaing and for four days its leading troops—the 6th Brigade—had no contact with the Japanese who had laid mines and planted other obstructions along the road to delay its advance. The clearance of these obstructions had the effect of delaying the employment of Allied mechanical transport. The 6th Brigade, however, concentrated in Thetkegyin area at Point 1670 on 21 December. The move forward of the armoured column was held up by mines at some points. On 21 December, patrols of 2 Recce reached Point 1410 at SQ 0784, and on 22 December linked up with 13 KAR patrols moving down the Kanni Chaung from the northwest.[7] On 23 December, leading elements of the 6th Brigade, having advanced from Mutaik, passed through Pyingaing and by nightfall were established four miles east of the village.

[5] *Ibid*, pp. 5-6.
[6] 21 December according to Leese's Despatch, 19 December according to Corps account.
[7] XXXIII Corps Account of Operations Vol. III p. 6. Also War Diary XXXIII Corps for December 1944.

In the meantime, 4/10 Gurkha Rifles of the 100th Indian Infantry Brigade with the 32nd Indian Infantry Brigade (both of the 20th Indian Division) had marched cross-country from the Chindwin at Mawlaik to operate against the Japanese flank in the Pyingaing area. 4/10 Gurkha Rifles had been placed under the command of the 2nd Division from 21 December to assist the advance of the 6th Brigade, by establishing road-blocks and ambushes to the east of the Japanese lines. This move of 4/10 Gurkha Rifles from one side and of the 2nd British Division from the other, forced the Japanese out of Pyingaing, but the two Allied forces were not yet able to contact each other. Pyingaing had been taken and on 24 December the advance was continued towards Wainggyo. It was reported that the Japanese were avoiding contact with the Gurkhas.[8]

To Wainggyo

At mid-day on 24 December, leading elements of the 6th Brigade reported contact with the Japanese dug in on a high ground at SQ 542577. They were dug in on both sides of the road covering bridges at 534574 and 537575.[9] The task for 25 December was that the 6th Brigade would overcome opposition and advance to the Wainggyo area. The key-point of Japanese resistance was a hill feature immediately south of the road. This was physically, but not numerically, strong as it was expected that there were only about 100 men holding it. If the 6th Brigade could take this, the road could be opened and contact with 4/10 GR gained.[10] This position was pin-pointed at 545578. Clearance of this feature could not be effected on 25 December, but was accomplished successfully on 26 December by 1 R Berks. The opposition encountered was less than expected and the total Japanese strength was now estimated at 40 only.[11] Mopping up of the Japanese and consolidating the feature was done on 27 December, and the plan for 28 December was that the brigade would move forward, with 2 DLI in lead, to make firm contact with 4/10 Gurkha Rifles and advance to the Wainggyo area. At 0715 hours on this day, 2 DLI with armoured columns began moving to Wainggyo. At 0815 hours, leading troops of the 6th Brigade established contact with 4/10 Gurkha Rifles, 500 yards west of Wainggyo, where the latter had overrun two companies of the Japanese troops who had been in position in the area. An hour later the Allied troops were in occupation of Wainggyo.

[8] 2nd Div. Sitrep to 2200 hrs. on 24 December.
[9] *Ibid.*
[10] Summary of situation by Divisional Commander, dated 25 December. See appendix 63 to 2nd Div. W/D for December 1945.
[11] 2nd Div. Sitrep to 2200 hrs. on 26 December.

Capture of Kaduma

Kaduma was the next objective of the 6th Brigade. The axis of advance was to be Sipadon Chaung—main road via Paga, to be taken by 2 DLI, and via Inbya to Ywange to be taken by 2 Recce. The Durham Light Infantry moving along the axis Sipadon Chaung on 29 December, encountered no opposition until it had reached the area 6554 and west Paga 7153. Stiff opposition was, however, offered by the Japanese at Paga but the position was evacuated by them during the night. The armoured column advancing on the main road axis met opposition at point 964 at SQ 6549 and at SQ 7847. The latter position had been wired and mined and was fairly strong. But the Japanese, identified as *124th Regiment,* fled in disorder on being overrun by tanks. Another position, the strongest so far during the advance on this axis, was met on 30 December. During this attack the tanks were able to deploy for the first time and the position was easily liquidated. The situation during the night of 30/31 December was that the 2 DLI had reached the main road axis at Taunggyaung and was in contact with the Japanese there, and the armoured column and 1 R Berks were at Inye-O and 1 RWF about one mile west of Kaduma. The speed of the advance, it seemed, had not allowed the Japanese time to prepare elaborate defences as all their positions appeared hastily dug.[12]

On the last day of the year the 6th Brigade occupied Kaduma. On that day the Japanese staged two air attacks, one by 12 Oscars bombing and strafing Kaduma area at 0910 hours, killing two and wounding fourteen, and another by 6 Oscars at 1350 hours causing twelve casualties in the same area.

Kabo Weir

On 31 December at 1800 hours, the 2nd Division's Operation Instruction No. 8 ordered the 6th Infantry Brigade Group to advance on the axis Kaduma—Kabo to capture Kabo weir intact and secure an area east of the Mu river to enable the brigade to deploy there for an advance on Shwebo.[13]

The 5th Infantry Brigade Group was at the same time to advance on the axis Kaduma—Ye-U to capture Ye-U and secure an area east of the Mu river before commencing its advance on Shwebo.

In pursuance of these instructions, 1 RWF of the 6th Brigade (forming an armoured column with two companies, a half Squadron 3rd Dragoon Guards and artillery) advanced through Kaduma for over 20 miles and captured Kabo weir, the headworks of the irrigation system of the plain of Shwebo and Ye-U, at 1950 hours on 31 December 1944. Thus on the last day of the year, the Allied troops

---

[12] 2nd Div. Sitrep, 30 December 1944.
[13] XXXIII Corps OO No. 11.

made an entry into the Shwebo plain. The capture of Kabo weir intact was a great economic gain, since this weir controlled the irrigation of the Shwebo plain—an important rice growing area. The Japanese had planned to demolish the weir, but when their demolition party arrived they found the place occupied. The Allies had just forestalled them. If the demolition party had succeeded, it would have had the most serious consequences on the civil population and would probably have led to a widespread famine.

Ye-U

The 5th Brigade moved up from Kaduma the following day, and was firmly established at the canal five miles from Ye-U with patrols reported to be near the town. The positions on the Kabo weir were also consolidated by the 6th Brigade which concentrated in that area. One squadron of 2 Recce, proceeding on the axis Kaduma—Ye-U airfield, completed its advance by occupying Ye-U air-strip. The town itself was occupied on the morning of 2 January by the 5th Brigade. But it was not until the following day that the Japanese who had remained behind and fought a skilful delaying action at the town were completely overpowered.[14]

Crossing the Mu River

Despite heavy small-arms fire, reconnaissance commenced at once to find suitable crossings over the Mu river. During these operations five squadrons of Hurribombers supported the 5th Brigade by attacking Japanese positions in the villages of Yadaw and Thayetpinzu. On 4 January at 0700 hours, 2 Dorset supported by artillery established a bridgehead at Yadaw against resistance from two Japanese companies. The Camerons had also found a crossing place and established a bridgehead opposite Bitagaya against slight opposition. By 1730 hours, the Camerons' bridgehead was firmly established. On 5 January the Camerons, with 7 Worcesters following closely, started attacks northwards with a troop of tanks in support. At 1010 hours, 2 Dorset occupied Thayetpinzu. On 5 January, the bridgehead over the Mu river was firm with 1 Camerons at Myindaung, 2 Dorset at Thayetpinzu, one mile to the east of Ye-U, and 7 Worcesters at a road junction two miles west of Myindaung.

Whilst the 5th Brigade cleared Ye-U, the 6th Brigade in the Kabo area met Japanese opposition including 70-mm artillery from the village. But on 3 January, 1 Royal Berks was able to cross to the other side of the Mu river at Kabo. On the night of 4 January severe fighting took place at Thayetpinzu where the Japanese were

[14] XXXIII Corps Account of Operations, *op. cit.*

strongly entrenched. The position was however captured by 2 Dorset of the 5th Brigade and the Japanese were forced to withdraw hastily leaving much equipment. Simultaneously with the 5th Brigade's crossing of the Mu river, the 6th Brigade reduced the Japanese at Kabo and linked with patrols from the 19th Indian Division.

Due to a shortage of troop-carrying transport, the 4th Brigade remained in the Kabaw Valley until transport from the 5th and 6th Brigades could return to ferry it forward. It was only on 2 January that the 4th Brigade started moving up in the rear of the division to Kaduma.[15] But by 5 January, these measures, namely the capture of Pyingaing, Wainggyo, Kabo weir, Ye-U and the crossing of the Mu river, had given the Allied troops a firm footing in the plain. Though the rapid speed of the 2nd Division had been somewhat retarded by the opposition offered by remnants of the *Yamamoto Detached Force* the timely capture of Kabo weir had more than made up for the delay.

19TH INDIAN DIVISION FRONT

As described in Chapter VI, the 19th Indian Division had, by the middle of December, not only crossed the river Chindwin at Sittaung, but had penetrated further east. Pinlebu had been taken, though against weak opposition only, and a link-up with the 36th Division made at Indaw (rail) thus establishing a continuous Allied front from India to the Chinese border.

The Allied operations were being carried out in the area of the railway corridor as also on the lower Chindwin. There was thus a gap in the Japanese defences between the 19th Indian Division sector of operations in the north and the area of the lower Chindwin where the 2nd Division and the 20th Indian Division were operating. The Japanese *15th Division* was disposed to fill up this gap. Based on Wuntho, the dispositions of this division were sited to cover the passes over the Zibyu Daung Range and particularly the important junction of Pinlebu. When the 19th Indian Division took Pinlebu easily, the Japanese *15th Division* began to withdraw in a southeasterly direction with a view to crossing to the east of the Irrawaddy. To cover that withdrawal the *58th Regiment* of *31st Division*, some 2,000 strong, was made to face the Indian division in the area of Kanbalu. When the 19th Indian Division moved towards Kanbalu (after capturing Pinlebu), in the second half of December, it met with stubborn resistance from this regiment. But on 24 December the 19th Indian Division had been told to take

[15] *Ibid.*

"risks freely and without hesitation."[16] Two days later it came under the command of the XXXIII Corps in accordance with Lieut-General Slim's plan. By that time the results of its advance had been apparent in as much as the *15th Division* had been forced to withdraw, and the only reserve of the Japanese, the *31st Division*, was forced to deploy its troops on two fronts, namely against the 19th Indian Division and against the 2nd British Division. In accordance with the instructions the 19th Indian Division was now about to "take risks freely."

When this Indian division came under command of the XXXIII Corps, its brigades were disposed as follows:
98th Indian Infantry Brigade advancing towards Kanbalu,
62nd Indian Infantry Brigade moving on Sadwingyi,
64th Indian Infantry Brigade moving on to Baw.

Leiktu Taken

On 24 December the 98th Indian Brigade was ordered to advance to the line Kanbalu—Sabenatha—road junction SR 4675 and establish, as soon as possible, road-blocks at the last two places.[17] The advance was to be carried out on two axes—the right axis to move via Kyaikthin—Tebin—Kanbalu, and the left via Letpanda, Baw, road junction SR 4675. On the right axis 2 Royal Berks and 4/4 Gurkha Rifles moved towards Kanbalu but found the road heavily mined. The advance, however, continued and came up against a Japanese position three miles south of Thityabin on 26 December.[18] There were some minor clashes that day but the Japanese position was found evacuated next morning. The advance was continued on 27 December to be halted again towards the evening by a Japanese position at SR 173810. One company of the 2 Royal Berks therefore made an encircling movement and established itself in the rear of the Japanese. On the morning of the 28th it was found that the Japanese had abandoned the position during the night. Meanwhile, 4/4 Gurkha Rifles of this right column had overcome some slight opposition along the railway line. By the evening of 28 December 4/4 Gurkha Rifles and 2 Royal Berks were both advancing towards the Leiktu village.

Meanwhile the left column of the 98th Indian Infantry Brigade consisting of 8 FFR had moved east towards Letpanda,[19] where on their arrival on 25 December, the leading troops were told by the villagers that there were 30 Japanese in a dug-in position to the east of the village, but no contact was made. During the night of

---
[16] 19th Indian Division Op. Instruction No. 12 of 24 December 1944.
[17] WD 19th Ind. Div. 24 Dec. 1944.
[18] 98th Indian Infantry Brigade Intelligence Summary No. 5 dated 28 December 1944.
[19] *Ibid.*

25/26 December, however, one company moved to the south of the village and gained contact with the Japanese. The rest of the battalion advanced through the village which was found to be clear. The whole battalion then advanced against the Japanese position towards the south of the village where 8 FFR was relieved by certain elements of the 64th Indian Infantry Brigade who had arrived in this area and were to advance on the line Letpanda—Sabenatha. On being relieved the 8 FFR returned to join in the drive on the right axis which was being carried out by 4/4 Gurkha Rifles and 2 Royal Berks. The 64th Indian Infantry Brigade now continued the advance on the left axis unopposed, and having left a block at Ngapyawdaing, concentrated by 1 January 1945, ten miles further south from where patrols were sent east to the Irrawaddy.

Meanwhile, on the right axis 4/4 Gurkha Rifles and 2 Royal Berks had reached the outskirts of Leiktu where they encountered a Japanese strong-point on the night of 30/31 December, to the south of the village, and another on 31 December further to the east. The Japanese were also contacted by a reconnaissance party of the 64th Brigade Field Company in the area of the chaung, north-east of Leiktu. It was clear that the Japanese were determined to offer strong resistance here. All units of the 98th Indian Infantry Brigade were therefore ordered to move to encircle the place. In addition, harassing fire was carried out by the 4th Indian Field Regiment and the 115th Field Regiment on 30 and 31 December, and an air-strike on Leiktu was carried out on the New Year's day by Hurribombers.[20] The Japanese suffered many casualties, and after the air-strike Leiktu was found to be clear and was occupied on 1 January after five days of fighting.

The advance to Kanbalu was then continued but, although some slight opposition was encountered, it appeared that the Japanese had evacuated the general area of Leiktu—Kanbalu during the night of 31 December/1 January and were withdrawing towards the south and south-east. On arrival at Kanbalu on 2 January, some sporadic rifle fire was encountered but the place was quickly cleared by 4/4 Gurkha Rifles; and Kanbalu, the gateway to the plains, was in Allied hands.

Pinde

Meanwhile, by 26 December, the 62nd Indian Infantry Brigade Group had moved off, with Sadwingyi as its destination, but the advance was held up by small parties of Japanese troops in succcessive lay-back positions. One such party estimated at one weak company was encountered in the evening by 4/6 Gurkha Rifles in

---

[20] 98th Indian Infantry Brigade Intelligence Summary No. 7, dated 2.1.45.

bunker positions astride a track, half a mile north of Pinde. The initial attack delivered on the 26th failed to dislodge the defenders who offered stubborn resistance. By the night of the 28th, Pinde was, however, reported well surrounded by Rajputana Rifles and 4/6 Gurkha Rifles with stops astride all tracks leading out of the village. At 1530 hours in the afternoon of 29 December, an attack was mounted from the west by 2 Welch after accurate artillery concentration. By the evening one company had succeeded in establishing itself in the north of the village. But the other attacking company suffered casualties. On the next morning it was discovered that the Japanese who were estimated at two companies had succeeded in getting away during the night,[21] and once again the brigade was baulked of its prey.

Sadwingyi

The march south was resumed on the 30th. The same evening 3 Raj Rif was held up by the Japanese in a bunker position one mile south of village Sadwingyi (524086). A stiff battle ensued for this position and numerous casualties were suffered. While C Company formed up a stop in the rear of Sadwingyi on the Sadwingyi—Gada road, B and D Companies put in an attack from the right and left respectively, leaving A Company in reserve. The village was occupied by dark, though not fully cleared. During this operation the Japanese used phosphorous bombs which caused several casualties among B and D Companies.

On 2 January, 2 Welch of the 62nd Indian Infantry Brigade, having been in contact with the Japanese forces north of Gada, occupied that village, following evacuation by the latter of their positions. This brigade was then ordered to send patrols to Male and Thabeikkyin on the Irrawaddy, and relieve the 64th Indian Infantry Brigade of the responsibility of probing that area. Meanwhile, the 64th Brigade had reached Sainggaung and its Gurkha battalion, 1/6 GR, was at Kongyi from where it was patrolling south-westwards towards Shwebo with a view to placing blocks on its eastern exits.

By 4 January, when the 2nd British Division was closing in on Shwebo, and its guns could be heard by units of the 19th Indian Division, the latter were cutting off Japanese escape routes from Shwebo leading east to the Irrawaddy and south to Mandalay. By 5 January the 62nd Indian Infantry Brigade had moved into the Myemun area and relieved the 64th Indian Infantry Brigade of the responsibility for probing the area of the Irrawaddy. During this time, the 98th Indian Infantry Brigade continued its push south and 2 R Berks entered Zigon against negligible resistance on 5 January.

[21] 3/6 Rajputana Rifles War Diary, 31 December 1944.

Thus by 5 January, all the three brigades had achieved their immediate objectives. The 98th had captured Leiktu and Kanbalu, had proceeded south from there and Zigon was in its hands; the 62nd had taken Pinde and Sadwingyi, and was sending patrols to Male and Thabeikkyin on the Irrawaddy; the 64th had reached Sainggaung and was concentrating for an attack on Shwebo, which one of its units, 5 Baluch, later entered. It is necessary here to interrupt the story of the operations of the 19th Indian Division for a while and see what was happening on other divisional fronts.

THE 20TH INDIAN DIVISION FRONT

Japanese opposition to the advance of the 20th Indian Division from Mawlaik to Pyingaing was offered by a part only of the *Yamamoto Force* which stretched in a thin screen from Indaw (oil) in the north to the Kanni Chaung in the south. These troops, dispirited and having a large proportion of sick and wounded, fell back rapidly before the 20th Indian Division and rejoined the main Japanese delaying force on the road Pyingaing—Ye-U.

No real opposition was offered in the later stages of the advance of the 20th Indian Division down the two banks of the Chindwin river. As a result, by 6 January it had debouched from the hills and was faced only by a part of the *33rd Division*, then in the process of concentrating in the area of Monywa and a small part of the *31st Division* which had withdrawn south from Ye-U.

20th Indian Division Operations

The 20th Indian Division, following a period of rest and refit, had concentrated in the Kabaw Valley by the beginning of December.[22] The 80th Indian Infantry Brigade was placed under Corps command and moved to the Kalemyo area where it assumed responsibility for the area south and east of the Myittha river. The 32nd Indian Infantry Brigade, with 4/10 Gurkha Rifles of the 100th Indian Infantry Brigade under command, was ordered to cross the Chindwin at Mawlaik and to advance on the axis Indaw—Chingyaung via the Pondaung Chaung. Its primary role was to clear the hill and jungle area on the right flank of the 2nd Division during its advance down the road. But when it was clear that the Japanese were withdrawing into the Shwebo plain, the brigade was ordered to concentrate at Pyingaing. The following plan was laid down for its operations:

    (a) The whole brigade to move on the axis of the Pondaung Chaung to the area of Kyaunggyigon;
    (b) On arrival at Kyaunggyigon, the brigade to be prepared

[22] XXXIII Corps Accounts of Operations, p. 11.

to operate north to clear any Japanese positions remaining in the area Indaw—Gas Spring and simultaneously to move at least one battalion to the area Chingyaung to establish a patrol base.

The crossing was successfully completed on 10 December.[23] After a very strenuous three days' march through thick jungle, along narrow tracks which followed chaung beds in places for many miles, the brigade reached Kyaunggyigon without opposition on 13 December. Here a few Japanese troops were met and some valuable documents captured. These clearly showed that the strength and direction of the advance was not appreciated by the other party.[24]

In the meanwhile, the leading brigade of the 2nd Division had started to advance out of the Shwegyin bridgehead along the main road to Ye-U via Pyingaing and the Wainggyo Gorge. This constituted a very difficult defile, easily defensible and difficult to turn.[25] On 14 December, therefore, the 32nd Indian Infantry Brigade was ordered to establish a firm base for further operations in the area of Chingyaung and send 4/10 Gurkha Rifles across the hills to block the easternmost exit of the Wainggyo Gorge.

To Pyingaing

On 16 December, the 32nd Indian Infantry Brigade completed concentration at Chingyaung. By 17 December, 3/8 Gurkha Rifles patrols were *en route* for SL 7303, and 4/10 Gurkha Rifles had reported that Mawtongyi was clear of the Japanese. On the following day, the operations against Pyingaing village were commenced. One company of 1 Northamptons moved south and established a base at Tegyi. The patrols moved into the area of Pyingaing Village and reported Japanese bunkers and foxholes to the west. One hundred and fifteen vehicles were seen moving east on the night of 18/19 December but only fifteen were observed moving west.[26]

On 18 December, 4/10 Gurkha Rifles moved from Chingyaung towards Pyingaing to establish road-blocks and prepare ambushes. On 20 December began the first of a most successful series of ambushes when a platoon put a block on the road east of the Wainggyo Gorge at SQ 538577. A large party of Japanese troops marching in column halted on a bridge which 4/10 Gurkha Rifles was covering. The patrol opened fire from a range of 25 yards, fifty[27] Japanese were killed and many more wounded. The Gurkhas

[23] *Ibid.*
[24] A Short History of 20th Indian Division by Major General D. D. Gracey (MSS), 601/1787/H.
[25] *Ibid.*
[26] XXXIII Corps Account of Operations, *op. cit.*
[27] Forty according to Corps despatch; fifty in 20th Division War Diary.

suffered very few casualties and the Japanese were taken completely by surprise. This action enabled the 6th Brigade of the 2nd Division to advance on to Ye-U against only minor opposition.[28]

As mentioned earlier, the tasks for the formations in the XXXIII Corps were defined on 20 December. According to that decision, taken by the Corps Commander in consultation with his formation commanders, the 20th Indian Division was to cross the Irrawaddy after capturing Monywa and then operate against Mandalay from the south-west.[29] Its Operation Order No. 7 was issued the next day to implement the above decision. The intention was that the division would capture Monywa and secure its airfield. The advance was to be carried out on two axes. On the left the 32nd Indian Infantry Brigade Group was to march by an easterly route, Pyingaing—Palusawa—Songon—Wetye—Budalin. On the right, the 20th Indian Division, less the 32nd Indian Infantry Brigade Group, was to move via Kalewa—Kado—Maukkadaw and thence by the line of the river Chindwin to Monywa. The 100th Indian Infantry Brigade was to lead the advance down the Chindwin and to concentrate in the area Maukkadaw. 2 Border was to move from Chaungzon to Maukkadaw. 4/10 Gurkha Rifles was to hold a firm base in the area Pyingaing until released by the 2nd Division, after which it was also to go to Maukkadaw. The Division Headquarters Group was to follow the 100th Indian Infantry Brigade Group to Maukkadaw. The 80th Indian Infantry Brigade Group was to remain where it was until ordered to move forward. Royal Engineers Group was also to move to the area Maukkadaw and improve the road Kado—Maukkadaw and then prepare to operate the river-craft and ferry service from Maukkadaw to the selected points of landing downstream.

To Maukkadaw

By 25 December, the 32nd Indian Infantry Group, having completed its concentration in Pyingaing, had reached Zalokma on the southward march to join the rest of the 20th Indian Division which had commenced to move forward from the Kabaw Valley.[30] The 100th Indian Infantry Brigade collected 2 Border which had been under the command of the Corps for traffic control at Chaungzon, and commenced its move towards Maukkadaw on the Chindwin, 17 miles south-west of Pyingaing on the 24th, reaching that area on the 27th. 4/10 Gurkha Rifles was to rejoin the brigade as soon as it was released by the 2nd Division. The divisional headquarters closed at Khampat on 25 December and left

---

[28] A Short History of 20th Indian Division, *op. cit.*
[29] See Op. Instruction No. 11 of XXXIII Corps.
[30] XXXIII Corps Account of Operations, Vol. III.

for Maukkadaw, but was held up by road demolition and could not open there till the morning of 31 December.

The 32nd Indian Infantry Brigade moving on all-pack basis reached Gwedaukkaing on 28 December and Palusawa without incident on 30 December, its advance being directed on Budalin, an important Japanese communication centre, 54 miles south-west of Maukkadaw. The Japanese did not oppose these columns with any show of force, and whatever troops were met on the route were probably withdrawing on Monywa.

As no threat could now be expected in the 80th Brigade area, the brigade group commenced its move to Maukkadaw on 29 December. To ensure the protection of the western flank of the 20th Indian Division, two companies of 3/1 Gurkha Rifles were ordered to move down the line of the Chindwin until they made contact with the IV Corps troops who were advancing down the Gangaw Valley. They moved across the very difficult country between Kalemyo and the west bank of the Chindwin, reaching the river at Mingin on 31 December. One company fought a very successful action at Myaunggon with a party of the Japanese troops and inflicted comparatively heavy casualties on them. After this the Japanese did not interfere with the 20th Indian Division's movements in this area.

Kyaukhlega

While these operations were taking place, the 100th Indian Infantry Brigade, Divisional Headquarters and later the 80th Indian Infantry Brigade were busy concentrating at Kyaukhlega on the east bank of the Chindwin, some 17 miles south of Maukkadaw. The concentration could have been accomplished easily if it had been possible to build a mechanical transport road along the east bank. But owing to some very hilly country intersected by numerous chaungs it was decided that the quickest way of getting from Maukkadaw to Kyaukhlega was by ferrying across to the west bank opposite Maukkadaw, driving down to opposite Kyaukhlega and then ferrying back to the east bank to Kyaukhlega itself.[31] This entailed crossing and recrossing the river, giving many Indian soldiers their first ride in amphibious craft or the Dukws. Animal transport, however, continued along the roadless east-bank to Kyaukhlega. Thanks to the magnificent work of all concerned, the concentration at Kyaukhlega, according to plan, was completed in the quickest possible time, and the 100th Indian Infantry Brigade was concentrated there by 3 January.

Whilst this operation (bisecting a loop in the Chindwin) was

---

[31] A Short History of 20th Indian Division, *op. cit.*

being carried out, one company of 3/1 Gurkha Rifles was given the detached mission of clearing the west bank of the Chindwin south of Kalewa. This company reached Kin on 30 December to establish a patrol base. Coming under the command of the 100th Indian Infantry Brigade, this company was known thereafter as 'Deancol' so long as it operated on the west bank.

Resistance at Budalin

Meanwhile, on the left, the 32nd Indian Infantry Brigade was making good progress in its advance towards Budalin. On 3 January it had been instructed to capture the place.[32] On that day one company of 9/14 Punjab was at Ledi with a patrol at Nyaunggon, and one company of 3/8 Gurkha Rifles was at Maungdaung with a patrol at Siba. The brigade was ordered to assemble in this area on 4 January. It made rapid strides, and while 9/14 Punjab's pursuit column had reached a point 8 miles from Budalin, on 3 January, the rest of the brigade also arrived in the area the next day. It was reported that the place was strongly defended, and that all residents had been cleared out and only Japanese soldiers were inside the town in bunkers.[33]

On 4 January, a patrol from 1 Northamptons drew fire from a position astride the road at 522188, and despatched a company to clear the position by dusk. This was done and the Northamptons continued to push on. Next morning their forward company (2 Company) was held up on the outskirts of Budalin by light machine-gun and grenade discharger fire from the direction of the Post Office area at 0900 hours. The attack was pressed on in this direction and the Northamptons made some progress but the Japanese continued to hold the position. On 6 January, however, the Northamptons made a surprise night attack, pushed back the Japanese outpost and seized the line of the railway and the railway station in the north of the town.

Meanwhile 9/14 Punjab had reached a point 4 miles to the south-west of Budalin, on the road to Monywa. Next morning they sent a message that a Japanese lorry was approaching their position from the direction of Monywa. It was later shot up and captured.[34] From the documents captured it was discovered that this was an engineer lorry which was on its way from Monywa to blow up the bridge between Budalin and Ye-U. Evidently it was too late.

Budalin Captured

While the Northamptons entrenched themselves in the north

---

[32] See Appendix D to 32nd Ind. Infantry Bde. WD for January, 1945.
[33] 32nd Ind. Inf. Bde. WD, January 1945.
[34] *Ibid.*, 5 January 1945.

of the town, and 9/14 Punjab held a position to the west, 3/8 Gurkha Rifles pushed to the south and south-east of the town to block the exits and stage attacks from that side. Thus, by 7 January, the town was completely surrounded. In an endeavour to deceive the forward troops the Japanese resorted to frequent changes in their positions, and for the next three days very little progress was made. The defenders, estimated at 200 strong, were skilfully disposed and well dug in, with extensive bunkers in and on the fringe of the town.

For the next three days skirmishes were reported, and the 32nd Indian Infantry Brigade was able to make very little headway. However, on the morning of 10 January, two platoons of 1 Northamptons, sweeping from the north of Budalin, reached 535181 without any contact with the Japanese. By 1050 hours Budalin was found clear. 1 Northamptons established itself in the west half of Budalin and 3/8 Gurkha Rifles in the east half with platoons at Myaukkyi, Thabyebindaw and Ywashe. In the 9/14 Punjab area Kyauk-o was found clear in the morning. Budalin then fell to the Indian brigade after a week's fierce fighting, but if armour were available the place would have fallen in 24 hours.[35] The success of this attack was largely due to a left hook put in on the town by 1 Northamptons which succeeded in exerting pressure in the rear of the Japanese, forcing them to give up their positions. They had resisted almost to the last man—only fifteen having escaped. But this garrison of a few determined men had held up the progress of a whole brigade for six days.

In the meantime 9/14 Punjab was busy clearing various Japanese patrols from the villages south and west of Budalin and north of the road, which was done in the course of the next few days.

The next task of the 32nd Brigade was defined as the capture of Monywa, while the 100th Brigade was directed on Ayadaw in the Shwebo plain.

THE FALL OF SHWEBO

Thus in the beginning of January, all was set for the capture of Shwebo. The position on 5 January may be summarised as follows:—

The 2nd Division crossed the Mu river after capturing Ye-U on 2 January. Kabo weir had been captured intact on 31 December and the 2nd Division was now ready to make a dash for Shwebo and attack it from the north-west.

The 19th Indian Division had taken Leiktu and Kanbalu. Zigon had been entered on the 5th, and the 64th Indian Infantry

---

[35] A Short History of 20th Indian Division. *Op. cit.*

Brigade had reached Kongyi. Patrols were probing the Male and Thabeikkyin area on the Irrawaddy. The 98th Indian Infantry Brigade was approaching Shwebo from the north, the 2nd Division from the north-west and west, and the 64th Indian Infantry Brigade from the east. Shwebo was thus surrounded practically on three sides. In fact a race was going on between the two divisions, the 2nd Division and the 19th Indian Division, for Shwebo.

At about this time, Major-General Rees had urged the 64th Brigade to Onbauk instructing it to patrol both westwards to Shwebo and eastwards to the Irrawaddy.[36] While engaged on this duty the brigade experienced stiff resistance in Myothit area where the Japanese had a dump. To overcome this opposition 5 Baluch was asked to do a left hook round Myothit. This move was successful and Myothit was captured the next morning by 1/6 Gurkha Rifles.

The way to Shwebo was now clear. Immediately after this, 5 Baluch was asked to proceed forthwith to Shwebo. The War Diary of the 19th Indian Division for 7 January records at 2110 hours: "64th Brigade ordered to instruct 5 Baluch to leave one company at their present location (Minbe) and move the battalion less that company into Shwebo immediately."[37] Perhaps it was not known at that time, that a patrol from 5 Baluch had already entered Shwebo from the eastern outskirt that afternoon. The next entry in the Diary says: "Patrol 5 Baluch entered Shwebo this afternoon. Stragglers only encountered so far." The rest of the battalion less one company moved into Shwebo the same night. The Baluch Regiment of the 19th Indian Division thus won the race for Shwebo, though only by a short-head, as the 2nd Division troops, now only a few miles from the town, entered it the next day from the north-west. The town was finally cleared by 10 January. In these operations the 19th Indian Division was provided excellent artillery support by the batteries of the 4th Indian Field Regiment.[38]

2nd Division Delayed

In fact it was intended that the 2nd Division would capture Shwebo, but it was delayed by a few hours. This is how it happened According to Operation Instruction No. 9 of 6 January, the plan for 6-8 January was that the 2nd Division would capture Shwebo by advancing on a two-brigade front, the 4th Infantry Brigade on the right and the 5th Infantry Brigade on the left. The 4th Brigade

---

[36] Verbal orders given to Commander 64th Brigade were:
    (a) As soon as possible establish 64th Brigade near Onbauk and get the air-strip ready for use earliest possible.
    (b) Send patrols to Shwebo and to Irrawaddy. (19th Indian Division War Diary Appx. A, January 1945).
[37] War Diary 19th Indian Division, 7 January 1945.
[38] 4th Ind Field Regt W/D January 1945, and Op. Instruction No. 7 of 9 January.

was to advance on the axis Bitagagya—Tonzu—Nyaungbintha—Shwebo, and the 5th Brigade on the axis Ye-U—Myindaung—canal and road crossing at 2420, and thence to Shwebo canal and Shwebo.

On the 6th, there was no opposition; the 4th Brigade advanced down the Ye-U—Shwebo road and captured the air-strip at SR 2012, while the 5th Brigade on its left flank had taken up the advance down the line of the main Shwebo canal. On the 7th, however, both brigades encountered some opposition, but nonetheless continued their thrust. First, the 4th Brigade met some 40 Japanese in a village and drove them from it. Advancing a little, it found another party at Payan and engaged it. Similarly the 5th Brigade reached Myingatha, 7 miles north-west of Shwebo, and having advanced 10 miles during the day, halted for the night. On the same day, the 2nd Division also suffered an air attack directed by the Japanese on 7 Worcester Regiment and on the Tank Column. Three persons were wounded and three vehicles damaged. It was because of this type of opposition met on the northern approaches to Shwebo that the 2nd Division had to halt a few miles short of the town on 7 January, while the 19th Indian Division troops entered it from the eastern side.

However, the 2nd Division entered Shwebo the next day (8 January) and between them the two divisions (the 19th Indian and 2nd British) started clearing the place. Meanwhile, on 8 January some troops of the 98th Indian Infantry Brigade (19th Indian Division) were moved on Yameiktha in order to block Shwebo from the north-east. 1 Assam was ordered to move in mechanical transport to Myothit and report to the 64th Indian Infantry Brigade for giving help to block Japanese escape route to the east and south from Shwebo. Meanwhile 5 Baluch less one company carried on mopping operations in Shwebo.

Mopping up in Shwebo

On the 2nd Division front 1 RS of the 4th Brigade cleared opposition at south Payan suffering the loss of one tank, and then pushed on for a mile or so when further resistance stopped its advance. During the day the 5th Brigade contacted the 48th Indian Infantry Brigade in the area of the road junction at SR 3610.[39]

On 9 January, the advance by the 4th and 5th Brigades continued, and by nightfall, the northern half of Shwebo was fully cleared. The defenders endeavoured to hold the line of the moat, which surrounded the town, but 1 RS advancing down the main road seized intact the bridge at SR 355008 and then came under heavy

---

[39] In the meantime, the 6th Brigade having completed their hand-over to the 268th Brigade at the Kabo weir, withdrew to concentrate in divisional reserve.

fire from the east. On the other axis, the 5th Brigade maintained steady progress along the old Mu canal until it reached the outskirts of the town, when machine-gun fire held it up in the area of the north-west corner of the moat, which it started crossing at 1345 hours. At 1550 hours two companies were across the moat with tanks in support, after clearing mines from the roads. Only sniper opposition was encountered here. By 1730 hours the Worcesters had cleared the north-west corner of Shwebo and contact was established with 5 Baluch of the 19th Indian Division, who had sent two companies to the western side of Shwebo. 1 Camerons, then clearing the line of the railway north of Shwebo, was held up by a position in Ta-Nawngwin at SR 3801, and in a chaung to the right of the railway. The 64th and 98th Indian Infantry Brigades of the 19th Indian Division also continued mopping up operations in their respective areas. In addition, 1 Assam cleared Shwebo airfield which was in the Allied hands by nightfall. The day's fighting resulted in 24 Japanese being killed and 4 taken as prisoners.

On 10 January, 1/8 LF overcame the resistance on the 4th Brigade front at Seikkun and pushing on to the crossroads at SW 3696 established contact with 1 RS operating on the left flank. The Worcesters continued to clear the town and liquidated all opposition inside it. By 1130 hours, the Shwebo area was completely cleared, the Japanese having lost another 34 killed and six taken prisoners. Meanwhile 1 Assam had continued to block the east and south exits from Shwebo.

19TH INDIAN DIVISION'S ACHIEVEMENT

The achievement of the 19th Indian Division up to the fall of Shwebo was a proud one. The capture of Shwebo marked the end of a 400-mile march from the Chindwin bridgehead at Sittaung. This remarkable march, completed in only five weeks and ending in the capture of Shwebo, sheds lustre on this Indian division, which had gone into action for the first time. It did not only fight its way through Japanese rear-guards, but also battled against natural obstacles and difficulties through one of the worst campaigning country in the world. It traversed the first half of the way not on a road but a Japanese-made track, long stretches of which had been washed away during the monsoon, and which wound through precipitous hills thickly covered with jungle. Often the men, British and Indian, manhandled guns and lorries for miles, and on one occasion mules were lowered down a cliff face by ropes. Supply was entirely by air.[40]

[40] XXXIII Corps, Account of Operations.

ACHIEVEMENT OF THE 2ND DIVISION

The 2nd British Division's performance was no less glorious. From the bridgehead over the Chindwin it had advanced 130 miles to the outskirts of Shwebo in 20 days inflicting 430 casualties on the Japanese in killed, wounded or captured and made its way round or repaired 226 damaged or broken bridges, cleared the road of 500 fallen tree obstacles, and built seven air-strips.

Before we close this phase of the operations up to the capture of Shwebo, it is necessary to mention briefly the role of two other units of the Fourteenth Army. Their role, though not very spectacular, was nevertheless important inasmuch as their supporting operations were essential for the success of the more forward formations. These two units were the 268th Indian Infantry Brigade and the 254th Indian Tank Brigade.

268TH INDIAN INFANTRY BRIGADE

Before the 268th Indian Infantry Brigade reverted from the IV Corps on 27 December, its task in its march from Yuwa on the Chindwin had been to clear the hill and jungle country between the axis of advance of the 2nd Division and the 19th Indian Division. By 28 December, the Tactical Brigade Headquarters with Mahendra Dal Regiment was at Kongyi, with one company moving on Kyunhla. 4/3 Madras was reported at Thetkegyin and was then moving on Kyunhla. On 31 December the Mahendra Dal made contact with the forward troops of the 19th Indian Division in the Kyigon area. It was common talk in the brigade (and no doubt a matter on which the men prided themselves) that the most difficult country fell more often to them than to any other formation.

On 4 January the brigade relieved the 6th Brigade of the 2nd Division in the area of the Kabo weir and passed under the command of that division. The brigade rested a few days at Kabo, battalions sending out patrols to reconnoitre the country ahead. During the long marches, unit transport consisted of mules and bullocks, and for some considerable time, even elephants.

254TH INDIAN TANK BRIGADE

During this phase of operations, the 254th Indian Tank Brigade had been assigned the task of concentrating two regiments of armour and the 18th (SP) Field Regiment Royal Artillery, less one battery, across the Chindwin. This was carried out by concentrating the brigade to the south of the Kabaw Valley in the Indainggale area and then moving up to Kalewa on tracks and then ferry to Shwegyin. This concentration was carried out as fast as conditions would permit, and by 30 December the two regiments of armour were complete at Mutaik.

On 2 January, the Fourteenth Army placed the 11 Cavalry under the command of XXXIII Corps and ordered it to concentrate at Kalewa forthwith. On the same day a signal was issued to the formations under command, stating that no sub-allotment of tank units would be made to formations unless a definite task was envisaged. This was necessitated by the need for conserving the already limited tank engine hourage and track mileage for the more decisive phases of operations to come. The tank brigade was, therefore, to move from Shwegyin to the Kaduma area on transporters. That this restriction was likely to impose a delay of up to 48 hours on local operations was accepted.

IMPORTANCE OF THE CAPTURE OF YE-U AND SHWEBO

With the capture of Ye-U and Shwebo, all the formations under the XXXIII Corps moved into the Shwebo plain and could now look forward to a period of operations away from the hill and jungle country through which they had fought continuously since the battle of Kohima in April 1944. If the Japanese army gave battle, here was the opportunity to defeat it in open country and to carry out Lieut-General Slim's intention, which was to bring the Japanese army to battle and to destroy it on the Mandalay plain.

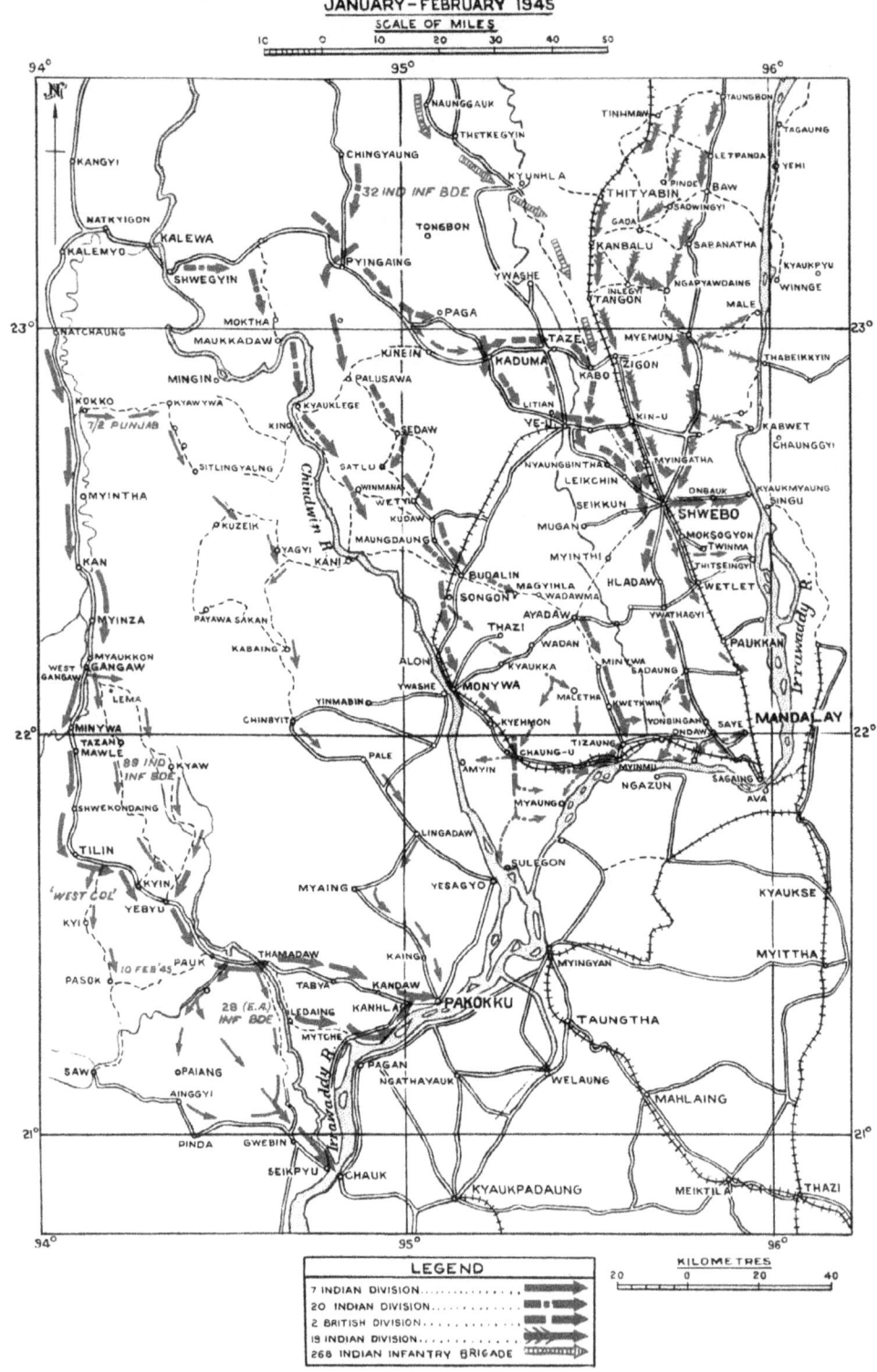

CHAPTER IX

XXXIII Corps Advance to the Irrawaddy (Contd.)

The advance of the 19th Indian Division towards Shwebo and the fall of Shwebo have just been described. This division had met with stubborn Japanese resistance astride the road and railway north of Leiktu, which had been overcome on 1 January by the 98th Indian Infantry Brigade. The other two brigades (62nd and 64th Indian Infantry Brigades) of this division had also moved south in parallel columns and had fought several actions, notably at Pinde, Baw and Sadwingyi. The 64th Indian Infantry Brigade, in the lead, had sent 1/6 Gurkha to block the eastern exits to Shwebo. This battalion had met and overcome considerable opposition at Myothit, but while the Gurkhas were thus engaged, 5/10 Baluch had entered Shwebo on 7 January, beating the 2nd British Division in the race for that town just by a day.

During its advance south, the 19th Indian Division had sent detachments eastwards to the Irrawaddy at Male and Kabwet. While Shwebo was being cleared by the 64th Indian Infantry Brigade, the troops of the 62nd Indian Infantry Brigade at Male and Kabwet had moved on to Kyaukmyaung, preparatory to crossing the Irrawaddy.

In the present chapter it is proposed to narrate the operations of the XXXIII Corps up to the eve of the main crossings in the second week of February. The actual crossings by the two Corps will be described in the next chapter. As, however, the 19th Indian Division crossings fall, chronologically, within the scope of this chapter, they will be noticed here.

JAPANESE DISPOSITIONS

The capture of Ye-U and Budalin must have led the Japanese to think that a full-scale attack on the Shwebo plain was impending with the crossing of the Irrawaddy and the capture of Mandalay as the main objectives. The capture of Shwebo town on 7/8 January must have confirmed this view. The Japanese *33rd Army* then comprised *15th, 31st, 33rd* and *53rd Divisions*. Of these, however, only the *31st Division* might be considered as comparatively fresh, with a strength of approximately half that of a full Japanese division. The *15th Division* had failed to check the advance of the 19th Indian Division and was sadly depleted in numbers, while of the

33rd Division only the *213th Regiment* and a small part of the *214th Regiment* remained on the east bank of the Chindwin (*215th Regiment* complete and the greater part of *214th Regiment* had been transferred to the Gangaw Valley). The *53rd Division* was described by NCAC as "a spent force", which had never provided stiff opposition during its steady withdrawal down the railway corridor, and even allowing for replacements and a certain amount of refitting, this division was not regarded as a formidable fighting force.[1]

These forces were disposed to make the best use of their scant numbers. The defence of the immediate approaches to Mandalay, with a forward line at Shwebo, was entrusted to the *31st Division*, as yet only lightly committed. The defence of Monywa and the western approaches was entrusted to the *33rd Division* whose only effective troops in this area were *1st* and *3rd Battalions* of *213th Regiment* strengthened by *1st Battalion 138th Regiment* of *31st Division*. The apparently simple task of holding the line of the Irrawaddy north of Singu (on the eastern bank) was allotted to the *15th Division* with the *33rd Division* in reserve, immediately north of Mandalay.

From these dispositions it was apparent that the Japanese had not fully appreciated the weight against them, particularly that of the 20th Indian Division which they had at first considered to be merely a detached column. It was also apparent that they had planned to preserve the line of the Irrawaddy river.

On the 2nd Division Front

The Japanese troops who had opposed the crossing of the Mu river at Ye-U fell back to cover the western approaches to Shwebo. These troops, *1st* and *3rd Battalions* of *124th Regiment*, amounted to less than 1000 men in all and after the capture of Shwebo they broke contact completely to fall back on prepared defences stretching from Legyi to the northern end of the Sagaing Hills. Here, in defences planned to accommodate much greater numbers, they joined the *138th Regiment* and were themselves joined by the *58th Regiment* (less three battalions) which had similarly broken contact with the 19th Indian Division at Shwebo. Opposition to the 2nd Division, therefore, after the capture of Shwebo was confined to minor action until the defensive line was reached.[2]

THE 2ND DIVISION AFTER THE CAPTURE OF SHWEBO

Since the Allied troops were advancing rapidly, the air force could not afford them close air support during the second week of

[1] XXXIII Corps, Account of Operations, Vol. III, pp. 14-15.
[2] Ibid.

January 1945. The Japanese air force took advantage of this fact and made several hit-and-run raids on Ye-U and Shwebo areas between 6 and 13 January. These raids were, however, abortive in the main. The bridge over the Mu river at Ye-U remained intact, though four Allied planes were destroyed on the ground on 12 January.

From 10 to 16 January the 2nd Division carried out wide mobile patrols. The 4th Brigade continued to advance on the axis of the Shwebo—Sagaing railway, and the 5th Brigade on the axis of the Shwebo—Mandalay road, with 2 Recce Regiment patrolling to the flanks on both the axes. The 6th Brigade concentrated forward into the Shwebo area and a carrier patrol contacted forward troops of the 20th Indian Division on the inter-divisional boundary at the road junction at SV 9398, on 13 January. On 14 January at 1630 hours, leading troops of 2 Reconnaissance Regiment occupied Sadaung position.

By 16 January, 2 Reconnaissance had patrolled into the villages east and west of the road and reported them clear, and made contacts with certain positions which appeared to be mere outposts. By the end of the day, two squadrons were established at Kyamingyi and one squadron moved to Samun. Patrols probing the line of the railway reached a point within 1,000 yards of Padu, but were forced to withdraw by heavy shelling from 105-mm guns.

On 17 January, the 6th Brigade concentrated at Taganan, and the following day, the 4th Brigade concentrated at Sadaung and the 5th Brigade at Wetlet. 2 Reconnaissance maintained continuous pressure on the Japanese positions contacted on the previous day, occupied them following the Japanese withdrawal, and reported that patrols from Padu in the east, to the Mu river in the west, had failed to make contact. By 18 January, the leading troops of the 2nd Division had reached the line approximately fifteen miles south of the position of the leading troops of the 20th Indian Division in the Monywa area, and approximately thirty miles south of the leading troops of the 19th Indian Division at Kyaukmyaung.

Although a counter-move by the Japanese was a remote possibility, nevertheless both flanks of the 2nd Division were dangerously open. The eastern flank was the more vulnerable. While the rest of the XXXIII Corps was progressing to the assault positions preparatory to crossing the Irrawaddy, the 2nd Division was directed, by Operation Instruction No. 11, dated 18 January, to give the Japanese no rest and to prosecute the offensive as vigorously as possible with the maximum of one brigade group. In order to carry out this task the following method was chalked out:— the 4th Brigade Group would assemble at Sadaung and advance to capture Ondaw. Bradforce, which had been formed on 12 January under Lt. Colonel J. M. K. Bradford, Officer Commanding, 2 Reconnaissance Regiment RAC, in order to maintain contact with the Japanese, would secure the eastern flank of the 2nd Division in the area Yemyet In Lake—northern end of Sagaing Taungdan Hills. 8 Gordons would advance on the axis Sadaung—Paukka to stop any Japanese withdrawal south along the river Mu or east of Myinmu. The 5th Brigade Group occupied positions in the Wetlet area and the 6th Brigade Group in the Hladaw area, and were responsible for the security of the divisional area within their respective boundaries.

On 19 January, the 4th Brigade commenced the relief of 2 Reconnaissance in the area west of the Yemyet and started its advance down the main divisional axis, with 2 Norfolk established one mile south of Yinmagyin. During the day, patrols reported the villages of Nyaungbinwun LF 67, and Legyi clear.

On 28 January 2 Norfolk leading the 4th Brigade advance, reached Wetthabok. The 5th Brigade, in the meantime, commenced patrolling the west bank of the Irrawaddy, in the rear of 2 Reconnaissance, in order to mop up any Japanese troops who might be left in this area, and to prevent infiltration from the east bank of the Irrawaddy.

On 21 January, 2 Norfolk met a little opposition in the Wetthabok and Yonbingan areas. This was rapidly liquidated, and Japanese artillery, hitherto little used, replied by firing 200 rounds, all of which fell wide off the mark and did no damage.

On the 5th Brigade front, 1 Camerons reported Kugyi and Yegamo to be clear.

At this stage, 100 Anti-Tank Regiment (Gordons) was used in an infantry role to operate patrols along the Sagaing—Monywa railway south-east of Ondaw. On 22 January they reported Ngatayaw railway station clear, and the 4th Brigade commenced patrolling in the area of Ondaw village, where the little opposition it met was confined to Japanese artillery fire. The gun positions located on the north-east corner of Ondaw area were bombed by 12 Hurribombers and 8 rocket-firing Hurricanes.

Japanese on the 19th Division Front

To enable the Japanese *15th Division* to escape across the Irrawaddy the defence of Kanbalu and the north and eastern approaches to Shwebo was undertaken by *1st* and *2nd Battalions 58th Regiment* and *2nd Battalion 124th Regiment* of the *31st Division*. After a determined resistance they were outflanked by the 19th Indian Division and broke contact after the fall of Shwebo. These troops, numbering in all some 1500 men, withdrew to prepared positions in the Sagaing Hills and then rejoined the remainder of the *31st Division* disposed for the defence of the approaches to Mandalay.³

As the 19th Indian Division turned its entire attention to the clearing of the west bank of the Irrawaddy from Thabeikkyin to Singu and the establishment of bridgeheads across the river, the Japanese were forced to distribute the already depleted *15th Division* on a wide front with *67th Regiment* and *1st Battalion 60th Regiment* in the area of Thabeikkyin, *51st Regiment* in the river bend between Kabwet and Kyaukmyaung and *2nd* and *3rd Battalions 60th Regiment* west of the river south of Kyaukmyaung. All crossing points were watched by Japanese patrols.

The reaction to the crossings at Thabeikkyin and Kyaukmyaung (described in the following paragraphs) was not immediate. This was due to the considerable dispersal of the Japanese troops and in some measure to their determination to maintain forces on the east bank of the river both in the neighbourhood of Kabwet and south of Kyaukmyaung. The reaction, when it did come, followed a typical pattern, that of piecemeal attacks as reinforcements arrived. The first really concerted effort did not take place until the night of 22/23 January by which time the 19th Indian Division was prepared to give it a hot reception.⁴

19TH INDIAN DIVISION CROSSES THE IRRAWADDY

We have described how on 6 January, the 64th Indian Infantry Brigade had met with opposition at Myothit, how 5 Baluch was sent round Myothit to do a hook, and how, after the capture of Myothit on 7 January by 1/6 Gurkha Rifles, 5 Baluch had gone to Shwebo and captured the town. During the next two or three days while 5 Baluch was engaged in mopping up operations at Shwebo, 1/6 Gurkha Rifles mounted a left hook and established blocks south of the town. The remainder of the brigade moved up to Minbe. Artillery support was provided by the 4th Indian Field Regiment. The 98th Indian Infantry Brigade was still some distance from Shwebo, but it moved towards Kin-U and captured it on 8 January after overcoming some resistance. The Japanese escaping from the village were caught at a road-block, one mile south of Kin-U, by 4/4 Gurkha Rifles. News from the 62nd Indian Infantry Brigade was not plentiful but it was established that two companies of 2 Welch were at Thabeikkyin on the west bank of the Irrawaddy, with one company at Kongyi. On 7 January, the 64th Indian Infantry Brigade was ordered to secure the west bank of the Irrawaddy at

³ XXXIII Corps, Account of Operations, Vol. III, p. 18.
⁴ *Ibid.*

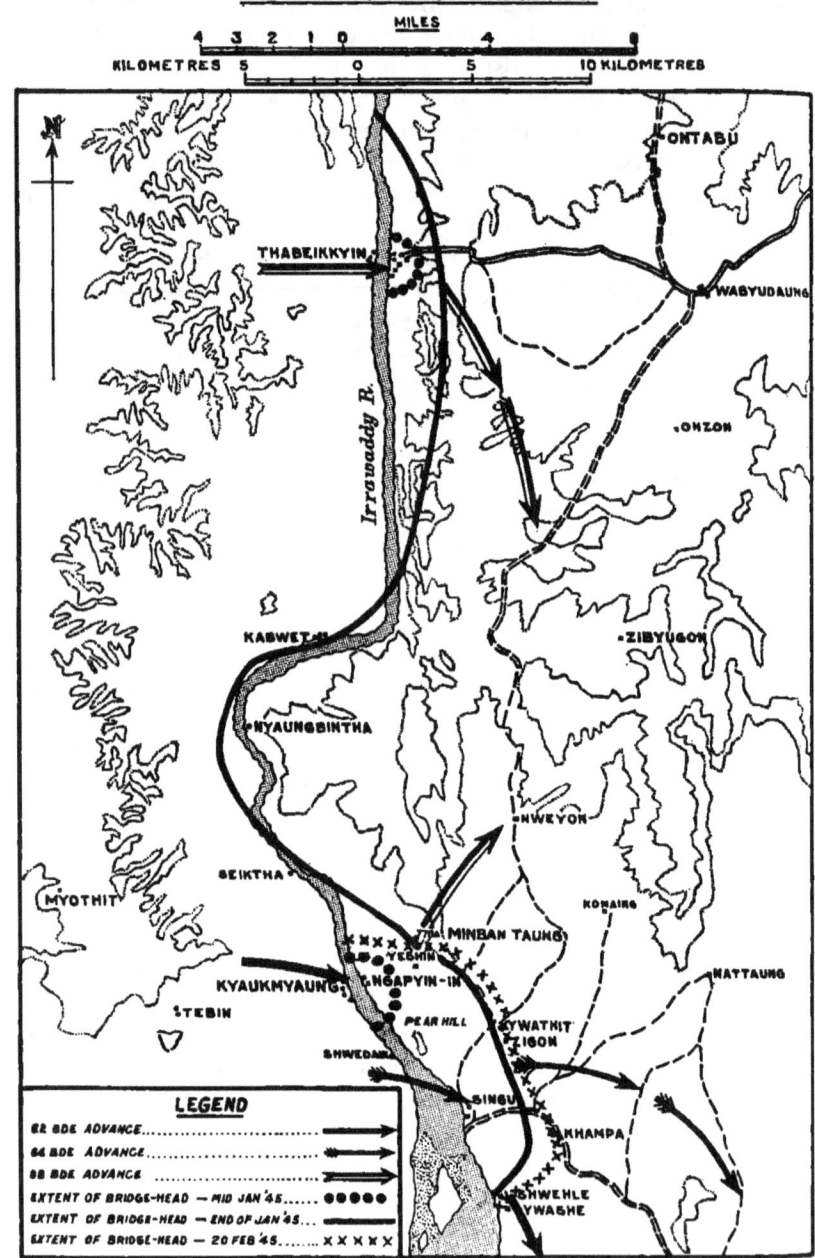

Kabwet. The following day 4/6 Gurkha Rifles was en route to Kabwet with the rest of the brigade closing on Kongyi.

On the 62nd Indian Infantry Brigade front, on 9 January, 3/6 Rajputana Rifles operating east of Onbauk had a clash with a platoon of the Japanese, who were established in a nulla west of the village. Two vehicles of D Company which were leading were knocked out and the company was held up. An attempt by B Company to carry out a right flanking move and come in from the rear was foiled, and both companies were meeting heavy machine-gun fire from an extremely well-sited position. The next morning, however, the position was found evacuated. 2 Welch pushed a patrol across the Irrawaddy at Thabeikkyin and encountered a Japanese bunker position with light machine-guns on the east bank of the river. A column of 4/6 Gurkha Rifles approached Kabwet village from the west but was held up by heavy machine-gun and rifle fire when 150 yards short of the first houses. After an intensive artillery bombardment, B Company attacked vigorously and killed seven Japanese and cleared 8 bunkers in west Kabwet. The Japanese, estimated at 50 strong, suddenly launched a furious counter-attack which was however beaten off at some cost to them.[5]

By 11 January, the 62nd Indian Infantry Brigade had probed the line of the Irrawaddy from Male to as far south as Makauk. On this day, 3 Rajputana Rifles entered Kyaukmyaung in the morning, having cleared out some Japanese who had held it the night before. Thereafter it was given the task of extensive patrolling north and south of Kyaukmyaung and observing and patrolling the far bank with a view to selecting a suitable crossing place for the 64th Indian Infantry Brigade, which was to cross over first and form the bridgehead. On this evening at 1800 hours the Brigade Defence Company, 1/15 Punjab, endeavoured to cross the river in country craft at Yadaw. The crossing was opposed and 1/15 Punjab suffered 3 casualties.[6]

The following day, 1/15 Punjab occupied Kyaukmyaung village and sent further patrols to the east bank, where, on encountering heavy fire, they withdrew. During the night of 12/13 January, C Company sent three patrols across the river. Two met with opposition but the third succeeded in penetrating inland for about 100 yards without hearing anything.

On 11 January, 4/4 Gurkha Rifles of the 98th Indian Infantry Brigade was ordered to relieve the 2 Welch detachment at Thabeikkyin. It was to patrol east of the river and establish a bridgehead on the east bank if no undue difficulty was encountered.

---

[5] 19th Indian Division War Diary, January 1945, and XXXIII Corps Account of Operations, p. 19.
[6] *Ibid.*

On the same day reports had indicated that a patrol from 2 Welch had crossed to Singu to investigate the village. It saw no movement in the area, and established a standing patrol on the Kyungyi Island at SW 7394 on the 13th.[7]

All this while the 64th Indian Infantry Brigade had been engaged in mopping up operations in the Shwebo area. On 11 January, it had also started a move towards Kyaukmyaung leaving 1/6 Gurkha Rifles to man the blocks south of Shwebo.

4/4 Gurkha Rifles had been ordered on 12 January to cross at least one company to the east bank as soon as possible. A plan had therefore been made to cross the river during the night of 12/13 January but had to be postponed owing to the non-arrival of boats at the rendezvous.[8] Nothing of importance happened during the day, 13 January, but things began to move rapidly during the night when the crossing commenced at 2300 hours, and C Company completed its crossing unopposed about a mile south of Thabeikkyin by 0300 hours in the early morning of 14 January. Other companies crossed later, and by midday on the 15th three companies were established there.[9] The leading company encountered a bunker position at 705379 just to the south of the village and cleared it. The Japanese withdrew to the village which was, however, captured on the next day (16 January) and a bridgehead was established.

The second crossing was made on the night of 14/15 January by two companies of 1/15 Punjab, the divisional reconnaissance regiment, two miles north of Kyaukmyaung at SR 680073,[10] where a bridgehead was established in the area SR 6807 and SR 6808. Previous observation had shown that this small area on the far bank was unoccupied. This was confirmed by patrols on the night of 13 January and the spot was selected for crossing.[11] The Japanese were taken by surprise and by 2000 hours on the 15th, the bridgehead was consolidated without interference. The 64th Indian Infantry Brigade, marching rapidly from Shwebo, had by then reached the west bank. 5 Baluch crossed to the bridgehead during the night of 15/16 January. Besides a patrol clash, no opposition was met on the first night. On 16 January again there were patrol clashes, but on the morning of 17 January approximately 150 Japanese in two parties attacked the bridgehead from the north-east and the south, but were beaten off, and withdrew at 1500 hours leaving some dead behind. Operations to extend the bridgehead then commenced. 1/6 Gurkha Rifles crossed from the west bank during the night of 16/17 January, and was in position in Minban

[7] XXXIII Corps War Diary for 11 January 1945.
[8] War Diary 4/4 Gurkha Rifles, 12 January 1945.
[9] *Ibid.*, 13-15 January 1945.
[10] 62nd Brigade War Diary, 14 January 1945.
[11] 1/15 Punjab OO No. 2 dated 14-1-45.

Taung area without having made any contact with the Japanese. On the 17th night the balance of the 64th Indian Infantry Brigade also crossed to the bridgehead, and the next day it was extended in the south to the area Ngapyin-In where some fighting took place, and clashes were also reported from the area of the high ground at Minban Taung where 1/6 Gurkha Rifles had succeeded in establishing two companies.[12]

In the north the 98th Indian Infantry Brigade was carrying out operations on both the banks of the Irrawaddy. West of the Irrawaddy, in the Kabwet area, 11 Machine-Gun Sikh Battalion was experiencing difficulty as its positions had been subjected to heavy fire. One company of 8 FFR and two companies of 2 R Berks were therefore sent to help clear the Kabwet area, where resistance was confined to the east end of the village. Accordingly on 17 January 2 R Berks started liquidating Japanese positions in the jungle east of Kabwet.

Enlarging the Bridgeheads

East of the Irrawaddy, 4/4 Gurkha Rifles occupied most of Thabeikkyin on 16 January, the Japanese having withdrawn slightly eastwards. During the night of 17/18 January a company of 8 FFR crossed to Thabeikkyin to join 4/4 Gurkha Rifles. Operations to enlarge the bridgehead were continued. On the 19th a Japanese position covering the road was located 1½ miles to the east and was subjected to an air-strike. During the night two parties of Japanese troops, approximately 30 men in each, attacked Thabeikkyin area.[13]

By 19 January, the 64th Indian Infantry Brigade had moved wholly to the east bank of the Irrawaddy and operations to extend the Kyaukmyaung bridgehead were progressing well. 5 Baluch reached Ngapyin-In village against considerable opposition, which began to increase and became almost continuous when the Japanese had reinforced their troops and artillery in an endeavour to throw the Allied troops back. A detachment of 1/6 Gurkha Rifles on Minban Taung was heavily engaged in the night of 19/20 January and the position had to be reinforced on the 20th. 2 Worcesters met fairly strong opposition midway between Ngapyin-In and Yeshin on 20 and 21 January. A company of 5 Baluch occupied hill SR 7201, named Pear, after a successful air-strike. They were later reinforced by a company of 4/6 Gurkha Rifles which brought rations for them.[14]

By 22 January the bridgehead included Pear Hill in the south and outposts on the Minban Taung Hill, and Yeshin.

---
[12] War Diaries of 98th Brigade, 64th Brigade and 62nd Brigade.
[13] War Diary 64th Brigade.
[14] 62nd Brigade War Diary, 21 January 1945, 601/346/WD/Pt. III.

While two companies of 5 Baluch were on the Pear Hill, 1/6 Gurkha Rifles on Minban Taung was operating southwards. Soon after dark several determined attacks were made on the bridgehead area but they were all beaten off. In the north on the west bank of the river, there was still no sign of the Japanese withdrawing from Kabwet, although their bunker positions to the east of the village were subjected to air bombardment and ground attack almost daily. At Thabeikkyin, 4/4 Gurkha Rifles was subjected by the Japanese to heavy attacks, all of which were repulsed. Thus, by 21 January, both the bridgeheads on the east bank were firmly established, one at Thabeikkyin and the other at Ngapyin-In. For the latter bridgehead, two outpost positions had also been established, one towards the north-east on the high ground at Minban Taung and the other on Pear Hill two miles south-south-east of Ngapyin-In.

The 62nd Indian Infantry Brigade was all this time responsible for the protection of the ferry area on the west bank. It was engaged in operations south and south-west of Kyaukmyaung to clear small parties of Japanese troops who crossed over to the west bank from the east with the intention of disrupting the administrative arrangements or determining the strength of the Allied troops likely to cross over to the east.

From the intensity of Japanese attacks, it was apparent that they expected this crossing north of Mandalay to be the main one across the Irrawaddy. They were reinforcing their troops as best as they could to oppose the drive on Mandalay from the north.[15] The ruse of the Allies was thus succeeding.

THE 20TH INDIAN DIVISION TO MONYWA

While the 19th Indian Division was operating on the west bank of the Irrawaddy and preparing to cross the river, the 20th Indian Division, on the right flank of the XXXIII Corps, had been advancing southwards, east of the Chindwin river. The object of this drive was to capture Budalin and Monywa, clear up the area to the north of the confluence of the Irrawaddy and the Chindwin rivers and then to cross to the south bank of the river.[16] In pursuance of this policy, Budalin had been captured on 10 January. The Japanese had failed to appreciate the weight of this advance in the Budalin and Monywa area, and that may account for the fact that only the *213th Regiment* of the *33rd Division* was disposed there to contain the threat. In addition one battalion of the *138th Regi-*

---

[15] XXXIII Corps, Account of Operations, p. 20. See also 62nd Brigade War Diary for 21 January 1945 which mentions "enemy arriving from south in transport and carts".

[16] Its task as defined in XXXIII Corps order No. 12 was the protection of the Corps' southern flank between the Chindwin and Mu rivers.

ment of the *31st Division* was stationed to guard the Myinmu crossing place on the Irrawaddy loop where the river runs from east to west. They had also strengthened the defences of Ayadaw and Monywa, but the lack of manpower made the task of holding these positions difficult. It was clear that the fall of Monywa and the encirclement of Myinmu would force the Japanese back to their last line—the Irrawaddy.[17]

To Monywa

As described earlier, Budalin had been taken on 10 January, and by 12 January 1 Northamptons and 3/8 Gurkha Rifles were firmly established there. The 20th Indian Division was therefore free to advance on to Monywa and the Irrawaddy river. The 32nd Indian Infantry Brigade moved towards its next objective, Monywa, while the 100th Indian Infantry Brigade moved eastwards to Ayadaw.[18] Advance towards Monywa over flat country riddled with bunkers and fox-holes was started, and on a report from a patrol of 9/14 Punjab that Alon, six miles north of the town, was clear, it was occupied.[19] The airfield at Alon also fell to the Punjabis. Monywa was known to be defended and patrols were immediately despatched to determine the extent to which the Japanese had prepared defences, which were thought to be very extensive.

The plan for the capture of Monywa was that 9/14 Punjab was to advance on 15/16 January down the main axis of the road, whilst 1 Northamptons would move along the railway axis and carry out a battalion hook to the left of the city through Ywadon, and thence through the Rifle Range and hospital areas at PK 5286. In their march towards the outskirts of Monywa, they were to exterminate some Japanese penetration groups and suicide parties, the presence of which had become known from the captured documents. 3/8 Gurkha Rifles was to operate east and south through Kaingdaw and Sagyingyi to establish blocks and cut possible escape routes to the south-east.

On 14 January, a reconnaissance patrol of 3/8 Gurkha Rifles was fired at from the positions east of Kothan. On 15 January one of its companies was established at Kyauksitpon while a company of 1 Northamptons proceeded to Kyweye and a platoon was at Palingon, which had a clash with the Japanese at Kothan. In view of the stubbornness of this position an air-strike was arranged to take place before the final assault was launched. Consequently, in the afternoon of 16 January twelve aircraft bombed and strafed Kothan. This was followed by an artillery concentration. The

[17] XXXIII Corps Account of Operations, p. 21.
[18] 32nd Brigade War Diary, 12 January 1945.
[19] *Ibid.*

Japanese however hung on. A patrol of 1 Northamptons which was sent to investigate the result of the air-strike was shot at. Again a company of the Northamptons *en route* to Ywathit sent a patrol into Kothan. This patrol was also fired on from the south-east corner of the village.

Similarly 9/14 Punjab, which had taken up position west of Gwegyi, met with Japanese counter-attacks, and its progress was held up. It was found that the Gwegyi area was strongly defended by the Japanese; hence an air-strike was arranged and Hurribombers bombed and strafed Gwegyi at 1015 hours on 18 January. Two companies of 9/14 Punjab then mounted an attack at 1100 hours and secured the village by 1210 hours without loss.[20] At the same time, 1 Northamptons occupied Ywathit village after slight opposition.

Similarly a commando group of 3/8 Gurkha Rifles, about 250 strong, with the aid of 11 Cavalry, had a brush with the Japanese at Kaingdaw, and the positions west of the village and on both sides of Buga Chaung were tackled. The Japanese attempted a futile attack on the Gurkha positions at 538842 but were repulsed with loss. At Monywa, 9/14 Punjab was actively patrolling to determine the extent of the hostile defensive positions to the north of the town, and had established its companies at Chadaung and Gwegyi. To block the escape of the defenders across the Chindwin, one company of 1 Devon came forward from the 80th Indian Infantry Brigade and established stops on the west bank of the river.

By 19 January the 32nd Indian Infantry Brigade was poised for a final assault on Monywa. The Japanese had built up strong defences covering the town from the north and from the east, for Monywa was their only remaining port and administrative centre on the Chindwin. In the north, a stone bund running from the river to the main road had been converted into a series of fire positions, whilst to the east, bunkers had been built in the stop-butts of the rifle range, and a two-company position had been sited in the area of the wood beside the Pongyichaung. The approach to all these positions was over open ground, and the defenders had considerable advantage over those attacking them. The Japanese, according to information available on 19 January, were disposed as follows:—

Facing 1 Northamptons there were four positions. Some were dug in on north slopes of the Rifle Range at 518859. At least fifty Japanese were around north and west side of the wood at 538856, with one medium machine-gun covering the road to the north-east and light machine-guns in the north-east and south-east corners of

---

[20] *Ibid*, 17 January.

the wood. 20 to 25 Japanese were reported at Ledi. Finally, a dug and wired position was seen along the north edge of an unnamed village at 526849 and some Japanese troops were seen there. The only known position on the 9/14 Punjab front was along the line Setyon—main road. Three light machine-guns were located at 505852 but the Japanese strength was not known. On the 3/8 Gurkha Rifles front, approximately 70 to 80 Japanese were known to be at Kaingdaw. There was a defended position on the railway east of the village Kadogon. Twenty-five Japanese with two light machine-guns were covering a road-block at 521827 and a new position was being made at 572820. Approximately twenty Japanese were reported in the last village.

It was evident that the positions might only be successfully assaulted if heavy supporting fire from all sources was used. Hence the attack on the town began with an air-strike by the Royal Air Force. On 17 January, three squadrons of Hurribombers had bombed and strafed known positions around Monywa. On 19 January, three attacks were delivered on the Water Tower area, east of the Rifle Range and the hospital area, respectively, by 24 Hurribombers. The Water Tower area and the Rifle Range were the targets a second time on the 19th. Another air-strike was planned for the 20th, the D-Day for the final assault. On that day at 1000 hours twelve Mosquitos bombed selected targets around the town. Between 1150 and 1250 hours, 82 Hurricanes and Thunderbolts continued the attack, in the course of which rocket projectiles were used for the first time on the XXXIII Corps front.[21]

At 1300 hours the assault began. All guns in the area opened up on the Japanese positions.[22] At 1305 hours the left hand company of 1 Northamptons captured the Ledi Rifles Range and the one from the right reached houses just north of Ledi at 1330 hours against heavy fire from the bunkers. Ledi itself was not occupied till 1630 hours. An attempt on the part of 9/14 Punjab to outflank the Japanese line confronting it was, however, unsuccessful due to heavy fire from the stone bunkers. In the meantime 3/8 Gurkha Rifles had cleared Kaingdaw at 1340 hours. The final entry into the town was a great anticlimax to the feverish fighting. On 21 January there were indications that the Japanese were clearing out of the town and, on the 22nd morning, 9/14 Punjab and 3/8 Gurkha Rifles entered it without any opposition. Thus, Monywa fell after a sharp three-day battle. The Allied troops could now see what had been holding them up. There was a high embankment running at right angles to the river bank and the main road. This had been

---

[21] War Diary 32nd Brigade says:—"1 Northamptons report rocket firing planes on Rifle Butts extremely accurate."
[22] *Ibid*, for 20 January 1305 hours.

erected by the Burmans to keep the Chindwin floods out and it formed a good enough natural defence line. Behind this the Japanese had prepared bunkers of stone and wood. On the side facing 9/14 Punjab the embankment wall was buttressed with heavy chunks of stone. Bombs and shells had made craters all around the bunkers, but the bunkers had remained undamaged.

From 18 to 22 January over 200 fighter-bomber sorties were flown by 221 Group in support of the 32nd Indian Infantry Brigade and over 100 were flown on the day prior to the capture of Monywa. The success of the brigade and the battering of the defences during the three-day battle were largely the result of an attack by Thunderbolts, Mosquitos and Hurricanes. Rockets were used for the first time on this front and had the effect of demoralising the defenders.

Capture of Ayadaw, Tizaung and Myinmu

While the 32nd Indian Infantry Brigade was concentrating south of Alon and probing into the Monywa defences, 4/10 Gurkha Rifles of the 100th Indian Infantry Brigade had moved to Budalin to take over from 3/8 Gurkha Rifles of the other brigade. On 13 January the Operation Instruction No. 5 was issued entrusting the brigade with the task of capturing Ayadaw. Two groups were formed. "A" group headed by 4/10 Gurkha Rifles was to be the spear-head of the advance while "B" group with 14/13 Frontier Force Rifles as its main component was to follow immediately behind and take charge of the rear positions as the Gurkhas marched forward. In pursuance of this plan 4/10 Gurkha Rifles moved to Thapan and thence to Magyihla on 14 January. On the 15th, 4/10 Gurkha Rifles made further progress and concentrated at Wadama. On 16 January, several parties of the Japanese were located in and around Ayadaw. To liquidate these positions 24 aircraft bombed Ayadaw at 1645 hours. The Japanese estimated at 300 thereupon withdrew during the night, but a party of 4/10 Gurkha Rifles moved and succeeded in ambushing a batch of about 100 Japanese troops moving down the road to Minywa and killing twenty-five and injuring many more. On 17 January, Ayadaw was occupied at 0900 hours while Minywa was occupied the next day. On 19 January, 4/10 Gurkha Rifles was at Kwetkwin and sent patrols to Tizaung where some Japanese troops were reported to be present. Three companies of 4/10 Gurkha Rifles had a grenade battle here on the 20th and captured the village. Myinmu was invested on the 21st. During the night of 21/22 January a party of the Japanese troops attacked C Company of 4/10 Gurkha Rifles, just north of Myinmu but they were repulsed and the Gurkhas gradually closed the ring round Myinmu with the assistance of armoured cars. On 22 January, there was an air-strike on the village and it fell on the 23rd. Much equipment including many important documents was captured. A look at the position of Myinmu on the map of Burma immediately reveals its importance to the XXXIII Corps at this stage. It is on the north bank of the Irrawaddy, where the river turns west before meeting the Chindwin, and it had been chosen as the point from where the 20th Indian Division was shortly to push across the Irrawaddy. From 22 January onwards, therefore, it became this division's main front, and a crossing was made three weeks later. (See Chapter X)

Although all organised resistance in this area, north of the Irrawaddy, had ceased, the brigades were ordered not to cross the Irrawaddy at this stage. On the other hand they were to clear the northern bank of any isolated resistance that might still be there.

14 Frontier Force Rifles

In the meantime, a company of 14/13 Frontier Force Rifles had moved forward to Wunbye, two miles north-west of Myinmu, on 22 January. The place was defended and so, prior to mounting an attack, aircraft bombed the defensive positions. The air-strike could not liquidate the defences and when the Frontier Force Rifles attacked the pagoda area it met with heavy opposition and had to withdraw after suffering some casualties. The village was however cleared the next day. The main body of the Frontier Force Rifles had meanwhile reached Allagappa, five miles west of Myinmu.

On 25 January a patrol of 11 Cavalry proceeded to Myaung where it found some Japanese, who were killed. Meanwhile, a company of 9/12 Frontier Force Regiment of the 80th Indian Infantry Brigade had encountered some Japanese at Pt 614 PK 7765, whom they attacked and defeated. Next day 14 Frontier Force Rifles was sent to assist 9/12 Frontier Force Regiment's company but the Japanese had withdrawn on the previous night.

32nd Brigade

Following the capture of Monywa, the 32nd Indian Infantry Brigade was ordered to clear south of the town. Though the Japanese had withdrawn, some snipers were still resisting there, with whom 3/8 Gurkha Rifles maintained contact. On 23 January, the Gurkhas captured Kanbyagale. The Japanese were entrenched in positions facing 3/8 Gurkha Rifles. At 1630 hours thirty-two aircraft hurled bombs and rockets on these positions. The strike was accurate and some casualties were inflicted but the defenders did not give up their positions and approximately twenty-five of them were reported to be present in the village at PK 548818, but the advance to the south continued.[23]

Lezin

To facilitate this advance towards Lezin, an air-strike on the defensive positions facing 3/8 Gurkha Rifles was arranged. From 1230 to 1630 hours the Japanese railway and road positions including an unnamed village at 548818 were bombed. The village caught fire; nonetheless the defenders still clung to Lezin. On 25 January, 3/8 Gurkha Rifles was relieved by 9/14 Punjab who occupied the village at PK 548818. An air-strike on Shabaukkon by twelve aircraft was followed by the evacuation of the village as also of Magyigan, Sagyingyi, and Kyaukpu. At 0938 hours, Lezin was reported clear by 1 Northamptons who then moved towards Kudaw. A patrol reaching there about 1600 hours was fired on from the north-east corner of the village. The same night 9/14 Punjab had a hand to hand fight with the Japanese at Kyabaing but could not dislodge them. Twelve aircraft bombed and strafed the village the next day at 1510 hours, and set the village on fire. By 0815 on the 28th it was reported clear.[24]

1 Northamptons was also meeting resistance at Kudaw and Payitkon. At 1330 hours twelve aircraft bombed and strafed Kudaw, Kyehmon and Payitkon. An hour later, the Northamptons attacked the Japanese positions with artillery support and occupied all the three villages before 1700 hours. The only organised resistance met during this period was in the area of the villages east of Kyehmon where air-strikes became necessary before the opposition was overcome. On 29 January the road was reported clear to PK 695642 and the 80th Indian Infantry Brigade moved forward, with the object of clearing the Irrawaddy-Chindwin confluence area.[25]

Capture of Letkapin by the 100th Brigade

Stung by the Allied action at Ayadaw, Wunbye and Myinmu, the Japanese High Command ordered two strong detachments back to the north bank of the Irrawaddy, and these occupied Letkapin and Satpangon, respectively. 4/10 Gurkha Rifles and a company of the Machine-Gun Jat Battalion proceeded thither without delay and by 29 January surrounded Letkapin before the Japanese had dug in.[26] The latter, numbering more than 100, offered strong resistance but the Gurkhas gave them no respite. Air-strikes were also delivered

---

[23] 32nd Brigade War Diary, *op. cit.*
[24] The policy laid down at this time was that no deliberate attack was to be made unless it was certain that it would succeed. Continuous harassing to Japanese was to be carried out while air and artillery pounded their positions. *Ibid.*
[25] XXXIII Corps Account of Operations, Vol. III, p. 35.
[26] A Short History of the 20th Indian Division, *op. cit.*

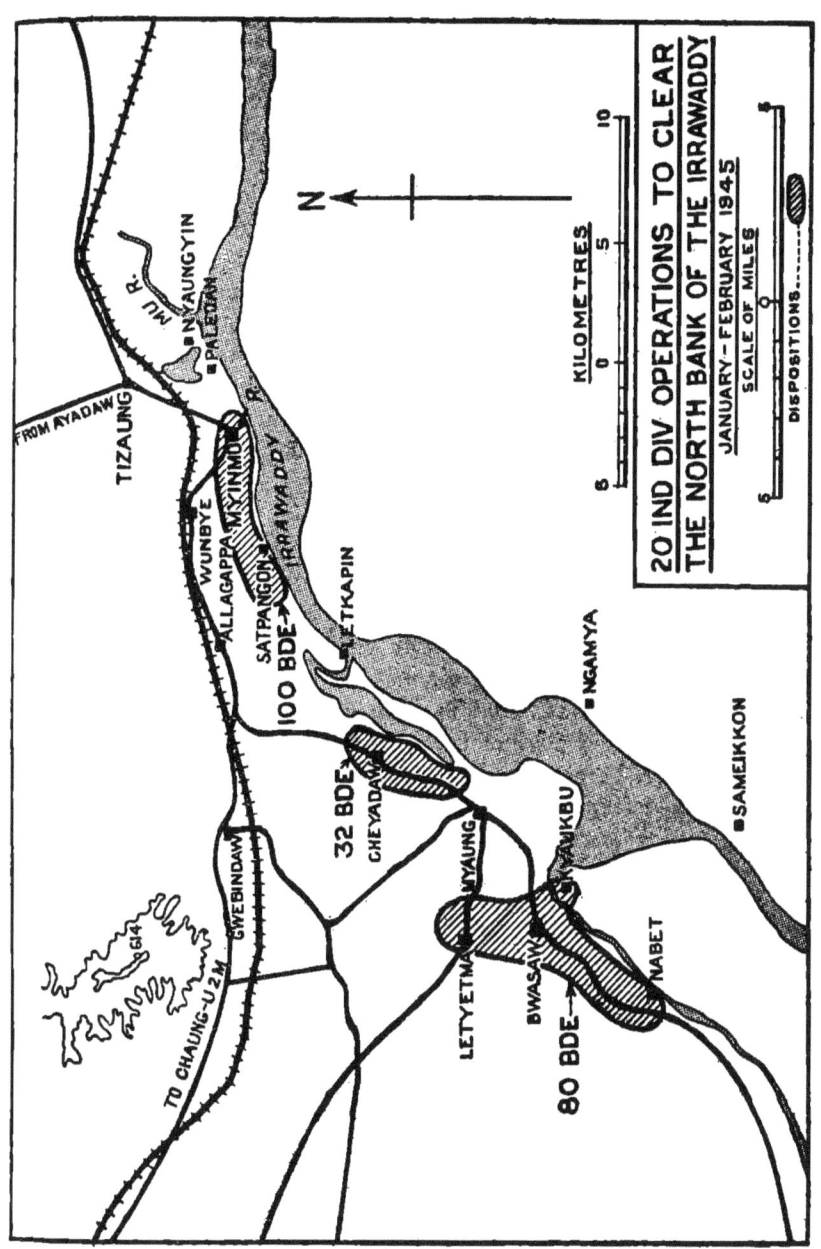

but the incendiary attack on the 29th did not appreciably affect the Japanese. The Gurkhas, however, maintained pressure and at the same time thwarted any Japanese attempt to cross the river to the east. Two boats, though hit by small-arms fire on the night of 29/30 January, succeeded in escaping, but out of five boats trying to cross on the morning of 30 January three were sunk. On 31 January again, two large boats, each containing twenty-five Japanese troops, were definitely sunk by machine-gun fire. In the meantime 4/10 Gurkha Rifles had infiltrated into Japanese positions during the night of 30/31 January and pushed them into a small area. The latter had no chance to escape and by 1700 hours on 31 January, all of them were liquidated and Letkapin—Thayabaung captured. The Gurkhas watched by moonlight the survivors in the village, about 25 Japanese officers and men, commit suicide by walking fully armed and equipped into the river.[27] Many wounded were thrown in by their comrades. Much equipment was captured. Gurkha casualties were negligible. A minimum figure of Japanese killed in this action was given as 150.

Battle for Satpangon

The liquidation of the Japanese at Satpangon was, however, a different affair. They occupied well dug-in positions obviously prepared some time before; and brick walls, pagodas and grave yards helped to nullify the effect of air-strikes and artillery. The Japanese machine-gun positions, sited in long grass, were difficult to locate and they had good field of fire over the surrounding paddy fields. The first clash here took place on 31 January when a patrol from 4/17 Dogra Defence Company encountered 20 to 30 Japanese troops and suffered a loss. An air-strike took place on 1 February and 2 Border[28] Regiment moved forward to deal with the Satpangon party supposed to be 100 strong. At 1400 hours on 2 February, 24 heavy bombers delivered another air-strike. In spite of it, 2 Border met with stubborn resistance on the fringe of the village, especially to the west and north-west. The opposition was fierce, but on 3 February after another air-strike the defenders were driven out of the north-east quarter of the village. The Border Regiment then encircled the village. Next day, again, after severe fighting, the eastern half of the village was captured. The entire village was cleared on the 5th.

The 100th Indian Infantry Brigade met with one more interruption in its preparations to cross the river when a strong Japanese raiding party crossed the Irrawaddy at approximately 0300 hours on

---

[27] *Ibid.*
[28] Border Regt. were undergoing river crossing training at this time, which they had to interrupt in order to liquidate the Satpangon position. See File No. 1787.

the night of 3/4 February, in the sector of the 2nd Division, east of the Mu river, and crossed to the west bank and came down on the rear and flank of a company of 14/13 Frontier Force Rifles guarding the flank. Luckily another company established in Nyaungyin—Aukkyin got scent of this crossing in time. Three fighting platoons of 14/13 Frontier Force Rifles located approximately 60 Japanese and engaged them throughout 4 February. Their attempts to enlarge the bridgehead, about noon, by a coastal thrust to Paledan were held up and by 5 February they were driven back across the Irrawaddy with many casualties inflicted by the Frontier Force Rifles, again ably assisted by air-strike and by a squadron of the armoured cars of the PAVO which had come through from Monywa.[29]

On 8 February, a patrol of 2 Border Regiment which had crossed the Irrawaddy five days previously, returned to the north bank. The patrol had penetrated to about six miles south of Myinmu and laid up, on one occasion, only ten yards from a Japanese gun position. However, very little movement was seen especially in the area of the south bank of the Irrawaddy.

The rest of the period on the 100th Indian Infantry Brigade front, up to 12 February, was marked by frequent Japanese reconnaissance patrols and jitter parties and spasmodic and occasionally heavy shelling on the brigade area, particularly Myinmu. By the afternoon of 12 February the brigade group, with 7 Cavalry less one squadron, was concentrated in the Wunbye area, preparatory to the crossing of the Irrawaddy.

80th Brigade

While the 32nd Indian Infantry Brigade was engaged in capturing Monywa, the 80th Indian Infantry Brigade was concentrating behind, as a preliminary to relieving the former and continuing the advance to the Irrawaddy. Its task was to clear the area of the confluence of the Chindwin and the Irrawaddy.

The brigade had concentrated at Kyaukhlega by 9 January, and began sweeping the country clear of the Japanese elements on both the banks of the Chindwin. It reached Kani on 13 January. No Japanese were met with on the east bank but their forward patrols on the west bank were driven southwards as the result of a series of clashes. By 25 January the brigade had concentrated in an area halfway between Budalin and Monywa in divisional reserve, 1 Devon being sent forward almost immediately to the 32nd Indian Infantry Brigade to take part in the impending operations for the capture of Monywa.

1 Devon less one company was made responsible for the protec-

[29] *Ibid.*

tion of the artillery area in and south of Alon, while one company was to cross the Chindwin and by a wide turning movement successively clear the high hill Letpadaung Taung overlooking Monywa and establish road-blocks on the Monywa—Salingyi road, and if possible on the western bank of the river some two miles downstream of Monywa.[30]

9 FFR of the brigade had, in the meantime, been sent in three company columns over the hills to the east of Monywa to cut off the retreating Japanese east, south and west of Chaungu. Operating 50 to 60 miles from their base, the columns fought two actions in which heavy casualties were inflicted on the vanquished. However, due to the size of the area in which 9 Frontier Force Regiment operated and the impossibility of keeping movement secret from the local inhabitants, the Japanese were able largely to evade these columns and slip away to the area of the confluence of the Chindwin and the Irrawaddy.[31] From here they moved on to an island whose bank became the forward area of the Japanese bridgehead across the Irrawaddy from Sameikkon, and it soon became evident that they were determined to hold it at all costs.

The Japanese defences consisted of firm bases in the groups of villages around Pozadaw, Thaunggyi and Ngabe, from which the intermediate villages were vigorously patrolled and jitter parties sent out to disturb the Allied positions. The only Japanese positions forward of the island were a number of bunkers near Subgeon, but as the 80th Indian Infantry Brigade had only two battalions of infantry in the area, it did not try to clear it completely. An additional difficulty was that the Japanese had arrived back at well-stocked ammunition dumps, and their artillery, operating from the island and from the east bank of the Irrawaddy, was very active and uncomfortably accurate. Efforts to bomb their gun positions were not yet successful.

On 1 February, the 80th Indian Infantry Brigade arrived at Letyetma and reported that Japanese occupation was on a very much lower scale, and that no large parties were in the area bounded by Zayatkon—Shwebontha. The brigade decided to infiltrate on to the island; 9 Frontier Force Regiment was to surround Kyaukbu in the Pozadaw group of villages, north of the confluence area, in order to keep the line of communication clear.

The 9/12 Frontier Force Regiment was therefore ordered to occupy Pauktaw and Zigon during the night of 1 February;[32] which was done, but Kyaukbu was reported occupied. An air-strike, in which 24 heavy bombers took part, was put down on Kyaukbu on

[30] Ibid.
[31] File No. 1787.
[32] 9 FFR, OO, No. 1 of 1.2.45.

2 February, and the place was set on fire.[33] Patrols were sent towards Pozadaw, but these were fired upon by the Japanese. Clashes and ambushes took place for about a week, after which Kyaukbu was reported clear and was occupied on 8 February, and Pozadaw on 9 February. Meanwhile, 3/1 Gurkha Rifles passing through Nabet, which had previously been reported as a Japanese concentration area, made contact at Taunggyi on 4 February. The village was strongly defended and the Gurkhas were held up. On 2 and 3 February air-strikes were directed on the defensive positions but without any appreciable effect. On the 5th, another air-strike was organised in which incendiary bombs were used. These were not as successful as was expected, and so, when the Gurkhas attacked after the air-strike, they suffered considerable casualties and were forced to withdraw back to Nabet. The Japanese followed up their success by accurately shelling the position of the Gurkhas at Nabet which resulted in 30 men being wounded. After further air-strikes on the 6th and 7th, 3/1 Gurkha Rifles made a fresh attack on the 7th with the support of the tanks of 7 Cavalry and captured the north end of the village, the tanks claiming 51 Japanese killed in the course of the action. By the 8th the whole of Taunggyi was cleared, although the Japanese reacted strongly with heavy shelling and a desperate counter-attack.

Whilst 3/1 Gurkha Rifles had been attacking Taunggyi, an expedition consisting of some infantry and armoured cars of 11 Cavalry penetrated south down the line of the Nabet river and engaged the Japanese north-east of Sulegon on 4 February, and expelled them from the village on the 5th. As the area could not be held by infantry, a second expedition went down a week later. The Japanese defended the position strongly and their bunkers were liquidated only after 7 hours of heavy fighting in which 9 Frontier Force Regiment and tanks took part. From 11 February onwards, the 80th Indian Infantry Brigade began to move up, leaving 11 Cavalry, a battery of 25-pounders and the Deception Unit to carry on the battle. It had however carried out the job, as approximately 40% of the infantry and 45% of the artillery available to the Japanese had been diverted from the eventual bridgehead of the Allies.

Thus, by the first week of February, the area to the north of the confluence of the Irrawaddy and the Chindwin had been cleared of all but small parties of Japanese troops, who were fully aware of the rapid build-up of the 20th Indian Division on the north bank of the Irrawaddy in the area west of Mandalay. They still believed, as Lieut-General Slim had hoped that they might, that the 19th

[33] WD. 9/12 FFR, Feb., 1945.

Indian Division, in its bridgeheads at Thabeikkyin and Kyaukmyaung, was under the command of the IV Corps. They, therefore, deduced that the 19th Indian Division's crossings were to be followed by the whole of the IV Corps; and that both the Corps were to the west of the Irrawaddy, massing for a drive to the north of Mandalay, and for another from a point immediately to the west of that town. They were further confused by the gradual southward advance of the 36th British Division which appeared to indicate a joint offensive by the Fourteenth Army and the NCAC forces. This led them to concentrate all their available forces against the 19th Indian Division. As NCAC had been weakened by the withdrawal of two Chinese divisions, the Japanese were able to divert the whole of their *15th* and *53rd Divisions* together with some of the tanks, against the 19th Indian Division before it could consolidate its bridgeheads.[34]

268TH INDIAN INFANTRY BRIGADE OPERATIONS[35]

During this phase of operations, the main task of the 268th Indian Infantry Brigade was the protection of the Kabo weir area, which it took over from the 6th Brigade on 8 January. On 16 January, orders were issued for it to take over from the 2nd Division operational responsibilities for the area west of the Mu river. Boundaries allotted to it were the line of the Mu river to Aungtha with the 2nd Division, and in the east with the 20th Indian Division the line of the main Ye-U canal. Within this boundary, the brigade was ordered to patrol all villages and to mop up any Japanese stragglers who might have remained in the area.

The brigade continued patrolling in the area west of the Mu river as ordered on 16 January, and by the end of the month this task was completed, and it prepared to move in to the Corps reserve at Shwebo, mostly providing troops for guarding the air-strips and patrolling the hills along the west bank of the Irrawaddy, south of Shwebo. From 8 to 13 February, the brigade continued to operate a patrol screen along the west bank of the Irrawaddy, north and south of Thitseingyi; but apart from minor clashes, no major contact was reported.

CORPS ADVANCE SLOWED DOWN—22 JANUARY TO 2 FEBRUARY

After the capture of Ye-U and Shwebo, it was necessary for the XXXIII Corps advance to slow down for a period of administrative build-up before the final phase of its operations—the capture of

---
[34] See Leese's *Despatch*, para 51, and Mountbatten's *Report*, para 127.
[35] XXXIII Corps Account of Operations, Vol. III, p. 36.

Mandalay.[36] It had to be so owing to the reduction of air supply, upon which the Corps was almost wholly dependent by reason of the length of the road from the railhead. Therefore, before any major battle could take place, it was necessary to re-stock the Corps and divisional dumps as fast as possilbe, and at the same time, limit current operations. The limitations placed on the formation commanders were that the 2nd Division would operate up to one brigade group and that the 19th Indian Division up to two brigade groups on air supply. Other divisions were of necessity restricted by the limits of their first and second line scale. Besides, the 254th Indian Tank Brigade was not expected to concentrate forward before early February and till then no offensive with armour was to be taken up.

The formation commanders were to operate boldly within the above limits, but to keep the following objects in view[37]:—

(a) Retaining the initiative.
(b) Maintaining contact on the Corps front.
(c) Locating main Japanese defences.
(d) Re-grouping and training for major offensive operations.

The objective of the Corps was to capture Mandalay as early as possible when a major offensive might be resumed after 1 February.[38] For this purpose the various formations were allotted their respective tasks:—

(i) The 2nd Division was to operate for locating the main Japanese positions north and west of the Irrawaddy, and to be prepared to effect a crossing on receiving orders from the Corps Commander. In addition, the 2nd Division was to operate one battalion in the Thitseingyi area with the object of leading the Japanese to believe that a crossing was to take place there.

(ii) The 19th Indian Division after establishing two bridgeheads, each of one brigade group, in the areas of Thabeikkyin and Kyaukmyaung, and after consolidating them by wide patrolling, was to advance on Mandalay from the north.

(iii) The 20th Indian Division, following the capture of Monywa, was to operate one brigade group in the area of the confluence of the Mu and Irrawaddy rivers. Subsequently, the division was to cross the Irrawaddy, west of Myinmu, with the object of isolating Mandalay from the west and south.

---

[36] XXXIII Corps Operational Instruction No. 24 of 17 January 1945, para 3. See also XXXIII Corps Accounts, Vol. III, p. 25.
[37] Ibid.
[38] XXXIII Corps Operation Instruction No. 24 of 17 January 1945.

(iv) The 254th Indian Tank Brigade was expected to concentrate in the Ye-U area, on or about 5 February, and the allotment of armour for the operations was:—

2nd Division	3 DG
19th Indian Division	Squadron 150 RAC
	Squadron 7 Cavalry
20th Indian Division	7 Cavalry less one squadron
	11 Cavalry less two squadrons.

To relieve the divisions of the responsibility for their rear, a Corps reserve was formed under the command of Brigadier R.L. Scoones, O.B.E. Commander 254th Indian Tank Brigade.

(v) The 268th Indian Infantry Brigade was placed in Corps reserve, when its task west of the Mu river was completed, with one battalion to operate in the Kin-U and Kongyi areas, to relieve the 19th Indian Division.

The rest of the Corps reserve was composed of the 150th Regiment Royal Armoured Corps less one squadron; and one squadron 11 Cavalry. The Commander 254th Indian Tank Brigade was ordered to assume operational command of all the troops in the Shwebo area with effect from 28 January, and be responsible for the co-ordination of all defences in that area, including airfields, against raids by small but determined Japanese raiding parties. In addition, the 268th Indian Infantry Brigade was to be prepared to relieve the 20th Indian Division in the Ayadaw area. This was subsequently found to be unnecessary, and the 268th Indian Infantry Brigade was ordered to relieve the 4th Brigade of the 2nd Division in the Sagaing area on 20 February 1945.[39]

JAPANESE PLANS AND DISPOSITIONS[40]

In order to keep their hold on central Burma, and the Lashio Road in particular, the Japanese *33rd Army* prepared to defend the line of the Irrawaddy river. For the maintenance of this front, stretching from Thabeikkyin in the north to Sameikkon in the south—a distance of some 120 miles—only the *15th, 31st, 33rd* and *53rd Divisions* were available, a total of less than 10,000 troops. No reinforcements had been received, and none were likely to arrive in view of the general pressure then being exerted by the Allied forces in every theatre of war against the Japanese.

Unmindful of the realities, the Japanese High Command had all along been busy planning a counter-offensive across the Irrawaddy

---

[39] *Ibid.* See also XXXIII Corps Operation Order No. 14 of 20 February 1945.
[40] XXXIII Corps Account of Operations, *op. cit.*, pp. 27-29.

—planning which was aptly described by a Japanese battalion officer as "pipe dreams." The High Command now found itself faced with the reality of two hostile bridgeheads established by the 19th Indian Division on the east bank of the Irrawaddy, in the areas of Thabeikkyin and Kyaukmyaung, and the imminent possibility of a further crossing in the general area Ngazun—Sameikkon. Of these, the most immediate threat came from the bridgeheads already established, and the main Japanese efforts were concentrated on an attempt to destroy, or at least neutralise, these positions; at the same time, efforts were made to build up a striking force on the south bank of the Irrawaddy, based on the village of Myotha and to dig and man defences on all likely crossing points. The immediate approach to Mandalay was rightly considered to be adequately protected by the positions centring around Sagaing.

The forces under the command of the Japanese *33rd Army* were therefore deployed as follows:—the *15th* and *53rd Divisions* (some 4,500 strong, with approximately 1000 held in reserve), were deployed against the 19th Indian Division bridgehead. Some 2000 men of the *31st Division* together with the *213th Regiment* of *33rd Division* held the western sector of the line against the 20th Indian Division. In addition, the Japanese at this time deployed some 20 guns of varying calibres against each of the three Indian and British divisions.

From these dispositions, it was apparent that the Japanese, although appreciating the gravity of the situation, were still determined to destroy the bridgeheads already established, and to prevent any further crossings of the Irrawaddy. After the fall of Shwebo, they had prepared an elaborate defensive plan covering the immediate approaches to Mandalay via Sagaing. They had withdrawn rapidly to positions north and north-west of Sagaing from where they could oppose the 2nd British Division. Although all the original positions were not manned as a result of shortage of manpower, the positions which extended from the tip of the Sagaing Hills to Ywathitgyi were extremely strong, and built to sustain considerable artillery and air attack.

These positions were held by the *2nd Battalion 58th Regiment* and *2nd* and *3rd Battalions 138th Regiment* both of the *31st Division* together with a proportion of anti-tank weapons and artillery. The total number of Japanese fighting troops did not exceed 2000, but the strength of the position they occupied made a full-scale frontal attack by the British division inadvisable. In consequence, although there was continuous fighting and the 2nd Division inflicted considerable casualties on them, the Japanese maintained their bridgehead substantially intact.[41]

[41] *Ibid.*

CLEARING THE SAGAING AREA

Kyaukse

As the Japanese withdrew from Shwebo towards their strongholds in the Sagaing area, a mobile column from the 2nd British Division followed up and overcame opposition near Sadaung. From there, the 4th Brigade took up the lead and drove the Japanese to Kyaukse. On 27 January, it was mainly engaged in re-grouping with a view to continuing advance south of Ondaw with the object of capturing Kyaukse and Ywathitgyi. The next day, while 2 Norfolk was established on the high ground at 3367 and 3467, 1/8 LF with tank support successfully engaged the Japanese in Kyaukse and strong fighting patrols of 2 Reconnaissance Regiment engaged the Japanese in Padu and Taungyin areas.

On 29 January, 12 Hurribombers attacked Padu. A little later 11 more Hurribombers attacked pagoda area. The next day again 12 Hurribombers and 9 Thunderbolts attacked Kyaukse area. The attack was successful and Kyaukse was finally captured on 4 February.[42]

Ywathitgyi

Meanwhile the 5th Brigade had advanced to the Irrawaddy and cleared the north bank from the Mu river on the west to (excluding) Ywathitgyi on the east. There was however no sign of the Japanese evacuating Ywathitgyi, although at other points they had been evacuating positions almost as soon as contact was made. On 31 January, an 'earthquake' attack was called for, and the village was bombed by B25s, Thunderbolts, and Hurribombers, following which, 1 Royal Scots supported by 3 DG occupied the eastern half of the village up to the main road in face of very strong opposition. The Japanese had made full use of stone buildings in siting defensive posts. The attacking troops were held up by opposition from the western half of the village.

On 1 February, patrolling to determine the extent of the remaining Japanese opposition in the village was carried out, and 12 aircraft attacked the positions located in the wood at the west end of the village. On 2 February, following another air-strike by three squadrons of Thunderbolts on the west half of the village, 1 Royal Scots occupied it by 1720 hours, against considerable opposition from numerous defensive posts. One boat-load of Japanese troops endeavouring to escape across the river was sunk, and a dump fired during the air-strike.

After the capture of Kyaukse and Ywathitgyi, the 6th Brigade

---

[42] This village of Kyaukse is not to be confused with another Kyaukse south of Mandalay.

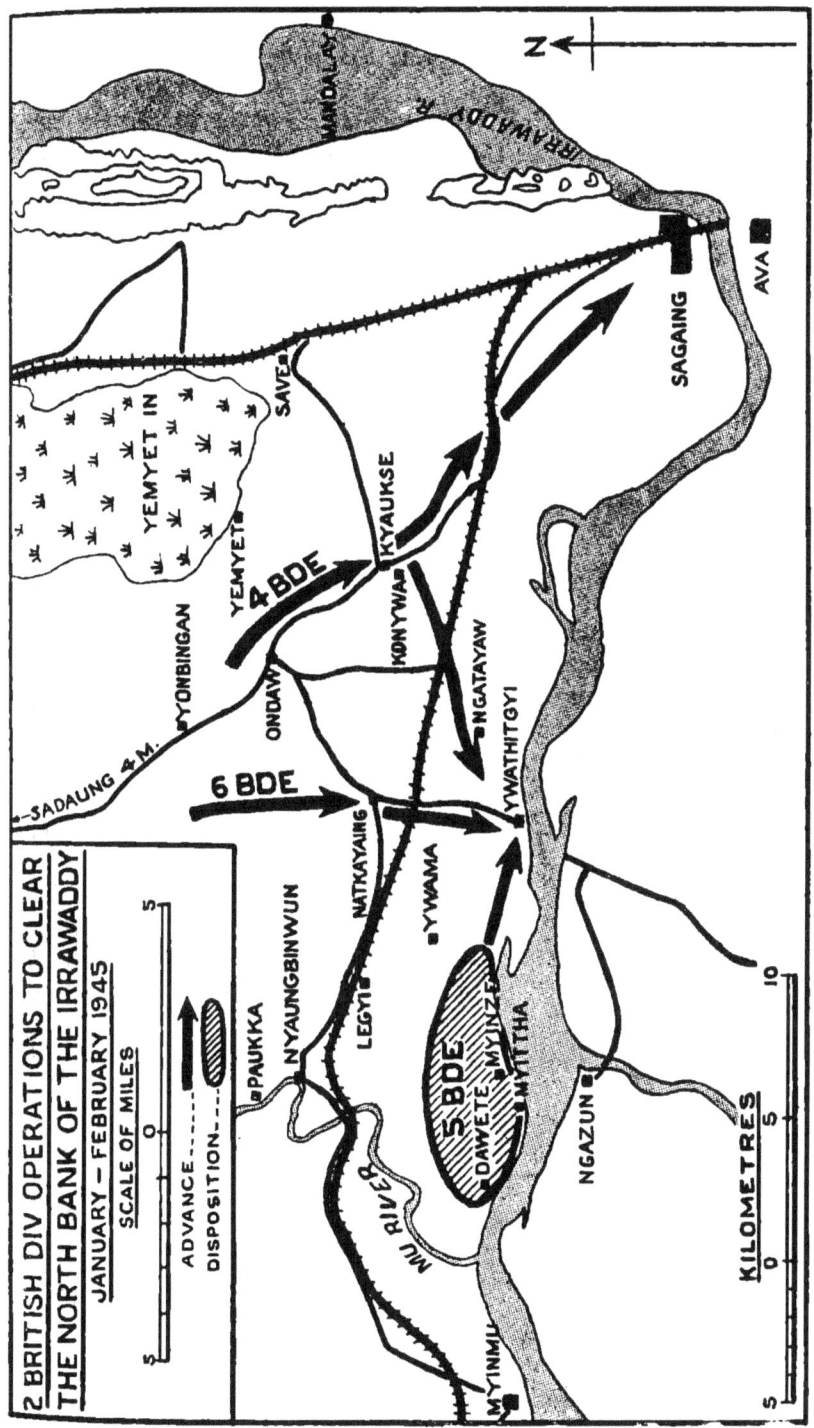

moved forward to the Ywathitgyi area, and along with the 5th Brigade prepared for the crossing of the Irrawaddy while the 4th Brigade continued to press the Japanese in their Sagaing positions.

During this period, the Japanese made frequent incursions from the south bank of the Irrawaddy to the Allied line on the north bank, but only one of these parties was markedly offensive; the remainder, for the main part, confining their activities to patrolling.

The 2nd Division Operation Instruction No. 14 was issued on 7 February. Its object was to establish a bridgehead south of the Irrawaddy river. The plan was that the 5th Brigade would assault from the general area Myittha and Tadaing, the 6th Brigade would concentrate within the bridgehead preparatory to a subsequent advance eastwards and the 4th Brigade with 2 Reconnaissance Regiment under command would contain the hostile force in the Sagaing area. The 4th Brigade was subsequently to be available for operations south of the Irrawaddy. The plan was to isolate Mandalay by a co-ordinate advance by the 19th Indian Division from the north, by the 2nd Division from the west and by the 20th Indian Division from the south and south-west.[43]

On 9 February, a directive was issued by the divisional commander. Since it was apparent that the Japanese would take offensive action with the double object of finding out the Allied intentions and hampering their preparations for the crossing of the Irrawaddy, the unit commanders were asked to ensure the defence of their respective positions by every means. Localities were to be wired to the maximum length of wire available. The north bank of the river was to be patrolled day and night. The Sea Reconnaissance Unit was to patrol the river nightly with the object of discovering Japanese activity and taking such counter measures as were within its scope.

JAPANESE EFFORTS TO DESTROY BRIDGEHEADS[44]

The main Japanese effort during this period was concentrated on an attempt to destroy, or at least neutralise, the two bridgeheads established on the east bank of the Irrawaddy. In addition, they attempted, without success, to maintain a bridgehead of their own in the area of Kabwet, which would prevent the union of the two main forces of the 19th Indian Division, and also act as a threat to its lines of communication, and to the division itself. This Kabwet bridgehead was held very tenaciously by approximately 500 men of

---

[43] See XXXIII Corps Op. Order No. 13 of 2 February 1945.
[44] XXXIII Corps Account of Operations, *Op. cit.*

the *51st Regiment* who occupied exteremely well-sited and well-prepared positions. It was not until three successive "earthquake" air attacks had been put in that on 1 February they were forced to abandon these positions.

In the meantime, the Japanese brought a considerable weight of infantry and artillery to bear against the Indian bridgeheads. Initially they disposed the *67th Regiment* and *1st Battalion 60th Regiment* of the *15th Division* against the 98th Indian Infantry Brigade at Thabeikkyin; this force was approximately 750 strong, but it made no real effort to do more than prevent the Indian troops from enlarging their positions. As it became clear that the main weight of the 19th Indian Division's attack was to be through the Kyaukmyaung bridgehead, some of these troops were withdrawn by the Japanese from Thabeikkyin to strengthen their forces in the more vital sector.

Realising that the real threat was to come from the Kyaukmyaung bridgehead the Japanese tried to liquidate the Indian forces in this area. This resulted in some of the bitterest fighting of the Burma campaign, particularly on and around Pear Hill. The Japanese used some thirty-four guns, including some medium ones, to add to the weight of their attacks on Allied positions. They did not mount a large-scale counter-offensive, as their forces were not sufficiently concentrated, but as reinforcements arrived, they were thrown into the continuous battle. Thus, although the Japanese finally succeeded in collecting a sufficiently strong force, all their attacks, except one, were of only one company strength or below. The most determined effort was made on the night of 30/31 January when more than two companies, with artillery support, managed to enter the perimeter of the 62nd Indian Infantry Brigade and engaged the brigade headquarters at point-blank range with two 70-mm guns. After the repulse of this attack at a loss to the Japanese of over 50 killed, it became apparent to them that the bridgehead was finally established; the Japanese, therefore, without ceasing their attacks, concentrated on the neutralisation of the bridgehead rather than on its complete extermination.

From the beginning of February, it became apparent that the Japanese were becoming worried by the potential threat of a crossing west of Mandalay, and they therefore re-dispositioned their forces to meet this eventuality. Artillery and certain other forces from the *15th* and *53rd Divisions*, facing the 19th Indian Division in the north, were withdrawn and sent to the south bank of the Irrawaddy. The Japanese were further confirmed in this view of the situation when on 12 February the 20th Indian Division crossed the Irrawaddy at Myinmu. This crossing made imperative the sending of reinforcements to the newly threatened sector, and still further weakened the Japanese forces available to operate against the 19th Indian Division.[45]

DEFENCE OF THE BRIDGEHEADS BY THE 19TH DIVISION

After the establishment of the bridgeheads, the position in Kyaukmyaung was that the original slender foothold, about a quarter of a mile in length along the eastern bank, was being slowly and painfully enlarged. First of all, two vital tactical features had to be secured. These were Minban Taung ridge and Pear Hill. The first of these was a finger of scrub-covered rock, 800 feet high, about three miles from the original bridgehead. This was covered by 1/6 Gurkha Rifles. The second was also essential for the defence and enlargement of the bridgehead. This feature was a bare barren peak rising sharply about 800 yards from the river bank and ran parallel to it. It was situated about 2½ miles from the main bridgehead and held a dominating position in the area. In fact, both these features were the key observation points of the Japanese, and deprived of them their artillery would be practically blind. Both these positions were in Allied hands before 23 January, but it will be interesting to note how Pear Hill was captured by two companies of 5 Baluch by a skilful surprise move on 21 January.

Capture of Pear Hill

The crest of the hill was stony with very little surface soil and thinly covered with thick jungle. A track ran up the north-west slopes and over the crest of Pear, eventually disappearing down the south-east slopes. Situated at the southernmost end of the hills were two small temples and a pagoda. A steep flight of steps went down from the pagoda south-westwards to the river.

It appeared that although the Japanese held the hill more strongly at night, it was but lightly held by day. A company of 5 Baluch was therefore ordered to capture the feature on the afternoon of 21 January. The attack was preceded by an air-strike which took place at 1630 hours. Soon afterwards one platoon of A Company went up the hill to reconnoitre in strength. It reached the highest point of the hill without opposition, but while doing further reconnaissance of its surroundings it discovered an Observation Post of the Japanese in which there were three officers, a captain, a lieutenant and a corporal. In a brisk engagement two men of the Baluch, using grenades and a sten gun, killed the three Japanese officers, and cut the telephone lines running away from the Observation Post. Meanwhile the remainder of the A Company came up

---

[45] XXXIII Corps Account of Operations.

and consolidated the position.[46] During the night C Company was ordered to reinforce A Company on the hill. It reached there next morning at 1100 hours.[47]

The position was vital as the hill commanded the whole of the bridgehead area and would have been a difficult and costly objective for an ordinary attack. The Japanese also were alive to the importance of this position. From the first night after its capture they subjected the hill to almost ceaseless shelling and nightly attacks which continued till 7 February but they failed to dislodge the Baluch, and later 3 Rajputana Rifles who relieved them, in spite of the fact that the feature was virtually cut off from the other Allied troops and had to be maintained by a daily carrier supply column.

The defensive layout was divided into two sectors, one company holding each, and was composed of a series of bunkers made of stones found locally. It was almost impossible to dig in to any great depth owing to the rocky nature of the feature. The perimeter did not embrace the pagoda area as troops were insufficient for taking in such a large area. Sited at either end of the perimeter covering the approaches from the north-west and south-east slopes was the 11th Sikh (MMG) Regiment. The whole of the perimeter was heavily wired in with booby-traps located round the perimeter outside the wire. Co-ordinated with the defences was a very comprehensive defensive fire plan embracing, if required, the whole of the divisional artillery.

The more vicious of the Japanese attacks against the Baluch took place during the early hours of 24 January and on the night of 25/26 January. On the former occasion the Japanese suffered eleven casualties (killed) against the Allied loss of fourteen killed and eight wounded.[48] In the latter action approximately 80 Japanese participated. The attack was preceded by a heavy concentration of artillery. The attack started at 2300 hours on the night of 25/26 January from the south and reached its peak at 0445 hours. Most of the night there was shelling and mortaring. The attack was repulsed, the Japanese loss being 1 officer and 14 other ranks killed; the Baluch casualties being 5 killed and 9 wounded. On the night of 26/27 January, further attacks were made against 5/10 Baluch but all were held. The following day, 27 January, saw the relief of the Baluch troops by two companies of 3 Rajputana Rifles.

Defence of Minban Taung Ridge and Yeshin

These attacks were in no way peculiar to the Pear Hill feature, as the Japanese, realising the extent of the bridgehead, attacked or

---

[46] WD 5 Baluch, January 1945, Appendix J. 7.
[47] Ibid, J.6.
[48] Ibid.

jittered all the Allied positions constantly. Other Allied positions which were particular objects of Japanese attention were Minban Taung and Yeshin. The former was held by a company of 1/6 Gurkha Rifles. This was attacked by about 40 Japanese on 26 January but they were driven back with casualties. There were two attacks on the 27th between 0400 and 0700 hours, the Japanese coming in massed waves, shouting.[49] The first wave consisted of men with automatics. The company of Gurkhas (C Company) holding Minban Taung ridge beat off all attacks, and in the morning found 13 bodies and estimated a further 20 casualties inflicted on the Japanese. During the night of 27/28 two platoons of the Japanese made another suicidal attack on this ridge under cover of grenade discharger and also threw a shower of hand grenades.[50] This attack was also beaten off with casualties on both sides. Full use of their artillery was also made by the Japanese during these attacks, and with one of the largest concentrations met in Burma up to that time they endeavoured, though without success, to force the troops in occupation to withdraw to the west bank of the Irrawaddy.

Northern Bridgehead

In the northern bridgehead in the Thabeikkyin area operations centred round sporadic Japanese attempts to dislodge the 98th Indian Infantry Brigade troops from their positions. The Japanese held the area round the Allied perimeter and carried on shelling of, and attacks on, the bridgehead. A heavy attack was made on 26 January when 4/4 Gurkha Rifles was attacked from the north by about 25 Japanese and by another party from the south. Thabeikkyin was again attacked from the south on the 28th. But these and other attacks were held, and the 98th Indian Infantry Brigade went on consolidating in this area. Here the Gurkhas had to face assault charges reminiscent of old time attacks led by Japanese officers, waving their swords.

Japanese Bridgehead on the Western Bank

While elements of the 19th Indian Division were resolutely holding on to their precarious foothold on the eastern bank and enlarging it, the Japanese were carrying on an interesting two-way traffic on the river. While to the north of Kyaukmyaung some of them were slipping eastwards across the river in country boats, further south some were filtering across to the west coast. Here (on the western bank) they had established a strong bridgehead at Kabwet in order to hold up the reinforcement of the Allied bridge-

---

[49] WD 1/6 GR, 27 January 1945.
[50] Ibid.

head. They fought with their wonted tenacity in an effort to hold on to their position. So stubborn was their resistance that even concentrated air-strikes totalling 180 tons of heavy and medium bombs failed to dislodge them completely from their strongly bunkered positions. The story of how they were finally liquidated after a struggle lasting for about ten days is briefly told below.

The Japanese had strong bunkered positions at Point 280 at 679208; on the ridge at 686207; and on its reverse slopes extending eastwards to 693210. Air-strikes on 21 and 22 January failed to dislodge them and patrols of the 2nd Battalion of the Royal Berkshire Regiment sent to recce the positions returned after suffering casualties. It was appreciated that considerable softening up of the bunkered positions was necessary before an infantry attack could be contemplated.[51] A heavy air-strike was therefore called for on 23 January, followed by intensive fire from 25-pounder and anti-tank guns on the bunkers. Some bunkers were destroyed and a few Japanese were flushed into the open and killed. But the Japanese improved their dug-outs overnight and their positions on the southern slopes of the ridge seemed still strongly held next morning.[52] Further air-strikes took place on the 24th and 25th, but the Japanese, ably supported by artillery, were not dislodged. The Allies, however, were able to make some headway on 29 January when a co-ordinated air and ground attack resulted in the Royal Berkshire Regiment capturing the western sector of Kabwet. The air-strike on the Japanese defences this day was very heavy and aircraft from Onbauk airfield flew 118 sorties in direct support which was well directed and proved very effective. Further territorial gains were made on the 30th, when 2 Royal Berkshire after another air-strike reached SR 690208, but they were unable to hold this position due to strong hostile fire from the south of the river. On 31 January, however, the Japanese resistance collapsed and Kabwet was completely occupied by 2 Royal Berkshire on 1 February.

Eastern Bank

Between 26 and 28 January the 64th Indian Infantry Brigade, less 1/6 Gurkha Rifles who remained on the Minban Taung ridge, was relieved by the 62nd Indian Infantry Brigade. 4/6 Gurkha Rifles took over the Ngapyin area and two companies of 3 Rajputana Rifles the Pear feature at SR 7201. Meanwhile the Japanese forces maintained a continuous pressure against the Allied bridgehead. Their attacks on Pear Hill, Minban Taung and Yeshin up to 27 January have already been described. The Gurkha position just north of Yeshin was again attacked early in the morning

[51] WD 2 R Berks, January 1945.
[52] *Ibid.*

of 28 January by a Japanese force of about 100, but the attack was beaten off. The position was again attacked by an estimated strength of one company from the south at 0045 hours in the night 28/29 January. The Japanese put in two bayonet assaults but achieved nothing beyond inflicting a loss of 2 killed, 4 wounded, and themselves losing at least 3 killed. On the 29th, a Japanese position was located at SR 723053 which was attacked from the air, but the strike proved abortive. On 30 January, the Gurkhas on Minban Taung drove the Japanese south after an air-strike. On this day 2 Welch, while advancing south-east from Yeshin, had a running battle with the Japanese but though they inflicted some casualties, they were obliged to return to Yeshin due to sniping and guerilla tactics.

On the Pear Hill feature the Rajputana Rifles suffered a loss of 1 killed and 7 wounded during the night of 29 January. There were two Japanese attacks. The first attack came from the north on C Company's perimeter at 0130 hours. The defensive fire quickly broke up the attack. A more serious attack came at 0215 hours from the south-east on A Company's sector. The Japanese freely used grenade dischargers besides light machine-guns. The attack was beaten off five hours later. The estimated strength of the Japanese in each of these attacks was over fifty. The Japanese were, however, found in occupation of the pagoda area on the southern slopes of Pear Hill. An air-strike was delivered in the morning, but they were not dislodged. At 0930 hours a mortar concentration was put in but they were not dispersed till about 1200 hours. On the night of 30/31 January, the heaviest and most determined attack on the bridgehead defence locality was launched by the Japanese. From 1800 to 2000 hours they heavily shelled the bridgehead and river crossings by 75-mm, 105-mm and 150-mm guns. As the shell fire lifted from the right sector at 1945 hours, a platoon of the Japanese troops attempted to cut the wire and break through, but they were met by heavy MMG and small-arms fire and stopped. About 40 of them, however, succeeded in infiltrating into and even going beyond a locality occupied by troops of the Assam regiment, crawling under their own barrage and MMG fire from the ridges all round the perimeter. They brought two 2-pounder guns right up to the perimeter about SR 702050, and fired into the brigade headquarters with the aid of red Verey lights. Other similar infiltrations were attempted from all sides except the north. The attacks were pressed home again and again throughout the night between the periods of shelling, mortaring and grenade discharger fire, but once their initial penetration had been pushed out they did not get in again. The engagement continued with short intervals until 0515 hours when the Japanese withdrew after suffering heavy casualties.

Some more were killed and wounded by a company of 4/6 Gurkha Rifles when the Japanese attempted to recover some bodies from the south of the bridgehead. This proved to be the last serious attempt by them to destroy the bridgehead.

The Rajputana Rifles on Pear Hill also had a trying evening, when at 1800 hours on 30 January, it was heavily and accurately shelled by 105-mm guns. At 1830 hours Japanese jitter parties were active on all sides of the perimeter using grenade dischargers freely. At 1854 hours they attacked the position from all sides, the main attack coming in on the south-east corner of the feature. A heavy and accurate defensive fire was brought down on the attackers but the Japanese succeeded, in spite of it, in penetrating the southern sector of the position of A Company. The whole feature was illuminated with numerous Verey lights and flares of all colours fired by the Japanese. Defensive fire on this sector was intensified. Under cover of this a counter-attack was put in by the reserve platoon of A Company at the point of the bayonet. After a sharp encounter which developed into a hand to hand fighting, the Japanese were forced to withdraw. By 2200 hours the main attack had spent itself. The Japanese then tried to give supporting fire, while their troops reorganised for a fresh attempt, but their shells, falling in their own assembly, caused a good number of casualties and after that only half-hearted attempts were made to get into the position from the east. The Japanese casualties in the Pear Hill area, in the course of this evening's attack were estimated at at least 40 killed, while earlier in the day they had lost 18 more in killed. The Rajput casualties during this night were 2 killed and 20 wounded, most of them suffered by A Company which was thereafter relieved by D Company on 1 February.

On the night of 31 January jitter parties were active all around the bridgehead. Pear Hill was also subjected to two attacks at 1800-2000 hours and 0500-0600 hours after artillery preparation. But both attacks were successfully beaten off.

At 0830 hours on 1 February, the Gurkhas on Minban Taung were relieved by 2 Welch and one company of 1 Assam. The features had been occupied on 18 January and since then held by two companies of 1/6 Gurkha Rifles against repeated attacks for nearly a fortnight. The position on the top being completely cut off from the bridgehead, casualties could not be evacuated and all supplies had to be air-dropped. The returning column met with stiff opposition on its way to Ngapyin. It by-passed one Japanese position at 699062 but struck against another in the area 702049, which was captured by a bayonet and Kukri charge. Yet another position was however encountered. The column wanted to break away but encumbered as it was with casualties and mules, it could not break contact and had to harbour for the night some 300 yards outside the bridgehead perimeter. Fighting was resumed in the morning of 2 February and continued till the force reached the bridgehead, after having suffered a loss of 25 killed and 35 wounded.

On the night of 1 February, Pear Hill was again attacked by two platoons of Japanese troops from the north at 1930—2000 hours, after artillery bombardment but the attack was repulsed with loss to the attackers.

5 Baluch, who had crossed to the west bank after handing over Pear Hill to the Rajputana Rifles now recrossed into the bridgehead area with half a squadron of tanks of 150 RAC. The remainder of the squadron crossed with 2nd Battalion the Worcestershire Regiment (2 Worc R) on 3 February. On the same day, 3 Rajputana Rifles detachment on Pear Hill was relieved by 2 Worc R, and an armoured column consisting of 4/6 Gurkha Rifles under the commander of the 62nd Indian Infantry Brigade and some tanks, moving from the bridgehead, reached Yeshin without incident at 0730 hours. On the following day, on its return journey the column was subjected to heavy and accurate fire. A company of 3 Rajputana Rifles supported by tanks moved from the bridgehead to contact the column and killed several Japanese by a bayonet charge. The loss suffered by the 62nd Indian Infantry Brigade (4/6 Gurkha Rifles and 2 Welch) during the fighting that raged for 48 hours in this area was heavy (over 100 killed) due almost entirely to heavy shelling. The force returned to the bridgehead next morning. There was a comparative lull in the fighting during the following two days and the Allied troops which had fought incessantly for about three weeks knew that the bridgehead had survived the crisis.

ON THE OFFENSIVE AGAIN

By this time it was clear that the Japanese, besides having suffered heavy casualties and considerable disorganisation in their repeated abortive attacks on the bridgehead, were seriously worried by the activities of the 2nd Division and the 20th Indian Division further south. This moment was considered opportune by the Allies for going over to the attack and resuming advance. On 6 February was issued the 19th Division's Operation Order No. 3 which laid down the enlargement of the bridgehead opposite Kyaukmyaung as the division's main task. The operation was to be undertaken in three phases. In the first phase the 62nd Indian Infantry Brigade would capture the ridge 7300-7301 by using one battalion. In the second phase, the 64th Indian Infantry Brigade would extend the bridgehead to the south of Kule and establish a defended locality including Thila. In the third phase, this latter brigade was to seize and hold Singu.

Prior to the attack on Kule and the east ridges numerous patrol parties were sent out for gathering information. Their reports all pointed to the fact that both the positions were strongly held and were not likely to be given up without a stiff fight.

The first signs of preparation for this attack were the intensive bombing and strafing of the villages Kule and Thila, between Pear Hill and Singu, and three wooded features called Able, Baker and Charlie to the east of Kule on 6 February. The outline plan for the capture of the positions was for 2 Worcesters to capture Kule on 7 February, followed the next day by an attack launched by 3 Rajputana Rifles on the east ridges with artillery, tank and air support.

On 7 February, the 64th Indian Infantry Brigade crossed to the east in accordance with the operation order and expansion of the bridgehead commenced. After some saturation bombing by the strategic air force in the afternoon, the 2 Worc R with a Squadron of 150 Royal Armoured Corps in support, attacked Kule. At first opposition was light but later it stiffened. By dark, the Worcesters had cleared the northern half of the village and captured a position 300 yards to the north-east. At night the Japanese counter-attacked from the south-east but were beaten off with air support. There was another attack from the south at 0730 hours on the next morning but the artillery broke it up. The Japanese had established well defended bunker positions in south Kule and this part of the village could not be cleared on that day.

Attacks on the east ridges were delivered on 8 February according to plan. The three features mentioned before, Able, Baker and Charlie, ran from north to south, parallel to the Irrawaddy. The Japanese had prepared defensive positions on these features and were manning them. A nulla running from the lake to the Irrawaddy was also held on both sides and was impassable for tanks without sapper help. All the tracks were held and booby-trapped. As the nulla appeared unfordable for tanks except near its estuary, and the crossing of it would be clearly seen if the attack was launched directly from Pear Hill, it was decided that 2 Worc R should seize Kule on 7 February, allow the sappers to make the nulla-crossing fordable for tanks, and establish a firm base for attack by 3 Rajputana Rifles on the 8th, which was to be made by three companies with one squadron of tanks in support of each.

The Worcesters crossed the nulla in the afternoon of 7 February but could not obtain a footing within the village of Kule which had been heavily reinforced the previous night. The nulla was however made fordable for tanks overnight and a precarious foothold was maintained on the far bank of it against strong Japanese opposition.

Attack on 8 February

In order to cover the approach of the tanks and to soften up Japanese defences an 'earthquake' air-strike was arranged. It started an hour before the H hour. It included 35 minutes bombing by Mosquitos, 12 minutes bombing by Thunderbolts and 20 minutes bombing and strafing by Hurribombers. Thereafter one squadron of Hurribombers remained on cab-rank duty. The H hour was 1100 hours.

Whilst this air bombing was in progress, 3 Rajputana Rifles with two companies up crossed the nulla safely. They were now to take a sharp left turn in order to reach their start line. But in view of the fact that the Japanese were still at Kule, the left wheel of 3 Rajputana Rifles naturally exposed its right flank to the Japanese at Kule and also to their machine-gun positions some way behind the nulla. Closer at hand Japanese snipers were located in the tall grass in front and in the palm trees. These took a great toll of the advancing infantry and had to be liquidated by tank-gun fire, tree by tree. Incendiary bullets also set fire to the grass, so that every vestige of cover was denied to the Japanese snipers. Once this obstacle was overcome, progress was comparatively easy and the features Able and Baker were occupied without further loss. It was found that the Japanese had withdrawn from these features down the east slopes during the air-strike.

No sooner had the two companies reached their objectives than the Japanese returned and put in a counter-attack on Baker. One tank from C Company troop which had reached the top of this ridge ably helped in beating off the counter-attack, and within half an hour both the companies had consolidated on Able and Baker.

Meanwhile A Company had got into difficulties in its march to Charlie. It had moved through the north-eastern corner of Kule to the right of the B Company and had come under heavy machine-gun fire and tree sniping from the chaung. It remained pinned down and the leading platoon suffered severe casualties. It was decided that the only possible way to continue the advance was for the troop of tanks to go ahead unescorted and engage the gun positions. The tanks did this job well and engaged every palm tree in sight which held a sniper and inflicted heavy casualties. A Company then advanced and secured Charlie.

The tanks were of considerable help through all the phases of these operations. They remained on the features while the infantry consolidated its positions, silencing a number of tree snipers on the southern end of Baker and firing at freshly dug positions in the defile between Baker and Charlie. After 1600 hours the tanks withdrew.

Meanwhile, the Worcesters were clearing the southern half of

Kule, and with the co-operation of a company of Mahrattas and a detachment of 150 RAC completely cleared Kule village in the morning of 9 February. After this 4/6 Gurkha Rifles relieved 2 Worcestershire Regiment in this village.

To Singu

During the operations on 8 and 9 February the Japanese had suffered fairly heavy casualties, a total of 70 bodies being counted. The expansion gained speed, and by 10 February 4/6 Gurkha Rifles, with air support, cleared Thila without opposition and the push continued down the river, toward Singu, with a squadron of 7 Cavalry in support. Singu was about 7 miles south of the bridgehead of the 19th Indian Division, and was a steamer station at the head of the metalled road to Mandalay. At the same time, 3 Rajputana Rifles moved out to the left flank to investigate Ywathit. A patrol went within 600 yards of this place and captured one 37-mm anti-tank gun, killing its crew. In the morning of 10 February, the Japanese had made two attempts to drive the Allies from the features 733015 and 733010 but both these were beaten off.

Continuing on 11 February, after an air-strike, elements of the 64th Indian Infantry Brigade fought their way into Singu from the north and by sunset had secured the northern part of the village against stiff resistance from tree snipers, machine-guns and one anti-tank gun. Japanese patrols continued their activity during the nights of the 11th and 12th. But by the 13th, 1/6 Gurkha Rifles was established in the village and was liquidating some of the defenders still lurking in the area. Singu was found burning when the Gurkhas entered it and the sound of explosions indicated that the Japanese were destroying their ammunition dumps before giving up the village.

2 Worcestershire Regiment and C squadron of 7 Cavalry, in the meantime, had overcome resistance in Myingyan area and the 62nd Indian Infantry Brigade was exploiting eastward. On 11 February Ywathit was seized against minor opposition by 4/6 Gurkha Rifles assisted by one company of Rajputana Rifles and a squadron of 150 RAC. During the next few days the Japanese carried out intense patrol activity in the brigade area, attacking 4/6 Gurkhas at Ywathit, and jittering in and grenading features 7300, 7301, Yeshin, Minban Taung and the tactical and brigade headquarters. But all these attacks were beaten off, though not without some loss to the defenders.

NORTHERN BRIDGEHEAD

All this while, the 98th Indian Infantry Brigade front in Thabeikkyin was comparatively quiet. Operations were mainly confined to patrolling and consolidating with Allied aircraft attacking hostile gun-positions and other targets. The Japanese on their part carried out patrolling from their bunker positions held round the Allied bridgehead perimeter, which extended from approximately SR 717394 to PT 868 at 830357 and thence south-east to Onzon Chaung. They had posts near Thabeikkyin, and moved frequently from one post to another.

By 12 February however, the Allied bridgeheads had been expanded, and consolidated, and the 62nd and 64th Indian Infantry Brigades were in position for the first stage of the final advance on Mandalay. By 17 February there were indications that the Japanese were definitely thinning out in Thabeikkyin area. The 98th Indian Infantry Brigade was then ordered to clear the areas between Thabeikkyin and the southern bridgehead, and to rejoin the remainder of the division for the push south. 4/4 Gurkha Rifles was to clear southward from the village, starting on 20 February through Chaunggyi, Wabyudaung and Kyaunggon, whilst 2 Royal Berks and 8/12 Frontier Force Regiment worked to the north from the Ngapyin-in area.

Thus, towards the end of the second week of February, the position on the different fronts in Burma was as follows:—

In the XXXIII Corps area, the 19th Indian Division had crossed the Irrawaddy in January, had established two bridgeheads on the east bank of that river, had foiled the Japanese attempts to exterminate the bridgeheads and after enlarging and consolidating them, was ready to march towards Mandalay—the "City of Kings". The 20th Indian Division, on the right flank of the Corps had taken Budalin, Monywa, Myinmu, Satpangon and Chaung-U. It had cleared the area to the north of the confluence of the rivers Chindwin and Irrawaddy, except for an isolated Japanese bridgehead opposite Sameikkon, and was getting ready to cross the Irrawaddy. In the area between these two divisions, the 2nd British Division had moved south, destroying Japanese opposition between the Mu and Irrawaddy rivers and was at this time at Ywathitgyi and near Legyi, to the north of the Irrawaddy, and was also preparing to cross this river.

In the IV Corps area, as described earlier, the 7th Indian Division had reached its first objective by this time and was ready to force a passage across the mighty Irrawaddy. The 17th Indian Division, which was to pass through the bridgehead of the former and make a dash for Meiktila, had also started its move. Thus the stage was set for an almost simultaneous crossing of the Irrawaddy at several places by both the Corps.

CHAPTER X

Crossing the Irrawaddy

In the preceding chapters, the advance of the IV and XXXIII Corps up to the Irrawaddy river has been described. The fighting was never on a large scale as the Japanese were only fighting rear-guard actions and were, on the whole, engaged in a withdrawal. But these operations have been described in some detail to give an idea of the tenacity and determination with which the Japanese then fought. The trend of these operations also indicates that they were as yet in the dark about the real intentions of the Allies, for they did divert some of their forces from the Meiktila area to the north of the Mandalay as they expected the main threat to develop in that region. Meanwhile Allied movements to cross the Irrawaddy south of Mandalay were proceeding according to plan.

The Irrawaddy

From Male in the north to Pakokku and Pagan in the south the distance is over two hundred miles. This wide frontage of the Irrawaddy was being approached by the two Corps by the middle of February. From Twinnge, seventy-five miles north of Mandalay, the river flows through thick forest and jungle for forty miles. Along twenty-four miles of this stretch between Thabeikkyin and Kyaukmyaung the course lies through a gorge, some 500 yards in width. Thereafter the country opens out as the river flows down-stream and the width at the confluence with the Chindwin, between Myingyan and Pakokku, varies between 2000 and 4500 yards. The current, which in the rains runs at five to six miles an hour, in the dry season is about two miles an hour in the wider stretches, but navigation is obstructed by islands and sand-banks which change positions after each monsoon. The difference between the minimum and maximum water-level at Mandalay is thirty-one feet and, in March and April, the river is liable to sudden rises. In general the south or eastern bank dominates the approaches to the opposite one, except in the stretch covered by the loop, where the Sagaing hills on the north bank dominate not only the east and south of the river but all approaches to it from the north. The Japanese held the Sagaing hills and by fortifying and defending them they' retained observation over the river on either arm of the great loop and all approaches to it from the north.

Altogether, the river Irrawaddy was one of the most difficult

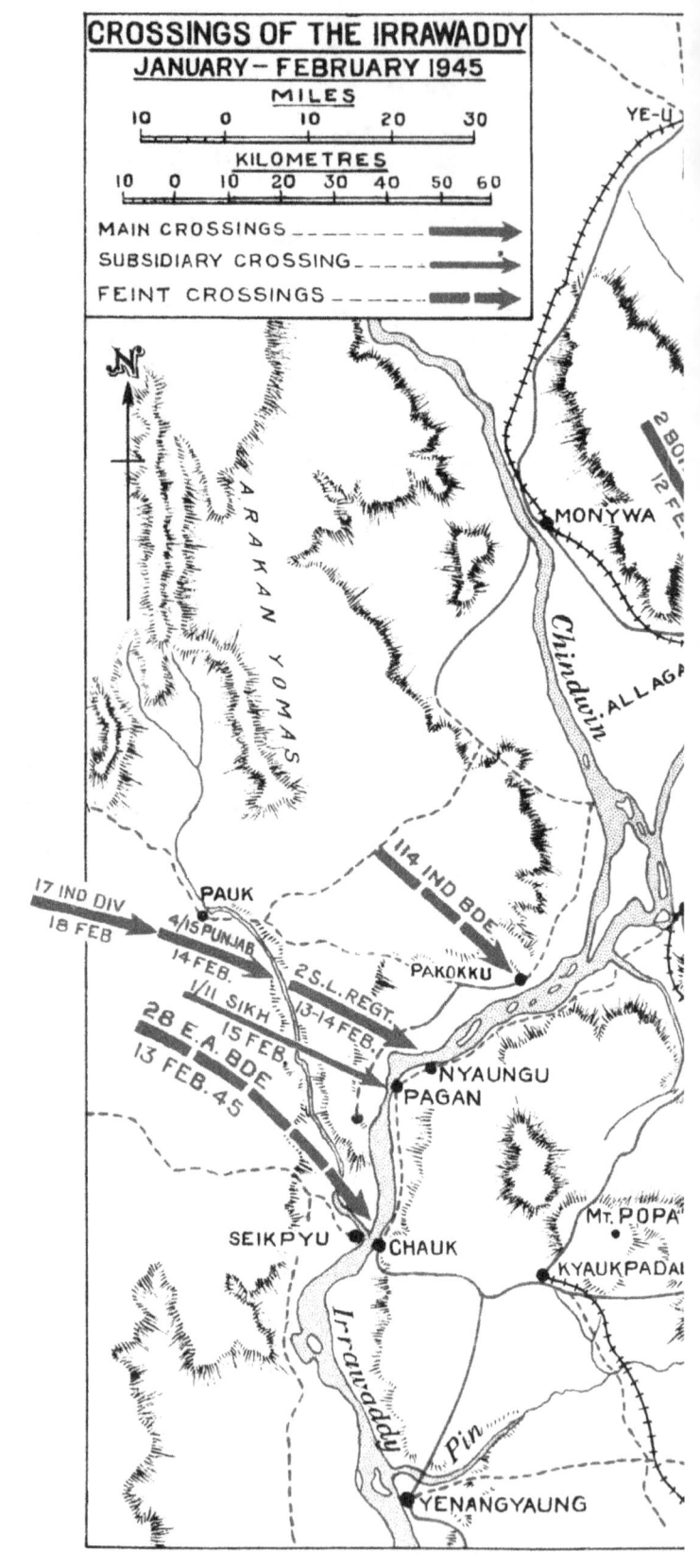

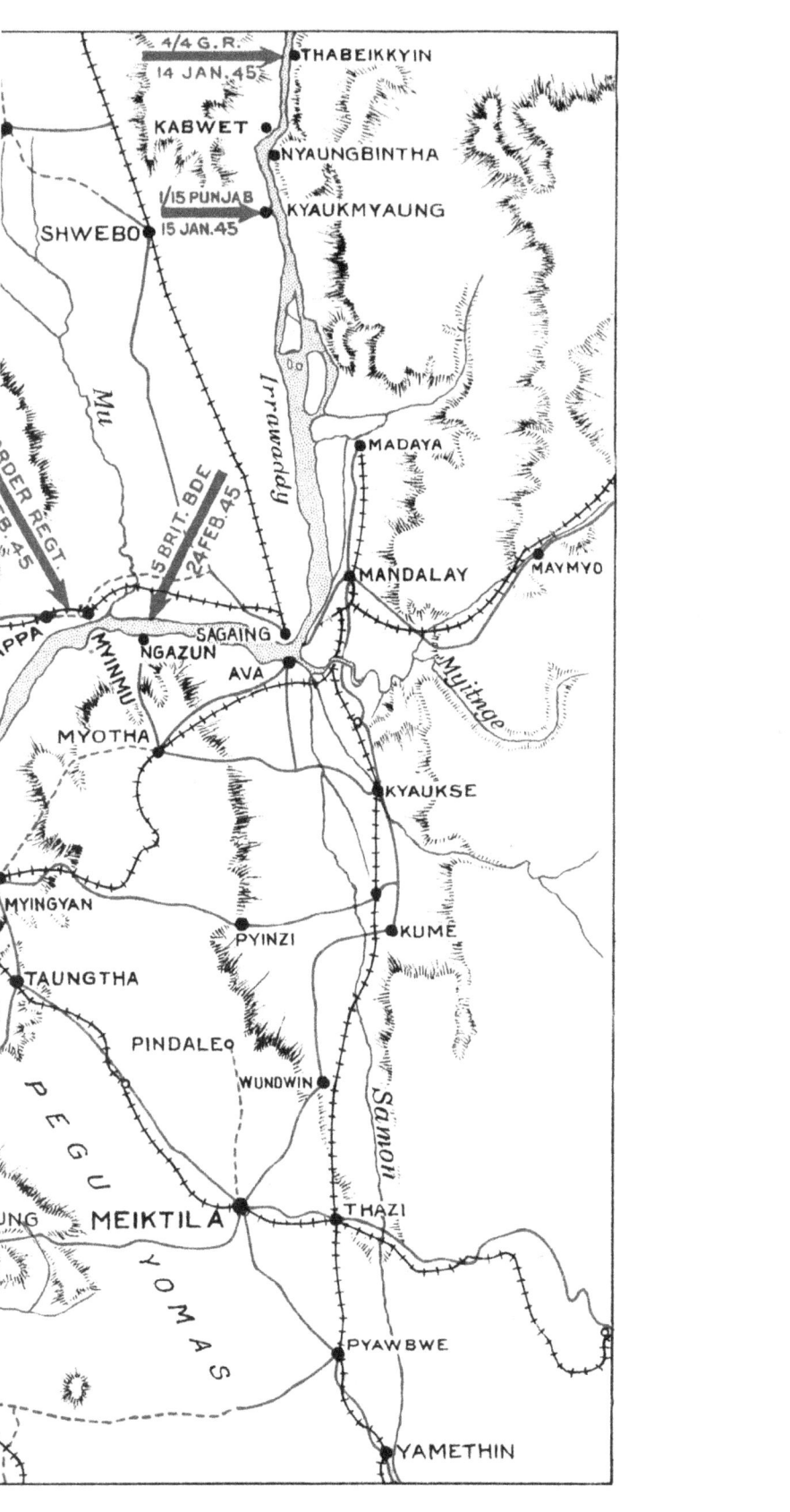

water obstacles that faced either side in the Second World War. Lieut-General Oliver Leese has summed up his impressions of 'this wide and treacherous river' by saying that he "could not imagine a more formidable military water obstacle."[1] To force the crossing of such a river against Japanese opposition required careful planning and preparation after reconnaissance, wise selection of the points of assault, deception, surprise, and swift action. Surprise is the secret of success and does more than anything else to make it possible for the assaulting infantry to cross over without meeting devastating hostile fire from air and ground. Speed was also enjoined in the British and Indian training doctrine, the object being to pass across to the further bank the greatest possible strength of all arms for securing a bridgehead, before the enemy might have time to react with superior force.

The Timing of Crossings

By the second week of February 1945, all was set for the crossing of the Irrawaddy by the IV Corps near Pakokku. The attention of the Japanese command had been successfully diverted from this point by the crossings made by the 19th Indian Division in January. They were lulled into the belief that this division belonged to the IV Corps, and, therefore, the rest of the Corps would follow the same line, and that the main Allied thrust would be directed on to Mandalay from that side. Lieut-General Slim had therefore to decide the delicate question of the priority of further crossings. There were three courses open to him, that either the XXXIII Corps or the IV Corps should cross first or that the crossings by both should be simultaneous. The advantage in adopting the first course was that it would fortify the impression that Mandalay was the main objective. On the other hand, it was realised that the Japanese would not be misled for long, and the advantage gained so far in deception would be lost unless the advance to Meiktila was made quickly and in strength. The disadvantage in adopting the second course—earlier crossing by the IV Corps—was that it would enable the Japanese to re-divert their forces from Mandalay to Meiktila. Lieut-General Slim, therefore, decided that one division from each Corps should cross simultaneously. In his own words, "the Japanese react slowly, and, even if they realised that the IV Corps crossing was the more serious threat, he would delay moving troops from XXXIII Corps front. Moreover it was necessary to secure the IV Corps bridgehead in good time as passing through the Striking Force for Meiktila might be a lengthy business."[2] In fact, this was the best decision calculated to leave the other side in

---

[1] Leese's *Despatch*, para. 77.
[2] Slim: *Campaign of the Fourteenth Army, 1944-45*, pp. 14-15.

to minds; and, for a time at least, they would not know from which side the real threat might develop. Hence it was finally decided that the 20th Indian Division from the XXXIII Corps and the 7th Indian Division from the other Corps should cross simultaneously. As will be described later, these two divisions crossed the Irrawaddy according to plan and within 24 hours of each other.

Administrative Build-up and Preparations

If the crossing of a river demands careful organisation and preparation when there is no enemy to oppose it, still more does this apply when the passage has to be forced. That the Irrawaddy was a formidable obstacle whose passage would be strongly contested was well recognised. It was clear that the operation would necessitate a specialised form of attack involving the closest co-operation between all arms, and elaborate preparations both in the base and forward areas. The India Command was made responsible for the rearward preparation. Consequently great attention was bestowed on training in India on rivers whose width approximated to some of the larger rivers in Burma, and experiments were made in the best method of crossing them. Past experience and lessons learnt in river crossings elsewhere during the Second World War were taken advantage of.[3] For example, the experience of the opposing armies in Russia which came up frequently against water barriers provided many useful lessons.[4] Again, the three Indian divisions in Italy had mastered the teachnique of river assaults by dint of serious study and practice. In particular the 8th Indian Division, between October and December 1943, had forced its passage across the rivers Biferno, Trigno, and Moro, as also in the following May when it successfully crossed the Gari and Melfa in Italy.[5] The preparations in India were therefore based on the latest experiences of the Indian and other Allied armies in different theatres of the war.

Though the arrangements for the actual crossings were left to the Corps and divisional commanders, the Army Headquarters in India provided all help in the shape of equipment, etc. The commanders had to decide upon the actual sites for crossing after detailed reconnaissances carried out by specially trained swimmers of the Inter-Service Sea Reconnaissance Unit. The equipment available was, however, by no means adequate. Many of the boats and much of the rafting stores had been brought over hundreds of miles of bad roads and had got damaged in transport. While there was a serious shortage of out-board engines, most of those which were

---

[3] Army in India Training Memorandum (AITM), March 1944, p. 49.
[4] AITM, April 1943, para 15.
[5] 17th Indian Inf Bde War Diary, May 1944, App. D.

available were not powerful enough for the purpose and some were unreliable. The equipment received was supplemented by a considerable number of pontoons captured from the Japanese, but these subsequently turned out to be unsuitable for anything but bridging. That, in spite of all these difficulties, the crossings were successfully made speaks highly of the capacity for improvisation and adjustment by all concerned in the operation. As the Army Commander has remarked: "The only equipment my army had in full supply was, as ever, brains, hardihood, and courage."[6]

The Japanese Plan

The Japanese had realised that the Fourteenth Army was about to cross over to the east bank, but it was not possible for them to cover the whole river front, over 200 miles in length. They appear to have been rather complacent about the southern (Pakokku) front, for it was in the beginning of February that they withdrew the *2nd Division* from that area and sent it to French Indo-China.[7] Nevertheless, they decided to concentrate over the likely crossing points and watch the intervening spaces, while keeping their reserves in the rear, ready to move to any threatened place. General Kimura inspected the defences, and "probably felt that while he might not be able to stop us crossing in places, he would be able to destroy rapidly, such forces as did manage to get over."[8] While he possessed what may be called this 'defender's advantage' in opposing the Allied crossings, he had the disadvantage of not possessing adequate air support. However, the Japanese were determined to use whatever aircraft they had "more boldly and more freely".

The Crossings

The following four main crossings of the Irrawaddy were decided upon and undertaken by the Fourteenth Army:

(i) The 19th Indian Division crossings north of Mandalay at Thabeikkyin and Kyaukmayaung in the second week of January. This division thus had the honour of being the first to cross the Irrawaddy. As has been narrated in an earlier chapter the Japanese had made several determined efforts to hurl it back but the division not only held on to its bridgeheads but also succeeded in expanding them.

(ii) The 20th Indian Division crossings near Allagappa, west of Mandalay, in the Myinmu area on 12 February with the object of advancing east along the south bank of the river towards Mandalay.

---

[6] Slim: *Defeat into Victory*, p. 410.
[7] Essays by Lt.-Col. Fujiwara Iwaichi, Seatic Historical Bulletin No. 240, p. 19
[8] Slim: *Campaign of the Fourteenth Army, op. cit.*, p. 15.

(iii) The 2nd British Division crossings on 24 February at Nagazun, a village between Sagaing and Allagappa.
(iv) The IV Corps crossings at Nyaungu to the south of Pakokku between 12 and 19 February.

19TH INDIAN DIVISION CROSSINGS

The crossings of the Irrawaddy by the 19th Indian Division have already been described and will not be dealt with here.[9] The only point to be noted here is the Japanese reaction to them. As was expected, they had thought these crossings to be the spear-head of the IV Corps' advance and had decided to destroy the 19th Indian Division before it could consolidate its bridgeheads. However, all their efforts proved abortive in spite of their concentrating the bulk of the *15th* and *53rd Divisions*, and very heavy artillery. Frontal attacks, suicide assaults, infiltration, bombing, in short everything was tried, but although the Indian division suffered casualties, it was not to be hurled back.

20TH INDIAN DIVISION CROSSINGS

After capturing Budalin, Monywa, and Myinmu, the 20th Indian Division spent some time in closing up to the north bank of the Irrawaddy. The remaining Japanese forces on the north bank were then cleared and some patrols were also pushed out across the river. The battle of the outposts was soon finished, and by the second week of February, the 20th Indian Division was poised for crossing the great river. Quite apart from meeting the opposition which the Japanese were likely to put up, the administrative problem itself was one of considerable magnitude. The area selected for the crossing was at the bend of the river, south of the village of Allagappa. The river in this area is very wide (1500 yards) and the current swift-flowing at the rate of three knots with steep banks which made evacuation of vehicles from the beaches difficult. Not being an ideal crossing place, it had, however, the advantage of being only lightly defended. Moreover, it lay at a point where the boundaries of the Japanese *31st* and *33rd Divisions* met, and this fact was expected to lead to some confusion in hostile ranks.

The assault crossing had to be effected with ranger boats, towed in a train, powered by out-board motors of an unreliable nature. There were no modern assault-craft available, and in the absence of complete surprise, it would have been difficult to get across on improvised rafts.[10]

[9] The first elements of the 19th Division to cross the river were 4/4 GR on the night of 13/14 January, and 1/15 Punjab on the night of 14/15 January 1945.
[10] A Short History of 20th Indian Division, *op. cit.*, and War Diary of the same division.

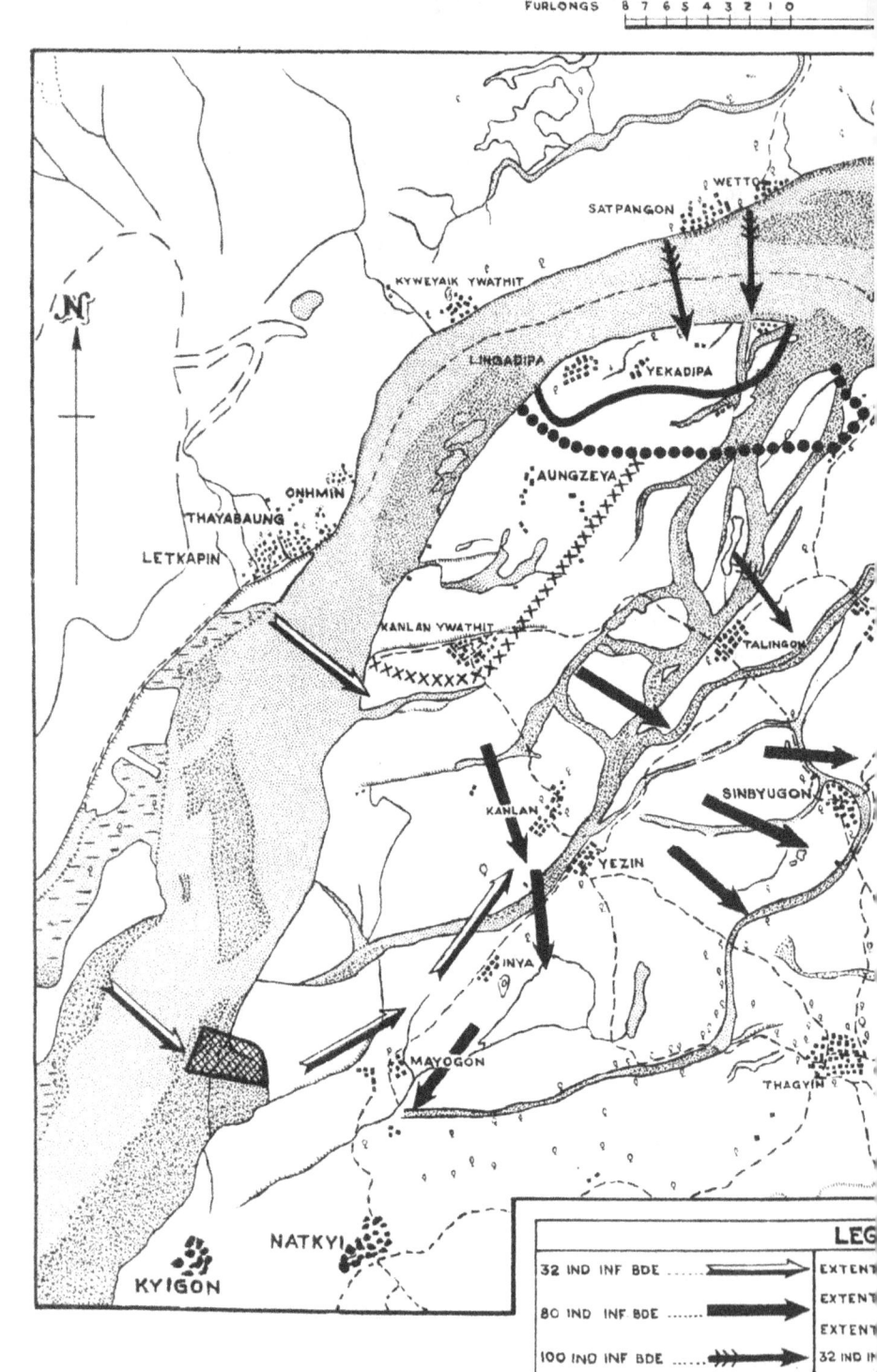

...WADDY BY 20 INDIAN DIV.
...ARY 1945

The Deception Plan

In view of the necessity of achieving surprise it was essential to deceive the Japanese as to the selection of the crossing places in order to make them not only dispose their reserves in the wrong place, and to disperse them, but also to prevent them from counter-attacking before the bridgehead had been firmly established.

There were two obvious crossing places at Sameikkon on the south bank and at Myinmu on the north bank as good roads or tracks led to and away from these on both the banks.[11] The plan decided upon was that some troops near these likely crossing places should be ordered to draw and contain the maximum strength of opposing forces. The 80th Indian Infantry Brigade was to deceive the Japanese into thinking that the division was going for the Sameikkon crossing, and the Devons attached to the 100th Indian Infantry Brigade were to behave as if they were interested in the Myinmu crossing, while a deception unit which had joined the 20th Indian Division was to build up a fictitious force in the confluence area west of Sameikkon. The 32nd Indian Infantry Brigade was to spread rumours of the division's intention to cross over to the west bank of the Chindwin. In addition, a faked sketch map, torn and charred, was passed on to one of the reliable agents of the Japanese showing the 5th Indian Division advancing astride the Chindwin on to their left flank.

Softening up by the Royal Air Force was, as far as possible, evenly spread to cover Japanese concentrations along the whole front, until the afternoon before the crossing when their gun area would be pounded by fifty Liberators.[12]

The Plan for Crossing

The plan for the actual crossing defined the tasks of the various brigades as follows:—

The 100th Indian Infantry Brigade was to cross at Satpangon, and establish its bridgehead up to a line running from Ywathit through Talingon, and Gaungbo to Alethaung. The crossing was to take place on the night of 12/13 February. The 32nd Indian Infantry Brigade was to concentrate secretly in the Cheyadaw area, and make a subsidiary crossing of not more than two battalions into a small bridgehead opposite Letkapin, and link up with the right of the 100th Indian Infantry Brigade bridgehead in the Kanlan-Ywathit area. The third battalion was to cross over into the bridgehead when sufficient depth had been attained. The 80th Indian Infantry Brigade was to continue active operations in the confluence area, but had to be prepared to move quickly into

---

[11] *Ibid.* See also Op. Order No. 13 of XXXIII Corps, 2 Feb. 45.
[12] *Ibid.*

the bridgehead of the 100th Indian Infantry Brigade preparatory to breaking out of it, leaving behind the PAVO and the Deception Unit in the confluence area to take its place and continue the jitter activities.[13]

100th Brigade Operations—First Phase

During the first twelve days of February patrols were active on the south bank of the Irrawaddy, trying to pin-point hostile positions. The Japanese guns were reasonably active during this period also, so that it was possible to make an estimate of the strength and location of their defensive artillery. The picture that emerged was of a light screen along the river bank, with the main body of infantry lying back to give them the best chance of deployment against the assault when it took place. The Japanese troops were disposed in a semicircle prepared to close in on any landing party. The medium artillery available for them was disposed in two groups. One, east of the Yazawin Chaung, was prepared to deal with any attack east of the confluence of the Mu river. The other, on the rising ground south of Kalaywa, dominated the river and the banks south and west of Myinmu, and had within its range the artillery areas of the 20th Indian Division, north of Myinmu.

The first essential preliminary to a successful crossing was, therefore, that the Japanese artillery be intensively pounded by the Royal Air Force. Hence on the afternoon of 12 February an attack was launched by fifty Liberators, and a squadron of Lightnings dropped flamethrowing bombs on the medium gun areas, which caused the destruction of four guns and the dispersal of the rest. The result of the operation was that the troops of the 100th Indian Infantry Brigade had a respite of 48 hours from heavy and organised shelling by Japanese artillery.

Operation Order No. 9 was issued on 11 February by the Headquarters 100th Indian Infantry Brigade giving detailed instructions for the crossing. According to it the 20th Indian Division was to establish a bridgehead south of the Irrawaddy with a view to cutting the road Mandalay-Meiktila in the Myittha and Kyaukse areas. The 100th Indian Infantry Brigade was to form the main bridgehead and the 32nd Indian Infantry Brigade the subsidiary one, and when this had been done, the 80th Indian Infantry Brigade was to pass through and move to the area Myittha—Kyaukse and cut the Mandalay—Meiktila road. As for the crossing by the 100th Indian Infantry Brigade was concerned, the 2nd Border Regiment was to form the spear-head, followed up immediately by the 14/13 Frontier Force Rifles.[14] The Border would establish a bridgehead from

[13] Ibid.
[14] See Appx. C to 100th Bde War Diary for February 1945. See also 14 FF Rif OO No. 1, dated 12 February.

including the bend in nulla PK 960567 to inclusive of Yekadipa 9456. The 'H' hours for the first crossing was to be 2300 hours on the night of 12/13 February, before which the Beach Recce Unit was to cross and guide the assaulting troops by lights. If possible the crossing was to be made in perfect silence. For purposes of deception the 114th Field Regiment was to fire smoke on Ywathit from 0645 hours to 0700 hours on the morning of 13 February.[15]

The crossing began on the night of 12/13 February, with 2 Border. It was an anxious night, for everyone was aware of the importance of surprise and of the frailty of the boats. Swimmers of the Sea Recce Unit, however, gave great encouragement by fixing guiding lights on the farther bank. Owing to the difficulty of warming the out-board motors before starting, and a high wind that was blowing at the time, the first flight was somewhat disorganised. A few boats swept some distance downstream, and some stuck in midstream on shifting sand-banks. But the second flight was more successful and they were in fact the first to land, near Yekadipa. The Japanese had by then opened up with a light machine-gun but clearly without any idea that anything more than a patrol was crossing. Through the early hours of the morning of the 13th, a ferry service worked very smoothly, and soon after daylight the whole of 2 Border had crossed, followed by 14 Frontier Force Rifles and one company of 4/10 Gurkha Rifles. All companies of the Frontier Force Rifles were across by 0900 hours on the 13th.[16] Some anti-tank guns and mortars and also some jeeps and two bulldozers were across, in a bridgehead already measuring some 2,500 yards by 1,000 yards.[17] This success, to a great extent, was possible because of the diversionary attacks by the 32nd Indian Infantry Brigade elsewhere which had succeeded in drawing some Japanese forces to itself. The heavy pounding received by the Japanese guns from air in the previous two days may also account for the comparatively unopposed landings.

Japanese Counter-Attacks

The Japanese had meanwhile discovered the fact of the landings and had begun to cover the beaches with mortars, and the following night their jitter parties were active trying to probe into the strength of the 100th Indian Infantry Brigade. On the other side, the British and Indian troops spent the night of 13/14 February in increasing the extent of the bridgehead eastwards as far as the sandy chaung. The patrols of 14 Frontier Force Rifles moving south

---

[15] *Ibid.*
[16] WD 14 FF Rif, 13 Feb. 1945.
[17] A Short History of 20th Indian Division, *op. cit.* Also 100th Bde WD/601/359, Part III.

towards Kanlan Ywathit bumped into many small parties of the Japanese troops but after an excellent air-strike the place was occupied. By the morning of the 15th, the brigade was firmly established across the Irrawaddy.[18]

32nd Brigade Operations—First Phase

Meanwhile the 32nd Indian Infantry Brigade had also begun to play its part in the plan by executing a subsidiary crossing further south. Its plan was that 1 Northamptons would first cross and establish a bridgehead in Kyigon area at the same time as the main crossing of the 100th Indian Infantry Brigade; and then the rest of the brigade, less 3/8 Gurkha Rifles in divisional reserve, would cross either through the bridgehead established by the other brigade or that formed by 1 Northamptons. It was also arranged that 9/14 Punjab would simultaneously send one company across the river from Letkapin to form a base near Mayogon. This company was to send out a gunbusting party in addition to acting as a left-flank stop to the Northamptons.

The object of this move was that the Northamptons, supported by 9/14 Punjab, should secure a bridgehead on the far bank, in the Kyigon area, with the object of acting as a 'stop' to Japanese attempts to interfere from the south with the main bridgehead of the 100th Brigade, and to divert pressure from the latter as long as possible.[19] At a later stage the two bridgeheads were to be linked up before the 20th Indian Division made its breakout. The location of the subsidiary bridgehead was to be in the neighbourhood of Kyigon and it was to be extended, opposition permitting, to include Natkyi.

The Northamptons made the crossing on the night of 12/13 February, but here again the first wave was unlucky; the out-board motor controlling the chain of ranger boats broke down in midstream and the whole party drifted about half a mile below the intended beach, landing under slight Japanese fire. The rest of them, however, managed after considerable difficulty to reach the proper beach and establish contact with the first party before dawn, by which time three companies and the battalion headquarters had also crossed.

A company of 9/14 Punjab had made an independent crossing at the same time, landing near Kanlan. The intention was that this company should rejoin the main body as soon as possible after completing its task of protecting the northern flank of the subsidiary bridgehead. These men unfortunately attracted the attention of the Japanese on landing who made a determined attempt, on the

[18] *Ibid.*
[19] 32nd Ind Inf Brigade, Op Instn. No. 9 of 8 Feb. 1945. Also WD 9/14 Punjab for Feb. 1945.

morning of 13 February, to burn the Punjabis out of the long grass and drive them into the field of light machine-gun fire on the beach. A lucky change of wind however turned the fire against the Japanese and relieved the Punjabis for the time being.[20] But the southern exits from the beaches were covered by machine-gun fire while, to the north, there appeared to be a confused movement of hostile troops moving up to attack the 100th Indian Infantry Brigade. This company was attacked again during the night of 13/14 February, and patrols sent north to contact 14 Frontier Force Rifles were unsuccessful. Ultimately, however, it established contact on the afternoon of the 14th and came under the command of 14 Frontier Force Rifles.

On 14 February, ferrying continued into the main bridgehead and the Northamptons completed their crossing during the day. They were followed by two companies of 9/14 Punjab before the morning of the 15th. At this stage it became necessary to get across the river some mortars and a forward observation party from 23 Mountain Battery to manipulate some direction-finding fire for the night of 14-15 February. But, in spite of a smoke screen put down very accurately by the Royal Air Force, these attracted hostile fire during the crossing and landed rather too far south where, throughout an uncomfortable afternoon, they remained pinned to the beach and rejoined the main body only after dark. By this time the Japanese guns had made daylight crossings very hazardous, hence the rest of 9/14 Punjab had to wait for the nightfall. But as this unit was crossing, the Japanese opened a fierce attack on the beaches, getting in behind the Allied defensive positions, and the boats came under heavy machine-gun fire, with the result that six of them were sunk. The Japanese overran an anti-tank gun and threatened the headquarters of 1 Northamptons but the situation was retrieved by a hastily organised counter-attack and the gun was recaptured. Another desperate Japanese attack by a party of about 100 men followed on the position of a company of 1 Northamptons at 904493, this time from the front, on the night of 16/17 February, with the result that they acquired a footing in its perimeter. Only a counter-attack in the morning helped to restore the position.

On 17 February again, the Japanese guns were busy against the beaches and the defences, which was followed by a third unexpected attack, heavily supported by artillery. Approximately 150 of them attacked 9/14 Punjab from the south during the night. The attack was pushed home with great tenacity, four Japanese soldiers penetrating the wire. ↓Of these, one was the commander of the *3rd Battalion 213th Regiment,* Captain Moritani—an indication that the

---

[20] See Appendix F 5 to 9/14 Punjab War Diary for Feb. 1945.

General view of one of the starting points on the river bank

Stuart tanks move up to cross the river

Men of 4 6 Gurkha and other Indian troops cross the Irrawaddy river during drive on Mandalay

Hoisting a section of the bridge into position in mid-stream

Gurkha patrol advances in Pakokku village area

Trucks go across the river on rafts as advance continues in Pagan area

Lieutenant
Karamjeet Singh Judge V.C.
4/15 Punjab

Captain Michael Allmand V.C.
3/6 G.R.

Naik Gian Singh V.C.
4/15 Punjab

Major Frank Gerald Blaker V.C.
3/9 G.R.

Japanese had withdrawn troops from their own Sameikkon bridgehead to throw the Indian troops out. All the four of them were killed. The Japanese casualties in the course of this raid totalled more than 40 dead.

There was a lull between 18 and 24 February, but life was made very unpleasant for the bridgehead defenders and for the troops manning the beaches, by the daily shelling which the Japanese, from higher ground, were able to put down very accurately. On the night of 24/25 February, they made their last attack with a very mixed force (believed to have included one tank) which was also repulsed with heavy loss.

All this prevented the troops of the 32nd Indian Infantry Brigade—9/14 Punjab reinforced by one company of 3/8 Gurkha Rifles—to make any advance outside their perimeter, as the Japanese held strong defences, had a superiority in artillery fire-power and excellent observation posts which enabled them to frustrate any aggressive movement by infantry alone (all the Allied tanks having been allotted to the main bridgehead).

On 28 February the Headquarters 32nd Indian Infantry Brigade moved into the main bridgehead in preparation for the second phase.

100th Brigade Operations—Second Phase

In the main bridgehead area also, by the morning of 15 February, the Japanese reaction became noticeable. The extent of their resistance at this stage may be judged by the fact that no less than twelve battalions were identified on the 100th Indian Infantry Brigade front. At 0730 hours sixteen Japanese aircraft (Oscars) made a dash at the beaches and the ferry, bombing and strafing. But they removed themselves in time before the Spitfires arrived to intercept them. The damage caused was however slight.[21] Also some Japanese attacking parties had infiltrated during the night of 14/15 February into the eastern flank of the bridgehead to a distance of about 20 yards from the perimeter of 2 Border[22] but they were driven out with severe losses. During the day, 14 Frontier Force Rifles occupied Kanlan Ywathit after an air-strike, but an attempt to exploit the area south of Kanlan was unsuccessful as the Japanese counter-attacked and forced one platoon to withdraw. During the night patrols went down to Talingon, which was found to be occupied.

The next day was utilised by the 100th Indian Infantry Brigade to consolidate its position when the ferries worked smoothly and the aerial cab-rank was ready to pounce on any Japanese attempt to

---

[21] Six persons were wounded and several vehicles slightly damaged as a result of the raid. 100th Bde W/D, 15 Feb. 1945.
[22] *Ibid.* 601/359/WD, Part III.

interfere. But with nightfall, hostile guns became active, harassing the beaches and the brigade headquarters perimeter. Jitter parties pushed in from the Alethaung side of the bridgehead; and the first heavy counter-attack was put in against 14/13 Frontier Force Rifles in Kanlan Ywathit by a combined force estimated at one battalion drawn from the *1st Battalion 215th Regiment* and the *1st Battalion 16th Regiment*. In this action Jemadar Parkash Singh[23] displayed a high degree of gallantry which won him a Victoria Cross. His platoon bore the main brunt of the night attack lasting over three hours. The Japanese had used artillery, mortars, machine-guns and even flame throwers. After the platoon havildar and the officer commanding were wounded, Jemadar Parkash Singh, though wounded, began to direct the action. He crawled forward on his hands and knees and reached a two-inch mortar post. Here with the help of his batman who was also wounded he continued firing until his ammunition was finished. Then he set about collecting whatever ammunition he could from the dead and wounded and distributed it to his few remaining supporters. Finally he got hold of a Bren gun but was wounded again. Wounded a third time, he stuck to his post and continued to encourage his men. A grenade burst near him and he was wounded a fourth time and died shortly afterwards, but not before assuring his company commander that he would look after himself.[24] The company fought on most gallantly against superior numbers, and only withdrew when its ammunition was completely exhausted. They killed 66 Japanese, their own casualties being no less than 42 killed and 48 wounded.

On the morning of 18 February, 4/10 Gurkha Rifles supported by light tanks of 7 Cavalry, attacked and captured Talingon. A large party of Japanese troops made prolonged attack on Kanlan Ywathit during the night and succeeded in establishing themselves on the north-east corner of the village, capturing two anti-tank guns. But the village was cleared after hand to hand fighting and the guns were recaptured. The Japanese tried to withdraw to Sinbugon, which was pounded by artillery and by the air force. At the same time 2 Border occupied Bethaung and pushed out patrols to Sindat. The sandy chaung was no longer a limit to the bridgehead. Air support throughout the day was magnificent, over 130 sorties being flown (a considerable figure for the Royal Air Force in Burma).[25]

It was the Japanese turn to be aggressive during the night. From that time up to 26 February there was a practically ceaseless struggle for Talingon—the Japanese counter-attacking by night, and

---

[23] Twenty-second Indian VC of the war.
[24] *India's VCs in two World Wars.*
[25] A Short History of 20th Indian Division, *op. cit.*

the Indian troops with tanks and wasps clearing them again by day.[26] At Kanlan Ywathit their desperate efforts had obtained for the Japanese a foothold in the north-east corner of the village, but in the morning they were again driven out. On the 19th, 14 Frontier Force Rifles was relieved in Kanlan Ywathit area by 3/8 Gurkha Rifles who made a raid into Kanlan on 20 February. Meanwhile 4/10 Gurkha Rifles had cleared Gaungbo, which gave some protection to their positions in front of Talingon. But the day's chief victory was that gained by the Royal Air Force. A Hurricane cruising over the field spotted a camouflaged tank near Paunggadaw. The cab-rank set to work and quickly destroyed this, and then more and more were picked out. A relentless search between Paunggadaw, Thagyin and Letpanlyin went on throughout the hours of daylight, and at the end of it at least 13 Japanese tanks were known to have been destroyed.[27]

This event had important results. On the previous night the Japanese had attempted to take medium tanks into Talingon. But owing to faulty preparations these were unable to cross a chaung to the south, and therefore had little effect on the course of fighting. At this stage, however, as the Allies had not any medium tanks across the river, and their anti-tank guns were to a certain extent vulnerable, both in attack and defence, the presence of Japanese medium tanks would have been prejudicial to the success of the 100th Indian Infantry Brigade. But as a result of the action taken by the Royal Air Force no Japanese tanks were used again on this front.

The Japanese infantry attacks continued around Talingon. The fighting was "confused and bitter".[28] The methods used were uniform and succeeding nights saw no change in the Japanese plan; every night they would raid 4/10 Gurkha Rifles positions, sometimes infiltrating and digging themselves in. While inflicting some casualties on the defenders they suffered heavy casualties themselves and achieved little.[29]

To the east of Talingon, 2 Border took the offensive and in two successful actions cleared the river bank to Sindat, inflicting heavy casualties. After a short rest, 14 Frontier Force Rifles had been switched on to this side of the bridgehead and began to patrol round Kalaywa (where the *124th Regiment* of the *31st Division* had its headquarters), preparatory to an attack supported by tanks and artillery, which succeeded in driving out the Japanese on 1 March, the fleeing Japanese being subjected to bombing and strafing. Headquarters 100th Indian Infantry Brigade had moved on 28 February

[26] *Ibid.*
[27] *Ibid.*
[28] See 100th Bde W/D for 24 February 1945.
[29] From 18 to 26 February, the Japanese lost more than 500 in dead in the actions around Talingon. 100th Bde W/D, *op. cit.*

to Sindat to make room for the 80th Indian Infantry Brigade in the rapidly expanding bridgehead.

Linking the Bridgeheads

While the 32nd Indian Infantry Brigade and the 100th Indian Infantry Brigade were establishing themselves across the river, the 80th Indian Infantry Brigade had begun to thin out from the confluence area. Its headquarters crossed to the main bridgehead on 21 February, having under it 1 Devon, 9 Frontier Force Regiment and 3 Gurkha Rifles (less two companies) and a company of 9/14 Punjab, under its command. The brigade was made responsible for operations in the Kanlan area, which were designed to push the Japanese finally out of the headland and to establish its troops across the sandy chaung at Yezin and Inya, preparatory to linking up with the bridgehead of the 32nd Indian Infantry Brigade.[30]

The situation when the 80th Indian Infantry Brigade crossed over was that two bridgeheads had already been established—the main one at Myinmu and a subsidiary one further down the river. The second bridgehead was part of the deception plan to force the Japanese to split their forces. But the latter had maintained a very heavy pressure on this and it was not possible to reinforce or withdraw the 32nd Indian Infantry Brigade, which was suffering considerable casualties and whose supplies were running short. The role of the 80th Indian Infantry Brigade, therefore, was to open communications with the 32nd Indian Infantry Brigade and destroy the forces between the two bridgeheads.[31]

On 23 February, 1 Devon, supported by 7 Cavalry, made a reconnaissance in force into Kanlan, inflicting many casualties. The Japanese reacted by shelling the tanks and inflicted some casualties on the company of Bombay Grenadiers which was escorting them. Infantry patrols during the next two days found Yezin and Inya strongly held and the chaung itself covered by defensive positions. 9 Frontier Force Regiment occupied Kanlan with two companies on 26 February against moderate opposition, and caught the Japanese in the open as they withdrew. The usual counter-attack against Kanlan developed during the night, but was not pressed home. The Japanese at this stage were described by the brigade commander as "young and timorous" and probably consisted of the last reinforcements which the *16th Regiment* could scrape together.[32]

Meanwhile the brigade area had been enlarged to include Talingon, which was taken over by 1 Devon; and 3/1 Gurkha Rifles also came across the river.

---

[30] A Short History of 20th Indian Division, *op. cit.*
[31] *Ibid.*
[32] *Ibid.*

.On 27 February, 9 Frontier Force Regiment received verbal orders to liquidate all the Japanese then hiding in tall grass between Kanlan Ywathit and Kanlan and capture Yezin and Inya. This operation was to be carried out in four phases.

Phase I, to attack the Japanese position south-west of Kanlan and clear the area west of the track between Kanlan Ywathit and Kanlan.

Phase II, to swing over to the left after Phase I and capture Yezin.

Phase III, after Yezin to capture Inya destroying the hostile force which was believed to be hiding in the nulla and grass astride the road leading from Yezin to Inya.

Phase IV, to clear the area east and south of Yezin by carrying out a sweep.

For this operation a squadron of 7 Light Cavalry (Stuart tanks) was placed under command. The divisional artillery was in support and a cab-rank at call.

The position is described by the local Diarist as follows:—

"It was believed to be the strongest Jap concentration facing the Division. The enemy was determined to prevent a junction between the two bridgeheads. Consequently his artillery had become more active and numerous. There were also signs of increased strength on his part.

"The ground was more favourable to the enemy. The tall elephant grass afforded him an excellent cover and prevented our tanks from seeing the enemy defences. He had camouflaged his dugouts very well. His O.P's could see our tanks or the dust raised by them from a long distance. To protect the tanks from tank-busting parties it was essential in such a thick country to keep the infantry close to the tanks. With artillery and other fire directed at tanks it was bound to cause casualties amongst the tank protecting infantry. But this risk had to be accepted as the squadron was already under strength regarding its tanks."

At 0900 hours on the morning of 28 February the C Company of the battalion began Phase I of the operations with the support of tanks provided by a squadron of 7 Cavalry. Artillery and air support was also made available. The Japanese were dug-in in strong bunker positions and could not be sighted from the tanks. They therefore employed their usual tactics of remaining silent as the tanks passed and opening up fire from the flanks and behind on the infantry following the tanks.[33] The only course open to the infantry was to charge them with bayonets. Most of the fighting therefore was hand to hand. Every Japanese position encountered

---

[33] W/D 9/12 Frontier Force Regiment, 28 Feb. 1945.

had to be eliminated completely before advance to the next was resumed. The result was that there was a considerable delay before Phase II could start.

In the meantime a heavy artillery concentration had been put on Yezin and Inya to pulverize hostile positions there. Tactical headquarters was also established at the south-west corner of Kanlan soon after Phase I had commenced. Cab-rank was usefully employed to keep the Japanese artillery quiet. But as the advance progressed Japanese medium machine-guns and artillery became more active and a number of casualties were suffered. It was found that C Company alone could not tackle the situation, hence B Company which was ready for such an eventuality, was also launched in its support. By then it was discovered that the main force on the other side was dug-in in very strong bunkers built in the lip of the Yezin Chaung, which were difficult for the tanks to tackle. All that was practicable was to employ the tanks to engage the hostile force and compel the Japanese to keep their heads down. For this task a few of the tanks were left there and the rest with D Company were ordered to commence Phase II, viz the capture of Yezin, which had been considerably delayed.

Between Kanlan and Yezin there was a stretch of open ground in full view of the Japanese force. D Company assembled in Kanlan under cover. When the tanks were ready they dashed across the open ground heading towards Yezin, at about 1500 hours. The artillery on the Japanese side opened up but luckily it was not effective. D Company reached Yezin without much serious opposition as the Japanese did not expect the attack from this direction. On arrival there, the Indian troops met heavy sniper fire from the trees and other covered positions. The main Japanese position was outside the village, but as soon as they saw D Company entering Yezin they tried to stage a come-back but were frustrated in their attempt and the tanks and the Indian infantry forced them to run away. Meanwhile the Japanese snipers had inflicted a few casualties but when they realised that they were surrounded and overwhelmed they also started running away, losing many in their withdrawal.

Capture of Inya

As soon as Yezin was consolidated and the tanks had reorganised, Phase III was put into operation. Instead of putting in fresh companies which would have imposed a further delay it was decided to continue the advance with C and D Companies. B Company was at the time to the south-west of Kanlan, where it had taken over operations from C Company, and A Company was further back in reserve.

About 1700 hours, C Company followed by D Company commenced its advance along the axis of the road leading to Inya. It encountered very heavy fire from the hostile bunkers in the nulla on the right and the fields on the left. As usual the Japanese held their fire till the tanks had gone past and then opened with everything on the infantry. And once again it developed into a close hand to hand fighting. Grenades were most effective in dealing with the Japanese bunkers.

In this advance a Japanese 105-mm gun which had been obstructing the move forward was overrun and the entire crew cut to pieces. Many Japanese machine-guns were knocked out. Just before dark C Company had succeeded in entering Inya, where soon after D Company also joined it. The Japanese put in a counter-attack, which was, however, successfully repulsed. A and B Companies spent the night 28 Feb./1 March in Yezin, C and D Companies at Inya.

In their advance from Yezin to Inya, the troops had suffered considerable loss, as the Japanese fire was heavy, accurate and devastating. Everyone of their weapon positions had therefore to be located and destroyed in turn. There was no other alternative. The tanks did not render much direct help as the Japanese showed themselves only when the tanks had passed. It was a pure and simple infantry-man's contest using bayonet and grenade. Although it was a costly method yet the men were determined to get through at all cost. Literally every inch of ground was contested most tenaciously by the Japanese as they knew it was their last chance to prevent the bridgehead from developing any further. The casualties on this side were gradually mounting up and C Company was specially getting thinner on ground as it had been in action the whole day. Nevertheless, the Indian troops unperturbed and shouting their war cries continued their excellent work with bayonets and grenades. They were also running short of ammunition towards the end, but the tank crew helped them liberally with their own stock.

The co-operation between the infantry and tanks was also very effective. The tanks were quick in dealing with any hostile resistance they could spot and their support to the infantry was prompt and unhesitating. The success of the operation was due mainly to the cold courage, iron determination and guts displayed by all ranks of the C and D Companies in the face of most stiff resistance. The battle having commenced in the morning went on till late in the evening without a pause. There were many individual acts of gallantry performed, some of which later received recognition too.

Phase IV was given up under the orders of the brigade as it was getting too late.

By this action 9 Frontier Force Regiment had linked up the two brigades, and the event was considered so important that the Corps Commander came down to Yezin to congratulate the battalion presonally on its, what he called, magnificent show. The battalion was relieved on 5 March by the 32nd Indian Infantry Brigade for the advance towards Central Burma.[34]

This attack was followed up the next day by 3/8 Gurkha Rifles, supported by tanks, who attacked Mayogon and occupied it later in the afternoon. The attack met with slight opposition from Japanese infantry, but their artillery began effective sniping with 75-mm guns. This uncomfortable sniping was a feature of the operations in the next few days while contact was being made with the bridgehead formed by the 32nd Indian Infantry Brigade; and even observation by aircraft did not help in keeping the guns entirely quiet.[35]. 3/8 Gurkha Rifles then reverted to the 32nd Indian Infantry Brigade which had moved into the main bridgehead to prepare for its second phase.

32nd Brigade Operations—Second Phase

It had been described earlier how the Japanese had contained 1 Northamptons and 9/14 Punjab of the 32nd Indian Infantry Brigade in their bridgehead at Kyigon and were fighting fanatically to prevent a link-up between the two bridgeheads. The 80th Indian Infantry Brigade was originally commissioned to make the link-up but the Japanese resistance and offensive action on its bridgehead did not allow it to spare any troops for the purpose. Hence the 32nd Indian Infantry Brigade was asked to cross over and was, assigned the task of making the link-up. This left the other brigade free to operate south from the bridgehead while the 32nd operated on its flank to the south-east.

Operations were continued to clear a passage from Mayogon southward and, on 4 March, 3/8 Gurkha Rifles made a raid towards Kyigon, while at the same time attacking and destroying a strong bunker position which separated it from the bridgehead. Japanese resistance had certainly decreased, their infantry had been thinned, and this action helped to create a gap between the *215th Regiment* and the *16th Regiment* which permitted the first patrols from 3/8 Gurkha Rifles to reach the Northamptons that evening. Both 1 Northamptons and 9/14 Punjab, together with anti-tank guns and mortars, were then evacuated under air cover, the former to Yezin and the latter to Kanlan.

The 32nd Indian Infantry Brigade then took over some of the

---

[34] The Episode of Irrawaddy Bridgehead in Feb. 45 by 9 Frontier Force Regiment. 601/7370/H.

[35] A Short History of 20th Indian Division, *op. cit.*

80th Indian Infantry Brigade area. On 6 March, 9/14 Punjab sent companies to Talingon and Gaungbo, itself moving next day to Talingon and sending forward a company to Sinbyugon. 3/8 GR moved a company forward to Nyaunglebin, battalion headquarters going there on 8 March with two companies at Paunggadaw. Patrols and air reconnaissances showed that the Japanese had begun to withdraw, and the only opposition to be met was from Natkyi and from small parties moving place to place on the road, around Thagyin and Magyigyat, in an effort to hide the fadeout.[36] The formidable Irrawaddy line was broken.

It may be noted that by this time, the IV Corps had crossed the Irrawaddy further south, and by the end of February fighting had begun in the Meiktila area. Hence troops from all the other fronts were being withdrawn by the Japanese in early March and sent for the defence of Meiktila,[37] and that explains the thinning out of the forces opposing the 20th Indian Division.

Meanwhile the 100th Indian Infantry Brigade had linked up with the 2nd British Division, 2 Border meeting patrols from the latter on the island north-east of Ywathit, and on 3 March on the mainland near Point 207. A lateral line of communication had begun to develop along the south bank. At the same time a new ferry was being prepared at Myinmu to take advantage of the existing road system, and on 9 March the original bridgehead ferry closed down.

Meanwhile moving southwards from Kalaywa, 14 Frontier Force Rifles had occupied Ywabo (south) on 4 March against slight opposition, and pushed on the next day scattering about 100 Japanese troops to capture Point 252. The same day divisional headquarters crossed the river to Alethaung.

Thus by 6 March the position on the 20th Indian Division front was as follows:—

The Japanese opposition was dying out; the 32nd Indian Infantry Brigade had broken out from its subsidiary bridgehead and was concentrated in the main bridgehead; the 80th Indian Infantry Brigade was operating on the right of the 100th Indian Infantry Brigade, and the following places were firmly in Allied hands: Paunggadaw, Nyaunglebin, Ywabo (south), Ywabo (north), Kalaywa and Ywathit. A link-up with the 2nd Division had been made north-east of Ywathit, and the stage had been reached when the 20th Indian Division might begin the next phase of its operations, namely to march towards Kyaukse, thirty miles south of Mandalay, and cut the road between Mandalay and Meiktila. This breakout

---
[36] *Ibid.*
[37] The Japanese Account of their Operations in Burma, Chapter 22, 601/8255/H.

from its bridgehead and further operations of the 20th Indian Division will be described in a subsequent chapter.

During the three weeks fighting in and around the bridgehead areas, the 20th Indian Division had played a vital role in the overall strategy of the Fourteenth Army. The Japanese command had already committed its maximum effort in the second half of January and early February against the bridgeheads established by the 19th Indian Division. The establishment of a new bridgehead by the 20th Indian Division was a shrewd move intended to further disorganise the Japanese defences and break their will to resist. In addition, the 20th Indian Division was able to draw off towards itself not only certain Japanese forces from Mandalay, but also some other forces which might otherwise have been used further south against the IV Corps bridgehead at Pagan. Thus the activities of this division to the south of the Irrawaddy indirectly helped the drive on Mandalay as well as Meiktila.

For the 20th Indian Division itself the establishment of the bridgehead marked its finest hour. In the bridgehead battle which lasted for three weeks before the breakout to the east began, this division had fought its most decisive action since the holding of the Shenam saddle. The fighting during this period from the middle of February to the first week of March was marked by bitter attacks by the Japanese, repelled only by the equal ferocity and valour of the Indian troops.

2ND DIVISION CROSSINGS

As described in the previous chapter, the 2nd British Division had, at the end of January and the beginning of February, swept the north bank of the Irrawaddy from the Mu river in the west to Ywathitgyi in the east. It encountered strong resistance at Ywathitgyi before capturing it on 2 February. Subsequently the 5th and 6th Brigades had concentrated in this area preparatory to crossing the Irrawaddy, while the 4th Brigade had been ordered to contain the Japanese in their Sagaing positions.

On 13 February instructions were issued for the crossing of the Irrawaddy. The 5th Brigade was to establish itself in a bridgehead across the river in the general area Ngazun-Ngalun-Thabyetha, 10 miles to the east of the bridgehead of the 20th Indian Division, prior to its advance eastwards on Mandalay. The plan was that by 17 or 18 February, the 4th Brigade should relieve the 6th Brigade on the north bank of the Irrawaddy, and the latter should then move into the bridgehead formed by the 5th Brigade. Actually, these crossings could not take place before the night of 24/25 February. This was so because the 4th Brigade was not in a position to relieve the 6th Brigade on the days agreed upon, owing to the Japanese activity in the Sagaing area. Moreover, considerable local patrolling was necessary throughout the divisional area, before a crossing was effected with safety. During the period from 14 to 24 February, therefore, active patrolling was carried out by all the three brigades, while the 4th Brigade, in addition, tried to capture some of the strong-points in the Sagaing area.

This long, active patrolling was rendered necessary by the frequent long-range Japanese patrols which crossed the Irrawaddy to ascertain the strength of the Allied concentration in the area east of the Mu river, as also to know whether there was to be another crossing in addition to those already made by the 19th and 20th Indian Divisions. The Allied patrols, however, did not confine their activities to the north bank of the Irrawaddy. On 15 February, 2 Durham Light Infantry crossed to Shwepyishin Island meeting with no difficulties in landing. On 17 February, the battalion sent another patrol, this time to cross to the south bank. Landing at LF 255575, it moved east to Letpanzin which was in Japanese occupation and then returned.

Offensive operations against the Japanese forces in the Sagaing area were also not neglected during this period. On 18 February, the 4th Brigade sent out an armoured patrol to test the Japanese defences in this area.. The patrol returned without meeting any opposition or suffering any casualties, but after having destroyed the Japanese outpost at 3963.

During the night of 17/18 February, a Japanese patrol, larger than the usual, crossed the Mu river at LT 105748 but it was engaged by 100 Anti-Tank Regiment in the Dibeyingwe area, before it could cross the river back again. Among the equipment carried by the Japanese were demolition charges and emergency rations for a fairly long period, indicating that they had an intention of carrying out a destructive raid in the Allied administrative areas. On the night of 19 February, again, a small party of Japanese raiders approached the company position of the Durham Light Infantry at 2760. They were engaged at close range and scattered in confusion.

On 20 February, following an accurate air-strike in which many Japanese bunkers were hit, and many effective strafing runs made, 2 Norfolk of the 4th Brigade supported by 3 DG captured Saye.

On 24 February the stage was set for the actual crossing. The 4th Brigade had been relieved in the Sagaing area by the 268th Indian Infantry Brigade on 23 February. It therefore moved to the 6th Brigade area to enable the latter to make the crossing along with the 5th Brigade. The site selected for the crossing was at Ngazun.[38]

---

[38] Operation Order No. 14 of XXXIII Corps, dated 20 Feb. 1945.

The river here contained many sand-banks and shifting shoals and varied in width between 1000 and 1500 yards. The current was quite swift (2½ knots). Three beaches were selected and it was planned to land on them simultaneously. Beach "A" (Dawete beach) was two miles west of Ngazun, beach "B" (Myittha) was about one mile from that village, whereas beach "C" was on the large island north of the village.

The crossings began on the night of 24/25 February by the 5th Brigade with 1 Royal Welch Fusiliers of the 6th Brigade under command. The first assault wave on to Ngazun Island ("C" beach) was fired upon, but one company and the tactical headquarters of the Royal Welch Fusiliers crossed to the island and charged through the hostile positions. The supporting wave however failed to land and the Japanese held their ground, pinning the first wave's boats to the beach by their fire and preventing their return. The assault on A beach was made by 7 Worc R. Immediately on starting, it had to encounter automatic and mortar fire. Seventeen of its boats were sunk and the force was obliged to return to the north bank. Thus the assault on "A" beach had also to be abandoned. The situation was serious and it looked as if the crossing would have to be abandoned. But there still remained the crossing site at Myittha, the "B" beach. Here the tactical headquarters, and two companies of the 1st Battalion the Queen's Own Cameron Highlanders succeeded in crossing to the south bank during the night against Japanese opposition, and navigational difficulties. The Camerons had the longest crossing to make, a diagonal course being adopted to avoid sand-banks, and that too in full view of the opposing forces owing to the moon.

Crossings to this beach under cover of smoke continued throughout the day of 25 Febuary and were supported by tank and artillery fire from the north bank and had excellent air-cover. Up to 1500 hours every flight had to cross a hostile belt of fire from concealed Japanese positions. River conditions made navigation for all craft except Dukws extremely difficult. Sporadic shelling of the north bank including Dawete and Myittha was also carried out by the Japanese, but their activities were mainly directed against the crossings. Nonetheless, by nightfall on 25 February, two battalions of the 5th Brigade were established on the south bank, and the remaining two companies of 1 RWF on Ngazun island. This was a remarkable feat of co-ordinated control, staff work, and discipline coming, as it did, after the confusion caused by the initial failure. The few troops who had crossed over during the night of 24/25 February, after the moon had set, were thus reinforced during the day (25 February) to maintain their hold on the precarious bridgehead.

On 26 February, the bridgehead was expanded further. The

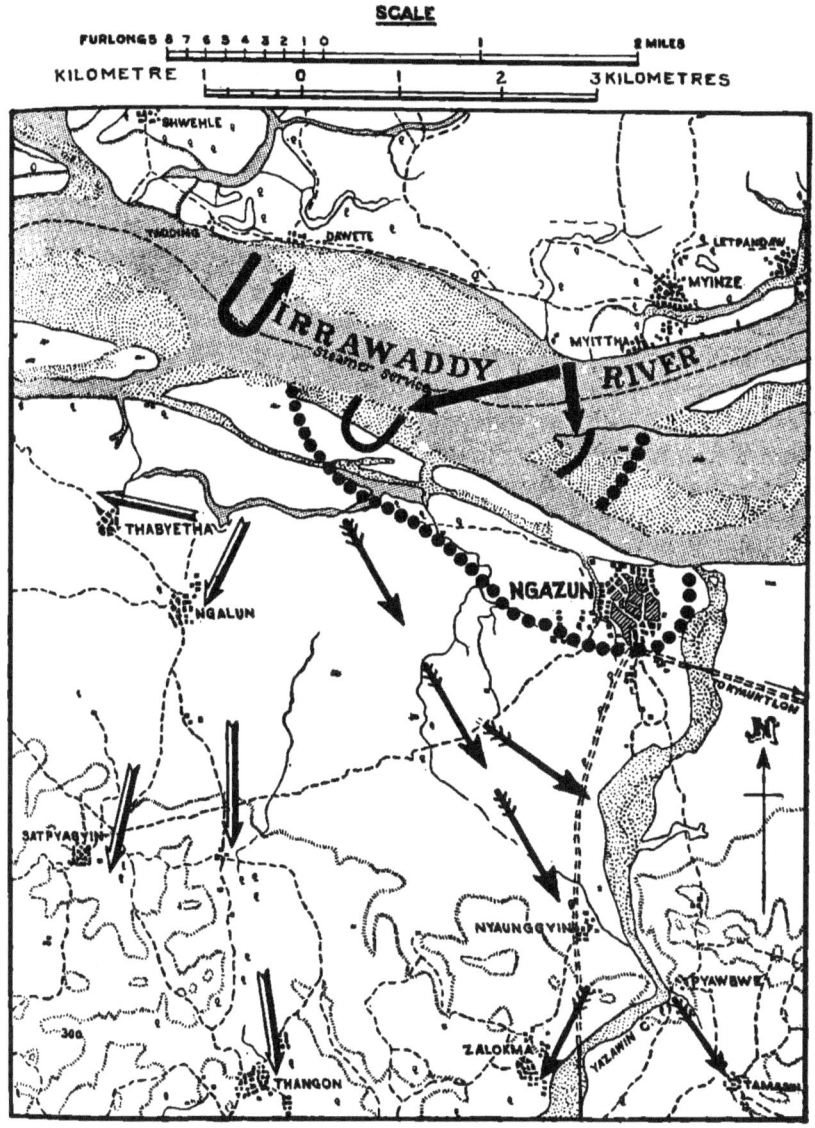

5th and 6th Brigades were completely across the river, and twenty tanks of 3 Dragoon Guards had been ferried across. Ngazun village was attacked by 2 Dorset and 7 Worcesters during the day, after the Japanese defences in the village had been thoroughly softened by aerial and artillery bombardment. The village was captured by the 5th Brigade without serious loss. In the 6th Brigade area snipers were active but the infantry and tanks carried out operations against them and soon succeeded in silencing them.

The 4th Brigade began its crossings on 27 February[39] while the 6th Brigade took to the expansion of the bridgehead with a successful attack on Nyaunggyin, which was captured. 1 R Berks and 2 DLI supported by 3 DG and 3/4 Bombay Grenadiers took part in this operation. They advanced south from the bridgehead, and while 2 DLI on the right overcame Japanese opposition on the high ground west of Nyaunggyin, including the reverse slopes, 1 R Berks supported by heavy artillery concentration and tanks cleared the village. Few defensive positions were encountered, opposition being mainly from a number of snipers many of whom as was usual with them went low to the ground on the approach of tanks, raised their heads when the tanks had passed and engaged the infantry which was following. In the 5th Brigade area the main effort was directed to regrouping and consolidating in the area Ngazun—Ngazun Island though some patrolling was also carried out. The bridgehead had been extended to a depth of 5 miles before the evening.

The following day, the main activity centred in the 4th Brigade area. 2 Norfolk began expanding the bridgehead to the west but was soon held up by heavy sniper opposition from thick and high grass. 1/8 Lancashire Fusiliers had more success. After an airstrike and heavy artillery concentration, with the tanks supporting, it attacked and captured some positions after overcoming determined opposition. 2 Recce less one squadron crossed the river and relieved 1 RWF on Ngazun Island. In the 6th Brigade area an important feature at LF 1352 was occupied. Throughout these operations the troops received strong air support and Ngazun was captured only after it had been set on fire by the Royal Air Force. Thus the position on 6 March, after one week of operations to expand the bridgehead, was that Nyaunggyin, Tamabin, Zalokma, Thangon and Thabyetha were in British hands and contact with the 20th Indian Division to the west had also been made.

7TH INDIAN DIVISION CROSSINGS

It may be recalled that the Fourteenth Army plan envisaged a crossing of the Irrawaddy in the Pakokku area by the 7th Indian

---

[39] 4th Bde had been relieved in the Ondaw area by 268th Ind Inf Bde and was therefore free to cross over.

Division, a part of the IV Corps. It was a vital move as with it was intimately related the proposed sudden attack on Meiktila. The plan had contemplated the establishment of a bridgehead by the 7th Indian Division through which the 17th Indian Division was to pass and capture that strategic city. As a deception measure, the 28th East African Brigade was to move to the south of the 7th Indian Division area to create the impression that the main objective of the Fourteenth Army advance was the Yenangyaung oilfields area.

The 7th Indian Division had concentrated itself in the area Kan—Gangaw by 17 January. Its 89th Indian Infantry Brigade made a flanking movement thereafter and reached Yebya on 25 February. Then it advanced by the main road via Kandaw and reached Myitche on 5 February. Meanwhile the other two brigades, the 114th and the 33rd Indian Infantry Brigades, had moved forward to make preparations for crossing the river at Nyaungu. Thus by 10 February 1945, the 7th Indian Division had reached the Irrawaddy and was prepared to take part in the Fourteenth Army's plan to assume offensive across the river and attack the Japanese. As early as 20 January, this division had been instructed by IV Corps to seize, as soon as possible, and not later than 15 February, a bridgehead over the river between Chauk and Pakokku, suitable for the passage of the 17th Indian Division in its advance on Meiktila. Hence the division decided that its 33rd Indian Infantry Brigade should make the initial crossing. While the rest of the division was moving forward, this brigade concentrated on training for the crossing with the divisional engineers at Gangaw.

The site of the actual crossing was to be at Nyaungu, roughly half-way between Chauk and Pakokku. Although this site, being the narrowest crossing and therefore obvious, was likely to be defended, it was chosen because of the dominant consideration of the rate of build-up of both the 7th and 17th Indian Divisions on the far bank and the shortest turn-round of the rafts. Nyaungu was also the junction of road communications leading eastwards and southwards from the Irrawaddy. Having chosen the most obvious place for crossing, the planners concerted elaborate deception plans to divert the attention of the Japanese. On the Corps level, the deception plan was to simulate the main crossing at Seikpyu,[40] opposite the important oil town of Chauk. The divisional deception plan was to launch a drive to Pakokku. Obvious preparations were made shortly before the real crossing, and at dawn on 13 February the 28th East African Brigade suddenly appeared on the west bank of the Irrawaddy opposite Chauk, after capturing Seikpyu.[41] Similarly the 114th Indian Infantry Brigade of the 7th Indian Division

---

[40] Seikpyu is about 40 miles down the river from Pakokku.
[41] The brigade was to attempt, if possible, an actual, though minor crossing.

appeared before Pakokku. Hurriedly, the Japanese sent reinforcements but the town was captured. The Japanese, however, entrenched themselves in an island in the river to oppose any possible crossing by this brigade. Thus, both these feints were entirely successful. The Japanese moved more troops towards these two places (Chauk and Pakokku) southwards and northwards from Nyaungu, thus leaving the real crossing place in the middle thinly defeated.

South of the confluence with the Chindwin, the Irrawaddy varies in width between three quarters of a mile and several miles, but at Nyaungu it was the narrowest, being under three quarters of a mile wide. Navigation straight across was not practicable owing to there being a 800-yard "beach" of soft sand between the banks. A diagonal crossing had therefore to be resorted to and the distance measured over a mile. Another topographical factor which determined the choice of the site was that, except for Nyaungu town, the far bank consisted of high cliffs intersected with dry chaungs (river beds) every few hundred yards, whereas the near bank was a lowland. The far bank appeared to afford complete observation over the near bank and, on account of the cliffs, landings would be confined to the dry river beds if vehicles were to be taken across initially.

There was a proposal to effect a silent crossing by an entire brigade during the hours of darkness. But in view of the risk of boats getting lost in the darkness it was given up. Instead, the plan was to have a silent flight at first light, with a quick follow-up in power-driven boats..

Deployment of the Division

Before the actual crossing is described, it is necessary to examine the dispositions of the various units of this division on 1 February 1945. On that date it was still spread out between Gangaw and Pauk, and some of its units which played an important part in the crossings were located as follows[42]:—

17 Divisional Engineers, from whom six field companies required for the task were to be formed, was established somewhere on the road between Imphal and Kan. Additional artillery units, required to support the crossing in case it was opposed, were also on the road between the same limits.

The 33rd Indian Infantry Brigade, which was to initiate the assault, was still at Gangaw and able to move forward only by using all available Corps transport. Headquarters IV Corps was therefore immobilised at Kan until about 5 February.

The forward airfield engineers had only just started to work on the main airhead at Sinthe through which the vital engineer stores

---

[42] F.601/234/WD/Pt. IV, p. 3, para 10.

and practically all the ammunition for the crossing had to pass. Fortunately the Sinthe site required very little work.

The bridging equipment was spread out between Kan and Gangaw and the medium tank regiment, 116 RAC (Gordon Highlanders), was also at Kan. It became apparent that the latter would have to do the remaining 150 miles to the river on tracks as the road was not fit for transporters. One sector of the road between Tilin and Pauk was causing grave concern for heavy vehicles.

There were three beaches on the near side: "A" beach PP 2176 the shortest crossing, "B" beach near Kukyon PP 2577 and "C" beach near Letpaugyon PP 2738. "A" beach was unusable without a lot of work on it and the approaches to "B" beach were also not good. On the far side there were four beaches, "B1", "B2", "B3", "B4" at PP 2275 to the north-east of Nyaungu. At least two of these were suitable for tanks and vehicles.

The plan drawn up was as follows[43]:—

Phase I. One battalion of the 33rd Indian Infantry Brigade was to carry out an assault crossing on a front 1500 yards wide on the night of 13/14 February, and capture four beaches ("B1", "B2", "B3" and "B4") under the cliffs, one mile north-east of Nyaungu.

Phase II. Remainder of the brigade was to reinforce this beachhead with a view to developing an attack on Nyaungu from the high ground which dominated it from the north-east.

Phase III. Capture of Nyaungu itself and a beach on the east bank at the shortest crossing place.

Phase IV. The expansion of the bridgehead to enable the remainder of the IV Corps to pass through.

The plan for the Assault Brigade was as follows:—

2nd Battalion South Lancashire Regiment

In view of its experience in handling boats during the combined operations training the 2nd Battalion of the South Lancashire Regiment (2 S Lan R) of the 114th Indian Infantry Brigade was to come under the command of the 33rd Indian Infantry Brigade for the assault crossing. One company of this battalion was to cross silently from "C" beach at 0400 hours on 14 February and arrive at the far beach by 0530 hours, i.e. half an hour before first light. This company was to seize the high ground above "B4" beach. The remainder of the fighting portion of the battalion was to leave "C" beach at first light. Two Harvard aircraft were to fly over the crossing area to drown the noise of the starting of the out-board motors. 2 S Lan R was to be followed by 4/15 Punjab. 4/1 Gurkha Rifles, 1 Burma and the remainder of the brigade group were to follow as

---

[43] Crossings of the Irrawaddy by the 7th Indian Division, War Diary of 7th Indian Division, 601/234/WD, Part IV.

craft became available. Besides the infantry, nine tanks of the 116 RAC (Gordons) and some jeeps and animals were to cross on the first day. After the crossing had been completed the plan was that 2 S Lan R would hold the beach area while 4/15 Punjab and 4/1 GR would occupy the high ground further inland. 1 Burma and the tanks were to be in brigade reserve for the attack on Nyaungu the next day.

Air Support[44]

Nos. 1 and 2 Air Commando Groups of the USAAF were to operate in support of the IV Corps for these operations. They were based in Arakan but had a tactical liaison with the Corps Headquarters. The squadrons available for service were two Mustang Squadrons, one flight of Mitchells and two Thunderbolt Squadrons. In addition there were one Spitfire Squadron (152) RAF, one Hurribomber Squadron (11) RAF and one Tac/R Flight (Hurricane) No. 1 IAF. The units were based on Sinthe.

The following air support was provided:

- D Day—one Harvard was used to drown the noise of the outboard motors starting up.
- 12 Hurricanes and 5 Mitchells attacked Japanese positions on the far bank directly after first light. For the rest of the day there were four Mustangs or Thunderbolts on cab-rank.
- D+1. 8 Thunderbolts or Mustangs remained overhead on cab-rank all day.
- D+2. The cab-rank was reduced to four aircraft.
- D+3. The cab-rank remained at four aircraft.

All concerned with the crossing were in their concentration areas by the evening of 12 February. Shortly before dark on the following day, organisation and signals moved down to the near bank beach and laid out the regulating headquarters. Assault troops and transport moved into their assembly areas without incident.

The rafting equipment available was as follows:—
- 120 Assault Boats with 9.8 HP out-board motors.
- 11 Class 9 Rafts with out-board motors.
- 7 Class 40 rafts with motor-boats and propulsion sets.

Special Boat Section and Sea Reconnaissance Unit detachments left early to carry out final reconnaissance of the far bank and returned at 0400 hours to report that all was clear. One party had encountered and shot two Japanese swimming in the river, and it was considered possible that this incident might have given the alarm.

[44] *Ibid.*

The crossing was a diagonal one of about a mile to a far bank 40 feet high, formed of cliffs intersected by deep chaungs every few hundred yards. The current was between 2 and 3 knots. One company of 2 S Lan R which had been ordered to effect a silent crossing left "C" beach at 0343 hours and reached the east bank at 0515 hours, after rowing for over an hour, and secured the high ground east of "B4" beach. At the same time a detachment of the Special Boat Section followed to mark the sand-bank "Z" and the beaches with lights. The rest of the battalion embarked from "C" beach at 0430 hours but then new difficulties began to appear. The launching of the boats proved more arduous than expected. The out-board motors failed to start in time as, owing to the need for maintaining silence, they had not been started up sufficiently beforehand to get properly warmed up. A number of boats were also found to be unserviceable when loaded, mainly because of their having been carried over long distances in mechanical transport by indifferent roads. There was considerable trouble with the motors as well, for while some failed to start, others broke down in midstream. As a consequence the boats which were scheduled to land at 0530 hours, were still approaching the far bank at 0610 hours, well after the first light. All boats except two were being rowed and many were in tow.[45]

When light came and the boats were still in the river, the Japanese opened up with a hail of medium machine-gun fire from the beaches "B2" and "B3". The situation appeared helpless. Many of the boats drifted down the stream past the Japanese positions, and suffered heavy casualties, but eventually beached on a sand-bank down the river from where they were recovered later. The current was strong and the control of any sort was exceptionally difficult. However, the boats finally moved back to "B" beach (near side) and many men had to swim back. Then the tanks and artillery on the near side opened up and B25s controlled by a Visual Control Post bombed and strafed Japanese positions on the far bank, which enabled the boats to make a covered withdrawal. It looked as if the crossing had failed.

At 0800 hours the situation remained much the same as it had been at 0530 hours, with one company only on the far bank. The outlook was gloomy. At this stage the brigade commander decided, on an offer being made by 4/15 Punjab, to put that battalion a little further upstream to cross to beach "B4" under air, artillery and tank cover. There was no need for silence now, a sufficient number of motors were started and warmed up and boats made serviceable. The leading company left "B" beach on the near side at 0945 hours

---

[45] Operations IV Corps, Oct. 44—May 45, p. 13.

and successfully crossed without any mishap. By 1140 hours the whole of 4/15 Punjab was embarked, and reached the far bank. The company of 2 S Lan R which had crossed earlier, now started operations. In an hour all the beaches on the far bank had been cleared of the Japanese and fighting patrols were well forward.

From 1300 hours onwards, everything went well and the available rafts were used to the maximum capacity to get the rest of the brigade across. Before dark practically the whole brigade had crossed over. Approaches for wheels and tracks were constructed across a wide sand-bank on the near side opposite Nyaungu itself, and ferrying continued during the next few days according to a priority list decided at a daily divisional "bidding" conference. It was found impossible to adhere to the original priorities owing to the changes in the situation. By 18 February, however, two brigades (33rd and 89th) of the 7th Indian Division were on the other side of the river complete with their transport and supporting arms, and 116 RAC less one squadron; and the bridgehead had been extended to a line Myinkapa—Thuhtekan—Nanthu—Kabani.

On 18 February the Corps took over control of the crossing and operated the main beach, while a subsidiary beach remained open under divisional control for maintenance, stores, baggage etc. By 19 February, the Sappers worked up to over 400 raft sorties a day enabling nearly 1000 vehicles being ferried across in a day.

Bridgehead Operations

The original plan of operations in the bridgehead was that 2 S Lan R after seizing the four beaches on the far side, would occupy the high ground which dominated the whole area and completely overlooked the town of Nyaungu. The next battalion, 4/15 Punjab, would deepen the bridgehead and turn towards Nyaungu. 4/1 Gurkha Rifles was to move south and cut the road from Nyaungu to Ngathayauk, about a mile and a half from Nyaungu. 1 Burma was to cross last on D Day and to clear the town.

Owing to the initial hitch in the plan, the bridgehead could not be expanded as deep as it had been hoped on the first day. Hence the night of 14/15 February was spent with the three battalions closely surrounding the landing beaches.[46] Early on the 15th the remainder of 2 S Lan R crosssed over into the 33rd Indian Infantry Brigade bridgehead, and the rest of the 89th Indian Infantry Brigade started to cross from "B" beach.

Meanwhile, in the main bridgehead of the 33rd Indian Infantry Brigade operations had been proceeding according to plan. 4/1 Gurkha Rifles, supported by tanks and artillery, had cut the

---

[46] So close were they in fact that it was not possible to put across as many mules as was intended.

THE CROSSING OF THE IRRAWADDY BY 7 INDIAN DIV. 14 FEBRUARY 1945

SCALE

LEGEND

33 IND. INF. BDE.

89 IND. INF. BDE.

17 IND. DIV.

EXTENT OF BRIDGE-HEAD ON 14 FEB. 45

EXTENT OF BRIDGE-HEAD ON 15 FEB. 45 ●●●●●●●

EXTENT OF BRIDGE-HEAD ON 16 FEB. 45 ×××××××

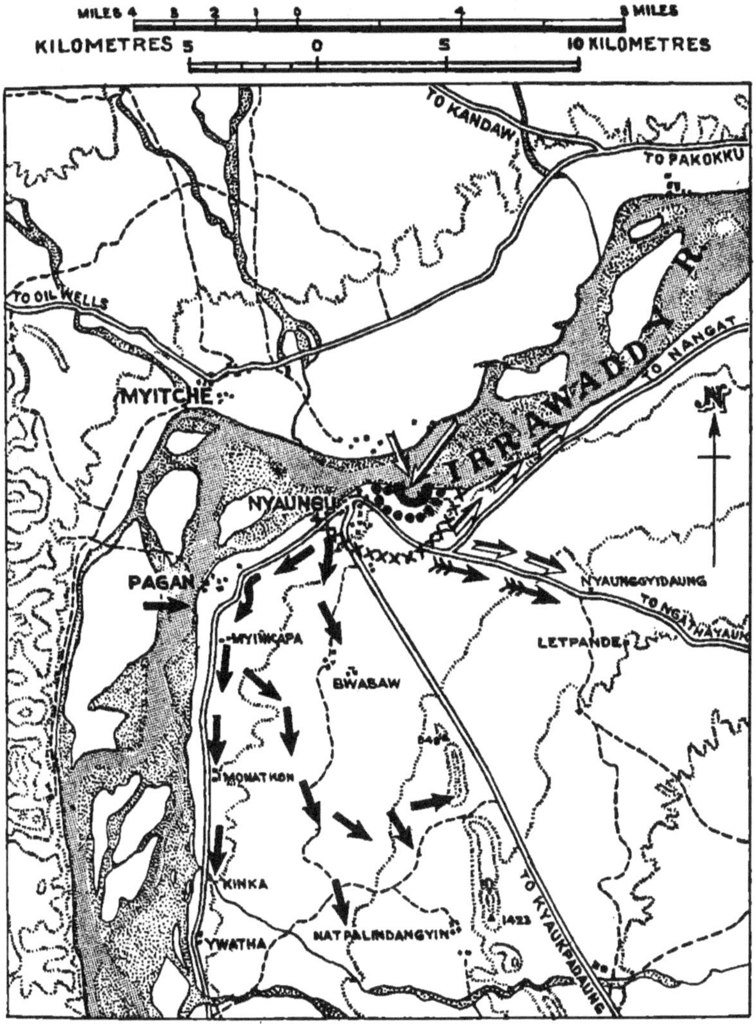

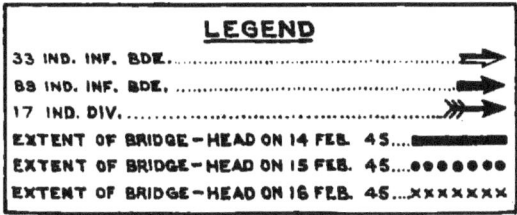

Ngathayauk road and was well established across it. Patrols to the south of Nyaungu found the road clear, but other patrols to the south-east encountered Japanese opposition about two and a half miles away.

On the river bank, the Japanese had withdrawn to some old catacombs which provided an extremely strong position covering Nyaungu town. 1 Burma attacked these tunnels at 1030 hours on the 15th. There was excellent support from artillery, tanks and air. Napalm fire-bombs were dropped and produced devastation in the town but the catacomb position proved intractable. It was then decided to seal the mouth of the catacombs and to carry on with the clearing of the town. By 16 February, the Japanese in the catacombs had all been killed or buried alive and Nyaungu was reported clear. 4/15 Punjab then moved to the south side of the town and the bridgehead was extended to Wetkyin. It was now 6000 yards broad and 4000 yards deep and vehicles were pouring into it.

Further enlargement of the bridgehead was then taken up and the plan was that the 89th Indian Infantry Brigade would take over the west and south flanks as far forward as Pagan, while the 33rd Indian Infantry Brigade would control the east and south-east with 2 S Lan R affording protection to Nyaungu town in divisional reserve. The 114th Indian Infantry Brigade less 2 S Lan R was still engaged in mopping up Pakokku. Meanwhile, the 17th Indian Division had also started crossing over on 17 February and concentrating outside the 7th Indian Divisional area, on the road to Ngathayauk. The extension of the bridgehead to the south and east proceeded simultaneously with the build-up of the 17th Indian Division.

The Japanese reaction to this situation was also swift. Oscars attacked the crossing on 17 February though they failed to inflict much damage. The *214th Regiment*, which was withdrawing from Pakokku, moved partly towards Nyaungu and encountered the 33rd Indian Infantry Brigade and suffered some casualties. The rest of the regiment on its way to Ngathayauk was routed by the leading armoured troops of the 17th Indian Division. In the Yenangyaung —Chauk area also the Japanese counter-attacked the 89th Indian Infantry Brigade on 19 February south of Pagan with the *72nd Independent Mixed Brigade* which was known to be in the oilfields area.[47] During the next few weeks, these counter-attacks became a common occurrence but failed to "drive the British back into the river and annihilate his forces in the Myitche area", as the Japanese had hoped.

---

[47] 89th Brigade's crossings are described in the next few paragraphs.

Subsidiary Crossings by 1/11 Sikh

It may be recalled that while the 33rd Indian Infantry Brigade was to carry out the real assault crossing of the river at Nyaungu, and preparations for two feint crossings were to be made at Pakokku and opposite Chauk respectively, a subsidiary crossing by 1/11 Sikh was also contemplated about six miles south of the main crossing. The purpose of this crossing was also the same, viz to divert the Japanese attention from the Nyaungu crossing. Since all assault craft had been allotted for the main crossing, the Sikhs were forced to rely on country boats and local boatmen, who were unwilling to row the patrols across. However, on 11 February, three days before the D Day for the main crossing, the boatmen were persuaded, with some difficulty, to take some patrols to the eastern bank. These patrols brought back the information that the southern end of Pagan on the far bank was not occupied by the Japanese. It was therefore decided to turn the feint crossing into a real crossing, which was to be carried out from an island in the middle of the river, to which the Sikhs moved over on the night of 12 February. In a pitch-dark night, three hundred yards of water were crossed in six country boats. From there all sorts of stores etc were carried over a long distance in the island and by the dawn the battalion was safely hidden in its concentration area. As the men were preparing to cross over to the east bank of the river, news was received at about 1100 hours (13 February) that Pagan, which was believed to be unoccupied on 11 February, had been occupied. "The Sikhs' attempt to attract the enemy's attention had met with unwanted success.[48]" Despite this it was decided to stick to the original plan.

At 0400 hours on 14 February, B Company set off in large, unwieldy country-craft. When nearing the far bank it met a hail of machine-gun fire. The following excerpt taken from Lt. Col. P. G. Bamford's book admirably sums up the rest of the story of this crossing[49]:

> "The local boatmen immediately panicked, stopped rowing and cowered in the bottom of the boats. Neither persuasion nor threats would induce them to go on, and the boats began to drift downstream completely out of control. The men did their best, but the boats were too unwieldy in the strong current for them to handle and they were carried away. After drifting for some time the boatmen were eventually persuaded to row and to take the Sikhs back to the island. "B" Company was very lucky to have only one man wounded, but it was quite obvious that it would not be possible to carry out a landing on the

---

[48] *1st King George V's Own Battalion, the Sikh Regiment*, by Lt. Col. P. G. Bamford, D.S.O.
[49] *Ibid*, p. 131.

opposite bank without some form of assault craft which could be handled by the men themselves.

However, this abortive attempt had drawn a large party of Japanese from the main crossing and had undoubtedly assisted the 33rd Brigade in establishing a bridgehead farther north."

On 15 February, however, Pagan was evacuated by the Japanese and occupied by the Indian troops.[50] The next few days were then spent by the battalion in clearing the Japanese to the south of the town and preventing them from moving north to reinforce their troops opposing the main bridgehead.

The success of the IV Corps was, to a considerable extent, due to the very elaborate deception scheme to mislead the Japanese regarding the intention of the 7th Indian Division to cross at Nyaungu. That would account for the weak and meagre opposition encountered in the crossing. In this respect the Corps was undoubtedly assisted by the fact that the place chosen for the crossing lay on the boundary between the Japanese *15th* and *28th Armies*. The fact that this boundary between these two armies passed through the eastern edge of Nyaungu was previously known to the Corps and did account for the selection of that place for the crossing. The trick played and the Japanese were taken completely by surprise.[51]

Thus having completely deceived the Japanese, a firm bridgehead had been established, and while the 7th Indian Division was still busy in expanding it, the 17th Indian Division with the 255th Indian Tank Brigade under command had commenced crossing the Irrawaddy at Nyaungu on 18 February for its dash to Meiktila. At the same time, on the front of the XXXIII Corps, the 19th Indian Division had taken the initiative and had resumed offensive operations preparatory to an advance on Mandalay. Thus both the Corps were poised for opening the operations for the capture of Meiktila and Mandalay which are described in the subsequent chapters.

---

[50] War Diary 7th Indian Div, 15/16 February 1945.
[51] General Kimura, GOC, Burma Area Army also admitted in his interrogation that the major crossing in the Nyaungu area which represented the boundary between the Japanese *28th* and *15th Armies* "caused complete confusion" among the Japanese staff.
See Interrogation of General Kimura, answer to question No. 10, file 601/7380/H

CHAPTER XI

Meiktila Recaptured

THE THRUST TO MEIKTILA

In the previous chapters has been narrated how, by the middle of February 1945, most of the crossings of the Irrawaddy had been effected and bridgeheads established towards the north and west of Mandalay and the west of Meiktila. General Kimura had made strenuous efforts to destroy such bridgeheads but had failed completely. By the end of February the scene was set for a breakout from the bridgeheads towards Mandalay and Meiktila. The decisive battle was imminent.

Three Indian divisions were already across the river. The 19th Indian Division was poised against Mandalay from the north and the 20th Indian Division from the west. The 7th Indian Division, to the south of the loop of the Irrawaddy, had established bridgeheads through which the 17th Indian Division had passed. The 2nd British Division also crossed a little later (24 February) against stiff opposition, and was established at Ngazun between Mandalay and the bridgehead established by the 20th Indian Division. In addition one more Indian Division, the 5th, entirely motorised or made airborne, was awaiting the signal to move to the front and put its well greased armour to the test.

In the present chapter will be described the thrust to Meiktila by the 17th Indian Division from its positions south of the loop of the Irrawaddy, a distance of about 85 miles covered in as many hours.

17th Indian Division Plan

The plan of operations for the capture of Meiktila by two motorised brigades of the 17th Indian Division together with 5 Horse and 9 Horse fell into six phases.

Phase I. Crossing of the Irrawaddy, capture of Ngathayauk and exploitation to Welaung and Seiktein.

Phase II. Capture of Mahlaing, sealing off or captutre of Taungtha, concentration of the division in Mahlaing.

Phase III. Capture of an air-strip at or near Meiktila for the fly-in of the 99th Indian Infantry Brigade.

Phase IV. Isolation of Meiktila.

Phase V. Capture of Meiktila.

Phase VI. Capture of Thazi.

Major-General D. T. Cowan, C.B., D.S.O., M.C., had been in continuous command of the division since the retreat from Burma in 1942.[1] This division (known as the Black Cat Division from its emblem) thus had the distinction of having fought against the Japanese throughout the Burma operations, namely in the withdrawal from Burma, in the Japanese offensive against India, and finally in the eventual reconquest of Burma. The Japanese had ousted the Black Cat Division from Meiktila in 1942, and it was in the nature of poetic justice that this division was selected to oust them from the same place in 1945. During its war record of three years (1942-45) it had won the largest number of Victoria Crosses of any Indian division, namely seven.

Close air support was to be directed by a tactical headquarters of the Combat Cargo Task Force situated at the headquarters of the IV Corps, which would also control the fly-in of the 99th Indian Infantry Brigade. This arrangement worked extremely well and was largely responsible for the speed with which opposition was dealt with throughout the operation.

Crossing of the Irrawaddy and initial Forward Deployment
Phase I

Having become motorised, the 17th Indian Division had secretly driven down the Gangaw Valley in the wake of the 7th Indian Division and was concentrated at Pauk, 40 miles west of Pakkoku, by 12 February. As has been described earlier, the latter had established its bridgehead at Nyaungu on 13 February. Five days later, on 18 February, the former division began its crossing of the Irrawaddy with a reconnaissance force of one squadron 11 Cavalry, some reconnaissance troops of the 255th Indian Tank Brigade and a motorised company of 6/7 Rajput. The 48th Indian Infantrty Brigade and the tank brigade crossed next, simultaneously, followed by the divisional headquarters and the 63rd Indian Infantrty Brigade. Time was not wasted in concentrating the whole division but reconnaissance was taken up immediately the first troops had crossed. Depth was essential both to gain speed in the movement forward and to avoid congestion. The first firm base was formed by 4/12 Frontier Force Regiment of the 48th Indian Infantry Brigade at

---

[1] The other commanders concerned were:—
  48th Brigade—Brigadier R. C. O. Hedley, D.S.O.
  63rd Brigade—Brigadier G. W. S. Burton, D.S.O.
  99th Brigade—Brigadier M. V. Wright, D.S.O.
  255th Tank Brigade—Brigadier C. E. Pert, D.S.O.
  5 Horse—Lieut.-Colonel M. R. Smeeton, D.S.O., M.B.E., M.C.
  9 R Horse—Lieut.-Colonel P. B. Sanger, relieved at the end of February by Lieut.-General G. H. Carr, M.B.E., M.C.
  CRA 17th Div.—Brig. H. K. Dimoline, C.B.E., D.S.O.
  IV Corps Operations, Oct. 44, May 45, p. 17.

Nyaungyidaung, seven miles from Nyaungu on the road to Welaung, on 20 February. Offensive operations began the next day.

Ngathyauk

On 21 February, the advance began with the 48th Indian Infantry Brigade leading on the axis of the main road to Ngathayauk (16 miles from Nyaungu) with the tanks on an axis south of the road through Wetlu. Since a long line of communication (82 miles to Meiktila) could not be maintained through hostile territory, the division sealed off its rear as it proceeded and subsisted on supplies dropped from the air. Armoured cars in front, then tanks and infantry, more infantry, then the 3,000 vehicles of the column and finally a rear-guard of infantry and tanks—such was the order of march. Every night the division went into harbour behind a perimeter bristling with weapons, which the Japanese in vain tried to breach.

Briefly the plan for the capture of the Ngathayauk group of villages was as follows[2]: —

(*i*) One squadron of the Royal Deccan Horse with the 48th Indian Infantry Brigade was to move along the main divisional axis of the road towards Seywa preceded by Tomcol.

(*ii*) The remainder of the 255th Indian Tank Brigade was to advance via Wetlu, south of the main road, to a point south-west of Seywa from which the Royal Deccan Horse was to attack Seywa.

(*iii*) On the capture of Seywa, Probyn's Horse with 6/7 Rajput was to move across country and attack Ngathayauk from the south. Mopping up operations were the responsibility of the 48th Indian Infantry Brigade.

Opposition was first met at Seywa, one mile west of Ngathayauk, where a combined infantry and tank assault helped to capture the village, which itself had been almost destroyed by previous air bombing and strafing. Thenceforward advance towards the Ngathayauk villages continued. From air reconnaissance it had appeared that the villages to be cleared, seven in all, were not extensive and cover was light. As the troops advanced from a nulla, just south of the group of villages, some small-arms fire was encountered from what was subsequently found to have been some Japanese troops withdrawing down the Seiktein road. The group of villages was entered and found to be empty. The villages contained thick trees and hedges, visibility being limited to 50 yards. On entering the villages it was found that control was extremely

---

[2] *An account of the operations in Burma carried out by Probyn's Horse during March and April 1945*, p. 2.

difficult, and made more so by the fact that a certain amount of prophylactic fire and grenading by the infantry had set fire to the bashas.³

Two-pronged Move on Taungtha

Three roads ran east from Ngathayauk: the southern to Seiktein, the middle to Welaung and the northern to Kamye. Reconnaissance showed that the Welaung road was narrow, deeply rutted and unfit for vehicles; accordingly it was decided to follow the other two routes. One column, consisting of the 63rd Indian Infantry Brigade with 5 Horse and artillery and reconnaissance troops, took the Seiktein Road while the rest of the force adopted the northern route to Kamye. This had two advantages; firstly it enabled the division to concentrate forward more quickly, and secondly it hid temporarily the real direction and objective of the main advance. But the basic idea was that the two movements should later converge on Taungtha resulting in a pincer movement against that place.

Oyin Captured

All moves were hampered at first by the wide sandy chaung half a mile east of Seywa. Taking the heavy vehicles over the sand presented difficulties which were however overcome, and the southern column⁴ was able to advance on 22 February. Soon it met fanatical resistance at Oyin four miles south-east of Ngathayauk. Nearly two companies of Japanese troops held the village and their bunkers were located on its south edge. A troop of tanks was despatched to cut off the southward retreat while the remaining tanks with infantry support attacked from the north. 5 Horse, with 6 Rajput, attacked at 1300⁵ hours and before dark the Japanese resistance had been broken and two guns and one light machine-gun captured. Only a few of them succeeded in withdrawing eastwards after blowing up their ammunition and petrol dumps.⁶ The casualties of 6/7 Rajput were not light either. There were a few instances of suicide gallantry shown by the Japanese troops. One of them got underneath a tank with a picric acid box and blew himself and the tank up, caving in the bottom plate, smashing the gear box and killing the driver. Some others attempting a similar trick however failed, as also did an attempt by one of them who got on to a tank and tried to open the turret to throw in his grenades. The attacking force harboured for the night south of the village and no Japanese troops

---

³ *Ibid.*
⁴ This consisted of Probyn's Horse (5 Horse), 6/7 Rajput and 59/18 Battery RA.
⁵ 1200 hours according to 17th Division War Diary (F.15).
⁶ 63rd Indian Infantry Brigade War Diary, 601/347/WD, Part III.

were found in the area next morning when advance to Seiktein was continued.

The northern column moved to Kamye on 23 February, behind Tomcol patrols, against only slight opposition, and the Sappers worked hard to get the Sindewa Chaung crossing fit for vehicles. Meanwhile, the southern column had reached Seiktein without incident by 1130 hours on 23 February. From Seiktein it turned northward to Welaung and fought several small actions on the way. Both columns crushed opposition as they moved forward, but found that water was their chief difficulty in this arid tract of Central Burma. Welaung was found evacuated but the 63rd Indian Infantry Brigade caught the Japanese at Kaing and inflicted a large number of casualties on them.[7] The progress of the brigade was however hampered as the road was found to be mined every five miles.

Capture of Taungtha and Mahlaing

The two forces rapidly converged on Taungtha. Sindewa Chaung, which had been made fit for vehicles by Sappers of the northern column, was crossed on the night of 23/24 February, and Taungtha was attacked on the 24th, mainly by the 48th Indian Infantry Brigade, the 63rd Indian Infantry Brigade not having arrived in the area until late in the afternoon. At 1200 hours, 4 Frontier Force Regiment in lead attacked Taungtha from the southwest with 9 Royal Horse in support. The resistance was lighter than expected and the town was taken without much opposition before 1400 hours. Late in the afternoon, the southern column (63rd Indian Infantry Brigade) also came up from the south having fought its way from Welaung. Both the forces having joined, the whole division started moving towards Mingan, 3 miles beyond Taungtha, to harbour for the night. For a brief period the whole division tore across country on a broad front, over bunds, cactus hedges and broken ground. These apparently proved no obstacle to a force animated by success. But the triangular area between the Mahlaing and Welaung roads was full of Japanese snipers, over 100 of whom had to be killed by 7/10 Baluch before harbouring was completed.

Air-strip Captured

On 25 February, the 48th Indian Infantry Brigade remained behind at Taungtha to collect the supply drop which was successfully made.[8] The rest of the force pushed on to Mahlaing which was taken at 0830 hours on 26 February, without opposition. On

---

[7] According to 63rd Indian Infantry Brigade War Diary, 158 casualties were inflicted on the Japanese at Kaing.

[8] 48th Brigade joined the main force at Mahlaing next day.

the same day by 0930 hours, some tanks and 9 Border had staged a wide left hook over difficult country via Kwawgaung and reached and captured the Thabutkon air-strip,⁹ 13 miles short of Meiktila, where work was taken up to prepare it for reception of troop-carrying aircraft. By midday of 27 February, the fly-in of the 99th Indian Infantry Brigade, the third brigade of the division, and attached troops had started and was pushed on so rapidly and efficiently that by the evening a complete battalion had been flown in. One squadron of Probyn's Horse was there to provide a protective screen for the landing.

Advance on Meiktila

The next phase of the advance was the move to Meiktila. On 27 February, the divisional headquarters and the 48th Indian Infantry Brigade remained at Sedaw, 16 miles from Meiktila, while one squadron of 16 Cavalry was sent forward for reconnoitring the approaches to the town. The first serious opposition was encountered at milestone 8 where the armoured cars of 16 Cavalry found the bridge demolished and mines laid, making it difficult to move forward. At 1100 hours, the 63rd Indian Infantry Brigade (one company of 9 Border and one company of 6/7 Rajput) was ordered to by-pass the road-block at milestone 8, move in a left hook and reach milestone 6. They succeeded in reaching milestone 6 but encountered another block there which was cleared. Tanks then smashed both frontally and from the north. The road nulla was found extensively mined and the north end of the nulla was defended by a sniper screen in the bushes. On the approach of tanks, the snipers fled back into the nulla and it was difficult to engage them on account of its steep banks. Eventually crossings were found on both sides of the bridge and a tank was driven down the bank of the nulla towards the bridge, "drumming up" the snipers on the way.[10] Other troops then crossed and moved up the road deploying on both sides of it. All hostile positions were engaged and destroyed, the Japanese offering no real resistance, at any rate nothing like the one encountered earlier at Oyin. Having brushed aside this opposition, the force harboured at milestone 6 and patrols to Meiktila reported that the Japanese were blowing up dumps everywhere.[11]

Meiktila

Situated on the Myingyan branch of the Burma railway, Meiktila is 320 miles from Rangoon and 75 from Myingyan. It

---

⁹ 63rd Brigade War Diary, 601/347/WD, Part III.
[10] *Operations in Burma by Probyn's Horse, op. cit.*
[11] Operations IV Corps, *op. cit.*, para 102.

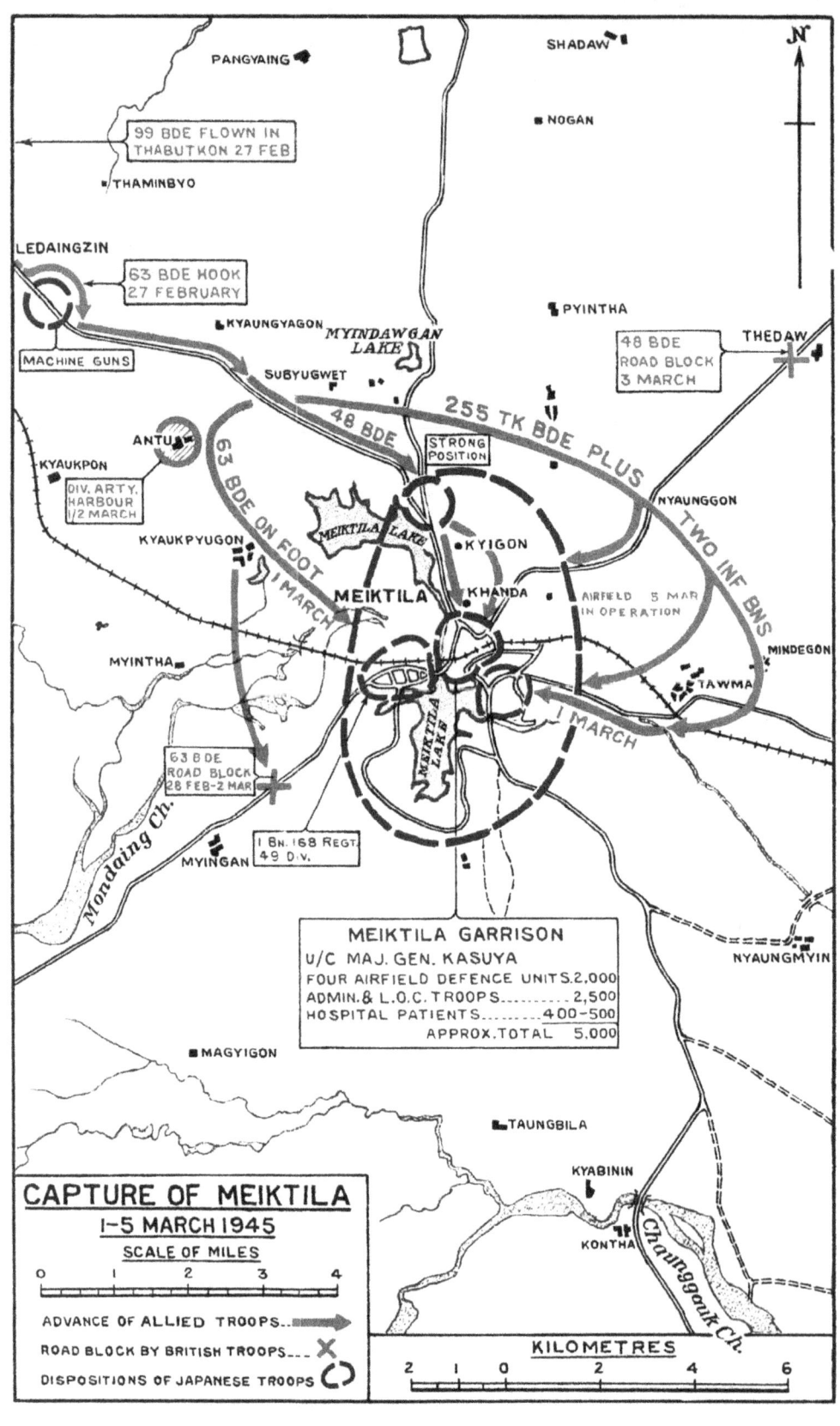

stands on the margin of a large artificial lake which is practically divided into two sheets of water, the north and the south lake. Over the strip of water uniting the two ran the railway bridge and a narrow wooden bridge which connected the town on the east with the civil station on the west.

As the centre of a group of forward airfields protecting the main line of communication up to the Irrawaddy, Meiktila was obviously an important town to the Japanese and identifications and dumps captured showed that the Japanese area headquarters at Meiktila controlled the main administration area of the *15th Army*. The Japanese had for some time been conscious of the risk of attack on Meiktila but had believed that the danger was from airborne operations. Captured documents dated 22 February, while the 17th Indian Division was still at Ngathayauk, showed that *1st Battalion 168th Regiment* of *49th Division* was ordered to come to the Meiktila area from Maymyo, while the rest of the regiment which had been somewhat depleted was to follow soon after. *1st Battalion* arrived in time to take up positions in the Kanna area (LL 2732) to the west of Meiktila, and took part in the defence of the town. Prior to the arrival of this reinforcement, the Japanese garrison of Meiktila had consisted of four airfield defence units, totalling some 2,000 men, a miscellaneous collection of administrative and line of communication troops nearly 2,500 and some 400 to 500 hospital patients, under the command of Major-General Kasuya who had been appointed area commander not very long before.

The Plan for Attack

The plan for the capture of Meiktila provided for a three-pronged attack. The 255th Indian Tank Brigade was to carry out a flanking movement to the north and east of the town and then to attack from the east, the 48th Indian Infantry Brigade was to attack from the north along the axis of the main road from Mahlaing, and the 63rd Indian Infantry Brigade was to move in.from the west . In addition all roads leading to Meiktila were to be blocked.

THE ATTACK

The attack on Meiktila began on 28 February, when the 63rd Indian Infantry Brigade moved forward towards Kyaukpyugon on foot, leaving almost all transport at Thabutkon. Only the very essential minimum fighting transport accompanied it. A divisional artillery harbour was formed at Antu, from which the guns could support an attack on Meiktila from any direction. Leaving one battalion to guard this harbour, the brigade sent out patrols to gather information about the strength of defence and the routes for launching an attack on Meiktila from the west. The reports indicated that the western edge of Meiktila was strongly defended. By the evening, the brigade was in harbour in the area of Kyaukpyugon. On the same day the 48th Indian Infantry Brigade, closing in from the north, had moved to milestone 3 on Mahlaing-Meiktila road. Its advance guard, 1/7 Gurkha Rifles, debussed and moved on foot along the road until they were held up by LMG and MMG fire from the area LL 2935.[12] On the way to this objective the Gurkhas found the bridge and the causeway partly demolished but sent two companies across the chaung at 2150 hours to get a foothold in Meiktila. But owing to darkness these companies withdrew to harbour north of the chaung. Entry into Meiktila was postponed till the next morning, but during the night one company of the Gurkhas was sent out to probe into Meiktila. This company was held up in the monastery area at LL 2933 and had to return.

The 255th Indian Tank Brigade with two infantry battalions was to attack the town from the east. These battalions had therefore to move round the north of Meiktila and then move south to attack from the east. Thus they had to cover the longest distance to reach their positions. Their first concentration area was at milestone 6, north-west of Meiktila, to which they moved as soon as a reconnaissance moving ahead had reported all clear. From here the main elements continued to move north, north-east and east of Meiktila by bounds. The idea of making this circuitous flanking sweep was to cut the roads to Thazi and Pyawbwe, capture Point 860 on the eastern shore of the southern lake, and then make a concentrated armour attack from the east. It was also hoped that attacking from the east would be like entering from the back door and might avoid minefields and fixed defences likely to be encountered on the west.

Two groups, A and B, each consisting of a squadron of 9 Royal Horse, a troop of armoured cars, two platoons of infantry and supporting arms, were assigned the task of reconnoitring the routes leading into Meiktila, from the north-east and east respectively.[13] A Group reached its objective, milestone 339½ on the road Meiktila-Mandalay without opposition on 28 February, and B Group also encountered little resistance until after it had crossed the airfield and was south of the railway line, due south of Khanda. B Group was closely followed by 5 Horse and 6/7 Rajput, who were to put in the attack astride the railway line from a forming up place at Khanda. In the meantime, B Group was hotly engaged south of the railway line. The opposition came from thick scrub covering

---

[12] WD 1/7 GR, 28 March 1945.
[13] 255th Ind. Tank Bde. Ops. Report for the period ending 5 March 1945.

the canal and the level-crossing area. The canal running south of, and parallel to, the railway line was found to be a complete tank obstacle. The infantry with the tank squadron began to suffer casualties. B Group commander was therefore asked to leave the infantry in a firm base covering the left flank, and to move to the high ground at Point 860 whence it was hoped the squadron would be able to give fire support to the attack by 5 Horse and 6/7 Rajput. The latter had decided to carry out their attack on a two-squadron two-company front. The right forward squadron and a company deployed at Khanda without incident, but the left squadron on moving across the railway line to deploy came under heavy machine-gun fire from the nulla, and the infantry suffered severe casualties and was unable to get forward. The left squadron commander then moved one troop forward on to the nulla line and a second troop on to the road running south of and parallel to the railway line. The Japanese ignited petrol drums all round the tanks on this road and the troop commander on opening up to see what was happening was shot through the head. Meanwhile the other troops engaged the Japanese bunkers in the nulla and destroyed several of them. The infantry tried again to get forward in the rear of this troop but suffered more casualties and withdrew.[14]

It was then too late to resume the attack that day in an extremely difficult area covered with thick scrub, trees, nullas and houses, in the face of strong opposition. The tanks then carried out a sweep of this area shooting up all Japanese positions they could see, after which 5 Horse and 6/7 Rajput retired to the harbour area, located about 400 yards north-east of the Khanda village.

Meanwhile 9 Royal Horse squadron in its advance on the ridge east of Point 860 engaged the Japanese in the broken nulla near that point. The nulla was untankable and one troop of tanks was ordered to cross the bridge over the nulla north of the Pagoda at Point 860. The leading troop crossed safely in spite of Japanese attempt to halt the tanks by igniting petrol drums on the bridge, but as it was getting late the tanks with the infantry were withdrawn to harbour for the night.

Just before last light the truck company of 6/7 Rajput and one troop of 16 Cavalry were established in the area of milestone 341 on the road Meiktila-Mandalay. This block was wired in and covered by mines. Also Japanese communications with Pyawbwe were cut, and Point 860 was captured, but mopping up of this sector and consolidation had to be left over for the next day, and the troops were ordered to withdraw for the night to Khanda.

During the night of 28 February/1 March, patrols were sent into Meiktila but they were all engaged by very strong Japanese

[14] *Ibid.*

posts. Meanwhile the divisional artillery had been active and added to the fires caused by the dumps ignited by bombing and Japanese denial plans. Thus at the close of the day on 28 February, the position on the different brigade fronts was as follows:—

The 63rd Indian Infantry Brigade had made some progress towards the western outskirts of Meiktila and was in harbour in the Kyaukpyugon area; the 48th Indian Infantry Brigade was to the north of the chaung LL 2935. It had not been able to capture the monastery on the northern edge of the town; the 255th Indian Tank Brigade had captured Point 860, but mopping up the area still remained to be done.

1 March

The first day of March saw some of the most bitter fighting on this front. As the 63rd and 48th Indian Infantry Brigades moved gradually forward, they met with increasing opposition, and the Japanese had to be pushed back slowly bunker by bunker. On this day, the tank brigade to the east of Meiktila was firmly established on Point 860. This feature had been reached on 28 February, but the troops had been withdrawn from there to harbour for the night at Khanda. On the morning of 1 March, A Squadron of 9 Royal Horse was ordered to seize this point again. This task was accomplished without much difficulty, but when one squadron of 5 Horse and a company of 6/7 Rajput were ordered to move forward and take over the position from 9 Royal Horse, they met with heavy sniping fire from Japanese bunkers hidden on the feature and from a nulla to the east of it. After one hour of fighting these bunkers were cleared and Point 860 was firmly in the hands of the Rajput company, which was reinforced by one more company towards the evening. After this the tanks came back from this point to the site of their harbour.

48th Brigade. In the north, 1/7 Gurkha Rifles of the 48th Indian Infantry Brigade with two squadrons of 9 Royal Horse had advanced on Meiktila, in the day, astride the Mandalay road on a two-company front, with two troops in support on the right and one on the left, to clear the area north of the lakes. Only light opposition was encountered up to the line of the monastery-Dak Bungalow. Thereafter heavy opposition developed in the monastery area, which was captured only after a Japanese 250-lb aerial bomb had exploded inside. The left troop was considerably delayed by aerial bombs on the road but finally it reached a position 100 yards north of the railway line, after neutralising several light machine-guns in the houses on the way. The troops on the right, after clearing considerable opposition, also reached this line. By this time it was getting late and as the area was still not fully cleared, orders were issued to withdraw at 1800 hours to Kyigon. An important feature of fighting in this thickly populated area was the presence of an unusually large number of Japanese machine-guns planted in houses. Another interesting feature was the deception devices employed by the Japanese. The area between the Dak Bungalow and the railway line seemed to be very heavily mined, but it was discovered that the majority of the minefields were mere deceptions consisting of bricks lightly covered with earth! Aerial bombs were also used for this purpose and some of them were buried to give the impression of mines, but no detonation device was attached to them.[15]

63rd Brigade. In the 63rd Indian Infantry Brigade area on 1 March, 1/10 Gurkha Rifles was ordered to attack Kanna, west of Meiktila. At about 1215 hours, after air-strike and artillery concentration, two companies of 1/10 Gurkha Rifles assisted by one troop of a squadron of 5 Horse attacked Kanna from the north. The tanks led the infantry and the village was cleared up to the main road. The infantry then proceeded along the road with one tank to protect each of its flanks. The left hand company was held up by sniping from the Jail but the area was cleared with the support of tanks. Meanwhile, the right tank directed by infantry, had been bunker-busting in the hospital compound which contained many bunkers. Here many Japanese were killed. An air-strike put the hospital on fire, and caused more casualties.[16] In the meantime the rest of A Squadron of 5 Horse had also arrived on the scene. It had been given the task of supporting an attack by one company of 7/10 Baluch on Magyigon village. After a short artillery concentration the infantry moved in and completely cleared it within half an hour without any loss.

The position on the night of 1/2 March was as follows:—The 48th Indian Infantry Brigade was harboured in Kyigon area, the 63rd Indian Infantry Brigade was on the outskirts of Meiktila west, and 255th Indian Tank Brigade was in Khanda area, the 99th Indian Infantry Brigade had arrived completely and was in Thabutkon area, but 1 Sikh Light Infantry from this brigade had been forward and was with the divisional headquarters about 1½ miles north of Meiktila. The divisional artillery was in Antu from where it could bomb in any direction. In the Thabutkon area, the chief threat to the air-strip was from the direction of Mahlaing. In order to defend the air-strip and the installations in the area, the 99th Brigade was to be supported by the 21 Indian Mountain Regiment.[17]

---

[15] 48th Indian Infantry Brigade War Diary, 1 March 1945.
[16] "50/60 Japanese were burnt alive in hospital". See 63rd Brigade War Diary, 1 March 1945, 601/347/WD, Part IV.
[17] 21 Mtn Regt, OO No. 2 of 2 March 1945.

During the night, the Japanese infiltrated back into certain areas from which the Indian troops had withdrawn at nightfall to harbour in safer places. On the perimeter of nearly all the harbours the Japanese jitter parties were active during the night but they could achieve nothing and suffered some casualties.

2 March

Offensive action against pockets of resistance was continued on 2 March. 4/12 Frontier Force Regiment, which had relieved 1/7 Gurkha Rifles, resumed the attack at 1015 hours from the north with the support of B and C Squadrons of 9 Royal Horse. B Squadron was on the right and C on the left. The right company found great difficulty in getting on against mines, medium machine-guns, light machine-guns and anti-tank guns in the area of the pagoda 297329. But the left company encountered less resistance. When the leading tanks of this company were 50 yards from the railway line they were fired upon by 75-mm guns in position south of the railway, and three tanks were knocked out before the guns were located.[18] The company, however, succeeded in crossing the railway line. The men were held up by the canal beyond, both bridges on which were heavily mined. One troop of C Squadron and a platoon of infantry thereupon proceeded east against stiff opposition and crossed the canal by the eastern loop road. The Japanese were slowly driven to the south-west of the town. At about 1700 hours the 48th Indian Infantry Brigade was ordered to withdraw to the monastery area. 4/12 Frontier Force Regiment withdrew to Kyigon harbour leaving one company less one platoon in the pagoda area.[19] 4 Frontier Force Regiment passed a night disturbed by Japanese jitter parties.

63rd Brigade. West of Meiktila, one company of 1/10 Gurkha Rifles with a squadron of 5 Horse in support started clearing the Jail area up to the causeway. A mortar concentration was put on the Jail and its wall was breached by the tanks. The infantry preceded the tanks and entered the Jail but found it empty.[20] The tanks then reached the causeway but were met by heavy fire from a 75-mm gun firing from the far end of the causeway, two tanks receiving direct hits. The attack was then switched on towards Kyaukpu area of the town, the route to which lay through dense thorn-thickets and well-built stone buildings, with many vehicle pits, fox-holes and air raid shelters. A divisional artillery barrage was put down but appeared to inflict no ostensible damage. As soon

---

[18] One tank was knocked out by mines and two damaged by anti-tank fire. 48th Brigade War Diary; 601/339/WD, Part II.
[19] *Ibid.*
[20] Many aerial bombs planted as mines were found in the jail. See 63rd Indian Infantry Brigade War Diary, 601/347/WD.

as the artillery had stopped, the tanks advanced. The infantry was unable to keep up with the tanks due to snipers and light machine-gun fire. The left troop of tanks entered a belt of scrub 150 yards deep and immediately came under a hail of small-arms fire. Two tanks were assaulted by tank hunters who placed a charge on the track and hurled petrol bombs on to the tanks. One tank was disabled but the other suffered no damage and they continued methodically to blast every bunker they could see. On emerging from the scrub they caught up with the Japanese in the process of withdrawing in the open and inflicted heavy casualties on them.

In the meanwhile the tanks on the right had been progressing steadily but slowly, destroying bunkers the whole way. The indefatigable cab-rank was always in support. Several snipers were knocked out of the trees by tank-guns. Resistance finally centered in one large red house with a deep air raid shelter, but the tanks drove at the Japanese who were engaged by a troop on the Kyaukpadaung road as they withdrew. Some Japanese withdrawing by the lake side were engaged by a troop of C Squadron (5 Horse) at Point 799 across the lake.

255th Tank Brigade—During the day, the tanks of the 255th Indian Tank Brigade had been busy in support of 6/7 Rajput in the Point 860 area, clearing up isolated pockets of resistance and maintaining one troop throughout the day on Point 799 overlooking the south and west sides of the lake.

As a result of the fighting on 2 March, having as its object the clearing of the pockets of resistance, the following areas were cleared: Meiktila west, Kanna, Magyigon, Kyaukpu and Thamangon. Cantonment area was also cleared and Point 860 remained in the hands of the Rajputs. However, certain areas still remained to be cleared, for example Paukchaung, Meiktila east and a few small pockets south of the railway. A feature of the day's fighting was the capture of 14 swords by the 63rd Indian Infantry Brigade.[21]

Night 2 March

During the night of 2 March the 48th Indian Infantry Brigade harboured in Kyigon area, but one company was wired in the area of the road-rail junction at LL 3033, and one company in the pagoda area, LL 2933. The 63rd Indian Infantry Brigade harboured in the area south of Kanna, with one company of 7 Baluch on the road-block at mile 9 on the Kyaukpadaung road, and one company of 9 Border at gun box at Antu (LL 2838). The 255th Indian Tank Brigade harboured at LL 3031 north of Point 860.[22] During this

[21] Sitrep to 1800 hours on 2 March, W/D 17th Division.
[22] *Ibid.*

night also, the Japanese jitter parties were active, especially in the nullas on the eastern outskirts of the town.[23]

3 March

The next day Meiktila east was cleared after some bitter fighting. 1 West Yorks which had relieved 4/12 Frontier Force Regiment launched the final attack on Meiktila. In the first phase one company of 1 West Yorks with A Squadron 9 Royal Horse advanced from the monastery at 0830 hours and reached the railway line against very light opposition. At 1015 hours the second phase commenced with one company of 1 West Yorks and B Squadron 9 Royal Horse crossing the railway line and the canal at the east end of the town and attacking from north-east to south-west after heavy air and artillery concentration. The advance on this axis could not be used for the whole attack as the 63rd Indian Infantry Brigade was holding the area immediately west of the lake and south of the railway line. This attack met with heavier opposition but it made good progress, and at 1300 hours the third phase was started when the right company crossed the railway line and advanced in conjunction with the left hook. A third company was deployed and the advance continued against extremely bitter resistance from the snipers in each block of buildings and from the bunkers which had to be cleared one by one. All objects looking like mines had to be lifted. Japanese 75-mm guns firing at point-blank range knocked out three tanks, two of which were completely burnt out. But opposition was, however, being gradually liquidated. Japanese guns on concrete emplacements on promontory at 299321 were finally eliminated at 1750 hours. About 50 Japanese jumped into the lake and were drowned or killed.[24] The town area was cleared by 1700 hours. The tanks and 1 West Yorks withdrew to harbour at 1800 hours, while 1/7 Gurkha Rifles was ordered to patrol the town area throughout the night.

Throughout the day while the above operations were going on, some parties of Japanese troops were seen in the area east of the town and west of Khanda in the drains, rifle-range hills and broken ground. These were wiped out by infantry, tanks, mortars, and machine-gun fire.

On this day, attacks on Meiktila were launched from several directions and the various columns were closing in the ring around the town. They were thus approaching near each other and the "overs" from the different attacking columns kept most people, including the divisional headquarters, on their toes. Luckily no loss was sustained.

[23] War Diary 17th Indian Division, 3 March 1945.
[24] Appendix H to 48th Indian Infantry Brigade War Diary for March 1945.

Thus by the night of 3 March 1945 Meiktila was bagged by the 17th Indian Division. Some of the most savage fighting had been witnessed during these four days. The Japanese asked for no quarter and every one of them had to be slain before resistance ceased. Several Japanese were found with aerial bombs between their knees and a brick in their hands, squatting in trenches waiting for a tank to run over the trench, and to strike the bomb detonator with the brick.[25] Every time the Indian and British troops withdrew from a forward position to harbour for the night in a safe place, the Japanese infiltrated back and the position had to be retaken the next day. Some captured documents were found to be full of exhortations to the Japanese soldiers to make a last-ditch stand, and there is no doubt that these were literally followed. It was estimated that about 2000 Japanese were killed in this battle, and 42 guns were captured or destroyed.[26] Deeds of great heroism and devotion to duty were performed by the Indian and British troops and two posthumous Victoria Crosses were won in the battle: one by Lieutenant W. B. Weston, the Green Howards, attached to 1 West Yorks, for superb gallantry displayed on 3 March, and the other by Naik Fazal Din of 7/10 Baluch Regiment for his gallant fighting a day earlier. A complete account of the action in which Naik Fazal Din's dauntless courage and heroism resulted in the elimination of an important and strong Japanese bunker is given thus in the citation:—

"Naik Fazal Din was commanding a section on 2 March 1945 during A Company's attack on the Japanese bunkered position at approximately 275320 (Meiktila map ·1.25,00). During this attack, the section found itself in an area, flanked by three bunkers on one side and a house and one bunker on the other. This was the core of the enemy position and had held a company attack made earlier in the morning. Naik Fazal Din's section was accompanied by a tank but, at the time of entering the area, it had gone on ahead. On reaching the area, the section was held up by Light Machine-Gun fire and grenades from the bunkers. Unhesitatingly Naik Fazal Din personally attacked the nearest bunker with grenades and silenced it. He then led his section in a blitz against the other bunkers. Suddenly six Japanese, led by two officers wielding swords, rushed at the section from the house. The Bren gunner shot one officer and a Japanese Other Rank but by then had expended the magazine on the gun. He was almost simultaneously attacked by the second Japanese officer who slashed with his sword and killed him. Naik Fazal Din went to the Bren gunner's assistance imme-

---

[25] Operations IV Corps, October 44—May 1945, p. 20.
[26] Sitrep 4 March War Diary 17th Division. The figure of Japanese casualties according to IV Corps account is 1600.

diately but, in doing so, was run through the chest by the Japanese officer, the sword point appearing through his back. On the Japanese officer withdrawing the sword, Naik Fazal Din despite his ghastly wound, tore the sword from the officer and slew him with it. He then attacked a Japanese Other Rank and also killed him. He then went to the assistance of a sepoy of his section who was struggling with another Japanese and killed the latter with the sword. Then waving the sword, he continued to encourage his men, thereafter staggering to Platoon Headquarters about 25 yards away to make a report. Here he collapsed and was evacuated to the Regimental Aid Post. He died here soon after reaching it.

"Naik Fazal Din's action was seen by almost the whole Platoon. Undoubtedly inspired by his glorious deed and taking advantage of the bewilderment created amongst the enemy by the loss of its leaders the Platoon continued the attack furiously and annihilated the garrison of this area which numbered 55. Such dauntless courage amounting to heroism, blazing determination to kill even when fatally wounded, supreme devotion to duty, presence of mind and sacrifice is seldom equalled in the annals of War and reflects the unquenchable spirit of a singularly brave and gallant Non-Commissioned Officer who, after being mortally wounded, killed three enemy and before this had personally eliminated the occupants of a large bunker. The whole Platoon was unquestionably fired by his magnificent conduct, inspiring it to annihilate the complete garrison and to reduce what was the strongest part of the enemy position. Naik Fazal Din's death, though sadly regretted, was a glorious one and is a magnificent inspiration to all ranks of the Battalion."[27]

During the night, 1/7 Gurkha Rifles sealing off the north and east ends of the town, carried out vigorous patrolling and disposed of a few stragglers, while one company of 4 Frontier Force Regiment established a road-block on the Mandalay road at milestone 344½.

On 3 March was also fought an action against some Japanese troops established at Shande near milestone 343. The force which participated in this action consisted of one company of Sikh Light Infantry, one of 6/7 Rajput, C Squadron of 5 Horse, and two troops of armoured cars besides other supporting arms. The plan was to direct a left hook on the road in order to take the Japanese in the rear. The infantry and the tanks assembled at 0700 hours, and reaching Nyaunggan village commenced to move to the road-junction and further south. They were engaged by two 37-mm and 75-mm guns from the south of the road. The tanks engaged both the guns and silenced them. Some tanks coming from the north were again heavily engaged by two 75-mm guns located on the road

---

[27] This was the sixth Victoria Cross to be won by the 17th Indian Division. See Appendix to 7/10 Baluch Regiment War Diary for May 1945.

Men of 4/12 Frontier Force Regiment charge burning remnants of a village during drive on Meiktila

3.7" Howitzer gun of 6 Jacob Mountain Battery, in action against the Japanese south of Meiktila

Rifleman Tulbahadur Pun V.C.
3/6 G.R.

Rifleman Lachhiman Gurung V.C.
4/8 G.R.

Naik Fazal Din V.C.
7/10 Baluch

Jemadar (acting Subedar)
Ram Sarup Singh V.C.
2/1 Punjab

at 70 yards range. The leading tank was burnt out but other tanks forced the Japanese gun crew to desert their posts. After an artillery concentration the Rajputs marched forward and found the road-junction deserted. The Sikhs pushed across the road to Shande village and found it clear. A new road-block was then established by 5/16 Punjab at mile 344½.

The town of Meiktila itself was divided into sectors and each sector was made ready to withstand a siege. It was expected that after recovering from the stunning effects of surprise, the Japanese would make every effort to re-take the town. All preparations to frustrate such a return were taken in hand and the different sectors were wired round. In addition, columns, usually of brigade strength (less one battalion left to guard the perimeter), were sent out on 4 and 5 March to carry out sweeps, to catch the Japanese forces unprepared and allow them no time to formulate plans of attack.

Meanwhile, the divisional headquarters, artillery and the 48th Indian Infantry Brigade moved into the cantonment area. The 63rd Indian Infantry Brigade remained in Meiktila west and the 99th Indian Infantry Brigade took over the Kyigon area. The fly-in of the 99th Indian Infantry Brigade, begun on 27 February had been completed by 2 March. It was therefore decided to abandon the Thabutkon air-strip for the bigger air-strip east of Meiktila. Infantry detachments remained at Thabutkon until all stores etc. were cleared off from the place. Meiktila main air-strip was quickly put in order and started operating on 5 March.

While the 17th Indian Division was busy capturing Meiktila, one of its brigades, the 99th, was being flown in at Thabutkon air-strip; and another division of the IV Corps, the 7th Indian Division, was active on the east of the Irrawaddy beyond its bridgehead. It may be convenient at this stage to recount their activities.

FLY-IN OF 99TH BRIGADE

It may be recalled that the 99th Indian Infantry Brigade of the 17th Indian Division had not moved forward with the other two brigades but had remained at Wanjing in the Imphal plain, practising emplaning and deplaning for the eventual fly-in to the front as soon as an air-strip west of Meiktila had been secured by its companion brigades.

The Thabutkon air-strip, as described earlier, was captured on 26 February, and the fly-in of the leading battalion[28] began the next day from Palel. By the evening the whole of the battalion was flown into Thabutkon air-strip by the U.S. Army Air Force.

---

[28] 1/3 Gurkha Rifles of 99th Brigade.

Earlier on the same day an American flying control team had been landed at Thabutkon air-strip by glider, followed by some Forward Airfield Maintenance Organisation detachments to hasten the unloading of supply aircraft. The whole operation, both at Palel and Thabutkon, was so perfectly organised that not a single mishap occurred.[29]

The fly-in of the other units of the 99th Indian Infantry Brigade continued during the next three days and was completed by 2 March in 353 Dakota sorties, without any interference by the Japanese and without the loss of a single aircraft or man.[30]

By 3 March, Meiktila had been taken, and the big air-strip to the east of the town was also in Allied hands. Hence the air-strip at Thabutkon was abandoned and the brigade moved to Meiktila on 4 March. This new air-strip was developed as the main supply base for the 17th Indian Division and started functioning on 5 March. The 99th Indian Infantry Brigade was made responsible for the defence of this air-strip for which it carried out intensive offensive patrolling. The Japanese penetrated to this airfield and on several occasions were in actual possession of it, but they were never able to use it for landing aircraft and were always driven back. But then, the Allies were not able to make use of it either.

ACTIVITIES OF THE 7TH INDIAN DIVISION

In Chapter X it has been described how the 7th Indian Division had established and enlarged the bridgehead at Nyaungu through which the 17th Indian Division had passed. For establishing the bridgehead, it had been necessary for the 7th Indian Division to divert the attention of the Japanese by two other moves, one by the 28th East African Brigade which appeared suddenly before Seikpyu on 12 February, and the other by 1/11 Sikh who attempted a feint crossing south of Pagan. The activities of these two units up to 14/15 February have already been described in the previous chapter. Their operations after that date may now be briefly noticed here, for, although not directly connected with the capture of Meiktila, they deserve a mention on account of the violent reaction they evoked in the Japanese which, as was intended, indirectly helped the operations against Meiktila.

In the 28th East African Brigade sector, the Japanese made repeated attacks on the morning of 15 February and again in the evening but were repulsed. Losses were suffered on both sides. In one of these attacks the Japanese tried to deceive the Africans by

---

[29] One plane came in the wrong way and landed in some scrub but there was no loss or casualties.
[30] Operations IV Corps, October 1944 to May 1945, para 110.

using Somali and Swahili phrases and were thereby able to get close to the African positions before being identified. The Africans were taken by surprise and suffered casualties. As a result of this Japanese artifice, the outlying platoons had to be withdrawn during the day. The two companies attacked were also withdrawn and the brigade was concentrated and reorganised at Gwebin. The Japanese succeeded in reoccupying the area vacated by the Africans. From its new position, the East African Brigade was asked to confine itself for the time being to patrolling activity and to harass the Seikpyu-Lanywa area. There were increasing signs of Japanese activity, but the brigade's task was to frustrate all attempts threatening the Nyaungu bridgehead from the south, and in this it succeeded.

On 19 February the Japanese launched another violent attack on the African Brigade's positions, and overran forward positions of 7 KAR. A small party of Japanese troops, at the same time, dug in behind some Africans in a position astride the Gwebin—Seikpyu road at PP 0243. Repeated attempts to dislodge them failed, though some casualties were inflicted. It was apparent that the Japanese had brought in reinforcements and were out for a showdown. The brigade administrative area was vulnerable and moreover there was a threat to its right flank. It was therefore felt that since the primary object of the advance, to threaten Seikpyu-Chauk-Sale area and divert the Japanese attention from the Nyaungu area, had been accomplished, it was not necessary to take a further risk. Hence it was decided to withdraw the brigade to a safer area, and on 20 February, the African Brigade Group less 46 KAR concentrated at Letse and 46 KAR at Ywathit. Its presence there invited Japanese counter-attacks, presumably under the impression that the oil area was threatened.

Meanwhile, in the Letse area the East Africans were forced by the Japanese attacks to shut themselves up in a defensive box where they were practically besieged. It therefore became necessary to send some troops from the 114th Indian Infantry Brigade to assist them. This brigade had by that time crossed the river and was holding the central portion of the bridgehead at Nyaungu and preventing Japanese infiltration from the Kyaukpadaung side. The 4/14 Punjab of this brigade was therefore detached and sent to the Letse area to help the East Africans. The Punjabis reached there on 22 February[31] and for about a month after that they fought many offensive and defensive actions against the Japanese. In the later stages of the Letse area operations 2 South Lancashire Regiment was also summoned and took over part of the defences from 4/14 Punjab.

While on the west bank of the river the Africans and the

---

[31] 4/14 Punjab War Diary, 601/5497/WD, Part II.

Punjabis were finding it difficult to clear the Japanese from the Letse area, on the eastern bank the 7th Indian Division was busy enlarging the bridgehead and clearing the area between Nyaungu and Meiktila which the 17th Indian Division had left uncleared in its hurried advance to Meiktila. The triangular area formed by Nyaungu, Myingyan and Taungtha contained many Japanese positions, Myingyan itself being held in sufficient strength. Myingyan occupied a strategic position as a strong hostile force from this place could prevent a contact being made between the Allied forces at Myinmu and Meiktila. It could also disrupt the Allied line of communication between Meiktila and the Irrawaddy. Moreover Myingyan was an important river port as also a railhead for the metergauge railway running south-east to Meiktila and beyond. Its capture was therefore considered to be as valuable for the Allies, as its retention was for the Japanese.

The 7th Indian Division was therefore assigned the following tasks:

    (a) to hold and enlarge the bridgehead,
    (b) to send back across the river a battalion to reinforce the East Africans who had been strongly counter-attacked at Seikpyu, and
    (c) to clear Myingyan of the Japanese.

These tasks involved the division in much hard fighting and gruelling work but the tasks were performed with commendable skill. This is clear from the fact that the operations to clear the approaches to Myingyan and to drive out the garrison brought two Victoria Crosses to the division—both awarded to 4/15 Punjab. We will now narrate briefly how these tasks were performed.

The various brigades of the 7th Indian Division were occupied as follows between 18 February and 6 March 1945:

The 33rd Indian Infantry Brigade continued enlarging the bridgehead by thrusting east along the left bank of the Irrawaddy. It was also given the task of capturing Myingyan to its north-east. The 89th Indian Infantry Brigade moved south from the area of Pagan. The 114th Indian Infantry Brigade sent one battalion to reinforce the 28th (East African) Brigade and the rest of the brigade took up close protection of the bridgehead area. This enabled the 33rd Indian Infantry Brigade to be directed north-eastward on to Myingyan.

33rd Indian Infantry Brigade

In order to carry out the task assigned to it, the 33rd Indian Infantry Brigade was divided into two columns. Column A consisting of the brigade headquarters, 4/1 Gurkha Rifles, 1 Burma Regiment, artillery and a squadron of Sherman tanks was to move along the road by the side of the river towards Myingyan via Palin-Letpanchibaw. Column B consisting of 4/15 Punjab, one battery of 139 Field Regiment and a troop of 16 Light Cavalry was to go towards Ngathayauk to block any Japanese attempt to escape from the direction of the advance of Column A.

Accordingly the 33rd Indian Infantry Brigade started its move on 24 February. The Japanese continued to oppose the advance of Column A (the main column) on the river-road, hence progress was rather slow. Here 1 Burma which had taken the lead after the capture of Palin reached Nyin and Tagaungde (both in PP 3378 area) on the direct road to Myingyan on 25 February. Meanwhile 4/15 Punjab of Column B had, with supporting troops, proceeded via the main road to Ngathayauk. In view of the resistance met by Column A on the river-road, 4/15 Punjab was asked to switch north along the Ngathayauk—Letpanchibaw road to make an out-flanking movement to cut off the Japanese retreat in front of the main column. It met with considerable resistance in the course of its march to Letpanchibaw. On 26 February the Punjabis encountered a Japanese position in the area of mile 5, but they deployed a company at each flank and succeeded in capturing the position after a stiff fight. On 28 February, it had cleared the road and moved north to link up with the main body of the brigade. Meanwhile, the Japanese had pulled out of Letpanchibaw, which was occupied by 4/15 Punjab. In order to gain contact with the Japanese, the Punjabis returned to Ngathayauk with a view to taking up the line of advance via Kamye. They were followed by 1 Burma and the brigade headquarters. The plan at this stage was for the main group of the brigade to move on the axis Ngathayauk-Kamye-Myingyan with only 4/1 Gurkha Rifles moving along the coast road.

The advance was made fairly quickly along both the axes. By the evening of 1 March the Gurkhas had reached Mala and 4/15 Punjab Kamye. The next stand by the Japanese was on the east bank of the dry Sindewa Chaung, south-west of Myingyan. The force moving north from Kamye met with opposition at the wide sandy Sindewa Chaung crossing. 4/1 Gurkha Rifles was likewise held up on the chaung crossing further north at PP 6596. Thus practically the whole brigade was disposed roughly on the line of the Sindewa Chaung from the Irrawaddy to the road junction at Taungtha. This chaung, though very wide, had no water at the moment. 4/15 Punjab while moving along the road Kamye-Myingyan preparatory to crossing the chaung clashed with a Japanese patrol on 2 March. One Japanese was killed and two wounded, but the rest of them ran across the chaung. The leading company—D Company—stopped on the near bank and started digging in. Meanwhile a small recce patrol was sent across to find out the exact position and strength of the Japanese on the other side. Before dark enough information had been obtained, and during the night C and D Companies made a right hook and cut the road behind the Japanese positions and established themselves at Point 276.[32]

On the morning of 3 March, A Company had to go across with the tanks. Everything was arranged properly and at the zero hour the tanks left the road and got into the chaung followed by A Company. After going about half way, they came under heavy machine-gun fire from the far bank. The tanks started blasting the position from which fire was coming and continued to move, though slowly, and finally reached the far bank and mopped up the area upto 1000 yards.[33] Here the Japanese had a strong position near a village towards which the Sikhs (A Company) now made a charge with loud war cries making the Japanese flee in confusion.

Most of the Japanese withdrew towards the village which was about 1200 yards from the road. One platoon of A Company was ordered to mop up the village. As they were moving forward, the section of Naik Gian Singh spotted a Japanese anti-tank gun which was firing at close range on the tanks.[34] The Japanese position was well concealed behind a cactus hedge. Naik Gian Singh ordered his gunners to cover as he rushed the Japanese fox-hole. The tanks also moved up but came under heavy fire. Naik Gian Singh who had sustained several wounds, again rushed forward and annihilated the Japanese anti-tank gun crew, capturing the weapon single-handed. He then led his section in clearing all Japanese positions. Later many Japanese bodies were found in this area. He was then ordered to the Regimental Aid Post, but although suffering considerable pains from his wounds he requested permission to continue leading his section until the whole action had been completed. The permission was granted, and later for his gallantry he was awarded the Victoria Cross.

After capturing the gun, A Company mopped up the village and moved forward to contact C and D Companies who had crossed during the previous night and were in position a mile ahead. It encountered some shelling on the way but suffered only slight casualties and finally contacted the C and D Companies.

In the meantime 4/1 Gurkha Rifles was also across the chaung but remained in Tanaungdaing area with the object of establishing itself to the rear of the Japanese front of 4/1 Gurkha Rifles. But on account of the supporting tanks having to withdraw to refuel

---

[32] WD 4/15 Punjab, 2 March 1945.
[33] *Ibid*, 3 March 1945.
[34] *Ibid*.

and heavy hostile shelling, operations were confined to patrolling until the return of the tanks on 5 March. On that morning after an air-strike, a company of 4/15 Punjab supported by tanks moved forward at 1000 hours but the progress was slow due to sniping. By 1500 hours, however, one company had reached its objective, the road junction at PP 7498, south of Myingyan.

Taungtha

Just when the troops were poised for an attack on Myingyan, it was found imperative to withdraw 1 Burma and 4/1 Gurkha Rifles from the area just south of Myingyan and to postpone the capture of the town. This was necessary in order to deal with a strong Japanese force which, escaping from the zone of the XXXIII Corps drive in the north, had firmly entrenched itself in the dominating high ground east and south-east of Taungtha, astride the Allied line of communication to Meiktila. Until this was cleared the large administrative base party of the 17th Indian Division, about to move from Nyaungu via Taungtha, could not reach Meiktila. In addition, there was the problem of the move forward of the IV Corps and the 5th Indian Division troops who were about to assemble in the bridgehead area via Monywa. A plan was therefore evolved whereby an armoured column of the 17th Indian Division was to open the road from Meiktila to Taungtha, while the 33rd Indian Infantry Brigade of the 7th Indian Division was to make the road safe for the administrative column to the west of Taungtha. The Burma Regiment, which had taken very little part in the battle for some time, was ordered to capture Taungtha while 4/15 Punjab contained the Japanese south of Myingyan.

1 Burma started its move towards Taungtha on 5 March. There was little opposition beyond shelling by the Japanese from Taungtha area. On 6 March the Burmese captured and consolidated Taungtha against slight opposition. The Japanese, however, continued to hold out on a hill feature (Point 676), one mile south-east of Taungtha. This position was attacked on 7 March by a company of 1 Burma with tank support. But the Japanese were securely dug in on the summit and the tanks failed to reach it. The battalion was under harassing shell fire throughout the day. Desultory fighting now ensued on this feature, which was subjected to shelling and air-attack and harassment by night, but the Japanese clung tenaciously to their position. On 12 March, 4/1 Gurkha Rifles took up the work of patrolling in this area prior to mounting an attack fixed for the 14th. The attack came off according to plan. 4/1 Gurkha Rifles supported by two squadrons of 116 RAC succeeded on 14 March in capturing this hill feature and clearing the area around it.

There was, however, another strong feature which remained to be cleared. This was Point 1788, a high feature to the north-east of Taungtha. This had been occupied by two platoons of 1 Burma on 7 March, but the Japanese had put in a fanatical attack and had forced the platoons to withdraw. Since the occupation of this dominating point gave the Japanese an uninterrupted view in all directions for many miles, it was decided to retake it. Many attempts were made but they were all unsuccessful. Meanwhile the 161st Indian Infantry Brigade of the 5th Indian Division had reached the area and relieved 1 Burma. This brigade, which had 4 Field Regiment RA under it, was then ordered to maintain the efforts to capture Point 1788. Tough fighting continued for several days, in which elements of the 161st Brigade and 33rd Brigade co-operated, supported by artillery of the 4 Field Regiment RA.[35] When finally on 30 March, 1/1 Punjab and 3/9 Jat advanced on the point from different directions, it was found that the Japanese had withdrawn during the night of 29/30 March having booby-trapped the area.[36] With the road to Meiktila now clear preparations were made by the brigade to move to Meiktila. The route for the 17th Divisions' administrative column, which was to move during the next few days, was also now clear.[37]

Capture of Myingyan

After the capture of Taungtha, the 33rd Indian Infantry Brigade (less 1 Burma) was free to devote its attention to the capture of Myingyan. 4/15 Punjab had been left alone in the Myingyan area to contain the Japanese while Taungtha was being cleared. It was now joined by 4/1 Gurkha Rifles and the attack against Myingyan began in right earnest.

The plan was that the Punjabis should force their entry into the southern outskirts of the town and from there move northwards, while the Gurkhas should make a right flanking move and attack from the east.

4/15 Punjab had already taken Saka on 11 March, which was about 4½ miles to the south of Myingyan; and its reduction was an essential preliminary to a march on Myingyan itself. Some Japanese troops established in a pagoda to the north of Saka were giving trouble by occasional shelling and grenading. But their bunkers were destroyed on 11 March and the Punjabis were ready to carry out the prescribed plan by entering the southern outskirts of Myingyan. Active patrolling was then taken up in the direction of Myingyan and a company was established at the cross-roads at PK 7601 on the 14th.

[35] WD 4 Fd Regt. RA March 1945.
[36] *Ibid.*
[37] *Ibid.*

Further advance was stayed by Japanese opposition at Shadaw. On the night of 16 March, however, 4/15 Punjab entered Shadaw. A Company of 4/15 Punjab and a squadron of tanks attempted to cross a chaung which flowed immediately south-east-south of Myingyan at a place south of Sunlun, but failed on account of the steepness of the banks. D Company of 4/15 Punjab thereupon moved to Shadaw and got across the chaung by 1730 hours on 17 March, and was almost at the gates of Myingyan.

It was at that time that 4/1 Gurkha Rifles, who had been asked to move to Myingyan area, also reached the scene of battle. The Japanese mounted repeated attacks to roll up the 4/15 Punjab D Company bridgehead at PP 767028. Attacks were delivered on the night of 17 March, and again once at 0930 hours and twice in the night on the 18th, but these were beaten off. Another company of 4/15 Punjab (C Company) and some tanks also crossed over on the 18th and started clearing the Cotton Mill area at 1000 hours. The advance was slow due to heavy shelling by Japanese guns, but the tanks bumped across the open ground while the infantry chased the Japanese from bunker to bunker. By 1530 hours the Mill area was cleared for the loss of 4 killed and 13 wounded. C Company then joined up with D Company north of the bridge at Sunlun.

It was believed that the Japanese guns which had been shelling the Punjabis were located in the area of the pagoda at PK 8103. On 20 March an attempt was made to shoot up this gun area. Two columns—one consisting of A Company 4/15 Punjab and a squadron of tanks, the other consisting of a company of 4/1 Gurkha Rifles and a squadron of tanks, moved forward about noon. The former reached the pagoda area without opposition except for some light machine-gun fire and shelling. By 1730 hours the company was established in the area 808038. The second column at the same time cleared Kyaukyan and was established at the railway station. The 33rd Indian Infantry Brigade then began converging on Myingyan from the south, east and north. While B and C Companies of 4/15 Punjab with tank support cleared the area bounded by 78 Easting line to the east and Paungbya Chaung to the north on 21 March, after overcoming sniper opposition, the company of 4/1 Gurkha Rifles crossed the Pyaung Chaung and after occupying Chaungdaung South started operations against Chaungdaung North. The Japanese had by then withdrawn from the southern and eastern parts of Myingyan across the Pyaungbya Chaung to the Jail area in the north of the town where they had established strong dug-in positions. But 4/1 Gurkha Rifles having crossed the chaung was advancing from the east. The Japanese bunker positions and snipers on the way could not stop its progress. Meanwhile an air-strike was put down on the jail, which was also bombarded by artillery and tanks. The Japanese fled westwards, as that seemed to be their only way of escape. Here too some tanks were lying in wait for them and they were shot up. By the evening of 22 March the entire town including the jail and the airfield area north of it were in the hands of the 33rd Indian Infantry Brigade. Thus the town fell after a battle lasting four days. It was during this fighting of four days, that Lieutenant Karamjit Singh of 4/15 Punjab won his posthumous Victoria Cross. While the Punjabis were on the outskirts of this city, he led charge after charge against the Japanese positions and wiped out many of them. Time and again he dashed forward to recall tanks to deal with hidden bunkers. Finally he was mortally wounded, but his men went on and cleared the area. The citation described him as an "outstanding leader of matchless courage", who "dominated the entire battlefield".

After the capture of Myingyan, it was decided to send some infantry and armoured columns to chase and destroy the retreating Japanese forces. On the 19th, an armoured column consisting of two squadrons of tanks and D Company 4/15 Punjab moved towards Natagyi and drove 25 Japanese out of Thitpinshe who were then caught in the open by artillery and a patrol of 4/1 Gurkha Rifles. The column then cleared Lethit against slight opposition and pushed on in two parties—one to Kinmagan and the other towards a pond, 8708. Both these places were cleared against slight opposition. Both parties then moved on a broad front to Nyaungbin and shot the village, leaving it in flames. A large number of stragglers were killed and several guns captured.

With the clearing of Taungtha hills and the capture of Myingyan, the road to Meiktila was opened and the 5th Indian Division started moving eastwards along with the Gordon Highlanders (116 RAC). The 161st Indian Infantry Brigade of this division which was at Taungtha also moved towards Meiktila on 31 March on being relieved by the 33rd Indian Infantry Brigade. As the latter was coming from the Myingyan side, it sent 4/15 Punjab on 29 March to Point 1788 and they found it unoccupied.[38] This was the point which had previously been stubbornly held by the Japanese. The brigade, after relieving the 161st Indian Infantry Brigade at Taungtha, stayed there a few days and then moved to Nyaungu for rest and refit.

The capture of Myingyan and the complete clearing of Taungtha hills came as a great relief to the Corps and Army administrative staffs. A steady stream of traffic soon started moving into Meiktila. The 17th Indian Division administrative base reached Meiktila as also the IV Corps Headquarters. The latter opened at Meiktila on

---

[38] WD 33rd Brigade and 4/15 Punjab.

4 April. The river port at Myingyan was quickly repaired and boats from Kalewa began to arrive there. Efforts were made to repair and use the Myingyan—Meiktila railway line also. "Bridges were rebuilt and even some of the captured and wrecked engines were patched to clank and rattle precariously over the rusty permanent way."[39]

BRIDGEHEAD AREA

We have described how Myingyan and Taungtha were captured by one of the brigades of the 7th Indian Division by the end of March and uninterrupted communications established with Meiktila. We may now turn to the 89th and 114th Indian Infantry Brigades of the same division and notice briefly the activities in which they were engaged.

Soon after the establishment of the bridgehead at Nyaungu in the middle of February, reports were received that the Japanese were collecting forces in the Chauk area with the idea of making an attack on the bridgehead from the south. 1/11 Sikh of the 89th Indian Infantry Brigade was thereupon given the task of protecting the right flank of the bridgehead.

On 17 February, as the Sikhs moved a few miles south of Pagan, their patrol working still further southwards reported that parties of Japanese troops were moving northwards. Apparently they were coming up with the intention of reinforcing their compatriots opposing the main bridgehead. Next morning therefore troops were sent down the Chauk road to drive them back. The Japanese withdrew to a large red pagoda, about half a mile farther south. Since the ground here was very open, tank support was requisitioned from the battalion headquarters. The tanks arrived at 1100 hours and B Company advanced. While the Japanese were driven back and were being pursued by B Company the commanding officer and mortars moved forward to the red pagoda. Here, on the right of the road, some Japanese were hiding behind some broken ground. As soon as they noticed that B Company had moved forward they debouched from their hiding place and attacked the Indian troops. Battalion headquarters and the mortars were completely surprised and were lucky to get away towards B Company in a 15-Cwt truck just as the Japanese closed in on the pagoda.

The commanding officer caught up with B Company, and ordered it to turn about, give up the pursuit of the retreating Japanese, and attack the pagoda. It was now the turn of the Japanese to be surprised, and they were driven out with great loss. This sally forth had broken up the Japanese column moving north

---

[39] Slim: *Defeat into Victory*, p. 457.

and had inflicted serious losses on them in their efforts to concentrate against the main bridgehead.[40]

On 19 February, 1/11 Sikh with tank support chased a Japanese force to Twinywa and inflicted severe casualties. On returning, however, to their own base, the Sikhs were heavily but unsuccessfully counter-attacked in Thuhtekan area. Approximately 200 to 300 Japanese troops approached the Sikhs and the brigade headquarters area from the south. The Sikh loss was 7 wounded against an estimated Japanese loss of 30. There was peace for a few days but on the night of 23/24 February the brigade headquarters and 1/11 Sikh were again attacked by about two companies of the *2nd Battalion 153rd Regiment,* supported by artillery and mortars. The attack continued for four hours before the attackers were driven off at about mid-night. The following day 2 King's Own Scottish Borderers with tanks attacked Nakyo-Aing, where the Japanese offered stout resistance from a well dug position but after some severe fighting, lasting for the whole day, the village was captured. Thereafter the 89th Indian Infantry Brigade started a slow but systematic advance down the road. On 26 February, Monatkon was entered and on 28 February 4/8 Gurkha Rifles occupied Kinka. The Japanese had suffered so much during these actions with this brigade that they gave up any further attempts to reinforce, from the south, their troops opposing the crossing farther north. The 89th Indian Infantry Brigade continued to push south towards Singu. On 2 March, 4/8 Gurkha Rifles occupied Ywathit, driving the Japanese further south into Milaungbya. Two days later, a company of 4/8 Gurkha Rifles while occupying a position PP 183485 near Milaungbya was attacked by about 300 Japanese troops. Although the company was surrounded, it beat off the attack, after some very heavy fighting. The Japanese were finally routed by artillery fire. Subsequently a successful air-strike was made on Milaungbya to which place they had retreated.

At this time the position east of the Irrawaddy was as follows:—The Japanese were holding the Singu—Chauk area in some strength, and some of their forces had been brought up to the Chauk—Kyaukpadaung—Mount Popa area, where they intended to hold out for the monsoon period. Leading elements of the 89th Indian Infantry Brigade were a few miles from Singu. The 114th Indian Infantry Brigade was in the bridgehead area in divisional reserve with part of 7/2 Punjab under command. The rest of 7/2 Punjab remained west of the Irrawaddy in the Pakokku area. The 33rd Indian Infantry Brigade was operating against Taungtha and Myingyan.

[40] Based on *The Sikh Regiment* by Lt.-Col. P. G. Bramford, D.S.O., Aldershot, 1948.

On 8 March, a company of 4/8 Gurkha Rifles made a successful attack on Milaungbya with B Squadron 116 RAC in support. It cleared both Milaungbya North and Milaungbya South against considerable opposition. It was not intended to hold the ground taken and so the company retired to the main battalion position before night. The Japanese reoccupied the place. Meanwhile 1/11 Sikh was operating on the east flank. On 9 March its patrols found Taungbi Ywathit and Pakokkukyun occupied, and successful airstrikes were directed against them. While returning from Taungbi Ywathit the Sikh patrol met a small party of Japanese troops just south-west of Tetma and killed several of them, while suffering some casualties itself. Tetma was found occupied and was attacked from the air on 11th and 12th as a result of which it was found evacuated on the 13th.

From 12 March onwards, for some time, the main feature in this area was the attempt by Major-General Yamamoto to attack the Nyaungu bridgehead and the Ledaing—Myitche area west of the river. Their plan as discovered later from some documents captured in an action at Tetma area was as follows[41]:—

The 187th Independent Battalion was to occupy Kawton, 20 miles west of Ywathit and protect the Japanese left flank. The whole of the *153rd Regiment* known as the "Left Column" was to advance to Myitche via Ledaing. One battalion of the *61st Regiment* known as the "Centre Column" was to advance from Singu due northwards and another battalion of the same regiment known as the "Right Column", was to advance northward from the Tetma area, the ultimate objective of the centre and right columns being Nyaungu. The date of the attack was not given but other evidence indicated that D Day was 12 March. The left column was to begin its advance on D minus 3 Day and the other column during the night of D Day. The plan miscarried in some details. The left column could not start its attack earlier than the night of 11 March; the right column also was behind time and mounted its attack as late as 15 March. Only the centre column's attack was delivered in time.

On the night of 12 March, according to plan, a company of Japanese troops moved forward and attacked 4/8 Gurkha Rifles forward company position in Milaungbya area. The attack was beaten off, several Japanese being killed, but the Gurkhas nevertheless withdrew.

The Right Column opened its offensive on the night of 15 March. About 100 Japanese attacked a company of 1/11 Sikh near Tetma at 2200 hours. The attack was beaten off. It was in this operation that the Japanese documents referred to above were captured.

---

[41] IV Corps Operation Instruction No. 135.

Since the failure of the Japanese attack in Milaungbya area, 4/8 Gurkha Rifles patrols found evidence of considerable Japanese build-up in that area. The village itself was believed to be used as a firm base and a gun area. An attack on this village was therefore expected to yield rich dividends. A co-ordinated plan of attack was formulated and on the morning of 18 March, immediately after two successful air-strikes, a company of 4/8 Gurkha Rifles with a squadron of 116 RAC in support attacked Milaungbya North. The opposition was strong but by 1530 hours the village was cleared.

The Allied troops again withdrew after this successful action and the Japanese again reoccupied the village. Another assault was therefore planned for 20 March to allow the Japanese no time to consolidate and to take them again by surprise. According to plan, two companies of the Gurkhas attacked the village on 20 March with the support of air, artillery and tanks but before the infantry could close in, the Japanese had retreated. By 1300 hours, Milaungbya North and Milaungbya South were cleared. This was a decisive victory in this area, and after this the Japanese did not return to it in strength. They occasionally moved back to Milaungbya South but were not allowed to stay long.

After their decisive defeat at Milaungbya, the Japanese morale in this area was shattered, and it was not expected that they would put in any more strong counter-attacks.. 4/8 Gurkha was therefore relieved by 1/11 Sikh who established a company patrol base outside Singu. In the middle of April, the Gurkhas came forward again and relieved the Sikhs, and after some confused fighting occupied Singu on 20 April. The result of the fighting in this area during the later half of February and the whole of March was that the Japanese attempts to attack the 7th Indian Division bridgehead were frustrated and the bridgehead was not only maintained but also extended.

DEFENCE OF MEIKTILA, MARCH 1945

We may now turn back to Meiktila area in the month of March 1945, when Japanese attempts to retake it were foiled and preparations were made to concentrate the whole of the IV Corps there (less the 7th Indian Division). The 5th Indian Division was at that time resting at Jorhat (on the Brahmputra) where it had been reorganised on a mechanised basis similar to that of the 17th Indian Division. It was to be brought to Meiktila (700 miles from Jorhat) from where it was to advance south towards Rangoon after the capture of Mandalay and Meiktila. In Meiktila itself, the task of the 17th Indian Division and other Allied forces was to hold the town and destroy "all enemy within striking distance."[42] The

---
[42] IV Corps. Op. Instn. No. 131, 11 March 1945.

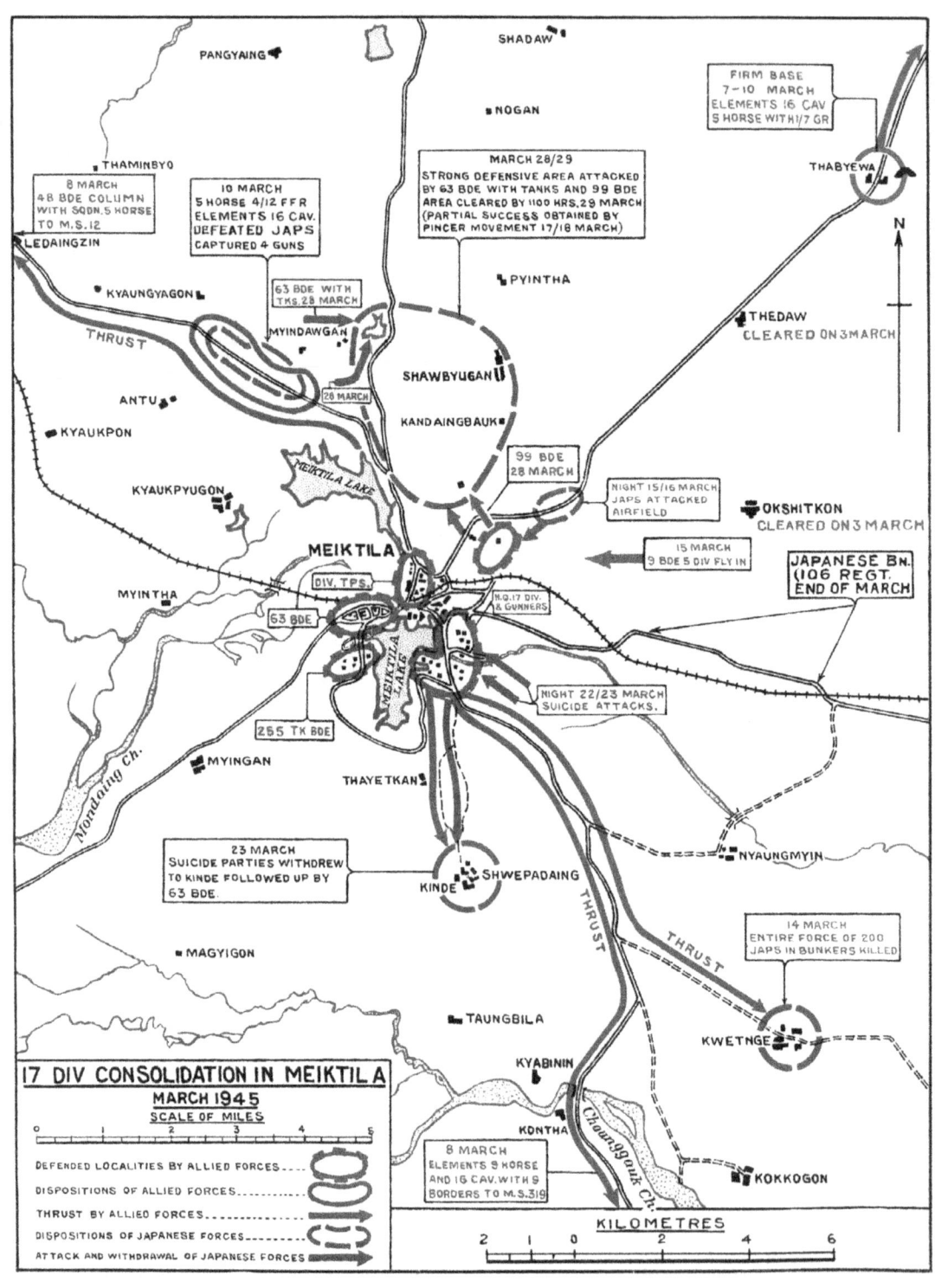

overall plan of course was, in accordance with operation 'Capital', to march south towards Rangoon after clearing Mandalay and Meiktila areas. The intention of marching to Rangoon was, however, not to be given out, and the impression was to be created, for purposes of deception, that "the time factor and shortage in air supply have reluctantly caused us to give up all hope of a move on Rangoon.[43]"

The Japanese reacted strongly to the capture of Meiktila and made efforts to retake it. A large force including the *18th Division*, less one regiment, *168th Regiment* of *49th Division*, and a part of *119th Regiment* with various units of *33rd Division* approached from the north and north-west while *106th Regiment* of *49th Division* moved up from the south.

The garrison in Meiktila was, in the first and second week of March, outnumbered by the Japanese around the town and those moving towards it from different directions. It seemed that they were determined to retake the town at any cost, and the only course for the defenders was to adopt offensive defence before reinforcements could arrive. Constant and vigorous action was therefore taken by the Allied troops and the initiative was never lost. The mode of action of the Indian formations was to organise sallies by very strong infantry and tank columns from the area of the town along the many roads leading from this vital communication centre.[44] A column returning from a sally was given two days' rest, which the men spent bathing in the lake, secure behind their wire, while other columns went out by turn.

The 99th Indian Infantry Brigade, which had been flown in to the Thabutkon air-strip between 27 February and 2 March, had moved into Meiktila and was given the task of holding the permanent defence of the town. The air-strip at Thabutkon was then abandoned and the one east of Meiktila was developed as the main supply landing ground, and maintenance of the force was started by air. But the Japanese soon established gun positions within the range of the air-strip and for some days made it impossible for the Allied planes to land. Consequently, dropping of supplies had to be resorted to. It was not possible to defend the air-strip properly with the troops then available, but the situation changed after the arrival of the 9th Indian Infantry Brigade (of 5th Indian Division) on 15 March.

There was constant fighting practically every day, between the Allied columns which went out of Meiktila and the Japanese in the outlying areas throughout the month of March, but only a few of the important engagements may be recounted below.

[43] *Ibid.*
[44] IV Corps Operations, para 118.

On 7 March an armoured column known as 'Ralphcol' composed of a battalion of Gurkhas (1/7 Gurkha Rifles) and some tanks and a company of 6/15 Punjab was sent out to reconnoitre the area Ywadan—Hanza—Thedaw—Wundwin. The force formed a firm base at Ywadan. A patrol from there went up to the causeway south of Shawbin. Another column composed of two companies of 1/7 Gurkha Rifles supported by one squadron of tanks cleared the railway station at Hanza and breached the line at four places. Besides contributing a company of 6/15 Punjab to this force, the 99th Indian Infantry Brigade, on its part, sent out three reconnaissances, on Mahlaing road, up Pindale road and on Thazi road. All these columns had minor clashes with the Japanese. During the day, the 48th Indian Infantry Brigade sent patrols down Pyawbwe road and the 63rd Indian Infantry Brigade patrolled up to milestone 23 on Kyaukpadaung road.

On 8 March, Ralphcol was split into two columns. One column—Chapcol—composed of one troop 5 Horse, one troop 16 Cavalry and one company of 1/7 Gurkha Rifles cleared Shawbin of all snipers as also two Japanese positions on the road between milestone 356 and milestone 358. The other—Fredcol—composed of 5 Horse less two squadrons and one company of 1/7 Gurkha Rifles formed a patrol base at Thedaw and then withdrew. The 99th Indian Infantry Brigade cleared a Japanese road-block near milestone 9 on the Mahlaing road and inflicted some casualties. On the Pyawbwe road the reconnaissance force met a minefield covered by fire at mile 319½, LL 4408. The position was found to be strongly held and was not attacked.

At 0900 hours on 8 March, Ralphcol withdrew to Meiktila having gained a considerable amount of valuable information. Two companies of 9 Border of the 63rd Indian Infantry Brigade supported by 9 R Horse less two squadrons, one troop of 16 Cavalry and attached troops moved out to the area of milestone 319 on the Pyawbwe road to deal with the Japanese opposition encountered there. The bridge at milestone 319 was found to be mined but this was cleared and the column advanced to Aungtha. After clearing opposition here the column moved further down to Wetlet where stiffer opposition was met. When the village had been set on fire, the infantry occupied it after stiff fighting. The retreating Japanese forces were engaged by the tanks. The force thereafter reconnoitred two villages beyond Wetlet and started to move back to Yindaw. But its return was obstructed by the Japanese who had in the meanwhile reoccupied Wetlet. An attempt was made to force a passage through Wetlet, but it failed, one tank being set on fire and two more damaged. The force therefore harboured south-east of Wetlet for the night.

On the Mahlaing road the Japanese were holding Yegyo area in some strength. A column composed of 1 West Yorks, 4 Frontier Force Regiment less two companies, one battery 21 Mountain Regiment and one squadron 5 Horse, moving out to reconnoitre the road, scattered opposition at milestone 6 and at Yegyo. The column pushed on, encountered stiff opposition from about 100 Japanese troops further on and after brisk fighting in which nearly 70 of them were killed and 3 guns destroyed, forced them to withdraw. After covering up to milestone 13, the column returned.

On the Pindale road a company of 1 Sikh Light Infantry (99th Indian Infantry Brigade) patrolling up the road ran into a strong Japanese ambush at milestone 13. The Japanese opened heavy fire and the company suffered considerable losses.

On 9 March, the 63rd Indian Infantry Brigade less 7 Baluch and 5 Horse set out from Meiktila in the morning to extricate the force cut off by the Japanese block at Wetlet and exploit towards Pyawbwe. By 1030 hours a junction had been effected with it and then patrols were sent towards Pyawbwe in the afternoon. They reported the presence of numerous small parties of the Japanese (totalling approximately one battalion) in all villages north of the town including the high ground and area to the west of the road. In the late afternoon, 100 Japanese soldiers were located in the area east of Yindaw. One company of 1/10 Gurkha Rifles supported by one troop of tanks and mortars attacked them. The village area where the Japanese had taken shelter was set on fire. In their attempt to escape the flames, they left their shelter only to fall victims to the Allied guns.

On 10 March, the 63rd Indian Infantry Brigade returned to Meiktila leaving a force consisting of 9 Border, a squadron of 9 Horse, one troop 82 Anti-Tank Regiment, one battery 21 Mountain Regiment and one platoon Medium Machine-Guns known as Sped Force at Yindaw. The Sped Force maintained vigorous patrolling for two days and gathered a great deal of operational and topographical information.

Action at Mahlaing—Meiktila Road

Meanwhile the Japanese had cut the road to Mahlaing and had also reoccupied Taungtha. It has already been described how the 7th Indian Division had cleared the road to the west of Taungtha (pp. 313-15). The portion of the road to the east and south-east of Taungtha and Mahlaing up to Meiktila was the responsibility of the 17th Indian Division.

Consequently, on 10 March the 17th Division despatched out of Meiktila a force consisting of B Squadron 5 Horse (12 tanks), one troop of A Squadron 5 Horse (5 tanks), three troops of 16 Cavalry,

4/12 Frontier Force Regiment less one company, one platoon 9/13 Frontier Force Rifles (Medium Machine-Gun), one platoon 4/4 Bombay Grenadiers and attached troops with the object of escorting some 400 soft vehicles from the Mahlaing area and clearing the road at milestone 5.

The force overran the Japanese position on both sides of the road at milestone 5 and then moved up the road. The infantry soon came under small arms and shell fire from an unlocated 75-mm gun. The advance was very slow. The main Japanese position appeared to be on the top of the high ground at mile $5\frac{1}{2}$. Two troops of tanks with 4/4 Bombay Grenadiers then moved north of the road and crossing it at milestone 6 came up on the right flank of the Japanese, who vacated their positions and commenced their retreat north across the road towards the village of Leindaw. But they came under heavy fire from the tanks and suffered many casualties. The two flanking troops of tanks reached the west of the hill and found many Japanese there in deep trenches. A company of infantry moved forward to help the tanks in clearing the position. They reached the top of the hill without opposition but withdrew as the Japanese opened up with 105-mm and 75-mm guns.

It was obvious that the Japanese gun positions which appeared to be somewhere in the Leindaw area would have to be silenced before the hill might be occupied. A company of infantry with the support of tanks accordingly commenced a wide sweep to the east side of Leindaw. They made good progress and destroyed one 37-mm and one 75-mm gun. Subsequent to an air-strike they were able to get up to the village but found it empty. They then withdrew to harbour at milestone 5.

Next morning, two troops of tanks accompanied by infantry moved in a left hook towards the hill which had been reoccupied by the Japanese early in the morning. The force had hardly moved forward when it was engaged by small arms fire from the left flank and a certain amount of 75-mm shell fire. One troop of tanks and one company of infantry proceeded to clear the left flank but it failed to make much headway against heavy gun fire. The other troop of tanks unsupported by infantry approached Leindaw but was hotly engaged by Japanese guns north of the nulla.

It was clear that the Japanese were in greater strength than was at first anticipated. Hence it was decided that the tanks alone should do a wide sweep to investigate the extent of the Japanese positions and destroy their guns. Before the operation commenced an air-strike was put on the top of the hill followed by an artillery concentration. The armour then moved off in a wide sweep to the left and came in slightly from the rear of the Japanese position. Upon this manoeuvre, the Japanese left their positions but while retreating they were caught by the artillery and suffered casualties. The tanks destroyed one 75-mm gun, and then proceeded up the road and turning right came to the north of Kyaungyagon village. In this village a 47-mm Japanese anti-tank gun was engaged and silenced. As the tanks passed north of Leindaw several of them were hit by another 47-mm gun sited in the village. An artillery concentration was then put down on the village and kept the gun quiet. The tanks, on completion of the sweep, returned to Meiktila.

Action at Kandaung

Another operation of note was carried out, south of Meiktila, by a force consisting of 1 West Yorks less one company, 1/7 Gurkha Rifles less one company, 9 R Horse less one squadron, two troops armoured cars, and one Indian Field Regiment less one battery. The object was to destroy the Japanese forces between Kandaung and Kwetnge. On 12 March 1/7 Gurkha Rifles received a warning order to be ready next day to move out to Kwetnge and Padwin if the Commando Platoon sent to that area located any Japanese there. The platoon returned from patrol next morning, but although it reported "no enemy seen," the Gurkha battalion was placed at two hours' notice to move.[45] Accordingly, at 0945 hours on the 13th, C Company moved out with the troop of armoured cars to Kandaung which had been held during the night by a company of 9 Border.[46] C Company's task was to send fighting patrols towards Kwetnge held in some strength.

Meanwhile, A Company was also sent out to patrol the area of the high ground at Point 801 and to establish a patrol base in the Myindawgan Lake area. While advancing in the area south of Myindawgan Lake this company came under shell fire and suffered casualties. It, however, established a company base, but was soon attacked and overrun. Two of its platoons however succeeded in reaching the 99th Brigade harbour and one found its way to the battalion next morning via the west of the lake.[47]

The Gurkhas had better luck on the 14th when the whole battalion, less A Company, moved out. Aircraft bombed and strafed Kwetnge, Padwin and Yewe in the morning after which B Company with tanks moved forward and occupied Kokkogaing. Later, patrols found Kwetnge also clear. Meanwhile at Hletaikon, the Japanese had established strong bunkered positions and fought desperately. A detachment from the column consisting of one company of 1 West Yorks and one squadron of 9 R Horse fought for 6 hours to clear this small village. Padwin West was also entered against some

---

[45] WD 1/7 GR 12-13 March 1945.
[46] *Ibid*, 13 March 1945.
[47] *Ibid*.

opposition. Another part of the column moved into Natkyigon after an air-strike and artillery concentration and cleared the opposition there. The column returned to Meiktila the same day.

During the next few days active patrolling was carried out on Mahlaing, Pindale, Wundwin, Thazi, Kyaukpadaung and Pyawbwe roads against Japanese attempts to close in on Meiktila. Outstanding among these was a sweep on 14 March by two squadrons of Probyn's Horse in an endeavour to destroy Japanese guns which were heavily shelling the Kyigon box. The tanks moved up the Wundwin road and then moved west from milestone 342 across Pindale road to Mahlaing road between milestone 6 and milestone 7. Several Japanese guns were destroyed as a result of this sweep.

Airfield Area

The Japanese had closed in on the main airfield east of Meiktila from the north side. On the night of 14 March, the airfield was attacked by one company of the Japanese troops but the attack was repulsed. On the morning of the 15th the western part of the airfield was shelled by the Japanese and several aircrafts were hit. Japanese camouflage was excellent and fire accurate. This curtailed the flow of supplies for some time but the fly-in of the 9th Indian Infantry Brigade of the 5th Indian Division continued without interruption. The Japanese guns shelling the air-strip were believed to be located in the general area north and north-west of the road junction at 2936. Tanks carried out a sweep of the area and located one gun area in pagoda 3039, which was cleared by the Gurkhas.

Japanese Attack the Airfield

On the night of 15 March, the Japanese were again active near the perimeter of the airfield. The Allied forward positions were attacked from the north and from the east along the railway axis. In the early morning of the 16th, some Japanese were found dug in the north-west corner of the airfield. By this time it had become impossible to land supplies which were dropped by parachutes. But the parachutes could not be returned and as their supply was running short, the situation became serious. Consequently, 6/15 Punjab with a squadron of 5 Horse swept the airfield and the area between it and Wundwin road, and 1/3 Gurkha Rifles established a company each at the north-east and south-east corners of the airfield. Airstrikes by cab-rank on the area north of the airfield and on Pindale road were most successful. The fly-in of the 9th Indian Infantry Brigade, interrupted in the morning due to intermittent shelling by the Japanese guns, was resumed later under the cover of counterbattery fire and air-strikes on gun areas. By 18 March the fly-in of the brigade was almost complete.

Kinlu

South-east of Meiktila some Japanese troops were found to be in the Kinlu group of villages. An air-strike on Mauklauk and an artillery attack on Chaukpin on 18 March inflicted a number of casualties on them. At the same time one company of 1/7 Gurkha Rifles put in an enveloping attack against these villages and cleared the area west of Kangyi Minor. More fighting developed in this area on the 19th causing casualties to the defenders.

AIRFIELD AREA AGAIN

In the airfield area the Japanese occupied some villages in the area 3532 during the night of 18 March and opened fire on the south-end of the air-strip on the morning of the 19th. Operations were undertaken against them but they were not dislodged.

While operations were taking place to oust the Japanese from the vicinity of the main airfield, an important operation was undertaken north and north-west of Meiktila. The guns which had been shelling the airfield were located in the area of Myindawgan, hence the 63rd Indian Infantry Brigade less 9 Border with the divisional artillery and two squadrons of 5 Horse in support were ordered to scour the area bounded on the west by the railway from Meiktila to Yegyo and on the east by the road Meiktila-Pindale. The sweep was to be carried as far north as Seywa. Simultaneously elements of the 99th Indian Infantry Brigade supported by one squadron of 9 R Horse were to attack Point 801 at LL 2938.

The force moved out at the break of the day on 17 March from its harbour area in Meiktila West and moved north on two axes— 1/10 Gurkha Rifles with one squadron of 5 Horse in support on the axis Inpetlet—Subyugwet on the right, and 7/10 Baluch with the other squadron of 5 Horse on the axis Kyaukpyugon—Antu—Kyaungpangon. The right column encountered resistance at Inpetlet. After an air-strike by sections of 134 Squadron on cab-rank duty[48] followed by an artillery concentration the village was attacked frontally by two companies while a troop of tanks moved round the left to give fire support. The tanks were engaged by three 47-mm anti-tank guns sited north of the road. These guns were knocked out by tanks and artillery fire but not before one British tank had been immobilised. After this the infantry and tanks slowly mopped up the village.

On the left, little opposition was met and Leindaw and Kyaungyagon were found to be clear. The force was however fired on from Subyugwet. But after an air-strike the village was cleared of all opposition. At the same time, some 105-mm guns pulling out from

---

[48] George Odgers: *Air War Against Japan*, p. 427.

the area Myindawgan Lake (LL 2839) were engaged by tanks and a battery from the west shore of the south lake.

After some further patrolling, the two columns harboured for the night in the areas Leindaw (left column) and Inpetlet (right column).

The plan for the following day was that the force on the left was to carry out a wide sweep north and east to Point 827 (LL 2743), and the force on the right was to mop the area between the two roads and south of Myindawgan Lake, but only after the 99th Indian Infantry Brigade had captured Point 801 to the east. The left force had a most successful sweep. It moved on to Point 827 and from there further up to cut the Pindale road at milestone 7. But owing to the failure of the 99th Indian Infantry Brigade to capture Point 801, the right-force was pinned down by Japanese artillery fire and was quite unable to achieve its objective. The following morning the whole force was withdrawn to Meiktila.

Operations by the 99th Brigade—18 March

While the above operations were proceeding, the 99th Indian Infantry Brigade with the support of one squadron 9 R Horse commenced its task of clearing the area Nyaunggon—Kandaingbauk—Shawbyugan—Kungyangon. The plan of operation was divided into four phases:

Phase I. The infantry was to clear the Japanese from the airstrip to the nulla running east to west, south of Nyaunggon.

Phase II. Capture of Kandaingbauk by infantry from the south with tank support.

Phase III. A combined infantry and tank attack on Kungyangon.

Phase IV. On the successful completion of Phase III, a combined tank and infantry attack was to be put in on Shawbyugan from the direction of Kungyangon.

The implementation of these different phases started on 18 March. There was some delay in achieving Phase I which was not reported as having been completed until 1200 hours. Owing to this delay the infantry brigade was ordered to carry out Phases II and III concurrently. As a result the infantry attacking Kandaingbauk had to do so without tank support. Advancing north to attack Kungyangon the infantry (two companies) was shelled by Japanese guns from Kandaingbauk. However, Phase III was completed without much opposition and the same troops proceeded to implement Phase IV at 1400 hours. It was proposed that the attack would go in the southern end of Shawbyugan village, but when it was known that the attack on Kandaingbauk (Phase II) had failed, it was switched to the north. It was preceded by an air-strike followed by an artillery concentration and smoke-screen. During the initial assault one tank was knocked out. The tanks and infantry were subjected to very heavy gun fire and small-arms fire from the north, from the west, from Kandaingbauk and from Shawbyugan itself. By 1730 hours both infantry and tanks had suffered several casualties, without achieving their objective. Therefore the attack was called off. Four tanks were destroyed by Japanese action and one tank had to be abandoned.

On 21 March a report was received that the group of villages around Shwepadaing was held by the Japanese in strength with a number of guns, and that the track running north to south through the village was mined.[49] Accordingly a plan was made for 9 R Horse supported by infantry to clear pagoda area north-west of Shwepadaing from the west and then to clear Shwepadaing itself from the north-west.[50] An air-strike had been made at 1030 hours on a village called Kangyi but this had proved ineffective. Consequently, an artillery concentration was directed half an hour later (between 1100 and 1110 hours) on the pagoda area, on Kinde and on the village of Shwepadaing itself. After this the force (9 R Horse and infantry) moved up, but encountered stiff opposition. Progress was very slow as the Japanese opened up with harassing mortar fire.[51] Another air-strike at 1620 hours and artillery concentration on the group of villages produced no results and the force withdrew at 1700 hours. On account of the failure of this attempt it was decided to attack the area with two squadrons and two companies of 1/7 Gurkha Rifles the next day.

22—23 March

Prior to the attack, medium machine-guns and mortars blocked all the possible avenues of escape and armoured cars covered the south-east flank. In the morning the attacking force concentrated at mile 334½ on the Pyawbwe road. At 1000 hours the two squadrons of tanks carrying their infantry moved off to take up positions on the east flank of the village. At 1030 hours, a heavy air-strike was put in. This was followed by an artillery concentration. At 1115 hours, B Squadron with one company of 1/7 Gurkha Rifles attacked and by 1135 hours had cleared an isolated basha area on the east flank. A Squadron and one company of Gurkhas then moved up on the left and both squadrons proceeded to attack Kangyi which was entered at 1140 hours. The attackers then proceeded to clear Kinde from the south-east to the north-east. B Squadron was held up by a nulla which it could not cross and which was strongly

---

[49] WD Royal Deccan Horse (9 R Horse) 20 March 45.
[50] *Ibid.*
[51] *Ibid.*

defended with mortars and at least one anti-tank gun. A Squadron made some progress on the left but the infantry was suffering heavy casualties from snipers and mortars. By 1500 hours very little progress had been made. Some tanks had suffered damage and some of the crew injured. The infantry was then pulled back and the tanks started putting down concentrated fire on a destroyed house and bund on the left flank which had proved to be the centre of resistance. One misdirected shell caused some casualties in the Indian ranks and delayed operations. At 1615 hours an artillery concentration was put on and the attack resumed. It was again held up by the same strong point which had remained undominated by the bombardment. By 1700 hours, it was obvious that the village could not be cleared. The force was thereupon withdrawn.

On 22 March, operations were directed to clear the group of villages at Nyaungbintha also. The 99th Indian Infantry Brigade less one battalion with B Squadron 5 Horse in support was entrusted with the work. At 0900 hours, two companies of 1/3 Gurkha Rifles crossed the line of the railway. After some time strong opposition was encountered and the infantry withdrew west of the railway line. An air-strike, mortar fire and the divisional artillery concentration were then put down on the village after which the two companies with the squadron of tanks less one troop were put through the village. One troop with one platoon 6/15 Punjab was ordered to move round the north of the village and take up positions covering the east of the village on the probable line of Japanese withdrawal. The group of villages was very thick and the frontage too wide for the small force, and the result was that the progress of the main drive was very slow, and the Japanese withdrawing on to the flanks of the two companies took them in the rear. By 1630 hours it was evident that the villages would not be cleared that day and so the troops were withdrawn. The troop of tanks and the platoon acting as a stop were mortared and sniped by the Japanese and the infantry sustained some losses.

ATTACK ON 48TH BRIGADE PERIMETER

On the night of 22/23 March, the Japanese made a suicidal attempt to get inside the 48th Indian Infantry Brigade perimeter. A party of about 500 of them made a fanatical attack on the southeast corner of the Meiktila defences where 1/7 Gurkha Rifles was located. The attack started quite early in the night with normal jittering, but the volume of fire increased and it became apparent that a heavy attack was pending. Two 75-mm guns opened fire. Then the infantry attacked 1/7 Gurkha Rifles and 4 Frontier Force Regiment perimeter. The attacks continued throughout the night but none developed into any serious threat to the wired-in positions. This attack cost the Japanese 195 dead—most being victims of artillery, mortar and medium machine-gun defensive fire. At 0400 hours they withdrew. Two battalions of the 63rd Indian Infantry Brigade with two squadrons of 5 Horse in support followed up the retreating remnants and found a large party dug in in the Kinde group of villages. A not very successful air-strike and an artillery concentration were followed by infantry and tank attack. These encountered determined opposition and made little progress. A further artillery concentration was tried to break the opposition, but by 1715 hours the village was not cleared and so the troops withdrew. One tank was destroyed and some others hit by Japanese artillery.

On 23 March two Allied aircraft were destroyed on the main Meiktila airfield at point-blank range by an anti-tank gun which the Japanese had moved under cover of darkness into a small nulla at the northern end of the strip.

48TH BRIGADE MOVES OUT

From 25 to 27 March, operations were directed to clearing the air-strip area. On 25 March, the 48th Indian Infantry Brigade less 1/7 Gurkha Rifles moved out of the Meiktila perimeter to clear the village of Kyigon as a preliminary step. One squadron 5 Horse and the divisional artillery were in support. 1 West Yorks was ordered to clear Kyigon and the copse, 1000 yards to the north-east. One Company of 4 Frontier Force Regiment remained behind with the tanks. 1 West Yorks moved forward with one company going towards Kyigon on the left and the other towards the copse. The company to Kyigon was held up on the southern edge of the village. The right company also came under fire on the southern edge of the copse. Considerable artillery and mortar fire held up further advance and one company of 4 Frontier Force Regiment and a squadron of tanks moved forward to clear the opposition at Kyigon.

The attack moved slowly against heavy shell and mortar fire, the tanks blasting the bunkers one by one. By 1630 hours, Kyigon was clear, about 50 of the defenders withdrawing into the villages just north of the road. These villages were thereupon subjected to an air-strike and artillery bombardment. The copse area could not, however, be cleared and the force withdrew for the day. Kyigon was finally reported clear, but the copse area was still held by the Japanese.

Next day the 48th Indian Infantry Brigade less 1 West Yorks with one squadron of 9 R Horse moved out again to complete the clearing of the air-strip. The plan was to sweep up to the air-strip. The advance was to be on two lines—the left column to advance from Kangalegon and the right from Khanda. 1/7 Gurkha Rifles moved through Kyigon towards the copse, which was held by the Japanese in some strength. At 1140 hours a heavy air-strike was put down on the copse but failed to silence the Japanese guns. Two companies of 1/7 Gurkha Rifles with two troops of tank following after the air-strike came under heavy shell and mortar fire. At 1400 hours the divisional artillery concentrated on the copse and accounted for one 47-mm gun.

In the meantime 4 Frontier Force Regiment with two troops of tanks was moving to the north-end of the landing strip with the intention of reaching the road in the area of mile 341. They were fired on by a 70-mm gun from the northern edge of the air-strip. They made progress against resistance and by 1225 hours reached the area LL 328349. There the tanks had a good shoot at the Japanese who were running away. By this time the Gurkhas also had made progress and the two sections eventually met between miles 340 and 341. The brigade then withdrew.

The task of clearing the airfield area was not yet completed and the brigade took it up again on 27 March. 1/7 Gurkha Rifles moved eastward astride the main road. 4 Frontier Force Regiment moved to the north edge of the landing ground and swung to the main road at milestone 341. Some carriers with rations for a company post of the 9th Indian Infantry Brigade, who had been isolated for three days at Nyaunggon at milestone 342, then attempted to go up the road. They were escorted by a troop of tanks but came under heavy fire from the pagoda area 342356 on the east side of the road and were forced to withdraw. The food was then transferred to the tanks which by-passed the guns by using the west side of the road, and after handing over the supplies to the garrison returned. Meanwhile, 4 Frontier Force Regiment infantry with the support of two troops of tanks was attacking a Japanese position just south of the air-strip. This position was liquidated and the sweep of the airfield began with 1/7 Gurkha Rifles supported by two troops of tanks on the east strip, and by one troop on the west strip. Heavy opposition was met from some bunkers about half way down the strip but this was overcome after heavy fighting with the support of tanks and the strip was cleared. After 1/7 Gurkha Rifles had got well clear, 4 Frontier Force Regiment started to pull out. The operation to clear the air-strip was only partly successful.

NORTH OF MEIKTILA, 27-29 MARCH

These operations marked the concluding stage of the Japanese attempt to recapture Meiktila. The Japanese must have long given up all hope of gaining their objective but still they continued their efforts to pin down the Allies in Meiktila area and prevent its airstrip from being used by aircraft. But after the operations of these days they realised the futility of their efforts and withdrew east and south.

During the past two weeks they had built up a strong defensive position in the Myindawgan Lake area and south up to the sluice just north of Meiktila at LL 293351. It extended east to Shawbyugan and Kandaingbauk. In this area at least 8 guns had been concentrated including 155-mm and 105-mm, which effectively shelled the air-strip so as to make it impossible for aircraft to land. The guns were so well concealed and dug in that air-strikes and cab-ranks failed to silence them, although some were knocked out. The Japanese position was an excellent one. The northern part was saucer-shaped and as soon as the Allied tanks and infantry appeared on the lip they were engaged on the skyline by artillery and medium machine-gun fire. The sluice area was very thick and much of it untankable, while the villages of Shawbyugan and Kandaingbauk were very densely populated.

One attempt to clear it, as has been seen, was unsuccessful though it had caused considerable damage. Air-strikes and counter-battery bombardment had failed to silence the guns which were shelling the main air-strip.

The new attack was carried out by the 63rd Indian Infantry Brigade with tanks from the west and north-west, and by the 99th Indian Infantry Brigade from the south and south-east. The preliminary phase was a tank sweep north of the Myindawgan Lake from the west in order to cut the Pindale road, and to destroy Japanese guns in that area. Two squadrons of 5 Horse with 6/7 Rajput were to carry out the task.

On the morning of 27 March A Squadron moved from the base at Leindaw to milestone 7 on Pindale road, while B Squadron with a company of 6/7 Rajput moved to the ring contour just west of mile 5½ on the same road. In spite of intense shelling A Squadron moved to Point 801 LL 2938. Japanese ammunition area was located at 3040 and 3141 in a nulla which was guarded by one Japanese medium tank which was knocked out, and a considerable amount of ammunition in the area destroyed by tank fire. Attempts of A Squadron to proceed south from Point 801 were foiled by heavy gun fire. Two Japanese guns were destroyed by air-strike and tank-gun fire but more guns were located on the east, south and west sides of the Myindawgan Lake. By the evening the attacking force returned to harbour.

Better success was achieved on 28 March when a converging movement on the Japanese defensive area was launched. This area, as has already been pointed out, had been turned into a strong position by the Japanese, a purpose for which it was well suited, being situated in a difficult tank-country and being flanked on one side by a water obstacle. Numerous nullas provided shelter for the defenders from attack from the air.

The plan of operations for 28 March was as follows: One Squadron of 5 Horse with a company of 7 Baluch would make a wide sweep east, on the north of Myindawgan Lake, and then proceed south. Another company of 7 Baluch with another Squadron would move east through Subyugwet to Myindawgan village, thence south down a nulla assisted by a third company to the Pindale road at milestone 4. 1/10 Gurkha Rifles was to move east from Inpetlet with one squadron of 5 Horse to the Mahlaing road at milestone 3 and then turn south. Meanwhile, 6/15 Punjab and 1/3 Gurkha Rifles of the 99th Indian Infantry Brigade would put in an attack in the broken area between the sluice and the north end of Meiktila North Lake from south-east, thus practically hemming in the Japanese.

According to plan one squadron of tanks with one company of 7 Baluch forced a crossing of the Pindale road north of Myindawgan Lake at mile 6. Mines were encountered on the way and one tank was damaged. One troop of tanks moved east towards Pyintha where large dumps were found and destroyed. The rest of the squadron proceeded to the Japanese ammunition area and completed the task left unfinished the previous day. By 1600 hours, this squadron had cleared the area north and east of the lake against light disorganised opposition.

C Squadron had in the meantime moved via Myindawgan village and emerged on the Pindale road at mile 4. From here it moved south towards the ring contour 850 at LL 288374. The tanks engaged this position from a range of 2000 yards, and by 1330 hours were advancing up to the crest of it. They destroyed a 75-mm gun on the crest and then withdrew to allow another gun position located nearby to be dealt with by artillery.

1/10 Gurkha Rifles also met heavy opposition in its move south along the Mahlaing road. An 'earthquake' air attack was put down on the broken ground east of mile 2 on this road, but it produced little impression on the defenders. 1/10 Gurkha Rifles had started east from the assembly area at Inpetlet at 1200 hours. On reaching the road the Gurkhas moved south but were held up by fire from the pagoda area LL 285362, despite the support by tank guns. The battalion then withdrew to harbour with tanks at Inpetlet.

The 99th Indian Infantry Brigade had been given the task of securing the area from the road and nulla crossing at 288359—293352 —287358 and destroying all the Japanese forces encountered during the advance. 6/15 Punjab less two companies assembled in the area

310350 and 1/3 Gurkha Rifles in the area 310358, early in the morning of 28 March. After an "earthquake minor" air attack and artillery concentration, the attack on the sluice area was put in. One platoon crossed the sluice near the west end and knocked out a light machine-gun post. But that was all the progress achieved. Both the battalions were held up by fire from strong positions at LL 303358, 301356 and 301355. Artillery concentrations were put down on these areas. Both battalions again moved but could not make any advance owing to fire from light machine-guns and many snipers hidden in thick scrub. The casualties of this brigade were heavy, 92 in all, including one company commander killed.

Though the attacks on this day failed to dislodge the Japanese from their defensive area, their spirit of resistance was broken, and during the night of 28/29 March the greater part of the garrison evacuated the area, moving north between the positions of the 99th and 63rd Indian Infantry Brigades and thence east through Kandaingbauk.

On 29 March, 1/3 Gurkha Rifles and 6/15 Punjab swept north of the sluice to the shore of the Meiktila Lake and as far north as the road-junction LL 290357 linking up with 7/10 Baluch in the area LL 299361. Elaborate bunker positions were found in the captured area which could easily hold 400 to 500 men.

As a result of all these operations in the Meiktila area in the month of March, the Japanese troops were kept away from the town and were not allowed to mount a serious offensive for retaking it. They had, however, successfully prevented planes from landing on the air-strip for a considerable time, and it was not before 31 March that the supply dropping was discontinued and the planes began to land again.

The Japanese reaction, as mentioned earlier, to the loss of Meiktila had been relatively quick to develop and they had thrown in, against the town, all the available reserve of the *Burma Area Army*. However, there was very little co-ordination between the Japanese to the north of the town and those to the south. But their individual efforts made it quite clear that their intention was to retake the town and not merely to contain the Allied troops inside it. In fact their intention was to defend their two main lines of communication running east and south from Meiktila at any cost and continue the "battle of the Irrawaddy shore". For this purpose it was necessary to recapture Meiktila, and the Japanese were prepared to make any sacrifices for achieving this object. The march of events was however against them; the Fourteenth Army had brought almost all the forces of the XXXIII Corps and the IV Corps into the battle area of the Irrawaddy shore and their overwhelming air superiority was something which the Japanese simply could not cope with. A Japanese withdrawal and an Allied march to Rangoon were both inevitably in the logic of history.

OPERATIONS WEST OF THE IRRAWADDY 6 MARCH—4 APRIL

While the 17th Indian Division marched towards Meiktila, captured it and defended it against the Japanese in the month of March and the 7th Indian Division cleared Myingyan, certain other units were still operating on the west bank of the Irrawaddy. Notable among these were the Chin Hills battalion and the 28th East African Brigade. The former was attacked on the night of 7/8 March in the area of Kazunma, but it drove off the attackers inflicting 25 casualties. After this it had no major engagement but continued active patrolling particularly southward where it dispersed a few Japanese at Thamingan on 12 March.[52]

During the whole of March and early April, until the 28th East African Brigade was withdrawn, the East Africans bore the brunt of Japanese attacks round Letse area. The Allies had established strong positions and from here they carried on defensive—offensive operations against the Japanese who endeavoured without success to overrun the defences and push north as part of their overall plan to capture the Nyaungu—Pakokku area and thus cut off the Allied line of communication at this vital spot. Persistent efforts were made by the Japanese to capture the brigade administrative box at Letse while the Allies on their part tried to occupy Subokkon area, north-east of Ywathit and another defended feature known as Kidney. Both sides defended stubbornly and suffered and inflicted heavy losses.

Letse Area—The administrative box at Letse was the target of Japanese attention almost every night after 4 March. The usual tactics was to send small jitter parties armed with grenades and small arms who would try to create confusion. Occasionally more serious attacks were launched. On the night of 19/20 March the Japanese attacked the box in about a battalion strength with the support of gun and mortar fire. A platoon position was overrun and they penetrated 200 yards inside the perimeter. But the situation was restored by a counter-attack by 71 KAR in which the Japanese were driven out at bayonet point by 4/14 Punjab, then under command of the 28th East African Brigade. The seriousness of the attack may be gauged from the fact that 251 Japanese dead bodies were counted after the attack and 2 prisoners were taken. Much equipment including 19 light machine-guns, 2 medium machine-guns, and other equipment and many documents were captured. The defenders on their part suffered casualties in 40 killed and 113 wounded. It was

---

[52] Operations IV Corps, *op. cit.*, para 133.

later learnt that this strong attack was the left prong of the Japanese advance on Nyaungu—Pakokku.

Kidney and Point 436—As remarked earlier 4/14 Punjab of the 114th Indian Infantry Brigade had been sent to this area in the last week of February to help the 28th East African Brigade, which was then practically besieged in its defensive box at Letse. The Punjabis not only helped in defending the box but also engaged in offensive operations in order to dislodge the Japanese from their strong points in this area. One such point was the feature Kidney. After an air-strike in the morning of 7 March, 4/14 Punjab raided the Japanese positions. Some initial success was achieved, five bunkers being destroyed and some Japanese being killed, but heavy defensive fire prevented further advance. As the feature was strongly occupied, it was decided to leave it alone for a while with a view to attacking it later at an appropriate time. A few days later one of the patrols of the Punjabi battalion walked into the Japanese position while they were having tea, had a good view and quickly walked back after picking up an unattended light machine-gun. This seemed the appropriate moment and a two platoon attack was launched with artillery support. The attack was perfectly executed and led to the capture of the whole feature by the Punjabis. A party of some forty desperate Japanese, after leaving the feature, unwisely set up their medium machine-gun in full view on the plain below. These were 'taken on' by the mortar platoon which liquidated them by a well-aimed salvo, killing thirty-nine. The only survivor blew himself up with a hand grenade.

Another strong-point—Point 436, north-east of Ywathit was, however, liquidated early. The position was behind the brigade forward posts and likely to be a source of nuisance. An "earthquake" air raid was delivered on 8 March which was followed by an attack by three companies of 71 KAR. The forward positions were captured and Japanese counter-attacks were broken up. The Japanese suffered heavy casualties.

Point 534—Later, the Japanese established another strong-point at Point 534 (PO 9675) uncomfortably close to the brigade box at Letse. It defied attacks of different Allied units for a considerable time. The first attack on 21 March by two companies of the 28th East African Brigade was unsuccessful.[53] An air-strike was made on 22 March; a patrol then advanced to attack but it could do no more than overrun one bunker position. After a successful air-strike on this point on 23 March, C Company of 4/14 Punjab was ordered by the East African Brigade Commander to attack it, supported by two platoons of other Punjabi companies. There was very little

---

[53] 28th EA Bde WD 21-3-45.

time for reconnaissance but, when the attack went in at 1530 hours, good headway was made in the beginning. Later, however, tougher opposition was encountered and the attack was called off. Point 534, however, continued to be invested and patrol clashes occurred on 25 and 28 March. A more serious attack was delivered on 31 March when, after heavy fire by the artillery and mortars, two companies of 2 S Lan R, who had come in replacement of 71 KAR on 22 March, proceeded to attack. The troops advanced along the ridge from the north but after they had covered two-thirds of the distance they were held up by snipers. One company advanced from the south and dug in towards the south of the ridge. On 2 April the ridge was found abandoned, and was occupied by the Allies.

Subokkon—Another strong Japanese point in this area was Subokkon, north-east of Ywathit which 46 KAR tried to liquidate unsuccessfully. This battalion made repeated attempts to capture Subokkon but failed. On 8 and 10 March, the Africans supported by artillery advanced on the Japanese positions but on each occasion defensive fire accompanied by an encircling move forced them to withdraw. Casualties on both sides were fairly heavy on the 10th. Further attempts on 14 and 15 March and the following days yielded no results, though the attack on 15 March was preceded by an air-strike. Subsequently Subokkon was found evacuated on 27 March.[54]

The fourth phase of IV Corps operations was completed by the end of March and there remained the advance on Rangoon. The brunt of the fighting had fallen on two of its divisions (the 7th and the 17th Indian Divisions) and the 255th Indian Tank Brigade. All had done magnificently including the 7th Indian Division which had advanced swiftly despite great topographical difficulties to Pakokku. Its planning of the Nyaungu bridgehead operation and its instant recovery after a disappointing start while crossing the Irrawaddy were beyond praise. All of its brigades had shared in these exploits, the 33rd in the bridgehead and at Myingyan, the 89th in many actions south of Pagan to Singu and the 114th in a variety of places from Pakokku to Letse.

The hardest fighting had however, fallen to the 17th Indian Division whose casualties between the crossing of the Irrawaddy and 5 April mounted to a total of 465 killed (including 28 officers) and 1402 wounded (including 45 officers).[55]

The success which attended the operations up to the capture of Meiktila and subsequently its defence throughout one month of furious counter-attacks by the Japanese was due in no small measure to the fact that they were at last being fought in a country which

[54] *Ibid*, 2 April 45.
[55] Operations IV Corps, *op. cit.*, p. 26.

allowed the Allies to manoeuvre their armour and to bring to bear on the Japanese the full weight of air power. After such a long period of jungle warfare, in which both jungle and mountains had given the Japanese a high degree of immunity from the Allied tanks and aircraft, they were unbalanced at last by being caught in the open by these weapons of swift movement.[56]

CAUSES OF THE SUCCESS OF MEIKTILA OPERATIONS

The capture of Meiktila in the short period of three weeks after the first crossing of the Irrawaddy at Nyaungu by the forces of the Fourteenth Army, was a remarkable feat of military strategy and tactics. There were various causes and a combination of circumstances which contributed to this great achievement. These may be summarised as:

(a) Speed and surprise,
(b) Use of tanks by the Allies, and
(c) Allied superiority in air power.

It will be interesting to analyse their respective share.

Speed and Surprise

Emphasis on speed and surprise had been laid from the very beginning of the movement of the IV Corps from the north to the south. The deception measures adopted en route to the Pakokku area have already been described. These measures were eminently successful, and even when the Japanese knew that crossings had been made at certain places, they could not get any clear idea of either the intention or the strength of the Allied forces. Their own account says:

> "The English troops that had crossed the Irrawaddy near Nyaungu on 14 February made a dash into the Meiktila area on 27 February from Taungtha area."[57]

This clearly shows how baffled the Japanese intelligence system was, for right up to 17 February and even for sometime after that they did not know that the troops which made a dash towards Meiktila (17th Indian Division) were other than those that had crossed at Nyaungu (7th Indian Division). The Japanese were making their own preparations for a counter-offensive to be launched in March (against the 19th Indian Division, 20th Indian Division and 2nd Division) north and west of the Irrawaddy, but the sudden and speedy march of the IV Corps from Nyaungu to Meiktila area resulted in its being postponed. Hurried redispositions of their

[56] *Ibid.*
[57] *The Japanese Account of their Operations in Burma*, p. 30.

troops were made and "the main force of the *53rd Division* was ordered to proceed to Taungtha; *18th Division* was ordered immediately to Meiktila where it was to attack the English troops there with the co-operation of *168th Regiment* (*49th Division*) which was then gathering around Meiktila."[58] But it was too late! As the Japanese account puts it, "the English[59] mechanised troops advancing from Taungtha began their attack on Meiktila on the evening of 27 February, and on the afternoon of 28 February entered and captured the town."[60] The Japanese thought that "either 5th or 7th Division supported by one armoured brigade had occupied Meiktila."[61]

It is surprising that even after this, the Japanese measures to retake Meiktila were unco-ordinated. It seems that although General Kimura realised the gravity of the loss of Meiktila, he still intended to prosecute what he called the "decisive battle of the Irrawaddy shore", namely the battle in the north.[62] No doubt he diverted some forces intended for fighting against the XXXIII Corps on to Meiktila, and ordered General Yamamoto in the Yenangyaung area to recapture Pakokku and cut the IV Corps communications. "But he gave no orders to his forces who were about Mandalay or south of the river to withdraw, evidently considering he could restore the situation about Meiktila while continuing the battle in the north. Here, as so often before, the Japanese underestimation of their enemy was to prove fatal to them."[63] The measure of the Japanese underestimation and ignorance of the Allied strength is also the measure of the poverty of their intelligence system as well as of the success of the Allied strategy aiming at speed and surprise.

Throughout the battle of Meiktila, before and after 28 February 1945, the 17th Indian Division, the 9th Indian Infantry Brigade and the 255th Indian Tank Brigade remained unidentified by the Japanese. The original battle picture given to the *18th Division* before it came to Meiktila remained substantially unaltered, namely that either the 5th or 7th Indian Division had occupied Meiktila. The Japanese took no Allied prisoners from whom they could get some information, and a few trucks captured by them during this period were without markings. Local reports revealed nothing of importance to them, and no locals were employed to go into Meiktila as spies, nor were disguised Japanese used for this purpose. After 27 February, locals of the villages around Meiktila fled and it was difficult for

---

[58] *Ibid*. Chapter 22, para 2.
[59] All Allied troops are referred to as 'English troops" by the Japanese.
[60] *The Japanese Account of their Operations*, chapter 22, para 3.
[61] Payagyi Interrogation Report No. 7, para 3.
[62] This was to be an offensive from Madaya and Sagaing towards Wetlet on the Shwebo railway line against XXXIII Corps, beginning on 10 March. See *Air War Against Japan*, (Australia in the War of 1939-1945), p. 425.
[63] Leese's *Despatch*, para 109.

the Japanese to find any one to enter Meiktila and bring in reports. Thus the Japanese remained ignorant of the strength and names of units fighting against them and holding Meiktila.[64] Observation from high points, with all its limitations, was the only source of Japanese information.

One illustration will suffice to show how disorganised was the Japanese system of intelligence and interunit liaison. The Japanese *18th Division* knew that the *49th Division Headquarters* was at Yindaw, but liaison did not extend beyond this awareness. One day towards the end of the battle, after Allied transport planes had ceased to use the air-strip, the Japanese *18th Division* observers saw a column of smoke from an area to the south-west of the Allied gun positions, where supplies were being dropped by parachutes. There was the sound of explosion from time to time. The Japanese (*18th Division*) ascribed this activity to their *49th Division* and were consequently pleased.[65] The more prosaic but real explanation was an accident, purely domestic in origin, on the dropping ground.

Use of Tanks

The Japanese felt that Meiktila was essentially a tank battle, and they 'complained' that the *18th Division* had had no time to prepare for anti-tank combat. Not that they could have brought any new anti-tanks methods into use; far from it. But there was possibly some injured vanity in their wishing to prove what the *18th Division* could have accomplished with well trained Nikuhaku-kogeki ("human combat") teams against Shermans if they had been given the time. In the event, their anti-tank methods consisted of fire from a few anti-tank weapons, or from field, mountain and regimental guns used in an anti-tank role. Hollow-charge shells were also used for the first time in Burma, though not on a considerable scale. It is worth remarking that a hit from one of these usually knocked out a Sherman.

The Japanese considered the tanks as the most lethal of all the weapons brought into use at Meiktila, to which could be ascribed most of their casualties. To them, the speed of the advance to Meiktila had suggested a lightly equipped force, which they thought would soon be in difficulties over the question of heavy repairs. They were naturally surprised when they saw no obvious reduction in the number of tanks used against them in the succeeding actions in and around Meiktila. Another thing that surprised them was the continuous activity of tanks in spite of high temperature. The Japanese were plagued by the heat on the barren treeless slopes north of Meiktila and wondered why it did not deter the tank crews of

[64] Payagyi Interrogation Report, Summary No. 7, para 14.
[65] *Ibid*, para 15.

the Shermans. During the interrogations after the war, one Japanese officer asked, "Did the tank unit at Meiktila come from the Western Desert?"

The Japanese had very few tanks in this sector and they were too light to engage the armoured fighting vehicles face to face, and it was never intended that they should. They were mainly used in dug-in positions, under camouflage as anti-tank pill boxes.

There is no doubt that the Allied superiority in the quality and number of tanks was one of the decisive factors in the Meiktila battle.

Air Superiority

In the battle of Meiktila, direct effect of attacks by Allied aircraft, that is casualties directly attributable to action from the air, was not very great. It is a well understood maxim that an undeveloped country presents fewer chances for air action than a developed theatre. But bombing and gunning from the air can do much to counter-balance the lack of artillery fire due to difficulty of bringing up many guns and the ammunition for them. Moreover, the Japanese had learned by experience how to put up defensive earthworks to protect themselves. In spite of the hardness of ground the *18th Division* was well dug-in, though their earthworks were not so elaborate as had been intended. They felt, however, that they had achieved a sufficiently high standard of passive air-defence during this battle.

In spite of all this the strain on the Japanese from Allied air attacks was very great. Considerable man-hours of labour were spent by them in precautionary measures at the cost of their fighting energies. Elaborate arrangements had to be made during the nights to move men and equipment. On the Allied side, such moves could take place in broad daylight with perfect impunity. No wonder the Japanese began to regard dusk as their ally and dawn as their enemy. The psychological effect of air action was very unnerving, particularly that of strafing. A few Japanese however maintained (during interrogations) that heavy bombing rather than strafing held the most fears for them.

The Allies made the maximum use of air-supply and no words are sufficient to appraise correctly the value of such aid. It is enough to say that without air supply the success in this and later battles in Burma could not have been achieved in the time available. In Meiktila, the Japanese were pleased to have stopped—temporarily—the Allied use of the airfield, but were disappointed to see the alternative supply-dropping arrangements.[66] The close-support

---

[66] *Ibid*, para 19.

afforded to ground troops by the cab-rank method also had its effects on the outcome of the battles.[67]

While emphasising the role of these factors in the achievement of victory, it must never be forgotten that there was a great deal of hard infantry fighting in and around Meiktila. In this area there was much broken and tank-proof ground of which the Japanese soon learnt to make full use. The infantry had to fight continuously and with very little rest, to clear such positions. In fact, the best summing up of the position would be to say that the issue was decided as a result of the brilliant team work of infantry, artillery, sappers, tanks and aeroplanes.

---

[67] During the course of the narrative reference has often been made to 'cab-rank' method of attack and 'earthquake' strikes. A brief explanation of what these words mean is given below:

Cab-rank: During the drive on Meiktila, it was found that after the submission of a demand for an air-strike, considerable time elapsed before the attack from air could materialise on the target. This delay was due to the fact that the air squadrons had to study maps and photographs before they could reach and bombard the exact position. In order to shorten this period between the demand made by the advancing ground forces and the air-attack, the system of 'cab-rank' was introduced whereby two to eight aircraft took to air simultaneously with the move of the ground forces. These aircraft remained high up in the sky and were available at call, always ready to come down and attack a target. They were of course constantly in touch with the forward troops through radio telephone which was operated, on the ground, by Visual Control Posts (V.C.P.). The aircraft remained aloft, waiting for a call from a V.C.P. until relieved by a fresh 'cab-rank' flight. This method was no doubt uneconomical in aircraft and oil, but was perhaps the only way of providing constant and immediate close-support to a rapidly advancing army.

Earthquake strikes: "Earthquake" strikes were regularly planned, heavy air-attacks meant to be delivered against positions of great tactical importance held by an enemy offering stubborn resistance to the ground forces. The attacks were made by a large number of medium or heavy bombers (three or four squadrons) which came from bases located up to 300 miles away from the target. An 'earthquake' strike was immediately followed by an artillery concentration and an advance of the troops on to the position. An earthquake was different from a cab-rank in two material ways, firstly because it required a larger number of aircraft and secondly because it required a detailed study of maps and photographs necessitating a delay of about 48 hours.

CHAPTER XII

To the City of the Kings

With the fall of Meiktila the way was opened for the capture of Mandalay, which was the next objective of the Fourteenth Army. In the middle of February, the Japanese were not only determined to hold the line of the Irrawaddy but were also planning to launch an offensive to prevent the Allies from reaching Central Burma. Within a fortnight, however, Meiktila had fallen and the Allied forces were marching against Mandalay—the City of the Kings—from the north. In another fortnight Mandalay city had also fallen and Fort Dufferin been besieged. Another week and that Fort too was in Allied hands. After the irretrievable loss of these two cities, the Japanese defences completely broke down and the battle of Burma developed into a hasty retreat. No doubt, General Kimura's avowed object even now was to bar both the routes of Allied advance on Rangoon, but he could not carry out his plan. Why?

The answer is not far to seek. One reason no doubt was the fall of Meiktila and the baffling effect it had on the Japanese intelligence system and High Command. As General Leese put it, "to say that our capture of Meiktila came as a surprise to the enemy would be an understatement."[1] In February, all the Japanese dispositions were based on the assumption that the Allied attack would come from the north and west of Mandalay. The new situation created by the attacks of the IV Corps therefore baffled them so much that they found it difficult to readjust their positions. General Kimura quickly made a new plan, no doubt; but his communications were so badly cut by the armoured columns of the Fourteenth Army that the plan for readjusting his positions, however feasible on paper, could not actually be carried out. The general counter-offensive planned for early March to the north or west of the Irrawaddy was completely out of the question with Meiktila in Allied hands. If only Meiktila could be retaken and the 19th Indian Division bridgeheads to the north of Mandalay eliminated, the situation might perhaps be stabilised. But they failed in both these objects. In addition, the 20th Indian Division had established a bridgehead at Myinmu and the 2nd British Division had also crossed the river on 24 February and captured Ngazun. These two divisions also presented a threat to Mandalay. Hence the

[1] Leese's *Despatch*, para. 109.

Japanese launched suicidal attacks against them, but after the fall of Meiktila they were fighting practically on four fronts, namely north of Mandalay against the 19th Indian Division, west of Mandalay against the 20th Indian Division and the 2nd British Division, in Meiktila against the 17th Indian Division, and west of Meiktila against the 7th Indian Division, from Pakokku to Chauk. Thus, at the beginning of March they were definitely outnumbered and by forces superior in equipment. This was the second reason for the sudden breakdown of their offensive and defensive structure though not of their morale.[2]

19TH INDIAN DIVISION FRONT

The Fourteenth Army plan of operations for the capture of Central Burma prior to an advance on Rangoon had assigned the northern zone for operations by the XXXIII Corps. In that area as has been mentioned earlier, the 19th Indian Division had crossed the Irrawaddy in January and established two bridgeheads on its eastern bank and was ready to make a dash for Mandalay. The other two divisions, the 20th Indian Division and the 2nd Division, were not far and had moved across the river. Meanwhile the IV Corps had succeeded in capturing and holding Meiktila and sending its forces to the region of the oilfields. The two arms of the pincer were thus extending to encircle the Japanese forces. Mandalay, because of its strategic position was the immediate-objective, for which the 19th Indian Division had been preparing itself.

Before proceeding with the account of the operations for Mandalay, we may assess the strength of Japanese opposition facing the 19th Indian Division about the middle of February. Certain troops of the *31st* and *15th Divisions*, numbering about 750, had been withdrawn from the general area of Wabyudaung and re-formed with the balance of the *15th Division* in the area south and east of Singu,[3] a little to the south of the 19th Indian Division's bridgehead at Ngapyin-In. At the same time, some other units which had originally faced this Indian division, such as the *151st Regiment* of the *53rd Division*, were withdrawn and sent to the area threatened by the 20th Indian Division, to the west of Mandalay. The *119th Regiment* of the *53rd Division* was also withdrawn and moved south to conform to the new location of the division. "Therefore by the end of February, 19th Indian Division was faced only by the *15th Division*

---

[2] In the Japanese army, the common soldiers' morale remained high in spite of insufficient rations, disease and bad weather. Even in the later stages of the war, when defeat was certain, they fought well though their feeling was one of "anger at their lack of air support and general inferiority of weapons and ammunition". 12th Army Intelligence Summary No. 13, Report No. 5.
[3] XXXIII Corps Account of Operations.

and the *3rd Battalion 58th Regiment* of the *31st Division*—a total force of some 1500 front line troops."[4] This was not a formidable force, and once the Indian division broke out from its bridgeheads, there was nothing that would stop it from achieving its object of capturing the city of Mandalay and Fort Dufferin.

19TH INDIAN DIVISION OPERATIONS

In the second week of February, as has been narrated earlier, the 19th Indian Division had foiled the Japanese attempts to dislodge it from its bridgehead. On the positive side this division had occupied the Pear Hill and the features called Baker and Charlie, besides Singu,[5] where a firm base had been established for the drive on Mandalay. On 12 February, in a Special Order of the Day, the divisional commander had pointed to the task ahead and said:[6]

> "The Japanese expressed their avowed intention of defeating us, and driving us across the river. The fighting in the bridgehead has been hard and bitter. But you have held our gains with a dogged determination for which I express my unqualified admiration and I thank you.
>
> "And now you have enlarged our bridgehead and broken out. Your task now is 'on to Mandalay'."

Two days later was issued the Operation Instruction No. 14, giving instructions about the advance towards Mandalay. In view of the continued Japanese withdrawal on account of the danger of being cut off north of Mandalay, the 19th Indian Division was to move rapidly towards that city without, however, taking unnecessary risks.[7] The 64th Indian Infantry Brigade was to initiate the advance southwards. The 62nd Indian Infantry Brigade would secure the disembarkation and transit areas from the river to Singu and to clear the hinterland to the east of the above area. Then the 98th Indian Infantry Brigade was to hold the western Kyaukmyaung bridgehead with one battalion; another battalion was to hold the Yeshin—Minban Taung area to protect the rear of the 19th Indian Division and to be in readiness to liquidate the Japanese forces pushed south by 4/4 Gurkha Rifles, the third battalion, from Thabeikkyin bridgehead.

---

[4] *Ibid.*
[5] See Chapter IX.
[6] W/D 19th Indian Division, February 1945.
[7] In the words of the Operation Instruction: "If the Japanese are obviously pulling out fast, act boldly and go fast while the going is good, and take risks." But if the resistance was well organised and considerable the advance would be deliberate. "I do not intend to incur unnecessary casualties in any ill-prepared rushes at organised defences." (Major General T. W. Rees words). See Operation Instruction No. 14 of the 19th Indian Division.

64th Brigade

On the day the Operation Instruction was issued, 5 Baluch of the 64th Indian Infantry Brigade supported by a squadron of 150 RAC advanced south-east through Myingan area and established itself at Ywazintaw. Here the Baluch faced some opposition and suffered loss. The next day while advancing to Ywathitgale along the road to the south they met heavy opposition from snipers armed with rifles and machine-guns, but the battalion continued its advance. On 16 February, the opposition on their fronts was thinning out; nonetheless, the patrols found the village of Khanpa in Japanese occupation.[8] On the 17th, following an air-strike, 1/6 Gurkha Rifles attacked Khanpa from the west and captured it against slight opposition. Ywathitgale and Kulbintha were also cleared, the latter after a stiff fight. Thus by 17 February, Khanpa, Ywathitgale and Kulbintha were firmly in the hands of this brigade. The majority of the Japanese forces, however, escaped despite stops. A troop of 7 Cavalry which was guarding the right flank of 1/6 Gurkha Rifles caught a company of Japanese troops in the open at SW 812946 and inflicted some casualties. On 19 February, the Japanese made two counter-attacks in this area but without success. A party of 80 Japanese troops attacking the village from the west in the afternoon was driven off with the support of 7 Cavalry. Another strong party of approximately 200 advancing west from Kokko area in two columns was engaged by the entire divisional artillery. Finally, at 2230 hours defensive fire (DF) broke a third party of the Japanese troops forming up for an attack from the north. 1/6 Gurkha Rifles at Khanpa was also heavily shelled by the Japanese during the next few days and suffered losses. There was also an attack from the north which was broken up at 0300 hours on the 21st.

98th Brigade

Of the two other brigades, the 62nd was engaged on patrolling the area and had succeeded in clearing Zigon of hostile forces. The 98th Indian Infantry Brigade was operating in two areas, 8 Frontier Force Regiment in the southern bridgehead against the Japanese positions at the pagoda on Minban Taung, and 4/4 Gurkha Rifles in the northern bridgehead. The brigade headquarters was opened at Ngapyin-In at SR 6904 on 19 February. On the same day 4/4 Gurkha Rifles began operations to clear the area southwards from Thabeikkyin bridgehead towards the main divisional bridgehead at Kyaukmyaung, while 8 Frontier Force Regiment moved north to meet the Gurkhas. Opposition in that area grew less and less as the Japanese had given up all hopes of liquidating the bridgehead. 4/4 Gurkha

---
[8] War Diary XXXIII Corps.

Rifles patrols encountered little opposition and a company proceeding eastward along the road reached Wabyudaung on 21 February. The Gurkha battalion then moved south and making good progress, in spite of the difficult country through which it had to march, reached approximately 5 miles south of Wabyudaung on 22 February. On the same day, 8 Frontier Force Regiment reached Kyaunggon in its march northward, routing some Japanese troops on the way by a bayonet charge. The next day, 4/4 Gurkha Rifles was established at Chaunggy which was reached by a patrol of 8 Frontier Force Regiment the next day, and a contact between the two was established. The gap between the two bridgeheads was thus closed.

The situation at this stage was that the Japanese *15th Division* was reported regrouping in the general area east of Singu, probably to cover the withdrawal of the *53rd Division* which was disengaging from the Allied front and withdrawing to lay-back positions covering the approaches to Mandalay. The Japanese anxiety at this time appeared to be to ensure the safe evacuation of their stores and equipment from the area between the positions held by the 19th Indian Division and the hills to the east while maintaining a rearguard action to delay the Indian advance.[9]

On 23 February was issued the 19th Indian Division Operation Order No. 5, directing that the Japanese forces in contact would be destroyed before resuming advance to the south.[10] The objective was to block the main road to the south in the Nyaungwun area. To facilitate this task, Shwehle was to be seized as a gun area and later the chaung from LA 5027 to LA 5426 was to serve as a block to the south. Further advance on a broad front, it was hoped, would then be facilitated. The plan was that the 64th Indian Infantry Brigade would first seize and consolidate Shwehle on 23 February. It would then march east on 26 February with a view to securing a firm footing on the southern position of Gawuntaung Hill and then establish a block in Point 565—Nyaungwun area. The 62nd Indian Infantry Brigade would take over Shwehle from the 64th Indian Infantry Brigade and establish a bridgehead over a chaung LA 5027 —LA 5426 on 27 February.

According to this plan, 5 Baluch and three troops of 150 RAC captured Shwehle and Ywashe on 23 February against slight opposition; and, by 25 February, both the 62nd and 64th Indian Infantry Brigades were ready for the final break-through. Thereafter, the plan as outlined was that the 62nd Indian Infantry Brigade would advance down the east bank of the Irrawaddy, and the 64th Indian Infantry Brigade would clear the area up to the Gawuntaung feature, and advance south along the foothills. The 98th Indian Infantry

---

[9] War Diary 19th Indian Division for February 1945, Appendix A to OO No. 5.
[10] *Ibid*, OO No. 5.

Brigade, having cleared south from Thabeikkyin, was then to move further south to rejoin the rest of the division with all possible speed.[11]

64th Brigade

In pursuance of the above plan, 1/6 Gurkha Rifles, supported by armour, opened the offensive on 26 February and cleared the villages of Minywa and Htankobin and captured two Japanese guns. The brigade then continued to press on towards the south-east with the idea of cutting the Japanese line of retreat from the north. On 27 February, it succeeded finally in closing the escape routes immediately west of Gawuntaung Hill. This move was strongly opposed by the Japanese and the brigade encountered the heaviest mortar fire yet experienced, in addition to the resistance by anti-tank guns. But, with the support of C Squadron 7 Cavalry, 5 Baluch established two companies on the main hill at LA 595277, though two tanks were knocked out and another two damaged during the operations. 2 Worcestershire Regiment then advanced southward to Ngwedaung and occupied it in the face of severe opposition, on 28 February. Then followed a period of hard fighting with the Japanese rear-guards in the rocky area of Gawuntaung feature, but by 1 March, 5 Baluch had captured Point 565, and the Allied troops dominated the whole area up to the Shwepyi Hill.

Nyaungwun was occupied on the morning of 2 March without opposition. The main body of the Japanese force withdrew due south followed by 1/6 Gurkha Rifles with 2 Worcestershire Regiment hooking east via Pyindaung. This last place was captured on 3 March by 2 Worcesters who then advanced south and assisted 1/6 Gurkha Rifles in occupying Shwepyi, Zegon and Zayatkon. At the same time, 1/15 Punjab at Taung-In came under the command of the 64th Indian Infantry Brigade. During the night of 3/4 March, the Punjabis occupied the summit of Point 850 from its north-east corner without opposition. Owing to the rocky nature of the ground they could not dig in. At daybreak they discovered that the Japanese held positions on all higher features to the south of this point, and that small hostile groups were all around the company perimeter. The Punjabis soon came under heavy fire and experienced great difficulty in evacuating their casualties. They also ran short of ammunition and had to use bayonets to drive away the opposition. But clinging on to a precarious position for 12 hours, they were eventually relieved in the evening by 1/6 Gurkha Rifles.

62nd Brigade

The plan for the 62nd Indian Infantry Brigade was to take over Shwehle from the 64th Indian Infantry Brigade and then establish

[11] XXXIII Corps Account of Operations, Vol. III, p. 40.

a bridgehead over the chaung at LA 5027—LA 5426. Shwehle having been captured on 23 February by the 64th Indian Infantry Brigade and handed over to the other brigade, the latter was soon ready to cross the chaung and move down south along the river bank while the former moved round along the foothill.

On 27 February, 3 Rajputana Rifles supported by a squadron of 150 RAC cleared Chaungywa while 2 Welch drove out the Japanese from Nyaunggon. 3 Rajputana Rifles then crossed the chaung LA 505279 against heavy opposition from Taungbetywa. But the battalion finally succeeded in capturing Taungbetywa and then pushed on to Sethi. With continuous tank support, the advance was maintained, and by the evening of 1 March, 2 Welch had captured Taung-In after an air-strike and artillery concentration, and 3 Rajputana Rifles had cleared the area up to the Tongyi Chaung in the south, after overcoming slight opposition at Yedaw. Notwithstanding heavy mortar fire the battalion established a bridgehead across the Tongyi Chaung, north of Tongyi. On the next day, 4/6 Gurkha Rifles passed through this bridgehead and cleared, in succession, the villages on the Irrawaddy south of Tongyi. 1/15 Punjab, in the meantime, had crossed to the Ketthin Island (formed by a bifurcation of the Irrawaddy) and having occupied Ketthin, on 28 February, occupied Letpangon. 1 Assam then took over from the Punjabis and cleared Paukkon, following an artillery concentration. The 62nd Indian Infantry Brigade then commenced to clear the island from Wetpaung.

On 1 March, the divisional commander had put into operation a plan which was intended to cause bewilderment to the Japanese who undoubtedly expected the 19th Indian Division to use the only apparently passable road, the one through Shwepyi, Pinle-In and Yenatha as the main axis of advance, and had made preparations to stop the Indian Division on the 'pig-hill' feature, called Kidney, between Shwepyi and Pinle-In. In this area the Japanese troops numbered approximately 500 while there were only 300 in the area Yedaw—Ketthin Island—Tongyi Chaung. The plan decided upon for further advance was that only the 64th Indian Infantry Brigade would operate on the left along the road axis and move forward maintaining pressure. The main drive of the division, with the tanks in front and the major portion of the artillery behind it, was directed down the water-logged, apparently impassable strip of land, between the Kidney feature and the Irrawaddy. The Divisional Base Area was to be responsible for the Base Area and for operations on Ketthin Island. The 62nd Indian Infantry Brigade was to be the spear-head of advance on the main line, and the 98th Indian Infantry Brigade, which had been advancing through the area Taung-In, was to follow.

The plan laid for 2 March was that one battalion (8 Frontier Force Regiment) of the 98th Indian Infantry Brigade would debouch from 3 Rajputana Rifles bridgehead during the night of 1/2 March and avoiding the east bank of the river, strike in a direct line to Shwegon, and thence on to Shwegondaing. The main body of the brigade was to operate in Yedaw and from there move south-east to Taung-In and further south. The 62nd Indian Infantry Brigade would march south along the east bank of the river; the overall intention of the 19th Indian Division being to "advance south with all speed".[12]

According to this plan, 4/6 Gurkha Rifles (62nd Brigade), with tank support, passed through 3 Rajputana Rifles and cleared, in succession, the villages on the Irrawaddy from Tongyi southwards. 8 Frontier Force Regiment of the 98th Indian Infantry Brigade was at Taung-In on 2 March, and 4/4 Gurkha Rifles advancing through Taung-In, captured Shwedon. The Gurkha battalion with 2 R Berks to its north formed a block to intercept the Japanese forces attempting to escape eastward from the grip of the 62nd Indian Infantry Brigade.

On 3 March, 3 Rajputana Rifles and 4/6 Gurkha Rifles crossed the island opposite Sagyetkon and pushing south cleared up to a line Athingon-Wetpaung-Nyaungbinywa.[13] Next day the 62nd Indian Infantry Brigade with the assistance of a troop of tanks cleared the island up to the gridline 07. Stubborn resistance was encountered at Kyaungi. The entire Sambo island was cleared the next morning and the 62nd Indian Infantry Brigade started concentrating in Shanywa area.[14]

The 98th Indian Infantry Brigade, which had been asked to capture the Kidney feature, also made rapid progress. On 3 March, 2 R Berks with tank support pushed south to intercept the Japanese force which was expected to cross from Kaukyobon. 4/4 Gurkha Rifles also reached Point 1320 from the north against slight opposition, and had little difficulty in capturing Harlech, on 4 March. 8 Frontier Force Regiment in the south seized Point 1487 (LA 6010) and Point 1120 (LA 6111) against slight resistance. 2 R Berks made a long march and captured Kadozeik astride Chaungmagyi river (LF 5499). On 5 March 1/15 Punjab, after having seized Sitkonywa and Hngethyizin the previous day, attacked a Japanese party at Hngethyizin Hill with the support of tanks, but the latter fought stubbornly all day and refused to be dislodged. 1/15 Punjab was then relieved by 2 Welch and formed a mobile column, named Stiletto, with C Squadron 7 Cavalry (less one troop), one troop of 150 RAC and

---

[12] 19th Division Operation Order No. 7, Appendix B to W/D for March 1945.
[13] 19th Division W/D, 2000 hours, 3 March.
[14] W/D Headquarters 19th Indian Division.

supporting arms, for operations south of Chaungmagyi Chaung. 2 R Berks extended the bridgehead at Kadozeik and drove the Japanese troops from Udein and also occupied the Marble Quarries at 5701. During the night Stiletto completed its concentration in the Kadozeik—Udein area.[15]

The final phase of the advance on Mandalay had now begun. On 5 March, the 64th Indian Infantry Brigade moved south from Shwepyi, 5 Baluch in the lead, and captured Magwe-taya and Point 625 to the south, against stubborn resistance, whilst 1/6 Gurkha Rifles occupied Point 850 (LA 5919), Point 1110 (LA 6018), and Point 1062 (LA 6118). 2 Worcestershire Regiment followed through on 6 March and completed the clearing of the road Shwepyi—Pinle-In, and by nightfall, after an advance of 14 miles reached Yenatha to find the 62nd Indian Infantry Brigade already there.

Thereafter, the 62nd Indian Infantry Brigade, following the passing through of the 98th Indian Infantry Brigade, pushed eastwards. 4/6 Gurkha Rifles moving east from Shanywa captured Yenatha in the morning of 6 March when a small Japanese concentration north of that place had been dispersed by artillery fire. By nightfall, 4/6 Gurkha Rifles had reached Myodin further to the east. On 7 March, the Gurkhas captured Ohnmin and were astride Mandalay canal. The troops were in excellent spirits in spite of fatigue.[16]

At this stage it was realised that a small motorised column with armour and artillery support would be the best means of exploiting the success already gained, and the most rapid means of following up the Japanese rear-guards. Such a column, known as Stiletto, had already been formed on 5 March and had pushed on down the east bank of the Irrawaddy to Powa Taung and Mayabin on 6 March. This last place was only about three miles west of Madaya.

Madaya

The situation on 6 March, therefore, was that while the 62nd Indian Infantry Brigade was at Yenatha, some eight miles north-east of Madaya, and the 98th Indian Infantry Brigade was at Chaungmagyi, also to the north of Madaya, only the Stiletto Column was west of that place. Madaya was an important place and was connected with Mandalay by railway and a good road motorable in dry season. Its capture was, therefore, essential prior to resuming the advance to Mandalay. As Madaya was also connected by a motorable road running north in which direction most of the 19th Indian Division troops were concentrated, the Japanese expected that it would be attacked from that side. They had some carefully prepared

[15] *Ibid.*
[16] *Ibid.*

OPERATIONS IN MANDALAY AREA

MARCH—APRIL 1945

ADVANCE OF ALLIED FORCES SHOWN THUS ➞

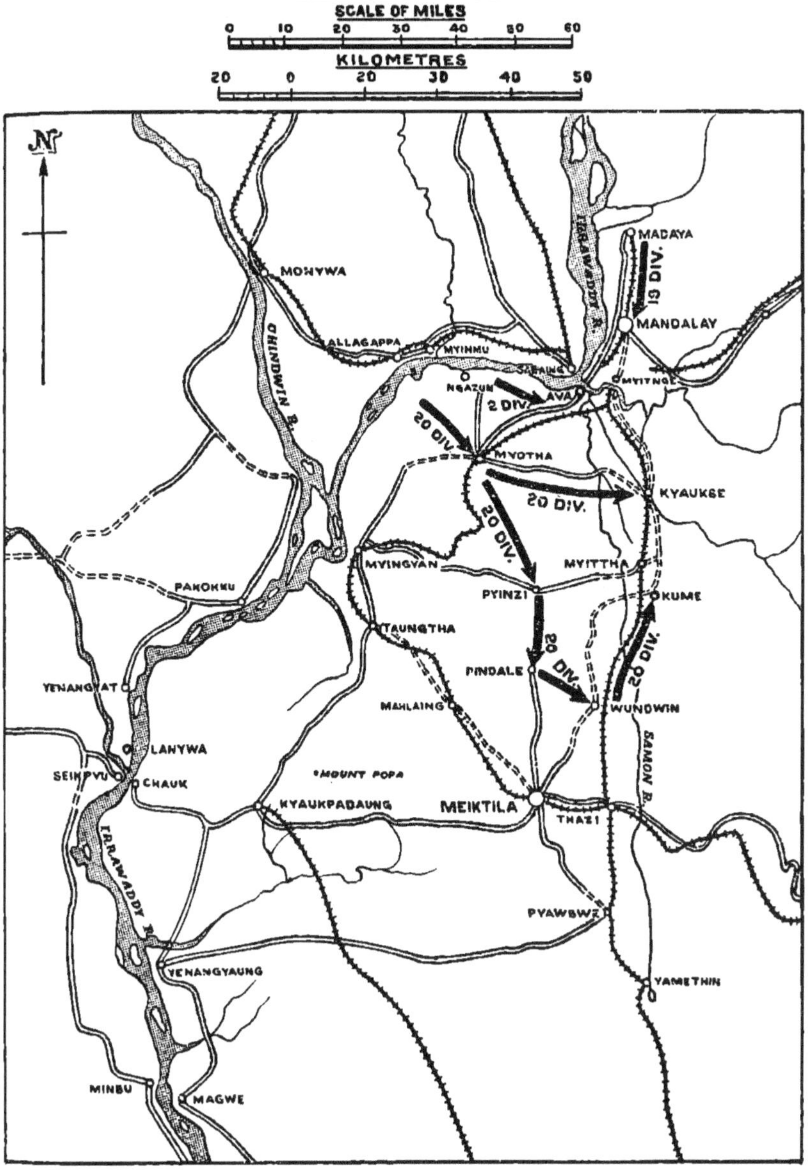

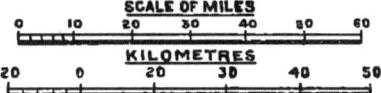

positions around that place, particularly in the north, and their intention was to fall back on these positions and make a stand there. Major General Rees however had different ideas, and succeeded in capturing Madaya without much fighting on 7 March. To achieve this end he decided to give up advance along the dusty road leading to Madaya which would have led to the north of that place. Instead "General Rees switched his armour there, made a swift punch, smashed through the Jap suicide parties in the burning Burmese village down the bank of the Irrawaddy on the road to Mandalay and entered Madaya from the west instead of the north."[17] What is still more remarkable about this operation is the fact that the 98th Indian Infantry Brigade entered Madaya before the Japanese, who were attempting to fall back on the prepared positions in this area, could reach it. The village was captured by 2 R Berks of the 98th Indian Infantry Brigade after some street fighting, in the course of which 3 Japanese were taken prisoners. With the capture of this place the 19th Indian Division was within 15 miles of the outskirts of Mandalay.

After the capture of Madaya, the advance south towards Mandalay continued rapidly, the 98th Indian Infantry Brigade moving in the middle on the railway axis, the 64th Indian Infantry Brigade about a mile to the east of it and Stiletto through the intricate country to the west.[18] "Stiletto continued their spectacular dash towards Mandalay"[19] and occupied Sinywagale and Kabaing, having overcome some opposition en route. Japanese prisoners captured during these days stated that the advance by the 19th Indian Division was too rapid for their *15th Division*.[20]

On 6 March, the 64th Indian Infantry Brigade had moved from Yenatha. On the 7th, it encountered little opposition and by the time Madaya was cleared by the 98th Indian Infantry Brigade, it was approximately one mile east of it. On 8 March, Stiletto occupied Obo railway station, gained contact with the Japanese position on Mandalay hill and occupied a feature (Pimple) to the north-west of it. Meanwhile, the 98th Indian Infantry Brigade, following fast behind it, also reached Obo railway station in the afternoon, and took upon itself the task of completely capturing and clearing the Mandalay Hill, a corner of which had been occupied by Stiletto. This hill had many pagodas and was studded with monastery buildings which dominated the city.

During the night of 8/9 March, 4/4 Gurkhas of the 98th Indian Infantry Brigade scaled the north-eastern end of the Mandalay Hill

---

[17] *Dagger Division*, p. 32.
[18] 62nd Brigade was not moving on Mandalay, as it had been asked to make a diversion towards Maymyo and cut the road from that place to Mandalay.
[19] War Diary XXXIII Corps.
[20] War Diary 19th Indian Division.

in the dark. In the morning of 9 March, the Gurkhas put in an attack with drawn kukris and reaching the summit established two companies there. But although they were established on the summit, the hill was by no means completely cleared of the presence of Japanese troops. The next eleven days were spent in clearing the hill and other areas around the fort and in breaching the walls of the fort by artillery fire and bombing from the air.

Fort Dufferin

Meanwhile 8 Frontier Force Regiment had cleared the area southwards up to the line of the northern moat of Fort Dufferin. This fort was overlooked by Mandalay Hill and covered an area of about 2000 square yards. At that time it contained the Palace, Government House, the Jail, the Club, the Polo ground and some other government buildings. It was covered by a moat, about 75 yards wide, with a wall on the inner side. Each wall had a main gate in the centre, set obliquely on the bridge leading to it and protected from direct fire by a massive buttress on the moat side. The wall was constructed of brick and was about 30 feet thick at the bottom narrowing off to about 12 feet near the top, forming a ramp protected by brick castellations two to three feet thick. It was about 23 feet high and buttressed every hundred yards.[21]

On 9 March, after the Gurkhas had established themselves on the summit of Mandalay Hill and were patrolling its southern portion (facing the fort) they were engaged by gun and machine-gun fire from inside the fort. 8 Frontier Force Regiment, who had reached the northern moat, attacked the fort with two troops of medium tanks in an endeavour to gain entry into it from the north gate. They encountered heavy opposition including much sniping, and one tank was immobilised by a direct hit. The Japanese force staged a counter-attack from the south end of Mandalay Hill but it was broken up by Defensive Fire (DF).[22] It was apparent that the attempt to force an entry into the fort had failed. The attack was therefore called off, and 8 Frontier Force Regiment dug in 50 yards from the wall opposite the north gate. Meanwhile, 2 R Berks had reached the outskirts of Mandalay during the day and cleared Japanese stragglers from Chaung Seaford area at 609704, killing a large number of them.[23] Meanwhile the 64th Indian Infantry Brigade also had neared Mandalay. 5 Baluch cleared Kyaukthanbat and the brigade, less 2 Worcestershire Regiment, faced the Japanese resistance at Patheingyi. The British battalion on its part took to clearing the area of the ridge from Point 1002 LF 6780 to LF 6876.

[21] An account of the breaching of the walls of Fort Dufferin—Mandalay—by the medium artillery of XXXIII Corps, File 601/9612/H.
[22] Headquarters 19th Indian Division War Diary, 9 March 1945.
[23] *Ibid*. The Japanese soldiers appeared to be in an exhausted condition.

Thus by 9 March, the Allied troops were hammering at the gates of Mandalay, and the situation as it emerged was that 2 R Berks was meeting heavy opposition on the lower slopes of Mandalay Hill, whilst 8 Frontier Force Regiment was deployed along the northern edge of the moat around Fort Dufferin, with 4/4 Gurkha Rifles trying to push down the eastern edge, on which side the opposition was the heaviest. The 64th Indian Infantry Brigade, to the east, was in contact with 2 Worcestershire Regiment on Point 1002 at LF 6780, and the rest of the brigade was in the Patheingale area.

It was evident that the Japanese had been completely surprised by the speed of the advance of the 19th Indian Division from the line of Chaungmagyi Chaung, as no serious opposition was met until the outskirts of Mandalay were reached, apart from the brief fight for Madaya. Many small parties of Japanese troops were, however, found wandering from village to village, with no idea of the situation or of the dispositions of their own troops. But in the city, Mandalay Hill was strongly held, and Fort Dufferin was heavily defended.[24] Even the demoralised parties outside were considered "capable of preliminary dangerous resistance which soon crumbles under skilful attack".[25]

On 10 March, 2 R Berks with tank support started clearing the southern slopes of the Mandalay Hill. The Japanese, entrenched in concrete strong-points and tunnels, offered stubborn opposition. During the day the Berkshires liquidated one strong-point and then started operations against another. In the meantime two of their companies with tank and artillery support had cleared the western side of the fort to its southern edge. 4/4 Gurkha Rifles cleared up to the cemetery in the south-west corner of the Mandalay Hill. 8 Frontier Force Regiment with tank and artillery support again made a very gallant effort to enter the fort but without success.[26] Meanwhile, 1/15 Punjab had moved eastwards to reach south of the fort with the intention of clearing that area next day (11 March) and blocking exits.

The fight for clearing the hill was continued the next day also. 2 R Berk was held up at 609691 and the pagoda to the south, but the obstacles were overcome during the day. Some of the defenders barricaded themselves in one of the tunnels but they were liquidated by rolling petrol drums into the tunnel and flinging grenades at them. As the petrol caught fire, they were burnt out.[27] Although nearly half of the Japanese on the hill had been killed by this time, they obstinately clung to their positions and their snipers continued to fire

---

[24] XXXIII Corps Account of Operations Vol. III.
[25] 19th Indian Division Operation Order No. 10, dated 9 March.
[26] 19th Indian Division War Diary, 10 March.
[27] The War Diary for 11 April says, "Garrison (of) one tunnel liquidated with grenades and petrol". 601/277/DW, Part II.

Major-General
D. T. Cowan
Commander
17th Indian Division
16 Nov. 43—30 May 45

3″ Mortars near Madaya open fire on Japanese position north of Mandalay

Brigadier (later General) K. S. Thimayya
Commander 36th Indian Infantry Brigade

from behind the pagodas. The Mandalay Hill was not completely cleared till the 12th, on which day the Japanese force, holding on to the pavilion at LF 608692 and two pagodas immediately south, was destroyed with "beehives" by 2 R Berks less two companies. The two companies operating apart from the main body had reached near the railway station at 584649 to the south of the fort. One reason why the clearing of the hill had proved so difficult was that Major-General Rees had decided not to bomb the sacred places, the pagodas, though lot of machine-gun fire was poured on the garrison from the air.

8 Frontier Force Regiment with tank support cleared the area north of the fort and 4/4 Gurkha Rifles who were deployed east of the fort, cleared to the line Ashebyin—Bugon. 1/15 Punjab, then established to the south-west corner of the fort, was relieved on 12 March by 1/6 Gurkha Rifles of the 64th Indian Infantry Brigade in the area of the Roman Catholic church.

The 64th Indian Infantry Brigade occupied Point 1002 (LF 6780) and Point 1335 (LF 7169) against slight opposition, and patrolled the eastern exits of the town. On 12 March, the brigade, less 1/6 Gurkha Rifles, moved east towards the Mandalay canal, and 5 Baluch occupied a pagoda feature at LF 6765, east of Mandalay, without opposition, following a successful air-strike which resulted in the position being obliterated and the majority of the garrison being destroyed. On the 13th, 5 Baluch reached Kyaukmiywa, one company was established at Tonbo without opposition and another at Maingleze with the intention of encircling Mandalay via the southern cross-roads.

On 12 March, in the fort area, 4/4 Gurkha Rifles was in contact at Ashebyin on the east, and 1/6 Gurkha Rifles was in the Roman Catholic church area, but there was no sign of the Japanese withdrawing from the fort, although they were rapidly becoming encircled. An air-strike on the Government House (inside the fort) and on the Jail area was very successful but the brewery was not attacked. In spite of all this it seemed the Japanese were determined to hold on.

BLOODLESS CAPTURE OF MAYMYO

It is necessary here to interrupt the story of the fall of Mandalay Fort for a while to describe how, marching three days and nights, over an opium smugglers' trail, another brigade of the 19th Indian Division captured Maymyo, a hill station in the Shan mountains, and the summer headquarters of the Burma Government in peace-time.

While the 98th and 64th Indian Infantry Brigades were engaged in Mandalay area, and Major-General Rees was wondering how to seize Fort Dufferin with its 30-foot thick walls, the 62nd Indian

Infantry Brigade was marching towards Maymyo. By Operation Instruction No. 17, dated 8 March, it was ordered to cut the road Maymyo-Mandalay to the west of Maymyo and prevent the Japanese movement from the north-east towards Mandalay. Occupation of Maymyo was of secondary importance and was to be attempted only if much opposition was not expected. The ultimate object was to get the brigade astride the road Lashio-Mandalay as soon as possible. When this had been achieved, offensive action could be taken. The route selected was east-south-east from Yenatha, over the Chaungmagyi Chaung and the Mandalay canal to Kyunbin, thence south through Zibyubin to Taunggaung and east over the hills to enter Maymyo from the north-west. Naturally only pack transport was possible, and supply was to be from the air. The brigade was told to "travel as light and as fast as possible."[28]

4/6 Gurkha Rifles, which had been organised on all-mule basis on 7 March, took the lead moving half a day's march ahead of the brigade. The Gurkhas reached Thapankaing on the 8th morning where they overcame opposition by a few Japanese to the south-west of the village.[29] They then pushed on to Taunggaung (via Kyobin) arriving there at 1200 hours on the 9th.[30] From here the route to Maymyo through Khadaw was over a difficult mountain country, the track being very steep and consequently dangerous for both men and mules. But the Gurkhas accomplished a truly remarkable feat in making their way through and reaching the outskirts of the Maymyo Cantonment by 0700 hours on 10 March.[31] They then concentrated near the north-east cantonment, blocked the Lashio road there and established a post at the railway station. The brigade column, less 3 Rajputana Rifles, reached Maymyo on the morning of 11 March to find it undefended. It was then occupied without any opposition, the Japanese having retired from it earlier. "Such was the speed of this swoop that the Japanese were completely surprised and those in the town took flight in a train which departed only a few minutes before the Gurkhas entered."[32] The brigade rested here for six days.

Whilst the Gurkhas led the way into Maymyo, 2 Welch proceeded to push south-west to establish a block on the Mandalay road. The battalion found Point 3780 held by some Japanese troops and proceeding further south-west was astride the road west of Maymyo at milestone 39. Here it ambushed a large Japanese convoy during the night and captured 36 trucks, 9 staff cars, 1 jeep, one 75-mm gun, 1 light machine-gun, besides two swords, much ammunition and

---

[28] 19th Indian Division Operation Instruction No. 7.
[29] WD 4/6 GR, March 1945.
[30] Ibid.
[31] Ibid.
[32] Dagger Division, p. 36.

documents.[33] During the next few days there was only normal patrol activity.

On 17 March the brigade, less 2 Welch, left in Maymyo for rest, marched down the Mandalay road to join the 64th Indian Infantry Brigade in completing the capture of Mandalay. It reached Tonbo, south-east of Mandalay, on 18 March and took 1/15 Punjab under command.

FALL OF FORT DUFFERIN

We may now resume the story of the attack on Fort Dufferin. On 13 March the situation was that two companies of 2 Royal Berkshire Regiment were established at LF 567640, and 4/4 Gurkha Rifles was held up by Japanese strong-points at Taiktaw. The 64th Indian Infantry Brigade was covering the eastern exits from the town with 5 Baluch at Tonbo, Maingleze and the road and railway crossing at LF 6953. The 62nd Indian Infantry Brigade after taking Maymyo was resting there prior to moving to rejoin the 19th Indian Division in the Mandalay area.[34]

In the Fort area at Mandalay, the officer commanding 8/12 Frontier Force Regiment asked the battery captain of 498 Battery to arrange for some guns to be brought up on 12 March to breach holes in the north wall of the fort. A 5.5" Howitzer was brought into action about 500 yards from the north wall slightly to the west of the north gate entrance. More guns were brought in during the next few days which witnessed a curious blend of the methods of Napoleonic wars with modern technique.[35] Constant efforts were made for eight days to breach the walls and enter the fort. The progress was gradual and may be estimated from the following diary:

12 March—A good breach was made in the north wall by a 5.5" Howitzer using about 30 rounds fuze 231.

13 March—Three 5.5s were sent up. One made another breach in the north wall, one breached the west wall, and the third made two breaches in the east wall. Twelve Thunderbolts bombed the bridge on the south side of the moat, whilst 8 Frontier Force Regiment patrolled to the north gate but drew no fire. In the southwest corner of the fort, 1/6 Gurkha Rifles with tank and artillery support attacked the Japanese in the area 579662, but the Gurkhas were stopped by gun fire which damaged their tanks. The Japanese were still holding the Roman Catholic church and the railway station.

The 98th Indian Infantry Brigade group had been engaged in

---

[33] War Diary 19th Indian Division *op. cit.*
[34] Incidentally, 62nd Brigade's presence in Maymyo became the cause of an interesting treat for the local population who were thrilled to see Dakotas dropping supplies to the troops.
[35] Account of the breaching of the walls of Fort Dufferin. *Op. cit.*

some very hard fighting and it was decided that the 64th Indian Infantry Brigade would take over in the city and fort areas, whilst the 98th Indian Infantry Brigade would move out to the east and south to block all Japanese lines of retreat from Mandalay.[36] The 4th Field Regiment, I.A., was to move with it and assist it in the task.[37]

14 March—14 March was spent in patrolling and probing for the Japanese weak points. In the fort area, the railway station was reported to be clear of Japanese troops though not the surrounding buildings. 1/6 Gurkha Rifles smoked bunker positions west of the moat near the west gate and forced the Japanese to withdraw but they returned again. 4/4 Gurkha Rifles was still in contact to the east of the fort. 5 Baluch patrolled to Wayonbin and ferry LF 5045.

15 March—The relief of the 98th Indian Infantry Brigade by the 64th Indian Infantry Brigade in the fort area was in progress and all exits from the fort had been blocked. 1/6 Gurkha Rifles was made responsible for the west side of the fort. 2 Worcestershire Regiment took over from 4/4 Gurkha Rifles in the Ashebyin area. Two companies of 2 Royal Berkshire Regiment secured the cross roads LF 594639 south of the fort, after having almost nightly scraps with the Japanese forces in this area. 5 Baluch under the command of the 98th Indian Infantry Brigade was established at Wayonbin and sent patrols to the Myitnge river with the object of discovering the Japanese withdrawal routes across the river.

On this day the two 6" Howitzers went into action. The task of the first one was to destroy the railway gate at the north-west corner of the fort wall. The second was to breach the west wall about 300 yards from the north-west corner. Both the guns were successful in carrying out their tasks.

The battle was now being fought primarily for the reduction of the fort and closing all Japanese escape routes south and south-east from the city. Despite constant bombardment, the Japanese remained entrenched behind the moat, and the high walls, behind which 50-ft. of earth had also been heaped. The masonry of the walls gave way to bombardment, but the shells were swallowed by the earth behind them.

16 March—Three 6" Howitzers were ordered out, one to breach the east wall and two to breach the north wall. Three breaches in the east wall and four in the north wall were made—the best breaches made till then. The guns were in open position but surprisingly enough there was no sniping from within unlike the previous days. The work of the gunners was, however, interrupted for several hours by air-strikes on the wall.

---

[36] The change over was completed by 15 March.
[37] WD 4th Fd Regt, IA, 15 March 1945.

Night of 16-17 March—'Exercise Duffy'. On 16 March the 64th Indian Infantry Brigade was ordered to carry out a surprise assault during the night with the object of achieving a silent night entry into the fort through one or more breaches in the wall. As a preliminary to this operation, Royal Air Force Hurricanes and Thunderbolts with 500-lb bombs damaged the wall during the day, but could not breach it. Nine P 47's caused a breach after a further air-strike, and preparations were completed for the night assault.

The object of "Exercise Duffy", as the operation was called, was to achieve a silent entry into the fort and then exploit this success to secure a foothold inside it consisting of an east to west belt including the north-east and the north-west bastions. This belt would include the north gate which might be secured, after which other forces could move in. The success of the operation would no doubt depend on surprise. As Major-General Rees put it in his instructions:[38]

> "The operation I intend is one of surprise; a silent start and rapid seizing of the bridgehead, NOT the forcing of an entry at all costs by bludgeon methods. If the surprise operation at reasonably light cost is not possible owing to enemy vigilance and preparations, then it will not be pressed home at all costs."

The battalions selected for this operation were 1/15 Punjab and 8 Frontier Force Regiment, who were to begin the move at 2200 hours. The moat separating the attackers from the wall had of course to be crossed first in boats.

B Company of 8 Frontier Force Regiment commenced crossing the moat from the north-east corner at the appointed hour and all went well for some time. Within one hour, but for one platoon, it was across, but it was suspected that there would be opposition as the left hand platoon had seen some movement of the Japanese within the breaches of the wall. This apprehension proved correct and at about 2315 hours the Japanese started firing. It was now apparent that surprise had been lost. However, by 0050 hours (17 March) the remaining platoon had also started to cross. It was then discovered that all breaches were held by the garrison who started grenading the battalion headquarters area to the north of the moat. Increasing activity was heard inside the fort towards the north-east corner as if reinforcements were arriving. B Company made several attempts to rush the breaches but these being filled with rubble were difficult to climb. Three light machine-guns were reported firing from the breaches and a fourth from the flank. In spite of this, further attempts were made to rush the breaches but without success. By 0340 hours it became apparent that the possibility of effecting an

---

[38] 19th Division Operation Instruction No. 18 of 16 March 1945.

entry from that sector was remote. The attempt was called off and B Company withdrew by 0545 hours.

On the north-west corner, 1/15 Punjab had still worse luck. Its leading platoon of C Company, after experiencing difficulty in getting boats into water due to thick mud, embarked at 2230 hours, half an hour later than scheduled. The boat carrying scaling equipment capsized and, leaving the equipment in the mud, floated away. Second platoon embarked at 2320 hours, but immediately came under heavy fire which sank its leading boat. The platoon then returned and it was decided to cross at a new place, 150 yards further west from the Government House. Boats were collected there and two sections crossed over. They were however immediately fired upon. The leading patrol was pinned down by the Japanese fire from the north-west corner. Others investigating the breaches found them all held. Eventually it was realised that no entrance could be effected from this sector also. Order was given for the company to withdraw at 0430 hours and this was successfully carried out under artillery cover. Each company had flame throwing detachments with it but these could not be used owing to the difficulty in approaching close enough to the targets. Both the gallant attempts to find an entry into the fort thus failed.

17 March—On this day it was decided to make so many holes in the walls that the Japanese would find it impossible to cover all by fire. A reconnaissance for gun positions was made on the 17th and 18th, but the big attack came on 19 March. Meanwhile, on the 17th an attempt by a patrol of 1/6 Gurkha Rifles to penetrate a road-block south of the Roman Catholic church had also failed as the area was strongly held.

On the same day, however, after an air-strike by 23 Thunderbolts, 2 Worcestershire Regiment cleared Taiktaw and rescued 160 internees from the leper asylum. During the night, patrols attempted to cross the moat on the east side of the fort on a silent reconnaissance of possible entrances but were not successful. Attempts were also made opposite Taiktaw but were unsuccessful owing to thick weeds in the water.

18 March—Three more attempts were made to cross the moat on 18 March. 2 Worcestershire Regiment made repeated attempts to cross it between the north-east corner and the eastern gate, but without success owing to weeds and strong opposition from the defenders which prevented wading or swimming. 2 Royal Berkshire Regiment tried to cross from the south and 1/6 Gurkha Rifles company from the west below the mosque at LF 581667, but both these attempts failed due to heavy fire. Not only did the Japanese hold the Allied attacks but they also attacked 2 Worcestershire Regiment company position at the junction of the road and canal at 617637 during the night inflicting some casualties. 2 Royal Berkshire Regiment forward company position at crossroads LF 594638 was also attacked.

19 March—This was the big gun-day of the siege of Fort Dufferin. Early in the morning four 6" guns were taken up and began blasting the north wall making 16 holes. Two 5.5" Howitzers were also pressed into service and they made some holes in the east and west walls. On the same day a company of 3 Rajputana Rifles took over the road and canal junction at 617637 from a company of 2 Worcestershire Regiment. Three B25s carried out an experimental attack on the north-western corner of the Fort with 2000-lb bombs, using skip bombing technique, and a 15-ft hole was blown in the wall.

During the night of 19/20 March, there was much Japanese activity both inside and outside the fort, mechanical transport, bullock carts and probably tracked vehicles were heard moving in the area of the south-east corner of the fort by patrols of the 62nd Indian Infantry Brigade.[39] This Japanese column was actually moving out of the fort in a south-easterly direction. On being engaged by 3 Rajputana Rifles patrols it changed direction and moved towards the east. In the 64th Indian Infantry Brigade area about 25 to 30 Japanese had moved out of the fort from the north gate and jittered 1/15 Punjab position. In the south-west corner also considerable movement was heard. It was later learnt that the Japanese were preparing to abandon the fort.

20 March—On 20 March again four guns went up to the north wall, the intention being to make up the number of holes in the wall to 40. Firing was interrupted at 1030 hours for an air-strike by medium bombers (B25s) which attacked the northern end of the fort, and two squadrons of Thunderbolts which attacked the north wall with success. After the air-strike, four Anglo-Burmans carrying a white flag and a Union Jack, came out of the northern gate and reported that the Japanese had moved out during the night. 1/15 Punjab then entered the fort from the north at about 1330 hours, and hoisted the battalion flag whilst 3 Rajputana Rifles entered it from the south soon after. The Japanese had gone but large quantities of food and stores had been left behind.

With the capture of Fort Dufferin the battle for Mandalay was virtually over. On 21 March the city was declared clear. Mr. Churchill announced it in the House of Commons saying: "Thank God they have got a place whose name we can pronounce." The Union Jack was hoisted on Fort Dufferin by Lieutenant General Slim in the morning of 21 January when Lieut.-General Messervy and divisional commanders from IV Corps and staff officers were also present.

---

[39] 19th Indian Division War Diary, 20 March.

Their presence was significant in that it showed that the capture of Mandalay was a joint army effort in which both Corps and all divisions had had their share, though the honour of actually seizing it fell, no doubt, to the 19th Indian Division. Lieut.-General Leese, the Commander-in-Chief ALFSEA, accompanied by the Governor of Bengal had visited the 19th Indian Division Headquarters on the 20th, and Lord Louis Mountbatten visited the division on 22 March accompanied by Major-General H. H. Fuller, Deputy Chief of Staff SEAC and Air Marshal Sir Keith Park. Congratulations of the Supreme Allied Commander, the Commander-in-Chief of the Army, and commanders of the IV, XV and XXXIII Corps were conveyed to the 19th Indian Division in a special order of the day by Major-General T. W. Rees on the "symbolic honour of capturing Mandalay itself, the ancient capital of Burma and all it stands for".

As it must have been seen from the account given above, the Japanese had resisted fiercely. Although so many holes were made in the north-east and west walls by heavy artillery, and so many airstrikes had taken place, they continued to hold the fort for eleven days. This was due mainly to the fact that the Army Commander, Lieutant-General Slim, had instructed both Lieut-General Sir Montagu Stopford and Major-General Rees not to risk heavy casualties in trying to take the fort by assault. There, is, therefore, no doubt that the Japanese could have held it for a few days longer if they had not suddenly decided to leave. Therefore the question naturally arises, why did they leave? The answer no doubt lies in the fact that the fall of Meiktila had affected the Japanese defensive system so vitally and adversely that to hold the fort for a days longer could not possibly have helped them materially. Moreover, the 20th Indian Division and the 2nd Division were fast approaching Mandalay, each "fiercely seeking the honour of leading Stopford's Corps into the city of the Kings,"[40] and this might have also influenced the Japanese to some extent. In any case, the fort was bound to fall even without the approach of these two divisions, and the Japanese decision to withdraw was as wise as that of the Fourteenth Army Commander not to risk heavy casualties in capturing it. In fact their decision to abandon Mandalay had been taken on 17 March (as revealed later by Lieutenant-General Numata Takazo) and was solely the decision of the *15th Army*.[41] How timely was this decision is clear from the fact that while the 19th Indian Division entered the fort on 20 March, the 2nd Division and the 20th Indian Division linked up with it on 21 March only to find that the fort had already

---

[40] Frank Owen: *Campaign in Burma*, p. 124.
[41] SEATIC Historical Bulletin No. 242, page 69-70. The decision to give up Central Burma altogether and withdraw to south Burma was taken (according to General Kimura) on 10 April.

been taken the previous day. Though deprived of the honour of being the first to enter Mandalay, the 2nd Division and the 20th Indian Division can legitimately claim their share of the credit for the fall of Mandalay fort.

One more fact about the capture of Mandalay needs to be mentioned. While the 19th Indian Division was pressing the attack with guns, which were having no effect in spite of so many breaches in the walls of Fort Dufferin, Major-General T. W. Rees was planning to capture the fort from beneath. "He recalled how once, as a young officer attached to the Government of Burma's Staff, he had explored a culvert which burrowed beneath the walls of the Fort and the moat itself. He sent a party of sappers to make a reconnaissance. By night they waded thigh-deep through the slime and water into the enemy camp. Had the Japanese fought a few days longer, Rees might have captured from Dufferin from beneath".[42]

With the capture of Mandalay, the Allied position in Burma had become quite strong, and the Fourteenth Army now dominated the central regions. At this stage we may analyse the strategic position. The XXXIII Corps had, within a year from its being engaged on the relief of Kohima, driven back the Japanese forces from an area of 35,000 square miles.[43] Nearly 20,000 of them had been killed, 720 taken prisoners and over 250 guns captured or destroyed.[44] The various divisions of the Corps were, at the end of March 1945, engaged in mopping up operations south, south-west and south-east of Mandalay. The 20th Indian Division was moving against Kyaukse, an important road junction and railway station on the line between Mandalay and Thazi; the 19th Indian Division was clearing the areas around Mandalay and preparing to move south towards Meiktila; the 2nd British Division, which had been operating in the Sizon-Ava area with the object of closing Japanese escape routes to the south, had linked up with the 19th Indian Division and was preparing to hand over that area to the latter and concentrate in the general area Tada-U. The IV Corps units had no less brilliant record. They had taken Meiktila and frustrated the Japanese attempts to retake it. After the capture of Myingyan and the opening of the road between it and Meiktila the formations of this Corps were busy mopping up east of Pakokku, Pagan and Chauk, and its patrols had penetrated up to Popa Hill and Kyaukpadaung. Thus the whole of Central Burma was practically free from Japanese control and the stage was set for the Allied advance on Rangoon.

In fact Lieut-General Slim had already directed his two Corps Commanders, several weeks earlier, to seize a port in South Burma,

---

[42] Frank Owen: *Campaign in Burma*, p. 124.
[43] Leese's *Despatch*, para 130.
[44] *Ibid.*

by which he could have meant either Rangoon or Moulmein. He now received a directive from the Commander-in-Chief ALFSEA to capture Rangoon before the monsoon. He had only five weeks in which to do it, but his plans for the drive south were ready and they were put into execution early in April.

Japanese Difficulties

The prospect for the Japanese was, however, as dark as it was bright for the Allies. They had not been able to retake Meiktila, and even Mandalay was gone. Whatever troops remained of the *15th Army* were trying to escape to the east of Mandalay—Thazi road and then turn south along the foothills. The *53rd* and *28th Armies* had also suffered severe casualties, but their fighting value was still considerable, and General Kimura's plan was to regroup and reorganise them in South Burma and prevent a land-advance against Rangoon. As he revealed afterwards, he had drawn up a plan to hold South Burma on the Allanmyo-Toungoo line. In his own words this plan was as follows:[45] "28 *Army* was to be based on Allanmyo, and *15* and *33 Armies* on Toungoo. I regarded Toungoo as a natural strong-point, since it was the narrowest gap between two mountain ranges. Strategically I never considered Mandalay worth any serious defence; the only reason, it was held at all, was for its prestige value." In addition General Kimura thought that tactically South Burma was easier to hold than Central Burma since it had the natural defence of the Pegu Yomas.[46] Whatever their plans, the Japanese could not possibly have entertained any high hopes of holding South Burma, especially in view of the fact that their air strength in Burma was daily declining.[47]

Another development which aggravated the difficulties for the Japanese was the revolt of the Burma Defence Army (BDA) towards the end of March. This force had been raised by the Japanese after their occupation of Burma, but the men did not like the long foreign rule and the nationalist elements among them were growing restive. Just at this time, their leaders were secretly in touch with the British and they decided to revolt and co-operate with the Allied forces. Lieut-General Leese, Commander-in-Chief ALFSEA was of the opinion that although this rising was in no way decisive, it "proved of great value to our operations and forced the enemy to divert forces

---

[45] SEATIC Bulletin No. 242. General Kimura's view, however, does not accord with the stubborn resistance which the Japanese put up in Fort Dufferin.

[46] *Ibid.*

[47] Major Okamoto of the *5th Air Division* revealed during interrogation that it had been decided in the beginning of 1945 to withdraw certain air force units from Burma to French Indo-China where aircraft were urgently needed for protection of convoys up the coast of FIC. See Interrogation reports of Japanese, SEATIC HS File No. 601/7779/H.

to deal with it."⁴⁸ But the Japanese maintained that the revolt did not affect the military situation as "the fighting spirit, training and quality of BDA was not of a very high order."⁴⁹ However, they feared that from the political point of view the revolt might lead to an estrangement of feeling between the Japanese and Burmans.⁵⁰ General Kimura also admitted that the Burma Defence Army managed to cut some of their communications and prevent the Japanese from getting supplies from the villages, and that it delayed considerably the transfer of four battalions of the *55th Division* from Arakan to Central Burma, at a time when their presence was very necessary.⁵¹ General Slim would also seem to agree with the Japanese estimate of the negligible effect of the Burma Defence Army on operations. He, however admits that "they proved definitely useful in giving information and in dealing drastically with small parties of Japanese".⁵² Whatever the tactical importance of the revolt, there is no doubt that its moral and political effect was considerable and it made the overall picture of the Japanese position in Burma gloomier.

---

⁴⁸ Leese's *Despatch*, para 128.
⁴⁹ SEATIC Bulletin No. 242.
⁵⁰ *Ibid.*
⁵¹ *Ibid.*
⁵² Slim: *Defeat into Victory*, p. 520.

CHAPTER XIII

The Dash to Rangoon—XXXIII Corps

With the fall of Mandalay and Meiktila all eyes turned towards the Burmese capital, Rangoon, 300 miles to the south. "The whole army was determined to go all out for Rangoon."[1] However, before the Fourteenth Army could march to Rangoon, the big Japanese concentration between the areas held by the two Corps had to be liquidated. Hence Lieut-General Slim decided to stage another rapid link-up between the two Corps. This took place south of Kyaukse in the first week of April when the XXXIII Corps struck south and the IV Corps struck north to meet each other. Thousands of Japanese lost their lives as the two Corps drew closer and closed the gap. Three Japanese divisions, or rather remnants of these divisions, abandoned all their equipment and dashed into the hills east of the Mandalay—Meiktila railway.[2]

Although the advance south was very rapid, it was at this time not fast enough to ensure the fall of Rangoon before the advent of monsoon. It was feared that should rains come with Rangoon still in Japanese hands the problem of supplying the Fourteenth Army would become insuperable. Already the supply services were taxed to the limit and were finding it hard to keep pace with the rapidly moving forces. Practically all forward formations of the Fourteenth Army were being supplied from the air, and this arrangement had to continue until the port of Rangoon might be opened to Allied shipping.[3] But the difficulty in continuing this arrangement was that only a few of the airfields from which the supply planes took off were of the all-weather variety, and it was certain that many of them would go out of commission with the onset of the monsoon.[4]

Thus it became essential to capture Rangoon in the next six weeks, and at the same time to disperse a big concentration of the Japanese forces in the Yenangyaung oilfields. Hence the plan was that while the IV Corps would make for Rangoon down the road and railway axis, the XXXIII Corps would destroy the Japanese forces in the oilfields area and then try to reach Rangoon by the river axis, if possible before IV Corps.

[1] Slim's words in *Campaign of the Fourteenth Army*, p. 28.
[2] *Burma—A Miracle Military Achievement*, p. 21.
[3] The backward formations, about half of the army in ration strength, were being supplied all the time by MT on the road by the magnificent Indian MT companies.
[4] *Burma—A Miracle Military Achievement*.

SUPPLY

But the crucial problem was that of supplies. How would these forces moving faster and faster and deeper and deeper into Burma be supplied even during the pre-monsoon period? The Fourteenth Army had been pressing the SEAC and ALFSEA authorities for the capture of certain air bases in Arakan from where the advancing forces might be supplied. The difficulty was resolved by the farsightedness of ALFSEA authorities who had appreciated the Fourteenth Army's view and had provided for it in their plans.

In the beginning of 1945, supplies were flown from east Bengal aerodromes and from Imphal. However, the importance of Imphal from the supply point of view went on diminishing as the Fourteenth Army moved forward. Simultaneous with the advance of the fighting troops, the supply and administrative services had also to move forward, and Chittagong replaced Imphal as the supply base when the Fourteenth Army advanced on Meiktila. To provision the forces south of Meiktila was, however, beyond the capacity of aircraft operating from Chittagong. The supply services had to establish a base further southward at Akyab. From here, too, it was considered that supplies would be economically transported only up to Toungoo. Hence another move to Ramree was essential to keep the forces supplied in the Rangoon area. The Fourteenth Army had therefore been pressing for the capture of Ramree and Chiduba islands so that air bases could be established there in time. In order to achieve this, Lieut-General Leese had opened the last Arakan Campaign in the middle of December 1944. The object of this campaign was twofold: firstly, to secure the bases for supplying the Fourteenth Army and, secondly, to release the Arakan forces for operations elsewhere. The XV Corps succeeded in achieving both these objects by its successful campaign down the coast of Arakan.[5]

CENTRAL BURMA

With the problem of supply bases during the dry season thus solved and Mandalay and Meiktila in Allied hands, there was nothing to stop Lieut-General Slim from launching his twin drive on Rangoon in an effort to reach there before the start of the rainy season. Lieut-Generals Leese and Slim both hoped that the Fourteenth Army would accomplish the task in time, despite the difficulties facing it.[6] Nevertheless, the possibility of failure had also to be taken into account. The results of such a failure would, no doubt, have been disastrous. In the words of Lieut-General Leese:[7]

---

[5] See *Arakan Operations*, published by C.I.S.H.S.
[6] Leese's *Despatch*, para 220.
[7] *Ibid.*

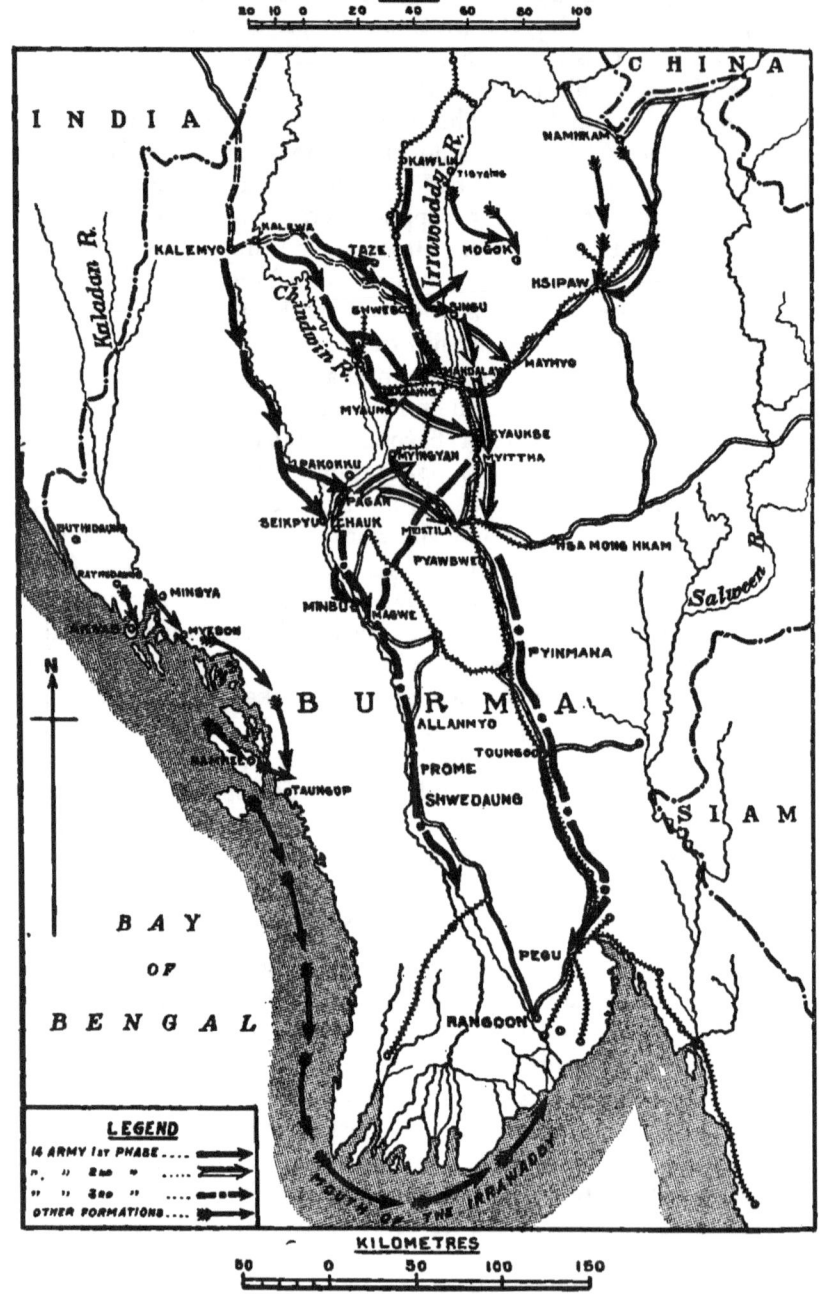

"The long land L of C—it is over 600 miles from MANIPUR ROAD railhead to MEIKTILA—was not designed to withstand monsoon conditions, as an important length of the road, running from KALEWA to SHWEBO, about 108 miles, was constructed to fair-weather standard only. Air supply on a considerable scale was in any case essential to supplement what came by land and river. But during the monsoon, flying conditions were often hazardous, and would certainly interrupt air supply altogether for periods, at a time when our land L of C was interrupted and possibly the I.W.T. traffic on the Chindwin was reduced too. Moreover, I knew, and the Americans had been quite candid and warned me, that if we did not get into RANGOON by June, their American transport aircraft which formed a large proportion of the theatre resources, would be taken off to CHINA. Thus we might well have the position where our troops, halted only a comparatively short distance from RANGOON by the monsoon rains, would have to be withdrawn back to MANDALAY or even to the CHINDWIN, with all the attendant losses in vehicles and morale, for reasons of supply."

Mention has been made earlier of an amphibious plan for the capture of Rangoon known as 'Dracula'. This was to be a combined operation but it had been postponed as the amphibious resources required for it were not available from the European theatre. In order to cover the possibility of the Fourteenth Army's failure to reach Rangoon from the north it was at this stage decided to carry out 'Dracula' in a modified form, with whatever resources were available. Details of this operation will be given in a following chapter;[8] it is sufficient here to mention that it was thought that with Rangoon in Allied hands, the forces in Lower Burma would not be stranded owing to lack of supply during the rainy season.

THE PLAN FOR THE DASH TO RANGOON

The Fourteenth Army had its own plan, operation 'Sob' for the capture of Rangoon by land.[9] The original intention was to advance down the two axes, the Irrawaddy and the railway in about equal strength. This was, however, ruled out owing to the difficulties of transport and shortage of aircraft. It was clear that it would be better to concentrate on one axis. The question was, which?[10] Since speed was essential, only a fully mechanised force could achieve

---

[8] See chapter XV.
[9] Slim: *Defeat Into Victory*, p. 482.
[10] *Ibid*, p. 483.

the object in time. Of the two axes, the eastern, along the railway line, seemed better suited for a mechanised force and was therefore selected for the main thrust. The plan in brief, for the capture of Rangoon from the north, was twofold:

(1) The 5th and 17th Indian Divisions were to lead the advance. These two divisions were to operate down the one main road between Mandalay and Rangoon along the railway axis. They were to adopt a method known in military parlance as "Leap-frogging" i.e. taking the lead by turns; the 17th Indian Division to move out first followed by the 5th Indian Division, one brigade of which had been flown to Burma for the second time, and the other two had come by road. The 19th Indian Division should arrive in Meiktila and take over from the 5th Indian Division, which should follow the 17th Indian Division. This was to be the main axis of advance to be conducted by the IV Corps, because it was already concentrated in the Meiktila area, about 50 miles to the south of the other Corps. Moreover the proposed route of the 5th and 17th Indian Divisions lay through a country suitable for fast moving tactics and both these divisions were already organised on a mechanical and air-transportable basis.

(2) Meanwhile the 7th and 20th Indian Divisions of the XXXIII Corps were to move along the river axis to capture Seikpyu and Chauk first, and then capture in succession Magwe, Yenangyaung, Prome and finally Rangoon, if possible before the other Corps.

In the words of Lieut-General Slim:

"It must not be thought that either of these axes was in any way ideal or comparable to the desert or Europe for rapid thrusts by mobile and armoured force. On each there was one single road off which it was often difficult to deploy even tanks. The open motorable country of the Central Burma plains had been left behind. Once the rains set in movement of wheels off the roads on both axes would be impossible. For the northern half of the two axes there was little to choose, but the farther south on the river axis the more the water crossings increased, all bridges would be blown, and unless an inordinate quantity of Bailey were carried serious delay must be expected there. The second factor was that the farther east we cut through the Japanese, the more of them would be left to cross the two Yomas, those jungle-covered jagged hills blocking their way either to Siam or South-East Burma. My aim was to reach Rangoon just before the monsoon. The Japanese west of the railway would then have to struggle out during the monsoon—a second retreat similar to that from Imphal to the Chindwin with, I hoped, the same consequences."[11]

Here the magnitude of the undertaking should be noted. "To reach Rangoon in time meant that the Fourteenth Army's advance had to average at least ten miles a day against opposition and despite demolitions—a formidable proposition".[12]

The new plan also involved a "Union Jack manoeuvre" which meant a cross-over of certain forces of the two Corps cutting each other's route diagonally. In order to bring the bulk of the XXXIII Corps on to the river axis, the 2nd British and 20th Indian Divisions had to move from north-east to south-west, whereas certain portions of the 5th Indian Division had to move from north-west to south-east to reach the railway axis. The 7th Indian Division of the IV Corps, which was already in the Irrawaddy Valley, was transferred to the XXXIII Corps and placed under its command on 29 March. The double object of this manoeuvre was to bring the two Corps into their separate areas of future operations and at the same time to comb out the areas on the routes of the cross-over.

SITUATION IN CHINA

Before we take up the narrative of operations of these two Corps, mention may here be made of another factor which threatened to disrupt the whole plan, namely a request made to the Supreme Allied Commander South-East Asia for the diversion of more troops and transport aircraft to China. We may describe this in the words of Lord Mountbatten himself:[13]

> "It was at this stage that it again became the turn of the Chinese to deal us our next routine blow. This time it was a serious threat of famine, and in order to relieve the famine the Generalissimo considered it necessary to reconquer vast areas of paddy fields to produce the necessary food. General Wedemeyer therefore asked me to send the American Mars Brigade (which had relieved Merrill's Marauders) and the remaining three Chinese divisions as well as all American air transport aircraft to China. I flew up and saw General Wedemeyer at Calcutta on his way to Washington, and then flew to Chungking to see the Generalissimo. After a series of talks we eventually hammered out a plan . . . I

---

[11] *Campaign of the Fourteenth Army*, op. cit., p. 29.
[12] Leese's *Despatch*, para. 218.
[13] *Strategy of the South-East Asia Campaign*, being a lecture by Admiral the Viscount Mountbatten of Burma to the Royal United Service Institute on 9-10-1946.

agreed to send back the American brigade to act as instructors to the Chinese and to pull out the other divisions as fast as the transport aircraft of the 14th U.S. Air Force could take them. The Mars Brigade were the only Americans we had fighting on land, and although they fought gallantly they required so much more air supply per man than a Chinese soldier that General Sultan agreed that they should be the first to be moved. I absolutely dug in my toes about releasing any further transport aircraft until we had reached Rangoon, which I prophesied would be by June."

SITUATION IN THE BEGINNING OF APRIL

Japanese Troops. After suffering heavy casualties at Meiktila and having lost a considerable portion of the Mandalay plain, the Japanese were engaged in a general withdrawal. The Japanese *15th Army* had suffered great losses and was scrambling back through the foothills, being chased and harassed by the Allied troops. The extent of the disorganisation in this army can be well illustrated by the contents of a captured Operation Order issued by its commander. One of its formations was directed in this order "to cope with any change in the situation". Such a general order is a clear evidence of the fact that the commander had lost control of the situation. Their other two armies *33rd* and *28th* were still effective fighting forces though most of their formations had lost much equipment, especially artillery.

Having realised that a situation would shortly develop in which there would be no strong field force between the Allied forces and Rangoon, *Headquarters 33rd Army* was hastily moved from northeast Burma to the railway axis south of Meiktila. Their object at this time was to collect the badly battered forces and reorganise them in two groups, one to dispute and prevent the Allied thrust towards Rangoon down the railway axis and the other to fight the Allied forces in the Irrawaddy Valley in an effort to keep them as far north as possible. The Japanese *33rd Army* was assigned the first task which it was to execute with the help of the *18th, 49th* and *53rd Divisions*. The second task of containing Allied forces in the Irrawaddy Valley was to be carried out by the *28th Army* with *Yamamoto Force* which was being steadily augmented by arrivals from other formations and from Arakan,. All were somewhat demoralised "but as always they would recover if allowed time."[14]

Allied Troops

Troops of the Fourteenth Army were, on the other hand, at the

[14] Slim: *Campaign of the Fourteenth Army*, p. 28.

EXPLOITATION PHASE
SITUATION 7 APRIL 1945

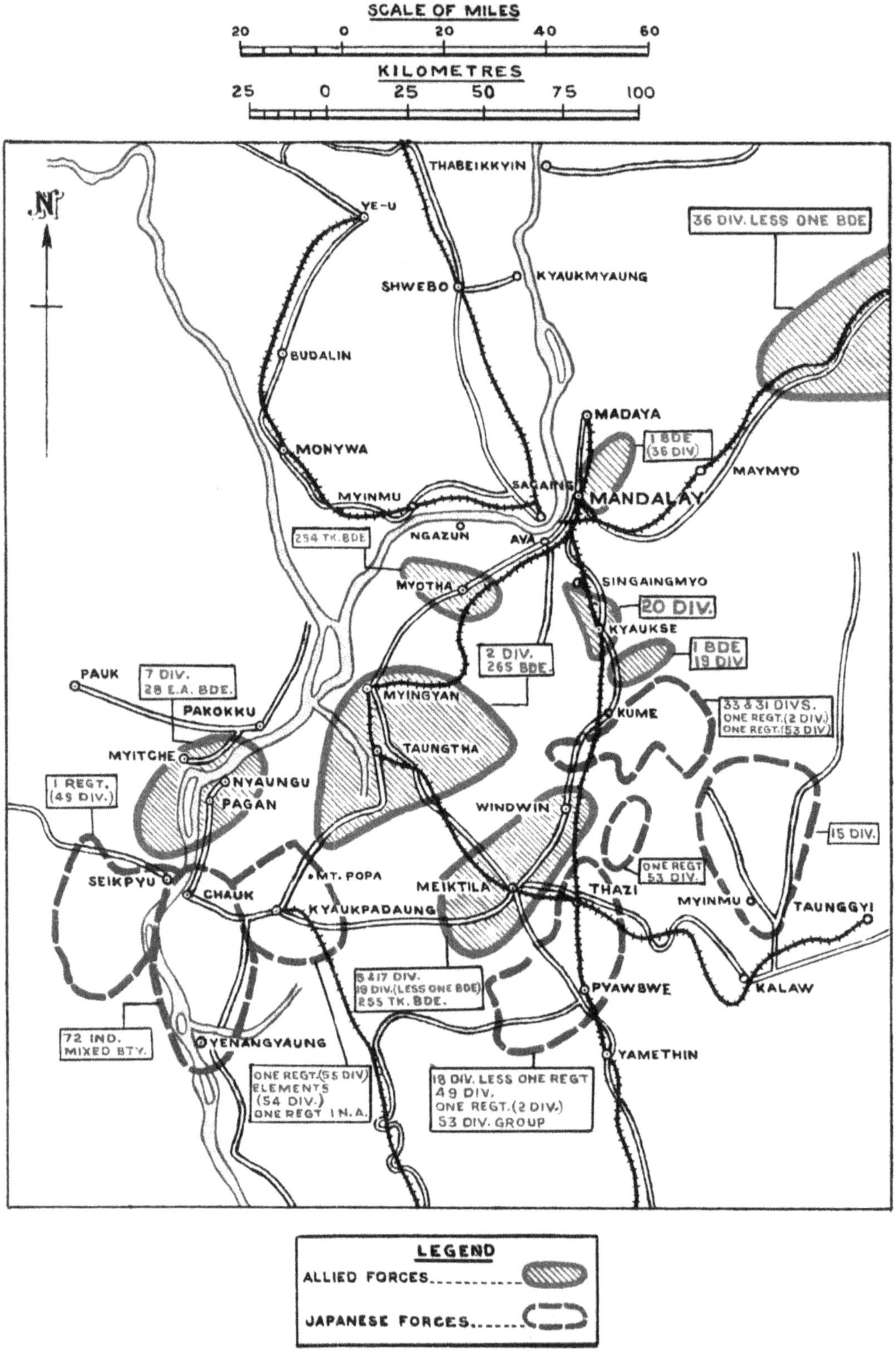

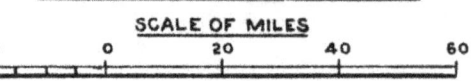

top of their form; "well trained, seasoned in battle, excellently led, and confident of their superiority over the Japanese."[15] They had fought and won victories. Their casualties, though considerable, had not been unduly heavy, and, in the case of Indian units, had been to a great extent replaced. The British battalions were reduced in numbers, but no guns had been lost either by the Indian or the British units.[16]

OPERATIONS

On 18 March 1945, Lieut-General Slim had issued an Operation Instruction to his Corps Commanders dividing the forthcoming operations into three phases: "the present battle, the regrouping stage and the advance south." The intention was stated thus:

"On completion of the task of destroying the Japanese forces in Central Burma, Fourteenth Army will:

(a) capture Rangoon at all costs and as soon as possible before the monsoon;
(b) capture Yenangyaung, Magwe and Prome;
(c) secure the area Myingyan-Mandalay-Maymyo-Chauk and the road and railway axis Meiktila to Rangoon."

The task of defeating the Japanese forces in Central Burma may be said to have been completed by the end of March 1954. The regrouping of forces and the plan of an advance to Rangoon on both axes was calculated to compel the Japanese either to surrender or, in the words of Lord Mountbatten, "run the gauntlet across the Irrawaddy valley, the Pegu Yomas, and the Sittang valley, before they could escape into Siam." The idea of Lieut-General Slim was "to throw a cordon round south-western Burma and lock up the Japanese during the monsoon, without supplies, and in highly malarial area."[17]

We may first describe the regrouping operations of the XXXIII Corps.

REGROUPING STAGE

2nd Division Operations to Capture Mount Popa. The 2nd British Division had broken out from its bridgehead in the beginning of March, and till the middle of the month was busy in mopping up to the south of Mandalay. On 26 March it commenced its move westwards towards Myingyan, preparatory to carrying out the crossover in accordance with the regrouping plan of the Fourteenth Army.

---

[15] Mountbatten's words in his *Report* to the Combined Chiefs of Staff, para 515.
[16] Slim: *op. cit.*, p. 28.
[17] Mountbatten's *Report*, para 520.

Having concentrated south of Myingyan by 28 March, its 5th Brigade moved south to Welaung as a preparation for the advance southwest towards Kyaukpadaung, in conjunction with the 7th Indian Division advancing on that place from the north.[16] The 268th Indian Lorried Brigade also moved southward simultaneously with the 2nd Division.

On 2 April, 2 Reconnaissance then leading the advance of the 2nd Division made contact with the Japanese at Legyi. Strong opposition was encountered there. In spite of an accurate air-strike on 4 April, the 5th Brigade failed to dislodge the hostile force which continued to resist for another five days. The terrain was such that the tanks could not give close support to infantry and the Japanese kept up jittering tactics. However, the place was finally taken on 9 April. By 12 April, 2 Dorset had reached and taken the high ground at PP 5844, against some opposition, and neutralised several Japanese bunkers by tank fire. Meanwhile the 268th Indian Infantry Brigade, starting its advance from Ngathayauk on 10 April, had reached the line of the road north-east of Kyaukpadaung on 12 April. There it came under the command of the 2nd Division, and co-operated with it in capturing Mount Popa.

Capture of Popa

Overlooking the road on which the 5th Brigade was moving was a high ground called Popa on which the Japanese were strongly established. Mount Popa is an extinct volcano about 500 feet in height whose steep slopes afforded excellent defence facilities. Here a force of about 600 Japanese disputed the passage of the 2nd Division and held out for about one week. Allied artillery and air-strikes continued to soften up the position until 20 April when information was brought that the position had been vacated during the night of 19/20 April. A column of the 5th Brigade then advanced without opposition down the road and made contact with the 268th Indian Lorried Brigade. The next few days were spent in putting stops south of Popa and in mopping up stragglers and stray parties of Japanese troops trying to escape south.

While the 5th Brigade was busy in capturing Mount Popa area, other elements of the 2nd Division were being flown out to India from Myingyan. The fly-out had begun on 11 April, and soon after the 5th Brigade and the remaining elements of the 2nd Division were all pulled back to that place and flown out. By 25 April, this division was completely out of Burma. There were two reasons for removing it from this theatre; firstly for administrative reasons it was necessary to reduce the forces in Central Burma by one division, and secondly this division was required as the follow-up division of the force for

---

[16] XXXIII Corps Account of Operation, Vol. IV, p. 151.

taking Rangoon from the sea and air to form part of the operation 'Dracula'. It was also during this period while the 2nd Division was engaged in the Popa operations, that the 7th Indian Division advancing south from Taungzin and down the east bank of the Irrawaddy had captured Kyaukpadaung on 12 April and Chauk on 18 April. By the clearing of Popa area, therefore, the left flank and rear of the 7th Indian Division were secured for the forthcoming advance towards Yenangyaung. Apart from this advantage, the capture of Popa bastion was not of much significance in itself. It was expected that in the event of a break-through in the east, on the main axis of advance, which was imminent, a complimentary withdrawal would be staged by the Japanese in the Popa area also.

Capture of Kyaukpadaung and Chauk

The tasks of the 7th Indian Division, as outlined in the orders received early in April, were (i) to capture the oilfields area and (ii) to clear the west bank of the Irrawaddy, southwards, and at the same time to cut off the Japanese Forces withdrawing eastwards from Arakan. In order to carry out these tasks, it was decided that the 33rd Indian Infantry Brigade should capture Kyaukpadaung and Gwegyo. The former was a strategically important place on account of its situation, almost in the centre of the valley. It was connected by road to many other important places in Burma such as Meiktila to the east, Chauk and Singu to the west, Nyaungu to the north-west, Ngathayauk to the north, Taungtha (via Welaung) to the north-east and Yenangyaung and Magwe to the south-west. It was also the terminus of a railway line which, passing through Myothit, linked it up with Pyinmana on the main Meiktila-Rangoon line, about sixty miles north of Toungoo. Moreover, only a few miles to the north-east of Kyaukpadaung lay Mount Popa also. Yenangyaung to the south-west was also well defended. The capture of Kyaukpadaung, (lying as it did between Mount Popa and the oil-town) would not only cut the link between two Japanese strong-points, but would place the 33rd Indian Infantry Brigade in a very suitable position from which it might attack Chauk from the south-east while the 89th Indian Infantry Brigade attacked it from the north. After the capture of Chauk a joint attack by the two brigades might be made against Yenangyaung. The divisional plan for the capture of these places was therefore chalked out as follows:

(a) The 33rd Indian Infantry Brigade advancing from Taungzin would capture Kyaukpadaung, turn west from there, capture Gwegyo and enter Chauk from the south-east.[19]

[19] OO No. 10, 8 April 1945: "33rd Indian Infantry Brigade Group will capture Kyaukpadaung with a view to subsequent operations against Popa or Gwegyo—Chauk."

(b) The 89th Indian Infantry Brigade, on the river axis, would move south and capture the northern end of Chauk while the 33rd Indian Infantry Brigade entered it from the south-east.[20]

Kyaukpadaung. On 11 April, the 33rd Indian Infantry Brigade reached the line Pyinma Chaung, some eight miles north-north-west of Kyaukpadaung without any opposition. This concentration was achieved undetected, by two night marches. To do this, the soldiers kit was cut down to the barest minimum and no lights were allowed at night.[21] It was however not considered desirable to attack the place from the north as all approaches from that direction were overlooked by Mount Popa which was at that time in the hands of the Japanese. Hence, during the night of 11/12 April, a company from 4/15 Punjab made a flanking move west of Kyaukpadaung, successfully avoided Japanese patrols and took the high ground PP 4727—an isolated feature to the south of the town. From there an excellent view of the area was obtained and artillery fire directed accurately against the Japanese positions.

On the morning of 12 April, 4/1 Gurkha Rifles cleared the Japanese from the outskirts of the town, who were surprised as they had not expected the attack to come so early. They were, however, strongly entrenched in a rocky feature called Pagoda Ridge, immediately to the west of the town and dominating the road to Chauk. This feature was attacked by 4/1 Gurkha Rifles at 1400 hours under cover of heavy artillery and mortar fire, and captured after two hours of fighting, the Japanese garrison of nearly two companies being completely wiped out.[22] Meanwhile 4/15 Punjab attacked the town from the right flank of 4/1 Gurkha Rifles and took Point 1886 while the Queens had executed a left hook. The patrols found the town clear during the night, and on the 13th morning it was in Allied hands.[23] Large stocks of equipment and ammunition were also captured including an howitzer in working order with eighty rounds of ammunition. Some new engineer equipment was still in camouflaged crates under trees by the side of the road when the victorious troops entered the town. It was clear that the Japanese had left in a great hurry. A light air-strip was built in the place the next day. In the meantime other troops had occupied Ingyaung and Sebauk, five miles north-east of Kyaukpadaung, having overcome resistance by small parties of hostile troops on the track from Ngathayauk.

---

[20] While this move against Chauk was being made by these two brigades, 114th Brigade on the west bank of the river was to continue advancing southwards, and 268th Brigade (as described already) was to co-operate with the 2nd Division and operate towards Popa.
[21] 33rd Indian Infantry Brigade Admn Order No. 8, 7 April.
[22] 7th Division History (Draft) 601/8445/H.
[23] 33rd Indian Infantry Brigade War Diary, 601/324/WD

Gwegyo. The next objective of the 33rd Indian Infantry Brigade was Gwegyo, a small village on the road connecting Yenagyaung to Chauk. It was expected that strong resistance would be met at this place so as to hold the road open long enough for the Japanese forces in Chauk to withdraw towards Yenangyaung. On the night of 13/14 April, a company of 1 Queens with observation post successfully infiltrated into the southern group of hills overlooking Gwegyo, and found it unoccupied. By first light on 14 April, 4/15 Punjab had established a secure base one and a half miles from Gwegyo astride the Gwegyo-Kyaukpadaung road. In this were concentrated the artillery supporting the attack. At 0800 hours 1 Queens less one company in lorries supported by a squadron of tanks entered Gwegyo after a wide outflanking move from the south along the Yenangyaung road. After a short sharp fight Gwegyo was captured, and the whole garrison, bewildered by the sudden sweep, annihilated with the exception of one who was taken prisoner.[24] The loss of this place was also a severe blow to the Japanese as Gwegyo controlled the road junction through which all mechanical transport between Yenangyaung and Chauk used to pass.

SINGU, CHAUK AND SEIKPYU

With Gwegyo and Kyaukpadaung in Allied hands, a two-brigade attack on Chauk could be made, by the 89th Indian Infantry Brigade from the north and the 33rd Indian Infantry Brigade from the southeast. Considerable hostile activity was reported between Chauk and Sale but there was no indication of a Japanese pull-out from Chauk or Singu. Operation Instruction No. 94 was issued on 17 April ordering the capture of Singu, Chauk and Seikpyu. Accordingly the 33rd Indian Infantry Brigade handed over the responsibility for the protection of Gwegyo to 7/2 Punjab and moved on Chauk to attack it from the south and south-east, while the 89th Indian Infantry Brigade moved to capture Singu. The oilfields of Chauk were situated amongst a spine of hills running north and south with ribs stretching towards the Irrawaddy and ending in low cliffs. Deep, steep side nullas separated the ridges breaking the intervening area into a mass of broken ground. In the south-east corner of the oilfield lay a hill feature which dominated the area of Chauk and also the main road from Gwegyo. On the night of 16/17 April, 4/15 Punjab succeeded in infiltrating patrols on to the hill feature, which was found to have been evacuated by the Japanese. The patrol was at once built up to a company strength. 4/1 Gurkha Rifles and 4/15 Punjab then moved forward during the day and built up in strength

---

[24] 7th Division History, *op. cit.* 601/8445/H. The 33rd Indian Infantry Brigade War Diary however mentions 5 Japanese taken prisoners. 601/324/WD/Pt. II.

on the hill. At first light on the 18th, these two battalions moved forward with tank support towards the town of Chauk itself. However, it was found that the Japanese had evacuated the town the previous night, escaping by boat across the river to Seikpyu and over land through Palin towards Yenangyaung.[25] Singu was captured without opposition on the same day by the 89th Indian Infantry Brigade which established contact in the evening with the leading troops of the other brigade which had captured Chauk earlier. The latter found a considerable quantity of equipment left behind by the Japanese in Chauk.[26] Sale was also occupied by 7/2 Punjab on the same day, thus closing all the routes leading south from Chauk.

The occupation of Chauk on 18 April was followed two days later by the occupation of Lanywa and Seikpyu, without opposition, on the west bank of the Irrawaddy by the 114th Indian Infantry Brigade, the gun captured at Kyaukpadaung being used for bombarding it. Seikpyu, it may be recalled, was the place from where the Japanese had driven out the East Africans in February towards Letse.

CAPTURE OF YENANGYAUNG

The 33rd Indian Infantry Brigade then started regrouping for further operations on the road Gwegyo—Yenangyaung. But in view of the fact that the Japanese had been completely surprised, it was ordered to move at once towards Yenangyaung with 7/2 Punjab protecting its left flank.

The oilfield of Yenangyaung lay within an area about six miles long and four miles wide, surrounded by bare eroded hills, rising to a height of six hundred feet and ending in low cliffs on the Irrawaddy, which formed the fourth side of a rectangle. Within the circumference of the hills lay numerous deep nullas, ravines and precipices, which separated three main spurs which ran across the area from east to west. A network of excellent roads covered the whole area. The oilfield installations comprised a mass of oil derricks, smashed buildings, destroyed power houses and storage tanks and a large built-up area in Yenangyaung itself. The circumference of hills, and the spurs overlooking the main road junctions throughout the area, were covered by a mass of trenches and dug-outs. Along the river side, except at possible landing beaches, the defences were less strong. The road from the north crossed a ridge at mile 370 and dropped slowly to the Pin Chaung which was easily fordable. Thence it

---

[25] 7th Division History, F 601/8445/H.

[26] 33rd Brigade War Diary gives the following items captured: one river steamer sunk in shallow water, three 75-mm AA guns, three 15-mm guns, 40 lorries, one gun tractor, one diesel tractor, six staff cars and three jeeps, large dumps of ammunition and much oil machinery and equipment. 601/324/WD, Part II.

climbed steeply through a defile to the village of Twingon, just north of Yenangyaung.[27] In view of the potential strength of the defences, the divisional plan was that the 33rd Indian Infantry Brigade would establish a bridgehead on the hills surrounding the oilfields, while the 89th Indian Infantry Brigade would carry out an encircling move to cut the main road south of Yenangyaung, and then strike simultaneously with the other brigade into the main oilfields.

On the morning of 19 April, 1 Queens was moved in lorries to mile 376, on the Gwegyo-Yenangyaung road, while the rest of the brigade moved from Chauk to Gwegyo. During the night, 1 Queens established a patrol base two miles north of the Pin Chaung, on which the rest of the battalion closed. On the early morning of the 20th, patrols had reached the Pin Chaung. The battery of the 139th Field Regiment, which was supporting the Queens, fought a successful duel with the Japanese 75-mm guns which were covering the chaung crossing. Soon afterwards, 4/1 Gurkha Rifles arrived from Gwegyo and set off across country to Sale, a village on the Irrawaddy bank, eight miles north of Yenangyaung. No opposition on the ground was met, but the Japanese fired air bursts from anti-aircraft guns, which might indicate shortage or lack of artillery.[28] Dense columns of smoke were rising from the oilfields area, and it was obvious that the Japanese were carrying out demolitions on a big scale. The Queens patrols crossed the Pin Chaung and found that the far bank was not held in strength, and in view of this information, all available transport was rushed back to Gwegyo and 4/15 Punjab was embussed immediately and brought forward to mile 370. The artillery was also ordered to concentrate forward with the utmost speed.

As soon as the leading company of 4/15 Punjab had debussed, 1 Queens was ordered to cross the Pin Chaung and secure the crossing. Information was received from the locals that the Japanese were pulling out, hence it was decided that the 33rd Indian Infantry Brigade should attack Yenangyaung forthwith without waiting for the other brigade to move up. The Queens was then ordered to attack Twingon on a three company front, the two outside companies making a wide half circle with a view to establishing themselves astride the Twingon ridge. The centre company with tank and artillery support was ordered to capture the defile. The reserve company would then pass through and capture Twingon. The Japanese held strong positions in the defile, which was also blocked by a mass of heavy oilfield machinery. The initial attack was

---

[27] 7th Division History, *op. cit.*
[28] War Diary XXXIII Corps. 601/195/WD, Part II. See also 33rd Ind Inf Bde War Diary for 20 April.

successful and after considerable fighting the defile was captured, where were found a series of forty-gallon drums of petrol which the Japanese had hoped to roll down the road on the advancing tanks. However, the tanks had not fallen into the obvious trap and had succeeded in by-passing it. By 1730 hours, Twingon and the ridge were captured and a bridge secured from which attacks were launched to complete the capture of Yenangyaung.

Meanwhile, 4/1 Gurkha Rifles had reached Sale and had moved down the river bank to the mouth of the Pin Chaung. The Gurkhas were ordered to cross the chaung and infiltrate on to the ridge on the south bank, clearing it if possible by first light. This was successfully accomplished. On the early morning of 21 April, 1 Queens was firmly established at Twingon and 4/15 Punjab moved up a little later to join it. Both the battalions then cleared a corridor down which 4/15 Punjab passed round the eastern outskirts of the town and established itself to the south of the town, behind the Japanese forces, to prevent them withdrawing on to Magwe. Thus by 1700 hours the Japanese in Yenangyaung were completely surrounded on all sides except the Irrawaddy, which a large number of them succeeded in crossing during the night. Next morning the Gurkhas started to clear the villages north of the town and by midday they had made contact with 4/15 Punjab in the southern portion of Yenangyaung. The opposition had been intermittently fierce, but by the end of the day all the main features had been gained.[29]

With the exception of mopping up stray parties of Japanese troops, found hiding in caves and dug-outs, which went on for another two days, the capture of the oilfields had been completed. Much equipment, ammunition, guns and vehicles were captured in the town. Opposition, though fierce, had been much less than what had been anticipated and an operation which was expected to have required a division had been accomplished by a single brigade group. Only thirteen days had elapsed between the date the 33rd Indian Infantry Brigade had left the concentration area at Nyaungu and the final capture of Yenangyaung. During this time it had advanced a hundred and ten miles and fought three major engagements.

The speed of the advance of the 7th Indian Division had taken the Japanese completely by surprise and plans were quickly made to chase them and exploit the success. The plan thenceforward was:—

> (a) the 89th Indian Infantry Brigade to cross the river Irrawaddy at Kyaukse and advance on Salin from the south,

[29] XXXIII Corps War Diary, *op. cit.*

(b) the 114th Indian Infantry Brigade to advance as rapidly as possible on Salin from the north,

(c) the 33rd Indian Infantry Brigade to consolidate Yenangyaung and send strong fighting patrols with tanks towards Magwe, and

(d) the Chin Hills Battalion and Lushai Scouts to continue the advance southwards.

Before we take up the operations of the 7th Indian Division in pursuance of the above plan, it is necessary to see how the regrouping of the Fourteenth Army had taken place during April. As mentioned earlier in this chapter, the "Union Jack" manoeuvre involved the switching over of the 2nd British Division, the 20th Indian Division and the 268th Indian Infantry Brigade from the north-east to south-west across the lines of communication of the IV Corps. The moves of the 2nd Division and the 268th Indian Infantry Brigade leading to the capture of Mount Popa have already been described. It now remains to describe the movements of the 20th Indian Division during April 1945 to complete this phase of operations.

20TH INDIAN DIVISION

Capture of Kyaukse

After breaking out from its bridgehead on the south side of the loop of the Irrawaddy river early in March, the 20th Indian Division had moved towards Kyaukse, about 30 miles south of Mandalay on a two-brigade front. The third brigade (the 100th Indian Infantry Brigade) had moved south of Ngazun towards Myotha, which had been captured by it without much difficulty on 13 March. It then concentrated at Chaunggwa, 15 miles to the east on 18 March. From here the brigade was ordered to move southward to Wundwin area with the object of relieving pressure on the hard pressed troops in Meiktila. It moved 81 miles in three days, and passing through Pyinzi and Pindale reached Wundwin on 21 March. By this time, however, the Japanese pressure against Meiktila was relaxing and the 100th Indian Infantry Brigade was required to move north towards Kyaukse where the other two brigades of the division were meeting steadily increasing resistance. Thus by 27 March, all the three brigades were operating against that town and the villages around it.

The two brigades (32nd & 80th Indian Infantry Brigades) had already inflicted considerable losses on the Japanese troops in this area, but had been unable to take the town. On the arrival of the third brigade, they redoubled their efforts, the Japanese resistance began to decrease and, on 30 March, the 80th Indian Infantry Brigade with 9/12 Frontier Force Regiment captured Kyaukse without much opposition.

With the capture of Kyaukse, the Japanese intention to withdraw troops down the railway to Rangoon was defeated. The area between Mandalay and Meiktila having been cleared, the 20th Indian Division continued to drive the Japanese into the hills to the east of the road, until relieved by the 36th Division of General Sultan, which had now been put under the Fourteenth Army.

Under the new plan the next phase of the operations by the 20th Indian Division was to cut the Japanese communications to the oilfields area, to seize Magwe and link up with the 7th Indian Division to complete the switch over from the north-east to the south-west in accordance with the XXXIII Corps Operation Order No. 19 of 29 March 1945. It started its advance from Kyaukse area on 10 April. The divisional commander's plan was to advance as fast as possible down the axis of the road westward from Meiktila to Zayatkon and thence south to Magwe and Allanmyo. For a rapid advance two of its brigades were organised on a motor transport basis. This quick reorganisation was made possible by the fly-out of the 2nd British Division whose vehicles were made available to the 20th Indian Division.[30] The roads which the division had to use were little better than cart tracks and passed through a barren and rocky country, and considerable engineer work was required to make them fit for mechanical transport. Lack of water was another serious problem requiring careful planning in all the moves.

Before this phase of the move began, the 20th Indian Division had a few days' rest, though some of the troops continued the mopping-up operations. "Visits were organised to Mandalay and Maymyo and concert parties toured the divisional area."[31] The constitution of the division also underwent a change during these days, for all the British battalions were transferred to the 36th Division and the Indian battalions taken over from it.[32] The 1 Northamptons, however, remained under the command of the 32nd Indian Infantry Brigade for the first stage of the new advance.

The move began on 10 April, Major-General D. D. Gracey's task being to "strike at the Japanese rear at Magwe and Allanmyo."[33] The first objective was Taungdwingyi, 43 miles east-south-east of Magwe and roughly half-way between the main railway line and the Irrawaddy, and about 65 miles from the starting point of the 20th Indian Division. The 32nd Indian Infantry Brigade led the advance, and moving west and south from Zayetkon reached Kangyingon,

---

[30] Only a part of the 2nd Division was engaged in Mount Popa area as described earlier.
[31] A Short History of 20th Indian Division by Maj.-General D. D. Gracey. 601/1787/H.
[32] Ibid. The Indian battalions of 36th Division taken over by the 20th Indian Division were 2/8 Punjab, 1 Hyderabad and 1/1 Gurkha Rifles.
[33] Slim: *Defeat into Victory*, p. 491.

without making any contact with the Japanese. Contact was, however, established with some Burmese Guerillas of Aung San's army, which was then hostile to the Japanese, who stated that Natmauk was clear. Thereupon a part of the brigade moved towards Natmauk, which it reached and occupied on 12 April. Kyaungon was occupied on 13 April and Taungdwingyi reached on 14 April. The last place was an important road and rail junction of the Japanese communications linking their east and west fronts.[34] But the place was weakly held by some INA troops, the Japanese having considered a sudden attack here improbable on account of the bad roads and barren country between Taungdwingyi and the Allied troops.

Satthwa

Having completed the capture of Taungdwingyi, the 32nd Indian Infantry Brigade continued its advance southwards and reached Satthwa (17 April), some ten miles further south and found it unoccupied. But it pushed on without occupying it. On 18 April it was learnt that the Japanese had again occupied the place. The Royal Air Force made attack on the Japanese positions around Satthwa which was again reported to be clear on 24 April, and the advance to Allanmyo was then resumed.

The Japanese intention at Satthwa appears to have been to hold up the advance of the 20th Indian Division for a few days to gain time for their forces to withdraw further south. Their defences at this place were well prepared and possible reinforcements were pushed in for an offensive—defensive action. They, however, did not meet with much success as the 32nd Indian Infantry Brigade started an encircling movement to contain them while the 100th Indian Infantry Brigade continued the advance. Before they could be completely encircled, they pulled out of the village which the former brigade occupied.

From its bases at Taungdwingyi and Satthwa, the 32nd Indian Infantry Brigade sent out columns to secure the Japanese retreat routes from Magwe. The first, called Hobforce, consisting of 9/14 Punjab with a squadron of armoured cars and some artillery, established a firm base 15 miles south of Magwe on 15 April, and patrolled forward to the Yin Chaung crossing at PU 4341. A second armoured column, called Daveforce, consisting initially of a company of 4/2 Gurkha Rifles with the Deception unit and some medium machine-guns and anti-tank guns got into Myingun, on the east bank of the Irrawaddy without opposition, to control all the river craft. This column shot up and sank three boat loads of the Japanese troops trying to escape across the river to the west bank

[34] Leese's *Despatch*, para 230.

on 18 April. This force was strengthened and during the next two or three days it created considerable havoc on the river and on the east bank.[35]

CAPTURE OF MAGWE BY 80TH BRIGADE

The 80th Indian Infantry Brigade was in this interval ferried forward from Kyaukse through Meiktila to the Natmauk area, and from there it advanced down the road to Magwe on 17 April.[36] No exact information about Japanese strength was available, but opposition was not expected to be strong. The primary consideration in this move was to capture the airfields east of Magwe and to block the road Magwe-Yenangyaung, prior to the occupation of Magwe itself.

The advance guard, consisting of 150 RAC with 4 Dogra and a battery of 114 Field Regiment moved forward on 19 April and reached the causeway across the Kadaung Chaung. Opposition was very slight, 3/1 GR marching along the road occupied Nyaungbinywa. Two companies of the Bombay Grenadiers and a squadron of tanks of 150 RAC then swept into Magwe. Three anti-aircraft, one 75-mm and one anti-tank gun were captured during the day.[37]

Although Magwe had been captured on 19 April, the Japanese outside the town were ignorant of the fact as was proved during the night. The 4 Dogra Regiment laid a successful ambush during the night of 19/20 April at the causeway PU 3155 and an unsuspecting Japanese convoy, consisting of mechanical transport and bullock carts, moved into the trap.[38] They had no idea that Magwe had already been captured.

Mopping up and patrolling continued for the next few days during which some shelling of Magwe was carried out by the Japanese from the west bank of the river on 21, 23, and 24 April.[39] South of Magwe a hospital was found in which the patients refused to surrender and died resisting. At Kyingun PU 2243 there was another hospital where 53 patients—in the last stages of starvation—surrendered. These had been evacuated by the Japanese two or three months earlier from Arakan. Small parties of stragglers were caught from time to time, but on the whole it was considered a waste of time to search for them as they were so split up as to be of

---

[35] A Short History of 20th Indian Division *op. cit.*
[36] Composition of 80th Brigade for capture of Magwe was: HQ 80th Indian Infantry Brigade with Signals Section and Def. Coy. 9 Frontier Force Rifles, 4 Dogra, 1 Hyderabad, 3/1 Gurkha Rifles, 150 RAC (with two companies Bombay Grenadiers), one Squadron 11 Cavalry, 114 Field Regiment, VCP and tentacle.
[37] War Diary XXXIII Corps, Part VI.
[38] War Diary XXXIII Corps, Part VI.
[39] "80th Brigade received a little attention from Jap artillery causing three killed at Brigade Headquarters in Magwe." War Diary for 23 April, 601/196/WD

no effective nuisance value. It was therefore decided that Magwe should revert to Corps control and the 80th Indian Infantry Brigade freed to continue the pursuit further south.[40] This was effected on 24 April.[41] In other places also the 20th Indian Division was progressively relieved of responsibility; as it marched forward the newly taken places in the rear were handed over to the Corps troops.

The 20th Indian Division and the 7th Indian Division operations by this time had resulted in the oilfields area being cleared of Japanese hold. Large numbers of them were forced to the west bank of the river and those that remained on the east bank were split up into very small groups trying to escape. Their pursuit by the Allied troops continued.

On 21 April, XXXIII Corps' Operation Order No. 20 had been issued which laid down that the 20th Indian Division "will capture Prome with maximum speed." The task was assigned to the 100th Indian Infantry Brigade, which took over the 32nd Indian Infantry Brigade's transport for this purpose and prepared to move towards Prome rapidly supported by 3 DG.[42]

TO ALLANMYO

The advance to Allanmyo by the 100th Indian Infantry Brigade began on 24 April from Satthwa which is at milestone 270 on the the Magwe-Rangoon road. The brigade was split up into two groups for this operation.[43] Group "A" marched 20 miles to Pozut on 25 April without opposition. Here about 100 Japanese fought a rearguard action with them. One of the tanks accompanying the group was knocked out by fire from a Japanese 75-mm gun in the initial stages of the engagement. The opposition was however easily overcome by 4/10 Gurkha Rifles (with tank support). The column advanced two more miles further south before harbouring for the night. Another 18 miles were covered on 26 April, some delay being caused on account of a demolished bridge on the way. The advance continued next day also when the column reached the outskirts of Allanmyo, having overcome some opposition at Shwenyaungbin with the help of a cab-rank air-strike. Real opposition was encountered

---

[40] Responsibility for Magwe was taken over by 101 HAA, 44 LAA and the Chamars under the command of CCRA.

[41] Another reason for relieving 80th Bde was that the brigade headquarters was sited on a too visible hill in a pagoda and had to fight frequent gun-duels with the Japanese across the river.

[42] 32nd Brigade and 100th Brigade were at this time in the Tangdwingyi and Satthwa area from where strong columns were already probing towards the west and south-west.

[43] Group A consisted of 4/10 GR, One Sqn & One TP 11 Cav, One Sqn 7 Cav, One Tp A/TK and One Troop Fd Arty. Group B consisted of Bde HQ, 14 FFR, MG Coy, One Sqn 11 Cav less one Tp, FD Regt less One Tp, and One Bty A/Tk less One Tp. 1/1 Gurkha Rifles remained at Satthwa.

at milestone 224 on the outskirts of Allanmyo, where the advance was again held up by an extensive minefield where two tanks were knocked out in the area of milestone 224. Next day (28 April) the battle for the town of Allanmyo was joined in right earnest and the Japanese resisted stubbornly. The Allied tanks were unable to find a way round to the east but their frontal pressure supported by 14 Frontier Force Rifles steadily pushed the defenders out. Nearly a hundred Japanese lost their lives and five guns were captured or destroyed. By the evening of the 28th two-thirds of the town had been occupied by the 100th Indian Infantry Brigade and the advance continued towards Prome on the 29th after clearing Allanmyo completely.[44]

TO PROME

Resistance was again met at the Bwetgyi Chaung, 12 miles south of Allanmyo on 29 April. This was broken and a decisive defeat inflicted on the Japanese troops who were skilfully encircled. A cab-rank provided by the aircraft of 11 Squadron was in attendance and carried out offensive patrols against targets indicated by VCP on the ground. The advance to Prome was resumed, and in spite of many destroyed bridges on the way, and the Japanese shelling from both banks of the river Payalo, MS 207 was reached on 30 April, and MS 195½ on 1 May, from where Prome was only about 15 miles. Next day, during the last lap of the advance to Prome no opposition was met on the way and the town itself was found clear of the Japanese, except for some isolated stragglers who were mopped up. On the 3rd, much to their surprise, the 100th Indian Infantry Brigade troops entered Shwedaung (10 miles to the south of Prome) without any opposition at all. In the meantime, behind this rapid advance, the 20th Indian Division build-up was going on in Allanmyo. The 32nd Indian Infantry Brigade had concentrated forward close behind the 100th Indian Infantry Brigade, and the 268th Indian Infantry Brigade had also reached Allanmyo on 30 April, and the divisional headquarters opened there on 1 May 1945. The position on this front on 1 May was as follows:—

(1) 20th Indian Division was concentrating in Allanmyo and had already started to advance south with the object of taking Prome (taken on 2 May).
(2) 268th Indian Infantry Brigade was concentrated in Allanmyo preparing for operations west of the Irrawaddy.
(3) 7th Indian Division less two brigades was established in Magwe.
(4) Corps artillery in an infantry role was responsible for the area Natmauk—Taungdwingyi—Satthwa.

[44] WD 20th Ind Div, April 1945.

(5) Corps Headquarters was at Magwe.
(6) 32nd Indian Infantry Brigade of the 20th Indian Division was preparing to take over from the 100th Indian Infantry Brigade and lead the advance along the Prome—Rangoon road.

We may now leave the XXXIII Corps at this stage and turn back to the main offensive of the Fourteenth Army by the IV Corps down the Meiktila—Rangoon railway axis.

CHAPTER XIV

The Dash to Rangoon—IV Corps
(Along the road and railway axis)

While the XXXIII Corps moved down the river axis in April 1945, the IV Corps drove rapidly along the primary axis of the southward drive, namely the road and railway between Mandalay and Rangoon. This axis was selected for the main thrust because of the possibility of speedier advance on this than on the river axis. On the other hand, it was certain that the Japanese would resist fiercely on this route and do all in their power to prevent the Fourteenth Army troops from reaching Rangoon before the monsoon.[1] They had, at this time, in the whole of Burma, one division completely intact and eight weak divisions;[2] thus the total strength of their infantry was estimated to be equivalent to about four and a half Indian infantry divisions. Though not inconsiderable in numbers, the Japanese troops were showing signs of tiredness, their supply system was rather shaky and there was little hope of reinforcements or equipment reaching them from outside. In addition, the local population was gradually turning hostile. The Japanese were, however, hopeful of holding southern Burma, since, as General Kimura put it, "tactically we considered south Burma much easier to hold than central Burma, since it had the natural defence of the Pegu Yomas."[3] The essential thing, therefore, from the Allied point of view was not to allow the Japanese any time to reorganise their men and defences, and to reach Rangoon before the monsoon. This would explain the emphasis on speed in the Operation Instruction of 5 April issued by the IV Corps: "Speed is all important and risks must be accepted to obtain it. Every day is precious."[4] Hence the instruction "to secure Toungoo with all possible speed as a preliminary to further operations southwards."

The divisions mainly involved in this advance to Rangoon were the 5th and the 7th Indian Divisions. The first stage of the advance to Toungoo was divided into three phases:—

(i) Capture of Pyawbwe by 7 April. This was to be accomplished by the 17th Indian Division with a squadron of 16 Cavalry, tanks and artillery.

---
[1] This was the IV Corps appreciation of Japanese intentions on 5 April 1945. See Appendix A to IV Corps Operation Instruction No. 139.
[2] *Ibid.* The one intact division was the *55th Division* located in south-west Burma.
[3] SEATIC Bulletin No. 242, p. 70.
[4] IV Corps Operation Instruction No. 139.

(ii) The 5th Indian Division (less the 9th Brigade Group)[5] to pass through the 17th Indian Division positions in Pyawbwe and secure an airfield at Pyinmana by 15 April. The 17th Indian Division would then follow up and take over the protection and further development of Pyinmana.

(iii) The 5th Indian Division to proceed towards and capture Toungoo by 25 April, the 9th Brigade Group being flown in from Meiktila for its assistance.[6]

All forces during these operations were to be supplied entirely by air. The plan for maintaining the forces during the rapid advance was that units would move with the maximum supplies that might possibly be carried in the vehicles allotted. Airfields were to be captured or constructed on the way and the daily maintenance collected from there, if these were within the range of the mechanical transport of a unit. If not, their daily supplies were to be dropped until a new advanced airfield was secured or constructed.[7]

17TH INDIAN DIVISION MOVES OUT

Leaving a garrison in Meiktila, the 17th Indian Division set out on 30 March for Pyawbwe, a distance of about 24 miles to the south-east. It had good natural defensive positions, and the Japanese, realising the impracticability of making any determined stand against the Allied forces at any place south of Pyawbwe, had made every endeavour to collect as much of their forces as possible to defend this place. The Commander *33rd Japanese Army* withdrew the *18th Division* through Thazi to take up positions to the north of Pyawbwe. The *53rd Division* of the *15th Army* was ordered to occupy positions west of Pyawbwe while the *49th Division* was to act as a rear-guard and delay the advance from Meiktila. Further to the east, the *15th Division*, after extricating itself from the Mandalay-Meiktila area, was expected to take up defence of the Thazi-Loilem road or reinforce the defences on the railway line.

The plan of advance by the 17th Indian Division to move down on Pyawbwe from three directions was as follows:

Firstly, the 99th Indian Infantry Brigade Group was to move east from Meiktila and attack Thazi, whence it was to advance south parallel to the main road and seize the high ground north of Pyawbwe, between the main road and the railway.

---

[5] 9th Brigade Group was to be air-transported afterwards.
[6] While the 17th and 5th Indian Divisions advanced south, the 19th Indian Division was to remain behind and destroy any Japanese still remaining in the areas around Meiktila such as Thazi or Wundwin. It was also to take up from the 5th Indian Division the duties of protecting the air-strips at Meiktila and Thedaw and patrol on Meiktila-Kyaukpadaung road up to mile 24.
[7] Para 34 of Operation Instruction No. 139 *op. cit.*

Secondly, the 48th Indian Infantry Brigade Group was to move on the main road followed by the divisional headquarters and the 63rd Indian Infantry Brigade. The latter was to leave the main road south of Yindaw and proceed via Yanaung securing P 900, south-east of Yanaung, and then attack Pyawbwe from the west.

Thirdly, Claudcol,[8] an armoured column, was to secure Yanaung, if possible earlier than the 63rd Indian Infantry Brigade, and then proceed to Ywadan where it was to split into two, the main force cutting the main road at MS 306 and a detachment proceeding to Yamethin at MS 300.

The 99th Indian Infantry Brigade moved towards its objective on 31 March. 1/3 Gurkha Rifles reported the area up to mile 10 on Thazi road clear of Japanese occupation. During the night of 31 March/1 April, 6/15 Punjab pushed forward of Kungyanyo and in the morning about 100 Japanese troops were located at LL 500293 and considerable movement was observed towards Kanzwe. Airstrikes were put down on Kanzwe and Katkyi-in, and these villages were freed from hostile occupation by midday. In the afternoon, 6/15 Punjab moved forward establishing platoons at these two villages and Segyi. The rest of the brigade concentrated at Pyinthe (MS 7). 1/3 Gurkha Rifles patrols pushing south reported that Thazi village and pagoda area (LL 426270) were occupied by the Japanese, where it appeared they had a fairly strong force. Hence the 99th Indian Infantry Brigade was ordered to leave a holding force in the area of Katkyi-in and attack the Japanese forces in Thazi village and Okpo. Consequently on 2 April, one company of 6/15 Punjab was left at Katkyi-in and the rest of the brigade moved forward. 6/15 Punjab (less one company) supported by a squadron of 9 R Horse consolidated in the pagoda area, but an advance further south was opposed by gun fire from a nulla LL 4325. 1/3 Gurkha Rifles also met with opposition from a channel north of Okpo where 300 Japanese troops were believed to be entrenched.

During the night of 2/3 April, the Japanese advanced close to Kanzwe and began digging in. This compelled the independent company of 6/15 Punjab to withdraw west of Kungyanyo. On 3 April, 1/3 Gurkha Rifles cleared Okpo and captured a 75-mm mountain gun. 6/15 Punjab then attacked Zidaw late in the afternoon, without being able to capture it. As a result, the 99th Indian Infantry Brigade could not rapidly move south if time were wasted in further attempts to capture Thazi. Hence, on 4 April, the brigade was ordered to contain Thazi and move south clearing all the villages in its path.[9] It left the Okpo area and moved across country parallel

[8] Under Brig. Claud Pert.
[9] Capture of Thazi was entrusted to a Brigade of 19th Division with 21 Mountain Regiment in support. Isolated pockets which could not be cleared were often by-passed in this campaign in order to maintain the rapidity of the advance.

Men of the 1st Sikh Light Infantry crawl up a nullah prior to dislodging the Japanese from a hill position south of Pyawbwe

Allied convoys driving on Rangoon frequently met with blown-up bridges. They forded the rivers helped by bull-dozers.

Major-General
E. C. Mansergh
Commander
5th Indian Division

Tanks and troops of 4/7 Rajput advance on a village during Fourteenth Army drive on Rangoon

to the main road while the 48th Indian Infantry Brigade moved down the road axis followed by the 63rd Indian Infantry Brigade.

Kandaung and Yewe

On the main road, the patrols of the 48th Indian Infantry Brigade found Kandaung occupied by the Japanese. A company of 4/12 Frontier Force Regiment based on MS 333 tried to get into the village on the night of 1/2 April, but was unable to penetrate it as it was strongly held, especially from the south end. On 3 April, the brigade left its harbour at Lungingyi to attack Kandaung. An air-strike was put down on the village at 1000 hours followed by an artillery concentration. The infantry attack went in at 1300 hours. Some progress was made towards the evening into the southern part of the village but there was little time to clear the whole village. During the night of 3/4 April, however, the Japanese kept up jittering the 4 Frontier Force Regiment position, and at 0430 hours they put down a heavy defensive fire lasting for 15 minutes preparatory to evacuating the village. At 0500 hours they had moved out of Kandaung taking at least three guns with them, though arrangements had been made for 1/7 Gurkha Rifles to attack Kandaung from the east on the morning of 4 April. The village was found to be heavily mined and booby-trapped and three lorries were blown off as they entered it.[10]

1/7 Gurkha Rifles moved up to Yewe on 4 April, where it was believed the forces withdrawing from Kandaung had retired. Stiff resistance was met in this area but by 1700 hours two-thirds of Yewe was cleared by the Gurkhas. Fighting continued until dark but the Japanese held on to the remaining one-third area and the Gurkhas harboured for the night in the occupied area. Row after row of bunkers were encountered in the village and the tanks and infantry approaching these positions came under heavy and accurate mortar fire.

Next day, 5 April, a squadron of Deccan Horse attacked the remaining uncleared portion of Yewe in support of 1/7 Gurkha Rifles and the place was finally cleared towards the afternoon. Some Japanese troops managed to break to the south but suffered considerable loss in men; some guns and wireless sets were also captured. 1 West Yorks with tank support occupied Kalaywa, just north of Yindaw, on the same day, but the latter was strongly held by the Japanese and patrols failed to get into it.[11]

Yindaw By-passed

Yindaw was a natural defensive position with a high bund

---

[10] 17th Indian Division War Diary. 601/254/W.D. Part III.
[11] Brief account of 17th Indian Division Operations, 5 March-6 May 1945, 601/254/WD Part III.

running all round it. One side of the village was on a lake and there was no tankable area apart from the main road. It was garrisoned by probably 1000 Japanese troops who were determined to carry out their orders to delay the advance until the rains broke. They were prepared to die to the last man and were particularly strong in anti-tank guns, which, during the next three days' fighting, never fired a round against infantry. All this was later borne out by captured orders and maps and the statement of a prisoner of war. For three days Yindaw was bombed from the air and shelled from the ground almost incessantly but the place did not fall. Then, in order to avoid further delay, it was decided to by-pass it altogether; the 99th Indian Infantry Brigade to the east and the remainder of the 17th Indian Division moving round the west. This was completed by 8 April.

During the process of by-passing Yindaw, the 99th Indian Infantry Brigade moving east of Yindaw contacted some Japanese in Kyattwinkala and killed many and captured some guns and swords. Meanwhile, the 48th Indian Infantry Brigade had again reached the road (south of Yindaw) and found Sadaung too strongly held by the Japanese for advance columns to deal with. 4 Frontier Force Regiment attacked Sadaung and a group of villages along the road axis and cleared Sadaung by 1600 hours on 8 April. About 100 Japanese broke and ran south out of the village, and infantry and tanks had 'rough shooting' in flat scrub country. Myenigon, however, could not be cleared that day and some Japanese troops also remained in some other villages of that group. During the night they left their positions leaving much equipment and stores. The divisional headquarters and the 48th Indian Infantry Brigade harboured at Sadaung, where they were jittered most of the night.

Meanwhile Claudcol whose task it was to capture Yanaung and then move on to Ywadan, had reached a nulla 2 miles north of Yanaung on 7 April. Here a bridge had been blown up and a deep nulla had made diversion impracticable without considerable labour. This was, however, accomplished and Claudcol captured Yanaung and Pt 900 (LQ 4191) on 8 April. On the far side of Pt 900 many Japanese troops were seen hiding in deep nullas. Mortars caught them as they tried to get out of the nullas and many were killed. On 9 April, Claudcol completed its move to cut the main road south of Pyawbwe and sent a detachment to Yamethin. Meanwhile, the 63rd Indian Infantry Brigade moving across difficult country had reached Kyauktaung and by 9 April Pyawbwe was encircled on three sides, leaving only a small escape route to the south-east. Some Japanese were understood to have used that route and escaped.[12]

---

[12] 17th Division flash to IV Corps at 1300 hours on 9 April. See IV Corps War Diary G Branch.

Pyawbwe

On 9 April, the 99th Indian Infantry Brigade advanced and 1 Sikh Light Infantry captured the high ground north of Pyawbwe, without much trouble, but was shelled from the south by two 75-mm guns. The troop of tanks which had supported this action went south towards the airfield area LL 5000 and made contact with the Japanese troops established in a bunker in the waterworks area. At 1300 hours, the Japanese shelled the position held by the Sikhs and caused fairly heavy casualties. By dusk, however, one company of 6/15 Punjab was established on Pt 796 as also a patrol base by 1/3 Gurkha Rifles at Pt 825.

Meanwhile 1/7 Gurkha Rifles of the 48th Indian Infantry Brigade, after clearing the Dahatkan group of villages, moved further south along the road to Kinda. But one 15-cm and two 75-mm guns fired by the Japanese from Pyawbwe side prevented movement of vehicles on the road from Nyaungnwe Taung onwards. The Gurkhas were, therefore, forced to withdraw and harbour with the rest of the brigade to the north of Nyaungnwe village.

On the morning of 10 April, 1 Yorks swept southwards on the west side of the road but was held up by heavy sniper and light machine-gun fire from the east of the road near Pt 770. This prevented the British troops from making any movement past MS 314½ even by organising wide detours to the west of the main road. Thereupon 6/15 Punjab and 1/3 Gurkha Rifles of the 99th Indian Infantry Brigade attacked Pyawbwe waterworks and Pt 770 respectively. In the initial sweep to the waterworks, 6/15 Punjab brushed aside opposition and drove away many Japanese troops towards the east where they were caught in the open by a squadron of tanks which had been sent on an independent mission to cut the road eastward from Pyawbwe. The waterworks area itself was, however, heavily defended. Here the country was very thick and water channels were untankable. The first attack failed to capture the waterworks but one company of 6/15 Punjab was established at the Pagoda LL 513002. In the afternoon another attack was launched, but the troops failed to enter the waterworks. Meanwhile, 1/3 Gurkha Rifles moving towards Pt 770 found that area to be a virtual maze of deep nullas teeming with Japanese troops in trenches and fox-holes. The infantry worked with grenades, mortars were extensively used and 21 Mountain Regiment gave magnificent support. 1/3 Gurkha Rifles gradually pushed its way towards Pt 770. Two 47-mm guns west of this point, which held up the vehicles, and numerous light machine guns which had held up the infantry of the 48th Indian Infantry Brigade along the main road, were captured and over 100 Japanese troops were driven to the south-west in front of the 48th Indian Infantry Brigade. It took 1/3 Gurkha Rifles one whole day to clear the area up to Pt 770. The next morning, 11 April, found the waterworks deserted by the Japanese, and 6/15 Punjab entered unopposed. The 99th Indian Infantry Brigade thereupon concentrated in this area and left Pt 770.

As mentioned earlier, the 48th Indian Infantry Brigade had been held up on the road by the Japanese guns fired from Pt 770 Once these guns were overcome by 1/3 Gurkha Rifles, it continued its advance. Meanwhile 4 Frontier Force Regiment with tanks had carried out a sweep south and cleared the whole of Pyawbwe cantonment up to the railway, and 9 Border had completely overcome Japanese opposition in the railway station and railway embankment area. The 63rd Indian Infantry Brigade had occupied the western half of Pyawbwe on the 10th, and when the Japanese left on 11 April the whole area to the south was also occupied by this brigade. Claudcol went smashing its way to Yamethin, found it unoccupied and withdrew to join the main body. The battle for Pyawbwe and the surrounding area was thus completed by 11 April 1945, and the first task of the "Black Cat" division was over. During these operations, the 17th Indian Division claimed that more than 1000 Japanese had lost their lives, and it had captured or destroyed eleven guns in addition to some tanks and other equipment.[13]

The fight for Pyawbwe was the last big clash with the Japanese which sealed the fate of Rangoon. Many other sharp engagements took place before Rangoon was captured on 2 May, but it was at Pyawbwe that the Japanese offered any organised resistance. Their *33rd Army*, rapidly reorganised after the fall of Mandalay and Meiktila, was completely defeated here and suffered heavy losses in men and materials. The later fights on the way to Rangoon were directed against forces thrown piecemeal on to the railway axis, which were, at best, intended to delay or obstruct the advance to Rangoon, whereas at Pyawbwe a determined attempt was made to halt the advance.

5TH INDIAN DIVISION TAKES THE LEAD

Henceforward the plan was that the 17th Indian Division should halt at Pyawbwe for about a week while the 5th Indian Division would pass through it and continue the advance south towards Pegu. This division commanded by Major-General E. C. Mansergh, comprised the 9th, 123rd and 161st Indian Infantry Brigades. Leaving the 9th Indian Infantry Brigade at Meiktila under the command of the 19th Indian Division, the remaining two brigades of the 5th Indian Division marched out towards Pyawbwe to take over the lead from that point, with the immediate object of capturing Pyinmana and Toungoo.

---

[13] Sitrep from 17th Division to IV Corps up to 1800 hours 10 April.

It may be recalled that while advancing from Meiktila to Pyawbwe, the 17th Indian Division had by-passed Yindaw where the Japanese were strongly entrenched and had a garrison of about 500 men.[14] It was necessary, before the 5th Indian Division could advance that the few Japanese troops who still remained at Yindaw should be dealt with. The 161st Indian Infantry Brigade was detailed to operate against them. On 8 April, an airstrike was also delivered on Yindaw after which a company of 4/7 Rajput went out to reconnoitre the village and was engaged by more than forty Japanese in the outskirts; many more were supposed to be in the village. During the night of 8/9 April, stops were placed on all roads leading out of the village to prevent the Japanese from escaping in any direction. Much activity was however seen in the village and some Japanese troops did manage to escape, and a platoon of 3 Jat bumped against about twenty of them who were moving southeast. The garrison having thinned out during the night, there was no opposition when two companies of 4/7 Rajput attacked Yindaw on the morning of 9 April and occupied it.[15] Next day the 123rd Indian Infantry Brigade with the armoured column moved forward towards Pyawbwe to pass through the 17th Indian Division.

Yamethin

On 11 April, the 5th Indian Division began its operation to pass through the 17th Indian Division. In the lead was the 123rd Indian Infantry Brigade with, under command, tanks of the 7 Cavalry and 116 RAC, and the 18 Field Regiment. The brigade was divided into nine separate columns and numbered over 1200 lorries and tanks, trucks and jeeps, armoured cars and bridging vehicles.[16] Two squadrons of 116 RAC preceded by armoured cars reached a point south of Yamethin (300 miles from Rangoon) after passing through the town without any incident. But in the evening, as the next group—two batteries of guns and a company of 3 Jat—was entering the place, it was shot at and had to withdraw to harbour north of the town. It seemed that some Japanese troops had slipped into the town after the armoured column had passed through and dug themselves in the houses from where they offered stubborn resistance.[17] During the night of 11 April, therefore, the armoured column harboured to the south of the town and the infantry to the north. All around the hastily prepared positions of the split-up brigade, the Japanese jitter parties were most active.

Early in the morning of 12 April, four Japanese aircraft

---

[14] 5th Div Sitrep to 0900 hrs 9 April.
[15] 5th Division Log for April 1945 Sheet No. 86.
[16] Anthony Brett—James: *Ball of Fire*, p. 414.
[17] Signal message from 5th Indian Division, 2045 hrs, 12 April.

appeared and started strafing and bombing the rear columns of the 123rd Indian Infantry Brigade, north of Thitson Chaung. Flying low over the road these aircraft destroyed 12 ammunition lorries. At 1000 hours two companies of 7 York and Lancaster probed forward east of the road, but were held up at 601782 by heavy fire and compelled to withdraw at 1345 hours. Shortly after, a heavy concentration of artillery fire was put down upon Yamethin and 7 York and Lancaster Regiment supported by two squadrons of 116 RAC, advanced to attack again from the roadside. Meanwhile, 3 Jat was clearing the town west of the main road and nearing the rail and road crossing. By 1600 hours a company of 7 York and Lancaster on the right flank had reached the hospital area while the company on the left flank advanced only about 300 yards from the area of the road south of Yamethin. But at this point this company ran into trouble, suffering heavy casualties, as a result of which all troops were ordered to withdraw, and the Japanese continued to hold the southern end of Yamethin.[18]

The 3 Jat positions at the cross-roads were attacked twice during the night of 12/13 April from the north-west and south-west by a party of about 40 Japanese troops with two light machine-guns, after which jitter parties were also active. It appeared that they were probably removing their casualties. The 7 York and Lancaster area was also jittered four times during the night, but early in the morning the British battalion again probed forward, meeting with no opposition for some time. At 0935 hours, however, it encountered strong opposition from a white house at 600781 and was ordered to withdraw. The Jats had better luck and by 1010 hours had secured the railway station and the road-crossing in the centre of the town. 2/1 Punjab had, that morning, formed up in an area north of Yamethin. This battalion was now ordered to clear the remaining Japanese troops from the town. Two of its companies began an advance southwards on either side of the road through Yamethin at 1130 hours, and by 1215 hours had cleared up to a line level with the hospital in the centre of the town. The hospital area was then cleared and the different companies of the battalion moved towards the end of the town clearing on both sides, east and west. Stiffer opposition was, however, met from the south-east side where some 300 to 500 Japanese troops were holding out with the help of guns and two light tanks.[19] At 1430 hours, two companies, B and D, were sent in that direction but suffered a few casualties as a result of running into a minefield and because of the Japanese fire coming from the market area. As the Japanese were in a strong position, the companies were withdrawn to enable a divisional

[18] Signal message from 5th Indian Division, 2045 hours, 12 April.
[19] 5th Indian Division Sitrep to 1800 hours, 13 April.

artillery concentration to be put down to destroy the minefields. Thereafter the battalion consolidated the position astride the road and a harassing artillery fire was put down on the south-east corner during the night.

In spite of this fire and a heavy air-strike next morning, opposition was reported from the south-east corner of the town. The Punjabis thereupon formed up for an attack, which went in successfully and by 1210 hours on the 14th they were in the general line of the market, supported by two companies of 1/17 Dogra in the rear. Advance to the east edge of the town was made quickly and by 1420 hours Yamethin was in the hands of the 5th Indian Division. A large amount of equipment, stores and ammunitions left behind by the Japanese was taken.[20]

In offering stubborn resistance at Yamethin the Japanese were no doubt continuing their overall policy which they had followed since the loss of Meiktila, namely that of yielding no ground until thrown back. The impression gained from interrogations of many Japanese prisoners taken on the railway axis was that they were philosophically resigned to being killed but were determined to fight on till the last.[21] Their higher command knew all the while that it was the only method of gaining some time for organizing their defences further south and preventing the fall of Rangoon before the monsoon.

Shwemyo Village and Shwemyo Bluff

While the Japanese were resisting at Yamethin, the Allied engineers were busy constructing a by-pass road to the west of the town for the use of the 161st Indian Infantry Brigade which was approaching it via Wayindok and Wetlet. It reached Yamethin on the evening of 12 April, where 4/7 Rajput helped in clearing north of the town on 13 April. Leaving the 123rd Indian Infantry Brigade to mop up south-east of the town, the 161st Indian Infantry Brigade pushed forward along the newly constructed diversion west of Yamethin on 14 April, and reached Tatkon before nightfall. So far very light opposition had been met, and Tatkon was cleared in the morning of 15 April. But slightly heavier opposition was encountered on the general line of the Sinthe Chaung, just south of Tatkon and four miles north of Shwemyo. The brigade orders at this time were to by-pass Shwemyo Bluff and push on down south on the main road while containing the bluff till relieved by the divisional troops.[22] The first step, therefore, was to secure a crossing over the Sinthe Chaung and a bridgehead across it. On 15 April, a

---
[20] *Ball of Fire, op. cit.*, p. 415.
[21] IV Corps Isum to 20 hours 13 April.
[22] 161st Brigade Group Instruction No. 10 of 14 April 1945.

company of 4 Punjab advanced towards the Sinthe Chaung crossing site at 6836 and began to dig-in in the area of the bridge which had been destroyed earlier by the Japanese. Although some crossings over the Chaung were secured to the west of the main road, the brigade harboured to the north of it when the tanks were shelled by the Japanese. On the same day D Company of 1/1 Punjab had also been sent forward to establish a firm base as near as possible to Shwemyo bluff and to patrol the foothills. But having come under heavy fire from the area of the bridge, it had withdrawn and established itself at milestone 273.[23] On 16 April, the brigade pushed forward and captured Shwemyo village at approximately 1230 hours, but the position remained fluid for some time. The Japanese avoided the tanks and cavalry but small parties moved about and engaged the infantry and sappers.[24] Snipers were also active against the sappers of a Field Company who were preparing a track west of the railway line south of Sinthe Chaung.

Meanwhile, the 123rd Indian Infantry Brigade, having completed the mopping up in Yamethin, had also moved forward and reached Shwemyo bluff, eight miles south of Tatkon. This hill feature bordered the eastern side of the road in this area for a few miles. As it afforded an excellent view of the road which it dominated, it was expected that the Japanese would offer stubborn resistance here. They were in fact reinforced from the south and did offer opposition, but, on 17 April, the 123rd Indian Infantry Brigade made a wide left hook on to the bluff from the east, and captured Points 850 and 875 on it. It was not possible for the 161st Indian Infantry Brigade to continue its move south until this feature had been completely cleared. This was accomplished by the 123rd Indian Infantry Brigade on 18 April, but meanwhile the advance of the other brigade and armour had continued towards Pyinmana.[25] There is no doubt that the Japanese had intended to delay the Allied advance on the line of the Sinthe Chaung but the speed of the 5th Indian Division had caught them unprepared.

It was fortunate that this place fell so easily for it is certain that if it had been held strongly and resolutely, it might have delayed the advance of the 5th Indian Division considerably. The Japanese had received some reinforcements (*114th Regiment* of the *55th Division*) only a short time earlier but these had no time to establish themselves fully.[26] Nor were they able to appreciate the speed of Allied advance for otherwise they would have prepared more positions in the general area of the bluff than were actually encountered.

---

[23] 1/1 Punjab WD, 15 April 1945.
[24] 161st Brigade War Diary, 16 April 1945.
[25] Operations IV Corps Oct 1944 to 6 May 1945, para 174.
[26] *Ibid*, para 175.

Another reason for the ease with which Shwemyo bluff was captured may be the fact that the Allied troops had broken the Japanese left flank and by-passed the bluff by moving down the railway axis.

Pyinmana and Lewe

After clearing the Shwemyo bluff area of all opposition, the 161st Indian Infantry Brigade handed it over to the 99th Indian Infantry Brigade of the 17th Indian Division, which came up to take over this area. Meanwhile the 9th Indian Infantry Brigade of the 5th Indian Division, which had been left behind at Meiktila, also moved up from that place by road and concentrated in Tatkon area on 17 April.[27] Thus by 18 April all the three brigades (9th, 123rd and 161st) of the 5th Indian Division were again free to proceed south with all speed, their next immediate objective being Pyinmana and its two air-strips.[28]

On 18 April, the tanks led the way towards Pyinmana, but their progress was slow on account of the demolitions carried out by the retreating Japanese forces and the constant sniping encountered on the way. The armoured column, however, reached MS 263 on that day. Early on 19 April, the armour struck rapidly south and making swift progress against little opposition it reached Sinthe Chaung bridge at MS 248, four miles from Pyinmana. Here, the bridge over the chaung was found intact although demolitions had been prepared. The demolisher was found asleep.[29] The opposition offered by the Japanese from Shwemyo to Pyinmana was confined to sniping and eight rounds of gun fire.[30] It was decided to leave one battalion to carry on operations against the town while the tanks moved south by a diversion made by bull-dozers. In doing so some opposition was encountered but was effectively dealt with by the tanks, and the main road was finally reached at MS 240, four miles south-west of Pyinmana. Part of the armoured column secured the airfield at Lewe (LV 5978) which was quickly made ready for the fly-in of gliders of the Forward Airfield Engineers, on 21 April. While one battalion of the 161st Indian Infantry Brigade was attacking Pyinmana from the north, the 123rd Indian Infantry Brigade moved up to MS 248 (Sinthe Chaung) and the 9th Indian Infantry Brigade, moving south from Tatkon and advancing rapidly along the railway axis reached north of Pyinmana on 20 April. Here it learnt that there were a few small parties of Japanese troops, mostly to the west of the railway line, who raided villages for food at

---

[27] 9th Indian Infantry Brigade Summary of Intelligence for April 1945.
[28] Signal Message from 5th Indian Division to its Brigades, 2150 hours, 17 April.
[29] 5th Division Intelligence Summary No. 2, 31 March to 21 April.
[30] *Ibid.*

night.³¹ The reduction of Pyinmana began on the morning of 21 April when forward companies of 3/2 Punjab captured the north edge of the town up to the rail and road bridges over the chaung. All bridges had been destroyed by the Japanese and mines laid to the south of the chaung. Meanwhile troops of the 63rd Indian Infantry Brigade (of the 17th Indian Division) also reached Pyinmana and entered the town from the east. The Royal Engineers constructed a diversion bridge over the chaung and 3/2 Punjab moved down to occupy the southern half of Pyinmana without opposition. Meanwhile 1 Burma moved further south and occupied the airfield there.

During the fighting at Pyinmana and Lewe, the Headquarters Japanese *33rd Army* narrowly escaped capture. From this point onwards the surviving troops of this army took no part in the battle but retreated southwards in a disorganised manner, hotly pursued by the IV Corps.³²

It may be recalled that the 161st Indian Infantry Brigade and the tanks had by-passed the town of Pyinmana by a diversion made to the east of it by bull-dozers. Pyinmana had not been completely cleared of the Japanese, but as the 63rd Indian Infantry Brigade of the 17th Indian Division had already reached the town, the leading troops of the 5th Indian Division continued their advance south without worrying about the road behind them.

Towards Toungoo

The next important point on the road to Rangoon was Toungoo, some sixty miles from Pyinmana and only 187 miles from Rangoon. The plan, after the capture of Pyinmana, was that the 123rd Indian Infantry Brigade and the armoured column of the 255th Indian Tank Brigade should capture Toungoo, followed by the 161st Indian Infantry Brigade, leaving responsibility for the airfield to the 63rd Indian Brigade of the 17th Indian Division.³³

The 161st Indian Infantry Brigade concentrated at Thawatti when it was re-grouped and divided into four groups to continue the advance as the leading brigade after Toungoo in the rear of the armoured column. It is remarkable that even on 22 April, when the Japanese were supposed to have been defeated, a few of their Oscar fighter-bombers appeared in the sky and strafed the 161st Indian Infantry Brigade at Thawatti early in the morning.³⁴ The rapid advance of the 5th Indian Division, however, continued. The

---

³¹ War Diary 9th Indian Infantry Brigade April 1945.
³² Operations IV Corps Oct. 1944-6 May 1945, para 179.
³³ 161st Indian Infantry Brigade Movement Order Nos. 9 & 10 of 21 and 23 April.
³⁴ 161st Indian Infantry Brigade War Diary for 22 April. Even on 24 April 6 Oscars bombed the 123rd Brigade area near Toungoo.

armour had already reached Yedashi on 21 April brushing aside slight opposition on the way, followed by the 123rd Indian Infantry Brigade, the next day. The Japanese were unable to hold the advance of tanks and all that they could do was to destroy bridges as they retreated. At 0930 hours on 22 April it was reported by Tactical Reconnaissance that the tanks had reached MS 177, two miles north of Toungoo, after overcoming some opposition at MS 184. At 1040 hours, Toungoo airfield was occupied without opposition, while 7 York and Lancaster who had rejoined the brigade swept the town behind the tanks. Two of its companies then moved forward and by 1700 hours had occupied Oktwin, without suffering any casualties, while 2/1 Punjab and 1/17 Dogra guarded the airfield,[35] which was of considerable importance as it was only about 166 miles from Rangoon and the fighter aircraft based on it could easily cover the distance. The air-strip was quickly repaired.

All this while, the 161st Indian Infantry Brigade was following close behind the 123rd Indian Infantry Brigade, as it was to take the lead again from Toungoo. After a day's pause on 23 April, for regrouping and maintenance, the 161st Indian Infantry Brigade led the advance on 24 April.[36] The order of march was 255th Armoured Brigade with the 161st Indian Infantry Brigade in the lead, followed by the 123rd Indian Infantry Brigade. The Japanese again strafed the airfield area inflicting about 40 casualties, but the brigade advance continued. The tanks went through with 4 Royal West Kent and reached Pyu, the next town down the road and railway. But the rest of the column was held up by the bad state of crossing at a destroyed bridge owing to heavy rainfall the previous night.[37] A pontoon bridge was constructed and the brigade moved forward during the night, taking advantage of a full moon,[38] and harboured at Kywebwe, MS 157. Pyu was captured on 25 April. After clearing some opposition in the villages east of Pyu on 25 April, the brigade concentrated in the Pyu area halting there to allow the 17th Indian Division to pass through. The armoured column with 1 Dogra, however, passed through Pyu on the same day and reached as far south as Penwegon where it, too, halted to allow the 17th Indian Division to pass through.

17TH DIVISION IN THE LEAD AGAIN

The 17th Indian Division took the lead again from 25 April. This division had left Pyawbwe on 17 April and had been following

[35] 123rd Brigade War Diary, 22 April.
[36] The Air Force made a fortunate error on 23 April. This lay in dropping "thousands of eggs on to the troops, so that men could go about ordering omelettes made from ten eggs". *Ball of Fire*, p. 418.
[37] WD 123rd Indian Infantry Brigade, 24 April.
[38] *Ball of Fire, op. cit.*, p. 418.

the 5th Indian Division in its rapid drive southwards. The drive was to become still more rapid henceforward as it was known that a parachute landing south of Rangoon was to be made at the entrance to the Rangoon river to enable the 26th Indian Division of XV Corps to capture Rangoon from the sea. The troops of IV Corps were still about 144 miles from Rangoon and they decided to make a gallant effort to cover this distance in 6 or 7 days to have the honour of being first to re-enter the port. The advance therefore became a race now.

The plan of advance was that the 17th Indian Division would march as rapidly as possible and after capturing Pegu and the airfield area, develop the airfields. It would then move on towards Zayatkwin and then press on towards Rangoon on the axis Hlegu—Taukkyan.[39] The 5th Indian Division (less the 9th Indian Infantry Brigade)[40] was to follow up and attack Rangoon from the north-east and east via Zayatkwin-Sadalin-Ledaunggan.[41] Meanwhile the 9th Indian Infantry Brigade was to fly in from Pyinmana and take charge of Pegu.

On 25 April, the 17th Indian Division began its move and by the evening the armoured column had advanced about 33 miles. Its other units including 1/3 Gurkha Rifles and 6/7 Rajput followed by the 63rd Indian Infantry Brigade, Divisional Headquarters and the 48th Indian Infantry Brigade and finally the 99th Indian Infantry Brigade (less 1/3 Gurkha Rifles) had also moved through the 5th Indian Division position. On 26 April the advance column had reached Kaukkwe, two miles north of Nyaunglebin, without opposition. Here contact was made with some retreating Japanese troops, mostly horsed cavalry who were either killed or scattered. Some railway wagons full of rations and a few prisoners were also captured. The armoured column pushed on and by the evening of 26 April was far south at Daik-U, only 85 miles from Rangoon; the 63rd Indian Infantry Brigade was at MS 99.5 near Nyaunglebin. The next stop of the armoured column was at Pyinbongyi, MS 68½ on 27 April, where fairly heavy fighting ensued and lasted for the whole day.[42] North of the village Japanese suicide parties attempted to destroy the tanks with pole-charges. The village had high bunds and thick clumps of under-growth which made the use of medium tanks difficult, but the opposition was overcome by 1/3 Gurkha Rifles and 6/7 Rajput with heavy casualties to the Japanese, some of whom were also taken prisoners. Some Japanese snipers were also encoun-

---

[39] See IV Corps Operation Instruction No. 142.
[40] It will be remembered that 9th Brigade was left behind at Pyinmana from where it was to fly-in later to an airfield further south with the task of securing the Sittang river crossing at Shweguin QG 37 and Mokpalin QG 31.
[41] IV Corps Operation Instruction No. 142.
[42] IV Corps Sitrep No. 32.

tered at MS 70, hidden in thick scrub. These were silenced by the tanks and infantry.

Payagale

The force then moved on to Payagale on 28 April. A road-block was encountered at MS 64 but was easily destroyed. At MS 63 obstacles were again met. Here too the area was thickly mined, mostly with aerial bombs, and suicide tactics with pole-charges were repeated, and two tanks were destroyed by mines. Mines were cleared but opposition by suicide squads continued throughout the day. Although some opposition was still being met here, the troops moved on towards Payagyi and established a road-block on the Payagyi-Waw road, three miles east of Payagyi. It consisted of one company of 1/3 Gurkha Rifles, one troop of armoured cars and one of Stuart tanks.[43] Many Japanese troops were supposed to be escaping to Moulmein via this road, which was the only road across the Sittang river, and it was essential to cut it off. During the night an unsuspecting Japanese staff car and two trucks drove into the block. These were destroyed at almost point-blank range and all the occupants killed which included some high ranking Japanese officers.

Payagyi

It was reported that Payagyi was occupied by the Japanese forces, hence a heavy air-strike followed by an artillery concentration was put down on it on 29 April. Subsequently the 63rd Indian Infantry Brigade put in a full-scale frontal attack, which went in exactly according to plan and was a perfect example of tank and infantry co-operation. But there was no opposition in the village and when the troops moved in they found it had been vacated earlier. It seemed the Japanese had evacuated overnight. In the village itself large dumps of mechanical transport, spares and medical equipment were captured, and it was obvious that the garrison had made a hasty exit. The 63rd Indian Infantry Brigade, therefore, continued the advance towards Pegu with 5 Horse; and by 1500 hours one column had reached MS 53 and another was moving east of Pegu to reach south of the town with the intention of cutting the road Pegu—Thanatpin. The column on the main road, which had reached MS 53 on the northern outskirts of Pegu, returned to MS 55 where it harboured for the night.

Pegu

Pegu was held by a battalion of *24 IMB* which the Japanese had brought up from Moulmein a few weeks earlier, and by some line

---

[43] *Ibid*. Sitrep No. 35.

of communication troops from Rangoon, hastily organised into a series of *ad hoc* infantry units.

The town of Pegu was situated on both the banks of the Pegu river which ran through it. The main road coming roughly from the north-east cut right through the town and joined its eastern part with the western through the road bridge over the river. The outskirts of the town began at mile 51 where the road may be said to enter the town, whereas the main bridge was at MS 49. A force attempting to take the bridge along the road from that side had to pass through a maze of houses and the hospital area over a distance of more than one mile before it reached the bridge. There were also two railway bridges. One of these was about three miles to the north of Pegu at 9108, where the main Burma railway crossed the river from the east to the west bank, and another at 9104, only about half a mile from the northern outskirts of Pegu where the railway line from Moulmein crossed the river. The railway station was in the western part of Pegu and was located in an easily defensible position.

On the evening of 29 April, while the 63rd Indian Infantry Brigade harboured at MS 55, a company of 1/10 Gurkha Rifles was immediately sent to try and seize the main bridge, but it was unable to do so owing to stiff opposition. It remained, however, in observation as a patrol base at MS 51.7 during the night of 29/30 April. Next day a little more patrolling established the fact that this bridge had been completely destroyed. The Allied troops were to the east of the river, hence the immediate task for them was to capture the eastern part of the town, seize a bridge, cross-over to the western part and destroy the opposition there, before they might continue their advance further south. In addition, a high ground to the north-east of Pegu had also to be captured as also a few hill features around the place. Pegu was thus a hard nut to crack.

The high ground was taken on the evening of 29 April by 7/10 Baluch against moderate opposition, but on account of sniping fire and growing darkness, the force had withdrawn to harbour at MS 54.

The plan for the capture of Pegu, to be put into operation was as follows:

> 4 FFR of the 48th Indian Infantry Brigade was to cross the Pegu river in the area of Okpo, advance south down the west bank and capture Pegu railway station.
>
> The 63rd Indian Infantry Brigade with a squadron of Royal Deccan Horse was to retake the high ground attacked on 29 April and exploit down the main road as far as the road bridge over the river.
>
> The 255th Indian Tank Brigade less 116 RAC (Gordon Highlanders) and one squadron of Royal Deccan Horse, with

under command 18 Field Regiment Royal Artillery, 1/3 Gurkha Rifles and composite squadron of 7 and 16 Cavalry, was to move south-east from the road at MS 53½ across country to attack Kamanat, and other villages to the south and then attack north-east to meet up with the 63rd Indian Infantry Brigade on the road bridge.

Thus Pegu was to be attacked from three sides simultaneously. Each attack is described below separately.

Attack From the North. This attack was aimed at capturing the western portion of Pegu. At 1030 hours on 30 April, 4 FFR received orders to establish a bridgehead at 916035 (on the Pegu river), with a view to the subsequent crossing of this water obstacle by the 17th Indian Division, and thereafter to proceed down the west bank to capture the railway station and the western portion of Pegu. The battalion moved off at 1300 hours and proceeded along the branch railway line, newly constructed by the Japanese, towards the railway bridge (QF 9108). A Company was in the lead, while D Company was sent to clear the villages on the east bank of the river as far south as Okpo.

As A Company approached its objective, the Japanese blew up the bridge and started shelling the leading troops from dug-in positions on the far bank. The A Company commander,[44] put down a second platoon on the near bank 400 yards south-east of the bridge and opened fire to distract the Japanese attention while he himself went forward to examine the situation. He discovered that there were still two girders intact on the southern one of the two bridges, and that it was possible for men to cross at this point in single file. Realising that speed was essential if his men were to get across the river before being discovered by the Japanese, he ordered a demonstration to be made by his second platoon which was lining the river bank and called for artillery fire on the bridgehead area. Accordingly fire was quickly brought to bear. Under cover of this fire one platoon quickly got across the girders by ones and twos and established itself on the far bank. The platoon had suffered some casualties but the platoon commander organised his men and put in a bayonet attack at the centre of the main Japanese position. The attack went home and the platoon established itself in the trenches.

The Japanese reacted violently and a hail of fire was directed on to the area and all attempts to get another platoon across failed. By nightfall however the second platoon was also able to get across and join the leading platoon to form the bridgehead. In the meantime, at about 1600 hours, while the above action was being fought, D Company made an attempt to cross the bridge at 915044. This

[44] Major Amrik Singh.

bridge was also found to be blown and the Japanese were holding the far bank supported by two tanks on the railway line due west of the bridge. A crossing was impracticable and D Company harboured for the night on the east bank.[45]

The two companies being thus established on the far bank the business of supplying them with food, ammunition, wire and entrenching tools commenced. It had been possible to get a few vehicles up to A Company with stores across country before dark, and the route being established, their supplies were completed and casualties evacuated by jeep. A Company was twice counter-attacked during the night but all Japanese attempts to retake the bridgehead were beaten off. The Japanese slipped away at first light and the whole area was cleared of snipers on the morning of 1 May.

A Company then advanced south down the railway on the west bank of the Pegu river to assist the rest of the battalion in making a crossing by the southern bridge in D Company's area. The combined threat from the north and east was too much for the Japanese, and D Company had already crossed to the west bank by the time the battalion arrived on the scene. The plans for the advance on the railway station were therefore at once put into effect.

At 1000 hours orders were issued for an attack south on a two-company front with C Company astride the railway line and B Company[46] on the right with the additional task of protecting the right flank. The attack went forward without opposition as far as the nulla and track-junction at 906036 when B Company was held up by mortar and medium machine-gun fire. An artillery concentration was put down and this opposition was cleared and the advance continued.

On reaching the area where the railway line crossed the nulla at 910033, C Company again came under considerable fire from the railway station area and houses to the north-east of it. An artillery concentration was called for on the railway station while C Company attacked the Japanese in the built-up area north-east of the station. This attack was successful and the few Japanese troops who were holding this area fled westwards. The railway station area was consolidated and both B and C Companies harboured there for the night.

During these operations many Japanese were killed and much valuable equipment and arms captured in the railway station including long-range wireless transmitting equipment, together with other dumps and stores. The river crossing action was remarkable for the enthusiasm and ingenuity shown by all ranks in the manhandling and ferrying across of stores and vehicles on improvised rafts, and the use made of the railway line as a means of transportation for

[45] D Company was led by Major Peyton.
[46] B Company was led by Major Khushal Singh and C Company by Major Virk.

both stores and personnel. After the capture of the railway station arrangements were immediately made by the Sappers for the repair of the two blown bridges and the first elements of the division began to cross by 1200 hours on 1 May.[47]

Attack from North-East. While, 4 FFR was carrying out the action described above, on 30 April, 1/10 Gurkha Rifles moved up to the area where one of its companies had been held up on 29 April, in the area of the main bridge. Many attempts were made to seize the vital bridge by infiltration attacks, but these were unsuccessful although many casualties were inflicted on the defenders. 7/10 Baluch also met with a stiff opposition. Although the southward advance had been held up by fire from hill features at QF 945043 and 945038, some platoons of this battalion, moving north, secured the whole of the north-east part of Pegu comprising the residential area. Meanwhile 1/3 Gurkha Rifles attacked from the east of the town, and 4/4 Bombay Grenadiers (less three companies), to conform with the movements of 1/3 Gurkha Rifles, had advanced down the axis of the road. 1/3 Gurkha Rifles and 4 Bombay Grenadiers were however held up and could not enter the town from the east against an exceedingly strong position. Finding this approach impracticable a new hook was put on and the tanks were ordered to move round to the south and attack Shwemadan area from the rear. Here, too, Japanese 75-mm guns were encountered, one of which was knocked out. But the light was failing and the tanks were withdrawn. So late was it in fact that the tanks had to be guided into their night harbour at MS 55 by jeep head-lights.

Attack from South. Meanwhile, the Royal Deccan Horse and the composite squadron of 7 and 16 Cavalries carried out their task, meeting with only minor opposition. But they were also unable to reach the road bridge owing to a very deep nulla on the way. Hence they returned to the brigade harbour. The 63rd Indian Infantry Brigade reached and consolidated the area of the Golf Course but was unable to exploit further south.

During the night of 30 April/1 May, many patrols were sent to probe into and locate Japanese positions in Pegu east. They reported that half of the area was clear and that numerous vehicles had been observed moving to and from the main road bridge over the Pegu river. Guns were also seen being towed away to the west, and many positions which had held up the advance were being vacated. In view of these reports, the plan of attack on 1 May was kept in abeyance and more patrols were sent early in the morning to ascertain whether east Pegu was clear. It was found that the Japanese had completely withdrawn from this area and had established

---

[47] Based on F601/7371/H.

themselves on the west bank of the Pegu river and in the railway station area where 4 FFR was engaging them. The 63rd Indian Infantry Brigade then swept the area and cleared it of mines and booby-traps. On 2 May, the area west of the river was cleared and the division re-grouped for a further advance.

Pegu was captured by 2 May but the advance by the IV Corps had been held up for two days at this place by the stubbornness of the opposition and by the blowing up of the bridges by the Japanese. These two days were vital for the troops of this Corps, for they had advanced over 300 miles in three weeks to a distance of only 50 miles from Rangoon, just to find that, after all, they would not be able to take Rangoon, the honour of capturing which rightfully belonged to them, but it would go to XV Corps which was scheduled to take this port by way of the sea early in May. The rains had already begun and were likely to slow down the advance, and yet speed was at no time more desirable than during the last two days, if the 17th Indian Division or the 5th Indian Division of IV Corps were to reach Rangoon before the 26th Indian Division took it.

Hlegu

For the dash from Pegu onwards the 17th Indian Division was re-grouped. The armoured column was split up, the armoured cars and tanks joining the 48th and 63rd Indian Infantry Brigades and 1/3 Gurkha Rifles reverting to the 99th Indian Infantry Brigade. The last brigade was left behind to hold Pegu but the rest of the division continued its advance south on 2 May.

4 FFR with a squadron of 5 Horse and 16 Cavalry less one squadron moved forward and reached mile 41, where it met with slight opposition and harboured for the night. The remainder of the 48th Indian Infantry Brigade and 5 Horse and the main divisional headquarters reached mile 47½ in torrential rain and harboured there. Earlier in the day, they had crossed the Pegu river by the Bailey bridge built over the rail alignment at approximately 1130 hours. But the 63rd Indian Infantry Brigade which was to cross last could not do so as the rain rendered the mile long approaches on either side of the bridge impassable, and it was marooned on the other side.

The advance guard having crossed the bridge had reached as far south as MS 40 on that day. Opposition covering the road, which was extensively mined, was encountered at MS 39½. An attack was put in at 1430 hours, but the position was only half cleared when darkness fell and the force had to withdraw to harbour for the night at MS 40. Two 47-mm anti-tank guns and two 75-mm guns were found abandoned though in perfect condition. Obviously, the Japanese must have been in a great hurry since they were unable to move or spike these guns. The Japanese withdrew from MS 39½ position during the night in heavy rain.

From MS 40 to Hlegu, progress was very slow. The road and side tracks were very heavily mined and booby-trapped. Apart from these obstacles the opposition was negligible. Between the 40th and 36th milestones alone nearly 700 mines had to be cleared on 3 May, but once the mines were lifted, the patrols dashed forward.

A road-block was encountered at MS 38. This was cleared and Intagaw was reached by 1/7 Gurkha Rifles with 16 Cavalry and one platoon 70 Field Company. The road up to Intagaw was heavily mined.

One troop of 7 Cavalry and one troop of C Squadron 5 Horse pushed through Intagaw without infantry and advanced to MS 32½ where they found that the bridge was completely demolished but not held. The remainder of the Squadron also advanced to the bridge and having established there a detachment of 6/7 Rajput withdrew to harbour at MS 36 where it was joined after dark by the rest of the Regiment. Owing to heavy rain it was not possible to harbour away from the road, with the result that the following morning the road was found to be crammed with transport. All troops were feeling the nearness of their goal and there was a tense atmosphere of great expectancy. Hopes of reaching Rangoon were however finally shattered when it was learnt that the 26th Indian Division coming from the sea, had captured it without opposition on 2 May.

On 4 May, a reconnaissance was made for a Sherman tank crossing of the chaung, south of the bridge, at MS 32½ but without success. Heavy rain delayed work on the crossing, hence infantry was ordered to advance on foot to link up with the 26th Indian Division which, having taken Rangoon from the south, was advancing northwards. Most of the battalion crossed by swimming or using a bamboo foot-bridge on 4 May, some used the low-level bridge on 5 May, and advanced towards Hlegu. The bridge at Hlegu had also been blown up and the Japanese held the west bank. But they left on the approach of the 26th Indian Division from the south and the meeting between the two divisions took place on 6 May at Hlegu, 28 miles north of Rangoon.

On 5 May orders were received that the 17th Indian Division was not to go to Rangoon, there being insufficient material to build a strong bridge over the chaung; and it being unnecessary now to move to Rangoon, it was decided on 6 May that the forward troops of the 17th Indian Division should move back to Pegu where sufficient accommodation was discovered for the men to live under cover as the monsoon had begun in right earnest. Mopping up of stray Japanese troops however continued. The 48th Indian Infantry

Brigade was, at this time, at Intagaw and the 63rd Indian Infantry Brigade in the area of mile 41. Both these brigades carried out extensive patrolling in all directions.

This closed the story of the attempt to capture Rangoon from the north. The attempt cannot be said to have failed for it was the momentum of the final advance from Pegu which induced the Japanese garrison in Rangoon to withdraw. The actual entry into Rangoon was however from the south, and the next chapter will tell the story of that remarkable 'triphibious' operation in which all the three services co-operated to make it a success.

CHAPTER XV

Operation 'Dracula' and the Fall of Rangoon

During World War II amphibious operations were employed initially in Europe and later more extensively in the Pacific theatre, but it was not until the early part of 1944 that the possibility of such operations in the Burma theatre was conceived. The term 'amphibious operation' had been applied in the past to a combined operation 'connected with both land and water'. In the Second World War, however, combined operations were no longer confined to land and water alone, but also included air. A unique technique of co-ordinating the activities of all the three fighting services was developed for offensive warfare which rendered the term 'amphibious', an anachronism, as applied to these operations. There is no new word which can correctly describe such operations unless we accept the word 'triphibious' invented by Mr. (now Sir) Winston Churchill in a jocular mood. This word, 'though of dubious etymological authenticity, has the merit of being expressive'[1] and rhymes with 'amphibious'. The phrase 'conjunct operations' is also used. Anyhow the three expressions, combined, amphibious or triphibious operation as used in connection with the Second World War, mean only an operation in which the army, the navy and the air force, all co-operate to make it a success, and these phrases are used in that sense in the following pages.

The story of amphibious operations in Burma is one long story of plans and their cancellations. It is not intended here to go into all its details but to indicate briefly how plan after plan was made for amphibious operations, only to be cancelled at the last moment. A few minor and truncated operations did, however, take place and 'Dracula' occupies a pre-eminent position among them. The chief reason for the cancellation or postponement of these operations, no doubt, was Burma's low priority in the matter of receiving allocations of equipment from the Allied pool of resources. Lord Louis Mountbatten, the Supreme Allied Commander for South-East Asia, referred to this in the following words:

"But this over-riding factor condemned our strategy to being planned against a background of perpetual uncertainty about higher policy. Allocations which appeared to be "firm",

[1] Ian Hay: *Arms and the Men*, p. 294.

were often to be revoked soon afterwards; and even from our slender resources, we were occasionally ordered to divert landing craft and ships, transport aircraft, artillery ammunition, and other materials, to theatres with a prior claim. More than once, when our detailed plans were cancelled at the last moment, we were to be compelled to improvise; and it was not easy to decide, at short notice, how to make the best use of what remained."[2]

Even before the arrival of Lord Mountbatten on the scene, the possibility of capturing Rangoon in the dry season of 1943-44 by a sea-borne assault had been examined, as early as January 1943, by the Joint Planning Staff, but they had come to the conclusion that such an operation was 'impracticable'.[3] The chief reason for such a conclusion even then was the lack of adequate resources.

From the very beginning of his appointment as the Supreme Allied Commander of South-East Asia, in the autumn of 1943, Lord Mountbatten had considered that a "sea-borne and airborne assault from the south would greatly help the advance from the north." Writing to Field Marshal Smuts, Mr. Churchill had written that "the appointment of Mountbatten heralds an amphibious operation of novelty and far-reaching scope; which I am pressing with all possible speed . . ".[4] In fact the British Prime Minister's Directive, dated 23 October 1943, to Lord Mountbatten specifically instructed him to use the sea and air power at his disposal to seize some strategic point or points.[5] For this he was promised a battle fleet of "sufficient strength" to engage any force which the Japanese might possibly divert from the Pacific theatre.[6] In addition to

[2] Mountbatten's *Report*, part B, para 4.
[3] "We have given particular consideration to the possibility of capturing Rangoon by means of a direct seaborne attack. This, if successful, would simplify our operations to recover Burma, but we have come to the conclusion in which DCO (India) concurs, (that) the operation is impracticable". JPS Paper No. 47 para 3, dated 26 Jan 1943.
[4] Churchill: *Closing the Ring*, p. 115.
[5] "The sea and air power, which you will have at your disposal are to be utilised by you to the fullest advantage, by the seizure of a point or points, which will not only bring about a powerful Japanese reaction but which will also provide you with the choice of several possible counter-strokes to this reaction. In your formulation of plans for amphibious operations in 1944, therefore, you will decide on the point which when attacked appears to you best calculated to provide the above requirements, and you will carry out whatever operation is approved. Further for the second phase of your operations in 1944 you will draw up your plans in the light of the reaction which has been induced in the enemy." Mountbatten's *Report*—Appendix C, para 3, p. 226.
[6] "H.M. Government will make available to you, at least four weeks prior to the first major amphibious operation, a battle-fleet of sufficient strength to engage any force which the Government considers the Japanese might be in a position to disengage from the Pacific theatre. The base of this battle-fleet will be Ceylon. With this object in view as many armoured fleet carriers as can be made available together with not less than ten escort carriers will be attached to the Eastern Fleet". Mountbatten's *Report*—Appendix C, para 4, p. 226.

Troops of 10th Gurkha search Pegu, last big town taken before the recapture of Rangoon

Part of the force consisting of warships of the Royal Indian Navy on their way to the mouth of the Rangoon river

Civilians help in disposal of supplies dropped by air to liberated Rangoon

The first paratroop jumps—some have already landed
and others are swarming down to the ground

Jemadar Parkash Singh V.C.,
14/13 Frontier Force Rifles

Jemadar Abdul Hafiz V.C.
3/9 Jat

Major General
H. M. Chambers
Commander
26th Indian Division

Major-General
W. A. Crowther
Commander
17th Indian Division
22 June 45—31 May 46

'Dracula', which was to be an amphibious operation for the capture of Rangoon, there were many other amphibious plans conceived by the South-East Asia Command, of which 'Culverin' was perhaps the earliest. This was a plan for an amphibious operation to be carried out against northern Sumatra. But the resources available for this operation were limited to "those which at the Casablanca Conference had been allotted to India Command and the Eastern Fleet for amphibious operations against Akyab and Ramree island".[7] But with such resources it was not possible to carry out 'Culverin' and hence the operation was cancelled in October 1943.

The Joint Planning Staff, who had, in January 1943, considered the idea of capturing Rangoon by a sea-borne assault as 'impracticable', was again instructed by the Chiefs of Staff, in October 1943, to prepare an appreciation and outline plan for the recapture of Burma in the dry season of 1944-45. In their new appreciation, dated 8 October 1943,[8] while emphasising the difficulties of capturing Burma from the north,[9] the Joint Planning Staff opined that operations in the south (capture of Rangoon) would be the 'decisive ones'. They, therefore, produced a plan for combined operations against Rangoon, but this was based on the assumption that "Germany has been defeated by November 1944," and as a consequence "naval and air forces can be made available to the extent required." As it was too optimistic an assumption, the plan was carefully studied but shelved for the time being.

The idea of an amphibious operation was revived next month when Marshal Chiang Kai-shek insisted at the Cairo Conference (November 1943) on such an operation being carried out against the Japanese. In spite of Mr. Churchill's arguments, President Roosevelt had promised the Chinese a considerable amphibious operation across the Bay of Bengal within a few months.[10] In fact, the entry of the Chinese Expeditionary Force from Yunnan into Burma was made conditional upon this demand being accepted. Earlier Marshal Chiang Kai-shek had mentioned to Lord Mountbatten also that he would allow the Chinese Expeditionary Force to take part in the land operations in Burma *only* if these were supported by an amphibious operation. The Generalissimo was given an assurance that an amphibious operation would be launched, and that a fleet would soon be in the Bay of Bengal. The SACSEA had considered various plans and had decided upon an operation against the Andaman Islands. This plan was called operation 'Buccaneer', which, it was believed, would be carried out with the resources then available in

---

[7] Mountbatten's *Report*, para 10.
[8] See JPS Paper No. 100.
[9] *Ibid.* "We do not consider that we could ever recapture Burma by an overland assault from the north".
[10] Churchill: *Closing the Ring*, page 290.

South-East Asia, or allocated to that theatre. Though not likely to provoke a powerful reaction from the Japanese, this operation, it was hoped, would serve the useful purpose of providing a base for future operations. In addition, since the islands lay "in the middle of the enemy's outer perimeter of air and naval bases, which stretched from Southern Burma to Sumatra; the seizure of the airfield at Port Blair would breach this perimeter and afford shore-based fighter cover for amphibious convoys passing through it. It would also provide a base for reconnaissance of the Kra Isthmus, Malaya, and Sumatra; and, more important, for bombing the recently completed Bangkok-Moulmein railway, and shipping in the Gulf of Siam. Port Blair Harbour would also provide a valuable advanced naval base for light forces and landing craft".[11]

The planning for such an operation had far advanced when the Teheran Conference was held soon after the Cairo Conference. Marshal Stalin was present at this Conference but not the Generalissimo. Here the Russian leader, "possibly prompted by the Americans, had flatly stated that Russia's entry into the war against Japan must be conditioned on the effectiveness of the British and American effort to finish the war in Europe first".[12] This implied that the largest forces available must be used against Europe. In spite of this, President Roosevelt wanted that Lord Mountbatten should be told to go ahead with his plans for operations in the Bay of Bengal. Mr. Churchill, however, thought that it might be necessary to withdraw resources from South-East Asia in order to strengthen the proposed operations in the European theatre. The President was not willing to give in on this point, but finally agreed to call off 'Buccaneer' when he learnt that 50,000 men would be required for it.[13] Lord Mountbatten's 'structure of hope began to crumble' when on 5 December, he was informed that operations in Europe would receive overriding priority and that the bulk of his landing craft might be withdrawn. Some triphibious resources had slowly been collected in the ports of India, but these were to be of no use to him now, and he had to cancel the Andamans operation off his list. Force 'G', comprising nearly two-thirds of the amphibious resources of the South-East Asia Command, was soon ordered to be sent back to Europe.

Lord Mountbatten was then asked to suggest some other operation, as an alternative to 'Buccaneer', on a smaller scale. He replied that "no considerable operation in support of our amphibious strategy now appeared possible".[14] However, to keep faith with the

---

[11] Mountbatten's *Report*, Para 11.
[12] *The Last Viceroy*, p. 177.
[13] Churchill: *Closing the Ring*, pp. 361-4.
[14] Mountbatten's *Report*, para 21.

Generalissimo, the possibility of some minor amphibious operation on the coast of Arakan began to be investigated. A minor operation styled 'Pigstick' was planned to be carried out with the remaining resources. 'Pigstick' had for its object the landing of 20,000 troops on the southern part of the Mayu Peninsula, behind the Japanese dispositions in the northern part of the Peninsula, where they were facing the XV Corps. It was hoped that this might satisfy the Gerneralissimo. The latter, however, refused to accept it as a substitute for 'Buccaneer', and considered himself released from his obligation to send the Chinese Expeditionary Force from Yunnan.[15]

He stuck to his decision for sometime, but was finally persuaded, though not before 21 April 1944, to order his troops in Yunnan to move into Burma.[16] Nevertheless, the preparations for 'Pigstick' continued and the Chiefs of Staff were asked for their sanction in December 1943. They replied that in view of the combined operations planned for the European theatre, all such operations in South-East Asia should be abandoned. Early in January 1944, therefore, even 'Pigstick' was cancelled. More than that, even the meagre remaining amphibious resources were ordered to be sent to the European theatre, and all hope of an amphibious operation in South-East Asia in the pre-monsoon period of 1944 was over.[17]

Dracula

After the decisive defeat of the Japanese in Imphal and Kohima during the spring of 1944, plans for the reconquest of Burma overland from the north were considered and finally adopted. The enterprise appeared long and arduous while the Japanese forces were maintained and supplied through well organised lines of communication, running north from Rangoon. The idea of an amphibious operation was therefore revived. The object was to capture Rangoon, then clear southern Burma of the Japanese forces and to advance north to link up with the two Corps then moving south, thus sandwiching the Japanese between the two Allied forces advancing from opposite directions.

A plan was therefore drawn up for a combined airborne and sea-borne assault on Rangoon and sent to the Chiefs of Staff for consideration in July 1944, along with the plans for the land operations. The combined operation against Rangoon was called 'Dracula' and the plan for land operations was styled 'Capital'. Lord Mountbatten was of the view that 'Dracula' would enable him to exploit fully his predominance over the sea, and thereby compel

---

[15] *Ibid*, para 23.
[16] Churchill: *Closing the Ring*, p. 502.
[17] Mountbatten's *Report*, paras 24, 25.

the Japanese to divert their forces to the south of Burma, thereby ensuring the success of the land operations in the north.[18] It was estimated that five divisions would be needed for 'Dracula' of which three might be withdrawn from Burma and two would have to be found elsewhere. Both men and material were required from Europe. It was expected that the effect of the withdrawal of three divisions from Burma would be to slow down the implementation of 'Capital', and it was not known how the Americans would view this. In August, Major-General Wedemeyer (Deputy Chief of Staff SEAC) was sent to America to find out the views of the U.S. Joint Chief of Staff on the proposed operations. He discovered that they would give favourable consideration to the amphibious operation, provided the land operations in Burma were pressed to the utmost. At the same time, both the British and the U.S. Chiefs of Staff considered that five divisions were not adequate for 'Dracula' and suggested seven. This meant, on the one hand, that three divisions would not be withdrawn from Burma, if the land operations were to be pressed to the utmost, and, on the other, that six divisions (and not two) had to be found elsewhere for 'Dracula'. Germany was expected to capitulate by the end of 1944, and Lord Mountbatten was promised all the necessary resources in men and material for 'Dracula' from the European theatre. Meanwhile, India was to be prepared for receiving forces and materials from Europe for the attack, tentatively scheduled to be launched in March 1945. The India Command readily agreed to make all preparations to accept the additional reinforcements within the necessary period.

At the second Quebec Conference (September 1944) plans for strategy in South-East Asia were considered, and it was decided that both the operations, 'Capital' and 'Dracula', should be put into effect as soon as possible after the 1944 monsoon, which was due to end in October. But the British Prime Minister advised Lord Mountbatten to make his bill for 'Dracula' as low as possible.[19] In accordance with this advice plans for 'Dracula', based on reduced scales, were completed by the end of September. In the meantime, the Combined Chiefs of Staff also gave their approval for the execution of 'Dracula' before the monsoon of 1945, with a target date of 15 March 1945.

All this, however, depended on the expected capitulation of Germany in October 1944, for only after that event could the resources be diverted to South-East Asia. This expectation was soon belied and by October it was clear that no resources would be available for 'Dracula' in time to launch the operation in the spring of 1945. Since amphibious operations are not possible during the long

[18] *Ibid*, para 224.
[19] *Ibid*, para 259.

monsoon period, the earliest date when Dracula could be put into effect was perforce postponed to the autumn of 1945.

DRACULA SHELVED

This was confirmed when Lord Mountbatten received a radio message[20] from Mr. Churchill to meet him at Cairo, where he told him that Marshal von Rundstedt was putting up stiffer opposition than anticipated, and that he (Mountbatten) would therefore not get the necessary resources to implement Dracula for some time to come. Mr. Churchill, however, invited him to discuss any other pre-monsoon operation that might be launched with the resources then available locally. As Lord Mountbatten's biographer puts it:[21]

> "Operation Dracula" was now nothing but an empty shell. Here, then, was yet another disappointment; and yet another operation to be shelved; and one more substitute to be effected whereby the best use could be made of the landing-craft then in the theatre. Mountbatten decided that all he could do in the way of an offensive was to clear the Arakan by a 'combined' operation. The area of the Arakan was becoming of increasing importance, due to the need of the Allies for control of some territory in Burma on which to build air bases from which to supply the advancing Allied forces in central Burma. As it was, the troops spear-heading the attack hurled southward from Kohima were beginning to get beyond the 250-mile range of the planes based on Assam."

COMBINED OPERATIONS IN ARAKAN

Consequently, on his return from Cairo, Mountbatten submitted a programme of operations which included the following in addition to the land operations in pursuance of Capital:—
   (*i*) Operation 'Talon' for the capture of Akyab;
   (*ii*) an amphibious operation by two divisions in March 1945, to establish a forward naval and air base on the Kra Isthmus before the 1945 monsoon;
   (*iii*) Dracula after the 1945 monsoon; and
   (*iv*) another amphibious operation against the coast of Malaya in spite of the monsoon.

The Arakan operations were planned with a dual purpose: firstly, to clear Arakan to a line Akyab-Minbya in order to release troops for other operations and, secondly, to make provision for air bases much further south than the existing ones in Assam for

---
[20] 9 October, 1944.
[21] Ray Murphy: *The Last Viceroy*, p. 201.

supplying the Fourteenth Army. It may be recalled that the Fourteenth Army was advancing rapidly all this time, and it was but natural that the difficulties of supplying it should increase in direct proportion to the length and speed of the advance. In the middle of November 1944, therefore, the XV Corps was ordered to provide troops for an amphibious assault on Akyab, on or about 15 January 1945. The series of minor amphibious operations undertaken in Arakan during the early part of 1945 need not be described here in detail as they have been described in a separate volume.[22]

DRACULA PROPOSED AGAIN

During January 1945 nothing was heard of, or said about, Dracula which was as good as shelved for the time being. But troops of all arms in Arakan got some very useful experience of amphibious operations during this month, and the operations both in Central Burma and Arakan proceeded very well. It was hoped that the Fourteenth Army would reach Rangoon before the monsoon, but in case it could not, Lord Mountbatten had always considered that it might become necessary to mount an amphibious operation in support of the Fourteenth Army, and in February he informed his Commanders-in-Chief that a modified pre-monsoon Dracula might be planned. The existing plan was that after the capture of Rangoon another operation (Roger) should be undertaken for the capture of Phuket Island, and after this an assault would be made on Singapore. Dracula at this stage would mean postponing Roger, but the success of the Fourteenth Army operations, and the clearing of Burma were considered all important at this stage. Lord Mountbatten held a meeting of his Commanders-in-Chief on 14 February at which these questions were discussed. The view was then expressed that a highly mobile, air-supported and air-supplied column might reach Rangoon overland by the middle of April, a month before the monsoon, and that Dracula would not be necessary. No decision to cancel Dracula altogether was however taken at this meeting. On the other hand, the Joint Planning Staff was directed to work out a plan by which either Roger or Dracula, whichever might be ordered on 23 February, would be carried out.

DRACULA SHELVED AGAIN

The decisive meeting was held on 23 February in Calcutta.[23] About this meeting Lord Mountbatten writes: "Lt.-General Leese

---

[22] *Arakan Operations*, published by CIS Historical Section (India & Pakistan).
[23] The meeting was attended by Lt.-Gen. Wheeler, all three Cs-in-C, Lt.-Gen. Sultan and Major-General Stratemeyer. Mountbatten's *Report*, para 405.

reported great satisfaction with the Fourteenth Army's progress, and still keenly supported the policy of Operation Roger. While sharing my repeatedly expressed wish to press on with the assault on Malaya, he considered that this would best be achieved by relying on the overland thrust, which would avoid the inevitable delay to the target date for the capture of Singapore, which the diversion of the amphibious force from Roger to Dracula would cause."

Air Marshal Garrod, supported by Major-General Stratemeyer, confirmed that air arrangements for supporting the overland thrust would be made. Lt.-General Leese, therefore, thought that Rangoon should be taken without the help of 'Dracula', before the monsoon. 'Dracula' was therefore again shelved and 'Roger' decided upon,[24] and orders were issued for all priority to be given to the latter operation. The only factor that was not taken into account in arriving at this decision was the possibility of the stubbornness of Japanese resistance to the advance of the Fourteenth Army. Within a month from the meeting described above, events proved that after all it might not be possible to reach Rangoon overland before the monsoon which was expected to begin in the second week of May. The Japanese were resisting more stubbornly than anticipated.

DRACULA INEVITABLE

At a meeting held in Monywa on 22 March, when the Japanese were still fiercely opposing IV Corps around Meiktila, Lt.-General Leese pointed out that the operations in Burma were somewhat behind schedule, and that he was not sure whether Rangoon would be reached before the rainy season. Soon afterwards (26 March), he asked for an immediate study to be made of the possibility of launching a modified Dracula against Rangoon. This meant changing the whole programme and time-table for launching 'Roger', but the decision was made to take Rangoon from the sea. There was only one month to complete the details of the operation, but preparations for an emergency amphibious operation, with part of the resources collected for 'Roger', were started. Even originally 'Dracula' was not planned on any ambitious scale, but its modified version now proposed was a very much reduced operation. It was also less difficult of execution now, because the Japanese army was more or less broken up and the Fourteenth Army's threat to the city was expected to increase daily. On the other hand, there were some difficulties inherent in the new operation: firstly, because there was a shorter time available for preparations, and secondly, because it was timed to take place in May when the weather conditions were likely to be worse on account of the monsoon.

[24] *Ibid*, para 406.

The XV Corps held the Arakan front and lay rather nearer to Rangoon than the other two Corps. At the same time it had undertaken some amphibious operations and had turned Akyab into an excellent air base. It was therefore decided that the operation Dracula should be mounted from Akyab and Kyaukpyu. The assault was to be made by one division, supported by armour and a composite battalion of air-borne troops, some time in the first week of May. Another division would follow up, if necessary. Provisional plans were prepared by 9 April and approved by Lord Mountbatten on 16 April. Dracula, though badly truncated, was after all going to be launched.

PREPARATIONS AND PLAN FOR DRACULA

Preparations for the operation began early in April, when on the Ramree Island, the 26th Indian Division started getting ready for the assault. At the same time the Fourteenth Army was asked to capture Pyinmana and Toungoo airfields to the north of Rangoon, by 25 April to give air-support to Dracula and take all risks to achieve this object. A highly integrated plan involving co-operation between the three services was evolved between Sir Arthur Power, Commander-in-Chief of the East Indies Fleet, Sir Oliver Leese and Sir Keith Park. A great fleet of ships of war, transports and landing craft was assembled. The D-Day was fixed for 2 May 1945, 'the latest date the weather would allow.'[25] The navy, army and air forces were all quickly made ready for D-Day, a great achievement by Rear Admiral Martin, Lieut-General Christison, and Air Vice-Marshal the Earl of Bandon, the responsible commanders.[26]

The plan envisaged that a day prior to D-Day the troops of 2/3 Gurkha Parachute Battalion were to be dropped in the area of centre point 651930 at 0630 hours near Elephant Point. This course was necessary to neutralise the defence which was presumed to be well entrenched on the line up the river from the sea to the city of Rangoon, a distance of ten miles cut up into norrow channels and shifting shoals. This portion was supposed to be guarded by well placed entrenchments and pill-boxes. In addition, the river was heavily mined by the Japanese as well as by the British mine-laying aircraft. A mine sweeping operation was difficult, if not impossible, owing to opposition from Elephant Point, which was believed to be strongly defended. "Owing to the difficulties of approach to the mouth of the river, it was not practicable to neutralise these (defences on the river bank) by fire, nor was a sea landing at the Point itself possible at this time of the year".[27] Hence the decision

---
[25] Slim: *Defeat into Victory*, p. 506.
[26] *Ibid.*
[27] Leese's *Despatch*, para 258.

was taken that paratroops should capture the Elephant Point on 1 May, and thereby enable naval craft and mine sweepers to enter the Rangoon river as from 0400 hours on 2 May. The capture of Elephant Point was all the more essential because the assaulting troops approaching their objective in landing craft could not expect any covering fire from the warships which would have to stay at least 25 miles away from the beaches on account of the shallowness of the sea near the coast.

The final plan was that 2/3 Gurkha Parachute Battalion would be mounted from Kaliakunda (80 miles north of Calcutta), leaving there in 40 Dakota aircraft of the USAAF Air Commandos on 29 April for Akyab. After stopping at Akyab for a day it would leave at about 0230 hours on 1 May for the objective near Elephant Point, landing there at about 0630 hours the same day. Its primary task was "the destruction of any Japanese who are occupying the Elephant Point area, so that craft and mine sweepers can enter the Rangoon river as from 0400 hours on D-Day."[28] It was further instructed to destroy gun and searchlight positions.[29] After performing these primary tasks it was to leave a part of the battalion at Elephant Point and exploit north-west towards Sadainghmut. The object of this secondary task (clearing of the west bank between Elephant Point and Sadainghmut) was to "prevent enemy interference with the movement of our craft in the Rangoon river, which must, of necessity, keep to the western channel". In case the Gurkhas were unable to complete their primary task of capturing Elephant Point by 0400 hours on D-Day, they were to do their utmost "to keep such defences occupied, distracted and subdued during the passage of the Assault Convoy."[30] In the event of meeting more serious opposition they could call upon a reserve of two more parachute companies at Akyab.

While the Gurkhas engaged themselves in neutralising the Japanese defences in and around the Elephant Point on the west bank, the minesweepers would enter the river and "sweep a channel up the river as far as its junction with the Bassein Creek at Thakutpin . The way being thus opened for the first flight of assault troops, the 36th Brigade of the 26th Division were to land half way between Elephant Point and the Bassein Creek on D-Day".[31]

Burma Defence Army to Co-operate with the Gurkhas

The Gurkhas were also to be supported by the Burma Defence Army (BDA), or Burma National Army (BNA), in revolt against

---
[28] 26th Indian Division Operation Instructions No. 19 of 19 April, Historical Section File No. 8252.
[29] *Ibid.*
[30] *Ibid.*
[31] Leese's *Despatch*, para 259.

the Japanese since 27 March. With the co-operation of Force 136 and the Anti-Fascist Organisation (AFO) four parties were planned for helping the Gurkha paratroops on D minus 1 Day. These were named 'Dog', 'Panda', 'Yak' and 'Cow'. The first named party (Dog) was to be parachute-landed into Payapon area (UD 9677) where Panda was already working. After receiving Dog, it was planned that Panda would move to the Elephant Point area with fifty guerillas and co-operate with the Gurkhas. Yak which was then operating in the Mingyangon area was to reach Thilawa area on the east bank of the Rangoon river by D-Day and receive Cow which was to be parachuted into that area. These four parties were to perform the general role of: (i) collecting information of Japanese movements and dispositions, (ii) harassing them and (iii) sabotage. In addition Panda was given the particular task of receiving 2 Gurkha Parachute Battalion on D minus 1 Day by moving into the Dropping Zone area 651930, some time prior to D minus 1, with a party of about fifty armed guerillas, and of passing to the Gurkhas the latest information regarding Japanese dispositions.

On D minus 1, a deception plan[32] was also to be brought into effect to assist the landing of the parachute battalion and its attack on Elephant Point. It was believed, on the strength of intelligence reports, that there were possibly two Japanese groups of uncertain strength in Twante and Kungyangon. Hence the plan was to drop deception devices west of the Twante hills to cause the Japanese groups either to deploy in a westerly direction before the real parachute landing or to remain in the Twante hills, uncertain as to whether they should move east or west. This implied that they (the Japanese group at Twante) would move against the rear of the parachute battalion on D minus 1 Day. Smoke screens, dropping of dummy paratroops, harassment by Burma Defence Army troops and diversionary movements to attract attention of the garrison at the Elephant Point in the wrong direction—all these devices were planned and later employed.

The sea-borne expedition was to "proceed down the coast of Arakan for a distance of some hundreds of miles south of Akyab, round the southern extremity, past the Irrawaddy Delta, and into the Gulf of Martaban, there to effect an assault landing upon Rangoon itself".[33] It is not necessary here to go into the details of the assault plan. Suffice it to say that it comprised landings in the estuary of the Rangoon river (in addition to paratroop landings on Elephant Point) leading to the eventual occupation of Rangoon and a link-up with the Fourteenth Army approaching from the north. A number of ships, principally HMS *Largs*, HMS *Phoebe* and HMS

---

[32] Issued with 26th Indian Division Operation Order No. 17 of 22 April 45.
[33] Ian Hay: *Arms and the Men*, p. 295.

Royalist, were to be used for the convoy in addition to a large number of smaller craft. The 36th Indian Infantry Brigade (of the 26th Indian Division) was to land on the west bank of the river whereas the 71st Infantry Brigade was to land on the east bank on D-Day. One battalion of the 71st Indian Brigade was then to exploit towards the village of Kyauktan which was supposed to be defended, though not strongly. But the town of Syriam on the Pegu river was reported to be strongly held. Hence the plan was that the 4th Brigade would also land on the east bank on D plus 5; and these two brigades (the 71st and the 4th) would, after the fall of Kyauktan, move north towards Syriam and invest or capture the town. Other elements including beach groups, administrative units, infantry regiments etc. were to follow on D plus 8 and later. The initial plan also envisaged a follow-up by the 2nd British Division on D plus 9. One brigade of this division was to relieve the 71st and 4th Brigades, in order to release them for the capture of Syriam, while the other two brigades (of the 2nd Division) were to move towards Rangoon and assault it.[34] Headquarters XV Corps was also to be established in the recaptured territory on D plus 21.[35]

DRACULA BEGINS, 1 MAY

Before the parachute battalion was dropped, all known defences on both the banks of the river were subjected to heavy attacks from the air. Subsequently the parachute battalion was successfully dropped at 0630 hours. Soon after it proceeded to its objective, the Elephant Point, and by nightfall captured it against slight opposition.[36]

Operations D-Day (2 May)

Leaving Kyaukpyu on 29 April, the assault convoy reached a point seven miles from the mouth of the river on 2 May. This was the point where the troops were to be transferred from the ships into landing craft. While still at sea they learnt that the Gurkha paratroops had overcome all opposition and had captured Elephant Point, commanding the entrance to the Rangoon river, and that the Japanese gun sites had been put out of action. To neutralise the wholesomeness of this news torrential rain began to fall and continued

---

[34] The 2nd Division was at this time in India and had to be re-equipped for taking part in operation Dracula. Although the whole of this Division was not, in the event, sent to Burma, it was re-equipped by GHQ India in record time.

[35] As a consequence of Japanese withdrawal this plan was altered later on. Of the 2nd Division only the foremost brigade, namely, 6th Brigade, landed on D plus 8 but the remainder of the Division remained in Calcutta. The move of HQ XV Indian Corps was also cancelled.

[36] WD 36th Indian Infantry Brigade for 1 May mentions that the Para Battalion killed forty Japanese in the process of capturing Elephant Point.

to pour until the evening of 3 May.[37] The monsoon had begun ten days earlier than expected.

Earlier intelligence reports had indicated the presence of considerable Japanese forces in and south of Rangoon,[38] and all planning had proceeded on the basis that heavy ground opposition, supported by artillery, would be encountered. But the last minute reports showed that the Japanese were possibly withdrawing or had already withdrawn. These reports came however too late to enable any important change to be made in the plan. Nor was the untimely rain allowed to interfere with it, "and the assault troops, seasick but indomitable, set off up the estuary on their twenty-four mile journey to Rangoon".[39]

During the first assault one landing craft, whose passengers included key medical and engineer personnel and which was carrying two 15-Cwt trucks, was blown up by mines. There were very few survivors and all officers aboard were killed.[40]

71st Brigade. The 71st Indian Infantry Brigade was to assault-land on the eastern bank of the river in the Hmawwun Chaung area with the intention of capturing Kyauktan—Thilawa and thence exploiting to the general line Payagon—Seikgyi.[41] After covering the distance from the outer anchorages to the place where the Hmawwun Chaung joins the Rangoon river, it reached the south bank (Mike Beach) of the chaung at 0715 hours. A company of 1 Lincolns landed here while two other companies made an unopposed landing on the north bank, known as 'Roger' sector of the beach. By 0815 hours the whole of the beach-head was occupied by the Lincolns, some of whom had also moved east and captured a few villages,[42] where they learnt that the Japanese had left the area south of Rangoon in small boats five days earlier, and that the Burma National Army was already in Syriam. Though the beach-head was securely held by the 71st Indian Infantry Brigade the area selected for landing vehicles had been quite unsuitable for the purpose on account of heavy rains. The rain and sticky mud had made "going" across the paddy fields difficult even for infantry. However, a caterpillar tractor managed to pull the guns a few yards from the beach where they went into action. It was decided that Roger sector of the beach should be abandoned and move made to Kyauktan, which was reported to be clear of the Japanese. By 1630 hours, 5/1 Punjab and 1 Lincolns had reached that village and taken it without opposition. The

---

[37] The rains had in fact come earlier in the voyage, but the storm was at its height at the time when troops were to be lowered from the transporters into the landing craft.
[38] File No. 601/2961/H.
[39] Ian Hay: *Arms and the Men*, p. 296.
[40] File 601/2961/H.
[41] 71st Ind Inf Bde Op. Order No. 2.
[42] War Diary 71st Ind Inf Bde for 2 May 1945.

vehicles were unloaded there smoothly on 2 and 3 May.[43] Some opposition was met with on the night of 2/3 May from the south bank of the Hmawwun Chaung, but this was overcome easily and a few prisoners were taken.[44] After this, off-loading proceeded satisfactorily but landing was possible only for one hour before and after the high tide.

As mentioned earlier, the original plan was that Syriam was to be attacked after the arrival of the 4th Brigade on D plus 5. But since Kyauktan fell so easily and without opposition, it was decided to send one battalion (5/1 Punjab) immediately to that place. Patrols of 5/1 Punjab advanced up the excellent all-weather road to Syriam, oil refinery town, and the Allied forces were established there without opposition in the morning of D plus 1. Syriam Jetty was found undamaged but was unsuitable for major movement of landing craft. The population of Syriam gave a spontaneous welcome to these Indian troops. 5/1 Punjab searched the town for any Japanese troops who might be still lurking there, but found none. Patrols sent out towards Pandaw, however, found three Japanese, one of whom threw a grenade. They were chased and one was captured. 1/18 Royal Garhwal Rifles was then ordered to proceed to Rangoon. which it entered the next morning.

36th Indian Infantry Brigade

Simultaneously with the 71st Indian Infantry Brigade, the 36th Indian Infantry Brigade had also been transferred successfully from the Dracula convoy to the landing craft, early in the morning of 2 May, and by 0700 hours it had completed its 28-mile journey from the lowering positions to the assault beaches.[45] Assault waves of 8 Frontier Force Rifles were the first to land on Fox White beach at 0655 hours, followed a few minutes later by 5 Jat on George Green beach (west bank of the river) without any opposition. Other units of the brigade came up soon after and, passing through 5 Jat position, began patrolling west towards Bassein Creek. A solitary Japanese officer wearing Burmese dress was captured by 8 Frontier Force Rifles, but the flooded hinterland on both sides of the river prevented the landing of vehicles, guns and stores.[46] However, 8 Frontier Force Rifles moved north and occupied Thakutpin by 1600 hours.

RANGOON ENTERED, 3 MAY

Next morning a decision was taken to occupy Rangoon immediately. Leaving 2/3 Gurkha Parachute Battalion in occupation of

[43] *Ibid.*
[44] The prisoners taken 'seemed dejected and disspirited.' The villagers had beaten up some of the prisoners before handing them over to the Allies. See File 601/2961/H and War Diary 71st Ind Inf Bde.
[45] War Diary 36th Indian Infantry Brigade, 2 May 1945.
[46] *Ibid.*

Elephant Point, and 1/8 Gurkha Rifles to hold the area south-west of Rangoon, the brigade, with 1/18 Royal Garhwal Rifles, sailed for Rangoon at 1500 hours, while 5 Jat moved north overland.

Thus in spite of bad weather, parts of both the brigades were moving up the soggy beaches on either side of the river, as well as up the river itself, only ten miles below Rangoon. As they were advancing forward they were met by a Sampan coming downstream and containing two air force officers who told them that Rangoon was undefended. While flying low over the city, pilots had seen a sign on the jail roof announcing 'JAPS GONE'. The RAF Wing Commander had then force-landed at Mingaladon airport, borrowed a sampan and sailed down the river to contact the troops advancing up the two banks.

The 36th Indian Infantry Brigade (comprising 5 Jat, 8 Frontier Force Rifles and 1/8 Gurkha Rifles) was the first to reach Rangoon on the afternoon of 3 May to find that the Japanese had left the town on 28 April, in spite of the fact that General Kimura had been ordered by the Supreme Commander of the Japanese Expeditionary Force of the Southern Region, Field Marshal Terauchi, to hold Rangoon at all cost. He had ignored the order, presumably because he thought that Rangoon was lost after the capture of Toungoo by the Fourteenth Army. Referring to this, Lord Mountbatten has remarked, "on our side of the theatre, the Supreme Commander was obeyed better than that."[47] Later on General Kimura justified the evacuation of Rangoon on the ground that the order to hold on to Rangoon was fantastic as it would have resulted in making it the grave-yard of the *Burma Area Army*.[48]

The elements of the 71st Indian Infantry Brigade, moving up the eastern bank and comprising 1 Lincolns, 1 Punjab and Garhwalis with tanks of the 19th Lancers, reached Rangoon a little later to take the city in the flank. It seemed that the departure of the Japanese from Rangoon was the signal for an outbreak of looting which had been going on for the last few days, before the arrival of the units of the 26th Indian Division. Disorder began to die out as the division moved in, but the preliminary tasks of bringing back normal life into the city naturally took some time. Electric and water supply systems were disrupted and there was little hope of their early restoration. Most of the main buildings and the quay front were in ruins. Eden Street and Pongyi Jetties had, however, not suffered much and off-loading of stores and vehicles commenced in these jetties. A few vehicles came ashore at Monkey Point also.

Following the initial landing practically the whole of the 26th Indian Division concentrated in Rangoon, only 5/1 Punjab remained

---

[47] *Strategy of the South-East Asia Campaign, op. cit.*, p. 31.
[48] SEATIC Bulletin No. 242.

at Syriam and one company of 5/7 Rajput at Kala. Certain units of the division moved up through the outskirts of the city and linked up with the elements of the Fourteenth Army (1/7 Gurkha Rifles of the 17th Indian Division) at Hlegu on the Pegu road, north of Rangoon at milestone 29, on 6 May 1945 as related earlier.[49] At the same time, the 71st Indian Infantry Brigade (less 5/1 Punjab) moved northwards from Rangoon up the Prome road, rapidly securing Insein and Mingaladon air-strips (5 and 6 May). Advance continued northward through Hmawbi and Taikkyi, hampered only by the necessity of repairing roads and bridges, and a link-up with a tank column of the 20th Indian Division was made, 61 miles north of Rangoon, on 15 May.[50] This cut off the bulk of the Japanese *28th Army* to the west of the Irrawaddy, whereas some retreated without equipment into the Pegu Yomas.

Inside Rangoon itself, internal security arrangements were immediately taken in hand. The General Officer Commanding the 26th Indian Division acted as the Military Governor of Rangoon and allotted to each of his brigades an area of the city to administer and restore order.[51] Rangoon, the richest prize in South-East Asia, was in Allied hands and the 26th Indian Division had snatched it from the Fourteenth Army and hit the headlines in the world press. It was a fitting recompense "for the two gruelling years of obscurity in the Arakan where, though well out of the play of the limelight, the Division had been doing an indispensable job in disrupting the Japanese supply lines and building up the air and sea communications necessary to nourish the main body of South-East Asia forces fighting their way down the interior of Burma."[52] The easy capture of Rangoon is no doubt explained by the fact that the Japanese army had been thoroughly defeated by this time and the Fourteenth Army was posing a direct threat to the city.

---

[49] War Diary 71st Indian Infantry Brigade 6 May.
[50] The link-up was made when men of 1 Lincolns and 19 Lancers (26th Division) made contact with forward troops of 9/14 Punjab and Carbiniers.
[51] Certain elements of the follow-up convoy which had sailed from Kyaukpyu on 4 May by HMS *Glenroy* had also reached Rangoon by 6 May and were allotted areas with the task of preserving law and order and disarming elements of the INA. See WD 2/13 FF Rifles, May 1945.
[52] *Tiger Head*, p. 36. The Division handed over its responsibility for L of C to HQ No. 1 L of C area and started embarking for Madras on 28 May *enroute* to Bangalore for rest and rehabilitation.

CHAPTER XVI

Completing the Conquest

As has been described earlier, troops of the XV Corps linked up with the vanguard of the Fourteenth Army at two places: Hlegu, 29 miles north of Rangoon, on 6 May and Taikkyi, 60 miles north of Rangoon on the Prome road, on 15 May.[1] As a result of this link-up the Japanese *28th Army* was cut off from the remainder of the *Burma Area Army*, scattered throughout the Sittang Valley. The liquidation of these forces was henceforth the main task of the Fourteenth Army and 221 Group.

ALLIED FORCES

The position of Allied troops at the time of the capture of Rangoon, in the beginning of May, was as follows:—

XXXIII Corps

This Corps had under its command the 7th and 20th Indian Divisions, and the 268th Indian Infantry Brigade and the 254th Tank Brigade. As has been described in an earlier chapter, it had advanced down the axis of the Irrawaddy on both the banks and recaptured the Yenangyaung oilfields area, as also Prome, some 150 miles further south. Meanwhile, the Japanese forces retreating southwards had linked up with those retreating from Arakan, and plans for a combined crossing of the Irrawaddy were made by them. But the swift advance of the XXXIII Corps, resulting in the capture of Prome, had cut off their retreat. The 7th Indian Division, in the north, was successfully preventing them from escaping across the Irrawaddy into the Pegu Yomas. In the central sector the 268th Indian Infantry Brigade was holding them on the west bank around Thayetmyo, while in the southern sector, the 20th Indian Division had pursued them southward down the valley and down the Prome-Rangoon road, cutting them off to the west by linking up with the 26th Indian Division.

IV Corps Front

Troops of the IV Corps, consisting of the 5th, 17th and 19th Indian Divisions and the 255th Tank Brigade, were strung out on the railway axis (Meiktila-Pegu-Rangoon) with the 17th Indian Division

[1] 26th Indian Division now passed out of XV Corps and came directly under the command of the Fourteenth Army.

in the lead, when contact was made with the 26th Indian Division at Hlegu on 6 May. This Corps by its link-up with the 26th Indian Division had cut off a large number of Japanese forces, who had escaped from Rangoon or across the Irrawaddy axis in the hilly region of the Pegu Yomas, where its operations were in progress. At the same time it mounted its offensive operations towards the east. One brigade of the 19th Indian Division was advancing along the axis of the road Meiktila-Kalaw, while the rest of the division, based on Toungoo, was operating eastwards along the Toungoo-Mawchi road. One brigade of the 5th Indian Division was pushing out towards Waw on the west bank of the Sittang.

In Arakan, the 82nd West African Division was maintaining patrol activity along the coast and eastwards along the Taungup-Prome road. The operations in Arakan had practically come to an end. In addition, behind the Japanese lines, both 'V' Force and Force 136 were operating, the former with the role of collecting intelligence without fighting and the latter operating in a guerilla role under the British or, in a few cases, Burmese officers.

JAPANESE FORCES

It has been mentioned earlier how the Fourteenth Army by its advance in the month of April had split the Japanese forces into four isolated areas:—

(i) east of the Meiktila-Rangoon road;
(ii) around the estuary of the Sittang and down the Tenasserim coast;
(iii) between the Sittang and the Irrawaddy, mainly in the Pegu Yomas; and
(iv) west of the Irrawaddy and in the Irrawaddy Delta.

The first of these groups, comprising the remnants of the vanquished Japanese *15th* and *33rd Armies* had, after the defeat in the Mandalay plain, succeeded in escaping east into the Shan and Karen hills from where it continued to defend the routes into Siam through Kalaw and Loilem and Kemapyu. The total strength of troops in this group was estimated to be about 20,000, but they were split up into small parties, trying to re-form and escape southwards through the Kemapyu route.

The second group consisting mainly of the remainder of the Japanese *33rd Army* had withdrawn south along the main road and railway and crossed to the east bank of the Sittang to continue its move southwards to Moulmein via Shwegyin-Mokpalin-Kyaikto. The total strength of this force was probably 7000, plus some line of communication troops. "It was clear (and post-war interrogation of Japanese generals confirmed it) that the enemy was laying special emphasis on escape routes to the south; and that General Kimura,[2] planning to hold us for as long as possible on the west bank of the Sittang, so that we should not cut the Mawchi-Papun-Moulmein routes, intended to concentrate what was left of his broken armies on the Tenasserim coastal strip. The Japanese *15th* and *33rd Armies* organised strong flank and rear-guards covering the Meiktila-Taunggyi and Toungoo-Mawchi roads; and although we realised that their main intention was to keep these escape routes open, it seemed likely that they would attempt a counter-offensive in order to interfere with our land line of communication between Rangoon and the north, and also to assist the break-out of elements of the original Rangoon garrison, which was cut off in the Pegu area west of the Sittang."[3]

The third group of the Japanese was in the Pegu Yomas trapped between the IV Corps to the east and the XXXIII Corps to the west. This comprised the *Headquarters 28th Army* and the remnants of the *55th Division* which had opposed the advance of the 20th Indian Division down the Prome road. In early May, these men were joined by the *72nd Independent Mixed Brigade* which crossed from the west to the east of the Irrawaddy (north of Prome) followed by the *153rd Regiment*. The latter formed a bridgehead on the east bank for the crossing of the *54th Division*.[4] Some troops had already escaped into the Pegu Yomas and others were preparing to do so. There was no reasonable alternative for the troops between the Irrawaddy and the Pegu Yomas but to retreat over the hills and either attempt to trickle eastwards across the Sittang Valley or make a concerted break-out. There were at the time a number of tracks across the Yomas of varying standards,[5] but none was fit for mechanical transport of medium artillery. No heavy equipment could, therefore, be taken across and only mountain guns carried on pack animals could accompany the columns.

The fourth group was still west of the Irrawaddy. It comprised the rest of the Japanese *28th Army* which was hoping to cross the

[2] Whose promotion from Lieut-Generalship was announced two days after the fall of Rangoon.
[3] Mountbatten's *Report*, para 554.
[4] *54th Japanese Div* crossed in the latter half of May losing nearly 1400 dead and 74 prisoners.
[5] Some of the important tracks used by the Japanese during May were:—
    (a) Paukkaung UE 8895—Kyetsha QA 4892—Oktwin QA 8684.
    (b) Paungde UE 8245—Sinzwe QA 1260—Kywebwe QA 8668.
    (c) Nattalin UE 8736—Kunzan QA 1240—down valley of the Kun chaung.
    (d) A track running due South through Sinzwe connected track 2 with track 3.
    (e) Okpo QA 0001—Pinmezali QA 3604—Theme QF 5590—Chaunggwa QF 7199—Penwegon QB 0410.
    (f) Letpadan QF 6858—Kodugwe QF 3465—Taikkyi QF 5054—Zaungtu QF 6438—Thitni QF 9140—Pyinbongyi QG 0232.
    (g) A north-south track connects Theme with Taikkyi.
    (h) Taikkyi QF 3102—Paunggyi QF 5608—Tandawgyi, QF 7624—Thitni QF 9140. IV Corps Account of Operations.

river and reach the Pegu Yomas, when the attention of the XXXIII Corps in this area was diverted.[6] The *28th Army*, commanding the *54th* and *55th Divisions*, had originally been responsible for the defence of the Arakan and Bassein coast line. In March, however, as elements of the *54th Division*, withdrawing eastwards across the recently constructed An pass, began to appear opposite Yenangyaung, the *28th Army* extended its command to include all troops south of the Pakokku-Tilin road, who were still to the west of the Irrawaddy. This brought the *72nd Independent Mixed Brigade* and the *153rd Regiment* of the *49th Division* under the *28th Army*. When Rangoon fell, the *54th Division*, *72nd IMB* and *153rd Regiment* were all to the west of the Irrawaddy.

All these Japanese units were disorganised and reduced in numbers. Their air-force still held some bases and airfields in Tenasserim and Siam but did not show much inclination to operate the few aircraft still remaining with it. As opposed to this the Allied air forces were fighting fit and the East Indies Fleet had undisputed command of the sea.

THE TASK FOR THE FOURTEENTH ARMY

The main task before the Fourteenth Army, at this stage, was to prevent the Japanese forces from leaving Burma and to liquidate them there. On this basis, the two Corps were assigned their respective tasks. The XXXIII Corps was commissioned to prevent the Japanese forces from crossing from the west to the east bank of the Irrawaddy or escaping into the Pegu Yomas, and further to pursue those who did manage to escape into the hills. The IV Corps was allotted the task of destroying all Japanese forces attempting to escape east from the Pegu Yomas towards the Sittang or across it. We shall now describe the operations of the two Indian Corps up to the end of May when a reorganisation of the higher command took place and the Twelfth Army took over the command of all operations in Burma from the Fourteenth Army.

XXXIII Corps Operations

The 20th Indian Division was commissioned to clear the road from Prome to Rangoon with the maximum possible speed, and was to be prepared to operate one infantry brigade group for capturing Bassein. The 7th Indian Division, meanwhile, was to operate one infantry brigade group to the west of the river Irrawaddy to destroy the Japanese forces to the south of the general line connecting Prome and Okshitpin. One brigade of this division was to operate east of the Irrawaddy and destroy the Japanese forces there, while the third

---
[6] Mountbatten's *Report*, para 555.

was to move to Dayindabo to come under the command of the 20th Indian Division. The 268th Indian Infantry Brigade was to complete the operations which it was then carrying on to cut the Japanese escape routes west of Thayetmyo and then concentrate in the Allanmyo area.[7]

As described in an earlier chapter, the 20th Indian Division had reached Allanmyo by the end of April 1945, where its concentration was progressing well and advance south towards Prome was begun by the 100th Indian Infantry Brigade on 29 April.[8] That day mile 211 was reached where some minor opposition was encountered and overcome. On 1 May, mile 195½ was reached though not without some opposition. Prome was reported clear of the Japanese forces by patrols on 2 May, and was reached the same day after the troops had been held up for a short while, four miles to the north of the town by a blown-up bridge. Next day the advance continued towards Shwedaung which was occupied, without any opposition.

After the capture of Prome the divisional plan was that while the 100th Indian Infantry Brigade would clear the area around Prome and Shwedaung and the east bank of the Irrawaddy, the 32nd Indian Infantry Brigade would capture Paungdi and thereafter advance on Rangoon.[9] But the weather started to deteriorate, and it became essential to open the road to Rangoon as soon as possible to enable the stores to reach the troops by sea. A rapid link-up between the 32nd Indian Infantry Brigade, moving south from Prome and the 71st Indian Infantry Brigade of the 26th Indian Division moving up north from Rangoon, was the only means by which this object could be achieved.

32nd Brigade Advance and Link-up with 71st Brigade

It had been anticipated earlier that the Japanese would put up a stubborn defence in the area between Prome and Shwedaung as a step towards their being able to retreat east of the Taungup road. Hence the 32nd Indian Infantry Brigade had planned to by-pass Prome to the east, via Paungdale and thence south to Paungde. Preliminary reconnaissance had shown that the only road available on this by-pass was in bad condition and the surrounding country so flooded as to make it easily defensible. The occupation of Shwedaung by the 100th Indian Infantry Brigade was therefore of great value.

The 32nd Indian Infantry Brigade thereupon passed through the 100th Indian Infantry Brigade on 6 May, and reached Paungde

---

[7] XXXIII Corps Op. Order No. 22, 6 May 1945.
[8] At this time 33rd Ind Inf Bde of 7th Div was operating west of the river with the role of preventing the Japanese escaping from that side to the east bank.
[9] 32nd Ind Inf Bde Op. Instn No. 14 of 4 May 1945.

without opposition. It found there many vehicles which had been destroyed by the Japanese before leaving. The next day milestone 120 was reached, again without opposition, but a minor clash occurred with some Japanese troops south of Okpo. Some parties of the Burma National Army helped by reporting to the Allied forces all along the road and advising them on topography and bringing reports of Japanese forces then retreating east from Paungde, Nattalin and Gyobingauk. The brigade patrols also went eastwards wherever possible, and on the road Okpo-Tanbingon clashes occurred with small parties of Japanese troops beyond Teinhmyok. As this road appeared, from local reports, to be an important escape route, 4/2 Gurkha Rifles was detached to explore it thoroughly.[10]

The first genuine opposition came at MS 104, where the Japanese had fortified the line of the Minhla Chaung, preventing movement either by road or railway. It was learnt that about 200 to 300 Japanese had arrived in the area, a few days earlier, from the south and had dug bunker positions along the chaung.[11] As this was clearly a flank protection for the movement of the *55th Division* and the *28th Army* troops out of the Irrawaddy Delta, via Bassein-Henzada-Letpadan, it was appreciated that a fully organised attack would have to be made to dislodge the Japanese forces which, it was later known, comprised a battalion of the *143rd Regiment* supported by 12 field guns, including 4 British 25-pounders and some anti-tank guns. This attack was planned for 11 May and was to be carried out by 9/14 Punjab supported by a squadron of 3 Dragoon Guards.[12] Meanwhile, active patrolling was continued on 9 and 10 May to find the flanks of the positions, and two Japanese guns were knocked out. The RAF also straffed those positions which had been pinpointed, but the artillery strikes on 8 May and during the night of 8/9 May caused no casualties, as the Japanese ran into the large bunkers which they had constructed on the chaung banks.[13] Meanwhile the harbour area at MS 107 was shelled daily by the Japanese. On the morning of 11 May when the main attack by the 32nd Indian Infantry Brigade was to be made, it was found that the Japanese had fled south-east after blowing the bridge.[14] On reaching the area the brigade troops found many bunkers and mines which were lifted. The Japanese own account states: "considerable alterations were inevitably given to the original transport plan . . . by such reason as . . . unexpectedly quick withdrawal of the defence unit around Minhla, where longer persistent fighting had been intended by the HQ".

[10] 32nd Bde Sitrep to 1900 hrs, 7 May.
[11] *Ibid*, 8 May.
[12] 32nd Bde OO No. 7 of 9 May.
[13] 32nd Bde Sitrep, 9 May 1945.
[14] *Ibid*, Sitrep, 11 May 1945.

The 32nd Indian Infantry Brigade thereafter continued its advance and reached Letpadan on 12 May where it encountered some gun-fire though no other opposition. 3/8 Gurkha Rifles was left there and 9/14 Punjab was attached to the advance guard. On the 13th, Tharrawaddy was reached, but the destruction of the important bridge at Thonze prevented further advance that day. The next day, despite a heavily mined road, the troops went through Okkan, which was found clear; but a party of about 150 Japanese troops on the nulla east of the village was observed and driven away. It was presumed to consist of the garrison of Okkan and some other Japanese troops who had fled from Taikkyi on the approach of the 71st Indian Infantry Brigade which was advancing from the south. At this time the 32nd Indian Infantry Brigade was separated from the forward troops of the other brigade by a distance of only about fourteen miles.[15] On 15 May the advance continued and at MS 62 some Japanese naval personnel were engaged and chased off the road towards Palon. The same day two miles further south the troops of the two brigades linked up and the road to Rangoon was thereby opened.

89th Indian Infantry Brigade West of the River

While some of the Indian forces were sent to operate near the banks of the river Irrawaddy to prevent the Japanese troops from crossing the river and escaping into the Pegu Yomas, the 89th Indian Infantry Brigade of the 7th Indian Division had been sent to the west bank at the end of April 1945. Its object was to move further west and south-west into the countryside north of the Prome-Taungup road and destroy the Japanese troops and frustrate their plans of reaching the river.[16]

This brigade had successfully crossed the Irrawaddy at a place about ten miles north of Yenangyaung and had then moved south. While one of its columns had captured Minbu on the west bank of the river opposite Magwe, another had moved south-west. This latter column was engaged in many small actions on its way to the Sidoktaya-Padan road, a possible Japanese escape-route, which it cut. It had then returned to the Minbu area preparatory to another thrust south and south-west. as the Japanese troops were reported to be moving in that direction. Accordingly, handing over charge of the Minbu area to the 114th Indian Infantry Brigade in the beginning of May, the 89th Brigade set out on its long hook towards the south-west. The leading battalion, 1/11 Sikh, reached Yenanma by 6 May and then pushed on towards Shandatgyi, closely followed by 4/8 Gurkhas Rifles. Some Japanese troops found strongly entrench-

---
[15] *Ibid*, Sitrep, 14 May 1945.
[16] 7th Ind Div Intelligence Summary No. 8, from 27th April to 19th May 1945

ed near the village of Kaingngegyi were liquidated after a stiff action lasting for several hours. In their turn the Sikhs were later attacked by a strong party of the Japanese which had come from the direction of Yenanma. Fighting continued for several hours in the morning of 9 May during which desperate attacks and counter-attacks were made by both sides. The Japanese finally broke contact and withdrew westward towards the Taungdaw Valley through a difficult jungle route.

On 11 May, therefore, B Company of 4/8 Gurkha was ordered to move out and bar their route before they emerged from the jungle. All available information indicated that the Japanese were retreating down the line of the Yegyi Chaung. B Company, therefore, took up a position on the chaung at 884804 in the area of the village of Taungdaw by 1200 hours, and waited for the Japanese. By the same evening, C Company had also marched out and was established at a ridge overlooking the B Company's position.[17] The Japanese came, as expected, down the line of the Yegyi Chaung, and, finding the Gurkha troops established there, surrounded the two Gurkha companies and cut their line of communication. Thus surrounded, the Gurkha companies were isolated for three days during which the Japanese made repeated attacks with artillery, mortars and grenades to get their guns and transport through. It was during this desperate fighting that Rifleman Lachhiman Gurung won the Victoria Cross. This is how it happened. In one of their desperate attacks the Japanese came rushing towards the Gurkha position, throwing innumerable grenades. Rifleman Lachhiman Gurung picked up the grenades as they fell and hurled them back at the Japanese. While holding a grenade, the fingers of his right hand were blown off; but, disregarding his wounds, he started firing his rifle with his left hand. His courage so inspired his comrades that they fought with heroic determination and defeated the Japanese attempt to rush the position.

Attempts to relieve the surrounded Gurkha companies on the 13th and 14th failed. But on the 15th, a simultaneous attack by 1/11 Sikh from the north and the remainder of the 4/8 Gurkha Rifles from the east, was successful in relieving these companies.[18] The severity of the fighting can be judged from the fact that during these operations—from 10 to 15 May—the Japanese casualties were at least 339 killed and 19 taken prisoners, while the 89th Brigade suffered a loss of only 18 killed and 48 wounded.[19]

This action at Taungdaw broke up the Japanese retreat plan, and evidence from captured documents and prisoners of war showed

[17] W/D 4/8 Gurkha Rifles, 11 May.
[18] W/D 7th Ind Div, 14 and 15 May.
[19] W/D 7th Ind Div, 15 May.

that the Japanese were intending to withdraw to Thayetmyo or Padaung, below Prome. Both these places were held by Allied troops and the only place left to the Japanese was below Kama, where they had secured a bridgehead on the east bank and to which they were holding on with determination. Troops of the 20th Indian Division were to foil their attempts at crossing at these places.

The Japanese had selected three main crossing sites over the Irrawaddy; at Zalon, a village a few miles north of Prome, at Shwedaung south of Prome, and at Yegin between Shwedaung and Hangada. The 20th Indian Division at this stage was widely spread out (over a road-stretch of 135 miles); and in that area it had to face two main Japanese attempts at crossing—one, in the area held by the 80th Indian Infantry Brigade, at Kama-Zalon; the other, in the 100th Indian Infantry Brigade area, south of Shwedaung.

80th Brigade Operations Around Zalon

The 80th Indian Infantry Brigade was operating in the Zalon–Kama area, and had come down the east bank of the Irrawaddy with a strange assortment of horses, mules and bullock-carts as its mechanical transport had been withdrawn. Leaving 4 Dogra and 2/8 Punjab to patrol the road Magwe-Taungdwingyi, the brigade was ordered to move south and concentrate in the Allanmyo area.[20] While it journeyed towards that place, the units left behind had some very successful patrolling and skirmishing with the parties of Japanese troops in the area of the Yin Chaung, between 27 and 30 April, after which these units also moved down towards Allanmyo to rejoin the brigade.

The journey of the brigade to Allanmyo was largely uneventful, and after reorganising, it moved down on 4 May to Tititut (MS 188 on the Rangoon road) to take over the area south of the Bwetgyi Chaung to the Prome-Paukkaung road (but excluding Prome). Its instructions at this time to the various battalions under its command were to "take most vigorous action on all known or suspected enemy assembly areas and routes of (Japanese) withdrawal south, south-east and eastwards. The whole essence of this task is to range far and wide, to find the enemy and then to kill him . . . It is our task to kill him and so recompense ourselves for the disappointment of not making Rangoon first."[21] Meanwhile 4 Dogra, which had arrived in this area on 2 May, had once again come under the command of the 80th Indian Infantry Brigade, as also 2/8 Punjab which as Rocol, had reached the area opposite Kama, with a mountain battery, a platoon of medium guns and a section of anti-tank guns.

---

[20] 80th Ind Inf Bde OO No. 11 of 24 April.
[21] 80th Ind Inf Bde Operation Instruction No. 18, 6 May 1945.

In order to carry out the task defined above the various formations of this brigade were assigned the following duties[22]:—

   (i) 4 Dogra had to clear the road Tititut—road junction 5686-Paukkaung daily, and to carry on vigorous offensive action, ambushes etc., and destroy the Japanese in its area.
   (ii) 1 Hyderabad was sent east of the road to Wettigan to search for stragglers.
   (iii) 3/1 Gurkha Rifles remained in the northern part of the brigade area on the main road from Bwetgyi Chaung to Tititut, with the same object as that of 4 Dogra.
   (iv) Rocol was responsible for Zalon and Myinzu areas for blocking the Japanese escape routes from Kama eastwards and down the Irrawaddy.

It appeared then that Kama was the obvious place, where the Japanese would make an attempt to cross from the west to the east bank of the river. In fact they did try to send some boats across, but 3/1 Gurkha Rifles sank 6 out of 8 of them which were trying to set out from Pato village on 4 May. Two days later Rocol also sank seven boats opposite Kama. Moreover, the 268th Indian Infantry Brigade which was at Thayetmyo—north of Kama, but on the east bank—crossed two of its battalions to the west bank which began to push down towards Kama, threatening it from the north. It became clear to the Japanese, therefore, that Kama was not the ideal site to cross and that they would have to choose some other place. Hence they began to concentrate their troops further south, at Taukma. Zalon on the east bank had evidently been decided upon as a suitable place for a bridgehead. The first intimation which the Allied troops had of this was on 9 May when a company of Rocol at Kyawza (north of Zalon) was attacked by about 100 Japanese who pinned them down for twelve hours with mortar and grenade-discharger fire and then withdrew to the west bank. On 10 May, 3/1 Gurkha Rifles, which had moved south from Pyalo, engaged a party of Japanese troops (identified as part of the *154th Regt*) to the east of the main road at Sitsaba; and there was constant Japanese movement in this area during the next few days. Hence 2/8 Punjab was re-positioned further to the south, and found the Japanese holding strong defensive positions in this area. By 13 May they had managed to cross three 75-mm guns and one or two battalion guns to the east bank, and shelled the brigade positions at Kyawza, which was attacked by their infantry on 15 May.

At this stage the estimate was that at least 4,000 Japanese troops were waiting to cross; the 80th Indian Infantry Brigade was therefore strengthened by 4/1 Gurkha Rifles from the 7th Indian Divi-

[22] *Ibid.*

sion and by 44 LAA Regt of the Royal Artillery acting as infantry; the former being deployed along the main road north of Tititut (less one company which had been sent with a mobile column along the Allanmyo-Shwebandaw road), the latter covering the open country south of the Pyalo defile. A company of 4 Dogra which had been brought into brigade reserve was then employed to relieve pressure on 2/8 Punjab, by an approach to Zalon from the south. The Dogras entered Zalon on the 18th, but the Japanese reacted very vigorously to this dangerous threat and pinned them down by heavy fire, before launching counter-attacks. The company defended itself successfully before withdrawing, suffering very few casualties but for an unfortunate accident when the RAF attack in support caused the death of the company commander and the wounding of four other ranks.

Fighting in the Zalon area continued on 19 May also, but not with the same intensity as before. The village of Zalon was reported clear by 4/1 Gurkha Rifles but the Japanese continued to hold their positions on the chaung, where an air-strike was delivered.[23] Still, the Japanese hung on to their bridgehead and further fighting was inevitable. Before, however, the fighting could be renewed, the 80th Indian Infantry Brigade was ordered to move south to relieve the 71st Indian Infantry Brigade in the Taikkyi area, north of Rangoon, as the 26th Indian Division was being withdrawn from Burma. The responsibility for the Zalon area was taken over by the 33rd Indian Infantry Brigade of the 7th Indian Division.[24] On 21 May, when the 80th Indian Infantry Brigade started relieving the 71st Indian Infantry Brigade, the 33rd moved into the Zalon area and found that certain positions previously occupied by the Japanese north of Prome had been vacated, but in the Zalon bridgehead area itself there were still some Japanese troops. A patrol of 4/1 Gurkha Rifles was fired on in the village of Zalon which had been reported clear the previous day. Many small engagements took place on 22 and 23 May but the Japanese defended the bridgehead area with great determination. In these attacks against the Japanese bridgehead some companies of 2/8 Punjab, 4/1 Gurkha Rifles and 1 Queens were involved.[25] Sporadic fighting continued for five days more and the Japanese made determined attempts to break out east towards the Pegu Yomas. The bridgehead was, however, cordoned off and their attempts were only partially successful. They made a full-scale attempt on 28/29 May but suffered heavy casualties. Those that did succeed in breaking out escaped into the Pegu Yomas.

---

[23] War Diary 80th Ind Inf Bde, G Branch, 19 May 1945.
[24] 2/8 Punjab and 1 Hyderabad of 20th Div remained in the area under command of 7 Div for a few days more.
War Diaries of 33rd Ind Inf Bde and XXXIII Corps for May 1945.

Shwedaung

As mentioned earlier, the Japanese had selected three main crossing places over the Irrawaddy, Zalon, Shwedaung and Yegin. Their attempt at Zalon and how the 80th and the 33rd Indian Infantry Brigades foiled it has just been described. The second place was Shwedaung to the south of Prome where the 100th Indian Infantry Brigade (of the 20th Indian Division) was operating.

On reaching this area in the beginning of May, this brigade found that it had arrived just in time to prevent the Japanese from carrying out their plan. The latter after crossing the mountains from Taungup, were beginning to reach Padaung on the west bank of the Irrawaddy (opposite Shwedaung on the east bank). The brigade acted with vigour and immediately put stops along the east bank of the river from where the Japanese bank could be brought within the range of artillery. About 300 Japanese managed to cross the river on 5 May, but they were engaged by 4/10 Gurkha Rifles and got back into their boats and sailed down the river.[26] Seeing the east coast so well guarded, the Japanese, it appears, lost heart and a small party in Padaung tried to negotiate its surrender, but later changed its mind.[27]

The 20th Indian Division decided to send some troops to the west bank to deal with the Japanese in the Padaung area or those withdrawing from Taungup to this area. Accordingly on 10 May two companies of 4/10 Gurkha Rifles, and on the 11th a third company, were put across the river into Padaung, to patrol north towards Dandalun and on the Taungup road. They started with a successful ambush in which a Japanese light tank and two vehicles were destroyed. But they met severe opposition at Taungbwe on 12 May, the Japanese being supported by four light tanks and artillery; and the Gurkhas were forced north-east on to a high ground where they managed to dig in. For their support anti-tanks guns were shipped across during the night. The Japanese made another attack on the 4/10 Gurkha Rifles position on the high ground on the morning of 13 May but this too was repelled.[28] Meanwhile the anti-tank guns and another company of the Gurkhas had arrived on the scene and, after an air-strike, the village of Taungbwe was redeemed and Dandalun was also reported clear by patrols on 14 May. The Japanese had by then realised that the 100th Indian Infantry Brigade was too firmly established at Shwedaung to make it a profitable site for crossing. Moreover, 4/10 Gurkha Rifles was established on the west bank; hence they decided to move further south to select new

---

[26] 100th Bde War Diary, Sitrep for 6 May.
[27] A Short History of 20th Indian Division *op. cit.* by Major-General D. D. Gracey.
[28] 100th Ind Inf Bde War Diary.

crossing places. After 22 May, no further attempts were made by the Japanese in this area which was declared completely clear of them on that day. The Gurkhas returned to the east bank at the end of the month. Meanwhile on the east bank, 1/1 Gurkha Rifles and 14 FFR had been dealing with the Japanese troops who had managed to cross the river. Severe casualties were inflicted on them and only a few could escape eastwards from Shwedaung.

Yegin

After giving up the idea of crossing the river near Shwedaung the Japanese, as mentioned above, had moved down south towards Yegin where the 32nd Indian Infantry Brigade of the 20th Indian Division was ready to intercept them. In so far as the crossing of the river is concerned, the Japanese had better luck here. Many of them including a majority of the troops of their *121st Regiment* did cross the river at Yegin, but then their luck ended. As they attempted to cross the road at MS 110, their first convoy, including bullock carts, was ambushed on 23 May by 4/2 Gurkha Rifles.[29] The second convoy avoided all ambushes and managed to reach Tanbingon, where the Japanese were known to be concentrating and re-forming their units. Accordingly 4/2 Gurkha Rifles was despatched to investigate, and on 7 June, in a fierce action, cleared the village and swept the neighbouring jungle, which was very thick and prevented a lengthy pursuit. At least a hundred Japanese were killed, and a valuable patrol base was denied to them.[30] The rest moved into the Pegu Yomas.

Final Operations West of the Pegu Yomas

By the beginning of June, it was clear that most of the Japanese troops of the *28th Army* had, after suffering heavy casualties, succeeded in infiltrating into the Pegu Yomas after crossing to the east bank of the Irrawaddy. Their plan evidently was to reach the east of the hills, cross the plains and the Mandalay-Rangoon road and the railway line and reach the Sittang river. The coming battles in June and July were therefore to be fought in the area of the IV Corps operations on the road and railway axis, east of the Pegu Yomas and on the Sittang river. Hence the task of the 20th Indian Division during these months was to keep law and order between the Irrawaddy and the Pegu Yomas and to deal with any Japanese parties that might try to re-enter this area or pass through it. Naturally, the period was not a very eventful one and only a few clashes occurred. The troops generally remained in monsoon quarters and came out only when some Japanese party in strength was

[29] A Short History of 20th Indian Div., *op. cit.*
[30] *Ibid.*

reported moving about by Burma National Army men, who established an "Intelligence Service" of their own to bring in news. Incidentally, the Burma National Army underwent another christening and was now known as the Patriotic Burmese Forces (PBF).

IV CORPS OPERATIONS

After the fall of Rangoon, in the beginning of May, the entire road and railway from Mandalay to Rangoon was in the hands of the IV Corps, but the fighting was by no means over. The Japanese were cut off in different sectors, but although separated from each other, they were determined to put up whatever resistance they could and withdraw to the east of the Sittang and to Moulmein. Some remnants of the Japanese *15th* and *33rd Armies* were still withdrawing south astride the road and railway from Meiktila. The majority of them had already withdrawn east of the Sittang by 6 May and were heading for Moulmein, while certain other groups of these armies had gone east into the Shan and Karen hills. West of Mokpalin also, there were some Japanese troops on the Moulmein road, covering the approaches to the Sittang. Above all, there were remnants of the *28th Army* who, having escaped from the XXXIII Corps area into the Pegu Yomas, were planning to break out into the IV Corps area.

It is interesting to note from the Japanese sources that, even at this stage, the morale of the *28th Army* was not as badly shaken as was supposed by the Allies. It was disclosed by them, during interrogations after the surrender, that after gathering all units under its command in the temporary safety of the Pegu Yomas, the *28th Army* planned to combine intense guerilla activity with a bold attempt to recapture Rangoon.[31] According to them, this plan for recapturing Rangoon was given up only because of the lack of mechanical transport, and it was decided instead to break out of the Yomas to the Sittang plain and rejoin *Burma Area Army* by moving along the east bank of the Sittang to Moulmein.[32]

For the breakout, the Japanese had two courses open to them. They could wait in the malarial region of the Yomas during the monsoon and make an attempt when the weather cleared, or they might make an attempt during the rainy season in the hope that the Allies would be unable to intercept them on account of rains. They chose the latter course[33] only to find to their cost that the 19th and 17th Indian Divisions were not resting in their monsoon quarters but had come out to fight them.

[31] History of Japanese 28th Army, SEATIC Bulletin No. 243, p. 3.
[32] *Ibid.*
[33] They decided upon 20 July as the date on which the breakout operations were to start SEATIC Bulletin No. 243, *op. cit.*, p. 3.

Soon after the fall of Rangoon, the new tasks of the IV Corps were defined as follows:

"The IV Corps will destroy the enemy now attempting to make their escape out of Burma. The two main zones of destruction will be between the Pegu Yomas and the Sittang river and along the Martaban coastline between the Sittang and Salween rivers."[34]

Redeployment

To carry out these tasks a redeployment of the forces available was necessary. Since the Corps had not to advance to Rangoon, a speedy redeployment was rendered easier, and by 10 May all moves on the main road axis were completed. In the extreme south was the 5th Indian Division, from Hlegu northwards to Pyingbongyi, in the centre was the 17th Indian Division from Pyingbongyi to Pyu, and in the north was the 19th Indian Division, from Pyu to north of Toungoo, with one brigade in Meiktila area. An intelligence screen composed of Burma National Army and the local civilians had been organised east and west of the main road during the previous two weeks to obtain and bring news of the approach of Japanese parties to these divisions. This was organised by officers of Force 136, but V Force was also operating in the area and was directly under the control of the Corps.

Southern Sector

All the three divisions were engaged in sporadic fighting with the Japanese forces during the month of May. In the southern sector, the 5th Indian Division was assigned the task of securing Kyaikto on the east bank of the Sittang, 17 miles below Mokpalin. But prior to it, the Japanese forces between Waw and the river Sittang had to be destroyed.

The 9th Indian Infantry Brigade undertook this job and overcoming all opposition in the Waw area advanced towards the river On 10 May, the troops smashed their way into Nyaungkashe, and subsequently patrols were pushed forward to reconnoitre the approaches to the river and the area beyond. They reported that the only feasible access to the river was in the vicinity of the Sittang bridge, which had been blown by the Japanese. It appeared then that to capture Kyaikto, the IV Corps might have to wait till the monsoon had passed. Hence, the idea of launching an assault up the stream against Mokpalin was given up, but the 5th Indian Division was ordered to remain in readiness to occupy that town in case the Japanese showed signs of withdrawing from there.

Central Sector—17th Indian Division

In the central sector all brigades of the 17th Indian Division

[34] IV Corps Operation Instruction No. 145 of 7 May 1945.

patrolled extensively in their respective areas and a few clashes with the Japanese forces occurred now and then. Sitkwin village was occupied on 11 May, but no major engagement took place until 17 May when, in the 99th Indian Infantry Brigade area, 1/3 Gurkha Rifles fought a successful action with a party of Japanese troops, ten miles south-east of Pyu. Some other small actions were fought by 1/3 Gurkha Rifles and other units, south-east of Pyu, against parties of Japanese troops up to 1 June, but there was no sign of a concerted effort by the latter to break out of the Pegu Yomas, nor were any major concentrations of the Japanese troops encountered by the patrols of the 17th Indian Division during this period.

Northern Sector—19th Division Mawchi Road

In the northern sector, the 62nd Indian Infantry Brigade of the 19th Indian Division continued its slow advance on the Mawchi road east of Toungoo, against physical obstacles and the stubborn resistance offered by the Japanese *15th Division*, whose objective was, firstly, to cover the escape route of their parties still slipping south along the foothills in this area, and, secondly, to prevent the 19th Indian Division troops from reaching Mawchi before the Japanese forces then operating north of Kemapyu and Loikaw could escape either to Siam or southwards to Moulmein via Papun. However, by 10 May, this brigade had advanced up to MS 5½. By 16 May, the tanks were in action as MS 6½ where Japanese mortars and anti-tank guns were active. The leading tank was hit seven times without being holed. By a series of infantry hooks another mile was gained but many road-blocks and demolitions hindered the advance further. "Cracker" Force was formed from the Tactical Headquarters of the 62nd Brigade, 3/6 Raj Rif and 8/12 Frontier Force Regiment with artillery and machine-gun detachments which attempted a wide southern hook with the object of emerging on the main road, in the rear of the Japanese force at MS 14, while 2 Welch advanced along the road itself from MS 8. This force met strong opposition at Kwettaik Ale and was forced to withdraw. Subsequently the advance was taken over by the 98th Indian Infantry Brigade and by 28 May the Thandaung road junction at MS 13 was captured though some hostile parties continued to resist in the surrounding hills. An idea of the stubborness of the Japanese resistance can be had from the fact that during all this period of nearly three weeks, the 19th Indian Division was able to cover only about 13 miles eastwards from Toungoo on the Mawchi road.

Kalaw and The 'Staircase'

The 64th Indian Infantry Brigade of the 19th Indian Division had been left in the Meiktila area. It was directed to relieve the 36th British Division in the Kalaw area and to afford protection to the Meiktila-Lewe area.[35] But, on account of the stubborn resistance of the Japanese and the difficult mountainous nature of the country, the 36th Division was held up at MS 17 north of Kalaw. When the 64th Indian Infantry Brigade took up the line, it encountered equally strong opposition. The Japanese had occupied a formidable natural position on a high hill, bounded by steep chaungs, through which passed a snake-like twisting road. This was the famous 'Staircase' area, north of Kalaw. No movement up the road was possible as the Japanese had blown up the bridges and the tanks could not manoeuvre to go up and destroy their bunkers. On 17 May some local people brought the report that the Japanese had about 2000 men and 20 guns between the 'Staircase' and Kalaw and that the latter place itself was well guarded.[36] On 18 May when the 19th Indian Division resumed the command of the 64th Indian Infantry Brigade, the latter was still facing great difficulty in capturing the 'Staircase' area. 5 Baluch, however, patrolled the area extensively and sent long-range patrols behind the Japanese positions who brought some very useful information on which operation 'Staircase' was planned, and finally on 29 May, 5 Baluch was ordered to secure the area.[37] The attack was preceded by an air-strike, which was successful. The rifle companies then moved up and captured the 'Staircase' area, thus opening the way to Kalaw. By 3 June reports were received that Kalaw had been evacuated by the Japanese three days ago, i.e. soon after the capture of the 'Staircase'.[38] Kalaw was therefore entered by troops of 1/6 Gurkha Rifles and 2 Worcesters without opposition on 7 June.[39]

REORGANISATION OF HIGHER COMMAND

Meanwhile a reorganisation of higher command had been effected and forces in excess of the requirements in Burma were sent to India. The Fourteenth Army had transferred its headquarters to India, and a fresh army, the Twelfth Army, was organised to control the operations in the Burma region. It comprised:—

    7th and 20th Indian Divisions,

    82nd (West African) Division (operational command only),

    6th Infantry Brigade of the 2nd British Division,

    268th Indian Infantry Brigade (under the command of the 7th Indian Division), and

    IV Corps consisting of the 5th, 17th and 19th Indian Divisions and the 255th Indian Tank Brigade.[40]

---

[35] See IV Corps Operation Instruction No. 145.
[36] 64th Brigade Summary of Information, 17 May. The units principally involved in the staircase fighting were 5 Baluch and 2 Worc R and later 1/6 GR.
[37] 5 Baluch OO No. 6 of 29 May 1945.
[38] 64th Bde OO No. 12 of 3 June.
[39] 5 Baluch WD June 45.
[40] 26th Indian Division and 254 Tank Brigade were withdrawn to India.

In addition to the above regular forces the Twelfth Army was supported by V Force and Force 136 as intelligence screen and in guerilla role, respectively. The local Burmese forces, redesignated as the Patriotic Burmese Forces (PBF), also gave useful support by their patrolling and harrying tactics. Air support available to the Twelfth Army was supplied by 221 Group RAF, consisting of four squadrons of Thunderbolts, F/Bs (fighter bombers), one squadron F/R (fighter reconnaissance) for direct air support and two squadrons of Mosquitoes.

Its Tasks

The tasks allotted for the Twelfth Army were:—
"(a) to prosecute the war against the Japanese in Burma,
(b) to take over operational and administrative responsibility for liberated Burmese territory, and
(c) to be responsible for internal security and maintenance of law and order."

These tasks involved in particular the destruction of the large Japanese forces which had been by-passed by the rapid advance south to Rangoon; the reconquest of the Tenasserim Civil Division and of all those parts which were still in Japanese hands, and the early introduction of Civil Affairs Service (Burma), and the preliminary re-forming of the regular Burma Army. For implementing these tasks the following orders were given:—

(a) IV Corps was ordered:—
   (i) To patrol westwards into the Pegu Yomas to harry the elements of the Japanese *28th Army* still trying to escape towards the Sittang river.
   (ii) To block the main routes and exits from the Pegu Yomas.
   (iii) To advance with one brigade group on the axis Meiktila-Kalaw-Taunggyi.
   (iv) To advance on the axis Toungoo-Mawchi.
   (v) To maintain one brigade group in an offensive/defensive role on the west bank of the Sittang river.

(b) The 7th Indian Division with under command the 268th Indian Infantry Brigade was ordered to mop up stragglers in the area Allanmyo-Kama-Prome and to operate with offensive patrolling into the Pegu Yomas from the west.

(c) The 20th Indian Division was to patrol offensively into the Pegu Yomas from the area Paungda in the north to Hmawbi in the south and mop up stragglers in the vicinity of the road-railway axis.

(d) The 6th Infantry Brigade and the 255th Indian Tank Brigade were to be held in reserve in Rangoon, with the task of forming a mobile column in the event of a Japanese thrust towards Rangoon. In addition, the 6th Infantry Brigade was to maintain garrisons at Syriam and Bassein and to operate water-borne patrols in the Irrawaddy Delta area in conjunction with the Navy.

(e) The 82nd (West African) Division, under operational command only, was to remain in Arakan until the monsoon was over. There was no change in its role.

But operations in pursuance of the above orders were on a reduced scale, both on account of the monsoon and the fact that the amphibious operations 'Zipper' and 'Mailfist', then being planned in India, were receiving overriding priority.

Operations in June, 1945

In the Rangoon-Prome axis, the fighting had virtually come to an end when the Twelfth Army was formed on 28 May. Many Japanese had succeeded in escaping to the Pegu Yomas, as has been already described earlier; but they had suffered heavy casualties. Mopping up of some stray Japanese parties which still remained in this sector was continued for some days in June.

The 7th Indian Division with the 268th Indian Infantry Brigade under command was allotted the northern sector of this front stretching from Prome to Shwedaung. The 20th Indian Division was operating to the south from Shwedaung in the north to Yandon—Hmawbi in the south.

In the northern sector allotted to the 7th Indian Division, the 114th Indian Infantry Brigade moved towards Paukkaung in which direction some Japanese troops were believed to have escaped. As the brigade moved forward it had to face steadily increasing opposition which showed that the Japanese were probably making Paukkaung a rallying point for their scattered parties before finally escaping to the east. They held some strong defensive positions covering Paukkaung. Hence the brigade made preparations to make a direct attack, but orders were received at this time that heavy casualties were to be avoided. This compelled the brigade to adopt merely outflanking and infiltration tactics and to abandon a direct attack. By the time it had outflanked the Japanese positions and reached the flat-basin in which Paukkaung was situated, the Japanese had made their preparations, and after some fighting in the middle of June, escaped into the Pegu Yomas. Paukkaung was occupied on 18 June but the Japanese had already gone. This area was taken over by the 268th Indian Infantry Brigade which started patrolling eastwards.

Elsewhere in the area of the 7th Indian Division, the 33rd Indian Infantry Brigade maintained active patrolling in the area south of

Prome. It was given the task of operating eastwards into the foothills of the Pegu Yomas and mopping up the Japanese force east of Paungdi and Zigon. 4/1 Gurkha Rifles was sent into the hills east of Paungdi, where it fought many minor engagements with the Japanese and dealt with their raiding parties from 7 to 27 June. Towards the end of June, however, it was felt that their activity in this area had decreased so much that the 7th Indian Division might be safely withdrawn. Accordingly this division was moved to the IV Corps front to relieve the 5th Indian Division which was intended for operations then being planned for the invasion of Malaya. This move of the 7th Indian Division was completed by the first week of July, after which the only forces left on the Prome-Rangoon axis were the 268th Infantry Brigade and the 20th Indian Division with under command the 22nd (EA) Brigade.

Operations in IV Corps Area

In the month of June and July, the IV Corps troops were deployed from Rangoon to Meiktila as follows:—

In the southern sector was the 5th Indian Division from Hlegu to Pyingbongyi.[41] In the central sector from Pyingbongyi to Pegu was the 17th Indian Division and in the northern sector was the 19th Indian Division from Pyu to Toungoo with some units on the Mawchi road east of Meiktila. In the southern sector Japanese stragglers continued to be active on the Rangoon road, south of Pegu, particularly in the area of MS 40 where the jungle bordered the road. But in general, the Japanese troops trying to escape eastwards were only too glad to avoid trouble whenever possible. Operations against such hostile parties in the area continued throughout June but no major action was fought.

BATTLE OF THE SITTANG BRIDGE—NYAUNGKASHE

The Nyaungkashe area was also the responsibility of the 5th Indian Division which had planned to cross the river Sittang in May and attack the Japanese forces to the east of that river. This plan had to be given up owing to the flooded nature of the river and the expectation of heavy casualties likely to result from an opposed crossing. The 9th Indian Infantry Brigade of this division had therefore been given the limited task of clearing the left bank of the river. While engaged in this task it discovered that the Japanese forces on the eastern bank were contemplating a local counter-offensive across the Sittang. They were endeavouring to infiltrate forces on to the

---

[41] This division was, however, relieved in July by the 7th Indian Division as described above.

west bank, and, on 19 June, elements of the *18th* and *53rd Divisions* actually crossed the river north of Kyaikkatha. Their intention, it seems, was to launch an offensive with the object of attracting Allied troops from the 17th and 19th Indian Divisions, in the north, to enable the *28th Army* to escape east. Another object would be to form a corridor for the troops escaping from Rangoon (*105 IMB*) to cross the road in the area of Daik-u by pinning down the 5th Indian Division in the Pegu area.

In order to appreciate properly the nature of developments that occurred in this area from 20 June to 8 July 1945, it is necessary to have some idea of the topography and weather conditions under which the troops of the 5th Indian Division, and later of the 7th Indian Division, had to fight.

The country east of Pegu and stretching from the foothills of the Yomas to the Sittang river was extremely flat and highly populated. East from Pegu a railway line ran through Waw to Nyaungkashe, four miles from the Sittang. The railway then crossed over the river and turned south towards Moulmein. However, the bridge had been destroyed and the railway line was only serviceable upto Nyaungkashe. By 19 June the monsoon and the floods had converted the whole countryside east of Waw into one big lake, and the only means of communication was either along the railway embankment or by water transport. Many patrols had to wade through waist-high water in an area devoid of cover, whereas the Japanese on the high ground on the east bank could observe them from their vantage point.

The Battle of the Lower Sittang

On 19 and 20 June, Nyaungkashe was shelled by the Japanese. During the night of 19/20 June, a company of 1 Burma on the west bank opposite Mokpalin was also attacked after a preliminary artillery concentration; machine-gunning and mortaring of Allied positions continued throughout 20 June and by the evening a force of 100 Japanese was established at a place about 3 miles south-east of Nyaungkashe. This was the position when elements of the 89th Indian Infantry Brigade of the 7th Indian Division started taking over from the 9th Indian Infantry Brigade on 21 June. Soon after this, 4/8 Gurkha Rifles went into action. On 26th June, it attacked a Japanese party in a small village, one mile north of Nyaungkashe, at QG 3418. The action was fought throughout in two feet of water against the Japanese troops in bunkers, dug into the side of buildings. The village was cleared with close-support weapons only.

By 29 June, when the 7th Indian Division assumed complete command of the whole southern sector, the Japanese strength was

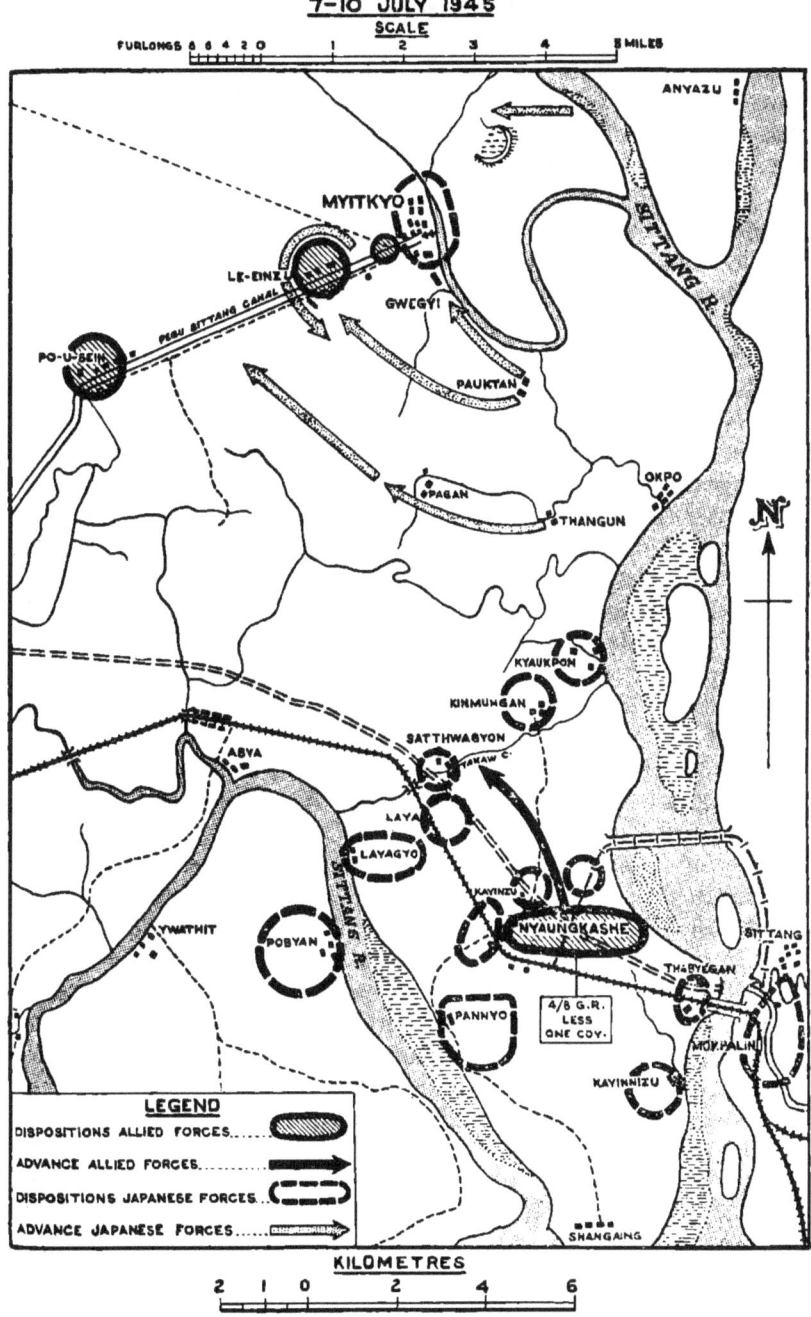

increasing in the villages north of Nyaungkashe at Kyaukpon[42] and Kinmungan and another party had again infiltrated into the village at QG 3418 cleared by the Gurkhas on 26 June. These few Japanese troops in the latter place began to strengthen their bunkers and occupied the important houses in the village under which bunkers were built and machine-guns sited. On 30 June, an air-strike on the villages was asked for by the Gurkhas, the demand was accepted but the strike could not take place on account of bad weather.

4/8 Gurkha Rifles, however, cleared Kinmungan on 1 July, but certain other villages—Panno, Pagan etc.—were occupied by the Japanese during the next two days and a considerable shelling of the Gurkha positions ensued near Nyaungkashe, indicating a possible offensive in this area. Further north the Allied troops in Pyinmagan were forced to withdraw by Japanese pressure. During the night of 3/4 July, Nyaungkashe was again heavily shelled by guns sited east of Sittang village (QG 3916). During the day on 4 July, the Japanese cut the canal line at 2732 and the railway line at 3020 and occupied the Pagoda at 305214. The pagoda position was attacked next day by 1 Sikh but it failed to dislodge the Japanese. Meanwhile the supply problem of the Gurkhas in Nyaungkashe was becoming more and more difficult. The railway and the canal lines were cut, the Gurkhas were surrounded on three sides and the supply dropping planes were able to drop only half-plane loads in the morning as the dropping zone was under fire. On 5 July, the Japanese were practically on all sides of Nyaungkashe as well as in the Pagoda, north of the railway line. 4/8 Gurkha Rifles (less one company) was completely cut off in Nyaungkashe with the Japanese in close contact with it, all round the perimeter. A patrol of 1/11 Sikh tried, unsuccessfully, to smash its way to the Gurkhas. All this while the number of Japanese in the villages around Nyaungkashe continued to increase.[43]

Meanwhile 4/15 Punjab of the 33rd Indian Infantry Brigade arrived at Waw and moved up to Abya to join 1/11 Sikh in that area. On 6 July, 3/15 Punjab left Abya at night by boat with the intention of entering Nyaungkashe from the south-west. However, the bank was held too strongly and any forced entry would have proved too costly an attempt, hence it was given up.

1/11 Sikh was then ordered to open the railway to Nyaungkashe, as that was probably the only way left to relieve the encircled

---

[42] "Local report: garrison at Kyaukpon reinforced by about 200 Japs with MGs and Mortars who crossed from east bank of Sittang in small boats during the day (28 June)", War Diary 89th Bde., 601/354/WD Pt. III.

[43] Meanwhile in the Myitkyo area the Japanese made an attempt to reach the line of the Pegu-Sittang canal running from Abya to Myitkyo and occupied Le-einzu QG 2833. But 3/6 GR cleared them from this place in hand-to-hand fighting. All aircraft available were switched to the support of 89th Bde and this deterred the Japanese from any further advance here.

Gurkhas. This could only be done, however, by first capturing the Pagoda position at 305214, which the Sikhs had failed to capture in their previous attacks. This position was again attacked twice on 6 July and also in the night of 6/7 July. But these efforts were unavailing; the planned air support did not materialise and the artillery support, already inadequate, was further limited by the shortage of ammunition. The situation was serious and the Japanese offensive, though local in character, had succeeded. On 7 July, the officiating divisional commander held a conference with the brigade commander, and at 1430 hours a message was sent to the besieged Gurkhas to destroy guns and equipment and withdraw from Nyaungkashe during the night of 7/8 July. The same evening, after dark, 4/15 Punjab and the company of 4/8 Gurkha Rifles which was not in Nyaungkashe established a firm base at Satthwagyon (3022) and formed a corridor extending south-east from that place, into which 4/8 Gurkha Rifles was to withdraw.

The withdrawal began during the night and surprisingly enough, although a few Japanese parties were contacted, no serious opposition was encountered. Carrying all their wounded and most of their equipment (except 3" mortar base-plates and three 25-pounder guns) the Gurkhas waded through the floods to Satthwagyon reaching there at dawn of 8 July. Although the water was sometimes chest-high and the rate of progress half a mile an hour, the withdrawal was carried out in good order.

After the Withdrawal from Nyaungkashe

By a strange irony of fate the weather began to clear on 7 July and the Royal Air Force support for ground troops increased just as the Gurkhas prepared to evacuate Nyaungkashe. This must have disheartened the Japanese and, on 8 July, when air operations flew as low as 100 feet they discovered that the Japanese had gone from Laya and the pagoda nearby. Nor was there any sign of their troops in Nyaungkashe. It would seem that they had withdrawn from their forward positions during the night of 7/8 July just at the time when the Gurkhas were withdrawing. Subsequently 1/11 Sikh went up and occupied the pagoda without opposition, and later reinforced the forward positions on the railway. When the Japanese realised that the Gurkhas had withdrawn from Nyaungkashe, they made fresh attempts to reoccupy their advanced positions but they were repulsed by the Sikhs on the night of 8/9 July.

The village of Myitkyo was also evacuated by the Allies. This was a large village but with the forces available it was not considered worth holding. A large party of Japanese troops entered it on 9 July but was badly harassed by the Royal Air Force whose attacks scattered them to the outskirts of the place where sporadic fighting continued for another week. But the Japanese thrust had been defeated and the majority of them had started withdrawing across the river towards the east bank, and no further attempts were made by them to advance west. Although it was not at first apparent, the Allied troops had achieved a major success even while engaged in the unsatisfactory fighting of the Sittang bend. It was confirmed by captured documents that the Japanese had aimed at capturing Waw in order to extricate their forces from the Pegu Yomas. This object was effectively defeated.

July Operations

By the middle of July 1945, the war position in Burma was as follows:—

To the west of the Pegu Yomas, on the Prome-Rangoon axis, the fighting had practically come to an end. Small Japanese parties occasionally came out of the hills foraging for food, but the 20th Indian Division was there to deal with them. In the hills of the Pegu Yomas the Japanese were making preparations to break out eastwards. To the east of these hills, on the Meiktila-Rangoon axis, the 7th, the 17th and the 19th Indian Divisions, while engaged in mopping-up operations, were also making preparations to meet the expected break-out of the Japanese forces from the hills.

To the east of the IV Corps axis, many Japanese troops had already escaped to the east of the Salween. The Allied forces had also given up the intention of crossing the Salween. The Japanese attempt to stage a counter-offensive in the Sittang river-bend at Nyaungkashe had failed in its object of diverting IV Corps towards the south to enable their forces in the Pegu Yomas to escape eastwards. The two-pronged thrust of the 19th Indian Division into the Shan Hills had only partly succeeded, that is, the Kalaw area had been cleared but operations on the Mawchi road had made very little progress.

The only point of interest therefore lay in the Pegu Yomas from which Japanese forces were expected to break out at any moment. Before we describe the actual attempt, it would be better to see what preparations the Japanese had made during a period of roughly about one and a half month preceding it. Of course during all this period—say from the beginning of June to 19 July—small groups of Japanese troops had continued to slip across the road at night and escape to the Sittang. In view of the length of the front and the number of troops available, it was obviously impossible to stop minor infiltration, but wherever the Japanese were encountered or seen they were engaged and casualties inflicted upon them. In these minor clashes, regular troops of the IV Corps as well as Force 136 and PBF took part.

Japanese Preparations

By the beginning of July detailed information of the disposition of the Japanese forces in the Pegu Yomas and their intentions had been obtained from the patrols sent by V Force. The information thus obtained was confirmed on 4 July when an operation order of the Japanese *55th Division* dated 10 June was captured. This order revealed definitely the dispositions and future intentions of the *55th Division* in detail and mentioned a D-Day for the break-out, but gave no indication of the date itself, which, from other sources, was believed to be 20 July. According to the information gleaned from all sources it appeared that the Japanese forces in the Pegu Yomas had formed themselves into five groups: *105th Independent Mixed Brigade, 55th Division, Headquarters 28th Army, 54th Division* and *153rd Regiment* and *Koba Heidan*.[44]

IV Corps Preparations

By early July, the IV Corps had completed its dispositions to counter the Japanese attempt for a break-out. In the southern sector of the Corps area, the 5th Indian Division had been relieved by the 7th Indian Division in the Pegu-Sittang area, but this division was allotted no part in meeting the Japanese break-out. The two divisions which were expected to face the Japanese were the 17th and the 19th Indian Divisions. Of these the 17th Indian Division was in the central sector, based on Penwegon, and the 19th Indian Division was to its north in the area Pyu Chaung to Toungoo.[45] In addition

---

[44] For details see Appendix 22. Japanese in Pegu Yomas before the break through.

[45] Detailed dispositions of these two Indian divisions were as follows:—
17th Div
 (i) 48th Bde was responsible from Kedok Payagyi MS 75 QG 0543 to MS 112½ QB ·1097. In this area *105 IMB* crossed the road to the north of the brigade area between MS 100 and 110 and the right-hand breakthrough unit of *55th* Div near Kukhram MS 113 on the brigade's northern boundary.
 (ii) 63rd Brigade was responsible from MS 112½ to exclusive Kun Chaung bridge MS 129½ QA 9720. In this zone the *55th Div* (Shinbu Heidan) crossed the road between Kyauktaga MS 115 QB 0901 and MS 130.
 (iii) Flewforce was responsible for inclusive Kun Chaung bridge to inclusive Pyu Chaung bridge MS 143 QA 8942. HQ *28th Army* and elements of the *121st Regt* (Saku Heidan) crossed the road between MS 130 and 136 whilst *54th Div* group (Tauwamono Heidan) crossed between Nayungbintha MS 135 and Pyu.
19th Div
 98th Bde was responsible for the area from Pyu Chaung bridge to Toungoo. In the area bends the elements of *Tauwamono Heidan* which crossed in the Pyu area, *153rd Regt* made an independent crossing between Pyu and Kywebe at MS 130 and the elements of *Koba* crossed in the area of Oktwin, MS 166.
See History of the Twelfth Army, p. 16.

an aggregate of four battalions and a field battery from the 20th Indian Division had been moved across at short notice from the west of the Pegu Yomas to strengthen the forces waiting to meet the Japanese east of the mountains.

THE BREAK-THROUGH

During the second and third week of July there was a temporary break in the monsoon over southern Burma and it was expected that the Japanese attempt to extricate their forces from the Pegu Yomas will be made with the return of the monsoon. The break-through attempt began on 19 July, and, as was expected, the larger part of it came into the 17th Indian Division area. These operations are narrated below.

17th Division Area

In the area of the 17th Indian Division, which extended between Pyu and Pyinbongyi on the main Mandalay-Rangoon road, full preparations had been made to meet the Japanese break-through. The intentions and plans of the latter were known more or less accurately from captured prisoners of war, some of whom had been sent out by the Japanese to reconnoitre and find out the gaps in the Allied line. Up to the middle of July, the Allied policy had been to let the Japanese cross the road and then to follow them towards the Sittang where an attempt was made to destroy them with artillery and air strafing.[46] Those who managed to reach the river were left to be dealt with by men of the Patriotic Burmese Forces who were watching the crossings on the river. Owing to the flooded nature of the country between the road and the river, it was not always possible to deploy armour effectively and prevent the escape of all Japanese forces. Many of their small parties therefore had succeeded in escaping without suffering much loss. The commander of the 17th Indian Division did not consider this method appropriate for dealing with the forthcoming large-scale Japanese attempt. In his own words: "I consider a better plan is to destroy the Jap as he crosses the road or comes within range of the road and then to follow the remnants up to the Sittang."[47] The main difficulty in this plan, however, was that the 17th Indian Division had a long stretch of 74 miles of the road to guard and it was impossible to watch every crossing place in strength. Therefore he ordered that likely places should be selected and strong ambushes laid there by night, which was the time that the Japanese might choose for crossing. These ambushes would also provide small patrols on the road

[46] 17th Ind Div Op. Instn. No. 17 of 16 July 1945.
[47] Ibid.

so that if the Japanese were seen crossing elsewhere, the ambush would be rapidly moved to the new place to hold them till the morning when mobile columns would arrive and destroy them.[48] To sum up, the new procedure to be followed was that ambushes were to be laid every night at all likely crossing places on the road, based on the information brought by V Force and locals and confirmed by the division's own patrol screen. Fighting was to begin as soon as the Japanese came within gun range, and those who did manage to cross the road were to be followed up to the Sittang by infantry, with artillery; and also air support if possible.

The Japanese, on their side, were planning to avoid fighting as far as possible, and to slip through the gaps between the Allied strong points.[49] For finding out these gaps active reconnaissance was carried out by them during the third week of July, but their plans and the likely crossing places were divulged to the 17th Indian Division, as has been mentioned, by certain prisoners taken during this period,[50] and it was fully prepared to checkmate the break-out.

In the area of the 48th Indian Infantry Brigade a platoon of 4/12 Frontier Force Regiment based at Pado was attacked on 19 July by a party of about 100 Japanese armed with machine-guns and rifles.[51] Fifty of them were forced to withdraw westward. Meanwhile another patrol of 4 Frontier Force Regiment making a sweep along the road to Pado from Peinzalok met approximately 25 Japanese in a nulla north-west of Pado. But the Japanese would not move from the nulla, hence 4 Frontier Force Regiment attacked them, and inflicted casualties on some. The rest then fled west and north-west.

The 'hide and seek' method during the next few days of fighting, of which it is difficult to give a coherent account, was for the Allied infantry to ambush all the probable approaches to the villages by night, to locate Japanese troops in the morning and to pin them down and to cut off their route to the Sittang. The Japanese on their part remained in the villages during the day covering the paths leading into them and tried to escape at night.

On the night of 19/20 July ambushes were laid and minor clashes with various Japanese parties occurred on 20 July at Maudan, Letpanbu Ale and at Peinzalok. In almost all the cases casualties were inflicted on them, and most of them were forced to withdraw to the west or north-west. Moreover, many local inhabitants were seen approaching the main road between Nyaunglebin and Peinzalok which indicated the imminence of the break-out attempt. The main

---
[48] *Ibid*.
[49] Appendix A to 17th Indian Div Op. Instn. No. 19 of 19 July 1945.
[50] Special Instruction, 17th Indian Div, 18 July.
[51] 17th Div Sitrep No. 169 of 20 July 1945.

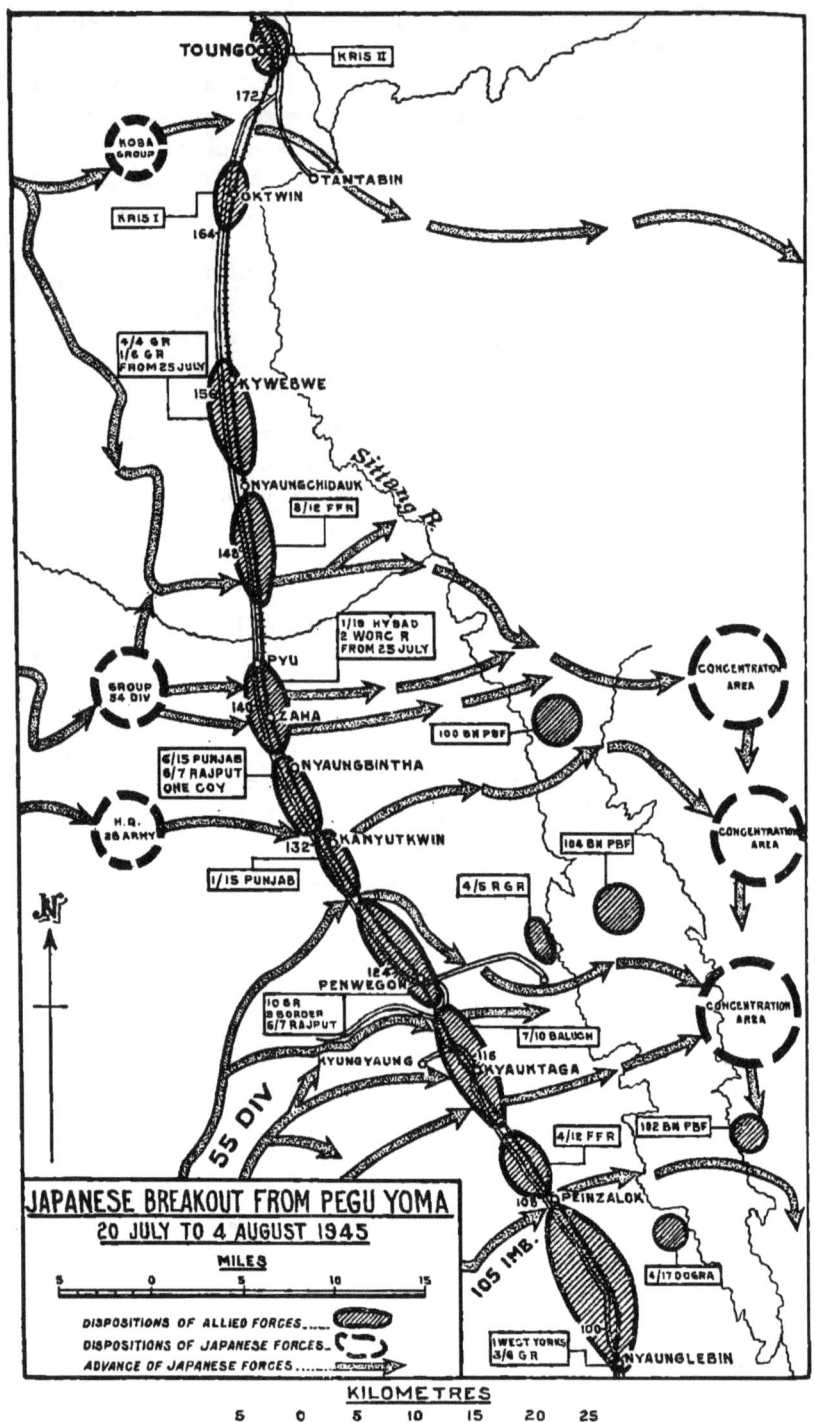

road north of Nyaunglebin was therefore immediately closed to all traffic.

Ambushes were again laid on the night of 20/21 July, and 4 Frontier Force Regiment made contact with the Japanese at many places. The break-out attempt was now in full swing. Next morning, 21 July, about 500 men of *105 IMB* were engaged between MS 103 and 107 on both sides of the road. All units of the 48th Indian Infantry Brigade contacted the Japanese troops in their respective areas and inflicted losses on them. It is not necessary here to describe the numerous killings and losses which the Japanese had to suffer. The fighting had deteriorated almost in a unilateral slaughter, as the fleeing Japanese troops were pursued and killed in every situation. The 48th Indian Infantry Brigade was responsible for the disaster of the Japanese in a large measure.

63rd Bde from 21 July—4 August

The experience of other brigades of the 17th Indian Division was similar. The 63rd Indian Infantry Brigade had been allotted the task of containing the break-through of the *55th Japanese Division*. This force had planned to cross the road somewhere between MS 112 and 129, without knowing that its plan had been captured. Hence, to their utter surprise they saw that the Allied force facing them was much stronger than they had anticipated. In this area, one of the crossing points chosen by the Japanese was at Kungyan which 1/10 Gurkha Rifles was watching. They attacked this area in suicidal waves and suffered heavy casualties at the hands of the Gurkhas. At 0300 hours on 22 July, another party came and made determined attacks in another place called Penwegon. They were repulsed and suffered many casualties, but spasmodic fighting continued till 0630 hours.[52] The Japanese broke battle at dawn and withdrew to the Pagoda area and Copse area 027093, but they were pursued and shelled by a platoon of Gurkhas. On the same day, 7/10 Baluch was in action at the bridge at QB 045045 just west of the road at MS 118½, where also the Japanese suffered severe losses.

During the night of 22/23 July, ambushes were laid and Japanese troops in small parties continued to bump against them. On the next day, 23 July, the Japanese came out along every escape route merely to be butchered. The final count showed that no less than 260 had been killed. The same story was repeated on 24 and 25 July. The morale of the Japanese forces fell, and those few who got across the road were harried by mortar and artillery fire and chased by infantry. Many who escaped fell into the hands of 4/5 Royal Gurkha Rifles on the river between Kyauksayit and Kungyaungwa.

---

[52] 17th Div Sitrep No. 173, 22 July 1945.

Mopping up of stragglers continued in the different sectors, but by 4 August only a few scattered parties had survived. Despite the fact that the *55th Division* must have realised from its first contact with the 63rd Indian Infantry Brigade on 21 July, that it was impossible to push any appreciable proportion of its troops across to the Sittang, it stuck to its original plan and suffered heavy casualties in the process. It was estimated that it lost 1621 as killed and 214 as prisoners in this sector from 21 July to 4 August.

Operations of Flewforce 20 July—4 August

In another sector Flewforce was operating from Kun Chaung bridge MS 129½ to Pyu Chaung bridge MS 143. Some troops of *HQ 28th Army* and elements of the *121st Regiment* tried to cross the road at MS 133 and MS 140 on 21 July, but suffered heavy losses. The monotonous tale of ambushes, killings, pursuits, drownings etc. was repeated in this area also till the break-out attempt had exhausted itself. On certain places the Japanese were too exhausted physically and were killed without offering any resistance.

98th Indian Brigade Area

To the north of the 17th Indian Division area was disposed the 98th Indian Infantry Brigade, blocking the Japanese escape route from Pyu Chaung Bridge to Toungoo. It expected the Japanese break-out to take place in Kywebwe, Nyaungchidauk and Zeyawadi areas within its sector.[53] In this sector also the Japanese began their attempt on the night of 20/21 July. Early in the morning of 21 July reports began to come in of the Japanese moving towards the Rangoon-Mandalay road and inquiring from the local population the route to the Sittang.[54] "Real, good monsoon rain during the night" prevented the air-craft to take off and attack the Japanese parties in the morning up to 1050 hours, but the ground troops moved into action immediately and engaged the Japanese. By 1233 hours the air operations also began[55] and an air-strike was put down at 942499 where a large party of Japanese troops was seen. Heavy fighting developed near the road at milestones 147, 168 and 172. Many were killed and those who succeeded in crossing the road were pursued. In Zeyawadi area to the east of the road, 8 Frontier Force Regiment engaged them and prevented them from reaching the Sittang. Nearly 600 casualties were inflicted in two days. On 23 and 24 July, the fighting shifted to the area east of Zeyawadi where also heavy casualties were inflicted on the Japanese.

On 25 July, when 4/4 Gurkha Rifles was clearing the northern

---

[53] 98th Ind Inf Bde War Diary. Op. Instn. No. 13 of 15 July.
[54] 98th Ind Inf Bde War Diary for 21 July.
[55] Ibid.

bank of the Pyu Chaung, 1–6 Gurkha Rifles less two companies concentrated at Pyu and by arrangements with Flewforce moved south of the Pyu Chaung to clear the area Wegyi—Okpyat, where a considerable number of the Japanese were reported. A cab-rank of Spitfires was in attendance and was asked to strafe Aukkon village. Instead it attacked another place called Leeinzu in error from where about 50 Japanese ran out. The Japanese in Wegyi, however, held out and fighting continued throughout 26 and 27 July. On the second day 4/4 Gurkha Rifles crossed the Pyu Chaung and attacked the Japanese in Obogon. Aukkon was captured by 1/6 Gurkha Rifles on 27 July causing further losses to the Japanese. Many Japanese crossed the road, but they were chased and hunted to the river. To the east of the river, Force 136 guerillas and PBF dealt with them, and thus only a few were able to escape.

The Japanese did not anticipate such heavy casualties in the break-out operations and considered this battle in July as one of their worst defeats in the Burma Campaign.[56]

The reasons for this defeat, according to them were:—
 (i) The reconnaissances carried out by them were not successful as most of the reconnaissance parties failed to return.
 (ii) The *28th Army* had no idea of the Allied dispositions and expected opposition only from scattered parties holding odd points.
 (iii) They were unaware that 17 and 19 Indian Divisions lay across their path. To the swollen chaungs, the rains and the artillery of these two Indian Divisions, they mainly ascribed their defeat.

As to why they decided on a concerted effort, instead of filtering out in small parties, the Japanese gave a very good reason. They thought that if the force was filtered out in small groups control would be lost after crossing the road and river. Hence they decided upon breaking through in an organised force on a fixed day.

Every man who came out of the Pegu Yomas carried a bamboo pole, which proved a hindrance on the march but was of great help in crossing the rivers; and, according to the Japanese, few men were lost by drowning.[57]

Starving, stricken by disease, harassed by the Royal Air Force and active patrolling by land forces with no cover from the unending rains, any other adversary would have surrendered his whole force. But Lieut.-General Sakurai, true to the traditions of his brave race—

---

[56] *Ibid.*
[57] But according to Allied sources the river must have taken a heavier toll, since it was swollen by rains and was flowing at a speed of 12 knots. Moreover it averaged more than 1000 feet in breadth at this time of the year.

not unlike the Rajputs of the Middle Ages in India—did not consider surrender and paid the price. Of his force, variously estimated from 16000 to 19000, only about 4000 to 5000 reached the east bank of the Sittang and made their way south. While marching towards Bilin they heard the news of the surrender of Japan on 15 August. And so ended the Burma Campaign.

APPENDICES

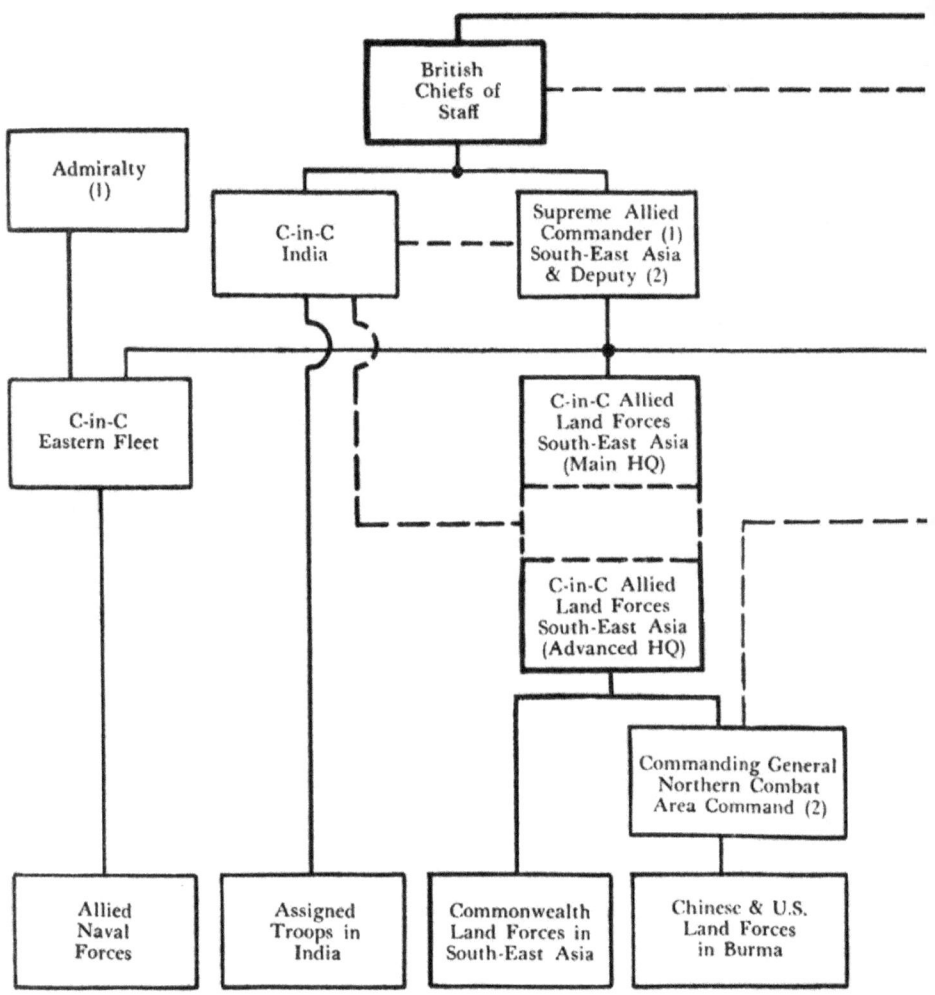

(1) During February and March 1945 the United States 20th Bomber Command of Super
    Supreme Allied Commander. He delegated his authority in these matters to the A
    of the Super Fortresses was vested in the Commanding General, Eastern Air Command

(2) Lieut.-General Stilwell was recalled to the United States on the 21st October 1944. He
    by Lieut.-General Wheeler. The China-Burma-India was divided into China (Lieut.-G
    Generalissimo. Lieut.-General Sultan also took over command of Northern Combat A

APPENDIX I

CHAIN OF COMMAND

After the Creation of Headquarters Allied Land Forces South-East Asia
12th November 1944.

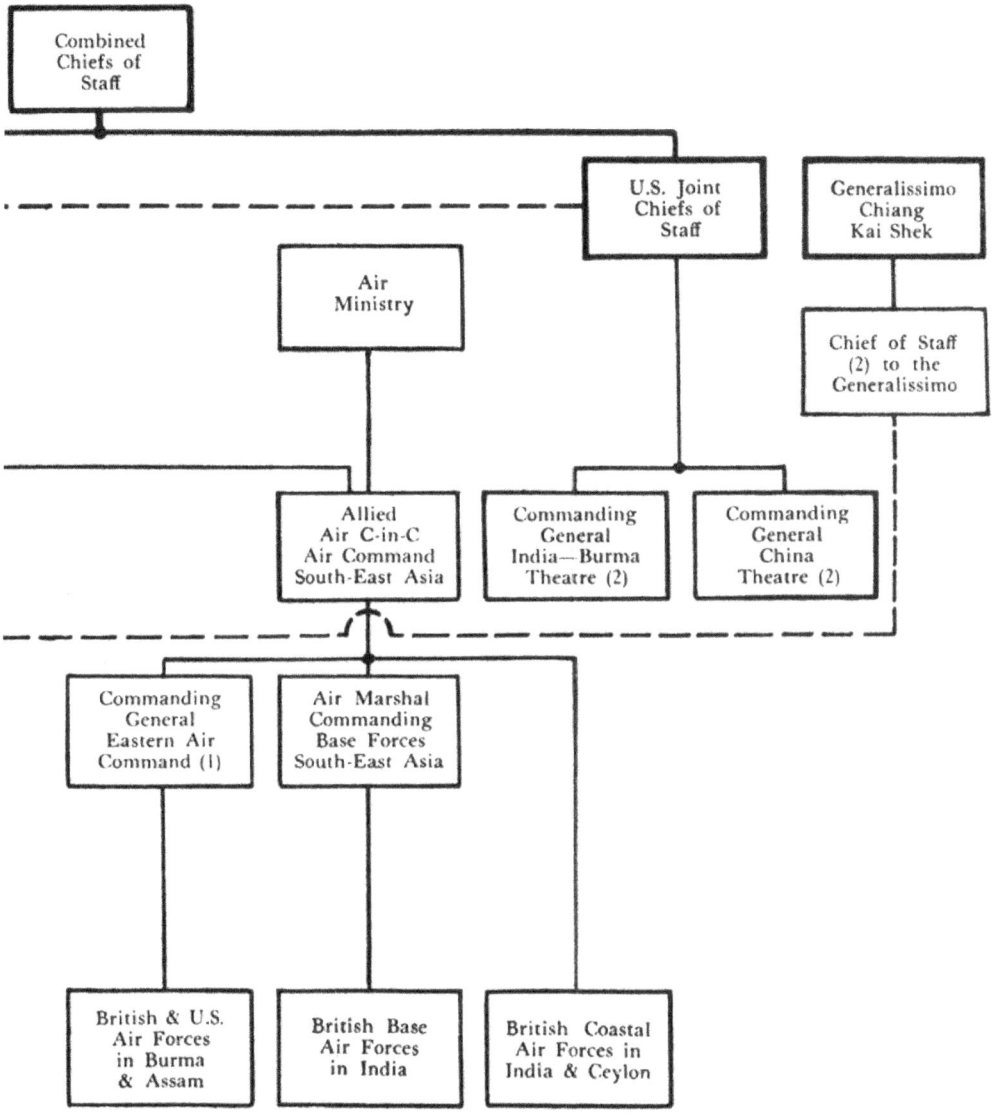

Fortresses (B-29) was put under the command of the
 llied Air Commander-in-Chief. Operational Control

was succeeded as Deputy Supreme Allied Commander
 eneral Wedemyer) also became Chief of Staff to the
 ea Command.

KEY
 Direct Command ... ─────
 Liaison ... ── ── ──

APPENDIX 2

ORDER OF BATTLE

33 IND. CORPS
1 AUG '44

UNIT	REMARKS
H.Q. 33 Ind Corps.	
H.Q. R.A. 33 Ind Corps.	
H.Q. 33 Ind Corps Empl Pl.	
H.Q. 33 Ind Corps Tpt Sec.	} G.H.Q. Tps.
5 S.W. Sec.	
201 S.W. Sec.	

CORPS TROOPS

ARTY.

1 Med Regt. Sig Sec & L.A.D.
8 Med Regt. less one Bty, Sig Sec & L.A.D.
67 Hy AA Regt. & Wksp Sec.
69 Lt AA Regt. & Wksp Sec.
78 Lt AA Regt. & Wksp Sec.
43/2 Svy Bty R.A.
44/2 Svy Bty R.A.
'D' Tp 44 Comp Svy Bty.   under comd 23 Ind Div.
1 (W.A.) H.A.A. Bty.
19/7 (Rajput) H.A.A. Bty less one Tp.
C.B. Staff.
3 Ind C.B. Tram.   under comd 23 Ind Div.

ENGRS.

H.Q. 33 Ind Corps Tps Engrs.
24 Ind Fd Coy.
67 Ind Fd Coy.
80 Ind Fd Coy.
362 Ind Fd Coy.
429 Ind Fd Coy.
332 Ind Fd Pk Coy.
1 Ind Div Br Pl.
Suket Div Br Pl.
10 (Pathan) Ind Engr Bn.
H.Q. 4 Corps Tps Engrs.
75 Ind Fd Coy.
94 Ind Fd Coy.   under comd 23 Ind Div.
424 Ind Fd Coy.
428 Ind Fd Coy.
305 Ind Fd Pk Coy.
15 Ind Div Br Pl.

SIGNALS

33 Corps Signals.
205 Ind Monitoring Sec.
241 W/T Sec.

UNIT	REMARKS
INF.	
H.Q. Assam Zone V Force.	
1 Det 3 V Ops.	
1 Det 4 Assam Rif.	
Burma Escort Coy (Kabaw Valley Det) (Kabaw Det Burma Regt)	under comd 23 Ind Div.
9 Jats M.G. Bn.	under comd 23 Ind Div.
80 Ind Inf Coy, 14 Punjab	
S.T.	
8 M.T. Regt. H.Q.	
37 G.P.T. Coy.	
40 G.P.T. Coy.	
64 G.P.T. Coy.	
160 G.P.T. Coy.	
164 G.P.T. Coy.	
904 Jeep Coy & Wksp Sec.	
905 Jeep Coy & Wksp Sec.	
H.Q. American Fd Services.	
1 M.A.S. (A.F.S.)	
2 M.A.S. (A.F.S.)	
3 M.A.S. (A.F.S.)	
4 M.A.S. (A.F.S.)	
61 M.A.S.	
78 D.I.D.	
312 Ind Sup Sec (POL)	
328 Ind Sup Sec.	
339 Ind Sup Sec.	under comd 23 Ind Div.
495 Ind Sup Sec.	
544 Ind Sup Sec.	
550 Ind Sup Sec. (POL)	
628 Ind Sup Sec.	
54 A.T. Coy.	
75 A.T. Coy.	
MEDICAL	
13 Ind C.C.S.	
16 Ind C.C.S.	
26 Ind C.C.S.	
20 Anti-Malaria Unit.	
33 Ind Anti-Malaria Unit.	
44 Ind Anti-Malaria Unit.	
55 Anti-Malaria Unit.	
68 Anti-Malaria Unit.	
69 Anti-Malaria Unit.	
3 Mobile X-Ray Unit.	
10 Mobile X-Ray Unit.	
82 Mobile X-Ray Unit.	
5 Ind Mob Surg Unit.	
9 Ind Mob Surg Unit.	
10 Ind Mob Surg Unit.	under comd 20 Ind Div.
14 Ind Mob Surg Unit.	
56 Ind Fd Hyg Sec.	

UNIT	REMARKS

7 Malarial Fwd Treatment Unit. (Dimapur)
8 Malarial Fwd Treatment Unit. (Kohima)
5 Fd Transfusion Unit.
27 Fd Transfusion Unit.
5 bearer Coy.
67 Ind Staging Sec.
76 Ind Staging Sec.
64 Ind Fd Amb.
67 Ind Fd Amb.
9 Ind Lt Fd Amb.
17 Ind Dental Unit.   under comd 23 Ind Div.
19 Ind Dental Unit.
44 Ind Sub Depot Medical Stores.
No. 1 ⎫
No. 2 ⎬ American Fd.
No. 3 ⎪ Service Pls.
No. 4 ⎭

PRO.
33 Ind Corps Pro Unit.

ORD.
19 Ind Ord Mob Cinema Unit.
25 Ind Ord Mob Cinema Unit.
36 Ind Ord Mob Cinema Unit.
5 Ind Ord Mob Laundry & Bath Unit.
11 Ind Ord Salvage Unit.
14 Salvage Unit.
19 Ind Ord Salvage Unit.
37 Ind Ord Salvage Unit.
H.Q. 4 Corps O.F.P.
4 Corps Tps & Army Tps Ord Sub Pk.
2 Div Ord Sub Pk.
5 Ind Div Ord Sub Pk.
11 Div Ord Sub Pk.
17 Ind Div Ord Sub Pk.
20 Ind Div Ord Sub Pk.
23 Ind Div Ord Sub Pk.

EME.
1 Inf Tps Wksp.
60 Ind Mob Wksp Coy.
81 Ind Mob Wksp Coy.
112 Ind Mob Wksp Coy.
328 L of C Rec Coy.
333 L of C Rec Coy.
24 Ind Bde R.A.S.C. Wksp Pl.
1067 Ind G.P.T. Wksp Sec.   att 33 Ind Corps Tpt Sec

REMOUNT & VET.
3 Ind Adv Remount Depot.
7 Ind Adv Remount Depot.
10 Ind Fd Remount Sec.
15 Ind Fd Remount Sec.
18 Ind Fd Remount Sec.
20 Ind Fd Remount Sec.

UNIT	REMARKS

3 Ind Saddle Fitting Team.
10 Ind Fd Vet Hospital.
21 Ind Adv Fd Vet Hospital.
22 Ind Adv Fd Vet Hospital.
25 Ind Adv Fd Vet Hospital.
21 Ind Fd Depot Vet Stores.
22 Ind Fd Depot Vet Stores.
1 Ind Mob Vet Sec.
15 Ind Mob Vet Sec.

Postal.

48 Ind F.P.O.

Int.

575 Ind F.S. Sec.
579 Ind F.S. Sec.
589 Ind F.S. Sec.
590 Ind F.S. Sec.
598 Ind F.S. Sec.
3 Mob Sec SEATIC.
2 Adv F.I.C.
3 Adv F.I.C.
Det No. 204 I.F.B.U.
51 Obs Sqn.

Survey

A.D. Survey & Pz.
Det 6 Fd Svy Coy.
33 Map Supply Sec.

P & L.

1340 Ind Pnr Coy.
1466 Ind Pnr Coy.
1467 Ind Pnr Coy.
1488 Ind Pnr Coy.

Mess Units

No. 3 Mess Unit.
No. 41 Mess Unit.
No. 138 Mess Unit.
No. 162 Mess Unit.
No. 163 Mess Unit.
No. 342 Mess Unit.
No. 336 Mess Unit.
No. 388 Mess Unit.
No. 1 Sjts Mess Unit.
No. 6 Sjts Mess Unit.
No. 62 Sjts Mess Unit.

Misc.

25 A.A.S.C.
115 P.W. Cage.
'E' Graves Registration Unit.
4 Corps Elephant Unit.

APPENDIX 2

254 IND TANK BDE.

UNIT   *REMARKS*

H.Q. 254 Ind Tk Bde.
254 Ind Tk Bde H.Q. Sqn Tk Tp.
149 R.A.C. (Less one Sqn) and L.A.D.
3 D.G. & L.A.D.
7 Cav and L.A.D.
3 Bombay Grenadiers and L.A.D.

ENGRS.
401 Ind Fd Sqn.

SIGS.
254 Ind Tk Bde Sig Sqn.

S.T.
609 G.P.T. Coy.
589 Tk Tptr Coy.

MEDICAL
14 Ind Lt Fd Amb less one Sec.

PRO.
254 Ind Tk Bde Pro Unit.

ORD.
104 Ind Ord Fd Pk (Tk Bde) less det.
Det 105 Ind Ord Fd Pk.

EME.
Det 2 Tk Rec Coy.
Det 4 Tk Rec Coy.
Sec 5 Ind Mob Wksp Coy.
74 Ind Mob Wksp Coy.
203 Mob Wireless Wksp Sec.

POSTAL
63 Ind F.P.O.

2 DIV.

HEADQUARTERS.
H.Q. 2 Div.
H.Q. R.A. 2 Div.
H.Q. 2 Div R.E.
H.Q. 2 Div R.A.S.C.
H.Q. 2 Div R.E.M.E.
H.Q. 2 Div Def & Empl Pl.

ARMD CORPS
2 Recce Regt, Sig Sec & L.A.D.
11 Cav.

ARTY.
10 Fd Regt, Sig Sec and L.A.D.
16 Fd Regt, Sig Sec and L.A.D.
99 Fd Regt, Sig Sec and L.A.D.
100 AA/ATK Regt, Sig Sec and Wksp Sec (B) (Less 2 AA Btys).

UNIT REMARKS

ENGINEERS
  5 Fd Coy.
  208 Fd Coy.
  506 Fd Coy.
  21 Fd Pk Coy and L.A.D. (B).

SIGS.
  2 Div Sigs and L.A.D. (A) (Less Inf Bde Sig Secs).

M.G. BN & INF.
  2 Manch M.G. and L.A.D. less one coy.

E.M.E.
  2 Div Tps Wksp.
  4 Bde Wksp.
  5 Bde Wksp.
  6 Bde Wksp.

MEDICAL
  4 Fd Amb.
  5 Fd Amb.
  6 Fd Amb.
  2 Fd Hyg Sec.
  44 A.M. Unit.

S.T.
  8 Inf Bde Coy R.A.S.C.
  24 Inf Bde Coy R.A.S.C.
  29 Inf Bde Coy R.A.S.C.
  387 Div Tps R.A.S.C.

PRO.
  2 Div Pro Unit.

POSTAL
  2 Div Postal Unit.
  131 Fd P.O.
  132 Fd P.O.
  133 Fd P.O.

INT.
  1 Brit F.S. Sec.

INF.
     4 Inf Bde
  H.Q. 4 Inf Bde & Sig Sec.
  H.Q. 4 Inf Bde Def Pl, and L.A.D. (A).
  H.Q. 4 Inf Bde R.E.M.E. and L.A.D.

INF.
  1 R. Scots.
  2 Norfolk.
  1/8 L.F.
     5 Inf Bde
  H.Q. 5 Inf Bde and Sig Sec.
  H.Q. 5 Inf Bde Def Pl and L.A.D. (A).
  H.Q. 5 Inf Bde R.E.M.E. and L.A.D.

| UNIT | REMARKS |

INF.
  7 Worc R.
  2 Dorset.
  1 Cameron.
  6 Inf Bde
  H.Q. 6 Inf Bde and Sig Sec.
  H.Q. 6 Inf Bde Def Pl and L.A.D. (B)
  H.Q. 6 Inf Bde R.E.M.E. and L.A.D.

INF.
  1 R.W.F.
  1 R. Berks.
  2 D.L.I.

5 IND DIV.

HEADQUARTERS
  Main H.Q. 5 Ind Div.
  Rear H.Q. 5 Ind Div.
  H.Q. R.A. 5 Ind Div.
  H.Q. 5 Ind Div R.E.
  H.Q. 5 Ind Div Sigs.
  H.Q. 5 Ind Div Regt R.I.A.S.C.
  H.Q. 5 Ind Div I.E.M.E.

ARTY. (5 IND DIV)
  4 Fd Regt R.A., Sig Sec and L.A.D.
  28 (J) Fd Regt. R.A., Sig Sec and L.A.D.
  56 AA/ATk Regt., Sig Det and Wksp Sec
  24 Ind Mtn Regt., Sig Sec and L.A.D.

ENGRS
  2 Ind Fd Coy.
  20 Ind Fd Coy.
  74 Ind Fd Coy.
  44 Ind Fd Pk Coy.

INF
  3/2 Punjab less three Coys   under comd 23 Ind Div.
  H.Q. 9 Ind Inf Bde, Sig Sec and L.A.D. (E).
  2 W. Yorks.
  3 Jat.
  3/14 Punjab.
  'D' Coy 3/2 Punjab.
  H.Q. 123 Ind Inf Bde, Sig Sec., and L.A.D. (E).
  2 Suffolks.
  2/1 Punjab.
  1 Dogra.
  'C' Coy 3/2 Punjab.
  H.Q. 161 Ind Inf Bde, Sig Sec, and L.A.D. (E).
  4 R.W.K.
  1/1 Punjab.
  4 Rajput.
  'A' Coy 3/2 Punjab.

UNIT   *REMARKS*

R.I.A.S.C.
  238 I.G.P.T. Coy.
  239 I.G.P.T. Coy.
  240 I.G.P.T. Coy.
  7 Ind Comp Issue Sec.
  60 Ind Comp Issue Sec.
  61 Ind Comp Issue Sec.
  62 Ind Comp Issue Sec.
  23 A.T. Coy (M).
  60 Mule Coy.
  66 A.T. Coy (M).
  74 A.T. Coy (M).
  82 A.T. Coy (M).
  5 Ind Fd Amb Tp Cl 1.
  22 Ind Fd Amb Tp Cl 1.
  23 Ind Fd Amb Tp Cl 1.

MEDICAL
  10 Ind Fd Amb.
  45 Ind Fd Amb.
  75 Ind Fd Amb.
  7 Ind Fd Hyg Sec.

PRO
  3 Ind Div Pro Unit.

IEME
  113 Ind Mob Wksp Coy.
  5 Ind Rec Coy.

VET.
  2 Ind Mob Vet Sec.

POSTAL.
  21 Ind F.P.O.
  22 Ind F.P.O.
  23 Ind F.P.O.
  169 Ind F.P.O.

INT.
  565 F.S. Sec.

7 IND DIV.

HEADQUARTERS.
  H.Q. 7 Ind Div.
  H.Q. R.A. 7 Ind Div.
  H.Q. 7 Ind Div Engrs.
  H.Q. 7 Ind Div R.I.A.S.C.
  H.Q. 7 Ind Div I.E.M.E.
  Div H.Q. Bn 7/2 Punjab (less one Pl).

ARTY
  Bty 21 Mtn Regt.
  25 Ind Mtn Regt, Sig Sec. & L.A.D.

ENGRS
  62 Ind Fd Coy.
  77 Ind Fd Coy.
  421 Ind Fd Coy.
  331 Ind Fd Pk Coy.

APPENDIX 2

UNIT	REMARKS

SIGS
  7 Ind Div Sigs.

S.T.
  20 A.T. Coy (M).
  57 A.T. Coy (M).
  63 A.T. Coy (M).
  65 A.T. Coy (M).
  60 G.P.T. Coy.
  130 G.P.T. Coy.
  30 Ind Comp Issue Sec.
  13 Fd Amb Tp.
  14 Fd Amb Tp.
  18 Fd Amb Tp.

MEDICAL
  44 Ind Fd Amb.
  54 Ind Fd Amb.
  66 Ind Fd Amb.
  32 Fd Hyg Sec.
  45 A.M. Unit.

PRO
  7 Ind Div Pro Unit.

EME
  7 Rec Coy.
  39 Wksp Coy.

MISC
  7 Mob Vet Sec.
  37 Ind Fd P.O.
  568 Ind F.S. Sec.
  37 Ind Salvage Unit.

33 IND INF BDE.
  H.Q. 33 Ind Inf Bde.
  H.Q. 33 Ind Inf Bde Sig Sec and L.A.D. (E).
  1 Queens.
  4/1 G.R.
  1 Burma.
  79 Ind Fd P.O.
  31 I.C.I.S.

89 IND INF BDE.
  H.Q. 89 Ind Inf Bde.
  H.Q. 89 Ind Inf Bde Sig Sec, and L.A.D. (E).
  2 K.O.S.B.
  1 Sikh
  4/8 G.R.
  94 Ind Fd P.O.
  32 I.C.I.S.

UNIT   *REMARKS*

114 IND INF BDE.
  H.Q. 114 Ind Inf Bde.
  H.Q. 114 Ind Inf Bde Sig Sec, and L.A.D. (E).
  2 S. Lan R.
  4/14 Punjab.
  4/5 G.R.
  39 Ind Fd P.O.
  29 I.C.I.S.

11 DIV.

HEADQUARTERS
  H.Q. 11 Div.
  H.Q. R.A. 11 Div and Sig Sec.
  H.Q. 11 Div R.E., Sig Sec and L.A.D.
  H.Q. 11 Div E.A.A.S.C.
  H.Q. 11 Div R.A.E.M.E.
  H.Q. 11 Div L.A.D.

ARTY
  302 Fd Regt EAA, Sig Sec and L.A.D.
  303 Fd Regt EAA, Sig Sec and L.A.D.
  304 ATk/LAA Regt and L.A.D.

ENGRS.
  54 Fd Coy E.A.E.
  58 Fd Coy E.A.E.
  64 Fd Coy E.A.E.
  62 Fd Pk Coy.

SIGS
  11 Div Sigs, Cipher Sec and L.A.D.

S.T.
  1 Inf Bde Coy.
  2 Inf Bde Coy.
  3 Inf Bde Coy.
  11 Div Tps Coy.

MEDICAL
  2 (Z) Fd Amb.
  6 (U) Fd Amb.
  10 Fd Amb.
  71 Fd Hyg Sec.
  60 F.D.S.
  61 F.D.S.
  2004 S.B. Coy.

PRO
  11 Div Pro Coy.

EME
  11 Div Army Tps Wksp.
  1 Inf Bde Wksp.
  2 Inf Bde Wksp.
  3 Inf Bde Wksp.

UNIT	*REMARKS*

INT
  5 Fd S. Sec.

POSTAL
  11 Div Postal Unit.

MISC
  12 Obs Unit.
  13 Fd Infs Pl.
  11 Div Salvage Unit.

21 INF BDE
  H.Q. 21 Inf Bde.
  21 Inf Bde Sig Sec, Cipher Sec. and L.A.D.
  2 (NY) Bn K.A.R.
  4 (U) Bn. K.A.R.
  1 N.R.R.

25 INF BDE.
  H.Q. 25 Inf Bde.
  25 Inf Bde Sig Sec, Cipher Sec and L.A.D.
  11 (K) Bn K.A.R.
  26 (TT) Bn K.A.R.
  34 (U) Bn K.A.R.

26 INF BDE.
  H.Q. 26 Inf Bde.
  26 Inf Bde Sig Sec, Cipher Sec and L.A.D.
  22 (NY) Bn K.A.R.
  36 (TT) Bn K.A.R.
  44 (U) Bn K.A.R.
  13 (NY) Bn K.A.R.

17 IND LT DIV.

HEADQUARTERS
  H.Q. 17 Ind Lt Div.
  H.Q. R.A. 17 Ind Lt Div.
  H.Q. 17 Ind Lt Div R.I.A.S.C.
  H.Q. 17 Ind Lt Div I.E.M.E.

ARTY.
  H.Q. 21 Ind Mtn Regt and Sig Sec.
  1 R. Mtn Bty.
  6 Mtn Bty.
  37 Mtn Bty (Mortar).
  H.Q. 29 Ind Mtn Regt and Sig Sec.
  9 Mtn Bty.
  14 Mtn Bty.
  38 Mtn Bty (Mortar).
  H.Q. 129 Fd Regt R.A. and Sig Sec.
  311 Fd Bty.
  312 Fd Bty.
  493 Fd Bty.

| UNIT | REMARKS |

H.Q. 82 L.A.A./A. Tk Regt R.A., Sig Det and Wksp Sec.
87 L.A.A. Bty.
88 L.A.A. Bty.
228 A. Tk Bty.
276 A. Tk Bty.

ENGRS
  H.Q. 17 Ind Lt Div.
  60 Ind Fd Coy.
  70 Ind Fd Coy.
  414 Ind Fd Pk Coy.

SIGS
  17 Ind Lt Div Sigs.
  48 Ind Lt Bde Sig Sec.
  63 Ind Lt Bde Sig Sec.

INF
  4/12 F.F.R. — Div H.Q. Bn.
  1 W. Yorks. — Div Sp Bn.
  7/10 Baluch. — Div Recce Bn.

H.Q. 48 IND LT BDE.
  9 Border.
  1/7 G.R.
  2/5 R.G.R.

H.Q. 63 IND LT BDE.
  1/3 G.R.
  1/4 G.R.
  1/10 G.R.

R.I.A.S.C.
  9 Ind Comp Issue Sec.
  10 Ind Comp Issue Sec.
  11 Ind Comp Issue Sec.
  17 Ind Fd Amb Tp.
  900 Ind Jeep Coy.
  901 Ind Jeep Coy.
  902 Ind Jeep Coy.
  906 Ind Jeep Coy.
  45 Ind Mule Coy.
  47 Ind Mule Coy.
  49 Ind Mule Coy.
  52 Ind Mule Coy.
  17 Div H.Q. Tpt Sec.

MEDICAL
  23 Ind Fd Amb.
  37 Ind Fd Amb.
  3 Ind Bearer Coy.
  4 Ind Bearer Coy.
  22 Ind Fd Hyg Sec.

PROVOST
  17 Ind Lt Div Pro Unit.

| UNIT | REMARKS |

ORD
  'B' Sec 51 Ord Fd Pk.
  33 Salvage Unit.

I.E.M.E.
  1 Ind Mob Wksp Coy.
  59 Ind Mob Wksp Coy.
  17 Ind Rec Coy.
  48 Ind L.A.D. Type 'F'.
  63 Ind L.A.D. Type (F).

VET.
  4 Ind Mob Vet Sec.

POSTAL
  82 Ind F.P.O.
  97 Ind F.P.O.
  100 Ind F.P.O.

INT.
  602 Ind F.S. Sec.
  4 Pl Burma Int Corps.

20 IND DIV.

HEADQUARTERS
  H.Q. 20 Ind Div.
  H.Q. R.A. 20 Ind Div.
  H.Q. 20 Ind Div Engrs.
  H.Q. 20 Ind Div R.I.A.S.C.
  H.Q. 20 Ind Div I.E.M.E.
  4 Madras less one Pl.   Div H.Q. Bn.

ARTY.
  9 Fd Regt, Sig Sec and L.A.D.
  114 (J) Fd Regt, Sig Sec and L.A.D.
  53 AA/ATk Regt and Wksp Sec.
  23 Ind Mtn Regt and Sig Sec.

ENGRS
  92 Ind Fd Coy.
  422 Ind Fd Coy.
  481 Ind Fd Coy.
  309 Ind Fd Pk Coy.
  9 Ind Div Br Pl.

SIGS
  20 Ind Div Sigs.

S.T.
  37 Ind Comp Issue Sec.
  38 Ind Comp Issue Sec.
  39 Ind Comp Issue Sec.
  45 Ind Comp Issue Sec.
  100 Ind G.P.T. Coy (15 cwt.).
  102 Ind G.P.T. Coy (15 cwt.).
  127 Ind G.P.T. Coy (3 ton).
  628 Ind Sup Sec.

UNIT	REMARKS

38 Bakery Sec.
3 Ind Fd Amb Tp.
14 Ind Mule Coy.
30 Ind Mule Coy.
43 Ind Mule Coy.
52 Ind Mule Coy.
55 Ind Mule Coy.

MEDICAL
  42 Ind Fd Amb.
  55 Ind Fd Amb.
  59 Ind Fd Amb.
  20 Ind Anti-Malaria Unit.
  26 Ind Fd Hyg Sec.

PRO
  20 Ind Div Pro Unit.

EME
  63 Ind Mob Wksp Coy.
  64 Ind Mob Wksp Coy.
  20 Ind Rec Coy.

INT.
  604 Ind F.S. Sec.

POSTAL
  76 Ind Fd P.O.
  120 Ind Fd P.O.
  122 Ind Fd P.O.
  123 Ind Fd P.O.

MISC
  13 Ind Mob Vet Sec.

32 IND INF BDE.
  H.Q. 32 Ind Inf Bde.
  H.Q. 32 Ind Inf Bde Sig Sec.
  H.Q. 32 Ind Inf Bde L.A.D. (E).
  1 Northamptons.
  9/14 Punjab.
  3/8 Punjab.

80 IND INF BDE.
  H.Q. 80 Ind Inf Bde.
  H.Q. 80 Ind Inf Bde Sig Sec.
  H.Q. 80 Ind Inf Bde L.A.D. (E).
  1 Devons.
  9 F.F.R.
  3/1 G.R.

100 IND INF BDE.
  H.Q. 100 Ind Inf Bde.
  H.Q. 100 Ind Inf Bde Sig Sec.
  H.Q. 100 Ind Inf Bde L.A.D. (E).
  2 Border.
  14 F.F. Rif.
  4/10 G.R.
  Pl. 4 Madras.

23 IND DIV.

UNIT   *REMARKS*

HEADQUARTERS
  H.Q. 23 Ind Div.
  H.Q. 23 Ind Div Def and Empt Pl.
  H.Q. R.A. 23 Ind Div.
  H.Q. 23 Ind Div Engrs.
  H.Q. 23 Ind Div R.I.A.S.C.
  H.Q. 23 Ind Div I.E.M.E.
  2 Hybad.   Div H.Q. Bn.

ARTY.
  158 (J) Fd Regt, Sig Sec and L.A.D.
  3 Ind Fd Regt, Sig Sec and L.A.D.
  28 Ind Mtn Regt, Sig Sec and L.A.D.
  2 Ind A.A./A. Tk Regt, Sig Sec and L.A.D

ENGRS
  2 Madras Engr Bn.
  68 Ind Fd Coy.
  71 Ind Fd Coy.
  91 Ind Fd Coy.
  323 Ind Fd Pk Coy.
  10 Ind Div Br Pl.
  Sec 442 Ind Quarrying Coy.

SIGS.
  23 Ind Div Sigs.
  3 Ind Cipher Sec.

S.T.
  H.Q. 23 Ind Div Tpt Sec.
  21 Mule Coy.
  24 Mule Coy.
  50 Mule Coy.
  61 Mule Coy.
  121 Ind G.P.T. Coy.
  122 Ind G.P.T. Coy.
  123 Ind G.P.T. Coy.
  12 Ind Comp Issue Sec.
  13 Ind Comp Issue Sec.
  14 Ind Comp Issue Sec.
  15 Ind Comp Issue Sec.
  7 Ind Fd Amb Tp.
  10 Ind Fd Amb Tp.
  18 Ind Fd Amb Tp.

MEDICAL
  24 Ind Fd Amb.
  47 Ind Fd Amb.
  49 Ind Fd Amb.
  23 Ind Fd Hyg Sec.
  68 A.M.U.

PRO
  23 Ind Div Pro Unit.

| UNIT | REMARKS |

EME

38 Ind Mob Wksp Coy.
61 Ind Mob Wksp Coy.
1 Ind L.A.D. Type 'E'.
37 Ind L.A.D. Type 'E'.
49 Ind L.A.D. Type 'E'.
23 Ind Div Rec Coy.
204 Wireless Wksp Sec Type 'A'.

VET

5 Ind Mob Vet Sec.

POSTAL

69 Ind F.P.O.
91 Ind F.P.O.
99 Ind F.P.O.
117 Ind F.P.O.

MISC

605 Ind F.S. Sec.
23 Ind Div Reinforcement Bn.

1 IND INF BDE

H.Q. 1 Ind Inf Bde.
H.Q. 1 Ind Inf Bde Sig Sec.
1 Seaforth.
1/16 Punjab.
1 Patiala Inf.

37 IND INF BDE.

H.Q. 37 Ind Inf Bde.
H.Q. 37 Ind Inf Bde Sig Sec.
3/3 G.R.
3/5 R.G.R.
3/10 G.R.

49 IND INF BDE.

H.Q. 49 Ind Inf Bde.
H.Q. 49 Inf Bde Sig Sec.
4 Mahrattas.
6 Mahrattas.
5 Raj Rif.

"253 SUB AREA"

18 Mahrattas.
27 Mahrattas.
1 Chamar.

"256 SUB AREA"

Kalibahadur Regt.

APPENDIX 3

4 CORPS OPERATION INSTRUCTION NO. 100

23 June 44

To: Major General D. D. Gracey, O.B.E., M.C., G.O.C., 20 Ind Div.

1. 31 JAPANESE Div appears to be withdrawing on UKHRUL. The elements of 15 JAPANESE Div escaping from the main rd KOHIMA-IMPHAL are attempting to do likewise. Both these moves are being covered from the south-west by a force of approx one regt 15 JAPANESE Div astride the rd IMPHAL-UKHRUL.

2. (a) 23 Bde is following up the withdrawal from the north and is moving on UKHRUL by the tracks leading south from KHARASOM RE 9144 via CHINGJUI RE 8636—PAOWI RE 8422 and KONGAI RE 9932—LONGBI KACHUI RE 9012. A detached force from 23 Bde is operating further to the east on SAIYAPAW SF 2398 from which place it will probably turn west against the JAPANESE main L of C.

   (b) 33 Ind Inf Bde of 7 Ind Div leaves MARAM RE 5236 on 27 Jun moving on UKHRUL via DINAM RE 6129—NGAWAR RE 6921—FUMI HUIMI RE 7516—TOLLOI RE 7610.

   (c) 89 Ind Inf Bde under comd 7 Ind Div moves via KANGPOKPI RE 3804 and CHAWAI RE 5301 and will have one bn in the area KHUNTHAK RK 6796 by the evening of 29 Jun. It will then be prepared to attack UKHRUL.

3. As soon as one bn of 89 Ind Inf Bde has arrived in KHUNTHAK as in para 2 (c) above you will employ 80 Ind Inf Bde to the best advantage with the object of assisting 100 Ind Inf Bde to reach the area of FINCH'S CORNER RK 7589 as early as possible. Meanwhile 80 Ind Inf Bde will occupy KHUNTHAK as early as possible.

4. As soon as 20 Ind Div reaches the area of FINCH'S CORNER you will be prepared to detach a force of up to one Inf Bde to cut the JAPANESE main L of C in the area south of GAMNON RK 9191. The remaining Bde will be prepared to attack UKHRUL from the south west on the general axis of the mian road.

5. It is important that the operation designed to assist the forward move of 100 Ind Inf Bde should be carried out as quickly as possible so as to avoid any delay in the attacks by the Bdes mentioned in para 2.

6. No firm date for the attack on UKHRUL can be given as much depends on weather and the state of tracks. Instructions for the coordination of the final movement will be issued later. The earlier that the L of C south of UKHRUL can be cut effectively the better.

7. The boundary between 4 Corps and 33 Corps will be—all incl to 33 Corps CHAWAI RE 5200—LEISHAN RE 6100—SIRARUKHONG RK 6795—RINGUI RK 6893—TUSHAR RK 7494—PHARUNG RK 7497. This boundary will come into force as the leading elements of 89 Bde reach the places named. The whole boundary will come into force at 1800 hrs 29 Jun.

8. Instruction regarding inter-communication between attacking forces will be issued separately.

9. ACK.

Sd/ G. Scoones
Lieut-General,
Comd, 4 Corps.

APPENDIX 4

5 INDIAN DIVISION LOCATION STATEMENT

19 August 1944

Ser No.	UNIT	LOCATION All map refs RK except where stated	
1.	MAIN HQ 5 IND DIV		RP 045895
2.	REAR HQ 5 IND DIV		101055
3.	HQ RA 5 IND DIV		100055
4.	TAC HQ RA 5 IND DIV		RP 045895
5.	HQ RE 5 IND DIV		RP 045895
6.	HQ 5 IND DIV REGT RIASC		RP 045895
7.	HQ IEME 5 IND DIV		101055
8.			
9.			
10.			
11.			
	Arty		
12.	4 FD REGT RA		3460
13.	28 (J) FD REGT RA		106154
14.	56 LAA/A TK REGT RA		310625
15.	24 IND MTN REGT IA		308625
16.			
17.			
18.			
	Engrs		
19.	2 FD COY IE	MS 47	RP 064912
20.	20 FD COY IE	MS 55	RP 016831
21.	74 FD COY IE	MS 55½	RP 010828
22.	44 FD PK COY IE	MS 49½	RP 041892
23.	No. 9 IND BR PL		354582
24.	No. 1 IND BR PL	Under comd 33 IND CORPS	
25.			
	Sigs		
26.	MAIN SIGS 5 IND DIV		RP 045895
27.	REAR SIGS 5 IND DIV		101055
28.	SIGS 4 FD REGT RA		3460
29.	SIGS 28 (J) FD REGT RA		106154
30.	SIGS 56 LAA/ATK REGT RA		310625
31.	SIGS 24 IND MTN REGT IA		308625
32.	SIGS 9 IND INF BDE	MS 69	RO 969665
33.	SIGS 123 IND INF BDE		105153
34.	SIGS 161 IND INF BDE		RP 019833
35.			
36.			
37.			

APPENDIX 4

Ser No.	UNIT		LOCATION All map refs RK except where stated	
	INF			
38.	2/1 PUNJAB less 4 Coy.			100053
39.	HQ 9 IND INF BDE	MS 69	RO	969665
40.	2 W YORKS		RO	973697
41.	3/9 JATS		RO	959635
42.	3/14 PUNJAB	MS 71	RO	959645
43.	B Coy 2/1 PUNJAB	MS 69	RO	969665
44.	HQ 123 IND INF BDE			105153
45.	2 SUFFOLK			122139
46.	3/2 PUNJAB REGT			114126
47.	1/17 DOGRA			107155
48.	C Coy 2/1 PUNJAB			105153
49.	HQ 161 IND INF BDE		RP	019833
50.	4 RWK		RP	025860
51.	1/1 PUNJAB REGT		RO	990822
52.	4/7 RAJPUT		RP	016831
53.	A Coy 2/1 PUNJAB		RP	019833
54.	D Coy 2/1 PUNJAB		RP	045895
55.				
56.				
57.				
58.				
	RIASC			
59.	238 IGPT COY (less 3 secs)		Under Comd 33 IND CORPS	
60.	239 IGPT COY		Under Comd 33 IND CORPS	
61.	240 IGPT COY		Under Comd 202 AREA	
62.	7 IND COMP ISSUE SEC			150385
63.	60 IND COMP ISSUE SEC			111085
64.	61 IND COMP ISSUE SEC			165418
65.	62 IND COMP ISSUE SEC			165407
66.	23 AT COY (M)			3659
67.	60 AT COY (M)		Under Comd 33 IND CORPS	
68.	74 AT COY (M)		Under Comd 33 IND CORPS	
69.	82 AT COY (M)		RP	010828
70.	5 IND FD AMB TP Cl I			3559
71.	22 IND FD AMB TP Cl I			146396
72.	23 IND FD AMB TP Cl II			3559
73.	FMC		MOIRANG	1824
74.				
75.				
76.				
	MED			
77.	10 IND FD AMB		RO	973747
78.	45 IND FD AMB			112076
79.	75 IND FD AMB		RP	020836
80.	7 IND FD HYG SEC			103057
81.	55 AMU			103057
82.	5 IND MOB SURG UNIT			020836
83.	45 AMU			103057

Ser No.	UNIT	LOCATION All map refs RK except where stated
	IEME	
84.	112 IND MOB WKSP COY	Under Comd 202 AREA
85.	113 IND MOB WKSP COY	3458
86.	5 IND REC COY	110086
87.	9 LAD 'E'	200480
88.	123 LAD 'E'	357607
89.	161 LAD 'E'	110086
90.		
91.		
	VET	
92.	2 IND MOB VET SEC	104057
93.		
94.		
	POSTAL	
95.	21 IND FPO	210480
96.	22 IND FPO	166416
97.	23 IND FPO	101053
98.	169 IND FPO	105153
99.		
100.		
	PRO	
101.	5 IND PRO UNIT	103057
	INT	
102.	565 F S SEC	RP 045895
103.		
	UNDER COMD OR IN SP	
104.	160 IGPT COY	350591
105.	37 IGPT COY	350591
106.	50 AT COY (less 4 tps)	350588
107.	544 ISS	MOIRANG 1824
108.	11 IND SALVAGE UNIT	132175
109.	47 AT COY	RP 022847

APPENDIX 5

WITHDRAWAL BEHIND THE IRRAWADDY, 1944

(Japanese view as disclosed in interrogations).[1]

Operations in Central and Southern Burma

Q. What were the motives behind the major reorganisation of the BURMA Area Army in Sep 44?

A. NUMATA
The underlying motives were to consolidate and reorganise the forces which were defeated at IMPHAL; the selection of the line connecting MANDALAY, the CHINDWIN and the DELTA to constitute the main line of defence thenceforth; suitably to prepare this area for defence purposes by a redisposition of forces and the enhancement of fighting power etc.

KIMURA
No specific reorganisation took place, other than the usual minor adjustments necessary from time to time. The reason was simply the prevailing lack of reinforcements.

NAKA
This reorganisation was a result of the great losses in fighting strength during the first half of 44.

KATAMURA
This was part of a general re-shuffle carried out after the battle of IMPHAL.

Q. What specific areas of BURMA were the Japanese hoping to defend against Fourteenth Army's advance?

A. NUMATA
The area south and east of LASHIO, MANDALAY and the IRRAWADDY especially the YENANGYAUNG oilfields and the BASSEIN DELTA, the granary of BURMA.

KIMURA
The general plan against XIV Army's advance was as follows:
  (a) To hold a line running SW from LASHIO and also along the entire IRRAWADDY axis.
  (b) To prevent any communication or link-up between the XIV Army and the Chinese-American forces.

NAKA
We were to hold the IRRAWADDY line, with particular reference to MANDALAY, MYINGYAN, PAKOKKU, YENANGYAUNG, PROME, and also TAUNGUP. Other plans dealt with the defence of the DELTA, RANGOON, MOULMEIN, and important points in TENASSERIM.

KATAMURA
Until 44, the line of the JUPI Mts.

[1] SEATIC Bulletin No. 242.

Q. In making his plan for the attack on Central BURMA, General SLIM calculated that they would disperse their main forces North of the IRRAWADDY and fight the major battle in the SHWEBO Plain so as to prevent us from cutting their communications from the North Burma front and keeping us out of the dry zone of Central BURMA. Is this an accurate appreciation of Japanese intentions in Sep 44?

A. NUMATA

(i) This is not an accurate appreciation. Rather than fight a decisive battle on the SHWEBO plain, the Japanese chose the banks of the IRRAWADDY instead.

(ii) Reasons.
1. With a view to repairing the various losses incurred in the retreat, the Japanese decided to make one complete action to withdraw the main body of their forces to the area east of the IRRAWADDY. Here it was planned to take advantage of the time so gained to augment and restore strength, and to engage and destroy the fast-pursuing British forces on the banks of the IRRAWADDY. The order involving the above plan was issued by the commander of the Area Army in Sep 44. However, the Japanese army attempted to draw the British Indian forces into thinking that the major battle would be fought north of the IRRAWADDY.

2. While the reason for selecting the banks of the IRRAWADDY as the site of the decisive battle was almost identical with General SLIM's appreciation, his judgement differed from the Japanese plan in that the Japanese, owing to the wide disparity in equipment, etc. between the opposing armies, considered it best to take full advantage of the barrier presented by the IRRAWADDY in the decisive battle. The 15 Army at the time was experiencing the greatest difficulty in concentrating its forces north of the IRRAWADDY and in establishing a position for a major battle.

KIMURA

Categorically—no. After the crossing of the CHINDWIN the Japanese Staff had NO intention of fighting a major battle North and West of the IRRAWADDY. The difficulties of supplying and reinforcing a large body of troops North of the river, particularly in view of the heavy opposition from the air, were considered insuperable.

NAKA

As General SLIM expected, we had from the beginning planned a defence line North of the IRRAWADDY, but from the point of view of reorganising fighting power and supply we recognised the difficulty of giving battle from those areas, so the plans were changed, and we decided to defend the line of the IRRAWADDY.

KATAMURA

At the time mentioned, General SLIM'S judgement was perfectly correct. The decision was changed later.

APPENDIX 6

TASKS OF THE LUSHAI BRIGADE

33 IND CORPS OP INSTR NO. 20 OF 6.10.44.

Ref Maps ¼" to one mile sheets 84 E, F, I, J.

To
    Major General D.F.W. WARREN, D.S.O., O.B.E.

The objective of this directive is to define the future tasks of the LUSHAI Bde, and should be read in conjunction with 33 Ind Corps Op Instr No. 14 dated 7 AUG.

INFM

Enemy
1. See current Sitrep and Int Summaries.

Own Tps
2. (*a*) 11 (EA) Div is op down the KABAW valley with first objective KALEMYO RU 56 ultimate objective KALEWA RU 86. The leading tps of 26 Inf Bde are in the area YAZAGYO RP 50.

(*b*) The composition of the LUSHAI Bde is shown at Appx 'A'.

TASKS

3. The future tasks of the LUSHAI Bde, in order of priority will be as follows:—

(*a*) Protection of the RIGHT flank of 5 Ind Div by operating on the axis of the MANIPUR R, and occupying the area FALAM RU 13—HAKA RU 00.

(*b*) As the adv of 5 Ind Div proceeds beyond KENNEDY PEAK RU 2081 the Bde will move into the MYITTHA VALLEY on a wide front.

(*c*) A block of not less than one bn will be est on the GANGAW PJ 39—KALEMYO rd, in the vicinity of GANGAW, as early as possible.

(*d*) On the occupation of the KALEMYO area, the task of the remainder of the Bde will be to dominate the area CHAUNGWA RU 84—MINGIN SQ 03—KANI PE 12—GANGAW. The object of this role, the effect of which can be much amplified by the spreading of calculated rumour, will be to compel the enemy EAST of the CHINDWIN to look for any further activities by us on a wide front.

4. The completion of these tasks will be carried out with the greatest vigour. Full advantage will be taken of the mobility conferred by air sup in monsoon conditions. Jap posns which cannot be assaulted will be out-flanked and the advance continued. Maximum use will be made of air sp.

ADM

5. Sup will continue by air under Fourteenth Army arrangements, until such time as the rd to KALEMYO-KALEWA is open.

Sd/ x x x x x
Lieut General
Commanding 33 Ind Corps

APPENDIX 7

33 IND CORPS OP INSTR NO. 23 DT. 1/12/44

Ref Maps: 1:1,000,000 ASIA, ASSAM Sheet

¼ inch to 1 mile Sheet 84 I.

To
    Maj Gen C. C. FOWKES, C.B.E., D.S.O., M.C.
    Comd 11 (E.A.) Div.

Establishment of bridgehead.

1. You will submit your outline plan for the est of a bridgehead over the R CHINDWIN as soon as possible.

2. In considering the disposition of your forces in the KALEWA and bridgehead areas you will take into account the following factors:—

    (a) the area immediately EAST and WEST of the crossing place must be left free as a transit area;

    (b) space must be allowed in the vicinity of the crossing for units such as R.E. bridging coys, A.A. btys, R.A.F. radar, etc., all of which must have priority;

    (c) an area within the bridgehead will be reserved for the conc of successive gps of 2 Div. In the first instance this area must be sufficient to accommodate one bde gp, div arty gp, one sqn tks and one tp S.P. arty.

As soon as possible after the crossing has been secured, a conference will be convened on the ground by this HQ, at which reps from your div and from Corps HQ and Corps Tps will be asked to stake their claims.

Subsequent role of your div

3. HQ Fourteenth Army has decided that, as soon as the present phase of ops permits, your div will be withdrawn into Army res for a period of intensive trg.

4. It is hoped to find an area, suitable from the climatic and trg aspects, in the vicinity of LAKHIPUR (Long 93" 3' Lat 24" 45') in the SURMA Valley; recce for this has been ordered.

5. From the administrative point of view it is necessary that the air sup commitment for this Corps should be kept at a minimum, and it will not be possible to complete the fwd conc of 254 Tk Bde until part, at least, of your div has been withdrawn.

6. The move of your div (less adv parties) will begin as soon as 2 Div has made sufficient progress EAST of the CHINDWIN to obviate the further holding of a bridgehead. The move will then be carried out as quickly as possible, by air and road, from a conc area about INDAINGGYI.

7. In order to facilitate the whole operation it is clearly desirable that, from now on, no tps, vehicles or installations which are not essential to your object—the capture and holding of a bridgehead—should be moved fwd of KYIGON.

8. Separate instns are being issued regarding the disposal of Corps Tps of E.A. origin and of other Corps Tps now in your area.

9. In considering your outline plan for the withdrawal of your div to the INDAINGGYI area, and for its subsequent move to its trg area, you may take into your confidence such of your comds and staffs as you consider necessary, provided that the procedure involved by the TOP-SECRET category is maintained until downgraded by this HQ.

Sd/ x x x x x x x
Lieut-General
Commanding, 33 Ind Corps.

APPENDIX 8

TASKS OF 33 INDIAN CORPS—DECEMBER 1944.

Minutes of a Conference held by 33 Indian Corps Commander with Divisional Commanders and heads of services at Corps HQ on 20 December 1944.

1. *PLAN*

The Corps Commander outlined 14 Army plan for operations to secure MANDALAY and thence to operate southwards.

The tasks of 33 Corps with under command
>   2 Div
>   19 Ind Div
>   20 Ind Div
>   254 Ind Tk Bde
>   268 Ind Inf Bde
>   Elements of 'V' Force

are as follows:—
   (a) To capture YE-U and SHWEBO
   (b) To capture MONYWA
   (c) To capture MANDALAY
   (d) To advance south on the Corps axis MANDALAY—YAME-THIN—NYAUNGLEBIN.

In implementation of this Divs will operate as follows:—

19 Ind Div—To capture SHWEBO. Right boundary will probably be incl railway KAWLIN—KANBALU—SHWEBO.

268 Ind Inf Bde—To patrol widely with the task of maintaining contact between 2 and 19 Divs. 268 Bde less two Bns will remain on road supply. (NOTE: The exact role of this Bde will be decided after discussion with Bde Comd on 22 Dec.).

2 Div—Will advance with all possible speed on the main axis east to SHWEBO.

20 Ind Div—Will capture MONYWA with all possible speed. 32 Inf Bde will be ordered to close on PYINGAING with a view to operating south across the main axis. A block of not less than one Bn will be retained at PYINGAING until 2 Div is through.

KABO. It is essential to capture this vital irrigation work intact. 2 and 19 Divs will be prepared to operate against it as soon as this is feasible. A decision will be taken as early as possible as to which Division is allotted this task.

(e) Further objectives. Following is the outline plan:—

19 Div will across the Irrawaddy after the capture of SHWEBO and will probably be directed on MAYMYO, thence to operate from the east on MANDALAY.

2 Div will operate south from the YE-U—SHWEBO area on MANDALAY.

20 Div will operate against MANDALAY from the south-west.

(f) This paragraph will be taken as a firm basis for planning and for deployment to secure the objectives indicated. Confirmation will be given in the form of an Operation Instruction, which will be issued as soon as 14 Army directive has been received.

APPENDIX 9

33 IND CORPS OP INSTR NO. 24 OF 17.1.45

Ref maps ¼ in. to one mile, Sheets—84 N, O.
93 B, C.

To: Maj Gen C. G. G. Nicholson, C.B.E., D.S.O., M.C.
    Comd 2 Div.

Maj Gen T. W. Rees, C.I.E., D.S.O., M.C.
    Comd 19 Ind Div.

Maj Gen D. D. Gracey, O.B.E., M.C.
    Comd 20 Ind Div.

Brig G. M. Dyer, O.B.E.
    Comd 268 Ind Inf Bde.

INFM

Enemy

1. (*a*) See Enemy Situation and Intentions paper dated 10 Jan 45, as supplemented by HQ 33 Ind Corps letter No. 1330/1/GSI(*a*) of 13 Jan 45, and current sitreps.

(*b*) All inf at present indicates that the enemy intends to make a determined stand on the gen line MYINGYAN PK 70—MANDALAY—MAYMYO LG 06. The JAPANESE, however, is NOT a passive enemy, and planning must envisage the possibility of a counter stroke in sp of his defensive posn with the object of slowing up our advance. The NORTHERLY moves of HQs 15 and 53 Divs, EAST of the IRRAWADDY, may constitute nothing more than positioning for the def of MANDALAY, but could indicate preparations for a counter offensive across the IRRAWADDY, in order to destroy maint airfields and to disrupt our L of C.

Own Tps.

2. (*a*) 268 Ind Inf Bde reverted to Corps res on 16 Jan and is moving to conc in area YE-U SR 0920—NYAUNGHLA SR 0908—TABAYIN SQ 9812.

(*b*) Corps bdys remain unchanged.

(*c*) 36 Div is op against MONGMIT SS 46 with 29 Bde advancing TWINNGE SR 76—WABYUDAUNG SR 83.

GEN

3. This Op Instr is issued in amplification of 33 Ind Corps Op Order No. 12 dated 5 Jan 45, and is designed to cover Phase II, and preparations for Phase III, of the Corps plan to capture MANDALAY.

4. Phase II is the period of adm build up for Phase III. During Phase II 2 Div will be allowed to op up to the equivalent of one, and 19 Ind Div up to two inf bde gps on air sup. The remainder of the divs will not operate beyond the limits of their own 1st and 2nd line tps.

254 Ind Tk Bde is unlikely to be conc fwd before early Feb.

Major offensive ops with full armd support cannot therefore be staged during Phase II.

Tasks in Gen

5. Fmns Comds will op boldly within the limitations outlined above with the following principal objects in view:—
   (a) retaining the initiative.
   (b) maintaining contact with the enemy on the Corps front.
   (c) locating main enemy defs.
   (d) regrouping and trg for major offensive ops.

6. In view of the possibility of a JAPANESE counter offensive or of raids by smaller but determined JAP colns all units, and especially those in rear areas, will be responsible for their own defs. Defs will be sited and dug to give all round protection, must be completely self contained and hold two days res rations at all times.

Tasks in Particular

Corps Plan

7. (a) The Corps plan is to capture MANDALAY as early as possible after the resumption of full scale ops.

The present estimate for the resumption of major offensive ops is 1 Feb, by which date 254 Ind Tk Bde may be conc fwd and sufficient res of amn, pet, bombs etc., built up.

(b) The capture of MANDALAY will be effected by co-ordinated outflanking movements by 19 and 20 Ind Divs, with 2 Div and the majority of the armour op to destroy the main enemy posns NORTH and WEST of the IRRAWADDY.

It is hoped that the continuous pressure by 2 Div will lead the enemy to believe that the main thrust is to take place towards SAGAING LF 45 thus distracting his attention initially from the outflanking movements of 19 and 20 Ind Divs against MANDALAY.

(c) Fmns Comds less 2 Div will prepare and submit outline plans on a D Day basis for the adv on MANDALAY, after concentration across the IRRAWADDY. D Day being the day on which the fwd move on MANDALAY begins.

8. *2 Div*

(a) 2 Div will op to locate the main enemy posns NORTH and WEST of the IRRAWADDY, and will be prepared to effect a crossing. No crossing in strength will be made until receipt of my further orders.

(b) 2 Div will op one inf bn in area THITSEINGYI LA 42 with the object of leading the enemy to believe that a crossing in strength is to be staged thence. The bn will not be est EAST of IRRAWADDY R but patrolling will be carried out on EAST bank.

9. *19 Ind Div*

(a) Will est two br heads each not in excess of one inf bde gp EAST of the IRRAWADDY in the areas THABEIKKYIN SR 73 and KYAUKMYAUNG SR 60. These will be strongly dug in in anticipation of enemy counter attacks.

Wide patrolling will subsequently be carried out from these br heads.

(b) The br head at THABEIKKYIN will be expanded to WABYU-DAUNG with the object of protecting the rear of the remainder of the Div when it begins its SOUTHWARD move on MANDALAY (Blocks will be set at THABEIKKYIN and WABYUDAUNG).

The bde gp will subsequently adv SOUTH continuing to protect the rear of the division.

For these operations the minimum number of guns and adm units and vehs will be committed EAST of IRRAWADDY R.

(c) KYAUKMYAUNG br head may be increased to two inf bde gps at the discretion of the comd 19 Ind Div provided the number of adm units to cross the IRRAWADDY is kept to the minimum.

(d) Will plan to isolate MANDALAY from the EAST with the div, less one inf bde gp, operating from KYAUKMYAUNG br head on my further orders.

(e) It is anticipated that the balance of vehs and adm units will cross the IRRAWADDY at SAGAING in rear of 2 Div.

10. *20 Ind Div*

After the capture of MONYWA, 20 Ind Div
  (a) will est one inf bde gp in the area of the confluence of the MU and IRRAWADDY RIVERS with the object of leading the enemy to believe that a crossing in force is to take place at MYINMU LF 06.
  (b) will plan to cross the IRRAWADDY WEST of MYINMU with the object of capturing KYAUKSE LF 62 and isolating MANDALAY from the SOUTH.

11. *268 Ind Inf Bde*
(a) 268 Ind Inf Bde will remain in Corps res.
268 Ind Inf Bde will plan to relieve 20 Ind Div in AYADAW area.

(b) If ordered to the AYADAW area 268 Bde will patrol widely with the object of dominating the area EAST to the MU R, WEST to WADAN PK 79, and SOUTH to a limit to be decided at a later date.

12. *254 Ind Tk Bde*
(a) *Estimated build up*—YE-U area

Available for	Date	Unit
2 Div	23 Jan	one sqn 3 DG
	24 Jan	one sqn 3 DG (to complete Regt)
19 Ind Div	25 Jan	one sqn 150 RAC
20 Ind Div	28 Jan	7 Cav less two sqns
	29 Jan	one sqn 7 Cav
Corps res	30 Jan	150 RAC less one sqn one sqn 7 Cav followed by remainder 254 Ind Tk Bde.

There is now only one sqn 3 DG fwd of MUTAIK. It is under comd 2 Div.

254 Ind Tk Bde will complete in YE-U area by about 5 Feb.

(b) Moves fwd of YE-U may be on tracks if operationally urgent. If not, tk tptrs will be used wherever possible.

(c) 11 CAV less one sqn is under comd 20 Ind Div. One sqn 11 CAV is under comd 19 Ind Div.

13. *RA*

Present allotments of Corps Arty in sp Divs is as follows:
1 Med Regt
2 Div	one tp
19 Ind Div	1 Med Regt less one bty
20 Ind Div ...	one bty less one tp

101 Hy AA Regt—in dual role
19 Ind Div	one bty
20 Ind Div	one bty less one tp
In Corps Res	one tp 7.2 Hows.

14. I wish Comds to exploit this period of adm built up to the fullest advantage in preparation for the early resumption of major offensive ops. The restrictions, which the recent rapid success of the Corps has brought upon us, do not in any way bring ops to a standstill.

Comds will act with vigour and boldness to secure the objectives given in this instruction.

Sd/- x x x x x
Lieut Gen
Commanding, 33 Indian Corps

APPENDIX 10

APPRECIATION OF THE SITUATION BY COMD 4 CORPS

19 JAN 1945

(Ref ¼" Map sheets 84 J, K, L, N, O and P 93 B-C)

OBJECT

1. My object is to get a sufficiently strong force to MEIKTILA IN TIME to be able to cut off all Jap forces retiring from the MANDALAY area and in conjunction with 33 Corps to destroy them.

CONSIDERATIONS

2. Enemy opposition up to the IRRAWADDY is likely to be offered only by the group now acting under 33 Div orders on our front. Estimated fighting strength 5 Bns. Subsequently enemy action against our advance may come from the YENANGYAUNG direction where by then 49 Div, less one regt, might be concentrated and form a garrison which will undoubtedly be detailed to hold MEIKTILA as our advance shows itself. MEIKTILA being a vital centre of communications, the enemy is likely to put at least one regt there before we can reach it.

Some tanks are also likely to be deployed against us as we advance from the IRRAWADDY on MEIKTILA. Numbers can only be guessed but the maximum is not likely to exceed 30 mediums and 10 lights.

I conclude from the above estimation of enemy opposition that 7 Div with 4 Inf Bdes at their disposal and, if necessary, a Tank Regtl Group and a Medium Bty in sp can seize PAUK first and then establish a bridgehead over the IRRAWADDY without undue delay.

Every effort must be made by rapid envelopment tactics to destroy and disintegrate enemy rearguards before the river is reached. Results have been disappointing till now, but the vigorous action on a wide front now in process should be more successful.

Once across the IRRAWADDY I must deploy a hard hitting force, strong in tanks and arty, against MEIKTILA while continuing to engage the enemy in the YENANGYAUNG area and preventing them from interfering with the crossing of the Corps or threatening the Corps administrative airhead.

Own Tps.

3. 33 Corps is to develop a double pincer movement against the Jap forces in the MANDALAY area.
    19 Div is crossing at THABEIKKYIN and KYAUKMYAUNG and is then to advance on MANDALAY from the North.
    20 Div is to cross at SAMEIKKON PK 83 and move on KYAUKSE.
    2 Div is to harass and pin the Japs in the posn covering SAGAING.

My advance on MEIKTILA from the PAKOKKU area fits in satisfactorily with 33 Corps plan, but I must be there IN TIME.

Time and Space

4. 33 Corps is to resume their advance in strength about 1 Feb and estimates to be in MANDALAY and KYAUKSE by 14 Feb. Therefore I must be in the MEIKTILA area as early as possible after that date.

The distances to be traversed are very great. 17 Div move 470 miles from DIMAPUR to PAUK. From PAUK to MEIKTILA is 120 miles and the R. IRRAWADDY has to be crossed.

There is only one way of achieving the necessary speed. Both air and MT must be employed to the maximum available extent to concentrate the Corps forward. This especially applies to 17 Div moves—and for a lightning thrust on MEIKTILA.

An estimate of fastest possible timings are:—

- 7 Div to seize PAUK area up to the Easternmost crossing of the YAW chaung by 1 Feb.
- 7 Div to have seized bridgehead over R. IRRAWADDY—probably in the NYAUNGU area by 15 Feb.
- 7 Div to have crossed IRRAWADDY less one Bde by 18 Feb and to have enlarged bridgehead by 19 Feb.
- 17 Div to start crossing mech force and Tank Bde less one regt on 19 Feb and to concentrate EAST of the IRRAWADDY by 22 Feb.
- The drive on MEIKTILA—80 miles—to start by 23 Feb and to reach MEIKTILA area by 25 Feb.

Airborne and air transported operations will help in the following main aspects:—

(a) Concentration forward of such elements of 17 Div as cannot be moved in MT.
(b) A glider borne operation to speed up the establishment of a bridgehead over the R. IRRAWADDY.
(c) Transportation of bridging material both in tpt aircraft to PAKOKKU airfield and in gliders to the bridging site.
(d) To build up 17 Div in the MEIKTILA area by air tpt of the non-mechanised portion of the Div.

5. *Surprise* must be attained by speed and deception. The main deception plan, already put forward, is to mislead the enemy as to place into the belief that our advance is on YENANGYAUNG, and as to time that we are being slowed up by administrative difficulties and lack of MT. Speed must be attained by the combined technique of an all mech and air advance. There is no place for mules in such a technique. It has therefore been decided to leave all mules of 17 Div in the DIMAPUR area.

6. *Country.* Once across the IRRAWADDY we will be in a country with supplies of water only just sufficient to meet the wants of the existing human and animal population. The implications have already been represented in a separate letter. Mules cannot be used for operations more than 5 miles from the river. This is an additional argument for the casting off of all animals from 17 Div. The loss in lift must be compensated for as far as possible by the hire of bullock carts and the use of A.T. carts instead of pack.

This dry zone is well suited to mobile operations and the best in BURMA FOR THE USE OF TANKS.

The lack of water and the suitability of the country for fast moving mech operations both strengthen my determination to make a rapid thrust from the River to MEIKTILA.

Plan

7. Outline has already been given in the Minutes of the Planning Conference held at this HQ on 18 Jan 45 and forwarded to all concerned.

8. Tasks and lay-out once the IRRAWADDY has been crossed are given below in more detail:—

   i. *CHIN HILLS Bn* with LUSHAI Scouts and one bty 25 Mtn Regt in sp moving on the general axis SAW (PO 37)—SIDOKTAYA (PT 48)—NGAPE (PT 63)—MINBU under orders from Corps.
   Tasks:—To clear any enemy opposition on this axis and develop a threat to YENANGYAUNG and MAGWE from this direction; to report enemy strength West of the IRRAWADDY in the general area SALIN (PT 99)—MINBU—NGAPE-SIDOKTAYA; to spread exaggerated reports of the strengths of the coln with a view to causing the enemy to hold his forces in the YENANGYAUNG area.
   This move will start as soon as TILIN is reached and will be on an all pack basis.

   ii. *7 Div* with under comd one Tank Regt Gp—one sqn Armd Cars one Medium Battery RA and one sec 7.2. Hows RA, Svy Bty RA (less det) and 5 Mahratta A Tk Regt in the general area PAKOKKU — KYAUKPADAUNG — CHAUK — YAW CHAUNG to PAUK.
   Tasks:—To protect airfields in use and the Corps airhead; to protect the Corps river crossing points; to advance to the general line SEIKPU (PP 03)—KYAUKPADAUNG and recce in strength up to YENANGYAUNG—PWINBYU (PT 97). All A.T. carts received will be issued to 7 Div to increase lift of mules and maximum use will be made of hired bullock carts—which are plentiful in this area.

   iii. *17 Div* with under comd 255 Tank Bde less one Regt Gp—16 Cav less one sqn—bty 18 Fd Regt (S.P. guns 105 mm) 8 Medium Regt less one bty—one Lt AA Bty—det Svy Bty R-28 (EA) Bde will be organised in two Gps.

   (a) *Mech Gp*—At least one Inf Bde and possibly two, plus 28 (EA) Bde—all Armd Corps and arty units less Div Mtn Regt.

   (b) *Air Gp*—At least one Inf Bde, and possibly two, with one A Tk Bty and Mtn Regt. The 1st line tpt for these units will move with the Mech Gp. Only minimum number of jeeps for immediate intercomn use on landing and for move of A Tk guns in emergency will be air transported. It is hoped that at least No. 1 and possibly Nos. 1 and 2, U.S. Army Air Force Air Commandos will be allotted as a special Task Force in sp of 17 Div.

Tasks :—
  (i) To seize MEIKTILA with utmost speed. The Mech Gp will move as one main striking force along one main axis so as to be able to crush quickly and completely any enemy opposition met. Minimum dets only will be detailed for moves by flanking routes for protective purposes.
  Considerations of ground and co-operation with 20 Divs move point at present to the most suitable axis as being HNAWDIN (PP 46)—WELAUNG (PP 76)—MAHLAING (LL 06).
  (ii) To destroy all forces withdrawing from in front 33 Corps.

iv. *Corps Tps*
  (i) A.A. protection of Corps river crossing points, Corps Airhead and PAUK-PAKOKKU airfields (if in use).
  (ii) RE construction and maintenance of airfields, running of Corps river crossing points and construction of main water points on East bank.

(Sd) F. W. MESSERVY
Lt. Gen.
Comd 4 Corps.

APPENDIX 11

DECECTION SCHEME "CLOAK"*

Information

1. The presence of 4 Corps in the GANGAW VALLEY is believed to be still undetected by the JAPS, but as soon as the Corps begins to emerge into the open country east of PAUK they will realise that we are a strong force and that we intend to cross the IRRAWADDY.

Intention

2. To continue to conceal from the JAPS for as long as possible the presence of the Corps in the GANGAW VALLEY.

3. Subsequently to mislead the JAPS about the Corps crossing place over the IRRAWADDY and bout the Corps objective east of the IRRAWADDY, at the same time misrepresenting to them the composition of the Corps.

Method in Outline

4. (a) To continue, as long as possible, the methods at present being employed to conceal the composition of 4 Corps and the presence of a Corps in the GANGAW VALLEY.
(b) To make a feint crossing at CHAUK, 3 or 4 days before our actual crossing elsewhere.
(c) To simulate preparations for crossing the IRRAWADDY at PAKOKKU shortly before our actual crossing elsewhere.
(d) To "sell" YENANGYAUNG to the JAPS as the objective of 4 Corps east of the IRRAWADDY.

Method in Detail

Concealment of the location and composition of 4 Corps

5. The present restrictions on the use of wireless will continue until relaxed by Corps HQ.

6. 17 Div and 255 Tk Bde will remain on wireless silence till deployed east of the IRRAWADDY.

7. No formation signs will be displayed on uniform, vehicles, notice boards or elsewhere until permission to do so is given by Corps HQ—but see para 9(a) below for special instructions for one bde of 7 Ind Div.

The feint crossing at CHAUK

8. As soon as possible after securing PAUK area 7 Ind Div will despatch one bde with some arty in sp, (28 (EA) Bde simulating 11 (EA) Div) down the YAW chaung towards SEIKPYU. During this advance, the bde will "sell' to the JAPS the bogus fact that it is a bde of 11 (EA) Div and that the whole of this Div is advancing by the same route. One sec D Force (from 11 (EA) Div) and 57 Coy D Force, will be under comd this Bde to assist in the deception. CSO 4 Corps is issuing separately details of the W/T deception methods to be employed as part of this "selling" of 11 (EA) Div.

*As given in 4 Corps Operation Instruction No. 124 of 25 January 1945.

9. Methods to be employed by this bde for simulating the presence of large numbers:—

- (a) They will wear on their uniform the signs of 11 (EA) Div. Corps HQ will arrange a supply of these.
- (b) Movement wherever possible by day.
- (c) Movement on a wide front, and widespread patrolling.
- (d) Faked dust clouds, simulating the movement of large columns of tpt or tps.
- (e) Wherever contact is made with the enemy, the use of tactical deception devices to simulate considerable firepower and strength.
- (f) The spreading of rumours that 20,000 EA tps are advancing down the YAW chaung axis, and that airborne troops will be cooperating in advance of them in considerable strength.

10. On arrival at the IRRAWADDY, preparations will be made for a divisional crossing, as described in paras 13 and 14 below.

11. At the appropriate moment this bde will carry out a diversionary crossing over the IRRAWADDY. At least one coy of inf will be employed for this crossing. The deception units with the bde will be able to assist in magnifying the strength of our force which lands on the far bank. This diversionary crossing will take place a few days before the real crossing by 7 Div elsewhere. To support the illusion that this diversionary crossing is the real thing, Corps HQ will arrange for dummy paratps and other deception devices to be dropped from the air on the east side of the IRRAWADDY to assist this diversionary crossing.

12. Only negligible engr assistance is likely to be available for this whole operation, since all available engr resources will be required for the main crossing.

Spurious preparations for crossing at PAKOKKU

13. These preparations will be made by 7 Ind Div, who will send one bde and engrs with river crossing stores into PAKOKKU itself. The activities of this bde will conform as nearly as possible to those of a bde which is, in fact, going to cross the river and will incl:—

- (a) Recces for crossing places by suitable recce parties. In addition to reconnoitring the near bank, some of these parties will recce the far bank at a number of different places during darkness, making sure that their presence becomes known to the locals.
- (b) Visits to selected crossing places by an officer wearing a red hat and red tabs.
- (c) Enquiries from local inhabitants concerning speed of current, sandbanks, nature of far bank, time required for crossing, exits from the river opposite PAKOKKU, enemy strengths and dispositions opposite PAKOKKU.
- (d) The "losing" on the far side of a marked map, showing a few sketchy details of projected recces and JAP posns. This map will be prepared at Corps HQ.
- (e) The collection of country boats from local boatmen—demands to be sufficient for the crossing of a whole division.
- (f) Work on the approaches to the river bank.
- (g) The establishing of dummy camps and dumps in the crossing area.

(h) Unloading bridging equipment from MT in the PAKOKKU area. If this can be arranged so that the local boatmen become aware of the activity or even so that the JAPS hear the work in progress, the effect will be improved.

14. Throughout these preparations, efforts will be made to confuse and jitter the JAPS on the far bank by dropping deception devices from the air and floating them downstream on rafts and boats at night and by any other means by which these devices can be usefully used.

15. 51 Coy, D Force, will be under comd 7 Ind Div to help carry out these various deception measures.

The "selling" of YENANGYAUNG as the 4 Corps objective

16. On arrival of 28 (EA) bde in the SEIKPYU area, a force of armd Cs and arty will operate south from there along the west bank of the IRRAWADDY, to simulate a threat to YENANGYAUNG. This force will:—

(a) Create a strong show of force wherever possible.
(b) Shoot up any JAP posns or movement seen on the east bank of the IRRAWADDY.
(c) Publish amongst locals rumours of large forces due to arrive from the PAUK area to operate on west bank of the river.
(d) Make enquiries concerning roads, water and enemy dispositions on both banks of the IRRAWADDY as far south as YENANGYAUNG.
(e) Make enquiries regarding suitable landing areas for airborne forces in the same area.

17. The CHIN HILLS bn moving on the general line TILIN-SAW-SIDOKTAYA PT 4886—NGAPE PT 7241, will also simulate a threat to YENANGYAUNG, by exaggerating their own strength and making similar enquiries about the area west of the IRRAWADDY as far south as MAGWE.

18. Corps HQ will arrange leaflet drops to indicate an interest in YENANGYAUNG.

19. An interest in YENANGYAUNG will also be "sold" to the JAPS through certain reliable secret channels. Corps HQ is arranging this.

Wireless Deception

20. The question of wireless silence and of a bogus network representing 11 (EA) Div have already been dealt with (paras 5, 6 and 8 above).

21. In addition Corps HQ will arrange for a few intentional mistakes, to be made in our own wireless transmissions with the object of supporting the overall deception. Details will be worked out at Corps HQ and notified to those formations required to participate.

22. Wireless activity by 28 (EA) Bde will show a considerable increase during the days immediately prior to the feint crossing at CHAUK. Details are being issued separately by CSO 4 Corps.

23. The armd C and arty force will maintain a high level of wireless activity from the time of their arrival at SEIKPYU onwards.

Air Activity

24. Dropping of deception devices to jitter the JAPS will be carried out under arrangements to be made by Corps HQ and on request from 7 Div in support of bogus activity and the feint crossing.

25. Air recce, air photography and air attacks will be asked for by Corps HQ in areas away from our real crossing places and objectives, in order not to draw the JAPS' attention to any particular area through undue air activity over it.

Date of crossing the IRRAWADDY

26. By other means arrangements are in hand to convey the impression to the JAPS that our crossing over the IRRAWADDY is going to occur one month later than we do, in fact, intend to cross.

SECURITY

27. The deception plan to be known by the code work CLOAK.

28. As far as possible everyone taking part in these deceptive activities should believe them to be genuine. Where the personnel involved are bound to guess that their activities are not entirely genuine, they may be told that confidentially—in order to obtain their wholehearted co-operation—that they are taking part in a deception.

29. Signal instructions with wide distributions will not be issued in connection with this scheme.

Sd/- E. H. W. COBB
B.G.S.
4 Corps

APPENDIX 12

33 IND CORPS OP ORDER NO. 13 FOR THE CAPTURE OF MANDALAY, 2 FEBRUARY 1945

Ref maps ¼ in. to one mile Sheets 84 M, N, O.
93 A, B, C.

Object

1. To capture MANDALAY as the first step in carrying out the Army Commander's intention of destroying the JAPANESE forces in the plains SOUTH of that city.

Infm

2. (a) *Enemy Strengths* (The detail of this statement is to be found in "Enemy Situation and Intentions" Paper of 1 Feb).

Area	Bns	Div	*Equivalent in Bns at JAPANESE WE of 1100*
(i) TWINNGE SR 76—	4	15	one bn
THABEIKKYIN SR 63	1	31	
(ii) KABWET SR 62—excl KYAUKMYAUNG SR 60	3	15	half a bn
(iii) Area KYAUKMYAUNG	2	15	
	6	53	two bns
	53 Recce Regt	53	
	53 Engr Regt	53	
(iv) Area MADAYA LF 69	3	53	one bn
In addition possibly two bns 34 Indep Mixed Bde under comd 53 Div			
(v) SAGAING Hills LF 47	3	31	one bn plus
Area KYAUKSE LF 62—SAGAING	2	31	one bn
(vi) Area YWATHITGYI LF 25	3	31	
LETPANZIN LF 25—	3	33	one and half bn
MYOTHA LF 13—NGAMYA PK 84	Possibly one bn 54 Div		

This makes a total strength of the equivalent of eight bns plus at establishment strength on the Corps front, omitting the possible bns of 34 Indep Mixed Bde.

Of the three div artys, present indications are that about 40% of establishment strength is deployed and it is unlikely that more than 50% is available for action. This gives us a considerable gun preponderance, which is very greatly increased by our available air effort.

The enemy will also have ancillary tps all of whom are capable of fighting hard.

In fighting value 33 Div is rated high: 15 and 31 Divs are only fair, 53 Div and 34 Indep Mixed Bde are rated low.

The estimated strength of enemy tks in MANDALAY is not in excess of 50 of all types.

The greatest enemy resistance is likely to be on NORTHERN approaches to MANDALAY, where we shall have an open left flank and rear which will be susceptible to attack from enemy forces which may withdraw SOUTHWARDS in front of N.C.A.C.

(b) *Own Forces*

Fwd conc of 254 Ind Tk Bde will be completed by 9 Feb. 268 Inf Bde less one bn will complete conc area SOUTH of Shwebo by 2 Feb. One bn is located at KIN-U SR 32.

33 Ind Corps RIGHT bdy—excl R CHINDWIN to confluence with IRRAWADDY R—MYINGYAN PK 70—thence incl NATOGYI LL 09—THABYEDAUNG LL 68.

33 Ind Corps LEFT bdy remains unchanged.

(c) *Geographical*

(i) R IRRAWADDY is to be crossed WEST of MANDALAY. Over the stretch MYINMU LF 06—SAGAING LF 45 the width varies 1,000 to 2,000 yds. At the broadest points cultivated sandbanks are almost invariably to be found in the centre of the stream. The current speed at this season is about 1½ knots.

The river line is easily defensible against assault and defences are already under construction on the SOUTH bank. Active patrolling will be carried out to mislead the enemy and to find places for unopposed crossings.

(ii) *SAGAING Hills.*

This feature on the WEST of R IRRAWADDY is about twenty miles long from NORTH to SOUTH. It is rarely more than two miles wide, has steep sides, and average height of 600 to 800 feet and a maximum height of 1330 feet. It covers the direct approach to MANDALAY from the NORTH, and dominates the approaches to the river from the WEST. Caves exist in this feature and it has been reported that they have been embodied in the defensive preparations which the enemy is believed to have made.

The feature is too narrow to permit the deployment of a strong force operating along its NORTH—SOUTH axis and would be very costly to assault frontally. It must, therefore, be isolated. Until cleared it will constitute a base from which the enemy can emerge to operate against us in the plain WEST and NORTH of R IRRAWADDY.

Water for the garrison will have to be brought from R IRRAWADDY, or from wells in the plain. This may prove a determining factor in the success of isolation.

(iii) *Tankable country.*

NORTH of MANDALAY there runs for approximately 30 miles a flat belt of country some ten miles wide. Obstacles are presented by the main canals and distributories of the MANDALAY irrigation system by the perennial CHAUNG MAGYI, by the bunds protecting MANDALAY (up to twenty feet in height) and by deeply eroded smaller chaungs which may have perpendicular band up to fifteen feet in height. Generally these obstacles run NORTH—SOUTH as far SOUTH as YENI CHAUNG LF 6170. SOUTH of this they run generally EAST and WEST.

An alluvial plain extends SOUTH from MANDALAY to 'MEIKTILA'. In this plain the following are the main rivers:
R. MYITNGE LF 82 (NOT fordable)
R. PANLAUNG ⎱ LF 43 (fordable in places with pre-
R. SAMON   ⎰ LF 50 paration of bed).

From these rivers irrigation canals and distributories are operated. The major ones are expected to provide tank obstacles. In general the country is a paddy growing area presenting NO obstacles to tank movement.

WEST of this alluvial plain the country alternates between low sandy areas and uplands. The sandy area is estimated suitable for tanks, though certain nalas may require ramping down of banks.

The nature of the uplands generally precludes tank movement except on certain "erosion" roads.

(iv) *Water*

Ample water is available in the plains NORTH of MANDALAY and between MANDALAY and MEIKTILA LL 23.

In the area WEST of the plain MANDALAY—MEIKTILA a dry belt exists; however, over all, enough water exists for operational purposes. In villages, which are on the alignment of chaungs, wells forty feet deep exist. Unless the dry season is protracted these wells will serve as unit water points without causing hardship to the local population. The following tanks or catchment areas are capable of providing formation water points throughout the dry season:—

PYOGAN	(Tank)	PK 9510
KANNA	(Tank)	LF 3204
POPA	(Catchment area)	PP 6239
PIN River	(Perennial)	PP 5925
MAHLAING	(Tanks)	LL 0560
TEZU	(Tanks)	LL 2462 & 2864
YINDAW	(Tank)	LL 3712
MEIKTILA	(Catchment areas)	LL 23

There is NO point in the area more than twenty miles distant from an adequate formation water supply.

The following headworks (weirs) are the main sources of irrigation in the strip of country MADAYA LF 69—MANDALAY—KYAUKSE LF 61—MYITTHA LL 69:—

SEDAW	LA 8505
NAUNGKON	LF 7904
KANDAW	LL 8278

It is essential that these are secured intact.

Plan in Outline

3. To isolate MANDALAY by coordinated advances by 19 Ind Div from NORTH, by 2 Div from WEST and by 20 Ind Div from SW and SOUTH.

As 19 Ind Div is the furthest from MANDALAY and is likely to meet the strongest opposition it is desirable that the operations of 2 and

20 Divs should develop as early as possible with a view to threatening the enemy's communications on the EAST bank of the IRRAWADDY and thereby compelling him to relax his pressure in front of 19 Ind. Div.

The initial crossing will be made by 20 Ind Div on D Day. My present intention is for 2 Div to cross when 20 Ind Div has reached or is close to MYOTHA LF 13, but this will depend upon the course of ops. Leading Bde Gp 2 Div will be at 24 hrs notice to cross wed $D+1$.

In order to mislead the enemy as to the crossing places over IRRAWADDY and to avoid expenditure of arty amn in covering bridgeheads for an unnecessarily long period, 2 and 20 Divs will patrol deeply and on a wide front across the river but will NOT establish bridgeheads until D Day. 20 Ind Div will also demonstrate across CHINDWIN R water front. D Day will be NOT before 10 Feb.

Plan For 20 Ind Div

4. (a) 20 Ind Div will establish a bridgehead on D Day on the SOUTH bank of the IRRAWADDY in a selected area opposite MYAUNG PK 84—MYINMU through which the Div will advance as early as possible with the primary task of establishing one bde gp in the MYOTHA LF 13 area.

(b) Steps will be taken to clear the area MYINMU—confluence of CHINDWIN and IRRAWADDY—MONYWA PK 58 as early as possible and a force consisting of one motorized bn will be retained in this area until 4 Corps has cleared the WEST bank of the CHINDWIN to PAKOKKU PP 48.

(c) 20 Ind Div will be directed on MYITTHA—KYAUKSE LF 62 in the first instance and may be called upon to cut the rd MANDALAY—MAYMYO with a mobile column at a later date.

(d) After crossing IRRAWADDY R steps will be taken to protect the outer flank of the division from counter attacks which might develop from the direction of MYINGYAN PK 70 and MEIKTILA.

(e) In principle 20 Ind Div, when moving EASTWARDS from MYOTHA, will be echelonned slightly in advance of 2 Div in order to cut enemy escape routes to the SOUTH before pressure from 2 Div makes itself felt.

(f) Plans will be prepared to seize the weirs at NAUNGKON LF 7904 and KANDAW LF 8278 in order to prevent the enemy from demolishing them.

Plan For 2 Div

5. (a) 2 Div will establish itself as early as possible on the line SAYE LF 4169—YWATHITGYI LF 2459—confluence MU and IRRAWADDY R. The EASTERN stop will be pushed further EAST if this can be effected without commencing major ops.

(b) A bridgehead will be established on D Day across the IRRAWADDY WEST of SAGAING in which the Div less one bde gp, will concentrate.

(c) Demonstrations will continue to be carried out against the SAGAING Hills and the country between this feature and YEMYETIN will be vigorously patrolled.

(d) When the Div crosses IRRAWADDY one bde gp will, in the first instance, be left to patrol and deal with possible enemy incursions in the area incl SHEMMAGA LA 40—SAGAING LF 45—confluence MU and IRRAWADDY. —THANIAYO LA 0405—excl WETLET LA 21. This bde gp will come under direct comd 33 Ind Corps at a date to be decided on later but will eventually revert to comd 2 Div.

Composition: One inf bde gp incl one tp 3 DG. A proportion of 2 Div arty will also be allotted if required.

(e) On a date to be decided on by me, 2 Div, less one bde gp, will advance from its bridgehead with the object of seizing the line rd junc LF 690495—AMARAPURA LF 55.

In order to ensure coordination of effort 2 Div is unlikely to be ordered to break out of its bridgehead until 20 Ind Div is established in the MYOTHA LF 13 area.

(f) After gaining its objective 2 Div may be called upon to cut the rd MANDALAY—MAYMYO LG 07.

Plan For 19 Ind Div

6. (a) It is anticipated that enemy will resist strongly any move SOUTHWARDS by 19 Ind Div and that he will probably counter attack fiercely from the NORTH and EAST.

(b) 19 Ind Div's first tasks are to clear the WEST bank of IRRAWADDY within existing div bdys, to patrol vigorously to a depth of at least 10 miles from the existing bridgeheads at THABEIKKYIN SR 63 and KYAUKMYAUNG SR 60 and to extend the THABEIKKYIN bridgehead to WABYUDAUNG SR 83.

(c) On a date to be ordered by me res bde less one bn will begin to concentrate on EAST bank of IRRAWADDY in the vicinity of the KYAUKMYAUNG bridgehead. One bn of res bde may be committed EAST of the river at discretion of div comd with task of expanding KYAUKMYAUNG bridgehead.

(d) When pressure of 2 and 30 Divs begins to make itself felt in the MANDALAY area, 10 Ind Div will be ordered to advance SOUTH on the axis NYAUNGWUN LA 52—MANDALAY LF 69 with a view to establish itself in the NORTHERN outskirts of MANDALAY and cutting escape routes to the EAST. During this advance special precautions will be taken to protect the rear and EASTERN flank of the Div.

(e) Plans will be prepared to seize the weirs at LA 8506 and LF 6985 in order to prevent the enemy from demolishing them.

268 Ind Inf Bde

7. Will conc less one bn by 2 Feb in the area SHWEBO and to the SOUTH and be responsible for patrolling WEST bank of the IRRAWADDY within operational bdys.

One bn will be located at KIN-U and will establish a patrol base of not less than one coy at KONGYI SR 51.

A patrol base of not less than one coy will relieve 2 Div at THITSEINGYI LA 42 on 2 Feb and will demonstrate and patrol EAST of the river with the object of persuading the enemy that a crossing is to be attempted.

268 Ind Inf Bde will assume responsibility for ONBAUK airstrip on 2 Feb and for SHWEBO airstrip under orders Comd SHWEBO Garrison on same date.

APPENDIX 13

4 CORPS OPERATION INSTRUCTION NO. 125
5 February 1945
Ref ¼" Map Sheets 84.N, K, O, L, and P, 93. B, C and D.

(NOTE: This Operation Instruction amends and supersedes Combined 4 Corps/Air/CCTF Outline Plan dated 28 Jan 45).

INFORMATION

1. *Enemy* as in current sitreps and summaries. Details in amplification are being sent separately to 7 Div, 17 Div and 255 Tank Bde.

Own Troops

2. 33 Corps is to develop, starting in the second week in Feb, a double pincer movement against the JAP forces in the MANDALAY area as follows:—

3. *20 Div.*
   (a) 20 Div with under comd 7 CAV (Stuart Tanks), (less one sqn) and 11 CAV (Armd C), (less two sqns), is to assault across the IRRAWADDY in the MYINBU area (LF 06) on about 12 Feb and move on the general axis MYOTHA (LF 13)—MYITTHA (LL 69)—KYAUKSE (LF 62). It may later be instructed to cut the main road MANDALAY—MAYMYO with a mobile column.
   (b) After 100 Inf Bde of 20 Div has secured the initial bridgehead, 20 Div is to advance as follows:—
   Right. 32 Inf Bde, with under comd 11 CAV, (less two sqns), and one Mtn Regt, advancing initially to the general line SAMEIKKON (PK 83)—NABUAING (PK 92) and later possibly towards MYINGYAN and NATOGYI (LL 09).
   Centre. 80 Inf Bde, with under comd 7 CAV (less one sqn), moving on the main div axis.
   Left. 100 Inf Bde moving on the general axis GYO (LF 34)—CHAUNGGWA (LF 42)—KYAUKSE (LF 62).
   (c) 20 Div has the special task of seizing the canal headworks at NAUNGKAN (LF 7904) and KANDAW (LL 8278) intact.

4. *2 Div* with under comd 3 D.G. is to assault across the IRRAWADDY WEST of SAGAING on about 12 Feb and to adv via TADAU (LF 44) and AMARAPURA (LF 55) on MANDALAY.

5. *19 Div* with under comd one sec 150 RAC and one sqn 7 CAV, is as soon as the presence of 2 and 20 Divs begins to make itself felt, to advance SOUTH on MANDALAY on the general axis NYAUNGWUN (LA 52)—MADAYA (LF 69).

6. *HQ 35 Corps* closes at 1200 hrs 6 Feb and opens in area SOUTH of SADAUNG (LF 28).

7. *Tac HQ Fourteenth Army* and HQ 221 Gp RAF open at MONYWA 9 Feb Main HQ Fourteenth Army joins Tac HQ on about 15 Feb.

8. *No. 1 and No. 2 Air Commando Groups* have been allotted as a U.S. Task Force of C.C.T.F., under the overall control of 221 GP RAF, in support of 4 Corps; No. 1 Gp from 7 Feb, No. 2 Gp from 15 Feb. For chain of command and organisation see Appx A'.

Intention

9. To seize the MEIKTILA—THAZI area in sufficient strength and in time to cut off all JAP forces retiring SOUTH from the MANDALAY area and in conjunction with 33 Corps to destroy them.

Method

10. The operation (MULTIVITE) will be phased as follows:—
    - (a) *VITAMIN 'A'*: Capture of PAKOKKU and concentration of 17 Div (less Airborne Troops) in the PAUK area.
    - (b) *VITAMIN 'B'*: Establishment of a bridgehead over the R. IRRAWADDY.
    - (c) *VITAMIN 'C'*: Concentration of the Corps on the left bank of the IRRAWADDY.
    - (d) *VITAMIN 'D'*: A lightning overland thrust assisted by an airborne build-up to seize the MEIKTILA—THAZI area, followed by the liquidation of any Japanese forces between 4 and 33 Corps.

11. *Speed and the utmost use of deception* are vital to the success of these operations.

12. Subsequently after all Japanese forces between 4 and 33 Corps have been liquidated, 4 Corps will probably be called on to advance Southwards with minimum delay.

Deception

13. Full details of the Deception Plan are given in 4 Corps Operation Instruction No. 124 dated 25 Jan 45 and in amended Appx 'B' issued under this HQ 257/10 G dated 2 Feb 45, which give details of the air dropping deception programme.

D Day

14. At this stage precise timings are impossible and are given in relation to D Day which is the day on which 7 Ind Div starts its assault across the IRRAWADDY in the NYAUNGU area (PP 27). Present target date is 12 Feb.

Vitamin 'A'. Capture of PAKOKKU—(Period D minus 7 to D minus 1)

15. 7 Div, with under comd:—
    One sqn 11 CAV
    28 (EA) Inf Bde Gp (until 1200 hrs 9 Feb)
    WESTCOL (until 1200 hrs 8 Feb)
and with in support leading Regtl Gp 255 Tank Bde will:—
   - (a) Capture PAKOKKU, clear the whole area WEST of the IRRAWADDY and Chindwin NORTH of MYITCHE (PP 18) by 10 Feb and push patrols across the IRRAWADDY between incl LETPANCHIBAW (PP 48) and incl MYINGON.
   - (b) Despatch 28 (EA) Bde, simulating 11 (EA) Div and operating on a broad front to SEIKPYU (PP 03), and to block the road SAW-SEIKPYU in the area KAZUNMA (PO 65).
   - (c) Despatch WESTCOL (CHIN HILLS Bn, LUSHAI Scouts and one bty 25 Mtn Regt) SOUTH on a broad front and on general axis SAW (PO 57)—SIDOKTAYA (PT 48)—NGAPE (PT 36), with the initial task of securing and clearing the area PASOK (PO 49)—KYAUKSWE (PO 46)—SAW (PO 37)—YAYMYO (PO 39).

(d) Assist in establishing, and protect, the Corps at SINTHE PJ 09).

16. 17 Div, fully mechanised, (less Airborne Bde Gp and attached troops concentrated for training at PALEL), will concentrate by road in the PAUK area by 15 Feb, with leading elements taking over from 7 Div by 0700 hrs 10 Feb the protection of SINTHE airhead.

17. 255 Tank Bde Gp will complete concentration in the PAUK area, leading Regtl Gp (116 RAC) in support 7 Div, by 8 Feb, and the remainder of the Bde Gp by about 11 Feb.

18. Corps will assume comd of 28 (EA) Bde Gp and ESTCOL at 1200 hrs 9 Feb.

Vitamin 'B' (Establishment of Bridgehead) (Period D to D plus 4)

19. WESTCOL will continue to show the maximum force in the SAW area and Southwards.

20. 2 to 3 days before D Day 28 (EA) Bde will push Mobile patrols Southwards in the direction of SALIN (PO 90) and will make a feint crossing near CHAUK, actually crossing if possible at least one company, and, with the aid of all possible deception methods, giving the impression that a major crossing is being attempted.

21. 7 Div will, if unopposed, cross one bn Gp at PAKOKKU as a feint, and will then, as rapidly as possible, cross in the NYAUNGU area (PP 27), if possible unopposed, and establish by D plus 2 a firm bridgehead with sufficient depth to enable the undisturbed concentration of the Corps on the left bank of the R. IRRAWADDY.

22. 20 gliders will be at call at PALEL from incl D day to fly in vital stores or equipment which cannot be dropped by air or supplied by road in time to the left bank of the river.

Vitamin 'C' (Concentration of the Corps in the Bridgehead area). (Period D plus 5 to D plus 10)

23. 17 Div (less Airborne Bde Gp) and 255 Tank Bde will cross and concentrate in the area HNAWDIN (PP 46). Target date for completion, D plus 10.

24. 7 Div will extend the bridgehead area (PP 4750), destroy any JAP forces in the MYINGYAN—TAUNGTHA area and seize KYAUK-PADAUNG (PP 43).

25. 28 (EA) Bde and WESTCOL, while continuing to demonstrate towards YENANGYAUNG and MAGWE, will secure the Corps right flank WEST of the river, reverting to comd 7 Ind Div at a date to be settled later.

26. Sqn 11 Cav, as soon as the leading Sqn of 16 CAV is deployed EAST OF THE IRRAWADDY, will revert to comd 33 Corps and rejoin 30 Div.

27. 4 Corps F.M.A. will be established in the bridgehead area.

Vitamin 'D' (Overland and airborne coup-de-main to seize MEIKTILA— THAZI). (Period D plus 10 to D plus 20)

28. 17 Div (less Airborne Bde Gp), with 235 Tank Bde (less one regt) and 16 CAV (Armd C) less one sqn, arty and other supporting arms under comd, will advance on MEIKTILA, with the maximum speed on the general axis WELAUNG (PP 77)—MAHLAING (LL 06).

29. 7 Div (with under comd one regt 255 Tank Bde and 28 (EA) Bde) will continue to protect the Corps bridgehead and airhead, capture

CHAUK, send mobile columns South towards YENANGYAUNG, feint from KYAUKPADAUNG towards MEIKTILA and destroy any JAP forces in the MYINGYAN area.

30. 17 Div will seize a suitable area for the construction of a fighter and C 47 strips, NW and close to MEIKTILA.

Two D8 Bulldozers and one Auto Patrol for work on the strips and a recce party from the American Aviation Engr Coy, will move with 17 Div.

31. Det U.S. Aviation Engr Coy with Airborne Regt will be flown in gliders from TILAGAON to the above area and will construct a C45 and a fighter strip. Target dates D plus 13 and D plus 18 respectively. Det will be flown out on completion of these tasks.

32. Immediately this airstrip is ready for C47's the 17 Div Airborne Bde Gp will be flown in with 20 jeeps as rapidly as possible direct from PALEL, followed by one fd coy and a very small number of misc troops from KAN. Target datestart D plus 13, completion D plus 16.

33. This Bde Gp will be followed by 17 Div Airborne Div Tps Gp about 100 C47 sorties. Target dates, start D plus 17, complete D plus 19.

34. Meanwhile 17 Div will surround and capture MEIKTILA (Target Date D plus 18) and THAZI (Target Date D plus 22).

35. 25 additional gliders will be at call at PALEL from D plus 10 to fly in vital stores or eqpt which cannot be dropped by air or supplied by road to the area MEIKTILA—THAZI.

36. Subsequently 4 Corps will—
    (a) In conjunction with 33 Corps advancing from the North, destroy all JAP forces NORTH of the line KYAUKPADAUNG —THAZI.
    (b) On completion of (a), prepare for an early advance Southwards by mechanised and airborne movement.

37. C.C.T.F. will continue to control all air transport operations in support of 4 Corps.

38. C.C.T.F. and U.S. Task Force organised and located as in Appx 'A' will together provide:—
    (a) Direct and indirect support of 4 Corps throughout MULTI-VITE from 8 Feb onwards.
    (b) Fighter cover over 4 Corps bridgehead area.
    (c) Air Transport and Glider lift as in Appx 'D'.
    (d) U.S. Aviation Engrs and eqpt for the construction or re-construction, with 17 Div's assistance, of airstrips in MEIKTILA area.
    (e) Assistance in L5s for Arty/R beyond the resources of 4 Corps Air O.P. Flt.

39. Bde Gp RAF will provide:—
    (a) Indirect support of 4 Corps throughout MULTIVITE.
    (b) Normal Tac/R, Photo and Arty/R.
    (c) Fighter cover over Corps FMA's, airheads and bridgehead area throughout MULTIVITE.
    (d) Dropping of deception devices as in amended Appx 'B' issued under this HQ 207/10 G dated 2 Feb 45.
    (e) Assistance to deception by strikes on CHAUK—LANYWA—YENANGYAUNG—MAGWE, rising to a peak 9-12 Feb to supplement the main deception plan and to cause losses to the JAPS in these areas.

APPENDIX 14

JAPANESE STRENGTH—15TH ARMY

March 1945*

The following is an extract from a captured 15 Army Staff Table dated 7 Jan. 45. The document was captured in Meiktila in March 1945.

		Code No.		Personnel
31 Div		RETSU	10720	
138 Inf Regt			10353	1733
33 Div		YUMI	10722	212
Div HQ			6820	212
213 Inf Regt			6822	464
214 Inf Regt			6823	425
215 Inf Regt			6824	564
33 Mtn Arty Regt			6825	232
23 Engr Regt			6826	249
Sigs Unit			6827	148
33 Tpt Regt			6828	489
Ord Duty Unit		(formerly	6829)	84
Med Unit			6830	165
No. 1 Fd Hosp			6831	204
No. 2 Fd Hosp			6832	206
Vet Depot ...			6833	41
Water Purification Unit		(formerly	6834)	86
Att Tps				
One Inf Regt of 53 Div				
1 Bn 124 Inf Regt			8906	530
One WT pl 19 Sigs Regt			10700	50
One pl Shipping Engr Regt ...			1750	—
22 Br Material Coy ...			1374	440
15 River Crossing Material Coy			3964	240
335 Indep MT Coy ...			12238	654
2 Coy 3 Special Water Tpt Regt			10438	50
One pl (less one det) YUMI of 38 Sea Duty Coy			5124	189
21 Special Sea Duty Coy ...			10393	52
One pl (less one sec) 53 Constr Duty Coy ...			6911	70
72 CCS (less one det—Tr) ...			6032	25
1 "Manufacture Materials" (SEI-SAI-Tr) Pl less two secs				
No. 1 Tpt Coy, 1 Div, INA ...				17
TOTAL str 33 Div and att tps				5859
53 Div		YASU	10016	
151 Inf Regt			10022	850

* Appendix A to 17 Div Periodical Isum up to 9 Mar. 1945.

APPENDIX 14

	Code No.	Personnel
Number of Guns—7 Jan. 45		
31 Div		
31 Mtn Arty Regt.		6 mtn guns, one 10 cm how
33 Div		
Div HQ	2 MGs	
213 Inf Regt	4 MGs	1 bn gun
214 Inf Regt	4 MGs	
215 Inf Regt	5 MGs	
33 Div Mtn Arty		4 mtn guns
33 Div Engr Regt	5 MGs	
33 Div Tpt Regt	2 MGs	
53 Div		
151 Inf Regt	9 MGs	6 A Tk guns, 2 Bn guns, 3 Regt guns.

Comparative figures for Guns as at end of Dec. 44
33 Div

92 Type	35
92 Type Inf Gun	11
94 Type A Tk Gun	5
41 Type Mtn Gun	2
94 Type Mtn Gun	7

Number of MT and AT in 15 Army

33 Div	205MT	283AT

APPENDIX 15

63 BDE OPS INSTRUCTION NO. 1

9 March 1945

Lt.-Col. C. M. R. Spedding
Comd 9 Border.

1. You will hold YINDAW to the last rd and the last man as a bastion on which the rest of the Div can deploy.

2. You will make YINDAW into as strong a bastion as possible.

3. You will retain in YINDAW BASTION only the following vehs:—
    Amm Trucks
    Cooks Trucks
    Mtr Vehs
    One or two vehs for truck patrols
    Remaining vehs will return to MEIKTILA this evening.

4. You will be responsible for Patrol Tanks as under:—
    (a) By day
        (i) NYAUNGYAN 5017 gp of villages and villages on the route thereto.
        (ii) KOKKOGON Gp 3817.
        (iii) Down to and incl all villages North of the line WETLET 4606—SHANZU 3802—YWATHIT 3406.
    (b) By night
        Only within 3000 yds of perimeter.
    (c) You will have a special patrol based and varied according to infn received to probe PYAWBWE from the North and West.

5. This will NOT be issued except:—
    (a) To extricate a patrol in difficulties.
    (b) To hit any small force reported by patrols which is not further out than a radius of 5 miles.

6. All patrols in addition to searching for enemy will give Topographical going reports for Tps and 4×4 vehs.

APPENDIX 16

4 CORPS DECEPTION SCHEME 'CONCLAVE'

INFORMATION

1. The enemy is aware of the presence of tps of 4 Corps in the MEIKTILA area. He does not know, however, that the whole Corps is concentrating there, nor does he know in which direction our next move from MEIKTILA will be made.

INTENTION

2. To conceal from the JAPS for as long as possible the fact that a force of the size of a corps is concentrating at MEIKTILA.

3. To conceal from the JAPS the direction in which our next move from MEIKTILA will be made.

METHOD

Concealment of the concentration of the corps at MEIKTILA

4. The minimum use of wireless will be made up to the time the southward adv of the corps from MEIKTILA starts. In particular 5 Div will remain on wireless silence until sanction is given by corps HQ for it to be lifted.

5. Until further notice no formation signs will be displayed on uniform, vehicles, notice boards or elsewhere except as in para 9 below.

Concealment of the direction of our adv from MEIKTILA

6. In outline, the method to be employed will be at first to emphasise the participation of 4 Corps in the destruction of the JAPS between MEIKTILA and MANDALAY, subsequently to persuade the JAPS that our future axis of adv is the rd THAZI—LOILEM.

7. Emphasis is already being laid on 4 Corps participation in the MANDALAY ops by press and wireless pronouncements. Propaganda leaflets dropped on the JAPS of 15 Army have also been designed to assist this emphasis.

8. The rd THAZI—LOILEM will be "sold" to the JAPS as our future axis of adv as follows:—

   (a) 17 Div will spread rumours by every possible means of a powerful eastward armd adv by ourselves starting at the end of Mar.

   (b) At least one sqn tks will accompany the force which moves EAST from MEIKTILA on to THAZI—HLAINGDET (LL 6524). As soon as troops are established in the HLAINGDET area, they will make enquiries as if preparing for an advance along the main road towards LOILEM.

   (c) Prior to the start of our adv south from MEIKTILA, a minimum of actual recce southwards will be carried out.

   (d) Extensive bombing, photo R and leaflet dropping on targets along the rd THAZI—LOILEM has already been started under Fourteenth Army/221 Gp arrangements.

   (e) Corps HQ will arrange tac R and further photo R along this rd.

(f) Pintails will be dropped under Army and Corps arrangements at suitable places to jitter the JAPS. Arrangements are already in hand and dropping will start about 29/30 Mar.

(g) Drops of paratroops will be realistically simulated east of YINMABIN LL 82 and SE of HOPONG LM 81 at the end of Mar. These will be followed up by actual supply drops, along their eastward axis, for a period of one full week.

(h) A map marked in a way which suggests a future adv along the rd THAZI—LOILEM will be planted on the JAPS in the MEIKTILA area. Corps HQ will prepare the map and send it in due course to 17 Div for planting.

(i) D Div are assisting the deception by their own methods, particularly by a notional airborne operation against the rd LOILEM—TAKAW, for which the notional D Day will be progressively postponed, until the operation serves NO further useful purpose, when it will be cancelled.

9. For the purpose of 8(b) above a notional armd bde is being "sold" to the JAPS as having already reached MEIKTILA; this formation is 51 Indep Tk Bde composed of 163 RAC, 42 Cav and 46 Cav IAC. The eastward recce in force will simulate this formation by every possible means—rumours, inclusion on map referred to in para 8(h), inclusion in distribution lists and if possible by vehicles showing the ordinary RAC sign of the "nailed fist".

Deception on Other Parts of Fourteenth Army Front

10. On 7 Ind Div front the threat to the oilfields will be continued. To assist in this threat, a bogus 18 Ind Div will be simulated advancing west of the IRRAWADDY, in place of the bogus 11 (EA) Div withdrawn to rest. Appx A, showing the notional order of battle of 18 Ind Div, is att for certain addressees only.

Full details of the deception on this axis will be issued later. In the meanwhile 7 Ind Div will continue to operate aggressively and will use wireless to as great an extent as possible to give the impression of impending activity on their front.

11. 33 Corps is to be publicized as being engaged in the MANDALAY ops and thereafter as operating eastwards in conjunction with NCAC.

Later Deceptions by 4 Corps

12. When 4 Corps reaches southern BURMA it is at present the intention to try to persuade the JAPS that the main weight of the Corps advance from NYAUNGLEBIN will be across the SITTANG towards MOULMEIN.

In conjunction with this, D Div are going to materialise a notional seaborne attack on MOULMEIN. The impression it is hoped to give the JAPS is that the main weight of 4 Corps is to participate in this attack on MOULMEIN.

This part of the deception is too far ahead to consider in detail now. It is probable, however, that a demonstration towards SITTANG will eventually be necessary.

Allocation of D Force Coys.

13. 51 Coy will remain under comd 7 Div.

14. 57 Coy will remain under comd 17 Div for the present, but will later be re-allocated by corps HQ when the situation requires this.

Security

15. The deception scheme will be known by the code word CONCLAVE.

16. Knowledge of the existence of the scheme will be limited to those who need to know in order to carry it out.

17. As far as possible everyone taking part in deceptive activities should believe them to be genuine. Where personnel involved are bound to guess that their activities are not entirely genuine, they may be told confidentially—in order to obtain their whole-hearted co-operation—that they are taking part in a deception.

APPENDIX 17
ORBAT 33 IND CORPS
31 Mar 45
HQ 33 IND CORPS

254 Tk Bde
150 RAC
3 DG
7 Cav
11 Cav
3/4 Bombay Grs

2 Div

Arty
10 Fd Regt
16 Fd Regt
99 Fd Regt
100 Atk Regt

2 Recce
2 Manch MMG Bn

4 Inf Bde
1 RS
2 Norfolk
1/8 LF

5 Ind Bde
7 Worc R
2 Dorset
1 Cameron

6 Inf Bde
1 RWF
1 R Berks
2 DLI

7 Div
(Came under Comd 29 Mar)

Arty
136 Fd Regt
139 Fd Regt
24 Atk Regt
25 Ind Mtn Regt

Inf
7-2 Punjab Div Recce Bn
13 FF Rif MMG Bn
2 Baroda Div HQ Bn

33 Ind Inf Bde
1 Queens
4/1 GR
4/15 Punjab

89 Ind Inf Bde
2 KOSB
4/8 GR
1/11 Sikh

114 Ind Inf Bde
2 S Lan R
4/14 Punjab
4/5 RGR

19 Ind Div
(Reverted to Comd Army 5 Apr)

Arty
4 Ind Fd Regt
115 Fd Regt
33 Atk Regt
20 Ind Mtn Regt

1/15 Punjab Div Recce Bn
1/11 Sikh MMG Bn
1 Assam Div HQ Bn

62 Ind Inf Bde
2 Welch
3/6 Raj Rif
4/6 GR

64 Ind Inf Bde
2 Worc R
5/10 Baluch
1/6 GR

98 Ind Inf Bde
2 R Berks
8/12 FF Rif
4/4 GR

28 (EA) Bde
7 Uganda Bn K.A.R.
46 (Tanganika Territory) Bn K.A.R.
71 (Somaliland) Bn K.A.R.

268 Ind Inf Bde
4/3 Madras
1 Chamar
Mahindra Dal

20 Ind Div

Arty
9 Fd Regt
114 Fd Regt
111 Atk Regt
23 Ind Mtn Regt

Inf
9 Jat MMG Bn
4/17 Dogra Div HQ Bn

32 Ind Inf Bde
1 Northamptons
9/14 Punjab
3/8 GR

80 Ind Inf Bde
1 Devon
9 FF Rif
3/1 GR

100 Ind Inf Bde
2 Border
14 FF Rif
4/10 GR

APPENDIX 18

SECURING TOUNGOO—4 CORPS OPERATION
INSTRUCTION NO. 139

5 April 1945

INFORMATION

Enemy

1. The JAPS have just suffered a resounding defeat in the battle for CENTRAL BURMA. Since 1 Jan 45 they have lost some 18,000 men (killed, wounded and PW) and about 255 guns, mostly from 15 Army.

At the same time as this has been in progress, 54 Div of 28 Army and 56 Div of 33 Army have been beaten and forced to retreat on both flanks of the JAP front in BURMA. 2 Div is thought to have left BURMA entirely, with the exception of 16 Regt, which is in 15 Army.

In consequence, there is at present only one JAP Div in Burma which approaches full strength; this Div is 55 Div, which is located in SW BURMA, less two bns in the Mt POPA area.

The overall result is that the Allied forces in BURMA are opposed by one intact div and eight weak divs. Taking into account two IMBs and the JIFs, the inf component of the JAP forces in BURMA is the equivalent of the inf of about four and a half divs. The condition of most of these troops is poor, however, and they are tired and dispirited; their supply system within BURMA is shaky, they have little hope of reinforcements or equipment reaching them from outside BURMA and that part of the population which has initiative to act is potentially hostile. The only help the JAPS can expect is from the many thousands of L of C troops which are spread over Southern BURMA.

The JAP situation and intentions are discussed in greater detail in Appx 'A'.

Own Tps

2. (*a*) 33 *Corps* on completion of the task of destroying all organised enemy resistance in the area MANDALAY—KYAUKSE—MYITTHA—WUNDWIN—MYINGYAN is operating to:—
    (*i*) Capture SEIKPYU (PP 03)
                 CHAUK (PP 13)
                 MAGWE (PU 24)
    (*ii*) Advance SOUTH subsequently astride R.IRRAWADDY.

(*b*) 7 *DIV* with 28 (EA) Bde (until flown out), Chin Hills Bn and Lushai Scouts under comd, is operating to capture CHAUK and SEIKPYU and thence to make junc with 20 Div at MAGWE. 33 Bde has been relieved in the TAUNGTHA area by 268 Bde and is moving to NYAUNGU.

    (*c*) 2 *Div*
        (*i*) 4 Bde Gp less 2 NORFOLK is concentrating MYINGYAN approx 7 Apr moving via PYINZI. 2 NORFOLK are moving to MYINGYAN from MAHLAING via TAUNGTHA on about 9 Apr.

(ii) 5 Bde Gp has reached WELAUNG (PP 76) and is advancing on axis KYAUKPADAUNG (PP 43)—CHAUK.
(iii) 6 Bde is already conc MYINGYAN. The withdrawal of 2 Div from the Army area by air is to be completed by 20 Apr.

(d) *268 Bde* has relieved 33 Bde of 7 Div in the TAUNGTHA area. Later, Bde HQ with MAHINDRA DAL Regt is to be prepared to cross R. IRRAWADDY, assume comd of CHIN HILLS Bn and LUSHAI Scouts under comd 7 Div, and move Southwards WEST of R. IRRAWADDY.

(e) *20 DIV* after a short period of rest and refitting is to move about 8 Apr on a semi-motorised basis and with an armoured coln on the axis MEIKTILA—NATMAUK (PU 76) to capture MAGWE, and is then to be prepared to operate either NORTH to effect junc with 7 Div, or SOUTH on ALLANMYO (PZ 55).

(f) *19 Div* has come under comd 4 Corps from 5 Apr. 64 Bde came under comd 4 Corps on 31 Mar and is moving on THAZI, 98 Bde is due to complete conc about 5 Apr at WUNDWIN, where 62 Bde will be moving after completion of relief by 36 Div.

(g) *18 Fd Regt* (less one bty already with 4 Corps) and *7 CAV Gp* (less one sqn) are moving to MEIKTILA under comd 4 Corps and come under comd OCRA 4 Corps and 255 Tk Bde respectively on arrival.

(h) 8 CAV is crossing R. IRRAWADDY at SAMEIKKON and moving via DWEHLA—WUNDWIN to MEIKTILA on about 6 Apr, coming under comd 19 Div on arrival.

(i) *Move of Army HQ*
HQ Fourteenth Army is likely to remain MONYWA moving to MEIKTILA area immediately HQ 4 Corps is clear.

INTENTION

3. To secure TOUNGOO with all possible speed as a preliminary to further operations Southwards.

METHOD

4. The operations will be phased as follows:—

(a) PHASE A   17 Div will capture the PYAWBWE area. Target date 7 Apr.

(b) PHASE B   5 Div (less 9 Airborne Bde Gp) will pass through 17 Div and secure an airhead at PYINMANA, (target date 15 Apr). 17 Div will move forward as close as possible behind 5 Div to PYINMANA and will take over its protection and further development.

(c) PHASE C   5 Div will surround and secure TOUNGOO, with the assistance of an airborne build up of 9 Bde Gp from MEIKTILA. Target date for capture of TOUNGOO 25 Apr.

5. Speed is all important and risks must be accepted to obtain it. Every day is precious.

APPENDIX 19

SECURING PROME—33 IND CORPS OP ORDER NO 21

30 April 1945

Ref map ¼ inch to 1 mile, Sheets 84 L, P
85 I, M, J, N, O.
All map refs PU except where stated.

INFM

Enemy

1. (*a*) The enemy forces in the IRRAWADDY valley comprise the following depeleted fmns:—
   (*i*) *54 Div.* Insignificant elements of this div remain in the ARAKAN. On 26 Apr 15 Corps estimated that they were opposed by 3 Bn 154 Regt in the AN PT 10 area and by two coys of 1 Bn 121 Regt, together with stragglers of 2 Bn 121 Regt, about TAUNGUP UO 39. Since that date there is evidence of further EASTERLY withdrawal from the ARAKAN.
   (*ii*) *55 Div*, less 144 Regt, 3 Sqn 55 CAV Regt (both of which are opposing 4 Corps) and elements of 143 Regt.
   (*iii*) 153 Regt of 49 Div.
   (*iv*) 72 Indep Mixed Bde.

   (*b*) These fmns are generally disposed as follows:—
   (*i*) *54 Div.* It is believed that 154 Regt, less 3 Bn, is finding the rearguard in face of the adv of 7 Ind Div. Z Force reports of a concentration in the gen area PADAN PT 72, of tps recently arrived from AN, must also refer to elements of 54 Div. There have been continued indications of withdrawal by tps of 54 Div on the axis AN—MINDON PY 95—KAMA PZ 31.
   (*ii*) The main body of 72 Indep Mixed Bde and of 153 Regt withdrawing steadily, are already SOUTH of MINBU 15.
   (*iii*) 20 Ind Div has lately been opposed by elements of 143 Regt and may be expected once again to meet 55 CAV Regt, less 3 Sqn, on its axis of adv.
   (*iv*) 112 Regt, less 3 Bn, withdrawing from the POPA area, is endeavouring to escape SOUTH in the hills WEST of SATTHWA 91.

   (*c*) Thus the IRRAWADDY valley presents a consistent picture of enemy withdrawal, apparently converging on the THAYETMYO PZ 44. It is evident that both PROME UE 58 and PAUNGDE UE 84 serve as assembly areas. Delaying actions as opportunities of terrain present themselves are to be expected on the routes to these two places. The enemy's overall intention is obviously to withdraw as much as is possible of the BURMA Area Army EAST over the SITTANG R, and he may be expected to defend RANGOON QL 53 for a period. Since his only land escape route is already seriously threatened, the possibility exists of a change of plan and of an attempt to pull out some of his forces in the IRRAWADDY valley by way of BASSEIN UO 94.

Own Tps

2. 17 Ind Div, leading the adv of 4 Corps, reached the outskirts of PEGU QF 90 during the morning of 30 Apr.

INTENTION

3. 33 Ind Corps will
   (a) seize PROME earliest possible.
   (b) destroy the enemy forces attempting to escape EAST.
   (c) adv with all speed on RANGOON with max force possible.

METHOD

Gen

4. (a) Deployment of 7 Ind Div, 268 Ind Inf Bde and Corps Tps RA in accordance with instrs already issued will be completed.

   (b) 20 Ind Div will continue adv SOUTH with max possible speed, and make fullest use of armour to maintain the momentum of the adv.

Bdys

5. (a) Between 7 Ind Div and CCRA incl 7 Ind Div TEWUN 57—GYOGYAGAN 56—MS 20 rd MAGWE 24—NATMAUK 76—KANTHIT CH 5053 to chaung junc 4944 thence excl YIN CH—incl MS 293 rd TAUNGDWINGYI 92—MAGWE—excl AINGZAUK CH 6923—incl track Pt 716 5914—SANMAGYI 6008—KYAUKPYUDAUNG PZ 5698—chaung junc PZ 5489.

   (b) Between 20 Ind Div and CCRA, initially, incl CCRA LINBAN C PZ 5189—KOBIN PZ 7192—NGADAN C PZ 8292 and, subsequently, incl 20 Ind Div KYINI C PZ 5257—YEZON C PZ 5856. Above bdys effective at times to be arranged mutually between 20 Ind Div and CCRA.

6. *7 Ind Div* will
   (a) op not more than one inf bde gp WEST of IRRAWADDY R SOUTH from MINBU on THAYETMYO.
   (b) op not more than one inf bde gp WEST of IRRAWADDY R SOUTH from area KYANGIN UE 51 with the object of destroying enemy wherever found.
   (c) be responsible for security area EAST of IRRAWADDY R within op bdy defined in para 5(a) above.
   (d) on conc Corps Tps RA area MAGWE (see para 9 below), secure area YENANGYAUNG 18—SATTHWA excl ALLANMYO PZ 55 with res ind bde gp. This inf bde gp will be conc for ease of sup and will be prepared to op small mot colns in a mopping up role.

7. *20 Ind Div* will
   (a) capture PROME as soon as possible.
   (b) op main effort on axis PROME—RANGOON by shortest route and with max speed.
   (c) op not more than one inf bde gp to clear area PROME—PAUNGDE—NYAUNGZAYE.

8. *268 Ind Inf Bde* will relieve 20 Ind Div in area ALLANMYO under orders 20 Ind Div. On completion of conc area ALLANMYO the Bde will revert to Corps control.

268 Ind Inf Bde will

APPENDIX 19   523

  (a) as early as possible op WEST of the IRRAWADDY R against area THAYETMYO with the object of cutting enemy escape routes WEST of THAYETMYO.

  (b) conc in area ALLANMYO on completion of task in para (a) above.

9. *Corps Tps RA* less units under comd divs will

  (a) take over in rear of 20 Ind Div as far SOUTH as excl KYINI C—YEZON C.

  (b) subsequently conc in area MAGWE on completion role in sub area (a) above and on orders from this HQ.

Rivercraft

10. (a) HM Gunboats PAMELA and UNA are being placed in sp 20 Ind Div for ops in the area ALLANMYO—NYAUNGZAYE at a date to be notified. These craft will subsequently sp 7 Ind Div ops SOUTH of PROME.

(b) Three powered crafts each capable of carrying one pl inf with pl weapons have already been allotted to 7 Ind Div.

Limitations on scale of ops

11. Available air sup places considerable limitations on the size of the force which can be operated SOUTH of MAGWE as all air sup beyond this airfd becomes increasingly uneconomical. Forces which can be operated are thus divided into:—

  (a) Fmns and units which can be maintained up to 100 miles by rd and 50 miles by IWT from MAGWE. Such tps, must except where ops demand otherwise, be located within 25 miles of MAGWE.

  (b) Fmns and units dependent on air sup SOUTH of ALLANMYO. These cannot exceed one div, with limited Corps Tps in sp, plus one inf bde gp. Of these tps up to two inf bde gps can be on SD at any one time.

  (c) Fmns and units which can be released for flying out as early as ops permit.

The conc of units already nominated for flyout will be expedited. All other non-essential units must be placed in category (a) above.

ADM

12. Adm instrs separately.

INTERCOMN

13. Sig instrs separately.

14. HQ 33 Ind Corps closes present location and opens at MAGWE at 1200 hrs on 4 May.

APPENDIX 20

ORBAT 33 IND CORPS

1 May 45

HQ 33 IND CORPS

RAC/IAC
102 Corps Del Sqn

254 Ind Tk Bde

7 Cav
3 DG
150 RAC
3/4 Bombay Grs

Arty
1 Med Regt
101 HAA Regt
44 LAA Regt
1 Ind Svy Regt

---

7 Ind Div

Arty
136 Fd Regt
139 Fd Regt
24 Atk Regt
25 Ind Mtn Regt

Inf
7/2 Punjab Div Recce Bn
13 FF Rif MMG Bn
2 Baroda Div HQ Bn

89 Ind Inf Bde
2 KOSB
4/8 GR
1/11 Sikh

114 Ind Inf Bde
2 S Lan R
4/14 Punjab
4/5 RGR

33 Ind Inf Bde
1 Queens
4/1 GR
4/15 Punjab

---

20 Ind Div

Inf
80 Ind Inf Coy (14 Punjab)

Arty
9 Fd Regt
114 Fd Regt
23 Ind Mtn Regt
111 Atk Regt

Inf
2/8 Punjab Div Recce Bn
9 Jat MMG Bn
9/12 FFR Div HQ Bn

32 Ind Inf Bde
4/2 GR
3/8 GR
9/14 Punjab

80 Ind Inf Bde
3/1 GR
4/17 Dogra
1/19 Hybad

100 Ind Inf Bde
1/1 GR
4/10 GR
14/13 FF Rif

---

33 Indian Corps Account of Operations, Vol. IV—20 March–28 May 1945, File 601/8758/H.

APPENDIX 21

EXTRACT FROM

INTELLIGENCE SUMMARY NO. 15*

18 May 1945

PSYCHOLOGICAL WARFARE

An interesting survey of JAPANESE PW captured in BURMA has been made. 100 JAPS captured in 1944 and 100 Japs captured in 1945 have been interrogated, to obtain a comparative estimate of JAP morale and reaction to our propaganda. The percentage of voluntary surrender is six times higher for 1945 than for 1944.

The following percentages are of interest:

	1944	1945
1. Considered it their duty to commit suicide if forced with capture	82%	75%
2. Did NOT consider it their duty to commit suicide	18%	24%
3. Gave up voluntarily	2%	8%
4. Did NOT resist capture ...	3%	21%

These figures obtained before the fall of RANGOON show that JAPANESE morale has suffered a severe shock.

*H.Q. 20 Ind Div "G" Branch, File No. 601/250/W.D./Pt. V.

APPENDIX 22

JAPANESE PLAN FOR BREAKOUT

July 1945

The following are extracts from a Japanese Operation Order issued by *Japanese 55 Div* for the break-out across the SITTANG River. It was in Allied hands by the 13th of July 1945.

"11. *Main body of the Heidan* This will be divided into 3 colns; the right coln will follow the route of the Right Breakthrough Unit; Central coln will follow the THATEGYI (QA 9902)—HMANDAN (QB 0402)—MANGO (QB 0703) route along the embankment of AINGDON Chaung, area KYAUKTAGA (QB 0801)—KYAUKSAYIT (QB 1803) rd; the left coln will proceed along the MAGYIBIN (QA 9705)—ALEGYIN (QB 0307)—ZAYATKIN (QB 0708)—ANAMBAW (QB 1611) rd. According to the situation after crossing the MANDALAY rd, they will proceed either along the South or North embankment rd.

The colns of the main body will, after their rear has crossed the rd, notify Right and Centre Breakthrough Units by means of sig pistol or by a picked officer. The Centre Breakthrough OC will notify the OC left Breakthrough Unit.

By the morning of X plus 1, OC Right Breakthrough will destroy the embankment rd in the area: LETKAN (QG 2199 and QR (about 3 Kms NNW of KYAUKTAGA); and will repel attacks by enemy armed Cs; at this time it must be made possible for pers and animals to cross, and also one Butai will be assigned to prevent repairs by the enemy.

Centre Breakthrough Unit will carry out demolitions in vicinity of TEGAU on the PENWEGON—KYAUNGYWA (QB 1609) rd, according to previous para.

Between 0630 and 0800 hrs on X plus 1 each breakthrough Unit will complete its preparation as follows:—

(*a*) Units that adv to WEST bank of the SITTANG, will disperse at 0700 hrs and conceal themselves in the jungle (or in a village if the river has overflowed its banks) and disperse themselves for def from attack from air or ground.

(*b*) Each unit of the main body, between the MANDALAY rd and the right bank of the SITTANG, at least in the area 2 Kms E of the rd, will, if attacks by tks are expected, avoid the rd and disperse in the jungle (or in a village if the river has overflowed its banks) and disperse themselves for defe from attack from air or ground.

(*c*) If any rear parties have not crossed the MANDALAY rd by 0600 hrs they will disperse in the jungle where the trees run close to the rd and make preparations against air and ground attacks. They will set out again on the evening of X plus 1.

(*d*) Each Breakthrough Unit will set a party at 0700 hrs to take up posn on the pts of the rd allocated to it while the main body disperses 2 Kms East of the rd in the jungle (or in a village if the river has overflowed its banks) and make preparations against air and ground attacks.

(e) The party left out for this purpose, according to last para, may be EAST of the rd and will secure their posn as best they can until the evening of the same day; to afford protection for the units, if the main body has adv East of the MANDALAY rd by the morning of X plus 1, the unit mentioned in para (c), besides preventing the adv of the demolition area and do their utmost to check the enemy WEST of the rd.

(f) Even if it is decided to act as in the preceding para, the Right Breakthrough Unit will be responsible for the def of the main body, according to the situation of the enemy in NYAUNGLEBIN and at the same time, according to the situation in KYAUKKYI, the centre Breakthrough Unit will allocate a party to the area of PENWEGON and KYAUNGYWA (QA 1609); its main force will attack the enemy in the area of KYAUNGYWA to facilitate the breakthrough of the main body of the Heidan.

Details to be carried out during the breakout

(a) After the breakthrough has started, an increase in the speed must be expected if circumstances demand. If any hitches occur, confusion must be avoided at all costs. Groups will band together into a temporary formation. Senior offrs will send advance parties in order to control the rate of advance.

(b) All units above platoon strength will send a party back under an officer or NCO to guide following units:

(c) Apart from units responsible for holding attacks and defence, formation will be in columns commensurate with the width of the route possible, Column comdrs, in case of night attacks during short halts, will allot defensive positions. Units responsible for holding attacks and defence will not fire at night except of necessity.

(d) In view of the character of the enemy, to maintain secrecy and prevent confusion among composite units, no firing will be permitted. Cold steel will be the order of the day.

(e) If enemy rifle or MG fire is encountered no halt will be made. In such circumstances coy comdrs or the equivalent offrs will send out a det to attack from flank or rear. If enemy gun fire is encountered coy comdrs etc. will cut across the line of fire and lead their units away, continuing their advance.

(f) In above circumstances, comdrs will send a party to collect casualties, stores and animals etc. after objective has been reached.

Crossing of the SITTANG

(a) KAMIKAZE Tac will send parties to guide each group and will collect country boats for the crossing.

(b) Main body of Meidan and each column must be prepared to cross the river under their own steam.

(c) Country boats and 3-4 men Sampans will be joined together by bamboo brought along with us and will be used to form rafts of three boats.

(d) Motor Car inner tubes and tyres, drums, and cans used in 'light' crossings will be taken along. Rafts and boats will be handed over to units following in rear.

(e) Bullocks and horses will cross as time permits.

Secrecy

12. In the move from No. 1 assembly point to the plain, recognised route will be avoided. East-West routes through mountain villages frequented by enemy agents will be cut across. The three columns will make a feint towards TOUNGOO. The general movement of the Heidan will be shortened by all means possible.

13. Speed and secrecy are essential in the move to the plain. Daring and boldness will be the rule in the move to the left bank of the SITTANG.

All preparations must be made in advance to counter any surprise collision with the enemy, or enemy knowledge of our plans.

By retaining the initiative, or regaining it if lost, by boldness, calmness, by clever and experienced comd, we may expect a successful breakthrough.

14. Comds will take responsibility for war diaries, records, orders and reports. Secret short term documents, except those absolutely necessary will be destroyed at the commencement of the operation.

15. Ammunition more than twice the prescribed quantity should be carried in the advance to the SITTANG."

Bibliography

This volume is based primarily on official records possessed by the C.I.S. Historical Section. Of these the most important are the war diaries of the various units which took part in the campaign for the reconquest of Burma. The Historical Section has an almost complete set of these diaries, particularly of the Indian forces.

In addition, there are a number of 'appreciations' written during the course of the war by military officers and men at the top. The contents of these appreciations must have formed the basis for strategy in Burma and a study of these is therefore essential.

The 'despatches' written by the different commanders soon after the completion of operations form another useful source for an understanding not only of higher policy but also of the administrative and logistical difficulties inherent in the conduct of a modern military campaign. It is not possible to give a complete list of all the diaries, appreciations and despatches consulted in the writing of this narrative but some of these are listed below.

Since ample documentary sources of a primary nature were available, much use has not been made of the secondary published sources or accounts, except perhaps for describing Allied strategy and diplomacy at the highest level. However, an illustrative list of these secondary sources which have been consulted is also given below.

WAR DIARIES

War Diaries of all units that took part in the campaign for the reconquest of Burma, and particularly of the following:—

IV, XV and XXXIII Corps; 5th, 7th, 17th, 19th, 20th, 23rd and 26th Indian Divisions; 2nd and 36th British Divisions; 11th East African Division; 1st, 9th, 32nd, 33rd, 37th, 48th, 49th, 62nd, 63rd, 64th, 80th, 89th, 100th, 114th, 123rd, and 161st Indian Infantry Brigades; 268th Indian (Lorried) Brigade; Lushai Brigade; 254th Tank Brigade, 255th Tank Brigade, 50th Parachute Brigade, 25th East African Brigade, 26th East African Brigade and 28th East African Brigade. Also War Diaries of smaller units comprised in the above.

DESPATCHES AND APPRECIATIONS

Lieut.-General Sir Oliver Leese's Despatch.

General Sir George J. Giffard's Despatch, 23 June 1944 to 10 November 1944.

"Operations IV Corps" by Lieut.-General Sir Frank Messervy.

"Operations XXXIII Corps" by General Sir Montagu Stopford.

Joint Planning Staff Paper 100 and 100A entitled "Operations in Burma 1944-1945".

South-East Asia Translation and Interrogation Centre Bulletin Nos. 240 and 242.

OTHER OFFICIAL DOCUMENTS

Japanese Account of their Operations in Burma.

19th Indian Division Engineers History.

War History 2 Welch.
Brigadier P. C. Marindin's Account of Lushai Brigade's Operations.
7th Indian Division History (Draft).
"A Short History of 20th Indian Division" by Major-General D. D. Gracey.
Payagyi Interrogation Reports.
History of the Japanese *28th Army*.
History of the Twelfth Army.
Outline History of 1st Sikh Regiment (1946) in the World War II.

PUBLISHED SOURCES

Churchill: *Closing the Ring*.
Mountbatten: *Report to the Combined Chiefs of Staff* by the Supreme Allied Commander, South-East Asia, 1943-45.
Slim: *Defeat into Victory*.
Slim: *Campaign of the Fourteenth Army, 1944-45*.
John Ehrman: *Grand Strategy*, Vol. V.
Ian Hay: *Arms and the Men*.
Roy Mckelvie: *The War in Burma*.
George Odgers: *Air War against Japan*.
Frank Owen: *Campaign in Burma*.
Anthony Brett-James: *Ball of Fire*.
Ray Murphy: *The Last Viceroy*.
Lt.-Col. P. G. Bamford: *1st King George V's Own Battalion, the Sikh Regiment*.
Oxford Printing Works, New Delhi: *Operations in Burma by Probyn's Horse, February—April 1945*.
India's VCs in two World Wars.
Historical Section, India & Pakistan: *Reconquest of Burma, Vol. I*.
Historical Section, India & Pakistan: *Arakan Operations*.

INDEX

Akyab: Operation 'Talon for the capture of, 417
Allanmyo: 385-6; battle for the town of, 386; 268th Indian Infantry Brigade at, 386
Allied Land Forces, South-East Asia: 10, 110
Allied Plan: in November 1944, 108-26; new plan, 162-5; progress of the new plan, 166-9
Allied troops: formations in the Assam-Burma theatre in mid-November 1944, 119-20; strategic tasks of, 124-6
American Chiefs of Staff: 4
Arakan: 1, 9-11, 97, 107, 111, 119, 126; combined operations in, 417
Army Ground Forces: 7
Arnold, General (Head of the American Air Force): offers to send reinforcements to SEAC, 4-5
Assam: 4
Aung San's Army: 383, *see also* Burma National Army and Patriotic Burmese Forces
Axiom Mission: 3-4
Ayadaw: capture of, 228

Baldwin, Air Marshal Sir John: 11
Bandon, Air Vice-Marshal the Earl of: 420
Ben Nevis Hill: 41, 45, 48-9, 52, 54-7
Bishenpur: 1, 13, 15, 63, 65-6, 69-70, 107
Black Cat Division: *see* 17th Indian Division under Indian Forces
Bradforce, Lieut.-Col J. M. K.: 218
British Army:
 Divisions:
  2nd: 14-17, 32, 35, 47, 72, 136, 149, 156, 158, 163, 193-5; advance in the Shwebo plain by, 195-200; capture of Wainggyo by, 197; capture of Kaduma by, 198; capture of Kabo Weir by, 198-9; Mu river crossings by, 199-200, 201, 203-4, 206, 210; summary of the achievements of, 213; after the capture of Shwebo, 216-18; *see also* 289, 337, 342-3, 362-3, 371, 374-5, 381-2, 423, 444
  36th: 1, 107-8, 110, 126, 129-30, 132-3, 137-8, 382, 443-4
 Brigades:
  4th: 14, 17-18, 72, 211, 217-18, 238, 240, 242, 274-5, 278
  5th: 14, 17, 18, 47-8, 53, 59-61, 72, 200, 211-12, 217-18, 240, 242, 274-6, 278
  6th: 14, 16-17, 158, 196-7, 198-9, 206, 213, 217-18, 236, 240, 274-8, 444-6
 Battalions:
  2 Border: 31, 206, 232-3, 262, 265, 267, 273
  9 Border: 65, 69, 323, 325
  1 Camerons: 199, 218, 276
  1 Devon: 20, 28-9, 31-2, 34, 36, 158, 226, 233, 268
  2 Dorset: 53, 199, 200, 278, 374
  3 D.G.: 40, 47, 71, 198, 238, 240, 275, 278
  2 D.L.I.: 196-8, 275, 278
  8 Gordons: 218
  13 K.O.S.B.: 20, 22-3, 184, 316
  1 L.F.: 211, 278
  1 Lincolns: 424
  2 Norfolk: 218, 275, 278
  1 Northamptons: 36, 65, 157-8, 205, 208-9, 225-7, 230, 263-4, 272, 382
  42 Queen's Royal Guards: 47
  1 Queens: 22-23, 33
  1 R Berks: 16, 196-9, 278
  2 R Berks: 201, 203, 223, 247, 254, 349-50, 352-5, 357-8, 360-1
  1 R.S.: 211-12, 240
  1 R.W.F.: 16-17, 196, 198, 276, 278
  4 R.W.K.: 66, 78-9, 82, 87-8, 104-5, 143, 401
  1 Seaforth: 42-4, 48, 53-6
  2 S Lan R: 281-4, 286
  2 Suffolk: 66, 70-1, 84
  2 Welch: 134-6, 138, 203, 219, 221, 248-50, 356-7, 443
  1 W Yorks: 65, 67, 69, 302, 323, 329, 391, 393
  2 W Yorks: 71-2, 74-5, 77
  1 Worc R: 17, 350, 353-4, 358, 360-1
  2 Worc R: 138, 140, 223, 250-1, 253
  7 Worc R: 199, 211, 276, 278
  7 York: 396
 Other Units:
  9 Field Regiment Royal Artillery: 47
  10 Field Artillery Regiment: 17
  16 Field Regiment Royal Artillery: 45, 47
  28 Field Regiment: 98
  114 Field Regiment: 262, 384
  115 Field Regiment: 202
  208 Field Company Royal Engineers: 47
  27 Light Battery: 45
  116 RAC: 281-2, 284, 396
  149 RAC: 45, 47-8, 53
  150 RAC: 238, 250-1, 253

2 Recce Regiment: 17, 196, 198, 217-18, 240, 278
British Chiefs of Staff: 3, 5, 7
'Buccaneer' (operation): 413-15
Budalin: Japanese resistance at 208; capture of, 208-9
Burma: strategic situation in, 1-3; 4, 35, 74; Japanese difficulties in the defence of, 364; war position in during July 1945, 452
Burma Area Army: 121
Burma National Army: 120-1, 421, 424, 441
Burma Road: restoration of, 3-4

Cairo Conference: 413
'Capital' (Plan): 114; an appreciation of the merits of, 117-19; 125, the three phases of, 126; *see also* 127, 141, 156, 158, 161, 165, 319, 415-16
Casablanca Conference: 413
Central Front: 1-2, 9-10, 13
Ceylon Army Command: 110
'Chapcol' (an armoured column): 320
Chiang Kai-shek, Generalissimo: 2, 116, 164, 413, 415
China: 3-6, 9, 126; diversion of aircraft to, 141; situation in, 371-2
China-Burma-India Theatre: 108-9
China Theatre: 109
Chin Hills Battalion: 173, 176, 178-9, 182-3, 185-6
Chinese Troops:
  Expeditionary Force: 6, 110, 126, 413, 415
  38th Division: 125
Chindwin (river): 1-2, 18, 37, 57-8, 72-3, 95, 107-8; Fourteenth Army crosses, 127-59; establishment of a bridgehead over, 148-9; crossing of, 149-51; 20th Indian Division crosses, 156-8; crossings of up to December 1944, 158-9; 255, 280
Chinese and American 'Mars' Task Force: 129
Christison, Lieut.-General Sir A.F.P.: 109, 420
Churchill, Sir Winston: 5, 119, 361, 411-14
'Claudcol' (an armoured column): 392
Columns (of L.R.P. Brigade):
  33 Column: 24-5
  34 Column: 22, 24-5, 33
  44 Column: 24-6
  55 Column: 14, 24-5, 33
  56 Column: 14, 24-6
  60 Column: 14, 24-6, 34
  76 Column: 24-6
  88 Column: 24-6
Combat Cargo Task Force: 10, 290
Combined Army Air Transport Organisation: 10-11
Combined Chiefs of Staff: 3-4; directive to SACSEA, 6
Comilla: 10
Coryton, Air Marshal W. A.: 11
Cowan, Major-General D.T.: 167, 290

Crete: 52-3, 55, 57
'Culverin' (operation): 413

Dagger Division (19th Indian Division): *see* Indian Forces
Dahforce: 17-18
Dalby, Colonel C.: 17
Dawson, Colonel I. A.: 10
Dimapur-Imphal Road: 32, 37
'Dracula' (for capture of Rangoon by sea): 114, 116; an appreciation of the merits of, 117-19; 124-5, 127, 369, 375, 411, 413, 415-17, 419; forces required for, 416; shelved, 417; proposed and shelved again, 418; inevitability of, 419; preparations and plans for, 420; begins, 423
Dufferin, Fort: 353, attack on, 357; captured by Allied forces, 361; Union Jack hoisted on, 361 *see also* 363
Dyer, Brigadier G. M.: 130

East African Forces:
  Divisions:
    11th: 57, 61-2, 72-3, 83, 97-8, 105, 107, 126, 142; operations of, 145-56; plan of actions for, 149; 156, 158, 186, 191, 195
  Brigades:
    21st: 146-50, 152-6
    25th: formations of, 146; entry in Kalewa, 148; 149-50, 153
    26th: formations of, 146; 149; starts to cross Chindwin river, 151; holding up of Chindwin Crossings by, 151-6
    28th: 127, 169, 172, 179-83, 186; Dimcol and Milcol, the two columns of, 186-7; 279, 306-8, 334-5
  Battalions:
    2 KAR: 147-8, 150-6
    4 KAR: 147-9, 151
    5 KAR: 147-8, 150-6
    7 KAR: 183, 187
    11 KAR: 143, 146, 155
    13 KAR: 153-5, 196
    22 KAR: 146, 152-4
    25 KAR: 155
    26 KAR: 146, 149, 152
    34 KAR: 146, 150-2
    36 KAR: 146
    44 KAR: 146, 152, 154-6
    46 KAR: 183, 186, 336
    71 KAR: 183, 334-6
    1 NRR: 147-8, 151-3, 155
Eastern Air Command: 10-11, 164
Elephant Point: 421-3, 426
Evans, Major-General G. C.: 80, 83, 89
Evans, Brigadier-General Frederick W.: 10

Falam Levies: 105, 145, 172-3, 176, 179; Japanese attack on, 185
Fazal Din, Naik (7/10 Baluch Regi-

ment): awarded posthumous Victoria Cross, 303-4
Finch's Corner: 26, 29, 33, 35
Fourteenth Army: *see* Indian Forces
Force '136': 422, 429, 442, 445, 453, 459
Fort White: 98, 103-4, 141-2, 146
'Fredcol' (an armoured column): 320
Fowkes, Major-General: 147-9
Fuller, Major-General H. H. (Deputy Chief of Staff, SEAC): 362

Galahad Force (American): 1
Gangaw: the plan of attack on, 174; attack on, 175-7
Garod, Air Marshal Guy: 419
Gian Singh, Naik (4/15 Punjab Regiment): wins Victoria Cross, 310
Giffard, General Sir George: 6-7, 10, 109-10
Gracey, Major-General D. D.: 27, 382
Gwegyo: 33rd Indian Infantry Brigade captures, 377

Haka Levies: 105, 144-5, 173, 176, 178-9
Hlegu: 408-9
Hollinghurst, Air Marshal Sir Leslie: 11

Imphal: 2, 3, 8, 11-14, 35, 37, 42, 57-8, 63, 69, 72, 83, 98
Indian Air Force: 282
India-Burma Theatre Command: 109
Indian Engineer Assault parties: 53
Indian Forces:
    11th Army Group: 7, 109, renamed ALFSEA, 110
    Twelfth Army: 431, 445-6
    Fourteenth Army: 2, 7, 10, 108-12, 125-7, 160-2, 166-7; deception plan of, 171-2; Operation 'Sob' of, 369; *see also* 178, 214, 258-9, 278-9, 342-3, 362-3, 366-7, 369, 371-3, 382, 388, 418-20, 422, 426-9, 431, 444
    Corps:
    IV: 1, 14-16, 18, 26, 39, 42, 65, 72, 109, 112, 127-31; advance to the Irrawaddy by, 160-92; Multivite plan of, 169-70; appreciation of the Commander of, 170-1; redeployment of, 172; Lushai Brigade placed under the command of, 176; *see also* 178, 182, 191-2, 207, 236, 254, 256, 259, 273-4, 279-82, 288, 311, 314, 318, 333, 336-8, 342-3, 361-3, 366, 371, 381, 387-8, 400, 402, 408, 419, 428, 430-1, 440-2, 444-5, 447, 452-3
    XV: 1, 26-7, 97, 107, 109-11, 124-6, 362, 367, 402, 408, 415, 418, 420, 423, 428
    XXXIII: 1, 13-16, 18, 24, 27, 32-3, 36, 42-3, 49, 67; charge of all operations on Imphal front taken over by, 72; 73-4, 89, 107, 112, 126-7, 139-59; plan of, 141-2; 143, 148, 156, 158, 163, 166, 168-9, 171, 176, 192, advance to Irrawaddy by, 193-255; redefined tasks of, 193; 194, 200, 206, 214-15, 217, 224; first use of the rocket projectiles on the front of, 227; 229; advance slowed down, 236-8; regrouping operations of, 373-4; *see also* 254, 256, 288, 311, 333, 338, 343, 362-3, 366, 370-1, 382, 385, 387-8, 428, 430-1
    Divisions:
    3rd: 2
    5th: 1, 13-14, 19, 66-7, 70-7, 81-3, 88-91, 94-5, 97, 100, 105, 107, 126, 142-4, 157, 168, 176, 191, 260, 289, 311-12, 314, 318, 324, 338, 370-1, 388-9; takes the lead, 394; *see also* 395, 397-400, 402, 408, 428-9, 442, 444, 447
    7th: 1, 14-15, 18-20, 22, 25-6, 33, 35, 72-3, 136, 139, 169-72; the move of, 172-3; 174, 179; forward concentration of, 180-2; the order of march of, 180-1; the tasks assigned to, 182; the plan of, 182-3; 187; clearing of the west banks of Irrawaddy by, 187-90; 192, 254; Irrawaddy crossings by, 278-88; deployment of the division's units on 1 Feb. 1945, 280-1; 284, 288-90; activities of, 306; *see also* 308, 311, 315, 321, 334, 336-8, 343, 370-1, 374-5, 380, 388, 428, 431, 434, 437-8, 444-6, 448, 452
    17th: 63-4, regrouping of, 65; 66-7, 70, 72-3, 167-8, 170-1, 182, 190-1, 254, 279, 286, 289; known as Black Cat Division, 290; *see also* 303, 305-6, 308, 311-12, 314, 318, 321, 334, 336-8, 343, 370, 388-9, 392, 394-5, 399-402, 405, 408-9, 427-8, 441-4, 447-8, 452-4, 457-9
    19th (or 'Dagger' Division): 128; the tasks assigned to, 129-30; 131-3, 137-40, 156, 163, 165-7, 171, 193-5; the front of, 200-4; comes under the command of the XXXIII Corps, 201; 203-4, 209, 211-12; summary of the achievements of, 213; 215, 217; Japanese on the front of, 218-19; 236-9, 242-3; defence of the bridgeheads by, 249-50; 253-4, 256, 258; Irrawaddy crossings by, 259; 274-5, 288-9, 337, 342-3; operations of, 344; *see also* 346, 348-50, 352, 354-5, 357, 362-3, 370, 394, 428-9, 441-4, 447-8, 452-4, 459
    20th: 13-14; placed under Lieut.-General Stopford, 15; 18, 20, 26-9, 32-3, 35-8, 72-3, 132, 136, Chindwin crossed by, 156-8; the

tasks assigned to, 157; 163, 181, 193; capture of Budalin by, 194; 195, 200; the front of, 204-9; moves to Pyingaing, 205-6; moves to Maukkadaw, 206; 216-17; moves to Monywa, 224-8; 237, 239, 242-3, 250, 254, 258; crossing of Irrawaddy by, 259; *see also* 260-1, 263, 273-5, 289, 337, 342-3, 362-3, 370-1, 381-2, 385-7, 427-8, 430-2, 436, 439-40, 443-6, 452

21st: 14, 16
23rd: 38-9, 42-3, 47, 55, 57-62, 72-3
26th: 402, 409, 420, 423, 426-9, 432, 438

Brigades:
1st: main task of, 38; 42-3; opening of the HQ of, 44; 48-51; penetration in the Jap Hill and Nippon Hill, 52; *see also* 54-7, 59-61
9th: 70-1, 74-5, 77, 88, 98-101, 103, 157; the tasks assigned to, 158; *see also* 319, 324, 330, 338, 394, 399, 402, 442, 447-8
23rd: 23, operation for the recapture of Ukhrul by, 24-6; *see also* 33
32nd: 15, 27, 36, 63-4; formation of, 65; 66-7, 157, 197, 204-6, 208-9, 226, 228-9, 233, 260, 262, first phase of the Brigade's operation to cross Irrawaddy, 263-5; 268, 272; second phase of the Brigade's operation to cross Irrawaddy, 272-4; *see also* 381-3, 386, 432-4, 440
33rd: advance from Maram, 15; advance to Ukhrul, 18-19; crosses the Iril river, 20; *see also* 22-7, 32-5, 185, 279-81, 284, 286-8, 308-9, 311-14, 316, 375-81, 438-9, 446, 450
36th: 200, 423, 425-6
37th: 38-40, 42-3, 49-52; opening of HQ at Malta, 53; *see also* 54-6, 61
48th: 63-4; formations of, 65; 66-7; locations of the Units of, 68-9; *see also* 191, 290-1, 293-5, 298-301, 305, 320, 328, 390-94, 402, 408-9, 455, 457
49th: 38, 40, 44, 48-51, 56-61
50th Parachute: 27; returns to Dimapur, 37; *see also* 63
62nd: 129-31, crossing of the Chindwin by, 131-3; to operate as Long Range Penetration group, 129-30; *see also* 134, 137-8, 201-3, 215, 219, 221, 224, 243, 250, 253-4, 344, 346-50, 355, 357, 361
63rd: 63-4; formations of, 65; the tasks of, 66-7, *see also* 69-70, 191, 290, 292-5, 298-302, 305, 320-1, 325, 329, 331, 333, 390-2, 394, 400, 402-4, 407-8, 410, 457-8
64th: 130-2, 134, 136-8, 201-4, 209-10, 212, 215, 219, 222-3, 247, 250-1, 253, 344-8, 350, 352-5, 357-9, 361, 443-4
71st: 423-7, 432, 434, 438
80th: 14-15, 20, 26-9, 31, 33, 36, 157-8, 204, 206-7, 226, 233-4, 260-1, 268, 272-3, 381, 384-5, 436, 438-9
89th: 14; moves from Kangpokpi, 15; 18; placed under the 7th Division, 19; 20, 22-3, 25-7, 32-5, 181-3; encircling movement by, 183-4; in the van, 184-5; *see also* 187-8, 279, 284, 286, 308, 315-16, 376-80, 434-5, 448
98th: 130, 132, 134, 136-9, 201-4, 210-12, 215, 219, 221-3, 243, 246, 253-4, 344-6, 348-50, 352, 355, 357-8, 458
99th: 191, 290, 294, 299, 305-6, 319-20, 323, 325-6, 327-8, 331-3, 389-90, 392-4, 399, 402, 408, 443
100th: 14-15, 26-9, 31-3, 36-7, 197, 204, 206-7, 209, 228, 230; capture of Letkapin by, 230-2; 260; first phase of the Brigade's operation to cross Irrawaddy, 261-2; 263; second phase of Brigade's Irrawaddy crossings, 265-8; *see also* 373, 381, 383, 385-7, 432, 439
114th: located at Kohima, 14; *see also* 19, 136, 139, 180-1, 183-5, 188-9, 279, 281, 286, 307-8, 315-16, 335, 378, 380-1, 434, 446
123rd: 66, 70-1, 75, 77; outflanking march by, 82-7; new units placed under the command of, 84; *see also* 88-90, 95, 98-101, 143, 395-401
161st: concentrating at Imphal, 14; placed under the command of 5th Division, 19; *see also* 66-7, 70, 76-81, 83-4, 87, 90-1, 94, 98, 100-1, 103-5, 143, 312, 314, 394-5, 397-401
254th Tank Brigade: 163, 213, 237-8
255th Tank Brigade: 127, 132, 167; 400 miles march by, 190-1; *see also* 288, 290-1, 295-6, 298-9, 301, 336, 338, 400, 404, 428, 444-5
268th (Indian Lorried): 14, 16, 47, 49, 52, 54-6, 59, 61, 128, 130-2, 134, 137-9, 163, 193, 213, 238, 275, 374, 381, 386, 428, 432, 437, 444-6

Battalions:
5/10 Baluch: 134, 215, 219, 222, 223-5, 250, 444
7/10 Baluch: 63-5, 293, 299, 321, 325, 333, 404, 407, 457
1 Bihar: 96, 105, 145, 174-6
2/4 Bombay Grenadiers: 45, 52, 61

3/4 Bombay Grenadiers: 278
4/4 Bombay Grenadiers: 132, 322, 407
5/4 Bombay Grenadiers: 47
1 Burma Regiment: 20, 22-4, 35, 281-2, 284, 286
1/17 Dogra: 66, 70, 87-95, 97, 99-100, 397
4/17 Dogra: 232, 384, 436-8
4/12 F.F.R.: 63, 65-6, 69, 290, 300, 302, 304, 321-2, 328-30, 391-2, 394, 404, 407-8, 455
8/12 F.F.R.: 201-2, 223, 254, 353-5, 357, 359, 443
9/12 F.F.R.: 27-9, 31-2, 36, 229, 234-5, 268-9, 272, 381
8/13 F.F. Rif: 77-8, 425-6
9/13 F.F. Rif.: 322
14/13 F.F. Rif.: 27-8, 31-2, 36-7, 228-9, 233, 261-2, 264-7, 273
2/3 Gurkha Parachute: 420-1, 425
1/1 G.R.: 440
3/1 G.R.: 27-9, 31, 158, 207-8, 235, 268, 384, 437
4/1 G.R.: 20, 22-4, 33, 35, 189, 281-2, 284, 309, 311-14, 376-7, 379-80, 437-8
4/2 G.R.: 383, 433, 440
1/3, G.R.: 65, 67, 69, 324, 328, 332-3, 390, 393-4, 402-4, 407-8, 443
3/3 G.R.: 42-5, 53, 55
1/4 G.R.: 63, 65
4/4 G.R.: 132, 134, 201, 219, 221-4, 246, 254, 344-5, 349, 352, 354-3, 458-9
1/6 G.R.: 130-1, 134-5, 203, 210, 215, 219, 222-4, 246-7, 249, 253, 345, 347, 350, 355, 357-8, 360, 444, 459
4/6 G.R.: 133, 135, 202-3, 219, 221, 247, 249-50, 253, 348-50, 356
1/7 G.R.: 65, 67-9, 296, 300, 302, 304, 320, 323, 325, 327-30, 391, 393, 409, 427
1/8 G.R.: 426
3/8 G.R.: 64-5, 157, 208-9, 225, 227-30, 263, 265, 272, 434
4/8 G.R.: 20, 22-4, 35, 184, 316-18, 434-5, 448, 450-1
1/10 G.R.: 69, 300, 321, 325, 332, 404, 407, 457
3/10 G.R.: 41, 43, 53, 55
4/10 G.R.: 28-9, 31-2, 36, 197, 204-6, 228, 230, 232, 262, 266-7, 385, 439
2/5 R.G.R.: 65, 68-9
3/5 R.G.R.: 39, 41, 43, 45, 53, 55
4/5 R.G.R.: 188, 457
1/18 Royal Garhwal Rifles: 425-6
1 Hyderabad: 437
2 Hyderabad: 43-4, 47, 52, 54, 56
1/9 Jat: 74, 76-7, 95-6, 104-5, 144-5, 174
3/9 Jat: 41, 48, 53, 71-2, 75, 77, 99-101, 103-4, 312
4 Madras: 28, 31, 138-9, 213
4/5 Mahrattas: 40-4, 50-1

6/5 Mahrattas: 40-3, 50-1, 58-9
152 Parachute: 27-8, 31, 33, 36-7
153 Parachute: 26-8, 32, 37
1/1 Punjab: 67, 70, 78-80, 82, 91, 93-4, 98-101, 103-5, 143, 312, 398
2/1 Punjab: 84, 87-95, 97, 99-101
5/1 Punjab: 424-7
3/2 Punjab: 66, 84, 87, 88, 90-101, 142, 400
7/2 Punjab: 172, 180-3, 185, 187, 316, 377-8
2/8 Punjab: 436-8
3/14 Punjab: 70-1, 74-6
4/14 Punjab: 185, 188, 307, 334-5
7/14 Punjab: 78, 80, 95-6, 105, 144, 176
9/14 Punjab: 36, 64-5, 208-9, 226-8, 230, 263-5, 268, 272, 383, 433-4
1/15 Punjab: 221-2, 347-9, 354-5, 357, 359-61
3/15 Punjab: 450
4/15 Punjab: 281-4, 286, 308-9, 311-14, 376-7, 379-80, 451
6/15 Punjab: 320, 324, 328, 332-3, 390, 393-4
1/16 Punjab: 38, 42, 44, 52, 54-6
5/16 Punjab: 305
3/6 Rajputana Rifles: 133-5, 203, 221, 245, 247, 250-3, 361, 443
5/6 Rajputana Rifles: 39-40, 43, 50, 57, 59
4/7 Rajput: 79-82, 103-5, 143, 395, 397
5/7 Rajput: 427
6/7 Rajput: 290-2, 294, 296-8, 301, 304, 331, 402, 409
1/11 Sikh: 20, 22, 34, 184, 187, 189, 287, 315-17, 434-5, 450-1
MG/11 Sikh: 223
Other Units:
  7 Cavalry: 345, 347, 349, 395, 405, 407, 409
  16 Cavalry: 294, 297, 309, 320-1, 388, 405, 407-9
  2 Engineer: 47
  10 Engineer: 47, 49
  17 Divisional Engineers: 280
  62 Field Company: 169, 184
  65 Field Company: 134
  68 Field Company: 53
  71 Field Company: 49
  74 Field Company: 84
  91 Field Company: 48
  94 Field Company Royal Engineers: 47
  45 Indian Field Ambulance: 84
  3 Indian Field Regiment: 45
  4 Indian Field Regiment: 219
  1 Medium Regiment Royal Artillery: 45, 47
  4 Jammu and Kashmir Infantry: 99, 101, 103-4, 142
  Kalibahadur Regiment: 39-40, 44, 57
  19 Lancers: 426
  Mahendra Dal: 138-9, 213
  6 Mountain Battery: 69

13 Mountain Battery: 45
15 Mountain Battery: 41, 49
16 Mountain Battery: 48, 52
23 Mountain Battery: 184, 264
21 Mountain Regiment: 299
24 Mountain Regiment: 84
25 Mountain Regiment: 18
28 Mountain Regiment: 45
India Theatre: 109
Indian National Army: 59-60, 120-1, 161
Inya: capture of, 270-2
Iril (river): 13-14, crossing of by the 33rd Indian Brigade, 20; see also 26, 32
Irrawaddy (river): 108, 127; IV Corps advance to, 160-92; Japanese withdraw behind, 160-3; XXXIII Corps advance to, 193-254; 19th Indian Division crossings of, 219-29; 236, 240, 242; Japanese efforts to destroy two bridgeheads on, 243-4; crossings of, 255-88; the timings of the crossing of, 256-7; administrative build-up and preparations to cross, 257-8; four main crossings of, 260-1, Indian troops cross, 290, position east of, 316; operations west of, 334-7

Japan: 96
Japanese Army:
 15th Army: 2, 35, 121-3, 128, 133, 140; tasks allotted to on 10 Oct. 1944, 140; see also 159, 161, 163, 193, 288, 362, 364, 371, 389, 429-30, 441
 28th Army: 123, 161, 288, 364, 372, 427-8, 430-1, 433, 440-1, 445, 448, 453, 458-9
 33rd Army: 123, 125; the plan and dispositions of to maintain Japanese hold in Central Burma, 238-9; see also 372, 389, 394, 400, 429-30, 441
Divisions:
 2nd Div.: 258
 4th Div.: 58
 15th Div.: 1, 13, 16, 26, 37, 72, 121-3, 128, 136-7, 161, 194-5, 200-1, 215-16, 218-19, 238-9, 243, 259, 343, 346, 352, 389, 443
 18th Div.: 1-2, 319, 338-40, 372, 389, 448
 31st Div.: 2, 12-13, 16, 37, 72, 121-3, 128, 160-1, 194-5, 200-1, 204, 215-16, 218-19, 238-9, 259, 267, 343-4
 33rd Div.: 1, 13, 63, 70, 75, 107, 121-3, 128, 161, 168, 191, 195, 204, 215-16, 229; 238-9; 259 319.
 49th Div.: 191, 319, 338-9, 372, 389, 431
 53rd Div. 13, 122, 128, 137, 161, 191, 194, 215, 238-9, 243, 259, 338, 343, 346, 372, 389, 448
 54th Div.: 13, 75, 123, 125, 430-1, 453

55th Div.: 123, 125, 365, 398, 430-1, 433, 453, 457-8
Brigades:
 34th IMB: 191
 72nd IMB: 161, 191, 286, 430-1
Regiments:
 14th Tank Regiment: 128
 16th: 266, 268, 272
 21st Field Artillery: 26
 51st: 21, 31, 219, 243
 58th: 16, 200, 216, 218, 239, 344
 60th: 16, 219, 243
 61st: 58, 191, 317
 67th: 16, 26, 219, 243
 114th: 398
 119th: 319, 343
 124th: 16, 65, 195, 198, 216, 218, 267
 138th: 16, 216, 224, 239
 151st: 343
 153rd: 191, 316-17, 430-1, 453
 154th: 75, 83
 168th: 319, 338
 213th: 146, 216, 224, 239, 265
 214th: 83, 188, 195, 216, 286
 215th: 83, 191, 195, 216, 266, 272
Japanese Strategy: in central Burma, 121-6
Japanese Troops: formations of in November 1944, 120-1; position of in December 1944, 161-2; dispositions of in mid-December 1944, 194-5; dispositions of on the 2nd Division's front, 216; morale of, 372

Kabaw Valley: 12, 61-2, 72-3, 83, 97, 107, 126, 181, 204
Kalemyo: 62-3, 73-4, 83; plan for the capture of, 89; 91, 95; pursuit to, 96-107
Kalemyo—Kalewa area: military importance of, 141
Kalewa: capture of, 145
Kamaing: falls to the Chinese, 2
Kandaung: action at 323
Kasuya, Major-General (Japanese): 295
Katamura, Lieut.-General (Japanese): 122
Kawabe, General (Japanese): 161
Kimura, General (Japanese): 161, 163, 192, 258, 289, 338, 342, 364-5, 388, 426, 430
Kohima—Imphal Road: reopening of, 16-18; 35, 73
Kohima: 2, 3, 8, 12-14, 37, 72
Kyaukse: capture of, 240
Kyaukpadaung: capture of by Allied troops, 376

Largs, H.M.S.: 422
Ledo Road: 4-5
Leese, Lieut.-General Sir Oliver: 7-8, 10; Allied division controlled by, 109-110; reason for the change of the HQ. of, 111; see also 124, 256, 342, 362, 364, 367, 418-420
Leigh, Mallory Sir Trafford: 109

Leiktu: capture of, 201-2
Letkapin: capture of, 230-2
Lezin: advance towards, 230
202nd Line of Communication Area: 110
Line of Communication Command: formed at Comilla, 110
Line of Communication (troops): 3
Litan: 1, 13-14, 29
Lokchao (river): 48; 1st Battalion on the other bank of, 51; 56, 58-9
Long-Range Penetration Brigade (23rd): 14-15, 22, 24, 32, 34-5; *see also* columns
Lushai Brigade: 72-4; placed under 5th Indian Division, 76; 78, 80; operation against the Tiddim—Falam area by, 91; Falam entered by, 95; review of the operations of, 95; new tasks allotted to, 95; fall of Haka to, 96; 97-8, 107, 127, 142; overall plan of, 144; 158, 167-9, 171, 173-5; comes under IV Corps, 176; 180, 183
Lushai Scouts: 145, 172-3, 176, 179, 182-3, 186
Lynch Hill: 52-3

MacArthur, General D.: 4, 96
Madaya: 350, 352
Magwe: 384-5, 387
Mahendra Dal: *see* Indian Forces
Mahlaing: captured by Indian troops, 293
Malta: 52-3, 55
Mandalay: 2-3; known as the city of kings, 342; Allied forces march against, 342; capture of by 19th Indian Division, 357; *see also* Dufferin, Fort
Manipur (river): pursuit to, 77-82; 78-83; crossing of, 87-90; 98
Mansergh, Major-General E.C.: 80, 394
Marindin, Brigadier P.C.: 176
Martin, Rear Admiral: 420
Maymyo: bloodless capture of by Allied troops, 355-7
Meiktila: the thrust to by Indian troops, 289; 17th Indian Division plan of operations for the capture of, 289; Indian troops advance on, 294; the attack on, 295-6; defence of by Allied troops, 318-21; Japanese attack the airfield at, 324-5; 48th Indian Infantry Brigade moves from, 329; causes of Allied success in the operations of, 337-41; 17th Indian Division moves out from, 389
Milaungbya: 4/8 Gurkha Riffes occupy, 318
Messervy, Major-General Sir Frank: 19-20, 169-70; 177-8, 361
Mintha: 56, 59-61, 73
Miyazaki, Major-General (Japanese): 13
Miyazaki Force: 16
Mogaung: 1-2

Morris Hill: 48, 53; 3/5 Gurkha Rifles at, 55; Japanese flame throwers and documents found at, 56
Mountbatten, Admiral the Lord Louis: 3-7, 9; visits London, 117; 118; visits 19th Indian Division Headquarters, 362; *see also* 371, 373, 411-12, 414-18, 420, 426
Mu (river): 57; 2nd Division crossing of, 199-200; *see also* 236, 240, 261, 274-5
Mutaguchi, General (Japanese): 2, dismissal of, 122
Myaukkon: 173-4, 177-80; final attack on, 178
Myindawgan Lake: 323, 326, 331-2
Myingyan: captured by Indian troops, 312
Myinmu: capture of, 228
Myitkyina: 1-3, 5-6, 9, 96
Myittha (river): 73, 95, 97, 150, 152, 155, 158, 176
Myittha Valley: Japanese forces in, 191-2

Naga Hills: 12
Ngathyauk: 291; plan for the capture of, 291-2
Nicholson, Major-General C. G. G.: appointed officiating Commander of 5th Indian Division, 80
Nimitz, Admiral Chester: 96
Ningthoukhong: destruction of the Japanese bunkers to the south of, 68
Northern Air Sector Force: 9
Northern Combat Area Command: 1, 8-10, 109-10, 113, 125, 129, 161, 164-5, 216
Northern Front: 1-2
Numata Takazo, Lieut.-General (Japanese): 362

Operations (Code names):
'Buccaneer': 413-15
'Capital': 114, 117-19, 125-7, 141, 156, 158, 161, 165, 319, 415-16
'Culverin': 413
'Dracula': 114, 116-19, 124-5, 127, 369, 375, 411, 413, 415-17, 419-20, 423
'Pigstick': 415
'Roger': 419
'Romulus': 119, 125, 127
'Sob':: 369
'Talon': 417

Pakokku: 166, 168-73, 176, 179, 181-2, 184-90, 255-6, 258-9, 278-80, 290, 363
Palel: 1, 15, 37; Japanese attack on, 42; 56, 60-1, 73
Park, Air Marshal Sir Keith: 109, 362, 420
Parkash Singh, Jemadar (14/13 F. F. Rifles): wins Victoria Cross, 266
Patriotic Burmese Forces (PBF): 441, 445; *see also* Aung San's Army and Burma National Army

Pauk: capture of, 185
Pear Hill: capture of, 244-5
Pears, Colonel: 131
Pegu: 403-4; plan for the capture of, 404-5; attack from the north, 405-7; attack from the north-east and south of, 407-8
Pegu Yomas: final operations west of, 440, Japanese preparations in, 453
Phoebe, H.M.S.: 422
Philippines: 96
Pierse, Air Chief Marshal Sir Richard: 109, 115
'Pigstick' (Operation): 415; object of, 415
Pinde: capture of, 202
Pinlebu: modified plan for the capture of, 132-3; the advance on by 19th Indian Division, 133-6; situation after the capture of, 136-40; plan of operations subsequent to the capture of, 137-8
Plan X (strategic plan of Allies): 112-13
Plan Y (strategic plan of Allies): 113-14; also known as 'Capital', 114; 116; appreciation of the merits of, 117
Plan Z (strategic plan of Allies): 114-16; also known as 'Dracula', 114; appreciation of the merits of, 117
Popa, Mount: 2nd Division Operations for the capture of, 373; final capture of, 374-6
Power, Sir Arthur (Commander-in-Chief East Indies Fleet): 420
Pownall, Lieut.-General: 7
Prome: 386; Allied advance on, 386

Quebec Conference: 118, 416

'Ralphcol' (an armoured Column): 320
Ram Sarup Singh, Jemadar (2/1 Punjab Regiment): wins Victoria Cross, 99
Rangoon: 4-5; XXXIII Corps dash to, 366; plan of operation in, 366; Lieut.-General Slim's twin drive on, 367; the plan for the drive to, 369-71; Operation 'Sob' for the capture of, 369; IV Corps dash to, 388-9; Operation 'Dracula' for the capture of, 415; Indian troops enter, 425-6; position of Allied troops in, 428
Rear Air-fields Maintenance Organisation: 10
Red Army: 96
Rees, Major-General T. W.: 131, 210, 352, 355, 359, 362-3
Roberts, Major-General: 43
'Roger' (operation): 419
'Romulus' (an Allied operation for Arakan): 119, 125, 127
Roosevelt, Mr. F. D. (President U.S.A.): 413

Royal Air Force: 10-11, 17, 48, 79, 87-8, 93-4, 100, 112, 260, 264, 266, 278, 282
Royal Deccan Horse: 291, 296-8, 300, 302, 320, 323, 325-7, 329
Royal Indian Army Service Corps: 181
Royalist, H.M.S.: 423

Sadwingyi: capture of, 204
Sagaing: clearing of the area of, 240-2
Sakurai, Lieut.-General (Japanese): 459
Sancol (a part of 153 Parachute Battalion): 28, 36
Satpangon: battle for, 232-3
Scoones, Lieut.-General Sir Geoffry: 72
Scotts Knob: attack on, 41-2
Seikpyu: capture of, 186-7
Shwebo: the fall of, 209-13; mopping up in, 211-12; importance of the capture of, 214
Sibong: the thrust to, 50-7; 59-60
Sittang (river): battle at, 447-8
Sittaung (village): 61, 73
Slim, General Sir William: 2, 7, 109-10, 112, 116, 127, 139, 141, 161-4, 166, 170, 178, 201, 235, 256; hoisted Union Jack on Fort Dufferin, 361; twin drive on Rangoon, 367; see also 362-3, 365-6, 370, 373
Smuts, Field Marshal: 412
'Sob' (operation): Fourteenth Army plan for drive to Rangoon, 369
South-East Asia: 1, 3, 6-7, 10-11, 109
South-East Asia Command: 2-6, 8, 108, 118, 160, 164
Special Combat Cargo Groups: 4
Special Force: 2-3, formation of, 110
Stalin, Marshal Joseph: 414
Stilwell, Lieut.-General J. B. (U.S.): 1-7, 9-10, 96, 108-9, 112, 116, 118
Stockades No. 2 and 3: 104, 105, 126, 143
Stopford, Lieut.-General Sir Montagu: 14, 35, 47, 57, 72-3, 83, 89, 179, 362
Strategy: see Plans *and* Operations
Stratemeyer, Major-General: 110, 419
Sultan, Lieut.-General Dan (U.S.): Commander NCAC and India-Burma Theatre Command, 8, 109-10, 115, 129, 164-5, 371, 382
Symes, Major-General G. W.: 110

'Talon' (operation): 417
Tamu: the regaining of, 38-62, the period of stalemate, 38-45; the plan of attack on, 45-50; 48, 56; the fall of, 57-60; the picture of Dante's 'Inferno' seen in, 60; see also 61, 83
Tarforce: 27-9, 31, 33, 35-7
Taungtha: two-pronged move on, 292; captured by Indian troops, 293; Japanese reoccupy, 321
Teheran Conference: 414
Tengnoupal: 56, 58, 60
Terauchi, Field Marshal (Japanese): 426
Third Tactical Air Force: 9-11

Tiddim: 12, 63; beginning of the advance to, 67-72; plans for the capture of, 67; 73, 75, 89; the fall of, 90-6; topography of the area of, 91; *see also* 98, 108, 142
Tilin: capture of, 183
Tizaung: capture of, 228
Toungoo: 400-1
Troop Carrier Command: 9-10

Ukhrul: the general situation in, 12-13; Allied plan for the recapture of, 13-15; plan to surround, 18; 22-3; recapture of by XXXIII Corps, 24; reopening of the Ukhrul Road, 26-32; mopping up beyond, 32-7; 72
United States Army Air Force: 2, 9-10, 97, 100, 113, 282, 305
United States Military Mission: 2

'Vanguard' (the earlier name of plan 'Dracula'): 118
'V' Force: 77, 84, 130-1, 138-9, 144, 153, 156, 167, 429, 442, 445, 453, 455
Vital Corner: 91, 93-4, 97-101, 103-4, 142

Warren, Major-General: 89, 95
Wedemeyer, Major-General (U.S.): 3, 7-8, 109, 118, 141, 164-5, 371, 416
West African Divisions:
  81st: 126
  82nd: 126, 429, 444, 446
Weston, Lieut. W. B. (1W Yorks): wins posthumous Victoria Cross, 303
Wetherall, Lieut.-General H. E. de R.: 110
Wheeler, Major-General R. A.: 7-8, 109
Whitworth-Jones, Air Vice-Marshal: 9
Woodforce: 63; formation of, 65, task assigned to and the disbandment of, 66

Yamamoto, Major-General (Japanese): 191, 317, 338
Yamamoto Force: 13, 38, 45, 47-50, 54, 56-8, 72, 121, 195, 200, 204
Yamethin: 395-6; capture of by the 5th Indian Division, 397
Yenangyaung: capture of by the Allied Forces, 378-81
Yunnan Force: 113, 116
Ywathitgyi: capture of, 240-2

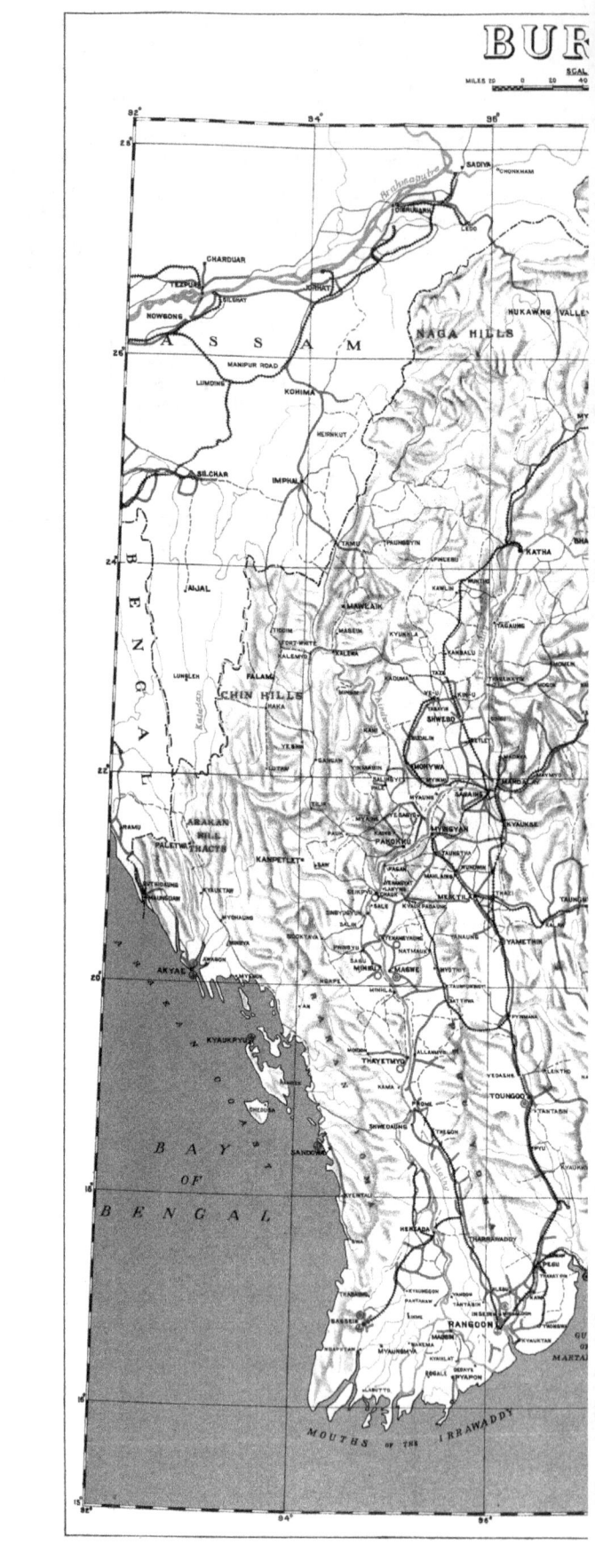

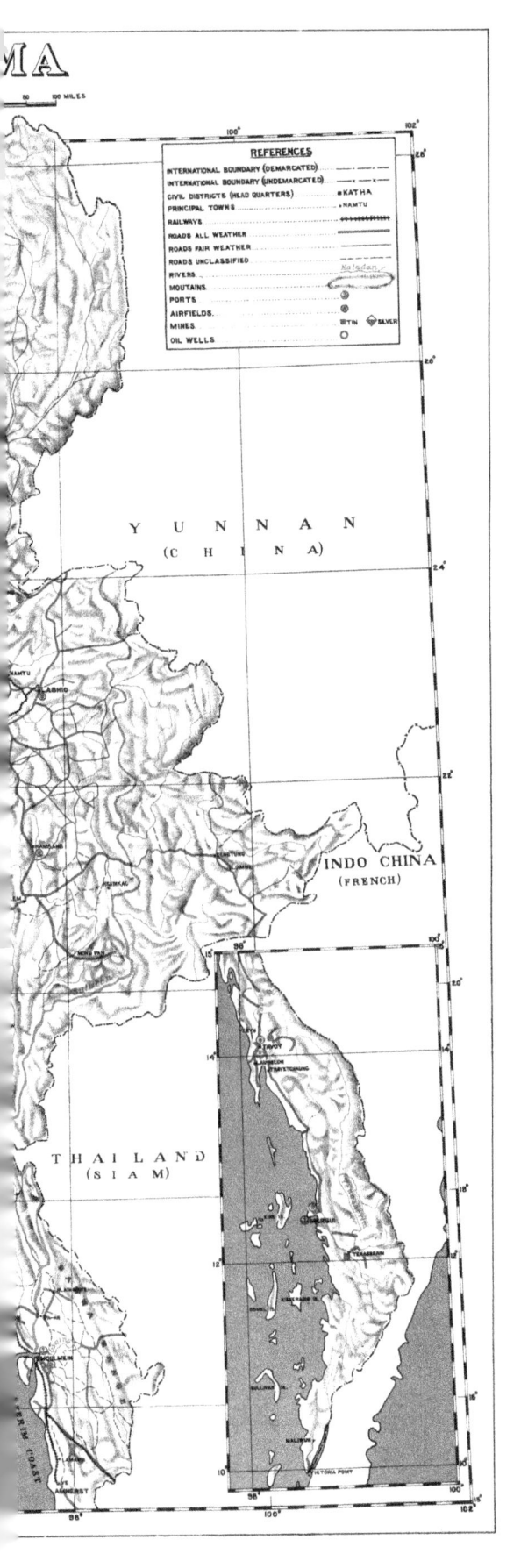

INDIAN DIVISIONS WON A FINE REPUTATION IN WORLD WAR TWO

Field Marshal Auchinleck, Commander-in-Chief of the British Indian Army from 1942, asserted that the British *"couldn't have come through both wars (World War I and II) if they hadn't had the British Indian Army"*.
British Prime Minister Winston Churchill also paid tribute to *"the unsurpassed bravery of Indian soldiers and officers"*.

Between 1945 and 1947, the Director of Public Relations, War Department, Government of India, published a series of short publications covering the individual histories of the WWII Indian Divisions. They followed a consistent format, having between 44 and 48 pages within illustrated soft card covers. They have an average of 50 monochrome photographic illustrations, and each has a full colour centrespread depicting a scene from the Division's wartime operations (drawn by official war artists). They were printed at various presses in Bombay and New Delhi, and each contains at least one map.

As condensed histories they are useful – particularly those which relate to Divisions for which no other record was ever produced.

The British Indian Army during World War II began the war, in 1939, numbering just under 200,000 men. By the end of the war, it had become the largest volunteer army in history, rising to over 2.5 million men in August 1945. Serving in divisions of infantry, armour and a fledgling airborne force, they fought on three continents: in Africa, Europe and Asia.

This Army fought in Ethiopia against the Italian Army, in Egypt, Libya, Tunisia and Algeria against both the Italian and German Army and, after the Italian surrender, against the German Army in Italy. However, the bulk of the British Indian Army was committed to fighting the Japanese Army, first during the British defeats in Malaya and the retreat from Burma to the Indian border; later, after resting and refitting for the victorious advance back into Burma, as part of the largest British Empire army ever formed. These campaigns cost the lives of over 87,000 Indian service-men, while another 34,354 were wounded, and 67,340 became prisoners of war. Their valour was recognised with the award of some 4,000 decorations, and 18 members of the British Indian Army were awarded the Victoria Cross or the George Cross.

RED EAGLES
The Story of the 4th Indian Division
9781474537520

During the Second World War, the 4th Indian Division was in the vanguard of nine campaigns in the Mediterranean theatre, Egypt, Eritrea, Syria, Tunisia, Italy and Greece. The 4th Division captured 150,000 prisoners and suffered 25,000 casualties, more than the strength of a whole division. It won over 1,000 honours and awards, which included four Victoria Crosses and three George Crosses. Field Marshal Lord Wavell wrote: "The fame of this Division will surely go down as one of the greatest fighting formations in military history."

THE FIGHTING FIFTH
History of the 5th Indian Division
9781474537513

As described in much greater detail in Anthony Brett James's book 'The Ball of Fire', the division saw active service in East Africa, North Africa and Burma.

GOLDEN ARROW
The Story of the 7th Indian Division
9781474537506

The role of this division is also duplicated by a much larger work the book by Brig. M. R. Roberts. However, this booklet gives a good account of Kohima and Imphal and the crossing of the Irrawaddy. In 1945, the division was flown into Siam, so becoming the first Allied formation to re-enter South East Asia.

BLACK CAT DIVISION
17th Indian Division
9781474537483

This formation was committed to Burma from the early days when the British were in full flight from the invading Japanese. It remained in Burma right through to the end, when the starving remnants of the Japanese Army were making their own desperate retreat.

ONE MORE RIVER
The Story of the 8th Indian Division
Inferno, Trigno, Sangro, Moro, Rapido, Arno, Senio, Santerno, Po, Adige

9781474537490

The 8th Indian Division started its overseas service in the Middle East in the garrisoning of Iraq and then the invasion of Persia to secure the oil fields of the area for the Allies, before moving to Italy in 1943. Landing at Taranto, it pushed up the length of the peninsula in a series of major battles: breaking the Sangro Line, forcing the Rapido and turning the defences at Cassino, breaking the stubborn German resistance at Monte Grande and, finally, forcing the Po River. It won four VCs, 26 DSOs and 149 MCs along the way. During the war the 8th Indian Division sustained casualties totalling 2,012 dead, 8,189 wounded and 749 missing.

TIGER HEAD
The Story of the 26th Indian Division
Arakan, Ragoon

9781474537452

This is a history of the division said later by the Japanese to have been the opponent which they most feared. The 26th held the Allied monsoon line in the Arakan during two such seasons, repulsing every attack launched against it. Later it made a series of leap-frog landings down the coast to clinch the issue in the Arakan. It was the first division to enter Ragoon, invading the city from the sea.

THE TWENTY THIRD INDIAN DIVISION
"The Fighting Cock Division"
Burma, Malaya, Java

9781474537469

The Fighting Cock Division is well recorded in the book by Doulton. This book gives coverage of the heavy fighting at the Kohima Battle, the capture of Tamu, the reoccupation of Malaya in August 1945, and then its strange role on the island of Java – concurrently disarming the Japanese garrison, fighting the insurgent Indonesian nationalists, and caring for 65,000 former internees pending the arrival of a new Dutch administration.

A HAPPY FAMILY
The Story of the Twentieth Indian Division,
9781474537476

One of the few Indian divisions in the 14th Army trained specifical for the war in Burma. Raised in Bangalore in 1942, it commence active operations in late 1943 and served from Imphal through to the end. It established the 14th Army's first brigade-head across th Chindwin and its second such brigade-head across the Irrawaddy. I final task was to round up the Japanese in French Indochina.

TEHERAN TO TRIESTE
The Story of the Tenth Indian Division
9781783317028

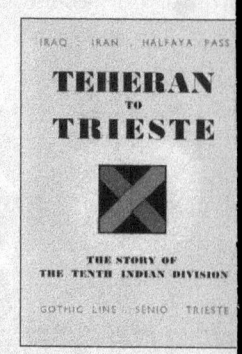

This History deals with the 10th Indian Div's exploits in Iraq (under Maj Gen "Bill" Slim) its role in the Libyan battles leading up to El Alamein, the following two years of garrison duties in Cyprus and Syria, and finally, its fighting services in the Italian campaign (from Ortona onwards).

THE STORY OF THE 25th INDIAN DIVSION
The Arakan Campaign
9781783317585

Formed in Southern India in August 1942 for defence of that area i case of Japanese invasion, the "Ace of Spades" Division had it baptism of fire in Arakan in February 1944. It served throughout th remainder of that campaign the climax being the battle of Tamandu Its victorious fight for the Kangaw roadblock was considered by man to have been the fiercest battle of the entire Burma war, while it liberation of Akyab was the first convincing proof to the rest of the world that the tide ha turned against the Japanese.

DAGGER DIVISION
The Story of the 19th Indian Division
9781783317035

Raised in the late 1941, the 19th was the first "standard" Indian Division. Its troops were the first to breach the Japanese defence line in Burma and to raise the flag at Fort Dufferin. It crossed the Chindwin in November 1944, driving on to Mandalay and Ragoon during seven months of continuous fighting. The 19th's exploits are graphically described also in John Masters' personal memoir, *The Road Past Mandalay*.

www.ingramcontent.com/pod-product-compliance
Lightning Source LLC
Chambersburg PA
CBHW060415300426
44111CB00018B/2856